WRESTED SCRIPTURES

A CHRISTADELPHIAN HANDBOOK OF SUGGESTED
EXPLANATIONS TO DIFFICULT BIBLE PASSAGES

by
RON ABEL

Revised and expanded by
JOHN ALLFREE

THE CHRISTADELPHIAN
404 Shaftmoor Lane
Hall Green
Birmingham B28 8SZ, UK

2011

*Republished in this considerably
revised and expanded edition:*
2011

©*2011, The Christadelphian Magazine and Publishing Association Limited*

ISBN 978 085189 194 1

Cover artwork by:
Justin Allfree

Printed and bound in Malta by:
GUTENBERG PRESS LIMITED

PUBLISHER'S FOREWORD

FOR forty years, *Wrested Scriptures* has been for many brothers and sisters what its subtitle describes: "A Handbook of Suggested Explanations to Difficult Bible Passages". Though it distilled ideas from various sources, it still bore the stamp of its major author and editor, Brother Ron Abel. He explains in his Preface (page iv), how the work came into existence and his own commitment to preaching the gospel in season and out of season. Material was gathered, and arguments sharpened, as Brother Ron taught, preached, debated and argued—always with the intention of uncovering the true message of the scriptures and upholding God's truth. For him, therefore, it was a workbook that he converted into a handbook for others.

With the passing years, the teachings of some groups changed, and the prominence of some others waxed or waned. It was thus evident that some revisions were needed. As Brother Ron fell asleep at the relatively young age of 44 in 1983, he could not do what was required, but one who was involved with him while *Wrested Scriptures* was still being prepared agreed to undertake the task. Brother John Allfree reviewed the whole work, identifying where further material was required, and in other places where revisions were needed. All this was done meticulously while his own health failed, but it was fully completed when he too fell asleep in 2007.

So now for a new generation there is an expanded Handbook, to be used with the same object in mind: to reveal the truths in God's word that are often misunderstood or misrepresented by other religious groups. It is a tangible testimony to the faith of two Bible students, and we pray it will lead and support others who look for the "faith in Christ Jesus".

Michael Ashton

2011

AUTHOR'S PREFACE TO THE FIRST EDITION

PETER commenting on the epistles of Paul, said that there "are some things hard to be understood, which they that are unlearned and unstable wrest, as they do also the other scriptures, unto their own destruction."[1] Since Peter's time, there have been few Christadelphians who have not at some time or another found themselves tangled up in discussion about some principle of the Truth, and there are few who have not been, at some time or another, compelled to admit, to themselves, if not to others, that they have been lamentably ill-prepared for such responsibility. As one Christadelphian of long preaching experience put it:

> "It is not sufficient, as one finds to one's cost, to be able to quote: 'The dead know not anything'. It is quite another matter that one should cope convincingly with the thief on the cross; the spirits of just men made perfect; Paul's desire to depart and be with Christ, and his manifest preference to be absent from the body and present with the Lord.
>
> It is one thing to know and believe: 'Hear, O Israel, the Lord our God is one Lord'. But to reason cogently concerning Isaiah's Messianic prophecy about a Mighty God, or with Thomas' confession, or with the copious pre-existence passages in John's gospel, is a different proposition altogether.
>
> Nor is it sufficient to fence with the copious problems of orthodoxy defensively. One must be able to carry the campaign into the home territory of ignorance and error. The chief function of light is that it shall shine in darkness.
>
> It becomes, therefore, the responsibility of all Christadelphians, and not only of those who are speakers or campaigners, to acquaint themselves with the best available means of quenching all the fiery darts of the enemy.
>
> [It should also be noted, that]…nothing imparts more confidence in controversy than a well-grounded knowledge of what the passage in question really does mean."[2]

This study commenced shortly after baptism and passed from personal needs to those of the contacts and new converts in Guyana (then British Guiana) during 1960–1961. Later, in Toronto, a number of preliminary copies were mimeographed and distributed to brethren throughout the ecclesial world. Their critical comments were solicited.

One unforeseen result of the distribution was the widespread interest in the project. The Spanish team working out of Bogota, Colombia, translated the section on "The Trinity" and young people in the Toronto area made copious notes from the sections on passages wrested by Pentecostals and Evangelicals in preparation for

---

[1] 2 Peter 3:16.

[2] H. A. Whittaker, "Wrested Scriptures", *The Christadelphian*, Vol. 94, (April, 1957), p.143.

open-air speaking in Allan Gardens, Toronto. The audiences, often numbering in the hundreds during a Sunday afternoon, presented problem questions, many of which found their way into this handbook. The instruction of these friends on a one-night-a-week basis resulted in the handbook being enlarged from a consideration of wrested scriptures to preliminary points and suggested strategies in reaching those with beliefs moulded by a religious organization.

Shortly after preaching work was undertaken in Allan Gardens, the Manitoulin Island Ecclesia (in Canada's Northern Ontario Region) began 'spying out the land' in the local churches in search of good and honest hearts. The brethren attended public meetings and at the conclusion of the services attempted to persuade preacher and congregation of a more excellent way. Knowledge of wrested scriptures played an important part in this venture.

In the Great Lakes area, a full page advertisement in the Toronto papers (during the June 1967, Arab-Israeli War) resulted in many requests for the Bible Postal Course. A.S.K. (Advancement of Scriptural Knowledge) workshops were enlarged to process the correspondence. Many of the questions asked were the same as previous ones (e.g., "Thief on the cross", "Rich man and Lazarus"). If a standard answer were drafted, the few brethren working to answer questions could give more time to those questions requiring detailed research. Again the usefulness of a handbook on wrested scriptures became apparent.

It is the design of this handbook to provide a ready reference source of suggested explanations and strategies especially for young Christadelphians. The study is not, however, intended to encourage "potted thinking". The solutions outlined are suggested solutions. Christadelphians will no doubt want to modify and enlarge the list of passages considered. Many an undiscovered vein of Scriptural treasure awaits the investigation of these students.

It will be apparent, especially to older Christadelphians, that much of the analysis is not original. It is a synthesis in which explanations gleaned from reading or discussion have been used without acknowledgement except where reference is made to copyright material. It should not, however, be thought that the problems and solutions are the result of "armchair theology". For the most part, they are the result of real life situations—West Indian town hall question periods, university campus discussions, and open-air disputations.

Ron Abel

1970

REVISER'S PREFACE

IT was with great pleasure that I responded to the publisher's invitation to assist in the preparation of a new edition of *Wrested Scriptures*. Many happy memories are associated with this book and its author.

I first met Brother Ron in the summer of 1963. We were living in Newfoundland and had the pleasure of an extended visit from him to help in our preaching work. At the time *Wrested Scriptures* was in its formative state, and much of our time together was occupied by energetic discussion on 'difficult passages', often taking the form of me being a hapless JW or RC against whom Ron would attempt (inevitably with overwhelming success) to quench the fiery darts that I sent in his direction! I certainly benefited from the experience.

Our visit to the local Kingdom Hall,[1] which resulted in us sitting in the middle of the hall with the congregation standing around us whilst the overseer allowed himself to be subjected to the same fearless treatment, is etched deeply into my memory. As also is the occasion, a year later, when a group of us visited a Pentecostal Rally. It was a 'hair-raising' experience with a congregation of about a thousand being skilfully manipulated by the fiery purveyor of their 'gospel' who just could not accept that we did not want 'to be saved'. However, the rest of the congregation obliged and by the end of the meeting people were falling down in the aisles—'slain by the spirit' and 'speaking in tongues'. When one of the fifty or so ministers on the platform began to 'speak with tongues', Ron climbed onto the platform and asked those adjacent to their incoherent colleague why they were allowing him to speak with tongues when there was no interpreter present! (1 Cor. 14:28). Ron was forcibly escorted from the assembly hall in such a way as to convince us that in that assembly there would be no intreating "by the gentleness of Christ" of this one who was "bold toward [them]"! (2 Cor. 10:1).

The revision has been carried out with the intention of retaining the original character of the book. Nothing has been changed that accuracy or clarity did not demand. It is still, for the most part, *Wrested Scriptures* as written by Brother Ron Abel. The layout has been changed a little to make it more consistent and 'user friendly'. Here and there an alternative suggested answer to a problem has been offered alongside those offered by the author.

A number of additions have been made, notably an entire chapter on "Islam" made necessary by the subtle appeal to the Bible by the adherents of Islam, as they seek to promote the Muslim cause in a floundering 'Christendom'—something that Brother Ron would not have encountered in the 1960s. A short section has been

---

[1] The JWs were of particular interest to Brother Ron at this time since, in the *Watchtower*, [August 1st, 1962, p.473], they had published an article entitled, "Christadelphianism: Of God or of Men?" Brother Ron had published a reply to this which he endeavoured to distribute to as many members of the sect as possible.

included (really as an appendix to Roman Catholicism) on the "Orthodox Catholic Church" since this appears to be spreading in the West and our preaching is extending into countries in the East. Extra material has been added to "Roman Catholicism" in Section One, and to "The Deity and Pre-existence of Christ" in Section Two. Also in Section Two, in view of the increasing importance of the subject in overseas preaching, "Demons and Demon Possession" has been enlarged and given a chapter of its own. In adding to the chapter on "The Holy Spirit" material that has to do with the wresting of scripture in support of evangelical teaching, I was fortunate to have in my possession notes on the subject given to me by Brother Ron in 1980 which I believe has enabled me faithfully to present his mind on the relevant scriptures.

Like Brother Ron I own up to the fact that much of the 'new' material is not entirely original. It, too, is largely a synthesis of material garnered over the years from exposure to the problems, reading around them and discussions with others. However, I am grateful to acknowledge the help received from others—to Brethren David Nicholls who submitted material for the chapter on "Roman Catholicism", Andrew Walker who made suggestions in connection with the section on "Inspiration" and John Thorpe who was very generous in his help with the chapter on "Islam" (more details of this will be found at the beginning of that chapter). The CMPA has been very patient as the revision has slowly come to fruition but without the help of Maureen, my wife, the process would have been even more protracted! As well as casting her critical eye over my typed manuscript she has rechecked every Bible reference in the book for accuracy of quotation.

I hope that all that is offered by way of new material would have been approved by Brother Ron. However, where it has failed to reach his high standard I know that he would have been very generous in his assessment and criticism.

There has never been a greater need for a book such as *Wrested Scriptures*. The extension of overseas preaching, and the increasing use of the seminar approach to preaching, means that the increasing number of those in 'the front line' need to be prepared to answer effectively those who oppose the Truth, and to respond to the questions of those who seek it. There can be no substitute for familiarity with the Scriptures themselves, but *Wrested Scriptures* can help us present our response in a logical and forthright way—to the glory of the God we serve.

John Allfree

2004

HOW TO USE THIS HANDBOOK

1. An explanation to a 'wrested scripture' can be found in two ways:

   a) At the front of the handbook, the *Table of Contents* is divided into four sections. These are as follows:

   Section 1— passages which are wrested uniquely by a religious group. For example, "Thou art Peter, and upon this rock I will build my church" (Matt. 16:18) is used uniquely by the Roman Church.

   Section 2— passages used by many different religious groups. For example, "Verily I say unto thee, To day shalt thou be with me in paradise" (Luke 23:43).

   Section 3— passages which appear to conflict with current scientific thinking. For example, "The sun stood still, and the moon stayed" (Josh. 10:13).

   Section 4— passages which appear to be inaccurate or contradictory. For example, the differing inscriptions on the cross.

   b) At the back of this handbook is a list of all the passages considered with the corresponding page number.

2. Certain abbreviations are used. These are as follows:

   AV—   Authorized (King James) Version of the Bible

   cf.—   Compare

   e.g.—   For example

   ibid.—   Quoted from the same source as the previous footnote

   i.e.—   That is

   JW—   Jehovah's Witness

   m.—   Alternative translation given in the margin

   OCC—   Orthodox Catholic Church

   RC—   Roman Catholic

   RSV—   American Revised Standard Version of the Bible (1952)

   RV—   Revised Version of the Bible (1885)

   SDA—   Seventh-day Adventist

   v., vv.—   Verse, verses.

TABLE OF CONTENTS

SECTION ONE: Passages uniquely Wrested by Religious Bodies
1. ROMAN CATHOLICISM

1.5. JEHOVAH'S WITNESSES

1.6. HERBERT ARMSTRONG'S "BRITISH-ISRAELISM"

1.7. THE CHURCH OF CHRIST

1.8. ISLAM

SECTION TWO: Passages Wrested by Many Religious Bodies
2.1. THE IMMORTALITY OF THE SOUL

xiii

2.8. DEMONS AND DEMON POSSESSION

2.9. PRE-EXISTENCE AND DEITY OF CHRIST

3.3. RADIOMETRIC DATING METHODS

3.4. THE DAYS OF CREATION

SECTION FOUR: Biblical Inspiration
4.1. PARTIAL INSPIRATION

4.2. NON-PROPOSITIONAL REVELATION

4.3. ALLEGED CONTRADICTIONS AND INACCURACIES

Scripture Index

1.1

ROMAN CATHOLICISM

PRELIMINARY POINTS:

In a Roman Catholic publication bearing the imprimatur[1] of the Bishop of Fort Wayne, U.S.A., the priest says: "I'll show you why you can't appeal to the Bible against the Church...In fact, I'll show you why the Bible is an authority only as long as the authority of the Church is admitted...Reject that authority...and the authority of the Bible as the inspired word of God falls to the ground".[2]

Sooner or later in his discussion with a RC one must settle the fundamental question of "authority" (i.e. as to whether or not the papal claim of infallibility is a valid one). The following dialogue illustrates this point:

Question:	"Mr. Roman Catholic, how do you know that purgatory really exists?"
Roman Catholic:	"Because my Church teaches that it does."
Question:	"But how do you know that what your Church teaches is right?
Roman Catholic:	"Because my Church has the Pope who is infallible on matters like this."
Question:	"But how do you know that he is infallible? (The discussion often terminates here if the RC insists that this must be accepted on "faith"). The discussion may, however, continue...
Roman Catholic:	"Because Jesus gave this infallible authority to Peter and his successors, the bishops of Rome, as recorded in Matt. 16:18; Luke 22:32, and John 21:15–17."

SUGGESTED STRATEGY:

1. The crucial question of authority must be settled. If the RC is agreeable, passages traditionally used by his church (and considered in this handbook) might be examined. In stressing the necessity of individual interpretation of the written Word the following might be helpful:

   a. Show that Jesus Christ appealed to the reason of his hearers in stating his case from the Scriptures:

---

[1] "Imprimatur" is an official license to print granted by the Roman Catholic Church. The reason for its use here is to indicate that the quotation cited has been officially sanctioned by the Roman Catholic Church.

[2] John A. Obrien, *What's the Truth About Catholics? An Exposition of Catholic Belief and Practice*, (Indiana: Our Sunday Visitor Press, 1950) p.90

       i. "Have ye not read …" (Matt. 19:4).

      ii. "If they hear not Moses and the prophets …" (Luke 16:31).

     iii. "Is it not written in your law …" (John 10:34).

b. The Apostle Paul likewise appealed to his readers' individual judgment of the Word:

       i. "These [Jews at Berea] were more noble than those in Thessalonica, in that they received the word with all readiness of mind, and searched the scriptures daily, whether those things were so." (Acts 17:11). This passage reveals God's attitude toward those who examine the Scriptures.

      ii. "I speak as to wise men; judge ye what I say." (1 Cor. 10:15).

     iii. "Prove all things; hold fast that which is good." (1 Thess. 5:21).

     iv. "…the holy scriptures, which are able to make thee wise unto salvation through faith which is in Christ Jesus. All scripture is given by inspiration of God, and is profitable for doctrine, for reproof, for correction, for instruction in righteousness: that the man of God may be *perfect* [complete], *throughly* furnished unto all good works." (2 Tim. 3:15–17).

[But be aware that the RC may well counter this approach by arguing that in addition to Scripture the apostles also appealed to "Tradition"—see page 5.]

2. It is sometimes helpful to show that support for the Roman position on Papal infallibility often rests on a *petitio principii* fallacy.[3]

a. The RC says: "I am absolutely certain that I am right in my religious views because I believe what the Pope says, and he is absolutely certain not to say what is wrong." But how can one be absolutely certain not to believe what is wrong? It is not possible to answer this question without arguing in a circle, i.e., stating one's own infallibility.

b. The RC may also say: "The Church is infallible because the Scriptures testify that this is so and the Scriptures testify this because the Church infallibly declares that such is their meaning." It is sometimes argued another way by the RC: "The Pope always speaks infallibly except when he makes a mistake. When he makes a mistake he is not speaking 'ex cathedra'." Both these arguments by a RC are tautological.

3. RC apologists[4] make appeals to the size and duration of the Roman Church as proof of its divine founding and guidance through the authority invested in the bishops. It is relevant to show that there is no necessary connection between size and duration of a religious organization and the truth of its claims. Jesus said, "Enter ye in at the strait gate: for wide is the gate, and broad is the way, that leadeth to destruction, and many there be which go in thereat: Because strait is the gate, and narrow is the way, which leadeth unto life, and few there be that find it." (Matt. 7:13,14). Judaism and Buddhism are both older than Roman Catholicism but this does not necessarily mean that their religious claims are true.

[3] A "petitio principii" is the logical fallacy of arguing in a circle and "begging the question".

[4] "Apologists", as used here, does not refer to Roman Catholics who regretfully acknowledge but rather to those who defend by argument.

2

4. Roman Catholic literature often points to the divisions within Protestantism (or even within the Christadelphian body) as proof of the inadequacy of the exercise of private judgment on religious questions. The Roman faith is presented by contrast as a haven of rest where uniformity of practice and loyalty of allegiance prevail. But this claim is inaccurate. Consider the following examples:

    a. During the Great Schism of the West (AD 1378–1417) there were three rival Popes, each claiming to be the real Pope, and each excommunicating the others.[5]

    b. Until recently the Uniat Church in Galicia was an integral part of the Roman Communion yet followed Eastern Orthodox rites and had a married priesthood.[6]

    c. The unity of the Roman Church is only superficially impressive. Conformity has often been achieved by scandalously unscriptural means.[7]

    d. The predictions of the coming apostasy within the early ecclesias (Acts 20:29,30; 2 Peter 2:1,2; 1 Tim. 4:1–3) conflict with the Romanist claim of "unity" and a "haven of rest". By the time John wrote his first epistle it was necessary for the believer to "try the spirits whether they are of God: because many false prophets are gone out into the world". (1 John 4:1).

5   Very devout RCs may be reticent to speak about their beliefs (especially in countries where illiteracy is high) through fear of excommunication. Heresy is considered a mortal sin for which the punishment is excommunication and relegation to the fires of hell for eternity. The bulls *In Caena Comini* or the annual cursings were renewed by the bull *Apostolicae Sedis* 1868. In this bull all who deny the Pope's universal authority and all who harbour the least doubt on any point which has been decreed by a Pope, are *ipso facto* excommunicated. This explains, in part, the difficulty in reaching some Roman Catholics. They fear to incur the mortal sin of heresy and consequent excommunication, if they listen, or if they entertain the slightest question as to any one of the decrees of the Pope.

---

[5] See, for example, William Shaw Kerr, *A Handbook on the Papacy*, (London: Marshall, Morgan and Scott, 1962), ch. 51.

[6] Alexander Stewart, *Roman Dogma and Scripture Truth*, (London: The Inter-Varsity fellowship, 1951), p.17.

[7] The Council of Ephesus is an example. Bethune Baker, in *Early History of Church Doctrine*, writes: "Dioscorus was attended by a strong body of Egyptians, bishops and monks, who all behaved with scandalous violence. The signatures of many other bishops were extorted by threats and physical force; it seems certain from the evidence, even when allowance is made for some exaggeration, that the result was only reached by insolent intimidation which proceeded to personal violence." p.284.

THE ALLEGED INSUFFICIENCY OF SCRIPTURE

2 Timothy 2:2

"The things that thou hast heard of me among many witnesses, the same commit thou to faithful men, who shall be able to teach others also."

1 Thessalonians 4:2

"For ye know what commandments we gave you by the Lord Jesus."

PROBLEM:

The RC Church teaches that the Bible does not contain all the information necessary for salvation and that "Tradition" is to be regarded as being on an equal footing with Scripture. "Sacred Tradition and Sacred Scripture make up a single sacred deposit of the Word of God, entrusted to the Church."[8] By "Tradition" the RC Church means "the writings of learned saints of all centuries from the time of the apostles…[and] the decrees of General Councils…the Tradition which we believe contains the word of God, is Divine Tradition, not human. Divine Tradition is the divinely revealed truth taught orally by Christ and His Apostles which is not found in the Bible, though recorded for all time by churchmen in the early age of the Church."[9] The above Scriptures are used to argue that Paul gave the early church oral teaching in addition to writing his letters. This shows that Scripture alone does not contain all that is needed for salvation.

SOLUTION:

1   The RC position is based on an unsustainable assumption that the oral teaching of the apostle contained saving truth that was additional to that contained in the completed Scriptures.

2   If "Tradition" is essential then it follows that the word of God given to us in the Scriptures is not sufficient to instruct men and women regarding God's salvation. This contradicts the teaching of Christ's apostles:

   a   "From a child thou hast known the holy scriptures, which are able to make thee wise unto salvation through faith which is in Christ Jesus." (2 Tim. 3:15). Thus the Scriptures are able to make wise unto salvation through faith (the word means simply "belief") in its message.

   b. This "faith" that leads to salvation, is a response to the word of God—"So then faith cometh by hearing, and hearing by the word of God." (Rom. 10:17). The RC will often point out that in past ages men could not read and did not possess a Bible, therefore they could not read Scripture and hence salvation does not come by reading Scripture. However, Scripture is

---

[8] *Dei Verbum*, art. 10; quoted in Michael Sheehan (Revised P. M. Joseph), *Apologetics and Catholic Doctrine*, (London: The Saint Austin Press, 2001), p.251.

[9] Most Rev. John Francis Noll & Rev. Lester J. Fallon, *Father Smith Instructs Jackson*, (USA: Nihil Obstat: Rev. Edward A. Miller, 1963), p.58.

WRESTED SCRIPTURES

$5

376

Clapham Public Hall, Meeting-place for the
South London Ecclesia in 1913

powerful to save whether read, or heard from those who "preach" the message.

c. "For I am not ashamed of the gospel of Christ: for it is the power of God unto salvation to every one that believeth; to the Jew first, and also to the Greek." (Rom. 1:16).

d. "Wherefore lay apart all filthiness and superfluity of naughtiness, and receive with meekness the engrafted word, which is able to save your souls." (James 1:21).

e. "For Christ sent me not to baptize, but to preach the gospel: not with wisdom of words, lest the cross of Christ should be made of none effect. For the preaching of the cross is to them that perish foolishness; but unto us which are saved it is the power of God." (1 Cor. 1:17,18).

2 Thessalonians 2:15

"Therefore, brethren, stand fast, and hold the traditions which ye have been taught, whether by word, or our epistle."

2 Thessalonians 3:6

"Now we command you, brethren, in the name of our Lord Jesus Christ, that ye withdraw yourselves from every brother that walketh disorderly, and not after the tradition which he received of us."

PROBLEM:

The RC will maintain that these Scriptures show conclusively that the apostle appealed to "Tradition" as well as Scripture in his teaching and therefore it is incumbent on the Church to do the same.

SOLUTION:

1. The word translated "tradition" in the above references refers simply to apostolic teaching whether preached on the occasion of his visit to Thessalonica or written in the epistle. 2 Thess. 2:15 is preceded by the reminder that they had been "called…by our gospel, to the obtaining of the glory of our Lord Jesus Christ. Therefore…stand fast and hold the traditions which ye have been taught…" There is nothing to suggest that "the traditions" (the Greek word means literally 'a handing down') refer to anything other than the content of apostolic preaching and writing.

2. It is worth noting the opinion of the Lord Jesus and the apostles with respect to those who added "tradition" to God's word:

   a. "Then came to Jesus scribes and Pharisees, which were of Jerusalem, saying, Why do thy disciples transgress the tradition of the elders? for they wash not their hands when they eat bread. But he answered and said unto them, Why do ye also transgress the commandment of God by your tradition? …Ye hypocrites, well did Esaias prophesy of you, saying, This people draweth nigh unto me with their mouth, and honoureth me with their lips; but their heart is far from me. But in vain they do worship me, teaching for doctrines the commandments of men." (Matt. 15:1–3, 7–9).

b. "Beware lest any man spoil you through philosophy and vain deceit, after the tradition of men, after the rudiments of the world, and not after Christ." (Col. 2:8).

c. "Forasmuch as ye know that ye were not redeemed with corruptible things, as silver and gold, from your vain conversation [way of life] received by tradition from your fathers; but with the precious blood of Christ, as of a lamb without blemish and without spot." (1 Pet. 1:18,19).

3. The appeal to "tradition" by the RC Church places them in the same position as the Pharisees whom Jesus accused of "making the word of God of none effect through your tradition" (Mark 7:13). E.g. "Tradition" teaches the doctrine of the trinity, which contradicts the Bible teaching about God. "Tradition" is responsible for incorporating the pagan teaching of the immortality of the soul into the beliefs of the church. "Tradition" alone is responsible for the strange and unscriptural teaching of transubstantiation. The RC teaching about the immaculate conception of Mary, her assumption into heaven and her work as Mediatrix are some of the grosser consequences of accepting human "Tradition".

THE PETRINE THEORY AND PAPAL INFALLIBILITY

Matthew 16:18

"Thou art Peter and upon this rock I will build my church."

PROBLEM:

The Roman Catholic interpretation of this is:

1. "Christ appointed the Apostle Peter to be the first of all the apostles and to be the visible Head of the whole Church, by appointing him immediately and personally to the primacy of jurisdiction.[10] According to Christ's ordinance, Peter is to have successors in his primacy, over the whole Church and for all time. The successors of Peter in the Primacy are the Bishops of Rome."[11]

2. "If anyone says that the blessed Apostle Peter was not constituted, by Christ our Lord, Prince of all the Apostles and visible Head of all the Church Militant [i.e., Church on earth]; or that he [Peter] directly and immediately received from our Lord Jesus Christ a primacy of honour only and not one of true and proper jurisdiction, let him be anathema."[12]

---

[10] "Primacy of jurisdiction" means that Peter received from Christ supreme authority to teach and to govern the whole church.

[11] DeFide, quoted in Ludwig Ott. *Fundamentals of Catholic Dogma*, ed. in English by James Canon Bastible, and tr. from the German by Patrick Lynch, (St. Louis, Mo.: Herder, 1954); Nihil Obstat and Imprimatur, (Oct. 7, 1954), pp.279-282.

[12] Vatican Council of 1870: Denzinger, par. 1823.

3. In summary then, the Roman Catholic position may be stated: Christ gave absolute spiritual authority in the Church to Peter. Peter passed this spiritual authority on to his successors—the Bishops of Rome. Therefore the Pope in any age has the right to spiritual authority over Christendom.

SOLUTION:

1. The rock on which the Church is founded is not Peter, but Peter's confession, "thou art the Christ". (Matt. 16:16) The following is the evidence:

   a. Matt. 21:42; Acts 4:11; 1 Cor. 10:4; Eph. 2:20; 1 Pet. 2:6–8 unambiguously state that Christ is the Rock. Paul explicitly states, "For other foundation can no man lay than that is laid, which is Jesus Christ". (1 Cor. 3:11). To take Peter as the foundation flatly contradicts this passage.

   b. The Roman Church emphasizes John 1:42 in stating that Jesus gave the name "Rock" (*Petros*) to Simon at the very start. But in Matt. 16:18 the Greek is: "Thou art *petros*, and upon this *petra* I will build my Church." Two different Greek words are employed with two different connotations:

   i. *petros* (masc.), detached stone.

   ii. *petra* (fem.), living rock, solid rock.[13]

   It is clear that a difference between Peter and the foundation is meant or the word "petros" would simply have been repeated. "Petros", therefore, shows Peter's instability, (e.g., Matt. 16:22,23) while "petra" indicates the immovable rock-like character of Christ, or the confession of Peter, "thou art the Christ".[14]

2. The power of the keys[15] given to Peter (Matt. 16:19) gave him no *unique* authority—no authority which the other apostles did not possess as well—Matt. 18:18 (cf. v. 1); John 20:22,23.

   a. "Keys"—keys to knowledge of the Kingdom (Luke 11:52; cf. Matt. 23:13). The keys were used by Peter in preaching to the Jews on the day of Pentecost

---

[13] Liddell, (authoritative lexicographer of classical Greek), *Intermediate Lexicon*, founded upon the 7th ed. of Liddell and Scott. Also, G. Abbott-Smith, (Professor Hellenistic Greek, McGill University), *Manual Greek Lexicon of the New Testament*, 3rd ed., and *Bullinger, Figures of Speech.*

[14] Some Roman Catholics may argue that the difference in Greek words is only for stylistic variation. But the burden of proof does not rest on the interpreter who says that two different words have at least connotative distinctions of meaning; it rests on the one who argues that the difference is of no consequence and that style explains all. Some argue that the use of two words in the Greek is of no consequence, for the original dialogue between Jesus and Peter took place in Aramaic, and undoubtedly but a single word (Kepha, "Cephas") was used in the Aramaic conversation. The fallacy in this argument (as in virtually all arguments based on proto-Aramaic New Testament conversations) is that it involves a reasoning from the unknown to the known rather than from the known to the unknown. The only means we have of knowing what in fact Jesus said to Peter on the given occasion is via the Greek record. Thus, if a valid distinction is made in the Greek, we must assume that a like distinction was made in the original conversation.

[15] Roman Pontiffs claim the custody of "Peter's Keys" i.e., the supernatural capability of opening the doors of life and death. It is inherent in the power claimed by the Bishop of Rome that he has "jus vertendi cardinus" - the power of "turning the hinge" of the doors of heaven and hades. The Pope is assisted by the Grand Council of State, or College of Cardinals. The name "Cardinal" is derived from "cardo", a hinge. Papal Cardinals are therefore, "priests of the hinge".

(Acts 2); to the household of Cornelius (Acts 14:27, cf. Acts 10); and to the Gentiles (Acts 11:18).

b. "binding"—e.g., Ananias and Sapphira—Acts 5. Here Peter's condemnation uttered on earth was immediately enforced in heaven.

c. "loosing"—e.g., palsied Aeneas loosed at Lydda. (Acts 9:32–35). Peter said, "Jesus Christ maketh thee whole", verse 34; Jesus in heaven "loosed" the paralytic. See also Acts 5:12–16.

d. "gates of hell"—the grave of Isaiah 38:10,17,18. Christ's Ecclesia will prevail against "hades"—(1 Cor. 15:53–55).

3. Peter did not receive infallible authority from Jesus, even in matters *ex cathedra*, for Paul wrote: "But when Peter was come to Antioch, I withstood him to the face, because he was to be blamed." (Gal. 2:11). Note how Christ also reproved Peter in Matt. 16:22,23.

4. There is not a particle of historical evidence that Peter passed on any authority to anyone; and, what is more important, there is *no New Testament evidence at all that Christ commanded Peter to pass on any authority*. Without such a clear command of Christ, the "successors" of Peter must be regarded as having arrogated authority to themselves, rather than having received it from Christ.

Some Additional Points:

5. The overwhelming majority of Popes, since the 15th century, have been Italian.[16] Why must the "vicar of Christ" generally be an Italian Pope? Is it not a claim of the Roman Church to be universal?

6. The Roman Church stresses the position of Peter but note the influence of Paul:

a. Paul went to Rome (Acts 28:14–31), but there is no certain Scriptural evidence of Peter having gone there.

b. Paul wrote to the ecclesia at Rome (Rom. 1:1,7), but Peter did not.

c. Paul had important jurisdiction and authority. For example:

i. 1 Cor. 7:17— "… as the Lord hath called everyone, so let him walk. And so ordain I in all churches." See also 1 Cor. 14:37,38.

ii. 2 Cor. 11:28— "… that which cometh upon me daily, the care of all the churches."

iii. 2 Cor. 13:10— "… according to the power ["my use of the authority"—RSV] which the Lord hath given me."

iv. Gal. 2:11— "But when Peter was come to Antioch, I withstood him to the face, because he was to be blamed."

7. Peter's primary responsibility was to the Jews (Gal. 2:9). The principle reason why Peter was involved in the taking of the Gospel to the first Gentile converts as recorded in Acts 10, was to pave the way for the work of the Apostle Paul and the acceptance of Gentiles into what was essentially a Jewish Church (Acts 10:45–47; 11:12–18). As a result Peter, who spoke with authority in the Jewish ecclesias, was later able to add his voice to that of James to support the work of Paul and convince the Jewish brethren that it was indeed God's will to "take out

[16] See William Shaw Kerr, *A Handbook of the Papacy*, (London: Marshall, Morgan and Scott, 1962), p.8.

of the Gentiles a people for his name". (Acts 15:7–14).

8. If the Roman Church is the custodian and preserver of absolute truth, why did it take nearly 1900 years, until this was officially declared in 1870?

9. Matt. 18:1; Mark 9:34; Luke 22:24 all record a dispute among the disciples as to who should be the greatest. This dispute is important for two reasons:

   a. It is apparent that if, in the prior events of Matthew 16, Peter had been given the kind of authority asserted by Roman Catholics then it is very unlikely that a dispute as to who was to be accounted the greatest would have arisen.

   b. Jesus' reply, in Luke 22:25–30, does not mention the primacy of Peter, and further suggests that there would be no distinction among the apostles, when they would "sit on thrones judging the twelve tribes of Israel". (v. 30).

10. A similar argument can be advanced, on the request of the mother of James and John, for the two highest positions in the kingdom. (Matt. 20:20–23). Would they be ignorant of Peter's appointment to the supreme place if this was in fact the case?

11. Peter never indicates any personal superiority in his epistles. He refers to himself as "an apostle" (1 Pet. 1:1), "an elder" ("a fellow elder", 1 Pet. 5:1 RSV), and instructs the elders not to be "lords over God's heritage," but to be "ensamples to the flock." (1 Pet. 5:3).

12. In the creed of Pope Pius IV (which is obligatory on all ecclesiastics and on all "who promise and swear that they will continue in obedience to Rome"), it is professed concerning Holy Scripture, "nor will I ever understand or interpret it, except according to the unanimous consent of the holy Fathers." Archbishop Kenrick, in his speech prepared for, but not delivered in the Vatican Council, but published at Naples in 1870, counts the following five different patristic interpretations of Matthew 16:18:

   a. "That St. Peter is the Rock, taught by seventeen Fathers;

   b. That the whole Apostolic College is the Rock, represented by Peter as its chief, taught by eight;

   c. That St. Peter's faith is the Rock, taught by forty-four;

   d. That Christ is the Rock, taught by sixteen;

   e. That the Rock is the whole body of the faithful."

   Several who teach a) and b), also teach c) and d), and so the Archbishop sums up thus: "If we are bound to follow the greater number of Fathers in this matter, then we must hold for certain that the word Petra means not Peter professing the Faith, but the faith professed by Peter."[17]

Luke 10:16

"He that heareth you heareth me; and he that despiseth you despiseth me; and he that despiseth me despiseth him that sent me."

---

[17] Friedrich, Docum ad illust. Conc. Vat. 1, pp.185-246. For a fuller elaboration of this point, see John Carter, *Parables of the Messiah*, (Birmingham: *The Christadelphian*, 1954), pp.118-123, and William Shaw Kerr, *A Handbook of the Papacy*, (London: Marshall, Morgan and Scott, 1962), pp.44-49.

WRESTED SCRIPTURES

PROBLEM:

This passage is interpreted by Roman Catholic expositors to support their position on papal infallibility. It is argued that the authority of Jesus Christ is guaranteed in this passage to the legitimate successors, i.e. the Bishops of Rome.

SOLUTION:

1. The above words are directed specifically to the seventy (vv. 1,17), not to a single supreme head and his "legitimate successors."
2. This passage has no application to the Roman Church since those to whom the words, "he that heareth you heareth me" were given, were instructed to:
   a. "Carry neither purse, nor scrip, nor shoes..." (v. 4). Is this the way RC emissaries are sent forth?
   b. "Heal the sick that are therein." (v. 9). Do the proselytizers of the Roman Church heal the sick in the cities they visit?
   c. Be "as lambs among wolves." (v. 3). Can it be said of the Roman Church that its Popes have been "lambs among wolves"? The facts of history as recorded by both RC and non-RC historians amount to a thorough refutation of the claim of the Roman Church to these words of the Lord.[18]
3. Even if this passage were intended to give unique authority to specially chosen successors, the Roman Church has no claim to this authority, since she has spoken contradictorily about the same things. Two examples illustrate the point.
   a. Eugene IV (1431–1447) condemned Joan of Arc to be burned alive as a witch, while another pope, Benedict XV, in 1920, declared her to be a saint.
   b. Sixtus V (1585–1590) recommended the reading of the Bible but Pius VII (1800–1823) condemned the practice.

Luke 22:32

"But I have prayed for thee, that thy faith fail not: and when thou art converted, strengthen thy brethren."

---

[18] The incompatibility of this statement of the Lord with the official practice of the Roman Church is borne out in the following quotation: "Those are not to be accounted murderers or homicides who, when burning with love and zeal for their catholic mother against excommunicated persons, shall happen to kill a few of them." This was the decree of Pope Urban II in AD 1088 and is embodied in the canon law of Rome, as Clause xxii quest. v., ch. 47, Excommunicamus from which the quotation is taken. When the canon law was revised by a commission of cardinals, under Pope Gregory XIII in 1580, this decree was left in, and was made an article of faith.

[19] "See" as it is used here, refers to that which is committed to a Bishop. The "Holy See", for example, refers to the Pope's court in Rome.

PROBLEM:

This is another passage considered by the RC to support the doctrine of papal infallibility. To put it in RC terminology: "Knowing most fully that the See[19] of Holy Peter remains ever free from all blemish of error according to the divine promise of the Lord our Saviour made to the prince of His disciples. I have prayed for thee that thy faith fail not, and when thou art converted confirm thy brethren."[20]

SOLUTION:

1. The New Testament word *sterizo*, translated in the AV "establish" or "strengthen", implies no unique authority for Peter since the word is used of other believers.
   a. Paul longed to go to Rome to "establish" (*sterizo*) the brethren. (Rom. 1:11).
   b. Paul sent Timothy to "establish" (*sterizo*) the faith of the Thessalonians. (1 Thess. 3:2).
   c. The angel (messenger) of the ecclesia at Sardis is commanded to "be watchful, and strengthen (*sterizo*) the things which remain, that are ready to die…" (Rev. 3:2).
2. The early history of the Ecclesia fails to vindicate the Romanist interpretation of this verse. No such primacy for Peter is recorded in Scripture. For example:
   a. Although Peter dominates the first chapters of Acts of the Apostles (at Pentecost and the opening of the door to the Gentile convert—Cornelius) he is *sent* with John *by the apostles* at Jerusalem to go to Samaria. (Acts 8:14).
   b. At the Jerusalem Council James, not Peter, presides and formulates the terms of the decision (Acts 15:13,19). This is noteworthy since Peter was sent specifically to those of the circumcision (Gal. 2:7). The decree indicates an astounding oversight of Peter's office if he were the "Pastor" and "Ruler" of the Ecclesia.
3. To see in these words of Luke 22:32 a guarantee that Peter was to be divinely protected from error is as foundationless as seeing in them a similar guarantee for the prelates[21] of the Roman See. It is probable that "faith", as used in the Lord's remark, "I have prayed for thee, that thy faith fail not", applies to Peter's trust in his Master and his faithfulness to his teaching. Subsequently Peter denied his Lord three times. (Luke 22:55–62).

John 21:16

"…Feed my sheep."

PROBLEM:

The Roman Church finds in this passage support for its papal doctrine of infallibility for Peter and his "legitimate successors", the bishops of Rome. The Vatican Decrees assert: "It was upon Simon alone that Jesus after His resurrection,

---

[20] Quoted in William Shaw Kerr, *A Handbook of the Papacy*, (London: Marshall, Morgan and Scott, 1962), p.50.
[21] A prelate is a high ecclesiastical dignitary, e.g. a bishop.

bestowed the jurisdiction of Chief Pastor over His fold in the words: 'Feed my lambs; feed my sheep'." [22, 23] The exalted status given to Peter by the RC Church should be noted. "Christ had spoken of himself as the Good Shepherd, the 'lambs and the sheep' being the Apostles and all who believed on him. But now he makes St. Peter the Good Shepherd in his stead. All, including the Apostles, are to listen to his teaching and obey his commands. This Primacy, like the Church herself, must last until the end of time, and must, therefore, be passed on to the successors of Peter."[24] On the basis of RC interpretation of this Scripture the Pope has replaced Jesus as the Good Shepherd!

SOLUTION:

1. This passage contains no such monopoly conferred upon Peter as decreed by the Vatican. Feeding the sheep is enjoined upon others as well as Peter:
   a. Paul instructed the elders at Ephesus, "Feed (*poimaino*) the church of God" (Acts 20:28).
   b. Peter exhorts the elders, "The elders which are among you I exhort, who am also an elder[25] ...feed (*poimaino*) the flock of God...neither as being lords over God's heritage, but being ensamples to the flock." (1 Pet. 5:1–3). Peter considers himself a "fellow elder" RSV, *not* the "Pastor" and "Ruler" of the ecclesia.
2. The word "feed" (*poimaino*) relied upon by RCs to establish unique authority for Peter is used by Peter of the elders to whom he writes. (1 Pet. 5:2). Why interpret it in John 21:16 as imparting exclusive sovereignty of jurisdiction and not in the other?
3. "Feed my sheep" gave Peter no superior jurisdiction over the rest of the apostles. It would appear that Jesus in this passage reconfirms Peter after his threefold denial (Matt. 26:33,34), hence Peter's threefold confession in this passage. The interpretation of his role as a *"fellow elder"* is in keeping with other New Testament references which give him a place of reward alongside the other apostles but not a position of superiority. For example:

---

[22] Quoted in William Shaw Kerr, *A Handbook on the Papacy*, (London: Marshall, Morgan and Scott, 1962), p.52.

[23] Note the circular reasoning involved in this interpretation of the words of Jesus. " 'Feed my lambs' said Christ to St. Peter, 'Feed my sheep'...If the Pope were to err in his ex-cathedra teaching, he would not be the pastor, but the poisoner, of his flock. Therefore, he must possess infallibility on these solemn occasions." (M. Sheehan, revised by P. Joseph, *Apologetics and Catholic Doctrine*, London: The Saint Austin Press, 2001), p.195. The infallibility of the Pope is assumed and then this scripture is used to prove his infallibility! However, by showing, on the basis of Scripture, that the Papacy has indeed been guilty of poisoning the flock by giving them wrong teaching then, from their own logic, it follows that he cannot be the divinely appointed pastor they claim him to be.

[24] M. Sheehan, *Apologetics and Catholic Doctrine*, (London: The Saint Austin Press, 2001), p.189.

[25] Roman Catholic writers dismiss this as merely an indication of Peter's humility. If Peter were commissioned to be Christ's vicar then it was his duty to make this known. If he had been appointed "Ruler" and "Teacher" why should he disguise what has been stridently proclaimed by his alleged "successors" as an essential part of God's plan for the salvation of the world?

a. In Matt. 19:27,28, Peter questions the Lord, "Behold, we have forsaken all, and followed thee; what shall we have therefore?" The Lord's answer contained no hint of any unique place reserved for Peter—nothing beyond what all the disciples were given. "Ye (plural) which have followed me, in the regeneration when the Son of man shall sit in the throne of his glory, ye also shall sit upon twelve thrones, judging the twelve tribes of Israel."

b. "The wall of the city had twelve foundations, and in them the names of the twelve apostles of the Lamb." (Rev. 21:14). Peter is a foundation-stone alongside the other apostles; he is not considered to be the cornerstone or even the chief foundation stone.

4. The role of Peter in the early ecclesia is one of prominence but not of monopoly:

a. Although Peter proposes that one be appointed to fill the place of Judas (Acts 1:15), he does not attempt to fill the vacant place on his own authority (as do the Popes of the Roman Church in appointing cardinals). After the exercise of the corporate mind of those gathered in the upper room, in choosing two possible candidates, the final selection was made by lot (vv. 22–26).

b. Peter expresses concern in his Epistle for the continuance of the purity of the gospel (2 Pet. 2:1,2), yet he never once exhorts the flock of a "legitimate successor" whom they were to follow when he passed away. (It seems Peter was nearing his death when he wrote this Epistle, see 2 Pet. 1:13–15. This would have been a most appropriate place for him to refer to his successor).

c. In Acts 6:2 it was the Twelve who called the multitude together and appointed the seven to administer the welfare needs. Peter is not singled out as having a monopolising voice in what was to be done.

d. Paul warned the Ephesian elders of heresies and disunity (Acts 20:29,30), but he omits to tell them to cling to Peter, the supreme "Pastor" and infallible "guide of the whole church militant."

5. The words of Scripture are clear with respect to the teaching that Peter and his successors have replaced Jesus as the Good Shepherd. Jesus was the Good Shepherd (John 10:14). He continued to be the Good Shepherd after his resurrection and ascension for, with clear reference to Isaiah 53, the apostle says of the believers, "Ye...are now returned unto the Shepherd and Bishop of your souls" (1 Pet. 2:25). He will still be the Good Shepherd at the time of his return, for, "When the chief Shepherd shall appear, ye shall receive a crown of glory that fadeth not away" (1 Pet. 5:4). There is not one shred of Scripture testimony to support the idea that Peter and the popes took over this work from Jesus. In connection with the Lord's future shepherding work see, for example, Ezek. 34:23; Isa. 40:10,11.

TRANSUBSTANTIATION

Matthew 26:26,28

"Jesus took bread, and blessed it, and brake it, and gave it to the disciples, and said, Take, eat; this is my body. And he took the cup, and gave thanks, and gave it to them, saying...this is my blood..."

1 Corinthians 10:16

"The cup of blessing which we bless, is it not the communion of the blood of Christ? The bread which we break, is it not the communion of the body of Christ?"

1 Corinthians 11:27

"Wherefore whosoever shall eat this bread, and drink this cup of the Lord, unworthily, shall be guilty of the body and blood of the Lord."

PROBLEM:

Roman Catholics understand these passages to teach that when the appropriate words are uttered by the priest, the wafer and the wine are changed into the real body and blood of Christ. This is the doctrine of transubstantiation.[26]

SOLUTION:

1. At the time these words were uttered Jesus was there present with the disciples; he had not yet died.

2. There is an abundance of passages, similar to this one, where the verb "to be" is used, for "to mean, to symbolize". For example:

   a. "I am the door." (John 10:7).

   b. "I am the true vine." (John 15:1).

   c. "That Rock was Christ." (1 Cor. 10:4).

   d. "The seven heads are seven mountains." (Rev. 17:9).

3. If the Romanist insists that "This is my blood" means literally that the wine is transformed into Christ's very blood, then "this cup is the new testament" (covenant) must mean that the literal cup becomes a literal covenant (1 Cor. 11:25).

---

[26] "Transubstantiation" means, "change of substance". See footnote 32, with reference to the meaning of "substance". The RC Church has its own unique understanding as to what constitutes "the substance" of the wafer and wine.

[27] This applies to the wine too. "As Body and Blood were united...in the living Christ, under the species of bread was the entire living Christ, true God and true man, and so too with the wine. At the last supper, as at Mass, the bread became the Body of Christ, and co-present were His Blood, soul and Divinity. The wine became the Blood of Christ, and co-present were His Body, soul and Divinity." (M. Sheehan, *Apologetics and Catholic Doctrine*, London: The Saint Austin Press, 2001, p.499).

4. The Lord's Supper is a commemoration of a sacrifice, not a repetition of it. Jesus said, "This do in remembrance of me" (Luke 22:19; 1 Cor. 11:24).

5. When it is realized that the doctrine of transubstantiation means that the wafer is changed into the whole Being of Christ,[27] which is then offered as a propitiatory sacrifice, it is important to point out that Christ has been offered "once for all" (Heb. 9:12 RV; 10:10; cf. 7:27). The sacrifice needs no repetition.

John 6:53

"Except ye eat the flesh of the Son of man, and drink his blood, ye have no life in you."

PROBLEM:

The Roman Church uses this passage to support the declaration of the Council of Trent that "by the consecration of the bread and wine, a conversion is made of the whole substance of the bread into the substance[28] of Christ our Lord, and of the whole substance of the wine into the whole substance of His blood;[29] which conversion is, by the holy Catholic Church, suitably and properly called Transubstantiation."[30]

SOLUTION:

1. The RC interpretation of this passage involves the impossible—to believe that the whole substance of his body and blood can be in every particle of the "consecrated" bread and wine on thousands of altars, while his literal body is in heaven at the *same time.*

2. The RCs (as did the Jews) misunderstand the teaching of Jesus in this passage. The question of the Jews was: "How can this man give us his flesh to eat?" (v. 52). Jesus did not reply by telling them that there would be a transubstantiation, i.e., that the literal bread would become his literal flesh throughout the ages; or that the literal wine (of which, however, the common people were not to partake) should similarly become his literal blood in quantities enough for thousands of mortals. Jesus suggested the explanation to his "hard saying" when he questioned: "What and if ye shall see the Son of man ascend up where he was before? It is the spirit that quickeneth; the *flesh* profiteth nothing: the *words* that I speak unto you, they are spirit, and they are life." (vv. 62,63).

3. Even if one could eat the literal flesh of Jesus and drink his literal blood, he would be no nearer the kingdom, unless he masticated[31] and assimilated the words which Christ spoke. Judas ate the passover but he was still a "son of perdition". (John 17:12). One can eat damnation to himself if he does not discern the Lord's body. (1 Cor. 11:29).

---

[28] See footnote 26.

[29] Not just his blood. See footnote 27.

[30] Session XIII, *On the Eucharist*, ch. 4. Waterworth's translation.

[31] The Greek word *trogo*, (John 6:57)—"So he that eateth me, even he shall live by me," means to gnaw, chew, devour"—Robert Young, *Analytical Concordance To the Holy Bible*, (London: Lutterworth Press, 1965).

4. The words, "except ye eat the flesh of the Son of Man and drink his blood ye have no life in you" are metaphorical for the words which Jesus Christ spoke. Consider the following:

   a. "The *words* that I speak unto you, they are spirit, and they are life." (John 6:63).

   b. Notice the relevance of Peter's comment, "To whom shall we go? thou hast the *words* of eternal life." (John 6:68).

   c. "Now are ye clean through the *word* which I have spoken unto you." (John 15:3).

   d. "This is life eternal, that they might *know* thee the only true God, and Jesus Christ whom thou hast sent." (John 17:3).

   e. "Sanctify them through thy truth: thy *word* is truth." (John 17:17).

5. The position of the Roman Church on transubstantiation casts serious doubt on its claim to authority. It was not until AD 1215 that transubstantiation was made an article of faith in the Roman Church. A doctrine which might be rejected with impunity prior to that date must now be accepted in peril of eternal damnation.

6. There is further reason for denying the doctrine of transubstantiation. The bread not eaten by RCs at masses becomes mouldy like any other bread, but the literal body of Jesus was preserved from corruption at death (Acts 2:31, cf. Psa. 16:10), and is not now corruptible. Therefore the interpretation placed upon this passage in John by RCs cannot be the one intended by Jesus.

7. There has not been any validated evidence that bread "consecrated" by a RC priest, when eaten by RCs becomes anything other than what it is—natural bread assimilated by the body. This amounts to a complete denial of the claim that the literal bread ever becomes the literal body of the Lord.[32]

8. The implications of insisting that John 6:53 refers to eating the bread and the wine are serious. By this interpretation of the passage it follows that RCs "have no life in [them]" unless they eat the bread *and* drink the wine. But RCs do not drink the wine—only the priests drink the wine. The decision to withhold the wine from the "laity" was made in contradiction of the instructions of Jesus. We are informed that Jesus "took the cup, and gave thanks, and gave it to them,

---

[32] This obvious fact is wrapped up in the very complicated language used to "explain" the supposed process of transubstantiation. The bread and the wine (like all other material things) are said to possess *substance* and *accidents*. The *accidents* of the bread and wine are the external qualities of shape, size, colour, weight and taste etc. These do not change during the ritual. It is the substance that changes! An illustration is given by M. Sheehan: "A bar of iron...has a certain size, shape, weight, colour, and hardness. None of these things makes it iron. Not its size or shape, for clearly, it may change in either respect and still be iron. Not its weight, for its weight depends on gravity, and varies according to the distance from the centre of the earth...Not its colour, for that changes with the temperature; under intense heat it will become red...Not its hardness for when it is cast into a furnace it becomes a liquid. If it is not iron because of its size, or shape, or hardness etc., what is it that makes it iron? It is its substance. The substance remains fixed amid many changes; it is an unchanging thing, whereas the changeable dress it wears constitutes its *accidents*...*Substance* is not a hard or heavy thing; it is something invisible, a power that supports the accidents." (*Apologetics and Catholic Doctrine*, (London: The Saint Austin Press, 2001), p.498. However, reason demands that if the

16

saying, Drink ye all of it". (Matthew 26:27). Mark records, "He gave it to them: and they all drank of it". (14:23). Later, Paul had to rebuke the Corinthian believers because of their behaviour at the memorial meeting. "Wherefore whosoever shall eat this bread, and drink this cup of the Lord, unworthily, shall be guilty of the body and blood of the Lord." (1 Cor. 11:27). Clearly they could not drink unworthily unless the wine was given to them.[33]

Psalm 110:4
"The LORD hath sworn, and will not repent, Thou art a priest for ever after the order of Melchizedek."

Hebrews 6:20
"Whither the forerunner is for us entered, even Jesus, made an high priest for ever after the order of Melchisedec."

Hebrews 7:17
"For he testifieth, Thou [Jesus] art a priest for ever after the order of Melchisedec."

Hebrews 7:24
"But this man [Jesus], because he continueth ever, hath an unchangeable priesthood."

Malachi 1:11
"For from the rising of the sun even unto the going down of the same my name shall be great among the Gentiles; and in every place incense shall be offered unto my name, and a pure offering: for my name shall be great among the heathen, saith the LORD of hosts."

---

substance of an iron bar were changed by a miracle, say, into aluminium then the *accidents* too would change—the bar would be lighter, and different in colour and hardness. If the *substance* of bread wafer were changed by a miracle into the Lord's body then its *accidents* too, logically, according to the above analogy would also change. If not then we are talking about two miracles not one—a change of the substance (transubstantiation) of the bread into the substance of the Lord's body, and a change of the *accidents* of the Lord's body into the *accidents* of a wafer. This cannot be. A wafer in its accidents and substance is corruptible. The Lord's body in substance and accidents is incorruptible.

[33] It was not until 1415 that the Council of Constance formally set out partial communion as a dogma to be observed by all. The Council of Trent (1545–1563) endorsed this, stating, "Though our Redeemer…did, in the last supper, institute this sacrament in two kinds, and thus delivered it to the Apostles, it must nevertheless be granted, that the true sacrament and Christ, whole and entire, is received in either kind by itself' (*Idem*, c. 1. Quoted by Charles Elliott, *Delineation of Roman Catholicism*, London: John Mason, 1844, pp.181-183). Thus, on their own admission, by their tradition of transubstantiation they make void the word of the Saviour.

WRESTED SCRIPTURES

PROBLEM:

RCs maintain that Melchizedek, of whom we read in Genesis 14:18–20 offering bread and wine, foreshadowed the priesthood of Christ. Using the above list of Scriptures it is said that Jesus inaugurated this priesthood at the Last Supper. In the Mass, Christ is both priest and sacrifice. Through the ministry of his ordained priest, Jesus the High Priest offers the sacrifice of his real body and blood in the transubstantiated bread and wine. The daily ritual of the Mass, conducted by RCs throughout the world, is a fulfilment of the words of Malachi.

SOLUTION:

1. It is indeed Scripture teaching that Melchizedek foreshadowed the priesthood of Jesus. It is testified that Jesus was appointed, by his Father, "a priest for ever after the border of Melchizedek" (Heb. 7:17,26–28). However, there is no Scripture testimony to the effect that the priesthood was inaugurated at the Last Supper.
2. The idea that Jesus repeatedly offers himself in the sacrifice of the Mass contradicts the plain teaching of Scripture—"But this man [Jesus], after he had offered one sacrifice for sins for ever, sat down on the right hand of God" (Heb. 10:12). The apostle in this chapter contrasts the priests under the Law Covenant who stood "daily ministering and offering oftentimes the same sacrifices, which can never take away sins" (verse 11), with the one effectual sacrifice of Jesus of which he remarks that "by one offering he [Jesus] hath perfected for ever them that are sanctified" (verse 14).
3. The idea read into Malachi 1:11 that in the daily sacrifice of the Mass the sacrifice of Jesus is offered throughout the world is a contradiction of the teaching of the New Testament: "For such an high priest became us, who is holy, harmless, undefiled, separate from sinners, and made higher than the heavens; who *needeth not daily*, as those high priests, to offer up sacrifice, first for his own sins, and then for the people's: for this he did once, when he offered up himself" (Heb. 7:26,27). Malachi 1:11 is looking forward to the future Kingdom of God on the earth when "they shall call Jerusalem the throne of the LORD; and all the nations shall be gathered unto it, to the name of the LORD, to Jerusalem: neither shall they walk any more after the imagination of their evil heart". (Jer. 3:17).

PURGATORY AND PENANCE

The RC Church teaches that the souls of the just who have failed in this life to pay their full debt to God's justice are cleansed in Purgatory, to fit them for admission to heaven. "The Church says this infallibly in the name of God. Hence God himself testifies, through the Church, to the existence of purgatory."[34] Thus the idea of purgatory is derived, not from the Bible, but from "the Church." Nevertheless the idea of purgatory is read into the following scriptures, which are then advanced to bolster the idea.

[34] Michael Sheehan, *Apologetics and Catholic Doctrine*, (London: The Saint Austin Press, 2001), p.632.

ROMAN CATHOLICISM

The Sacrament of Penance may be conveniently considered under this head since the RC Church teaches that the priest can forgive sins and reduce the amount of time to be spent in Purgatory.

Matthew 5:25,26

"Agree with thine adversary quickly, whiles thou art in the way with him; lest at any time the adversary deliver thee to the judge, and the judge deliver thee to the officer, and thou be cast into prison. Verily I say unto thee, Thou shalt by no means come out thence, till thou hast paid the uttermost farthing."

PROBLEM:

The RC sees this as an allegory referring to "a prison house in the other world, from which the soul will not be freed 'until thou hast paid the very last penny' ... no last penny needs to be paid in heaven, and from hell there is no liberation at all; hence this reference must apply to a third place".[35] This place, the RC maintains, is purgatory.

SOLUTION:

1. There is no suggestion in these words of Jesus of purgatory—the idea has to be read into the text. Further, since the idea of purgatory depends upon the unscriptural teaching of the immortality of the soul, it must be rejected for that reason alone.
2. There is nothing in the discourse that *demands* it be viewed as an allegory. The thrust of Jesus' teaching is that grievances that are allowed to run on can have irrevocable consequences.
3. However, it is possible that the words of Jesus had a deeper meaning (the context of "the signs of the times," supplied in the parallel passage in Luke 12:58,59, suggests this). By refusing the opportunity of reconciliation that God was offering them through His Son, the Jews turned God into their adversary. Little did they know that their nation was, even then, well on its way to the magistrate and would soon be brought before the court. The verdict against them was inevitable and the judge (Jesus, the supervisor of the AD 70 judgments) would find against them. Their nation would be overturned, the people scattered and "hid in [the] prison houses" of the diaspora (Isa. 42:22).

Matthew 12:32

"Whosoever speaketh against the Holy Spirit, it shall not be forgiven him, neither in this world, neither in the world to come."

PROBLEM:

It is argued by the RC that since sin against the Holy Spirit cannot be forgiven in the world to come, this implies that there are some sins that can be forgiven after death. Clearly the Lord assumed that his hearers understood about forgiveness in

---

[35] John Francis Noll & Lester J. Fallon, *Father Smith Instructs Jackson*, (USA: 1963), p.69.

19

the world to come. Only the very good go immediately to heaven after death. The wicked (those who die in mortal sin) go to hell for eternal torment. The righteous, dying with unforgiven venial sin or undischarged temporal punishment, go to purgatory where they undergo a painful purification before being fit for heaven.

SOLUTION:

1. Purgatory presupposes the unscriptural doctrine of the immortality of the soul. Show that there is no immortal soul then purgatory is seen to be an invention.

2. The assumption that "the world to come" means "life experienced by the soul at death" is a gross distortion of scripture truth. The word "world" (Gk. *aion*) means "age". "This age" denotes that period of time during which the nation of Israel was organized under the Law of Moses. That age was fast drawing to its close (Heb. 9:26) for the sacrifice of Jesus had rendered the Law Covenant obsolete. That age finally ended with the Roman invasion of Israel and the destruction of Jerusalem and its temple in AD 70. "The age to come" is the age of Israel's restoration and the establishment of Messiah's Kingdom.

3. There was no provision made under the Law of Moses for the forgiveness of the sin of blasphemy against the holy spirit. Neither will it be forgiven in "the age to come" when Jesus has returns to judge the living and the dead and to establish his kingdom.

Luke 12:42–48

"Who then is that faithful and wise steward, whom his lord shall make ruler over his household, to give them their portion of meat in due season? Blessed is that servant, whom his lord when he cometh shall find so doing. Of a truth I say unto you, that he will make him ruler over all that he hath. But and if that servant say in his heart, My lord delayeth his coming; and shall begin to beat the menservants and maidens, and to eat and drink, and to be drunken; the lord of that servant will come in a day when he looketh not for him, and at an hour when he is not aware, and will cut him in sunder, and will appoint him his portion with the unbelievers. And that servant, which knew his lord's will, and prepared not himself, neither did according to his will, shall be beaten with many stripes. But he that knew not, and did commit things worthy of stripes, shall be beaten with few stripes. For unto whomsoever much is given, of him shall be much required: and to whom men have committed much, of him they will ask the more."

PROBLEM:

The RC maintains that here the Lord refers to three classes of people.

1. Those who the Lord sets over the household are those who reign with Jesus in heaven.

2. Those who are appointed their portion with the hypocrites are the wicked who are consigned to hell.

3. The third class comprises two groups:

a. Those who knew the Lord's will but did not prepare themselves, are the repentant but guilty who will be beaten with many stripes in purgatory.

b. Those who knew not the Lord's will and committed sins of ignorance also suffer in purgatory, but less so.

SOLUTION:

1. Again the exposition is based on the unscriptural teaching of the immortality of the soul and can be rejected on this ground alone.

2. The Lord is not talking about what happens to the soul at death, but about what will happen to the individuals at Christ's coming—"Blessed is that servant whom his lord *when he cometh…*" (v. 43); "the lord *will come* in a day when he looketh not for him…" (v. 46). Conclusions based on such careless treatment of the record of Scripture may be safely rejected.

John 20:23

"Whose soever sins ye remit, they are remitted unto them; and whose soever sins ye retain, they are retained."

Matthew 18:18

"Verily I say unto you, Whatsoever ye shall bind on earth shall be bound in heaven: and whatsoever ye shall loose on earth shall be loosed in heaven."

PROBLEM:

The Roman Catholic Church uses these passages to justify its teaching that the key of purgatory lies in the hand of the priest. In this unseen region of suffering he is said to open and shut, bind and loose. It is also held to lie within the priest's power to forgive sins and lessen the duration and severity of the suffering. The remission of sins is secured by the Sacrament of Penance "…by which the priest remits sins committed after baptism to those who confess them with sorrow, and are willing to perform the works of satisfaction he imposes".[36]

SOLUTION:

1. The promise in these scriptures was to those immediate disciples of Jesus (Matt. 18:1; John 20:19) who, in Luke 6:13, he designated "apostles". If the Roman Church has any claim to the promise it must first demonstrate the existence of apostles in its midst. Paul instructed the Corinthians. "Truly the signs of an apostle were wrought among you in all patience, in signs, and wonders, and mighty deeds." (2 Cor. 12:12). Where is the RC priest who can, in God's name, strike an Elymas blind (Acts 13:11); raise a Eutychus from the dead (Acts 20:10–12); or suffer no harm after being bitten by a viper (Acts 28:3–5)? These were the signs of an apostle.

[36] M. Sheehan, *Apologetics and Catholic Doctrine*, (London: The Saint Austin Press, 2001), p.543.

2. Even the apostles did not claim the power to forgive sins as the RC priests do. They fulfilled the work of "binding and loosing" by preaching the gospel, belief of which resulted in men's sins being forgiven—e.g. Acts 26:17,18.

3. When claims to the tremendous power outlined in the problem are vested in the hands of ordinary men or, as may happen, in the hands of mercenary and unscrupulous men, imagination can scarcely comprehend the documented historical abuses.

4. The New Testament refers to only one sacrificing priest, Jesus Christ (Heb. 10:12) and to a "royal priesthood" of all believers. (1 Pet. 2:9). There is no exclusive order of priests officiating for a laity in New Testament arrangements.

5. Sins are forgiven upon repentance and confession to God. So says the apostle: "If we confess our sins, he is faithful and just to forgive us our sins, and to cleanse us from all unrighteousness." (1 John 1:9). No man can forgive what is only in the power of God to remit. Jesus himself taught men to pray to the Father for forgiveness—"After this manner therefore pray ye: Our Father…forgive us our debts, as we forgive our debtors." (Matt. 6:9–12).

6. The idea of performing "works of satisfaction" dictated by a human priest is totally alien to the teaching of Jesus and his apostles. The truth is that "the blood of Jesus Christ…cleanseth us from all sin". (1 John 1:7). "If any man sin, we have an advocate with the Father, Jesus Christ the righteous: and he is the propitiation for our sins…" (1 John 2:1,2). To argue that "works of satisfaction" are necessary for forgiveness is to argue that the sacrifice of Jesus is not enough, and to deny that "he is able also to save them to the uttermost that come unto God by him, seeing he ever liveth to make intercession for them". (Heb. 7:25). That true repentance of sin is to be reflected in behaviour, is another matter altogether.

Leviticus 13:2

"When a man shall have in the skin of his flesh…like the plague of leprosy; then he shall be brought unto Aaron the priest, or unto one of his sons the priests."

Numbers 5:6,7

"When a man or woman shall commit any sin that men commit, to do a trespass against the LORD, and that person be guilty; then they shall confess their sin which they have done."

Leviticus 6:1,6,7

"If a soul sin…he shall bring his trespass offering unto the LORD, a ram without blemish out of the flock, with thy estimation, for a trespass offering, unto the priest: And the priest shall make an atonement for him before the LORD: and it shall be forgiven him for any thing of all that he hath done in trespassing therein."

PROBLEM:

These Scriptures, and similar, are advanced by the RC to show that under the law the person who had leprosy (a symbol of sin) or who had transgressed the law, was required to present himself to the appointed priest and make confession. This was a pointing forward to confession to a priest and the Sacrament of Penance under the new arrangement established by Christ.

SOLUTION:

1. The visits to the priest under the law were not simply to make confession—they were to make repeated, ineffective, sacrifices "which [could] never take away sins". The sacrifice of Jesus was offered once and is continually effective (Heb. 10:11–14; 7:26,27). Jesus is the only appointed priest through whom men can approach God for forgiveness (1 Tim. 2:5,6; 1 John 2:1,2).
2. The Scriptures are silent with respect to confession to any priest other than Jesus. They never mention the Sacrament of Penance.

1 Corinthians 3:13

"Every man's work shall be made manifest: for the day shall declare it, because it shall be revealed by fire; and the fire shall try every man's work of what sort it is."

PROBLEM:

This passage is used to support the Roman Catholic doctrine of a discipline in purgatory, which takes place immediately after death, and endures for an unspecified and varying period.

SOLUTION:

1. Note the context; the passage is speaking about a "day" (although likely longer than 24 hours) and not a period of long duration. See the use of the same Greek word, *hemera* in Matt. 7:22; 12:36; John 9:4; 11:9; 12:48; 2 Cor. 6:2. This "day" is defined in Mal. 3:2; 4:1–3; cf. 2 Thess. 1:8–10.
2. The Roman Catholic argues for the burning up of the "wood, hay, stubble," (1 Cor. 3:12) as the purging of man's soul of all that is unworthy. A man in purgatory should be glad to get rid of these impurities, to be fit for eternal happiness, but Paul says he *"shall suffer loss"*. (1 Cor. 3:15).
3. What the passage does mean:
   a. There were divisions in Corinth and Paul discusses the relationship of a man and his converts to Christ. (1 Cor. 1:10; 3:3–8).
   b. "Every man's work shall be made manifest." *The Day of Judgment* will reveal the spiritual quality of a preacher's converts, whether it be gold, silver, precious stones, for the eternal temple of God, or cheap, unenduring wood, hay, or stubble.
   c. "If any man's work abide [if his converts endure to eternal life] he shall receive a reward" (1 Cor. 3:14)—the reward of seeing, in the Kingdom of God, the fruits of his labour and travail. (See 1 Thess. 2:19).

    d. "If any man's work shall be burned [if his converts are unworthy before the Judge of all] he shall suffer loss" (1 Cor. 3:15)—the loss of seeing his labour come to naught.

    e. "But he himself shall be saved; yet so as by fire." (1 Cor. 3:15). The same fire of judgment that devoured his converts will have to be endured by the preacher also. And even though all his converts should perish, he himself may yet stand approved, because of the faith and zeal with which he has lived and worked in all good conscience before God.

2 Timothy 1:16-18

"The Lord give mercy unto the house of Onesiphorus; for he oft refreshed me, and was not ashamed of my chain: but, when he was in Rome, he sought me out very diligently, and found me. The Lord grant unto him that he may find mercy of the Lord in that day: and in how many things he ministered unto me at Ephesus, thou knowest very well."

PROBLEM:

The RC sees in this passage Paul praying for the family of Onesiphorus who had obviously died. Then he offers a prayer for Onesiphorus himself—"The Lord grant unto him that he may find mercy of the Lord in that day." Here is an example of prayer being offered for the dead when they are in purgatory.

SOLUTION:

1. The idea of forgiveness of sins after death and the concept of purgatory must be read into the words of Paul—he mentions neither. Being grounded in the Scriptures nothing would have been further from the apostle's mind than the idea of purgatory based on the pagan concept of the immortal soul.

2. Even if Onesiphorus had died (probably the correct understanding of the text), the apostle is not praying for the speedy deliverance of his immortal soul from purgatory. He is expressing the desire that Onesiphorus would find mercy "in that day"—i.e. at the time of the second coming of the Lord Jesus and the resurrection and judgment. (2 Tim. 1:12; 4:1,8).

CELIBACY OF THE PRIESTHOOD

1 Corinthians 7:1

"...It is good for a man not to touch a woman."

PROBLEM:

"The Roman Catholic Church uses this passage to support its concept that celibacy is necessary for single-minded devotion to ministerial office."

SOLUTION:

1. Celibacy is *not* a necessary pre-requisite for single-minded devotion to ministerial office. Celibacy, in Scripture, is left to the *free* decision of those concerned, without forbidding those who marry to assume ecclesial offices. (Matt. 19:12; 1 Cor. 7:6–9).

2. Peter (the first Pope according to RCs) was married (Matt. 8:14); as well as other apostles. (1 Cor. 9:5).

3. There were also married bishops. (1 Tim. 3:2; Titus 1:6).

4. The Apostle Paul clinches the argument—"Now the Spirit speaketh expressly, that in the latter times some shall depart from the faith, giving heed to seducing spirits, and doctrines of devils; speaking lies in hypocrisy; having their conscience seared with a hot iron; forbidding to marry…" (1 Tim. 4:1–3).

5. The evil results of enforced celibacy are well documented. Fornication, adultery, homosexual practices and sexual abuse of children, have been commonplace throughout the history of the celibate priesthood of the Roman Church. With the decline in the influence of the clergy in the Western World abused individuals have been more willing to complain. In former years, and today in countries where the Catholic priest is still held in awe, people were afraid to complain. Some idea of the scale of the problem may be seen from the fact that as this revision is being prepared, the RC authorities in the archdiocese of Boston, USA, have offered £35,000,000 to settle lawsuits to compensate over 500 victims of sexual abuse.[37] Of particular note is the abuse of the "confessional" by priests who have used this relationship with vulnerable "penitents" to proposition them.

1 Timothy 3:2 (and Titus 1:6)

"A bishop then must be blameless, the husband of one wife, vigilant, sober, of good behaviour, given to hospitality, apt to teach…"

PROBLEM:

It is argued by the RC that the apostle in this advice to Timothy is speaking about a second marriage after widowhood. Such a second marriage was a sign that a man could not live in the dedication demanded of a cleric.

SOLUTION:

1. The apostle does not say that he is speaking about a second marriage after a man's first wife has died. If so he would have said, "A bishop must be a man who has married only once". He does not say this.

2. It is pertinent to ask the RC why the apostle in his list of qualifications for the office of a bishop at no point says the bishop should be, or preferably be, unmarried and celibate—surely a serious oversight on the part of the inspired apostle if the RC teaching about a celibate clergy is correct.

---

[37] *The Daily Telegraph*, 11 August 2003.

3. In the pagan world in which these early Christians were living it is possible that there were converts who, at the time of conversion, had more than one wife. If this were so the apostle does not tell us how this situation was to be handled. We can be certain that the problem would have been sorted faithfully and sympathetically. But an overseer in the ecclesia could not be such as this.

4. There would have been converts who had been divorced and remarried according to the custom of the times and who could therefore be said to have more than one wife. Again such a situation would have been handled faithfully and sympathetically. Such a brother could not be considered for appointment as an overseer in the ecclesia.[38]

5. The important element in the apostle's instructions regarding the appointment of overseers was that they be "blameless"—i.e. "beyond reproach" in the midst of the licentious pagan world. The instruction about marriage, and the other instructions that follow, served to reinforce this.

EXTREME UNCTION

James 5:14
"Let him call for the elders of the church; and let them pray over him, anointing him with oil in the name of the Lord…"

PROBLEM:

This passage is used to support the doctrine of "extreme unction". Extreme unction is described as "the anointing by the priest of those in danger of death by sickness, with holy oil, accompanied with a special prayer … It is called Extreme because administered to sick persons when thought to be near the close of life."[39]

SOLUTION:

1. The passage in James is no sanction for the RC practice for the following reasons:

   a. Extreme unction is administered only to those who are expected to die, not for those who are expected to recover, (it is intended as a preparation of the soul for its last passage). The purpose of the instruction in James is that the "prayer" of faith shall save the sick. (v. 15).

---

[38] There is some difference of opinion amongst Christadelphian writers with respect to the meaning of Paul's counsel that an overseer must be "the husband of one wife." A. H. Nicholls in *Letters to Timothy and Titus* opts for the view, mentioned in (1) above, viz. he was saying that an overseer must have been married only once. If this were the case it is difficult to understand why the apostle did not say this. Reviewing the articles in *The Christadelphian* that have commented on this, the majority view seems to be that the apostle was referring to the idea considered in (4) above, but some allow it might have been referring to the view mentioned in (3). For those who wish to peruse them, the most helpful references were 1874, p.479; 1922, p.457; 1950, p.105; 1972, p.158; 1994, p.466 and 1996, p.385.

[39] Loraine Boettner, *Roman Catholicism*, (London: The Banner of Truth Trust., 1966), p.248.

b. The concern, in the administration of extreme unction, is for the soul. The passage in James is concerned with physical infirmities. This is indicated by verse 15, "The prayer of faith shall save the sick, and the Lord shall raise him up; and if he have committed sins, they shall be forgiven him".

c. The Roman Church sends a priest. James instructs that the elders (plural) be called.[40]

Mark 6:13

"They cast out many devils, and anointed with oil many that were sick, and healed them."

PROBLEM:

According to RC teaching, the Sacrament of Extreme Unction (or Anointing of the Sick, their preferred title for this "Sacrament") was instituted by Christ. This view is based on "the solemn teaching of the Church, Sacred Scripture and Tradition". This verse from Mark is the one usually advanced to show from Scripture that Christ instituted the Sacrament, although the rider is added, "This was not the Sacrament itself, but prefigured it".[41]

SOLUTION:

1. Since the RC admits that "this was not the Sacrament", on whose authority must we accept that the Sacrament was prefigured by it? The circular argument again!

2. It is interesting (but no more than that) to note that Cardinal R. Bellarmine of the RC Church argued against the application of this Scripture to support Extreme Unction for the following reasons:

a. The anointing relates chiefly to the cure of the body, whereas Extreme Unction relates to the soul.

---

[40] The way in which the RC church rides roughshod over the clear teaching of Scripture is again seen here. Sheehan comments, "James, in speaking of 'presbyters' instead of 'a presbyter', did not absolutely require the presence of several priests for the valid administration of the Sacrament. If he did, very many Christians would die without its consolations." (M. Sheehan, *Apologetics and Catholic Doctrine*, London: The Saint Austin Press, p.568). The assumptions are made that "presbyter" = "priest" and that the consolation of a Sacrament called "extreme unction" is necessary for dying Christians. On this basis James didn't really mean what he said.

The proceedings of the Council of Trent on this are more direct. "If any shall say that the presbyters of the Church, whom James directs to be called for the anointing of the sick, are not priests ordained by the bishops, but elders in age in any community, and that therefore the priest is not the only proper minister of extreme unction, let him be accursed." (*Concil. Trident.* sess. xiv, c. i sq.; quoted McClintock and Strong, *Cyclopaedia of Biblical, Theological and Ecclesiastical Literature*, vol. 3, Grand Rapids, USA: Baker Book House, 1968, p.425).

It is worth noting that the RC Douay Rheims Bible renders James 5:14, "Let him bring in the priests…" However, *The Jerusalem Bible* (*Nihil Obstat*: Lionel Swain; Imprimatur: John Cardinal Heenan, New York: Doubleday & Co.,1966) translates it, "He should send for the elders of the church…"

[41] M. Sheehan, *Apologetics and Catholic Doctrine*, (London: The Saint Austin Press, 2001), p.568.

b. The apostles were not priests at that time and therefore could not confer Extreme Unction.

c. The apostles in Mark 6 anointed those who were not in danger of death, as probably the blind; but Extreme Unction is given only to those in danger of death.

d. The apostles probably anointed "infidels" whereas Extreme Unction is intended only for the baptized.[42]

WORSHIP OF MARY

1. HER IMMACULATE CONCEPTION

Genesis 3:15
"And I will put enmity between thee and the woman, and between thy seed and her seed; it shall bruise thy head, and thou shalt bruise his heel."

PROBLEM:
Mary is held to have been the child of Anna the prophetess and a man named Joachim. She was conceived in the usual way but from the very moment of conception God gave her soul sanctifying grace. Not only was she free from the stain of original sin but also throughout her life she remained free from the stain of all sin. In this regard Mary is considered to be the new "Eve" of Genesis 3:15 and the enmity between Satan and "the woman" set out there, demands that the woman (Mary) be free from Satan's dominion.

SOLUTION:
1. There is in fact no mention in the Bible of the circumstances of Mary's birth. There is not the slightest hint that she was immaculately conceived. We are not told that she was the daughter of Anna and this seems unlikely. Mary is presented to us as a member of the tribe of Judah being a descendant of David through her father Heli (Luke 3:23).[43]

2. It should be noted that nowhere in Genesis 3 is there mention of the RC "Satan"

3. The One who was to destroy the serpent was not the woman but the woman's seed. Jesus was the woman's seed—"God sent forth his Son, made of a woman..." (Gal. 4:4). By this means Jesus was a partaker of "flesh and blood" nature (Heb. 2:14) and was able to be "in all points tempted like as we are"

---

[42] Bell. De Ext. Unct., c.2. I, p.705, tom. 3. Prog 1721.

[43] Joseph was the son of Jacob (Matt. 1:16). The RC view is that Heli was Jacob's brother [both Heli (Luke 3:24) and Jacob (Matt. 1:15) appear to have been descended from Matthan] therefore Joseph was the result of a Levirate marriage. In this way Jacob having died childless, Heli, according to the law, took his wife and produced Joseph. However, this depends on Matthan (Luke 3:24) being the same person as Matthat (Matt. 1:15), which is by no means certain. Also there are other possible explanations; the most likely being that Matthew gives the legal and royal genealogy through Joseph whilst Luke gives Mary's genealogy through Heli.

(Heb. 4:15), although, unlike us, he never sinned. It was necessary that he be "in the likeness of sinful flesh" (Rom. 8:3) so that he could be tempted, resist temptation, and thus destroy the power of sin. What Jesus inherited from his mother was her "flesh and blood" nature; her "sinful flesh".

4. The Bible does not teach that sanctifying grace is given to souls—Mary's or anyone else's.

John 1:14

"And the Word was made flesh, and dwelt among us, (and we beheld his glory, the glory as of the only begotten of the Father,) full of grace and truth."

PROBLEM

Jesus derived his human nature from his mother. The RC then argues that since this was "full of grace and truth" it was clearly necessary that his mother be free of the stain of original sin.

SOLUTION:

1. It is not true that Jesus' "human nature" was full of grace and truth. Jesus human nature was "sinful flesh" (Rom. 8:3). It was this that he inherited from his mother. Having his mother's nature he could be tempted as all other members of the human race are tempted. But he overcame all temptation and showed forth the character of his Father to the point where he could say, "He that hath seen me hath seen the Father…" (John 14:9). It was the character of Jesus, developed during his life, that was full of grace and truth.

2. In order for Jesus to accomplish the purpose of God it was clearly necessary for Mary to have been a member of our race, a partaker of our sinful flesh, so that she could pass this on to her divinely begotten son.

Ephesians 5:27

"That he might present it to himself a glorious church, not having spot, or wrinkle, or any such thing; but that it should be holy and without blemish."

PROBLEM:

Mary is said to be the living image ("type") of the church, which is Christ's Bride, that Paul in this passage declares to be "without spot or wrinkle…holy and without blemish". Clearly Mary too must have had these characteristics.

SOLUTION:

1. Nowhere in the Bible is Mary said to be a type of the church, therefore to apply to Mary the attributes of the church is inappropriate.

2. The description of the church as not having spot, or wrinkle…holy and without blemish, is a description of the church when her redemption is completed. To apply this to the nature of Mary is to miss the point completely.

3. Mary was an ordinary member of the human race, as far as we know begotten in the normal way, descended from Adam and Eve (and therefore carrying their fallen nature) in the line of Abraham (Luke 3:34) and David (v. 31). In this way "Jesus Christ our Lord…was made of the seed of David according to the flesh" (Rom. 1:3). Apart from the Lord Jesus, "All have sinned, and come short of the glory of God" (3:23) and there is no scriptural reason to exclude Mary. There was nothing special about her nature.

2. MARY AS "THEOTOKOS" (MOTHER OF GOD)

Luke 1:43

"And whence is this to me, that the mother of my Lord should come to me?"

PROBLEM:

The RC doctrine was set out at the Council of Ephesus in AD 431. Mary's son, Christ, is God and so it follows that Mary is the Mother of God (Theotokos). Since Elizabeth hailed Mary as "the mother of my Lord", this is said to be proof from Scripture that Mary was the Mother of God.

SOLUTION:

1. The Bible teaching is that Mary was the mother of God's son. Jesus was conceived in her womb by the power of God (Luke 1:35; Matt. 1:20). He was thus the Son of God. Never is Jesus referred to as God the Son. Mary is never said to be the Mother of God or the Mother of God the Son.
2. The doctrine of the Theotokos depends on the pernicious doctrine of the Trinity which is not taught in Scripture.
3. Elizabeth describing Mary as "the mother of my Lord" in no way supports the doctrine of Mary being the mother of God, rather the reverse. Paul writes, "To us there is but one God, the Father…and one Lord Jesus Christ…" (1 Cor. 8:6). The Father is "the only true God" (John 17:3). Jesus is repeatedly referred to as "Lord" or "my Lord" (e.g. Matt. 8:2,6,21,25; John 20:13; Rom. 1:3; Phil. 3:8) but never as God the Son.

3. HER PERPETUAL VIRGINITY

Luke 1:31,34

"And, behold, thou shalt conceive in thy womb, and bring forth a son, and shalt call his name JESUS…Then said Mary unto the angel, How shall this be…?"

PROBLEM:

The RCs teach that Jesus was the only child of Mary and that she remained a virgin. At the time of her espousal to Joseph she intended to remain a virgin and, by an ingenious exercise of twisted logic, Luke 1:34 is advanced to support the idea. It is alleged that, "How can this be?" is a meaningless question unless she had intended life-long virginity."[44]

SOLUTION:

1. That Mary did not remain a virgin is indicated by the words, "Joseph...took unto him his wife: and knew her not till she had brought forth her firstborn son" (Matt. 1:24,25). The clear implication of this is that subsequent to the birth of Jesus, Joseph and Mary had a normal marital relationship.

2. Whilst it may be argued that the word "firstborn" is not present in many of the Greek manuscripts for Matt. 1:25, it cannot be denied that in Luke 2:7 all reliable manuscripts have, "she brought forth her firstborn son." The use of "firstborn", written from a historical perspective (as the Gospels were), implies that other children followed. Hence Mary could not have been perpetually a virgin.

3. The NT confirms that Jesus had brothers and sisters—"Is not this the carpenter's son? is not his mother called Mary? and his brethren, James, and Joses, and Simon, and Judas? And his sisters, are they not all with us?" (Matt. 13:55,56). Many ingenious attempts have been made to avoid the plain sense of these words.[45] From Thayer's Greek-English Lexicon we learn that the word brothers (Gk. *adelphos*) means, literally, "from the same womb."[46] Whilst the word can be used to denote members of a common race, i.e. "kindred" (e.g. "brother" in Matt. 5:22), its use here, as in many other scriptures, e.g. Matt. 1:2; 4:18 etc., should be understood in its literal sense.

4. "How can this be?" was Mary's bewildered reaction to the angel's announcement that she was going to have a son. The complete question was, "How can this be seeing I know not a man?"—How could she possibly be pregnant since she was a virgin? There is neither stated nor implied in these words that Mary intended to remain ever a virgin.

---

[44] Michael Sheehan, *Apologetics and Catholic Doctrine*, (London: The Saint Austin Press, 2001), p.393.

[45] E.g. they were the children of Joseph from a former marriage (Origen, Epiphanius and many of the so called "Church Fathers"); they were not brothers but cousins (Jerome).

[46] Joseph H. Thayer, *Greek-English Lexicon of the New Testament*, (Peabody, U.S.A.: Hendrickson, 1996), p.10. Thayer continues, "That 'the brethren of Jesus,' Matt 12:46,47; ... 13:55 f; Mark 6:3 (in the last two passages also sisters); Luke 8:19 f; John 2:12; 7:3; Acts 1:14; Gal. 1:19; 1 Cor. 9:5, are neither sons of Joseph by a wife married before Mary...nor cousins, the children of Alphaeus or Cleophas (i.e., Clopas) and Mary, a sister of the mother of Jesus...but his own brothers, born after Jesus, is clear principally from Matt. 1:25 (only in the *Textus Receptus*, Griesbach); Luke 2:7— where, had Mary borne no other children after Jesus, instead of *huion proototokon* (= firstborn son, JA), the expression *huion monogenee* (= only begotten son, JA) would have been used, as well as from Acts 1:14, compare John 7:5, where the Lord's brethren are distinguished from the apostles."

WRESTED SCRIPTURES

4. HER ASSUMPTION INTO HEAVEN

Revelation 11:19–12:1

"And the temple of God was opened in heaven, and there was seen in his temple the ark of his testament: and there were lightnings, and voices, and thunderings, and an earthquake, and great hail. And there appeared a great wonder in heaven; a woman clothed with the sun, and the moon under her feet, and upon her head a crown of twelve stars…"

PROBLEM:

This Scripture is advanced by RCs to support the dogma of the Assumption of Mary. By this is meant that at the end of her earthly life Mary was taken, body and soul, into the glory of heaven.[47] This teaching was not defined as a dogma until 1950 when Pope Pius XII put the stamp of papal infallibility to what had been accepted by many for centuries. Whether Mary died before her assumption into heaven is left as an open question.

In the passage from Revelation 11:19–12:1 it is maintained that Mary is the new ark of the covenant. Just as the ark of the covenant in the temple disappeared from the earth in a mysterious way, so Mary, the new ark mysteriously disappeared from the earth being assumed into heaven. Mary is also the woman in heaven in Revelation 12:1.

SOLUTION:

1. There is not one shred of Scripture evidence to support the idea that Mary was taken to heaven at the end of her life.
2. Revelation 11:19 is a prophecy of the time when, "The kingdoms of this world are become the kingdoms of our Lord, and of his Christ; and he shall reign for ever and ever" (verse 15) and has nothing to do with the end of Mary's life on earth.
3. The idea that Mary is the "new ark of the covenant" has no basis in scripture— it is a figment of ecclesiastical imagination.[48] To say that the first ark mysteriously disappeared "from the earth" is to overstate the case in order to support the myth of the assumption of Mary. It certainly disappeared, but the circumstances of its disappearance are not set out in scripture. Opinions vary as to what happened to it. Some think that it was hidden by the Jews, others that it was taken by the Babylonians when Jerusalem fell and was not present in the second temple. There is not the slightest indication that it was spirited away into heaven.
4. To equate Mary with the "woman in heaven" in Rev. 12:1 would be laughable were it not so serious a distortion of scripture. This woman is pregnant and in

[47] Michael Sheehan, *Apologetics and Catholic Doctrine*, The Saint Austin Press, London, 2001, p.393.

[48] The fact that the ark remained in the house of Obed-edom for three months (2 Sam. 6:11) and Mary stayed with Elisabeth for three months (Luke 1:56) is offered as supporting evidence!

the process of giving birth—in heaven (v. 2)! In heaven she is also confronted by a seven-headed, ten-horned dragon that is waiting to eat her son (vv. 3,4)! The RC says that Mary was on earth and went to heaven. Revelation 12 says the woman was in heaven and came to the earth for, having given birth to a son, the woman flees into the wilderness (v. 6). Her son, on the other hand, was "caught up to God and to his throne", which surely implies that, although she was "in heaven", the woman was not with God when she gave birth. Clearly this is apocalyptic language that must be interpreted in order to be understood. There is certainly nothing in the chapter to support the idea of the assumption of Mary; in fact it contains no reference to Mary at all.

5. Mary, like every other member of the human race, died and returned to the dust (Psalm 146:4). She now sleeps awaiting the resurrection (1 Cor. 15:22,23; 1 Thess. 4:14–16).

5. MOTHER OF THE CHURCH AND MEDIATRIX OF GRACE

John 19:26,27

"When Jesus therefore saw his mother, and the disciple standing by, whom he loved, he saith unto his mother, Woman, behold thy son! Then saith he to the disciple, Behold thy mother!"

PROBLEM:

When Jesus said to the disciple whom Jesus loved, "Behold thy mother", he was, according to RC teaching, speaking to all the elect. "Mary's motherhood, which becomes man's inheritance, is a gift: a gift which Christ Himself makes personally to every individual."[49] The motherhood of Mary began with the consent she gave to the Annunciation in Luke 1:38, and continues until all the elect are eternally fulfilled. In heaven she continues to procure for the elect the gifts of eternal salvation. It is through her intercession that Christians receive all the graces sought in prayer.

Pope Paul VI, who formalized this teaching in 1964, said, "[She] now continues to fulfil from Heaven her maternal function by which she co-operates in the birth and development of divine life in the individual souls of redeemed men."[50]

SOLUTION:

1. John 19:26,27 is saying no more than, for reasons that we may not fully comprehend, Jesus was committing his mother to the care of the beloved disciple.
2. The mother of the church, according to Scripture is Jerusalem, not Mary— "Jerusalem which is above is free, which is the mother of us all" (Gal. 4:26).

---

[49] Pope John Paul II, *Redemptoris Mater*, 1987, no. 45. (Quoted by Michael Sheehan in *Apologetics and Catholic Doctrine*, The Saint Austin Press, London, p.394.)

[50] Pope Paul VI, *Signum Magnum*, 13 May 1967, Part I. (Quoted by Michael Sheehan, *Apologetics and Catholic Doctrine*, The Saint Austin Press, London, p.394.)

WRESTED SCRIPTURES

3. The RC Church in exalting Mary to the position of Mediatrix usurps, on her behalf, the work of the Lord Jesus. He is the "one mediator between God and men" (1 Tim. 2:5).

4. The holy spirit gifts (Gk. *charismata*, graces) given to the first century church were given by Jesus, not by Mary—"Being by the right hand of God exalted, and having received of the Father the promise of the Holy Spirit, he hath shed forth this, which ye now see and hear" (Acts 2:33); "Unto every one of us is given grace according to the measure of the gift of Christ. Wherefore he saith, When he ascended up on high, he led captivity captive, and gave gifts unto men" (Eph. 4:7,8). There are no *charismata* available to Christians today (see page 325).

5. It is through Jesus, not Mary, that believers obtain forgiveness (1 John 2:1,2; Eph. 1:7) and "find grace to help in time of need" (Heb. 4:16).

WORSHIP OF SAINTS AND IMAGES

Luke 15:10
"Likewise, I say unto you, there is joy in the presence of the angels of God over one sinner that repenteth..."

Revelation 5:8
"And when he had taken the book, the four beasts and four and twenty elders fell down before the Lamb, having every one of them harps, and golden vials full of odours, which are the prayers of saints."

Revelation 8:3,4
"And another angel came and stood at the altar, having a golden censer; and there was given unto him much incense, that he should offer it with the prayers of all saints upon the golden altar which was before the throne. And the smoke of the incense, which came with the prayers of the saints, ascended up before God out of the angel's hand."

PROBLEM:

1. This collection of scripture passages is used by the RC to argue that in heaven the angels, represented in Rev. 5:8 by the twenty-four elders, present the prayers of the Christian faithful to God. Thus it is right to seek the intercession of angels and therefore it must be right to seek the intercession of the Saints in heaven.

2. This assumption is then bolstered by the argument that Paul wrote to the Colossians, "We...do not cease to pray for you" (1:9). If a Christian on earth can pray for others, why can he not pray for those who are in heaven?

SOLUTION:

1. Nowhere in scripture are we told to pray to angels. The verses quoted from the Revelation are couched in apocalyptic language that must be interpreted if it is

to be understood. For example, in Rev. 8:5 we are informed that, "The angel took the censer, and filled it with fire of the altar, and cast it into the earth: and there were voices, and thunderings, and lightnings, and an earthquake". Surely not a literal act!

2. The idea of praying to Saints in heaven is based on the pagan doctrine of the immortality of the soul that has been accepted and embellished by the Roman Church. A "saint" (Gk. *hagion*) is simply a description of one who has been baptized into Christ (e.g. Acts 9:13; Rom. 1:7; 1 Cor. 1:2; Heb. 6:10). All dead saints return to the dust and are said to be asleep awaiting the resurrection and judgment. (Psa. 146:3,4; Heb. 9:27; Dan. 12:2). The RC practice of canonisation is thus entirely without foundation in scripture.

3. Believers do not need to pray through Saints, Mary, or a priest: they have access to the Father through their Great High Priest, Advocate and Mediator, Jesus Christ (Heb. 4:14–16; 1 John 2:1,2; 1 Tim. 2:5).

Exodus 25:18–20

"Thou shalt make two cherubims of gold, of beaten work shalt thou make them, in the two ends of the mercy seat. And make one cherub on the one end, and the other cherub on the other end: even of the mercy seat shall ye make the cherubims on the two ends thereof. And the cherubims shall stretch forth their wings on high, covering the mercy seat with their wings, and their faces shall look one to another; toward the mercy seat shall the faces of the cherubims be."

Numbers 21:8,9

"And the LORD said unto Moses, Make thee a fiery serpent, and set it upon a pole: and it shall come to pass, that every one that is bitten, when he looketh upon it, shall live. And Moses made a serpent of brass, and put it upon a pole, and it came to pass, that if a serpent had bitten any man, when he beheld the serpent of brass, he lived."

PROBLEM:

These scriptures are cited in an attempt to support the practice of using images of Christ, Mary and the Saints in worship. It should be noted that, when pressed, RCs would claim that they do not worship the image, but use the image as an aid to worship. However, the distinction is not quite so clear. The 7th General Council in 787 decreed that it is legitimate to use and reverence images of Jesus, Mary, the Angels and Saints "since *the veneration of the image* refers to the original, and the one who *honours the image* honours the person of the one depicted in it."[51]

SOLUTION:

1. In the case of both the cherubim and the serpent of brass there were definite instructions from God that they should be made, together with instructions as to how they should be employed. This is not so with the images employed by RCs.

---

[51] DS 600–1, quoted by M. Sheehan, *Apologetics and Catholic Doctrine*, (London: The Saint Austin Press, 2001), p.470.

Israel in the Old Testament period were expressly commanded, "Thou shalt not make unto thee any graven image, or any likeness of any thing that is in heaven above, or that is in the earth beneath, or that is in the water under the earth: thou shalt not bow down thyself to them, nor serve them…" (Exo. 20:4,5). The RC will say that this was not a prohibition of the making of images, but of worshipping them.[52] However, the plain meaning of the text is that it was a command not to *make* images for the purpose of worship. The RC cannot show any scripture command to support the making of images of Christ, Mary, Saints or Angels.

2. The Cherubim were in the Most Holy Place in the tabernacle (and later in the temple). They were not even seen by the priests or the people and were certainly not venerated. The High Priest alone was able to enter the Most Holy Place once each year on the Day of Atonement. He did not venerate the Cherubim.

3. God condemned all examples of images made by man to assist them in worship: e.g., the golden calf (Exo. 32) and the images in Dan and Bethel set up by Jeroboam (1 Kings 12:28–30). The veneration of the serpent of brass (and offering incense to it) in the time of the Kings was displeasing to God and was destroyed by faithful king Hezekiah (2 Kings 18:4). The use of images appears to be the hallmark of apostate religion.

---

[52] J. F. Noll & L. J. Fallon, *Father Smith Instructs Jackson*, (USA: 1963), p.80.

I.1a

THE ORTHODOX CATHOLIC CHURCH

(Also known as the Orthodox Church, Greek Orthodox Church, Eastern Orthodox Church, Graeco-Russian Church, etc.)

PRELIMINARY POINTS:

The increase in our preaching activities into areas in which the Orthodox Catholic Church (OCC) is very active, and the spread of Orthodox activities into the western world (mainly as a result of the migration of its adherents), means that we shall be increasingly brought face to face with members of this group. A note about the OCC was therefore thought to be necessary.

The beliefs of the OCC coincide to a large extent with those of the Roman Catholic Church and the same Scriptures are likely to be used to support their beliefs. However, the Christadelphian venturing onto Orthodox territory needs to be aware of the following differences:

1. The separation of the Eastern Church from the Western (Roman Catholic) Church was a gradual process but the principle cause of the division was the unilateral action of the western churches (in AD 589 at the Council of Toledo) who included in the Nicene Creed what has become known as the 'filioque'. The Western Church maintains in its doctrine of the trinity that the Holy Spirit "proceedeth from the Father *and the Son…*" whilst the occ rejects this, teaching that the Holy Spirit "proceedeth from the Father" only.

2. The OCC claims to base its teaching on the Bible, but the Bible is held to be insufficient without 'the sacred Apostolic Traditions'. These traditions are principally the proceedings of church councils, especially those of the undivided church between AD 325 and 787. These are said to have guided the Church into "all truth" (John 16:13).

3. Great emphasis is placed on the mystical activity of the Holy Spirit in the church by means of which the believer is enabled to live the christian life.

4. The OCC does not accept the primacy of any one leader or the infallibility of any church leader. It maintains the 'infallibility of the church' which it believes is always guided by the Holy Spirit. It does not insist on the celibacy of its priesthood.

5. Mary is considered to be 'theotokos' (mother of God) but her immaculate conception and bodily assumption into heaven are denied.

6. In the celebration of 'the eucharist' the mystery of the change of the 'elements' into the body and blood of Jesus is accepted, although a full doctrine of transubstantiation has not been formulated. The OCC teaches a communion of both elements for laity as well as priest and they use leavened bread. All 'baptized' individuals, including young children, are allowed to celebrate the eucharist. Because of this they do not practise 'confirmation'.

7. Whilst accepting the ideas of heaven and hell, they reject the RC teaching about purgatory.

8. The use of icons (especially pictures of Jesus and the 'saints') is encouraged. Since Jesus is said to be "the image [Gk. *eikon*] of the invisible God" (Col. 1:15) it is argued that icons of Christ help believers to appreciate the incarnation of God.

INSUFFICIENCY OF SCRIPTURE

John 16:13

"Howbeit when he, the Spirit of truth, is come, he will guide you into all truth: for he shall not speak of himself; but whatsoever he shall hear, that shall he speak: and he will shew you things to come."

Acts 15:28

"For it seemed good to the Holy Spirit, and to us, to lay upon you no greater burden than these necessary things…"

PROBLEM:

For the OCC the Bible is insufficient as a source of truth. These passages are quoted to support the idea that over the centuries the church has been guided, and continues to be guided, by the Holy Spirit. As the Council in Jerusalem recorded in Acts 15 was guided by the Holy Spirit, so the councils of the undivided church, and the OCC since the division, have likewise been guided by the Holy Spirit into truth.

"The Bible, and more specifically the New Testament, does not contain all the doctrine and teachings of Christ…"[1]

"The promised gift of 'all the truth' came to the Church in the outpouring of the Holy Spirit, but it took centuries…to define it using man's limited concepts…we need the power of the Holy Spirit, which was given to the Church, to guide it to the truth and protect it…

The Bible by itself, without the Tradition as its living interpreter, is insufficient as a source of truth.

The fifteenth chapter of Acts tells of a meeting held by the Apostles, who announced their decision by saying, 'It seemed good to the Holy Spirit and to us…' Similar gatherings of the Apostles' successors, all the bishops of the Church, were held from time to time during the first millennium…"[2]

"The Holy Spirit is the Supreme Author and Guardian under Whose direction and protection the Scriptures *become* [emphasis mine, J.A.] the inspired and infallible source of faith and salvation…The Church is guided by the Holy Spirit, Who remains in it until the consummation of the ages."[3]

---

[1] Re. Maximos Aghiorgoussis, *The Dogmatic Tradition of the Orthodox Church*, Pittsburgh (Internet Edition).

[2] Archbishop Paul of Finland, *The Faith We Hold*, St. Vladimir's Seminary Press: New York, 1999, pp.16,19.

[3] Mastrantonis, Rev. George, *The Fundamental Teachings of the Eastern Orthodox Church*, Greek Orthodox Archdiocese of America: Internet Edition, 1996.

SOLUTION:

1. The promise of the Holy Spirit to guide into all truth was a promise to the apostles and was fulfilled on the day of Pentecost as described in Acts 2. This Pentecostal outpouring was for a specific purpose and for a specified limited period of time—"the last days" of the nation of Israel (Acts 2:16,17). For further details on this see Acts 2:38,39, on pages 79–82.

2. All the things that Jesus said the Comforter would do, were accomplished in the lifetime of the apostles. In particular the ecclesia was guided "into all the truth" (John 16:13, Gk.) so that the apostles were able to write:

   "[God] will have all men to be saved, and to come unto the knowledge of *the truth*." (1 Tim.2:4).

   "For if we sin wilfully after that we have received the knowledge of *the truth*, there remaineth no more sacrifice for sins." (Heb. 10:26).

   "For I rejoiced greatly, when the brethren came and testified of the truth that is in thee, even as thou walkest *in the truth*. I have no greater joy than to hear that my children walk in truth." (3 John 3,4).

   For more on the Comforter passages see pages 82–84.

3. To insist on the need for the Holy Spirit to guide into the truth is to deny the power of the gospel as God's appointed means of salvation: "For I am not ashamed of the gospel of Christ: for it is the power of God unto salvation to every one that believeth; to the Jew first, and also to the Greek." (Rom. 1:16).

4. The apostle commands: "Beloved, believe not every spirit, but try the spirits whether they are of God: because many false prophets are gone out into the world." (1 John 4:1). So we must apply the test and ask: Were the councils of the undivided church (AD 325–787) guided by the Holy Spirit? The apostle writes: "But to us there is but *one God, the Father*..." (1 Cor. 8:6). It was these councils that produced the doctrine of the trinity which teaches One God consisting of God the Father, God the Son and God the Holy Spirit. "Ye shall know them by their fruits" (Matt. 7:16). Since the conclusions of the councils contradict the simple teaching of the Scriptures they cannot be the results of Holy Spirit guidance.

   Anyone venturing onto OCC territory must be capable of demonstrating the doctrine of the trinity to be false—it is at the very centre of their theology.

THE NEED FOR THE HOLY SPIRIT IN THE EXPERIENCE OF THE FAITHFUL

2 Peter 1:3,8

"According as his divine power hath given unto us all things that pertain unto life and godliness, through the knowledge of him that hath called us to glory and virtue...For if these things be in you, and abound, they make you that ye shall neither be barren nor unfruitful in the knowledge of our Lord Jesus Christ."

39

WRESTED SCRIPTURES

PROBLEM:

According to the OCC, 2 Pet. 1:3,8 teaches that:

"Christ does not only offer us the forgiveness of our sins, but He also gives His divine power for our use and for our development so that we might not be 'ineffective or unfruitful in the knowledge of our Lord Jesus Christ' (2 Pet. 1:8)."[4]

"Orthodox Christians believe the biblical promise that the Holy Spirit is given through chrismation (anointing) at baptism (Acts 2:38). We are to grow in our experience of the Holy Spirit for the rest of our lives."[5]

SOLUTION:

1. There is tremendous emphasis on the work of the Holy Spirit (by which is meant the third person of the trinity) in the sanctification of the believer. This is essentially the doctrine of continuing grace as taught by many mainstream churches. See *The Gift of the Holy Spirit Subsequent to Conversion–Preliminary Points*, pages 326,327.

2. In this passage from 2 Peter 1 the "things that pertain unto life and godliness" are said to come to us "through the knowledge of him that hath called us" (v.3) and this in turn is the means "whereby are given unto us exceeding great and precious promises: that by these ye might be partakers of the divine nature…" (v.4). These promises are the focal point of the true Christian gospel and comprise the promises made to Abraham and David which are centred on the Lord Jesus, the promised seed. (Matt. 1:1; Rom. 1:3; Gal. 3:16). We can only know of these through the Scriptures which God has graciously given to us so that we might know them; not from an inner working of the Holy Spirit.

3. The believer is required to build upon the foundation of faith in these promises: "Beside this, giving all diligence, add to your faith virtue; and to virtue knowledge; and to knowledge temperance; and to temperance patience; and to patience godliness; and to godliness brotherly kindness; and to brotherly kindness charity. For if these things be in you, and abound, they make you that ye shall neither be barren nor unfruitful in the knowledge of our Lord Jesus Christ." (2 Pet. 1:5–8). Thus, "if these things be in you and abound", refers to the things the believer is required to add to his faith. There is no suggestion in the text that these things come by allowing the Holy Spirit to come into our hearts.

USE OF ICONS

Colossians 1:13,15

"His dear Son…who is the image [Gk. eikon] of the invisible God, the firstborn of every creature…"

---

[4] Archbishop Paul of Finland, *The Faith We Hold*, St. Vladimir's Seminary Press: New York, 1999, p.22.

[5] Bishop Alexander (Mileant), Ed., *Missionary Leaflet E2b*, Holy Trinity Orthodox Mission, La Canada, Ca. USA.

Hebrews 1:3

"Who being the brightness of his glory, and the express image [Gk. eikon] of his person, and upholding all things by the word of his power, when he had by himself purged our sins, sat down on the right hand of the Majesty on high."

PROBLEM:

The OCC believes fervently in the use of icons, mainly pictures of Jesus, Mary and 'the saints', and supports this by an appeal to these words from the New Testament.

"The Orthodox faithful prostrate themselves before Icons, kiss them, and burn candles before them…Icons have been used for prayer from the first centuries of Christianity…The Orthodox Church had a clear understanding of the importance of Icons right from the beginning; and this understanding never changed, for it is derived from the teachings concerning the Incarnation of the Second Person of the Holy Trinity—our Lord and Saviour Jesus Christ…He has revealed the Image or Icon of God. For being the brightness of [God's] glory, and the express image of [God's] person (Heb. 1:3), the Word of God in the Incarnation revealed to the world, in His own Divinity, the Image of the Father."[6]

Thus it is maintained that religious art is a form of pictorial confession of faith and a channel of religious experience and that, for example, images of Christ, as man, affirm what the OCC perceives to be 'the truth of God's real incarnation'.

SOLUTION:

1. Whilst the OCC insists that icons have been used from the beginnings of Christianity the New Testament is silent with respect to them.
2. It is easily shown that the doctrine of the incarnation as understood by the OCC is unscriptural.
   a. Jesus was "the seed of David according to the flesh"—truly a descendant of David through his mother. (Matt. 1:1; Rom. 1:3).
   b. He was conceived by the operation of the Holy Spirit on Mary's womb, and so God was his Father. (Matt. 1:18–21; Luke 1:31–35).
   c. He had no existence before he was born and his exaltation to the position of "Son of God with power" occurred at a definite point in finite time—"Thou art my Son, this day have I begotten thee" (Heb. 1:5).

   For further details see the chapter, *The Pre-existence and Deity of Christ*, page 276.
3. The icon is thus seen to reinforce a doctrine that is unscriptural and shows the wisdom enshrined in the injunction, "Thou shalt not make unto thee any graven image, or any likeness of any thing that is in heaven above, or that is in the earth beneath, or that is in the water under the earth: thou shalt not bow down thyself to them, nor serve them…" (Exo. 20:4,5). The Apostle Paul wrote concerning those who disobeyed this commandment, "Professing themselves to be wise,

[6] Bishop Alexander (Mileant), Ed., Missionary Leaflet E2b, Holy Trinity Orthodox Mission, La Canada, Ca. USA.

they became fools, and changed the glory of the uncorruptible God into an image [Gk. *eikon*] made like to corruptible man…Who changed the truth of God into a lie…" (Rom. 1:22,23,25). The OCC will protest that they do not worship the icon and that they are using the icon to help them worship Jesus. However, the Jesus they worship is not the Jesus of the Bible, and in confirming them in their belief of a false Jesus the icon is as reprehensible as the pagan images by which Israel were led astray.

4. The ornate and adorned icons of Jesus are said to be 'images of Christ as man'. Physically, Jesus was as described by the prophet: "He hath no form nor comeliness; and when we shall see him, there is no beauty that we should desire him." (Isa. 53:2). What Jesus revealed in his ministry was the moral image of God and it was in this sense that those who saw him, saw the Father (John 14:9). Believers are themselves "changed into the same image [Gk. *eikon*]" (2 Cor. 3:18) as they are influenced by the example of the Lord Jesus—"Lie not one to another, seeing that ye have put off the old man with his deeds; and have put on the new man, which is renewed in knowledge after the image [Gk. *eikon*] of him that created him…" (Col. 3:9,10). The only source of information about the character of Jesus and the Father whom he "declared" (John 1:18) is the Scriptures.

42

1.2

MORMONISM

PRELIMINARY POINTS

The Mormon Church was founded in 1830 by Joseph Smith and his followers. It was claimed for the church that it was a restoration of primitive Christianity as it had been lived in the time of the apostles, with the addition of more recent revelation.

Today, there are two major groups[1] claiming allegiance to Joseph Smith. The differences between the two groups are summarized as follows:

Church of Jesus Christ of Latter-day Saints (Brighamites)	Reorganized Church of Jesus Christ of Latter-day Saints (Josephites)[2]
1. Followed Brigham Young on the death of Joseph Smith.	Claimed that succession must be through the seed of Joseph Smith, therefore rejected Brigham Young and chose the son of Smith as head of the church.
2. Headquarters at Salt Lake City, Utah.	Headquarters at Independence, Missouri.
3. Believe in the revelations regarding polygamy (but do not officially practise it).	Reject polygamy and the Brighamite claim that Joseph Smith wrote "Revelation on Celestial Marriage".
4. Reject the official use of Joseph Smith's *Inspired Translation* of the Bible.	The *Inspired Translation*[3] is published and officially accepted.

[1] There are other factions, such as, "The Church of Christ" (Temple Lot or Hedrickite) with headquarters at Independence, Missouri. This group, though small, is vigorous and claims to be the only true church by reason of its possession of the temple lot designated by Joseph Smith in 1831 as the site of "the Temple of Zion".

[2] In Ontario, Canada, the Reorganized Church has membership in areas of Christadelphian ecclesias at Grand Valley and Manitoulin Island. A special responsibility is felt by Latter-day Saints to preach to their "Lamanite" brethren, the American Indian, purportedly apostate descendants of Hebrews to whom Jesus supposedly preached on this continent.

[3] Parallel translations of Gen. 2:5 illustrate the way in which the "Inspired" Version distorts Biblical passages:

Inspired Version	King James Version
"For I the Lord God created all things of which I have spoken, spiritually, before they were naturally upon the face of the earth ... in heaven I created them ..."	"And every plant of the field before it was in the earth, and every herb of the field before it grew: for the LORD God had not caused it to rain upon the earth, and there was not a man to till the ground."

It is apparent that the Inspired Version incorporates into the text the Mormon doctrine of pre-human spirits. Similarly, the life of Enoch in the Bible is expanded in the Inspired Version to give support to the communistic "Order of Enoch" attempted, but later abandoned, by Smith and Rigdon. (Rigdon was an ex-Campbellite of the Disciples of Christ and convert to Mormonism.) The account of Melchizedek and the Epistle to the Hebrews are likewise imaginatively enlarged to provide a "scriptural" basis for the Mormon priesthood.

5. Accept the Adam-god doctrine as taught in Doctrine and Covenants.	Reject the Adam-god doctrine but retain the belief in gods with flesh and bones. Reject Section 132 of *Doctrine and Covenants*.
6. Practise secret rites in temples.[4]	No secret temple rites. In the Kirtland Temple all meetings are open to the public.[5]

MORMON "REVELATION"

Continuing revelation is held by Mormons to be an essential characteristic of their faith. The following are considered to be divine sources of revelation:

1. *The Bible*—The official version is the Authorized King James Version. It is authoritative insofar as it is translated accurately.

2. *The Book of Mormon*[6]—It purports to tell the histories of two nations which flourished in America as descendants of small colonies brought from the "eastern continent". The first of these, the Jaredite nation, followed Jared from the Tower of Babel (2,250 BC). By 590 BC internal warfare led to the destruction of these people. The colonists are alleged to have crossed the Atlantic in eight cigar-shaped barges and settled in Central America.

   The second nation, the Nephites followed Nephi the son of Lehi, who (it is said) left Jerusalem in the time of Zedekiah and migrated to the American continent, arriving on the coast of Chile by 600 BC. The golden plates on which this story was written were hidden by the last surviving Nephite, Moroni (AD 421) in the Hill Cumorah in New York State. "In AD 1827, this same Moroni, then a resurrected personage, delivered the engraved plates to Joseph Smith."[7]

3. *The Doctrine and Covenants*[8]—All but two of the 136 sections are revelations allegedly given to Joseph Smith. A concluding "word and will of the Lord, given through President Brigham Young" is included. There is also an "official declaration" prohibiting polygamy, added by President Wilford Woodruff in 1890.

4. *The Pearl of Great Price*[9]—A small volume containing a "selection from the revelations, translations and narrations of Joseph Smith". It is usually bound with the *Doctrine and Covenants*. The thirteen Articles of Faith are included.

---

[4] The first Mormon temple in Canada was built at Cardston, Alberta. Cardston was founded by Charles Ora Card, who had three wives and trekked into Canada in 1886 (pursued by U.S. marshals) four years before plural marriage was ostensibly abandoned (*MacLean's Magazine*, Jan. 15, 1951).

[5] In the courts, the Reorganised Church was awarded the title to the Kirtland Temple as the legal successor to the original church founded by Joseph Smith.

[6] There were many errors and awkward phrases in the first edition of the work, but many of them have now been removed. See William Alexander Linn, *The Story of the Mormons*, (New York, 1902). For example: "And they having been waxed strong in battle"; "We did arrive to the promised land", p.260. "Yea if my days could have been in them days", p.449.

[7] *Book of Mormon*, preface.

[8] This is an edited and altered text of an earlier book of "revelation" called the *Book of Commandments*. The changes are noted in Thomas O'Dea, *The Mormons*, (Chicago: University of Chicago Press, 1957), p.162.

[9] "The Book of Abraham", included in *The Pearl of Great Price*, is claimed to be a "Translation of some ancient Records, that have fallen into our hands from the catacombs of Egypt. The writings of

5. *Pronouncements by the President*—The Mormon Church has twelve "spirit-guided apostles" and a president "like unto Moses...a seer, a revelator, a translator, and a prophet, having all the gifts of God which he bestows upon the head of the church."[10] The president is to Mormons what the pope is to Roman Catholics.

SUGGESTED STRATEGY:

The basic question of authority must first be settled with Mormons as with Roman Catholics. While it is claimed by Mormons that the Bible is the Word of God, the claim has little practical value since the real stress is placed on the later "revelations". A Mormon course of study for the Melchizedek priesthood gives the following instruction:

"In general, it is well not to use a single passage of scripture in proof of a point, unless it is confirmed by modern revelation. If a single quotation is confirmed by modern revelation, we may be sure of its interpretation..."[11]

It is not usually advisable to condemn Mormon books outright on the basis of Rev. 22:18, "If any man shall add unto these things, God shall add unto him the plagues that are written in this book". Mormons interpret this verse as only applying to the Revelation. Their stock rejoinder is to quote Deut. 4:2, "Ye shall not add unto the word which I command you, neither shall ye diminish ought from it..." They then ask whether or not the later writings of Joshua, Judges, the Prophets and the New Testament are accepted as inspired revelations.

A more fruitful approach utilizes the small common ground that a Christadelphian shares with a Mormon—the belief that the Bible is the Word of God. The Bible can then be used to test the claims of the *Book of Mormon*, the *Doctrines and Covenants*, and the *Pearl of Great Price*. This approach has the advantage of discussing the basic issues of Gospel doctrines rather than disputing, for example,

Abraham while he was in Egypt ... written by his own hand, upon papyrus." (*Pearl of Great Price*, p.29). The papyri were found in the wrappings of certain Egyptian mummies which Smith purchased from a travelling showman named Chandler. The mummy, on which the writings of Abraham were allegedly found, was claimed to be that of Pharaoh's daughter. Smith claimed to translate the Egyptian, but not by divine revelation, as he claimed for the *Book of Mormon*. The latter he is said to have translated, using two stones called Urim and Thummim, from "Egyptian characters" written on metal plates given to him by an angel called Moroni. Smith's claim to translate the Egyptian was credible since in 1820 an Egyptian grammar had not been published. By 1836, however, Champollion's grammar was published and subsequent Egyptologists such as Dr. W. Flinders-Petrie of London, Dr. James H. Breasted of Chicago, Dr. Arthur Mace of New York, and Dr. John H. Peters of the University of Pennsylvania (cited in Gordon R. Fraser, *Is Mormonism Christian?* [Chicago: Moody Press, 1965], p.29), have rejected Smith's translation as utterly incorrect. The Egyptologists have pointed out that Smith's papyri were no more than ordinary documents used in the funeral rites of the Egyptians. Thousands of these are in existence and displayed in museums. The Reorganized Church has recognized the force of these arguments and has ceased to regard the "Book of Abraham" as inspired.

[10] *Doctrine and Covenants*, Section 107:91,92, p.197.

[11] James L. Barker, *The Divine Church: A course of study for the Melchizedek Priesthood*. Quorums for the year 1952, (Deseret News Publishers), p.9.

whether or not the Indians of the Americas could have used steel swords.[12] The Christadelphian argues on his strong familiar territory, not on historical and anthropological details. Arguments about the latter inevitably degenerate into a battle of "authorities" with each citing what the "scholars" say.

BASIC APPROACH

1. Since Mormons and Christadelphians have the common ground of the Bible as an accepted authority, the Bible can be used as a criterion to test the validity of the *Book of Mormon*.

2. The Apostle John instructs, "Believe not every spirit, but try the spirits ..." (1 John 4:1), and Paul admonishes, "Prove all things; hold fast that which is good" (1 Thess. 5:21). This is the test to be applied to Joseph Smith's, *Book of Mormon*.

3. Contradictions Listed:

The Book of Mormon[13]	The Bible
1. *Man is an immortal soul tabernacling in a fleshly body*	*Man is mortal, does not have an immortal soul*
—"his immortal soul" (Mosiah 2:38, p.139).	—Word "soul" is used in different ways, but never in the sense of immortality.
—"the soul could never die" (Alma 42:9, p. 299).	—"utterly destroyed ... the souls" (Josh. 10:28).
—"their immortal souls" (Helaman 3:30, p. 365).	—"the soul that sinneth, it shall die" (Ezek. 18:4,20).
2. *Heaven promised to the righteous*	*Earth, not heaven promised*
—"those that keep the commandments of God ... if they hold out faithful to the end they are received into heaven, that thereby they may dwell with God in a state of never-ending happiness." (Mosiah 2:41, p. 139).	—"The heaven, even the heavens, are the LORD'S: but the earth hath he given to the children of men." (Psa. 115:16).
	—"...the kingdom *under* the whole heaven, shall be given to the ... saints" (Dan. 7:27).
	—"we shall reign on the earth" (Rev. 5:10).

---

[12] Many commentators have pointed out what appear to be anachronisms in the *Book of Mormon*. These have included the steel sword of Laban (592 BC, 1 Nephi 4:9, p.7), and the finding of horses in the New World. (It is generally accepted that horses were introduced by the Spaniards many years later.) It has also been pointed out that the American Indians (unlike the Jews of the Mediterranean) lack facial hair growth, and have distinctly different facial features (thereby indicating that the Jews of Palestine are not of the same racial stock as the American Indian).

[13] Unless otherwise stated, all quotations are taken from *The Book of Mormon: An Account Written By The Hand of Mormon Upon Plates taken from the Plates of Nephi*, translated by Joseph Smith, Jun., (Salt Lake City, Utah: The Church of Jesus Christ of Latter-Day Saints, 1964).

3. *Eternal hell-fire torment*

—"which lake of fire and brimstone is endless torment" (Jacob 6:10, p.122,3).

—"his final doom is to endure a never-ending torment" (Mosiah 2:39, p.139).

Annihilation of wicked

—"This is the second death." (Rev. 20:14).

—"The wicked ... shall be destroyed [not destroying] for ever." (Psa. 92:7).

—Since man does not have an immortal soul there is nothing to burn eternally.

4. *The devil is a fallen angel*

—"... an angel of God ... had fallen from heaven; wherefore, he became a devil ..." (2 Nephi 2:17, p.54).

—"...that angel who fell from before the presence of the Eternal God, and became the devil" (2 Nephi 9:8, p.67).

Devil—a term used to describe sin in various manifestations

—It is never used to describe a fallen divine angel.

—"wives be grave, not slanderers" (Gk. *diabolous*, devils) (1 Tim. 3:11).

—"Have not I chosen you twelve, and one of you is a devil?" (John 6:70).

5. *Pre-human existence of Christ*

—"Is the Son of God the very Eternal Father? ... Yea, he is the very Eternal Father of heaven and of earth ..." (Alma 11:38,39, p.223).

Christ did not have a literal pre-human existence

—His life began when born in the days of Herod: "thou shalt conceive", "shall be born", indicate beginning of life. (Luke 1:31,35).

4. Contradictions between other Mormon writings and the Bible:

Mormon Writings

1. *God, a progressive being*

—"What sort of being was God in the beginning? God himself was once as we are now, and is an exalted man and sits enthroned in yonder heavens." (Joseph Smith).[14]

—"As man is, God was. As God is, man may become." (Lorenzo Snow).[15]

—"Remember that God our heavenly Father was perhaps once a child, and mortal like we are, and rose step by step in the scale of progress in the school of advancement; has moved forward and overcome until he has arrived at the point where he now is." (Orson Hyde).[16]

The Bible

God, unchanging in nature

—"with whom is no variableness, neither shadow of turning." (James 1:17).

—"For I am the LORD, I change not." (Mal. 3:6).

[14] Joseph Smith, *The King Follett Discourse*, ed. B. H. Roberts, (Salt Lake City: 193?).

[15] Lorenzo Snow, quoted in Milton R. Hunter, *Gospel Through the Ages*, (Salt Lake City: Steven and Wallis Pub. Co.), p.105,6.

[16] Orson Hyde, *Journal of Discourses*, Vol. 1, p.123. Quoted in Gordon Fraser, *Is Mormonism Christian?*, (Chicago: Moody Press, 1965), p.43.

2. *Revival of the Aaronic Priesthood*

—"Upon you, [Joseph Smith and Oliver Cowdery] my fellow servants, in the name of Messiah, I [John the Baptist] confer the Priesthood of Aaron … and this shall never be taken again from the earth…" (*Doctrine and Covenants*, Section 13, pp.20,21).

Priesthood of all believers

—"Ye also…are built up a spiritual house, an holy priesthood, to offer up spiritual sacrifices…" (1 Pet. 2:5).

—In this dispensation the revival of the Aaronic priesthood is contrary to the teaching of Heb. 7:18,19; 10:1.

3. *Sabbath Observance mandatory*

—"And the inhabitants of Zion shall also observe the Sabbath day to keep it holy." (*Doctrine and Covenants*, Section 68:29, p.112).

Sabbath observance not binding

—"Let no man therefore judge you … of the sabbath days: which are a shadow of things to come…" (Col. 2:16,17).

—See also Rom. 14:5,6; Gal. 4:10,11.

4. *Restrictions on meats and drinks*

—"…flesh also of beasts and of the fowls of the air … should not be used, only in times of winter, or of cold, or of famine." (*Doctrine and Covenants*, Section 89:12,13, p.155).

—"That inasmuch as any man drinketh wine or strong drink among you, behold it is not good, neither meet in the sight of your Father … hot drinks are not for the body or belly." (*Doctrine and Covenants*, Section 89:5,9, p.154).[17]

Liberty is granted[18]

—"For every creature of God is good, and nothing to be refused, if it be received with thanksgiving." (1 Tim. 4:4).

—"The kingdom of God is not meat and drink; but righteousness, and peace, and joy in the Holy Spirit." (Rom. 14:17).

—See also Rom. 14:1–4,14; Col. 2:16,17, 20–22; Mark 7:19 RSV.

5. *Site of Zion to be Independence, Missouri*

—"…this is the land of promise, and the place for the city of Zion … Behold the place which is now called Independence, is the centre place." (*Doctrine and Covenants*, Section 57:2,3, p.89).

Site of Zion to be Jerusalem in Palestine

—"…Jerusalem; for it is the city of the great King." (Matt. 5:35).

—"…the law shall go forth of Zion, and the word of the LORD from Jerusalem." (Micah 4:2).

—Zech. 14:4,5,9,14–17 indicate that Matthew and Micah refer to Palestine.

6. *Resurrection of the non-responsible*

—"And then shall the heathen nations be redeemed, and they that knew no law shall have part in the first resurrection…" (*Doctrine and Covenants*, Section 45:54, p.72).

Resurrection is only for the responsible

—"For as many as have sinned without law shall also perish without law." (Rom. 2:12).

—"others which have no hope" (1 Thess. 4:13).

—"having no hope, and without God in the world." (Eph. 2:12).

—"They shall not rise." (Isa. 26:14).

7. *Will resort to force*

—"It has always been a well understood doctrine of the Church that it was right and praiseworthy to kill every person who spoke evil of the Prophet. This doctrine had been strictly lived up to in Utah, until the Gentiles arrived in such great numbers that it became unsafe to follow the practice, but the doctrine is still believed, and no year passes without one or more of those who have spoken evil of Brigham Young being killed in secret manner." (John Lee)[19]

—In The Mountain Meadows Massacre (1857) an entire group of non-Mormon immigrants on their way to California (during the gold rush) was murdered in Utah. The Government of the U.S.A. executed the Mormon, John D. Lee, in 1877, for his part in the massacre (Juanita Brooks).[20] A number of investigative writers believe that there is strong circumstantial evidence that implicates the Mormon President, Brigham Young, in the atrocity.[21]

In this dispensation the use of force by believers is condemned.

—"...resist not evil: but whosoever shall smite thee on thy right cheek, turn to him the other also." (Matt. 5:39).

—"Love your enemies, bless them that curse you, do good to them that hate you, and pray for them which despitefully use you, and persecute you." (Matt. 5:44).

---

[17] The Mormon theologian, Talmage, indicates the importance given by Mormons to dietary laws: "Through partaking of food unsuited to their condition [Adam and Eve] and against which they had been specially forewarned, the man and wife became subject to physical degeneracy." James E. Talmage, *The Vitality of Mormonism*, (Boston: Richard G. Badger, publisher, 1919), p.52.

[18] Drunkenness is condemned in Gal. 5:21, and respect for the prejudice of one's brethren is required in 1 Cor. 8:9–13.

[19] John D. Lee, *Mormonism Unveiled*, (Omaha, Nebraska: 1891), p.284. Lee was a Mormon who was executed by the U.S. Government for his part in the Mountain Meadows Massacre, and although he considered he was "sacrificed" in a "dastardly manner" by the Mormon Church, he never relinquished his faith in Joseph Smith.

[20] Juanita Brooks, *The Mountain Meadows Massacre*, (Palo Alto: Stanford University Press, 1950). In 1838 the Mormons set up a secret police movement to support the Presidency of the church. "This group became known as the "Danites", or Sons of Dan, or Avenging Angels, and Brothers of Gideon, as well as, somewhat inappropriately, Daughters of Zion. Shortly afterward the Danite bands were extended into the Armies of Israel or Host of Israel, which were organized into groups of tens, fifties, and hundreds, each with its captain. This was, in fact, a defensive army..." [In 1838 the Mormons engaged a hostile group of Missourians who tried to prevent the Mormons from voting. The result was] "Mormon leaders encouraged resistance and aggression, which they unquestionably saw, not without justification, as counteraggression. Danite bands raided and looted..." Thomas O'Dea, *The Mormons*, (Chicago: Univ. of Chicago Press, 1957), pp.46,47.

[21] E.g. Will Bagley, *The Blood of the Prophets*, (University of Oklahoma Press: 2002); Sally Denton, *American Massacre*: *The Tragedy at Mountain Meadows*, (Knopf, 2003).

5. These contradictions between the Bible and the *Book of Mormon* leave only three possibilities:

    i. The Bible is the Word of God.

    ii. The *Book of Mormon* is the Word of God.

    iii. Neither is the Word of God.

    There is no possibility that both the Bible and the *Book of Mormon* are the word of God. As Scripture asserts, "God is not the author of confusion." (1 Cor. 14:33). The Mormon claim that the *Book of Mormon* is inspired by God as is the Bible ("insofar as it is translated accurately")[22] is a completely untenable position.

6. Joseph Smith claimed that he received instruction from a divine messenger who said that the churches had creeds which were an "abomination in His sight".[23] Since Joseph Smith continued to teach the immortality of the soul, heaven as the home for the righteous, eternal hell-fire torment of the wicked, a fallen-angel devil (all of these doctrines Roman Catholicism shares with her Protestant offspring) then either Joseph Smith was a disobedient student or else he never received instruction from a divine messenger.

7. The King James translation was published in 1611, 200 years earlier than Joseph Smith's, *Book of Mormon* (1830). The King James translators did not claim divine inspiration for their translation, yet Joseph Smith copied this version word for word in many places. He claimed there were no errors in the *Book of Mormon* because he translated under the direct supervision of God. Notice the way the following sections have been copied from the King James Version:

    2 Nephi 12–24 from Isa. 2–14

    Mosiah 13:12–24 from Exo. 20:4–17

    3 Nephi 24, 25 from Mal. 3,4

    3 Nephi 12–14 (with slight variation) from the "Sermon on the Mount" (Matt. 5–7)

8. In passage after passage, the *Book of Mormon* reproduces the inaccuracies and peculiarities of the King James Version. For example:

    a. 2 Nephi 13:17–26 (except for the omission of the italicized words) is identical with Isa. 3:17–26. More recent Hebrew scholarship, however, has shown that the KJV rendering of this section is defective and the RSV makes considerable alteration in its translation.

    b. Isa. 6:13 (a very difficult Hebrew text to translate) contains no significant alteration in the *Book of Mormon*. (2 Nephi 16:13; cf. changes in RSV).

---

[22] The official position of the Mormon Church is given as follows: "We believe the Bible to be the Word of God as far as it is translated correctly, we also believe the Book of Mormon to be the Word of God". Article 8, "Articles of Faith", *Doctrine and Covenants*.

[23] "I was answered that I must join none of them, for they were all wrong and the Personage who addressed me said that all their creeds were an abomination in His sight ..." *Joseph Smith Tells His Own Story*, (Salt Lake City, Utah: Deseret News Press), p.4.

c. The KJV renders Isaiah 5:25 incorrectly as "and their carcases were torn in the midst of the streets." The Hebrew word *suchah* means "refuse" not "torn".[24] The RSV reads, "and their corpses were as refuse in the midst of the streets." The *Book of Mormon* in 2 Nephi 15:25 perpetuates the King James error.

Joseph Smith, working with a supposedly independent record in another language, dating from the 6th century BC, and "inspired" to translate, succeeds in reproducing the errors of the KJV. Just when one would expect illumination from an inspired independent translation, the Book of Mormon contains only the faulty rendering of the KJV.[25]

9. Joseph Smith (1841) insisted that "the *Book of Mormon* is the most correct of any book on earth, and the keystone of our religion, and a man would get nearer to God by abiding by its precepts, than by any other book."[26] But there have been more than 2,000 textual changes in the *Book of Mormon* since the original 1830 edition. Not all of these changes have been grammatical. Consider the following:

a. "Behold, the virgin which thou seest, is the mother of God." (1830 edition, p.25). "Behold, the virgin whom thou seest, is the mother of the *Son* of God, after the manner of the flesh." (1 Nephi 11:18, p.18, 1950 edition).

b. "And the angel said unto me, behold the Lamb of God, yea, even the Eternal Father!" (1830 edition, p.25). "And the angel said unto me: Behold the Lamb of God, yea, even the *Son* of the Eternal Father..." (1 Nephi 11:21, p. 19, 1950 edition).

c. "... that the Lamb of God is the Eternal Father..." (1830 edition p.32). "...that the Lamb of God is the *Son* of the Eternal Father..." (1 Nephi 13:40, p.25, 1950 edition).

d. "...king Benjamin had a gift from God." (1830 edition, p.200). "...king Mosiah had a gift from God." (Mosiah 21:28, p.176, 1950 edition).

e. "Yea, decreeth unto them that decrees which are unalterable..." (1830 edition, p.303). Completely deleted in current edition. (See Alma 29:4, p.267).

ALLEGED SCRIPTURAL SUPPORT FOR MORMON REVELATION

Deuteronomy 33:15

"And for the chief things of the ancient mountains, and for the precious things of the lasting hills..."

[24] Robert Young defines *suchah* as "filth, sweepings, scrapings". *Analytical Concordance to the Holy Bible*, (London: Lutterworth Press, 1965).

[25] Discrepancies also occur like "Son of Righteousness" rather than "Sun of Righteousness" when the Bible is quoted. See Malachi 4:2 KJV and compare with the Mormon quotation in 3 Nephi 25:2, p.447.

[26] Quoted in William J. Whalen, *The Latter-day Saints in the Modern World*, (Notre Dame, Indiana: Un. of Notre Dame Press, 1967), p.49.

WRESTED SCRIPTURES

PROBLEM:

The Mormons interpret this song of Moses as follows: When the descendants of Joseph were led to this land of America about 600 BC they were told that it would be a land choice above all other lands. The reading of Moses' blessing to Joseph indicates that Moses was impressed with this fact and attempted to so describe it. He further indicated that it would be in the "ancient mountains" and the "lasting hills." The land to which they were led was in the western part of South, Central and North America, in the Rocky Mountains, which accurately answers Moses' description.[27] Thus, it is said, the Bible endorses the teaching of the Book of Mormon.

SOLUTION:

1. Mormons assert that the ancient mountains refer to the Rocky Mountains, but what is required is *proof*.

2. Richards asserts that the "descendants of Joseph were led to this land of America about 600 BC", but how does he know this for certain? Principally because the *Book of Mormon* allegedly records this migration. It can be seen that the validity of the Mormon interpretation of this passage stands or falls with the *Book of Mormon*. Once it is shown that the *Book of Mormon* is not divinely inspired, doubt is cast on all Mormon interpretations based on the *Book of Mormon* which are not capable of independent verification.

3. The Revised Standard Version translates verses 13–15 as follows: "And of Joseph he said, 'Blessed by the LORD be his [Joseph's] land … with the choicest fruits of the sun, and the rich yield of the months, with the finest produce of the ancient mountains, and the abundance of the everlasting hills…'" Can the Rocky Mountains be described as an area which produces "the choicest fruits of the sun"? Much of the region is uninhabited *rock*, not fertile agricultural areas[28] "accurately" answering "Moses' description".

4. The mountains of significance in the Bible are those about Jerusalem. (Psa. 48:1,2; 125:1,2; Isa. 2:2,3; 11:9).

5. There is circularity in the Mormon use of this passage. When pressed for evidence that the Bible refers to the *Book of Mormon*, this reference in Deut. 33:15 is cited as allegedly referring to Nephite migrations to America. But the passage in Deut. 33:15 merely refers to "ancient mountains" and "lasting hills" which in itself offers no proof of the Mormon interpretation. Recourse is then taken by the Mormon to the *Book of Mormon* to show what Deut. 33:15 "really" means. If the Bible refers to the Mormon records, this must be established *independently* of the *Book of Mormon*.

---

[27] LeGrand Richards, *A Marvellous Work and A Wonder*, (Salt Lake City, Utah: Deseret Book Co., 1958), p.64.

[28] Even the Rocky Mountain Forest region which extends from northern British Columbia southward into Mexico, to below the Tropic of Cancer "is not important agriculturally". "North America, flora", *Collier's Encyclopedia*, (1964), XVII, 601.

Isaiah 29:4

"And thou shalt be brought down, and shalt speak out of the ground, and thy speech shall be low out of the dust, and thy voice shall be, as of one that hath a familiar spirit, out of the ground, and thy speech shall whisper out of the dust."

PROBLEM:

Mormons claim this passage refers to the plates allegedly found by Joseph Smith at Cumorah Hill, N.Y. State. A Mormon Presiding "Bishop" (1952), LeGrand Richards, comments as follows:

> "Now, obviously, the only way a dead people could speak 'out of the ground' or 'low out of the dust' would be by the written word, and this the people did through the *Book of Mormon*. Truly it has a familiar spirit, for it contains the words of the prophets of the God of Israel."[29]

SOLUTION:

1. Since the Mormons cite this passage as a prophecy of the *Book of Mormon* the onus of proof rests with them.
2. The following require answers:
   a. What proof is there from Isa. 29 that the people referred to (i.e., those who speak out of the ground) are dead?
   b. Since it is "obviously, the only way a dead people could speak 'out of the ground'", how is Gen. 4:10 to be interpreted?
   c. How is the term "familiar spirit" used elsewhere in Isaiah and in the Old Testament generally? (See 3.a, below).
   d. Since Isaiah used the terms "speak", "speech", "voice", "whisper", what proof is there:
      i. that these words refer to a book?
      ii. that the book referred to is the *Book of Mormon*?
3. The following information is useful:
   a. "Familiar spirit" is translated from the Hebrew word, *ob*, which means a necromancer[30] (the pretended power to foretell the future by communicating with the dead; magic). The expression "familiar spirit" occurs in Isa. 8:19,20 where the practice is condemned: "And when they shall say unto you, Seek unto them that have familiar spirits, and unto wizards that peep, and that mutter: should not a people seek unto their God? for the living to the dead? To the law and to the testimony: if they speak not according to this word, it is because there is no light in them." Under the Law of Moses death was the punishment for turning after familiar spirits. (Lev. 20:6). There is not one

[29] LeGrand Richards, *A Marvellous Work and A Wonder*, (Salt Lake City, Utah: Deseret Book Co., 1958), p.69. Richards was ordained as one of the "twelve apostles" of the Mormon Church.

[30] Robert Young, *Analytical Concordance to the Holy Bible*, (London: Lutterworth Press, 1965).

passage in the Bible in which "familiar spirit" occurs with the meaning given it by Mormons.

b. Isa. 51 is a commentary on Isa. 29. The following are the points of identification:

   i. The subject of the prophecies is Jerusalem (Ariel) or Zion. (Isa. 29:1 and Isa. 51:17).

   ii. Both passages refer to drunkenness but not with wine. (Isa. 29:9 and Isa. 51:21).

   iii. Both passages refer to punishments of God by means of invading nations. (Isa. 29:3,7 and Isa. 51:19,23).

   iv. Both passages speak of Jerusalem being debased to the ground. (Isa. 29:4 and Isa. 51:23).

The reason for the inhabitants of Jerusalem speaking "low out of the dust" is not because the *Book of Mormon* would be discovered but because they were being "brought down", beaten into the ground by their enemies. (Isa. 51:23). The "whispering voice" of a necromancer is contrasted with the lifting of the voice when Zion will again be redeemed. (Isa. 52:9).

Ezekiel 37:19

"...Behold, I will take the stick of Joseph, which is in the hand of Ephraim, and the tribes of Israel his fellows, and will put them with him, even with the stick of Judah, and make them one stick, and they shall be one in mine hand."

PROBLEM:

This passage is understood by Mormons to predict the coming of the *Book of Mormon*. The passage is interpreted so that the "stick of Judah" refers to the Bible, and the "stick of Joseph" refers to the *Book of Mormon*. A Mormon expositor, LeGrand Richards (ordained as one of the "twelve apostles" of the Mormon Church) puts it this way:

"In ancient times it was the custom to write on parchment and roll it on a stick. Therefore, when this command was given, it was the equivalent of directing that two books or records should be kept...Now, granting that the Bible is the stick of Judah where is the stick of Joseph?...It would naturally be a record kept in another land, since Joseph was to be 'separate from his brethren'...Could this promise be fulfilled in a more simple and perfect manner than it was through the coming forth of the Book of Mormon? God led a branch of the house of Joseph to America and commanded them to keep records all their days...Now, the two records have been joined together, constituting a complete fulfilment of another great prophecy."[31]

---

[31] LeGrand Richards, *A Marvellous Work and a Wonder,* (Salt Lake City, Utah: Deseret Book Co., 1958), pp.67,68.

SOLUTION:

1. The stick of Joseph and the stick of Judah are sticks, and not scrolls. The Hebrew word *ets* is translated "tree", "wood", "gallows" etc. but never scroll.[32] The Hebrew word for scroll is *sepher* (as in Isa. 34:4).

2. The sticks do not represent the Bible and the *Book of Mormon*. They represent the two divisions of the nation of Israel that came about in the reign of Rehoboam (1 Kings 12:16,17). These were the southern Kingdom of Judah and the northern ten tribe Kingdom of Israel, also referred to as "the house of Joseph" (e.g. Zech. 10:6). The joining together of the two sticks portrays the future restoration of these two divisions of Israel under one king, which is one of the major themes of Bible prophecy. Ezekiel is instructed to give this interpretation: "Thus saith the Lord GOD; Behold, I will take the children of Israel from among the heathen, whither they be gone, and will gather them on every side, and bring them into their own land: and I will make them one nation in the land upon the mountains of Israel; and one king shall be king to them all: and they shall be no more two nations, neither shall they be divided into two kingdoms any more at all." (Ezek. 37:21,22).

3. This passage offers no proof that the coming of the *Book of Mormon* is prophesied in the Bible.

John 10:16
"And other sheep I have, which are not of this fold: them also I must bring, and they shall hear my voice; and there shall be one fold, and one shepherd."

PROBLEM:

The Mormon interpretation of this passage is as follows:

"It should be noted that Jesus did not minister unto the Gentiles although he did send his Apostles unto them after his crucifixion. This leaves us with the question unanswered, so far as the Bible is concerned: Who were the other sheep he promised to visit? For this information we must look to the restoration of the gospel and the coming forth of the *Book of Mormon*.

"After Jesus had been crucified and had ascended unto his Father, he visited his 'other sheep' in America, known as the Nephites, and there chose twelve disciples and organized his Church, as he had done among the Jews, an account of which is given in some detail in Third Nephi of the *Book of Mormon*..."[33]

Again, according to Mormon teaching, the supposed "revelation" set out in the *Book of Mormon* is endorsed by the Bible. Further, Scriptures such as this can only be understood in the light of this new Mormon "revelation".

---

[32] Robert Young, *Analytical Concordance to the Holy Bible*, (London: Lutterworth Press, 1965).

[33] LeGrand Richards, *A Marvellous Work and a Wonder*, (Salt Lake City, Utah; Deseret Book Co., 1958), p.60. Richards refers specifically to 3 Nephi 15:11–24 in his identification of the "other sheep".

SOLUTION:

1. Using this scripture to endorse the divine origin of the *Book of Mormon* involves putting the cart before the horse. It is assumed that the *Book of Mormon* is inspired and then this Scripture is pressed into supporting that view.

2. Richards' suggestion that the identification of the "other sheep" is contained in the *Book of Mormon*[34] is worthless once it is demonstrated that the *Book of Mormon* is not an inspired revelation from God. This is done in the introduction to the Mormon section of this handbook.

2. The Mormon argument assumes that "they shall hear my voice" means Jesus would personally visit the "other sheep". But Jesus does not say he would personally visit the other sheep. Those who heard the gospel preached by the Lord's ambassadors heard his voice. Jesus said, "He that heareth you heareth me; and he that despiseth you despiseth me; and he that despiseth me despiseth him that sent me." (Luke 10:16). Paul said, "Now then we are ambassadors for Christ, as though God did beseech you by us: we pray you in Christ's stead, be ye reconciled to God." (2 Cor. 5:20).

3. The "other sheep" are the Gentiles. Jesus in his earthly ministry was sent to the lost sheep of the house of Israel. (Matt. 15:24). It was prophesied, however, "He shall bring forth judgment to the Gentiles" (Isa. 42:1), and that he would be given as "light to the Gentiles". (Isa. 42:6 RSV, cf. Matt. 12:18–21). The Gentiles heard the voice of the Shepherd through the labours of the Apostle Paul, a vessel specially chosen for this work. (Acts 9:15; 1 Tim. 2:7, cf. Acts 18:6). By about AD 63 (the time of Paul's letter to the Colossian brethren), Paul wrote that the gospel "was preached to every creature [i.e. to all nationalities] under heaven..." (Col. 1:23). No mention is made of "other sheep" yet to hear the gospel on the American continent.

4. Gentile sheep like Cornelius heard the voice of the shepherd and followed in the one fold. The same cannot be said for the Nephites. Sheep worship God in spirit and in truth. (John 4:23,24). The following references taken from 2 Nephi in the *Book of Mormon* prove the falsity of the Mormon claim that the alleged descendants of Joseph were sheep in America: The proof rests on the fact that the Nephite "sheep" never knew the "voice of the Shepherd." (John 10:16,27). The alleged covenant contains doctrines which are subversive of the truth taught by Jesus Christ. The following quotations are also an indictment of the Mormon claim that Jesus ever appeared to these "sheep".[35]

---

[34] All references to the *Book of Mormon* are taken from *The Book of Mormon: An Account Written By The Hand of Mormon Upon Plates taken from the Plates of Nephi*, translated by Joseph Smith, Jun., (Salt Lake City, Utah: The Church of Jesus Christ of Latter-day Saints, 1950).

[35] Jacob, the brother of Nephi, (2 Nephi 6:1), claims to be "called of God" and "ordained after the manner of his holy order." (2 Nephi 6:2). The quotations referred to are part of his alleged revelations from God. Jacob states his claim as follows: "And now, my beloved brethren, I have read these things that ye might know concerning the covenants of the Lord that he has covenanted with all the house of Israel—that he has spoken unto the Jews, by the mouth of his holy prophets, even from the beginning down, from generation to generation, until the time comes that they shall be restored to the true church and fold of God." (2 Nephi 9:1,2).

a. They misunderstood the nature of God and His relationship to his Son: "For it behoveth the great Creator that he suffereth himself to become subject unto man in the flesh, and die for all men..." (2 Nephi 9:5). The Shepherd said, "And this is *life eternal*, that they might know thee the only true God, and Jesus Christ, whom thou hast sent." (John 17:3).[36] Why were the "Joseph Sheep" in ignorance if Jacob (the alleged prophet who wrote this quotation) received his information by divine revelation?

b. They misunderstood the nature of angels, and the devil: "For behold, if the flesh should rise no more, our spirits must become subject to that angel who fell from before the presence of the Eternal God, and became the devil, to rise no more." (2 Nephi 9:8). An angel who fell and became the devil is never mentioned by the Good Shepherd in the New Testament.[37]

c. They believed in the pagan idea of the immortality of the soul and eternal hell-fire torment for the wicked: "And they shall go away into everlasting fire; prepared for them; and their torment is as a lake of fire and brimstone, whose flames ascendeth up for ever and ever, and has no end." (2 Nephi 9:16).[38] The Shepherd said that the wicked "have their part in the lake which burneth with fire and brimstone: which is the *second death*." (Rev. 21:8).

d. They were confused over the time of the judgment: "And it shall come to pass that when all men shall have passed from this first death unto life, insomuch as they have become immortal, they must appear before the judgment-seat of the Holy one of Israel; and then cometh the judgment, and then must they be judged according to the holy judgment of God." (2 Nephi 9:15). The Shepherd taught that immortality would only be given *after* judgment. (Matt. 25:31–46).

Nephite "prophets", if they ever existed, were wolves in sheep's clothing—false prophets speaking lies. Upon such, the indictment of inspired Scripture rests. (Jer. 16:19; Gal. 1:8,9).

Revelation 20:12

"And the books were opened: and another book was opened, which is the book of life..."

PROBLEM:

Joseph Smith and his followers interpret the reference to "the books" to be the Mormon records of proxy baptisms and other rites maintained by the secretaries in Mormon temples. Official Mormon "revelation" puts it this way:

[36] Scripture makes a clear distinction between Jesus whose literal origin began in the days of Herod when he was born (Luke 1:31–35, cf. Matt. 2:1) and his Father who is eternal. (1 Tim. 1:17, cf. 1 Tim. 2:5; 1 Cor. 8:6).

[37] The origin of sin in Scripture is the heart of man. (Matt. 15:19; James 1:13–15). The word "devil" is used of humans. (John 6:70; Titus 2:3—"false accusers" is translated from the same Greek word, *diabolos*; cf. 1 Tim. 3:11).

[38] See also Jacob 6:9,10.

WRESTED SCRIPTURES

"The books spoken of must be the books which contained the record of their works [the dead who die without a knowledge of the Mormon gospel], and refer to the records which are kept on the earth."[39]

SOLUTION:

1. The Mormon case rests on two prior propositions:
   a. That living persons can perform acts of eternal value for dead relatives.
   b. That dead persons who die in ignorance of the gospel have a hope of salvation (i.e., by conscientious Mormon relatives performing proxy baptisms).

   Mormons should be pressed hard for *Scriptural* justification for such beliefs.

2. The onus of proof rests with him who asserts. Mormons must, therefore, justify the following assumptions in the above argument:
   a. It must be shown that the books referred to by John are books kept by humans.
   b. It must be shown that the books referred to are kept on earth.
   c. It must be shown that the books referred to by John contain the works of those who died in ignorance of the gospel.

3. There is evidence against the Mormon interpretation. Scripture never presents the Judgment Day as depending on secondary sources of information (i.e., Mormon temple minutes). Consider the evidence:
   a. John, writing of Jesus' *earthly* ministry, says; "But Jesus did not commit himself unto them, because he knew all men, and needed not that any should testify [witness] of man; for he knew what was in man." (John 2:24,25). Jesus will not need to rely on human testimony when he comes to judge "the quick and the dead". Even in his earthly ministry he "knew what was in man".
   b. It is prophesied of the Messiah that "the spirit of the LORD shall rest upon him, the spirit of wisdom and understanding, the spirit of counsel and might, the spirit of knowledge and of the fear of the LORD; and shall make him of quick understanding in the fear of the LORD: and he shall not judge after the sight of his eyes, neither reprove after the hearing of his ears..." (Isa. 11:2,3).
   c. The Apostle Paul wrote: "Moreover it is required of stewards that they be found trustworthy. But with me it is a very small thing that I should be judged by you or by any human court. I do not even judge myself. I am not aware of anything against myself, but I am not thereby acquitted. It is the Lord who judges me. Therefore do not pronounce judgment before the time, before the Lord comes, who will bring to light the things now hidden in darkness and will disclose the purposes of the heart. Then every man will receive his commendation from God." (1 Cor. 4:2–5 RSV). Note the following differences between the Mormon interpretation and Paul's letter to Corinth:

---

[39] *Doctrine and Covenants*, Section 128:6–8, pp.232,233 (1952 ed.).

i. Paul says human judgment is unreliable. He hesitates even to judge himself because there may be things he ought to have done which he has ignorantly left undone. Mormons assert that the careful temple secretaries afford reliable information for judgment.

ii. Paul says that the Lord judges the purposes of the heart bringing to light the things now hidden in darkness. Granting the generous assumption that Mormon secretaries accurately record the minutes of secret temple rites, they are ineffective in discerning the secret purposes of the heart.

POLYGAMY (PLURAL MARRIAGES)

It is a fundamental belief of Mormons that God has worked with the development of the organization of the church through modern revelation. Restoration of Spirit-gift powers is taught in the *Book of Mormon*: "I speak unto you who deny the revelations of God, and say that they are done away, that there are no revelations, nor prophecies, nor gifts, nor healing, nor speaking with tongues, and the interpretation of tongues; Behold, I say unto you he that denieth these things knoweth not the gospel of Christ." (*Book of Mormon*, Mormon 9:7,8, p.476).[40]

A very strong argument against Mormon claims of modern revelations can be advanced on the basis of Mormon "revelations" on polygamy.

THE ARGUMENT

1. In 1830 Mormons were damned if they had more than one wife:
   a. "Behold, David and Solomon truly had many wives and concubines, which things were abominable before me, saith the Lord." (*Book of Mormon*, Jacob 2:24, p.111).
   b. "Wherefore, my brethren, hear me, and hearken to the word of the Lord: for there shall not any man among you have save it be one wife; and concubines he shall have none...Wherefore, this people shall keep my commandments, saith the Lord of Hosts, or cursed be the land for their sakes." (*Book of Mormon*, Jacob 2:27,29, p.111).
   c. See also Jacob 1:15; 3:5; Mosiah 11:2,4,14; Ether 10:5.

2. But in 1843 a "revelation" through Joseph Smith resulted in a "new and everlasting covenant" being proclaimed, in which those were damned who did not have more than one wife:
   a. "For behold, I reveal unto you a new and an everlasting covenant; and if ye abide not that covenant, then are ye damned; for no one can reject this covenant and be permitted to enter into my glory...And let mine handmaid, Emma Smith, receive all those wives that have been given unto my servant

[40] When the Kirtland temple was dedicated in 1836, some of the Mormons spoke of "seeing the Lord, others of seeing Moses, while those outside saw a pillar of fire resting on the temple." Thomas O'Dea, *The Mormons*, (Chicago: University of Chicago Press, 1957), p.44. Mormon accounts of visions, revelations, and miracles pervade their historical records. The 'miracles' have included the healing of sick horses by the laying on of hands and the arrival of seagulls which destroyed a devouring horde of crickets.

Joseph Smith...And if he have ten virgins given unto him by this law, he cannot commit adultery..." (*Doctrine and Covenants*, Section 132:4,52,62, pp.239,244,245, 1952 ed.).

b. "...I hold the keys of this power in the last days, for there is never but one on earth at a time on whom the power and its keys are conferred; and I have constantly said no man shall have but one wife at a time unless the Lord directs otherwise."[41] (*Joseph Smith's Diary*, Oct. 5, 1843).[42]

3. The American Congress passed a series of bills (The Edmunds-Tucker Act, 1887) prohibiting polygamy. The Mormons finally bowed to surrounding hostile non-Mormons and the Federal Government. Wilford Woodruff, the President of the "twelve apostles" and head of the Mormon Church, "prayed and feeling inspired" issued the following manifesto in 1890:

"Inasmuch as laws have been enacted by Congress forbidding plural marriages...I hereby declare my intention to submit to those laws, and to use my influence with the members of the Church over which I preside to have them do likewise." (*Doctrine and Covenants*, Official Declaration, p.257).

Polygamists, after this declaration, were excommunicated so that in 1907 it was stated that the church had respectfully submitted to the law enacted against plural marriages.

4. The Mormon claim that God commanded plural marriage through revelations to Joseph Smith can only be maintained if one is prepared to allow that God gave contradictory revelations within the short space of thirteen years. One in the *Book of Mormon* forbidding polygamy (1830), and the other, through Joseph Smith, commanding it (1843). It seems incredible that a God-inspired "new and everlasting covenant" could then be withdrawn by the same God because of a man-made decision of the Supreme Court.

5. Mormons still attempt to justify the polygamous revelations allegedly given to Smith on the basis of several passages in the Bible. The Christadelphian should be aware that polygamy is not an abandoned doctrine of a forgotten age of Mormonism. This point is acknowledged by secular writers. "...all Mormon doctrinal innovations were to fall into place around this new teaching on marriage...sexual relations and procreation the central role in man's

---

[41] The doctrine was at first communicated to a few select of the "inner circle" only. It was understood that this "strong meat" was not to be fed to the Gentiles who were to receive only the "first principles".

[42] Quoted in J. K. VanBaalen, *The Chaos of Cults*, (Michigan: Wm. B. Eerdmans Co., 1962), p.202. Joseph Smith claimed to have received a revelation which commanded his wife, Emma Smith, to submit to a polygamous relationship or be destroyed. "Verily, I say unto you: A commandment I give unto you...let mine handmaid, Emma Smith, receive all those that have been given unto my servant Joseph...And I command mine handmaid, Emma Smith, to abide and cleave unto my servant Joseph, and to none else. But if she will not abide this commandment she shall be destroyed, saith the Lord..." (*Doctrine and Covenants*, Section 132:51-54, p.244).

Smith is reported to have had 48 wives. See Fawn M. Brodie, *No Man Knows My History: The Life of Joseph Smith, the Mormon Prophet*, (New York: Alfred A. Knopf, 1946).

progression to divinity."[43] The following citations from Mormon writings prove this to be the case:

God

Mormons speculate about a divine mother in connection with God's fatherhood. The following are the words of a Mormon hymn:

In the heav'ns are parents single?
No! The tho't makes reason stare!
Truth is reason; truth eternal
Tells me I've a mother there.[44]

Jesus Christ

"Jesus Christ was a polygamist; Mary and Martha, the sisters of Lazarus, were his plural wives, and Mary Magdalene was another. Also, the bridal feast of Cana of Galilee, where Jesus turned the water into wine, was on the occasion of one of his own marriages."[45]

"We say it was Jesus Christ who was married [at Cana, to Martha and Mary] whereby He could see His own seed before He was crucified. I shall say here that before the Saviour died He looked upon His own natural children as we look upon ours. When Mary came to the sepulchre she saw two angels and she said unto them, 'They have taken away my Lord or husband'."[46]

Adam

"In the Heaven where our spirits were born, there are many Gods, each one of whom has his own wife or wives which were given to him previous to his redemption, while yet in his mortal state."[47]

"When our father Adam came into the garden of Eden, he came with a celestial body, and brought Eve, one of his wives, with him."[48]

"...Michael [the Archangel], or Adam, the father of all, the prince of all the ancient of days..."[49]

The Fall

"Adam found himself in a position that impelled him to disobey one of the requirements of God. He and his wife had been commanded to multiply and

---

[43] Thomas O'Dea, *The Mormons*, (Chicago: University of Chicago Press, 1957), p.60. O'Dea is a sociologist. (Early Mormon history contains sordid charges of seduction and rivalry for wives. See O'Dea, pp.61,62,104,110.)

[44] Eliza R. Snow, a Mormon poetess and plural wife of Joseph Smith. The poem remains a sacred Mormon song and is retained in *The Deseret Sunday School Songbook*, (No. 181).

[45] Brigham Young (the second president of the Mormon Church), quoted in Eliza Young's, *Wife No. 19*, Chpt. XXXV.

[46] 7 Orson Hyde, *Journal of Discourses*, Vol. 11, (Oct. 6, 1853). p.210. Quoted in Gordon Fraser, *Is Mormonism Christian?* (Chicago: Moody Press, 1965), p.63.

[47] Orson Pratt, *The Seer*, 1, 3, (March 1853), p.31. Quoted in Irving Robertson, *What the Cults Believe*, (Chicago: Moody Press, 1966), p.14.

[48] Brigham Young, *Journal of Discourses*, 1, 50, (April 9, 1852). Quoted in Irving Robertson, *What the Cults Believe*, (Chicago: Moody Press, 1966), p.15.

[49] *Doctrine and Covenants*, Section 27:11, p.41.

replenish the earth. Adam was still immortal; Eve had come under the penalty of mortality; and in such dissimilar conditions the two could not remain together, and, therefore, could not fulfil the divine requirement [i.e., to procreate]. On the other hand, Adam would be disobeying another command by yielding to his wife's request. He deliberately and wisely decided to stand by the first and greater commandment; and, therefore, with a full comprehension of the nature of his act, he also partook of the fruit that grew on the tree of knowledge."[50]

Ultimate Reward

"...would you, like your heavenly Father, prompted by eternal benevolence and charity, wish to fill countless millions of worlds with your begotten sons and daughters and to bring them all through all the gradations of progressive being, to inherit immortal bodies and eternal mansions in your several dominions?...The eternal union of the sexes, in and after the resurrection, is mainly for the purpose of renewing and continuing the work of procreation."[51]

Abraham's Faith

"Abraham received concubines, and they bore him children; and it was accounted unto him for righteousness, because they were given unto him, and he abode in my law..."[52]

6. It will be appreciated by those familiar with Biblical teaching that the Mormon claim to "believe in the Bible insofar as it is translated accurately" is worth very little in the context of Mormon distortion of Biblical accounts. Until the authority of Scripture is established and the polygamous interpretations eradicated, little progress can be expected.

7. Despite the official change in attitude by the Mormon Church, plural marriage continues to be practised in Utah. It is estimated that there are several thousand polygamists in Utah today.[53] Fundamentalists claim that for every "fundamentalist" Mormon discovered and excommunicated for polygamy there are ten Mormons in good standing who have more than one wife.[54] Whalen comments:

"Throughout the west, they say, thousands of women known outwardly as widows, divorcees, spinsters, or wives of travelling salesmen or servicemen are actually plural wives. Attorney General Walter Budge of Utah has

---

[50] James E. Talmage (a recognized Mormon theologian), *The Articles of Faith*, (Salt Lake City: Church of Jesus Christ of Latter-day Saints, 1901), p.68.

[51] Parley Pratt (a Mormon missionary), 1830. Quoted in J. K. VanBaalen, *The Chaos of Cults*, (Grand Rapids, Michigan: Wm. B. Eerdmans Publishing Co., 1962), pp.205,206.

[52] *Doctrine and Covenants*, Section 132:37, p.243.

[53] Thomas O'Dea, *The Mormons*, (Chicago: University of Chicago Press, 1957), p.248. In 2001 a self-confessed "fundamentalist" Mormon who lived with five wives and 29 children near Trout Creek, 125 miles south-west of Salt Lake City, was found guilty on four counts of bigamy. At that time the Associated Press reported, "An estimated 30,000 polygamists, most of them in Utah, live in the American West." (http://www.cnn.com/2001/LAW/05/19/utah.polygamy/index.html).

[54] William J. Whalen, *The Latter-day Saints in the Modern World*, (Notre Dame, Indiana: Un. of Notre Dame Press, 1967), pp.284,285.

estimated there are at least 20,000 men, women and children living in plural marriages in his state alone. *Newsweek* magazine agreed with this estimate in an article on the polygamous Mormons in 1955…It quoted State Attorney General E. R. Callister who said, 'Utah's jails aren't big enough to hold them all.'[55] *Newsweek* also observed that 'many a Utah Mormon takes quiet pride in his polygamous forebears and is inclined to be lenient toward the Fundamentalists'."[56]

Short Creek, Arizona, has been a famous Mormon Fundamentalist settlement. In 1953 warrants were presented for the arrest of 36 men and 83 women. Convictions resulted, but only suspended sentences were received since Arizona has no laws against polygamy. It is known that the Fundamentalists protect themselves by planting spies to tip them off about raids by the police departments.

8. Mormon missionaries distribute a publication, *The Challenge The Book of Mormon Makes to the World*. Many of the thirty claims made in this tract are easily answered but some involve historical information. For those wishing to analyse the historical information cited, the references given in the footnote will prove helpful.[57] They are listed in order of thoroughness of content.

Isaiah 4:1

"And in that day seven women shall take hold of one man, saying, We will eat our own bread, and wear our own apparel: only let us be called by thy name, to take away our reproach."

---

[55] *Newsweek*, (Nov. 21, 1955), p.99.

[56] William J. Whalen, *The Latter-day Saints in the Modern Day World*, (Notre Dame, Indiana: Un. of Notre Dame Press, 1967), p.285.

[57] It must, of course, be realised, that these writers are not Christadelphians, and references to Biblical teaching must be cautiously and critically evaluated. Men competent in archaeology and anthropology may have no credentials for expounding Biblical teaching.

O'Dea, Thomas. *The Mormons*. Chicago: The University of Chicago Press, 1957, p.288. This book is a sociological analysis (without the anti-Mormon sentiment characteristic of Sectarian publications). The book is similar in style and treatment to Bryan Wilson's, *Sects and Society*. (available from public libraries).

Whalen, William. *The Latter-day Saints in the Modern Day World: An Account of Contemporary Mormonism*. Notre Dame, Indiana: Un. of Notre Dame Press, 1967, p.319 (a paperback).

Fraser, Gordon. *What Does the Book of Mormon Teach? An Examination of the Historical and Scientific Statements of the Book of Mormon*. Chicago: The Moody Press, 1964, p.128 (a paperback).

Robertson, Irving. *What the Cults Believe*. Chicago: The Moody Bible Institute of Chicago, 1966, pp. 9-30 (available from public libraries).

VanBaalen, Jan Karel. *The Chaos of the Cults*. Grand Rapids, Michigan: Wm. B. Eerdmans Publishing Co., 1962, pp.188-218 (available from public libraries).

Fraser, Gordon. *Is Mormonism Christian?* Chicago: The Moody Press, 1965, pp.7-115 (a paperback).

WRESTED SCRIPTURES

PROBLEM:

This passage is cited by Mormons in an effort to find Biblical support for the doctrine of polygamy taught in Mormon "scripture".

SOLUTION:

1. This passage is cited for scriptural support for the Mormon doctrine of polygamy. But does the passage state that the seven women would *marry* the one man? The request is "let us be called by thy name to take away our reproach." Is this synonymous with a request for marriage? If so, why the statement, "We will eat our own bread, and wear our own apparel?" When were such requests made by Mormon women of Mormon men for the reason "to take away our reproach"?

2. In the passage in Isaiah it is the *women* who request of the man, "let us be called by thy name", but Mormon "inspired scripture" has the initiative resting with the *men*. The basis for Mormon teaching on polygamy is that God commanded Joseph Smith to take plural wives because of a new and everlasting covenant.[58] Rather than the woman making the request of the man, Joseph Smith's wife was told if she did not submit to a polygamous relationship, she would be cursed.[59] Is submission the same as request?

3. The geographical location of the prophecy is not Independence, Missouri, nor the area covered by the Mormon trek to Salt Lake City, in the 1800s, but Palestine. Consider the following evidence: Judah and Jerusalem (Isa. 2:1); "cedars of Lebanon" (2:13); "oaks of Bashan" (2:13); Jerusalem and Judah (3:1); "Judah is ruined and Jerusalem is fallen" (3:8); "daughters of Zion" (3:16); "he that is left in Zion, and he that remaineth in Jerusalem" (4:3); mount Zion (4:5).

4. There are two reasons implied in the context for seven women requesting to be called by the name of one man:

   a. So many young men had been slaughtered there was no longer enough males for the females. "Thy men shall fall by the sword, and thy mighty in the war". (Isa. 3:25).

   b. The females had been stricken with plagues (Isa. 3:16–24; "filth of the daughters of Zion", Isa. 4:4) which were so repugnant that no young man desired these women for wives. Hence the request to be called by a man's

---

[58] "For behold, I reveal unto you a new and an everlasting covenant; and if ye abide not that covenant, then are ye damned; for no one can reject this covenant and be permitted to enter into my glory...And let mine handmaid, Emma Smith, receive all those [wives] that have been given unto my servant Joseph...And if he have ten virgins given unto him by this law, he cannot commit adultery, for they belong to him, and they are given unto him; therefore is he justified." *Doctrine and Covenants*, section 132:4,52,62, pp.239,244,245 (1952 ed.).

[59] The following revelation is alleged to have been given Joseph Smith by God: "And let mine handmaid, Emma Smith, receive all those wives that have been given unto my servant Joseph... And I command mine handmaid, Emma Smith, to abide and cleave unto my servant Joseph, and to none else. But if she will not abide this commandment she shall be destroyed, saith the Lord; for I am the Lord thy God, and will destroy her if she abide not in my law." *Doctrine and Covenants*, Section 132:53,54, p.244 (1952 ed.).

name to take away the reproach, yet "we will eat our own bread, and wear our own apparel…"

Either, or both of these reasons are incompatible with the Mormon claim that polygamy was a "new and divine covenant" communicated by God through the "prophet" Joseph Smith.

Mormon communities have been noted for their patriarchal rule.[60] Mormon doctrine teaches that a woman cannot attain the highest glory for a woman, apart from a man.[61] But the context to the passage in question states, "as for my people…women rule over them". (Isa. 3:12). Since Mormon history is silent about rulership by women, this is further evidence that Isa. 4:1 is not prophetic of Mormon polygamy.

BAPTISM FOR THE DEAD

1 Corinthians 15:29
"Else what shall they do which are baptized for the dead, if the dead rise not at all?"

1 Peter 3:18–20
"For Christ also hath once suffered for sins, the just for the unjust, that he might bring us to God, being put to death in the flesh, but quickened by the Spirit: by which also he went and preached unto the spirits in prison; which sometime were disobedient, when once the longsuffering of God waited in the days of Noah…"

Malachi 4:5,6
"Behold, I will send you Elijah the prophet before the coming of the great and dreadful day of the LORD: and he shall turn the heart of the fathers to the children, and the heart of the children to their fathers, lest I come and smite the earth with a curse."

PROBLEM:

The doctrine of baptism for the dead is not mentioned in the *Book of Mormon* (which is said to contain "the fulness of the everlasting gospel")[62] but was allegedly given to Joseph Smith in a vision after the *Book of Mormon* had been translated. Scriptural support for the doctrine is derived solely from 1 Cor 15:29. 1 Pet. 3:18–22 is held to teach that Christ preached to the departed souls of antediluvian men and women during the three days of his sojourn in *hades*, thus showing that men can have "a second chance" after death. It is therefore pressed into use to

---

[60] See LeGrand Richards, *A Marvellous Work and a Wonder*, (Salt Lake City, Utah: Deseret Book Company, 1950), p.200.

[61] Ibid., p.195.

[62] In fact the general teaching of the *Book of Mormon* is against the idea of a second chance. E.g., "Behold, if ye have procrastinated the day of your repentance, even until death, behold, ye have become subjected to the spirit of the devil, and he doth seal you his…the devil hath all power over you and this is the final state of the wicked." (*Book of Mormon*, Alma, 34:35).

support baptism for the dead. Mal. 4:4–6 is said to speak of a "welding link between the fathers and the children" and this link is said to be baptism of the children on behalf of their dead fathers and of fathers for their deceased children.

Mormons spend great amounts of time looking up their genealogies. Some have been baptized[63] by proxy more than fifty times for the benefit of "Gentile" ancestors. The baptisms are always done within the secrecy of Mormon temples— support for this practice being taken principally from 1 Cor. 15:29. One Mormon put it this way:

> "Millions of earth's sons and daughters have passed out of the body without obeying the law of baptism. Many of them will gladly accept the word and law of the Lord when it is proclaimed to them in the spirit world. But they cannot here attend to ordinances that belong to the sphere which they have left. Can nothing be done in their case? Must they forever be shut out of the kingdom of heaven? But justice and mercy join in answering 'yes' to the first, 'no' to the last question. What, then, is the way of their deliverance? The living may be baptized for the dead. Other essential ordinances may be attended to vicariously. This glorious truth hid from human knowledge for centuries,[64] has been made known in this greatest of all dispensations..."[65]

SOLUTION:

1. Looking at the two ancillary quotations first:
   a. 1 Pet. 3:18–20 is considered in detail on pages 184, 302. It has nothing to do with the departed spirits of men being given a second chance. Such an explanation is ruled out by the clear teaching of Scripture that in death men return to the dust and are unconscious, e.g. Psa. 146:3,4 and Eccl. 9:5–10.
   b. To use Mal. 4:5,6 as referring to baptism for the dead is a gross distortion of Scripture. Malachi is saying that Elijah the prophet would be sent to Israel and he would "turn the heart of the fathers to the children, and the heart of the children to their fathers." The consequence of Israel rejecting this message was not hell fire because they had rejected the offer of a second chance, but the smiting of "the land [of Israel] with a curse".

2. It is apparent from Penrose's argument that the Mormon position rests on two prior propositions:
   a. That Mormon "scripture" is authoritative.
   b. That at death the real person departs to the spirit world.

   Since these two Mormon claims are considered in detail elsewhere in this manual, they are not examined here.

---

[63] Mormons baptize by immersion in water. Although infant baptism is rejected, Mormons consider the age of accountability to be eight!

[64] Other groups have practised baptism for the dead. Among these were the Marcionites and the Montanists. The Council of Hippo (AD 393) forbade the practice. See James Hasting (ed.) *Encyclopedia of Religion and Ethics*, Vol. 8, (New York, Charles Scribner's Sons), p.408.

[65] C. Penrose, *Mormon Doctrine Plain and Simple: or Leaves from the Tree of Life*, 1897, p.48.

3. The Mormon doctrine of proxy baptism rests on this one passage in the entire Bible. Any doctrine must be suspect which rests on only *one* verse. Much more so when the interpretation given to the verses violates the teaching of Scripture that in death responsible men and women are unconscious (asleep) until the resurrection and judgment[66], whilst death is eternal annihilation for those who die in ignorance of the gospel.[67]

4. But what does 1 Cor. 15:29 mean? A number of interpretations have in the past been proposed. The one which best fits the context is the following:

   "Else what shall they do which are baptized for the dead [Christ][68], if the dead [believers] rise not at all?"

   The argument being: "Why be baptized on behalf of Christ if he has not been raised from the dead?" (c.f. vv. 4–19; vv. 20–28 being read as parenthetical).

---

[66] For example Psa. 6:5; 1 Cor. 15:18; Heb. 9:27.

[67] For example Psa. 49:20; Eph. 4:18. This would include the "other lords" (Isa. 26:13,14) and the Babylonians (Jer. 51:39,57).

[68] It is sometimes argued that "the dead" cannot refer to Christ since the Greek word for dead, *nekron* is plural, not singular. But a check of the Hebrew word for "death" in Isa. 53:9 ("He made his grave with the wicked, and with the rich in his death"), indicates that the word "death" in this reference is also plural. The plural is in harmony with the argument of the Apostle Paul that "if one died for all, then were all dead". (2 Cor. 5:14). The death of Christ comprehended many deaths.

1.3

SEVENTH–DAY ADVENTISM

THE BIBLE AND THE SABBATH

THE "CEREMONIAL LAW" AND THE "MORAL LAW"

PROBLEM:

A distinction is made by SDAs between the "ceremonial law" (written in a book), which it is argued was done away with in Christ, and the "moral law" (inscribed in the tables of stone) which is said to be eternal and immutable. A SDA publication puts it this way:

> "We feel that there are ample Biblical grounds for making this distinction. The Ten Commandments, or the Decalogue, constitute in principle God's eternal law. Not only is this law eternal, but it is immutable."[1]

SOLUTION:

SDAs impose on Scripture a division not made by Scripture itself. Consider the following:

1. Hezekiah appointed "the king's portion of his substance for the burnt offerings …for the sabbaths, and for the new moons, and for the set feasts, as it is written in the law of the LORD." (2 Chron. 31:3). This passage indicates that the "law of the LORD" includes "ceremonial" aspects (i.e., feasts, burnt offerings) as well as "moral law". (SDAs teach that the "law of Moses" refers to the ceremonial aspects, whereas the "law of the LORD" refers to the moral law.)

2. In Num. 31:21 the ordinance of "the law which the LORD commanded Moses" is stated concerning the men who had returned from battle with the spoils of war. "The law which the LORD commanded Moses" is not, therefore, an expression exclusively used for the decalogue. The passage also indicates that "the law" cannot be divided between "ceremonial" and "moral aspects" since the above instructions regarding war had a moral intent.

3. In the New Testament "the law" is consistently spoken of as a single entity. For example, "The law was given by Moses…" (John 1:17). Never is a distinction made between the "moral law" and the "ceremonial law".

4. God's decree forbidding marriage with the alien is not specifically indicated in the decalogue, but is written in the "book of the law of Moses" (Josh. 23:6,12) and likewise contains a moral intent.

---

[1] *Seventh-day Adventists Answer Questions on Doctrine*: An Explanation of Certain Major Aspects of Seventh-day Adventist Belief, (Washington: Review and Herald Publishing Ass., 1957), p.129.

5. There is an inconsistency between SDA teaching and practice with respect to what they style "the ceremonial law". SDAs do not eat unclean meats. This practice is based on that ceremonial law which they accept was abolished by Jesus.

ORIGIN AND DURATION OF THE SABBATH LAW

PROBLEM:

SDAs argue that the Sabbath law was given to Adam and Eve before the fall and is eternally binding on all believers. The argument is stated as follows:

"But the Decalogue, sealed with the lip and finger of God, was lifted above all Jewish rites and ceremonies. This is evident from the fact that the Sabbath was established before man sinned, and therefore before he had any need of a Redeemer. It was not a part of the ceremonial regulations occasioned by the entrance of sin, and which were annulled by the death of Christ (Col. 2:17)."[2]

SOLUTION:

1. There is no passage of Scripture which explicitly states that the keeping of the Sabbath was binding on any prior to God's giving of the covenant to Israel. God "rested" (Gen. 2:2,3), but nowhere is it stated that Adam and Eve were commanded to observe the Sabbath.

2. Paul expressly states that "the law" (of which the decalogue was a part) "was added because of transgressions, until the seed should come." (Gal. 3:19). Since the law was added because of transgressions, then clearly it could not have been given to Adam and Eve before they sinned. In fact the apostle says that it was "added" after the giving of "the promise" to Abraham (Gal. 3:17). In the context he is clearly referring to the law, given at Sinai, which was "added" because of the transgressions of the people of Israel. The law was added until "the seed should come," which clearly implies that its provision had served its purpose when the Seed had come.

3. Even if it were true that the Sabbath law was in existence before the law of Moses, this does not necessarily make it binding today, since both animal sacrifices and circumcision were commanded by God in patriarchal times, but are not now binding.

4. If the Sabbath law were eternal, why did an alleged "ceremonial law"— circumcision, take precedence over Sabbath observance—a moral law? The law required that eight days after a child was born it must be circumcised (Lev. 12:3), but sometimes the day of circumcision would fall on a sabbath. A conflict of laws resulted—one demanding that circumcision should take place, and the other, that no work should be done. (See John 7:22,23). Circumcision took precedence because unless one was circumcised, the law could not be kept. Likewise, on the "sabbath days the priests in the temple profane the sabbath,

---

[2] *Seventh-day Adventists Answer Questions on Doctrine*, (Washington: Review and Herald Publishing Ass., 1957), pp.150,151.

and are blameless." (Matt. 12:5). Instead of the Sabbath being a day of rest to the Lord, their work was doubled. (Num. 28:9,10). All believers are a "royal priesthood" (1 Pet. 2:9) and as such, are exempt from one day Sabbath keeping.

5. Part of the Sabbath law was the penalty for its disobedience: "Whosoever doeth any work in the sabbath day, he shall surely be put to death." (Exo. 31:15). If the law commanding observance has not changed why has the penalty for its disobedience been changed by the SDAs?

6. The Sabbath law is expressly stated to be a sign between God and Israel: "It is a sign between me and the children of Israel for ever." (Exo. 31:17, cf. Deut. 5:15). The law was not given to the forebears of the Israelites since it is stated: "The LORD made not this covenant with our fathers, but with us, even us, who are all of us here alive this day." (Deut. 5:3). This is further suggested by the ignorance of Moses and Aaron as to what to do with the man caught picking up sticks on the sabbath: "And they put him in ward, because it was not declared what should be done to him." (Num. 15:34). Why would there be ignorance about the penalty for Sabbath disobedience if the law had been in force since Eden?

7. If the Sabbath law is eternal why is it termed (as part of the decalogue) "the ministration of death, written and engraven in stones" and the "ministration of condemnation"? (2 Cor. 3:6–9).

8. The Sabbath is termed a "shadow". (Col. 2:16,17). How can that which is a "shadow" be eternal? The Sabbath was designed to teach men to rest from the works of the flesh in anticipation of the great millennial rest which God would provide. "There remaineth therefore a rest to the people of God." (Heb. 4:9,11). The believer now rests every day from the works of the flesh, labouring "to enter into that rest". (Heb. 4:11). This parallels the change in circumcision—from a literal cutting off of flesh to "that of the heart, in the spirit and not in the letter." (Rom. 2:29)[3]

9. Judaising heretics who said that it was needful to keep the Law of Moses (Acts 15:1,24) subverted the Truth and received strong indictments from the Apostle Paul in his letter to the Galatian ecclesia. But no mention is made by the apostle of a binding Sabbath law to be observed by Gentile converts. Similarly, it is significant that the Council at Jerusalem (Acts 15) was convened to consider Jewish claims regarding the Law of Moses, but no mention was made of Sabbath keeping. If the Sabbath were eternal and immutable one would have expected that at this conference such would have been stated. Rather, Paul's letters leave Sabbath observance to the individual choice of believers. (Rom. 14:5,6; Col. 2:14–17).

10. There is further evidence that Sabbath observance is not mandatory for New Testament believers:

   a. The ten commandments were a part of the "old" covenant. (Exo. 34:28; Deut. 4:13; 1 Kings 8:9,21).

---

[3] Even now believers can partially experience the Sabbath rest of the millennium. Jesus said: "Come unto me, all ye that labour and are heavy laden, and I will give you rest." (Matt. 11:28). The Greek word, *anapausis*, translated "rest" is used in the Septuagint for the Old Testament Sabbath rest. (The Septuagint is the Greek translation of the Old Testament Scriptures in the third century BC.)

b. But the writer to the Hebrews states, with respect to the making of the new covenant, "he hath made the first old. Now that which decayeth and waxeth old is ready to vanish away." (Heb. 8:13).

c. Therefore, the law as given to Israel (which included the decalogue) is no longer binding upon New Testament believers.

11. It is sometimes contended that if the "old" covenant has been replaced by the "new" then it must now be permissible to steal, murder etc., but this is not so. The following tabulation shows that nine of the ten commandments have been reaffirmed in the affirmative form ("do" rather than "do not"). Sabbath observance is the one command of the law which is not reaffirmed.

	New Testament	Old Testament
1st	Eph. 4:6; 1 John 5:21; Matt. 4:10	Exo. 20:3
2nd	1 Cor. 10:14; Rom. 1:25	Exo. 20:4–6
3rd	James 5:12; Matt. 5:34,35	Exo. 20:7
4th	Abolished: Rom. 14:5; Col. 2:16,17; Heb. 8:13	Exo. 20:8
5th	Eph. 6:1; Col. 3:20	Exo. 20:12
6th	1 John 3:15; Matt. 5:21,22; Rom. 13:9	Exo. 20:13
7th	Heb. 13:4; Matt. 5:27,28; 1 Cor. 6:9,10	Exo. 20:14
8th	Rom. 2:21; Eph. 4:28	Exo. 20:15
9th	Col. 3:9; Eph. 4:25; 2 Tim. 3:3; 1 Tim. 3:8–11	Exo. 20:16
10th	Eph. 5:3; Col. 3:5	Exo. 20:17

12. The apostles gathered with believers on the first day of the week to remember the sacrifice of Christ and to take up the collection of money for the work of the Truth. (Acts 20:7; 1 Cor. 16:2). On the Sabbath they were engaged in contentious disputation with the Jews in the synagogues. Acts records: "And Paul, as his manner was, went in unto them [the synagogue of the Jews], and three sabbath days reasoned with them out of the scriptures." (Acts 17:2). Seventh-day Adventists have reversed this example. They gather with those of like belief on Saturday and proselytize on Sunday.[4]

---

[4] SDAs contend that the custom of holding the memorial service on Sunday owes its origin to the decree of Constantine in AD 328 in which it was commanded that the first day of the week should be kept holy by all "Christians". This SDA assertion is inaccurate. Historical records indicate that the custom went back to Apostolic times. Consider the following: a) "We do not regard circumcision, nor observe the sabbath, because such things as these do not belong to Christians" (Eusebius, about AD 324); b) "The obligation of the Lord's resurrection binds us to keep the paschal festival on the Lord's day" (Anatolius, AD 270); c) "Sunday is the day on which we all hold our common assembly; since it is the first day in which God made the world; and Jesus Christ, our Saviour, rose, on that day from the dead." "On the day called Sunday there is made a gathering into the same place of all that live in city or country, and the memoranda of the apostles, or the writings of the prophets, are read as long as may be. Afterwards, the reader having ceased, the president makes verbally the admonition and exhortation to the imitation of these excellent things. Then we all rise and pour forth prayers. Then the bread and wine are taken" (Justin Martyr, AD 140); "Those who were concerned with old things, have come to newness of confidence, no longer keeping sabbaths, but living according to the Lord's day, on which our life, as risen again through him, depends." (Ignatius, about AD 100). [Quoted from "How and When the Sabbath Should Be Kept", *Herald of the Coming Age,* XVIII, No. 6, (April, 1968), p.96].

WRESTED SCRIPTURES

Matthew 24:20

"But pray ye that your flight be not in the winter, neither on the sabbath day."

PROBLEM:

This passage is cited by SDAs in an attempt to prove that the Sabbath is binding upon believers. The question is pressed: "Why would Jesus instruct his disciples to pray that their flight be not on the Sabbath, if Sabbath observance were no longer binding?"

SOLUTION:

1. This instruction from the Lord was to his disciples and has to do with the Roman invasion of Israel in AD 69–70. They were to leave in haste at the first sign of the Roman legions.
2. Nehemiah had commanded that the gates of the city be closed on the Sabbath. (Neh. 13:19). The Jews, with veiled eyes, failed to respond to the teaching of Christ about the Sabbath. Consequently, if the Jewish believers fled Jerusalem on a Sabbath, they would be confronted by closed gates in those cities in which they sought succour as they headed into "the mountains" and by the wrath of the Jews.
3. A flight on the Sabbath would have involved more than the "sabbath day's journey" stipulated by Jewish tradition (cf. Acts 1:12). In the midst of the conditions then prevailing this would have been to invite death from the fanatical Jews.
4. A flight in the winter would bring its own obvious hardships.

THE DESOLATION OF THE EARTH DURING THE MILLENNIUM

The SDA Church teaches that at the second advent of Jesus the righteous will be taken to heaven. The wicked will be destroyed to await "the resurrection of damnation" at the end of the millennium. The earth will be made utterly desolate and will remain so for the duration of the millennium. A number of scriptures are said to support this teaching.

Isaiah 24:1,3,19

"Behold, the LORD maketh the earth empty, and maketh it waste, and turneth it upside down, and scattereth abroad the inhabitants thereof."

"The land shall be utterly emptied, and utterly spoiled: for the LORD hath spoken this word."

"The earth is utterly broken down, the earth is clean dissolved, the earth is moved exceedingly."

PROBLEM:

According to SDAs these verses support their belief that the earth will be desolate for a thousand years during which time Satan will be "circumstantially bound" on the earth. A SDA publication comments as follows:

"The implication is almost unavoidable that the destination of the righteous at the second advent is heaven—not the earth from which they are removed at the last trump."[5]

"Satan's followers have all been destroyed at the second advent. The righteous ...are removed from his [Satan's] domain. The earth is in utter desolation, with dead bodies everywhere...Satan is consigned by divine fiat to the earth, there for one thousand years to ponder on the results of his rebellion against God."[6]

SOLUTION:

1. If the earth is to become completely desolate who are the "few men left"? (v. 6). Why is every house shut up so that none can enter? (v. 10). Who is crying in the streets for lack of wine? (v. 11). Who is it that sings for joy? (v. 14).

2. Isaiah refers to the Lord of hosts reigning in Mount Zion, "and in Jerusalem, and before his ancients gloriously." (v. 23). This time is referred to by Isaiah in chapters 2 and 65. Both of these passages require the continued existence of mortal people on the earth. Note the following: Isa. 2:3 (these are not righteous immortals since they go to Jerusalem to learn, Zech. 14:17); Isa. 65:17–20 ("the sinner being an hundred years old shall be accursed" likewise indicates the continued existence of mortal nations on the earth).

3. The saints will not be removed to heaven. "They shall be priests of God and of Christ, and shall reign with him a thousand years." (Rev. 20:6). This reigning, will be on the earth: "And hast made us unto our God kings and priests: and we shall reign on the earth." (Rev. 5:10).

4. The apparently absolute expressions of desolation on the earth must, therefore, be read in a limited sense. This conclusion is further indicated by noting parallel expressions in Jer. 44:2,6 in which Jerusalem is referred to as a desolation with no man dwelling therein, yet Nebuzaradan the captain of the guard left certain of the poor of the land for vinedressers and husbandmen. (Jer. 52:16).

5. God will not leave the earth utterly desolate with no inhabitants since "the LORD said in his heart, I will not again curse the ground any more for man's sake; for the imagination of man's heart is evil from his youth; neither will I again smite any more every thing living, as I have done." (Gen. 8:21).

6. The words "the earth" throughout this chapter are the Hebrew words for "the land", as pointed out in the alternative translation in the RV (ASV). The "land" referred to is the land of Israel, which was made desolate when its people were scattered abroad (v. 1) in fulfilment of "the curse" (v. 6), as predicted in Deut. 28:15,25,64; Lev. 26:16,31–33.

---

[5] *Seventh-day Adventists Answer Questions on Doctrine*, (Washington: Review and Herald Publishing Ass., 1957), p.495.

[6] Ibid., p.492.

Jeremiah 4:7,23

"...and thy cities shall be laid waste, without an inhabitant."

"I beheld the earth, and, lo, it was without form, and void; and the heavens, and they had no light."

PROBLEM:

SDAs connect these verses with those in Isa. 24:1,3,19 to teach that the earth will be completely desolate during the millennium except for Satan who will be left to ponder on the results of his rebellion against God.

SOLUTION:

1. As in Isa. 24 "the earth" in this passage refers, not to the globe but to the land of Palestine. (v. 1–3,5,6).
2. The passage was fulfilled when Nebuchadnezzar took Jerusalem in 586 BC (Jer. 44:2,6; 52:5,7,8). Even then, some Jews were left to till the soil. (Jer. 52:15,16).
3. Even if there were a secondary application of this passage at Armageddon, positive evidence that mortals will inhabit the earth during the millennium is supported from the following passages:
    a. The saints are to be given power over the nations to rule with a rod of iron. (Rev. 2:26,27). But this time must be during the millennial period since the end of the millennium results in the end of sin and mortality. (1 Cor. 15:22–28).
    b. The saints are said to reign for a thousand years (Rev. 20:6). But who are they to reign over if removed to heaven? (cf. Rev. 5:10—"We shall reign on the earth.").
    c. See also Zech. 14:16,17; Isa. 65:17,18.

Revelation 21:10

"And he carried me away in the spirit to a great and high mountain, and shewed me that great city, the holy Jerusalem, descending out of heaven from God."

PROBLEM:

Seventh-day Adventists cite this passage in support of their doctrine that the rapture will take the saints to heaven for 1,000 years, after which the bride, represented as a city, will descend to the earth.[7]

SOLUTION:

1. The saints will not be in heaven for the 1,000 years period, therefore the passage cannot teach the literal descent of the saints to the earth. See Rev. 5:10—"and we shall reign on the earth." This reigning is during the 1,000 years as is

---

[7] See *Seventh-day Adventists Answer Questions on Doctrine*, (Washington: Review and Herald Publishing Ass., 1967), pp.504,505.

indicated in Rev. 20:6—"they shall be priests of God and of Christ, and shall reign with him a thousand years."

2. The Revelation which depicts the saints as a city descending from God out of heaven employs the language of theophany in which a manifestation of God is said to be God descending or coming down. See for example: Gen. 11:5; 18:21; Exo. 3:7,8. The saints are chosen in Christ "before the foundation of the world". (Eph. 1:4). Their origin is from heaven in the sense that they are new creations (James 1:18; 2 Cor. 5:17) born from above (John 3:3,7 RVm.) by the Spirit-given word. (John 6:63). Similarly the manna which the children of Israel ate in the wilderness was bread sent down from heaven. (John 6:31). "From heaven" emphasizes its divine origin without asserting that it was manufactured in heaven and floated down to the earth. Similarly, the bride descending out of heaven symbolically portrays her heavenly origin.

I.4

PENTECOSTALISM

PRELIMINARY POINTS:

Pentecostals[1] tend to be very difficult to engage in a reasoned Biblical discussion. Inevitably, the discussion becomes a stalemate when the Pentecostal asserts that he has had a personal experience with the Lord and is now led into all truth by the Holy Spirit. It has been said that "the man who has had an experience is never at the mercy of a man with an argument". The point is, there is no longer any common ground from which to reason from the accepted to the disputed. The non-Pentecostal is relegated to the position of a "natural man" who "cannot understand the things of the spirit" (i.e., the spiritual "truths" of Pentecostal teaching).[2]

One problem area in such discussions is that there is no common authority to which appeal might be made. It may at first be thought that the obvious authority is the Bible, but in actual fact this is seldom the case. The real authority is nearly always extra-Biblical, i.e., the Holy Spirit, or the "reality" of a personal encounter with the Lord. The apostolic instruction to "prove all things" (1 Thess. 5:21) is an objective basis for discussion, but Pentecostalism operates on the highly subjective basis of personal experiences and Holy Spirit guidance. The tragedy of such authorities is the way in which the Holy Spirit is, in effect, charged with errors taught in the name of Pentecostalism. It is not uncommon to find "Spirit-guided" Pentecostals

[1] There are many factions within the Pentecostal movement with differences of belief. Some are independent and known as "Jesus only" (denying the orthodox trinitarian belief), but all Pentecostals emphasize the "born-again" experience and the baptism of the Holy Spirit. The term "Pentecostal" is used in this analysis to include all groups within the general movement.

[2] *Time* called Pentecostalism the "fastest growing church in the hemisphere" ("Fastest Growing Church in the Hemisphere", *Time*, 80, Nov. 2, 1962, p.56). *Life* regarded it as "the third force", equal in significance to Roman Catholicism and historic Protestantism ("The Third Force in Christendom", *Life*, 44, June 9, 1958, p.113). When the first edition of *Wrested Scriptures* was published, A. A. Allen was one of the most popular Pentecostals in America. The A. A. Allen Revivals Inc., in 1968 grossed $2,692,342.00—not counting the salaries of Allen and his two associate preachers who took their cut directly from "their ministry"—printed 55 million pieces of literature; maintained daily radio broadcasts (58 stations), and weekly television programmes (43 stations). See "Religion: Faith Healers Getting Back Double from God", *Time* (Canadian edition), 93, No. 10, p.52.

[3] Historically, official differences have existed among Pentecostal groups. For example, the Elim movement and the Assemblies of God have these principal differences:

a) Whether the initial sign of "Baptism of the Holy Ghost" is necessarily speaking in tongues—affirmed by the Assemblies of God, whereas Elim has regarded tongues as only one of several possible signs. b) Whether there are apostles in the church today—asserted by the Apostolic Church. c) Whether there would be a total or partial rapture of the saints. d) Interpretations of Bible prophecy. This latter was a source of division within Elim itself. See *Elim Evangel*, 21, (1940), p.125. Referred to by Bryan Wilson, *Sects and Society: A Sociological Study of Three Religious Groups in Britain*, (London: William Heinemann Ltd., 1961), p.57.

76

repeatedly differing in their respective interpretations of the same verses.[3] Is the Holy Spirit power of Almighty God the author of confusion?

SUGGESTED STRATEGY

1. Christ predicted that miracles and prophesying would be done in his name, apart from his sanction or power. (Matt. 7:21–23; see also 2 Thess. 2:9). This is why an experience or miracle, no matter how great, cannot be appealed to as the sole judge of the source of that event. A discussion with a Pentecostal can often be more effective if a simple, yet important, ground rule is laid down at the beginning—that if anything is said in the discussion, even if attributed to extra-Biblical sources, it must stand the test of Scripture.[4] To assume such a posture in the discussion is to follow the instruction of the New Testament. Consider the following:

   a. Paul establishes the test of sound doctrine as the criterion by which claimants to Spirit-gift powers can be examined: "Now concerning spiritual gifts, brethren, I would not have you ignorant. Ye know that ye were Gentiles, carried away unto these dumb idols, even as ye were led. Wherefore I give you to understand, that no man speaking by the Spirit of God calleth Jesus accursed: and that no man can say that Jesus is the Lord, but by the Holy Spirit." (1 Cor. 12:1–3). The lord prominent in the first century was "my lord Serapis".[5] The Gospel challenged allegiance to this god through converts made to the Hope of Israel. No teacher with Spirit gifts would say "Jesus is accursed", but on the other hand, no teacher who followed the pagan cult would assert that Jesus was lord. The test of the claimant to Spirit powers, was, therefore, the test of the doctrine he taught.

   b. Similarly, John applied the test of sound doctrine: "Hereby know ye the Spirit of God: Every spirit that confesseth that Jesus Christ is come in the flesh is of God: and every spirit that confesseth not that Jesus Christ is come in the flesh is not of God..." (1 John 4:2,3). The test is the same—Is the teaching of the one who claims Spirit gifts in accordance with the revealed Word?

2. Now an area of discussion can be selected. But where should one start? The recurrent theme of Pentecostal services is the weight of man's sin, the suffering of Christ in vicariously atoning for man's guilt, and the debt of gratitude which all believers owe to Jesus who relieved them of their guilt. It is in this context that the Pentecostal evaluates Christadelphian teaching about the kingdom of

---

[4] The Bereans were commended as follows: "These were more noble than those in Thessalonica, in that they received the word with all readiness of mind, and searched the scriptures daily, whether those things were so." (Acts 17:11). If the inspired teaching of the Apostle Paul was put to the test of Scripture, how much more the statements of latter day claimants to Spirit gifts!

[5] This foreign god was imported to Egypt where in Alexandria it was regarded as a protector. A temple was built for Serapis which "rivalled the pride and magnificence of the Capitol". The god was similar in appearance to Jupiter and it was confidently affirmed by his votaries that if any impious hand should dare to violate the majesty of the god, the heavens and the earth would instantly return to their original chaos. See Edward Gibbon, *The Decline and Fall of the Roman Empire*, (New York: Harcourt Brace and Co., 1960 ed.), pp.415-417.

God and the nature of man—interesting discussion, perhaps, but, to the Pentecostal, hardly fundamental to the "gospel". It certainly could be effectively argued that both of these areas are *fundamentals* of the Gospel. There are times, however, when it is advantageous to work within the belief system of the non-Christadelphian and in so doing, become "all things to all men" (1 Cor. 9:22) that some might be saved. What better place to start than the nature, death and atonement of Christ?[6] The implication of such a discussion would be to imply, if not to state, that the Pentecostal claim to be led into all truth by the Holy Spirit is wholly unjustified, since the doctrines taught are unscriptural and therefore subject to the severe condemnation of Gal. 1:8,9 ("As we said before, so say I now again, If any man preach any other gospel unto you than that ye have received, let him be accursed").

SUBSTITUTION

Romans 5:6

"For when we were yet without strength, in due time Christ died for the ungodly."

Romans 5:8

"But God commendeth his love toward us, in that, while we were yet sinners, Christ died for us."

PROBLEM:

These verses are understood by Pentecostals (and others, such as Evangelicals) to mean that Christ paid Adam's debt by dying *instead* of the sinner. Therefore, salvation is offered by grace alone.

SOLUTION:

1. In the statement, "Christ died for us", "for" does not mean "instead of". See its usage in 1 Cor. 15:3; Gal. 1:4; Heb. 10:12; Heb. 7:25.
2. If Jesus died as a substitute for me, paying my penalty, then why should I die? Why is it that mankind die the same today as before this substitution took place? If I am sentenced to jail and a substitute takes my place instead of me, I do not then go to jail with him!

---

[6] The following is a brief outline of Pentecostal belief in these three areas, as defined by J. A. Synan et. al. (eds.), *The Pentecostal Holiness Church Manual*, (Franklin Springs, Georgia: Board of Publications, Pentecostal Holiness Church, 1965):

a) *Christ's Nature*—He was "a perfect, sinless human being...very God and perfect man." p.29.

b) *Christ's Death*—"Christ lived *in* a mortal body subject to suffering and death." "He 'dropped out' of the mortal body on the cross." p.25.

c) *Christ's Atonement*—"We believe, teach and firmly maintain the...doctrine of justification by faith *alone*...We do not believe that any sort or degree of good works can procure or contribute toward our justification or salvation; that this is accomplished solely and exclusively upon the basis of our faith in the shed blood..." p.31.

3. If the sacrifice of Christ were a substitute, how can there be real forgiveness with God. A creditor who releases the debtor because someone not his debtor pays the latter's debt, surely cannot claim to have *forgiven* the debt! If the debt is paid, then there is no longer need for forgiveness.

4. If Christ's death were a substitution, instead of the sinner, then the redeeming power lay in his death and not in his resurrection, yet Paul declares: Jesus Christ "…was delivered for our offences, and was raised again for our justification." (Rom. 4:25). Cf. also 1 Cor. 15:17—"If Christ be not raised, your faith is vain; ye are yet in your sins."

5. The Scriptural language is that Christ died that he "should taste death for every man." (Heb. 2:9). This is the language of representation exhibited throughout the types of the Law of Moses, not substitution.

GIFTS OF THE SPIRIT

1. GENERAL

Acts 2:38,39

"Then Peter said unto them, Repent, and be baptized every one of you in the name of Jesus Christ for the remission of sins, and ye shall receive the gift of the Holy Spirit. For the promise is unto you, and to your children, and to all that are afar off, even as many as the Lord our God shall call."

PROBLEM:

Pentecostals believe that the gift of the Holy Spirit is available today. Sooner or later, in discussion with the Pentecostal, the Christadelphian will be required to provide proof that the Spirit gifts are not available today. These verses from Acts 2 are frequently used to support the view that the promise of the Holy Spirit was for all believers and for all time.

SOLUTION:

1. Two important points should be noted from the context of these verses:
    a. Peter's remarks were addressed to Jews and converts to the Jewish religion (vv. 5–14).
    b. His remarks have to do with an event that is limited by the context to a period referred to as "the last days" (v. 17).

    Those parts of the New Testament that were addressed primarily to Jewish believers refer to this period on a number of occasions. E.g. "God, who at sundry times and in divers manners spake in time past unto the fathers by the prophets, hath in *these last days* spoken unto us by his Son…" (Heb. 1:1,2; see also James 5:3 RV; 1 John 2:18). The destruction of Jerusalem predicted by the Lord Jesus (Luke 21:20–22) was fast approaching. Those days were the "last days" of Israel under the Old Law Covenant.

79

This promise of the Holy Spirit was thus:

a. For Jews ("you and your children").

b. For Gentiles ("all [nations] that are far off"; cf. Eph. 2:13,17).

c. But not for *all* Jews and *all* Gentiles—only "as many as the Lord our God shall call".

d. And not for all time but for those Jews and Gentiles who were called during those "last days".

2. It is worth noting that, speaking to the Jews, Peter said, the gift of the Holy Spirit was promised "to you and to your children—two generations. These two generations would have taken the ecclesia up to the time of the destruction of Jerusalem—the end of "the last days" period. The ability to pass on the Spirit gifts seems to have been the special privilege of the apostles only (Ananias being a possible exception—Acts 9:17[7]). This is indicated by the fact that although Philip's preaching was accompanied by miracles (Acts 8:7), the apostles at Jerusalem sent Peter and John to Samaria to transmit the Spirit gifts by the laying on of hands. (Acts 8:14–18). Why should Peter and John be sent to Samaria to transmit Spirit-gift powers, if this power were available to all believers? (See also Acts 19:6 where Paul gave the Holy Spirit to the Ephesian believers by the laying on of his hands.) Hence, with the death of the apostles, there was no one able to transmit these gifts and so they ceased.

3. In 1 Cor. 13, the Apostle Paul contrasts the temporary character of the gifts with the permanence of faith, hope and love. "But covet earnestly the best gifts: and yet shew I unto you a more excellent way...Charity never faileth: but whether there be prophecies, [i.e., the *gift* of prophecy, 1 Cor. 12:1,9,10] they shall fail; whether there be tongues, [i.e. *gift* of tongues, 1 Cor. 12:10], they shall cease; whether there be knowledge, [i.e, *gift* of knowledge, 1 Cor. 12:8] it shall vanish away." (1 Cor. 12:31; 13:8). When was this to take place? Paul says, "But when that which is perfect is come, then that which is in part shall be done away." (1 Cor. 13:10). Two interpretations are usually given to this verse. Pentecostals argue that the "perfect" refers to the return of Christ, while others, such as the Christadelphians, argue that it refers to the maturity which came to the ecclesia with the completed Scriptures. If the latter could be proven, then, of course, this would amount to a proof that the Spirit-gift powers ceased about the end of the first century. The following is advanced in support of the latter interpretation:

a. The Spirit gifts would pass away before the advent of Christ since Paul says, faith and hope *abide* (v.13). But when Christ returns one will have no need of hope, for "hope that is seen is not hope: for what a man seeth, why doth he yet hope for?" (Rom. 8:24). Nor would one have need for faith, since faith is "the assurance of things hoped for, the conviction of things not seen". (Heb. 11:1, RSV). Therefore, there must be a period of time *after* the passing

---

[7] There is another way of looking at this Scripture. The normal way of using the gift of healing appears to have been by the laying on of hands: "They shall lay hands on the sick, and they shall recover" (Mark 16:18). Ananias may well have laid hands on Saul solely for the purpose of restoring his sight, the Holy Spirit being given later directly from the Lord. If this were not the case, and Saul received the Holy Spirit when Ananias laid his hands on him, then Saul received the Holy Spirit before he was baptized.

of the Spirit gifts in which faith and hope "abide". Hence the passing of the Spirit gifts cannot be at the return of Christ, but must be at some time prior to this.

b. The apostle stressed, "*Now* abideth faith, hope, charity..." (1 Cor. 13:13). This stress indicates that the apostle did not consider the Holy Spirit gifts would continue past his age.

c. The immediate context to verse 10, ("But when that which is perfect is come, then that which is in part shall be done away") is the knowing "in part" and prophesying "in part". The term "perfect" is, therefore, qualified by the subject in the context—the possession of the knowledge of the purpose of God. The impartation of this knowledge was dependent in the first century upon the presence of believers with the gifts of "knowledge" and "prophecy" until the completion of the New Testament. Since the completion of the New Testament no claimants to Spirit-gift powers have been successful in adding to the perfected[8] (completed) Scriptures. Why this lack of new knowledge, if in fact the Spirit gifts have been available from the first century until the present day?

d. The most frequent use of "perfect" (Gk. *teleion*) is for the maturity of believers.[9] It is sometimes used in contexts which imply that the maturity is reached before the judgment at the return of Christ. Note the following:

—"Howbeit we speak wisdom among them that are perfect [*teleiois*, "mature", RSV]..." (1 Cor. 2:6).

—"Let us therefore, as many as be perfect [*teleioi*, "mature", RSV] (Phil. 3:15).

—"...in understanding be men [*teleioi*, "mature", RSV]. (1 Cor. 14:20).

—"For every one that useth milk is unskilful in the word of righteousness: for he is a babe. But strong meat belongeth to them that are of full age, [*teleion*, "mature", RSV] even those who by reason of use have their senses exercised to discern both good and evil." (Heb. 5:13,14).

e. The use of the word "perfect" in Eph. 4 is particularly interesting. Having referred to the Spirit gifts of "apostles...prophets...evangelists... pastors ...teachers" (vv. 8,11) Paul says that they were given, "*Till* we all come in the unity of the faith, and of the knowledge of the Son of God, unto a perfect man, unto the measure of the stature of the fulness of Christ" (v. 13). Clearly the ecclesia attained to this "perfect man" state (F. F. Bruce renders this "the maturity of fullgrown manhood"[10]) otherwise there would still be "apostles" in evidence today. The state of maturity had to do with the church being "no more children, tossed to and fro, and carried about with every wind of doctrine..." (v. 14). The completed Scriptures provided them with the means to resist the winds of false teaching.

[8] The Greek word translated "perfect" in 1 Cor. 13:10 is *teleios* which means 'ended, complete'. Robert Young, *Analytical Concordance to the Holy Bible*, (London: Lutterworth Press, 1965).

[9] *Teleion* is used once in reference to the Scriptures in James 1:25—"The perfect [*teleion*] law of liberty".

[10] F. F. Bruce, *Expanded Paraphrase of the Epistles of Paul*, (Devon: Paternoster Press, 1965).

WRESTED SCRIPTURES

The purpose of the Spirit gifts was to confirm the word which was spoken (Mark 16:20), and to equip the saints for the work of the ministry and for edification (Eph. 4:12), but when the mature state of the ecclesia was reached with the completion of the New Testament Scriptures, that which was "in part" (the Spirit gifts, e.g. some had the gift of tongues, others the gift of prophecy, etc.) ceased.

An explanation must also be offered for two comparisons which the apostle makes:

a. "When I was a child, I spake as a child, I understood as a child, I thought as a child: but when I became a man, I put away childish things." (1 Cor. 13:11). The apostle's personal life illustrated the development of the ecclesia, (the comparison of the ecclesia to a human body is made in chapter 12; cf. also Rom. 12:4–8) from the immature state which depended on Spirit gifts, to the maturity reached with the completion of the Scriptures. There may be a subtle allusion to the gift of tongues ("I spake"), and the gift of knowledge ("I understood"), and the gift of prophecy ("I thought", "reasoned" mg.). These would "be put away"—rendered inoperative by maturity.

b. "For now we see through a glass, darkly; but then face to face: now I know in part; but then shall I know even as also I am known." (1 Cor. 13:12). By looking into the partially revealed Word, man obtained a partial picture of the revelation of God to himself, but with the completion of revelation, man could then see himself as he was seen by God in the divine purpose.

4. A reasonable case can be made from the testimonies of Justin Martyr, Irenaeus, Origen, Chrysostom, and Augustine that in the post-apostolic era (AD 100–600) the gifts of the spirit, including speaking in tongues, ceased.[11]

COMFORTER PASSAGES:

John 14:16

"I will pray the Father, and he shall give you another Comforter, that he may abide with you for ever…"

John 14:26

"The Comforter, which is the Holy Spirit, whom the Father will send in my name, he shall teach you all things, and bring all things to your remembrance, whatsoever I have said unto you."

John 16:13

"Howbeit when he, the Spirit of truth, is come, he will guide you into all truth: for he shall not speak of himself; but whatsoever he shall hear, that shall he speak: and he will shew you things to come."

---

[11] An excellent historical survey of "speaking in tongues" is developed in Robert Gromacki, *The Modern Tongues Movement*, (Philadelphia: Presbyterian and Reformed Publishing Co., 1967), pp.10-17.

PROBLEM:

Inevitably at some point in the discussion with a Pentecostal the Christadelphian will be faced with "the Comforter passages" from John's Gospel. They clearly relate to the outpouring of the Holy Spirit on the Day of Pentecost and the argument will be pressed by the Pentecostal that the Comforter was to remain with the church "for ever".

There may well be the added assertion that unless a person has the Holy Spirit he cannot come to an understanding of the "Truth" for part of the work of the Comforter, according to Pentecostal (and Evangelical) teaching, is to guide men and women "into all truth" (John 16:13).

SOLUTION:

1. It is worth pointing out that those to whom the Comforter was promised were told that they would do "greater works" than those done by Jesus (John 14:12). Which "miracles" done by the Pentecostal churches are greater than those done by Jesus?
2. In fact Jesus was speaking primarily to his immediate disciples not to disciples of today. It was to these disciples that Jesus promised the Holy Spirit, which, he said, would "bring all things to your remembrance, whatsoever I have said unto you" (John 14:26). Clearly Jesus has not said anything to us that can be brought to our remembrance. But the Holy Spirit did bring all things to the remembrance of the disciples and the things recalled were written down and form part of the New Testament.
3. The same applies to all the other things that Jesus said the Comforter would do. The Holy Spirit "[taught them] all things" (John 14:26) and guided them "into all the truth" (John 16:13 RV). These things were recorded for us in the New Testament so that Jude could speak of "the faith once for all delivered unto the saints" (v. 3 RV). The Holy Spirit also "showed them things to come"—New Testament prophecies such as 2 Peter 3 and the Book of Revelation—which also were written down for the benefit of subsequent generations. Thus it is clear that all the things that Jesus said the Comforter would do were done in the lifetime of those to whom the gift of the Holy Spirit was given.
4. The Holy Spirit is no longer needed to "guide into all the truth." "The gospel", recorded in the pages of the Spirit-given Scriptures, "is the power of God unto salvation to everyone that believeth" (Rom. 1:16). Belief (or faith[12]) comes from reading (or hearing preached), understanding and willingly accepting this gospel into "a good and honest heart" (Rom. 10:10,17; Luke 8:15).

---

[12] On the basis of 1 Cor. 12:9 it is often assumed by the Pentecostal that "faith" is itself a gift of the Spirit. The word "faith" in the NT means exactly the same as "belief", both being translations of the same Greek word *pistis*. It is necessary to use the word "believe" because there is, in English, no verb for "faith". So we have to say, "He that believeth…" rather than, "He that faitheth…" Whatever the gift of faith in 1 Cor 12:9 was, it does not refer to believing (i.e. showing faith in) the gospel for the Spirit gifts were given to those who had already believed the gospel and submitted to baptism (Acts 2:38,39).

WRESTED SCRIPTURES

5. The statement of Jesus that the Comforter would "abide with you for ever" (John 14:16) is often combined with Matt. 28:20 ("Lo, I am with you alway, even unto the end of the world") to argue that the gift of the Holy Spirit was for all time. Both of these statements were made to the immediate disciples of the Lord. The word "ever" in John 14:16 is the same as "world" in Matt. 28:20. Matt. 28:20 is correctly rendered in the RSV, "I am with you always, to the close of the age". The age of Israel under the Law Covenant expired in AD 70 with the destruction of the temple. This coincided with the death of the apostles (who alone were able to pass on the gifts) and the maturity of the ecclesia and the completion of the New Testament (the reason why the gifts were given).

Hebrews 13:8
"Jesus Christ the same yesterday, and to day, and for ever."

PROBLEM:

Since Jesus Christ is "the same yesterday, and today, and forever" (Heb. 13:8), the Pentecostal movement claims that the Spirit gifts must be available today. It is argued that Jesus can do today what he did in the first century—send the Comforter to divide "to every man severally as he will" (1 Cor. 12:11).

SOLUTION:

1. It is not a question as to whether Christ can make the Spirit gifts available today. He obviously has the power to do so. The question is rather, is it his purpose to make the Spirit gifts available today?
2. To argue that Christ must do today what he did in the past is to put a limitation upon his sovereignty. Jesus is immutable (unchanging in his character and person) as is his Father (cf. Num. 23:19; Mal. 3:6; James 1:17), but he is not confined to do in the present and the future what he has done in the past. To argue otherwise is to ignore the history of the relationship of God and Jesus Christ with men. Two examples illustrate this point:
   a. The disciples were told not to preach to the Gentiles—"Go not into the way of the Gentiles, and into any city of the Samaritans enter ye not: but go rather to the lost sheep of the house of Israel." (Matt. 10:5,6). After the resurrection of Christ, the disciples were told to preach the gospel to all nations. (Mark 16:15). Philip preached to the Samaritans (Acts 8), and Paul was specifically sent to the Gentiles. (1 Tim. 2:7; 2 Tim. 1:11).
   b. Nearly all Pentecostals would agree that apostles who are able to strike liars dead (Acts 5:3–10) and raise the dead (Acts 9:40) are no longer in existence. The fact that such are not in existence, does not reflect on the essential character of God, but rather indicates that the purpose which they served is now past.

2. HEALING AND TONGUES

Mark 16:17,18

"And these signs shall follow them that believe; In my name shall they cast out devils; they shall speak with new tongues; they shall take up serpents; and if they drink any deadly thing, it shall not hurt them; they shall lay hands on the sick, and they shall recover."

PROBLEM:

These verses are quoted by Pentecostals in support of their belief that the Holy Spirit gifts operate within the Pentecostal movement. Testimonies of "divine" healing are cited in proof of the existence of the gift of healing. Individuals said to possess this gift are sometimes referred to as "faith healers".

SOLUTION:

1. Today most claimants to Spirit powers stress the gifts of tongues and healing, yet the apostle says, "And God hath set some in the church, first apostles, secondarily prophets, thirdly teachers, after that miracles, then gifts of healings, helps, governments, diversities of tongues". (1 Cor. 12:28). Why the emphasis today on the gifts of lesser importance? It is significant that the gift of prophecy is seldom claimed today by Pentecostals, yet it is the most amenable to the test of truth or falsity. Its greater value is set forth by Paul, in its great benefit and profit in the development of faith and character. This would lead one to expect that if any gifts were present, this one would be.

2. The ability of God, if He wishes, to answer the prayer of faith to heal the sick is not in dispute. What the Pentecostal must provide is proof that Spirit-gift possession (e.g., the gift of healing, 1 Cor. 12:9) is available today. The Mark 16 passage states that the following signs would accompany those who believed:

   —demons could be cast out

   —believers could speak with new tongues

   —serpents could be taken up without hurt

   —deadly poison could be taken without hurt

   —hands could be laid on the sick for their recovery

   What is required is proof that the gift of healing can be demonstrated by these signs.

3. To deny the present day existence of the Spirit gifts is *not* to deny that some cures are effected at faith-healing meetings. Given sufficient mental excitement "miraculous" cures are not impossible, but this is not evidence of God's intervention, but rather to the "faith" of the patient. Roman Catholics and Pentecostals, with mutually antagonistic teaching, both claim miraculous healings,[13] and both have admitted that some "miracles" claimed divine are, in

---

[13] The curative powers of relics has been exploited to great profit by the Roman Church. The sick,

effect, not so. This is a significant admission. Recourse to divine healing is not needed to explain all claims.[14]

4. Pentecostals often catalogue testimonies of paralytics, the deaf, and drunkards as indications of the curative powers of the "Holy Ghost". The following comments by a medical doctor indicate that such examples are not proof of *divine* healing:

"Diseases may be divided into three classes: first, those which are entirely mental; second, those which are physical but tend to cure themselves; third, those which are physical but do not tend to cure themselves. Eighty to ninety per cent of all diseases belong to the first two classes. A man with a paralysis of his leg of mental origin, [or] with a head cold...gets well under the attention of a faith healer, a chiropractor, or even by taking patent medicine, and all but the paralytic will get well if nothing were done. On the other hand, such diseases as diphtheria, malaria, syphilis, cancer, diabetes, tuberculosis, and pernicious anemia do not get well with faith healing, chiropractic treatment, or psychoanalysis...Under the ministrations of a faith healer these patients would die. But even if they did, the faith healer's result would be still 80 or 90 per cent effective."[15]

"None of the parts of the body is superlative or independent; they are all dependent and correlated. Each organ of the body when disordered manifests a characteristic disturbance, and this disturbance involves all of the parts of the body which are dependent upon the functioning of that organ ... [16] The basis of faith healing lies in the influence of the mind on the activity of the body. The mind is a function of the brain and through the brain is a constant communication with every part of the body by means of the nerves which

who were benefited at the church, made payments, and in some cases great fortunes were amassed from these donations. Relics have included the following: wood of the "cross" (if the pieces scattered throughout Europe were collected there would be enough wood for many crosses); tears of the Saviour, the Virgin Mary, and Peter (allegedly brought back from the Holy Land centuries after their deaths); the blood of Jesus; one monastery in Jerusalem even offered for sale what was represented, to the gullible, as the finger of the "Holy Ghost", and another monastery claimed to have a feather from the same source; in the twelfth century the shrine at Cologne claimed to have obtained the skulls of the wise men of the East. See Howard W. Haggard, M.D., *Devils, Drugs, & Doctors: The Story of the Science of Healing from Medicine-Man to Doctor*, (New York: Pocket Books, Inc., 1959), pp.313,314. Relics have been effective in "curing" certain ailments even when it is known that the relics are counterfeit. For example the bones of "St." Rosalia, preserved in Palermo, Italy (a source of income for the Roman Church and town) have for many centuries been found effective in curing diseases; but when examined by an anatomist, turned out to be goat bones. See Bertrand Russell, *Religion and Science*, (Oxford: University Press, 1947), p 83.

[14] Many members of Pentecostal Churches claim "divine healing", but almost always these are obscure and self-diagnosed complaints such as "pains in the back", "stomach trouble" and "headaches". Others, often with better defined illnesses, ascribe their cure to divine intervention, even though they have received medical treatment, or even been in hospital. Large numbers of congregations offer testimony to confirm that God answers the prayers of the sick, but in practice they do not hesitate to seek medical care when seriously troubled.

[15] Howard W. Haggard, M.D., *Devils, Drugs & Doctors: The Story of the Science of Healing from Medicine-Man to Doctor*, (Pocket Books, Inc., New York, 1959), p.305,306.

[16] Ibid., p.304.

extend to and from the brain. The activity of every organ of the body is controlled by the nervous system."[17]

"Paralysis of a limb and lameness are common symptoms of hysteria[18]; the limb may be drawn up in a deforming contraction, or palsied. Persons with hysteria may become mute or blind, their sensations may be perverted, they may vomit obstinately or lose their appetite and waste away. Hysterical women may believe themselves pregnant and show all the signs of that condition, suppression of the menses, colostrum in the breast, morning sickness, and swelling of the abdomen. This may continue until the time for delivery has long passed and their minds have turned to some other manifestation."[19]

"Not all men and women who have responded to faith cures are hysterical. There are numerous cases of bedridden invalids crippled by rheumatism and unable for years to put a foot on the ground, who nevertheless under some great stress, such as the house burning down around them, have shown remarkable returns of activity. The rheumatism which had crippled them had been real in the beginning, but during a long illness they had got into the habit of believing themselves crippled even after they were well. They had lost confidence in themselves."[20]

5. Apparently "miraculous" results have been reported without the patients affirming belief in God. Some warts may be "charmed away" by pretending to pass under a ray, or simply suggesting to the patient that they will go away.

6. Even in the time of the apostles, some who failed to understand the truth in Jesus Christ, did not hesitate falsely to claim miraculous powers in his name: "Then certain of the vagabond Jews, exorcists, took upon them to call over them which had evil spirits the name of the Lord Jesus, saying, We adjure you by Jesus whom Paul preacheth." (Acts 19:13). Warning that such would be the case is explicitly indicated in the following references:

a. Jesus—"Not every one that saith unto me, Lord, Lord, shall enter into the kingdom of heaven; but he that *doeth* the will of my Father which is in heaven. Many will say to me in that day, Lord, Lord, have we not prophesied in thy name? and in thy name have cast out devils? and in thy name done many wonderful works? And then will I profess unto them, I never knew you: depart from me, ye that work iniquity." (Matt. 7:21–23). —"For there shall arise false Christs, and false prophets, and shall show great signs and wonders; insomuch that, if it were possible, they shall deceive the very elect." (Matt. 24:24).

b. John—"Beloved, believe not every spirit, but try the spirits whether they are of God: because many false prophets are gone out into the world." (1 John 4:1).

---

[17] Ibid., p.296.

[18] It should be noted that the word "hysteria" is used here in its medical sense and not in its common usage as when we speak of someone who is over-excited as becoming "hysterical".

[19] Ibid., p.300.

[20] Ibid., p.301.

    c. Paul—"This know also, that in the last days perilous times shall come…But evil men and seducers shall wax worse and worse, deceiving, and being deceived." (2 Tim. 3:1,13).[21]

7. Modern "faith-healers" cannot tell which of their patients will be healed and which will not. The miracles of the Lord Jesus and the apostles were not apparently subject to any such doubt.

8. This passage in Mark indicates that God confirmed the Word with signs. Today, the Word is complete and has been such since the completion of the New Testament. Spirit gifts such as healing have, therefore, been withdrawn, as Paul said they would (1 Cor. 13:8–12), and now the believer walks by faith in the perfected Word of God.

9. It is worth comparing an apostolic healing such as that in Acts 3:1-8 with the activities of modern "healers". The man in Acts 3 was a congenital cripple. He had never walked. Peter healed him with a simple command, with no build up of excitement, and no expectation of something unusual on the part of the person being healed. He was healed instantly and completely. There is no Pentecostal healer who can heal a congenital deformity or restore an absent limb. Their "healings" take place against a background of induced excitement and expectation. So often the subjects are sent away to let the body's healing processes take their natural course.

1 Corinthians 14:2

"For he that speaketh in an unknown tongue speaketh not unto men, but unto God: for no man understandeth him; howbeit in the spirit he speaketh mysteries."

PROBLEM:

Pentecostal "speaking in tongues"[22] is unintelligible speech uttered in a state of religious fervour. The justification for this practice is sought in this passage.

SOLUTION:

1. The tongues referred to in this passage are not unknown. The word "unknown" is not in the Greek text and is deleted in the RSV. (This is also indicated by the printing of "unknown" in italics in the AV.)

2. Pentecostals sometimes argue that since *glossa* (the Greek word for speech) is used in this verse, rather than *dialektos* (the Greek word for language), that the

---

[21] Some rather sensational claims are made in Pentecostal publications. In an article, "They Let God Be Their Dentist!" A. A. Allen reports the testimonies of six persons who allegedly had their teeth miraculously filled: "God filled four teeth for Beulah Clark as she sat in the audience", the article states, and "James drove all night in faith that God would do the work. He did! God filled three teeth." *Miracle Magazine*, 14, No. 9, (June, 1969), p.6. Only in small print in Allen's *Miracle Magazine* can a reader find the careful demurrer: "…A. A. Allen Revivals, Inc. and *Miracle Magazine* assume no legal responsibility for the veracity of any such report, nor do they accept responsibility as to the degree of permanency of reported healings, deliverances or miracles…" Ibid., p.3.

[22] More technically the phenomenon is referred to as "glossalalia" from *glossa*—tongue, and *lalia*—to speak or talk with.

unintelligible utterance is intended. This argument is shown to be invalid by the following:

a. *Glossa* and *dialektos* are used interchangeably in Scripture. In Acts 2:4 the word for "tongues" is *glossa*, but in verse 8 the word for "tongues" is *dialektos* (translated "language", RSV).

b. *Glossa* refers to foreign languages in the following passages: Rev. 5:9; 7:9; 10:11; 11:9; 13:7; 14:6; 17:15. *Glossa* also means intelligible speech in the following passages: Rom. 14:11; Phil. 2:11; 1 John 3:18.

3. When the disciples spoke in tongues as recorded in Acts 2, fifteen languages or dialects were spoken. "Every man heard them speak in his own language." (Acts 2:7,8). Galilean fishermen could speak the language of the Elamites although the language had never been the subject of study. But Pentecostal meetings are characterized by unintelligible speech, not by recognizable foreign languages.

4. In 1 Cor. 14, the following differences from Pentecostal practice are noteworthy:

a. Pentecostal women usually predominate in unintelligible utterances[23] and even preach during public assemblies.[24] But Paul says, "Let your women keep silence in the churches: for it is not permitted unto them to speak; but they are commanded to be under obedience, as also saith the law. And if they will learn any thing, let them ask their husbands at home: for it is a shame for women to speak in the church." (1 Cor. 14:34,35).[25]

b. Pentecostal meetings frequently have more than one person uttering unintelligible sounds at the same time, but Paul instructs that all things should be done "decently and in order" (1 Cor. 14:40), and that "if any man speak in an unknown tongue, let it be by two, or at the most by three, and that by course..." (1 Cor. 14:27).

c. Pentecostals seldom have any "interpreter" of the unintelligible speech, yet Paul says, "let one interpret. But if there be no interpreter, let him keep silence in the church..." (1 Cor. 14:27,28).

d. Many Pentecostals consider themselves *compelled* by the Holy Spirit to "speak in tongues"[26] yet Paul says, "the spirits of the prophets are subject to the prophets." (1 Cor. 14:32).

---

[23] Many writers have noted this. Bryan Wilson at one meeting counted twenty-five instances of "glossalalia" in one assembly, of which twenty-four were women. He noted that usually three-quarters of the audience consisted of women, and never much less than two-thirds. "In Pentecostal meetings, women tend to give vent to pent-up feelings—in tears, heavy breathing, groans, utterances of joy and rapture, and, of course, tongues." See Bryan Wilson, *Sects and Society: A sociological Study of Three Religious Groups in Britain*, (London: William Heinemann Ltd.), pp.302,303.

[24] For example, Allen commenting on his "miracle revival" in Naga City, in Southern Luzon states: "Sister Rogers preached a salvation message to a fine crowd each afternoon..." See *Miracle Magazine*, 14, No. 9, (June, 1969), p.17.

[25] Pentecostal preachers tend to disregard the apostle's instruction by a casual dismissal on the grounds that the church must "move with the times". It is noteworthy that the apostle's reason for this instruction is not founded on culturally relative grounds, but rather on the fall of Eve. (cf. 1 Tim. 2:11–15).

[26] In recent years within the Elim movement there is an opposite point of view—that tongues may deter possible converts. Speakers in tongues at revival meetings have often been silenced. A. A. Allen

WRESTED SCRIPTURES

It is also appropriate to cite Paul's instruction to the Corinthians: "If any man think himself to be a prophet, or spiritual, let him acknowledge that the things that I write unto you are the *commandments of the Lord*." (1 Cor. 14:37).

5. It is also relevant to emphasize that "glossalalia" occurs among those who practise voodoo in Haiti. It is not, therefore, a phenomenon peculiarly "Christian". This indicates that explanations other than God's Holy Spirit can account for "glossalalia". It is also noteworthy that "glossalalia" is now being practised by other denominations including Anglicans and Roman Catholics.[27] Do Pentecostals believe these religious bodies hold the truth of the gospel? This point is especially forceful when it is recognised that speaking in tongues is understood by Pentecostals as an initial sign of Holy Spirit baptism.

comments: "It's little wonder that many Pentecostal preachers today will not have speaking in tongues in their main assembly and under their tent. Too much of it sounds too downright silly, too obvious that it isn't genuine. It isn't real." *Miracle Magazine*, 14. No. 9, (June, 1969), p.11.

[27] That the gifts can be abused or imitated is acknowledged by some Pentecostals. A. A. Allen comments as follows: "I wouldn't give you two cents for what you call a Holy Ghost experience, if the only action you got was a few minutes of stammering lips: "Bla, bla, bib, gah, gah, goo!" My children said that when they were six months old! I have seen people do that when they are drunk ... I have seen many people whom I believe were merely 'trained' by those who prayed with them, to seemingly receive the Holy Ghost ... I believe some Pentecostal denominations are full of people who have never received the baptism in the Holy Ghost experience. They have just been patted on the back and shook on the chin, and told what to say, until they couldn't say anything but, "Bla, bla, gag, gag, goo!" And then somebody said, "You've got it!" The only action they got was when somebody shook them under the chin!" "The Book of Acts is Holy Ghost in Action", *Miracle Magazine*, 14, No. 9, (June, 1969), p.10.

Bre Peter Neate-Stidson (Yeovil)   SeeCAL'S diary under Yeovil
e Kevin Sweeney (Sapcote)   and Coventry East.

If any bro. would like info. or help with talking to JW's please
contact either Peter (a JW for 16 years) rising to the position of Elder.
— Bro. Kevin has researched JW's e their organisation for 35 years.

1.5

JEHOVAH'S WITNESSES

PRELIMINARY POINTS:

In discussions with Jehovah's Witnesses (JWs) a familiar pattern can be observed. What begins as a Biblical discussion on a point of doctrine, soon results in the JW sorting through his book bag for the appropriate Watchtower publication, which then serves as a prop throughout the remainder of the discussion. The pattern is indicative of the reliance placed on the Watchtower organization by the JW (in many respects comparable to the regard a Roman Catholic has for the hierarchy of his church). The following factors contribute to the trust an ordinary JW has in the Watchtower organization (and also suggests ways in which the organization is able to maintain its totalitarian-like control):

1. The organizational structure in Brooklyn, New York, is headed by those who claim to be among the 144,000 destined to reign in heaven at the instant of death.[1] These "anointed sheep" of the "remnant class" are said to be led by "Jehovah's spirit" to new "revealed" truths. These new truths are indoctrinated into JWs throughout the world by weekly classes in Kingdom Halls. Watchtower articles are studied in repetitive question and answer sessions similar to those conducted so effectively by the Jesuits of the Roman Church.[2]

2. Prophecies especially in Revelation are interpreted by the Watchtower as being fulfilled in the development of the organization. These interpretations are

---

[1] ~~Judge Rutherford's~~ *Hayden C. Covington* removal as vice-president in 1945 is stated in a JW publication to be for this reason: "(His) resignation was not an evasion of responsibilities, but was rather an effort to comply with what appeared to be the Lord's will, namely, that all the members of the directorate and the officers be of the anointed remnant (144,000). His hope was to be one of the 'other sheep'." *Jehovah's Witnesses in the Divine Purpose*, (Brooklyn, NY: Watchtower Bible and Tract Society, 1959), p.197. As of Jan. 1, 1969, 10,619 JWs now living claim to be among the 144,000. *The Watchtower*, (Jan. 1969), No. 1, Vol. XC, p.25. *Judge Rutherford died in 1942 as president*

[2] In the "Plan of Studies" of the Jesuits, "every main issue was settled, every procedure was already outlined…The Jesuit teachers depended in no small measure for their effectiveness upon constant repetition." Luela Cole, *A History of Education*, (New York: Holt, Rinehart and Winston, 1961), pp.317,322.

[3] *Babylon The Great Has Fallen! God's Kingdom Rules!* (Brooklyn, NY: Watchtower Bible and Tract Society of NY, Inc., 1963), pp.530–557. Another example further illustrates this point: Dan. 8:14— (the cleansing of the sanctuary) is interpreted to refer to the cleansing of the Watchtower organization when it changed from democratic election of officials to selection and confirmation by the society's executive or manager. A Watchtower publication comments as follows: "The announcement in the Watch Tower magazine of October 15, 1932, at the exact end of the time period mentioned in Daniel's prophecy, was the official notification made by Jehovah through his visible channel of communication that his sanctuary [i.e., the Watchtower organization] had been cleansed and had been restored to its rightful state as regards the elimination of this democratic procedure in electing elders." *Jehovah's Witnesses in the Divine Purpose*, (Brooklyn, NY: Watchtower Bible and Tract Society, 1959), p.127. *of the then president of the Watchtower Society and succeeded in 1942 by Nathan Knorr*

Chris Mag April 2015 p.151
See note at top.

"revealed" to JWs through the *Watchtower* magazine and other books. For example, the seven vials of Revelation 16 are related to seven Watchtower proclamations issued (1922–1928)[3], and the "times, times, and a half" (Dan. 12:7) is applied to the disruption of Watchtower activities with the sentencing of the president and other members of the Watchtower organization to eighty years' imprisonment.[4] Prophecy, therefore, gives sanction to the organization and serves to legitimize its activities.

3. To the ordinary JW the Watchtower organization is *the* scholarship centre. The library in the Gilead ministry training school, the numerous books released at past conventions, and the issuing of the *New World Translation of the Holy Scriptures*, provide guarantees to the JW that Watchtower materials have the backing of sound research.

4. Watchtower publications give prominence to persecutions suffered by JWs in the war years. Although JWs have fought many legal cases in the courts, persecutions are interpreted by Watchtower writers to indicate the self-sacrificing character of JW preaching and the divine nature of the work. Did not Jesus say that his followers would be persecuted?[5] Stress is also placed on the numbers attending conventions, number of books printed, and number of lands in which JWs are working: the effect of which is to confirm to the JW that the Watchtower must be a theocracy.[6]

SUGGESTED STRATEGY:

1. In view of the influence of the Watchtower organization, how can one engage in meaningful preaching activity with the JW who calls at the door? It would seem that a "psychological battle" must first be won. The JW at the door, or in the home study, considers himself to "have the truth" and, therefore, assumes the teacher role and the householder is deemed to be the student. At some point the JW must appreciate that with you the role is not that of a teacher-pupil relationship. The JW must also become the listener—the learner (which is not a relationship for which JWs are particularly well known).

2. How is this to be done? The Jew in the divine purpose affords an advantageous position from which a Bible student can assume the offensive. This topic has the following advantages:

   a. It affords a topic of mutual interest. JWs have challenged Christadelphian teaching on this subject in their *Watchtower* magazine, August, 1962,

---

[4] *Your Will Be Done On Earth*, (Brooklyn, NY: Watchtower Bible and Tract Society of NY, Inc., 1958), pp.330,331.

[5] See for example, *Babylon The Great Has Fallen! God's Kingdom Rules*, (Brooklyn, NY: Watchtower Bible and Tract Society, 1963), p.550; *Jehovah's Witnesses in the Divine Purpose*, (Brooklyn, NY: Watchtower Bible and Tract Society, 1959), pp.166-174,186,192.

[6] This point is illustrated in the following JW publication: "In the thirty-three years from 1919 to 1952 inclusive, Jehovah's Witnesses distributed more than half a billion bound books and booklets, hundreds of millions of oral testimonies, in over 90 languages. Only by God's spirit and power could this witness have been given in the face of worldwide opposition and persecution; and the witness still continues." *Let God Be True*, (Brooklyn, NY: Watchtower Bible and Tract Society, 1952), pp.200,201.

"Christadelphianism—Of God or Men?"[7] In this article, the Christadelphian teaching concerning the Jew in the divine purpose is misunderstood. Correction of the Watchtower mistakes is a useful way to chip away at the scholarship image the JW has of Brooklyn publications.

b. The JW approach to Biblical interpretation can also be challenged. JWs "spiritualise" passages in Isaiah, Jeremiah, and Ezekiel concerning the Jew to make them refer to the Watchtower organization. It requires stating plainly that a passage should be read literally, unless convincing evidence to the contrary can be produced. Otherwise, a passage can be read to suit nearly any presupposition. Little can be achieved until this groundwork is established.

c. Not being infallible, a Bible student may change his mind regarding an interpretation of an obscure verse or a highly symbolic prophecy, but when change of mind involves hundreds of passages, as it does with the Jew, (JWs once taught the literal restoration of the Jew to Palestine)[8] how can one claim to be Jehovah's witness? Can one witness contradict the statements of later witnesses on such a basic biblical theme, and yet both be Jehovah's witnesses?

d. A discussion of the Jew leads readily into a discussion of the return of Christ. The Jewish return to Palestine then becomes evidence for the future *visible* return of Christ (implying, of course, that he did not return invisibly in 1914, as JWs assert).

3. The Bible student can set a worthy example by knowing his Bible. The ability to flip to the desired passage on the spot (without taking recourse to other books) is cultivated by frequent use of the Word. This has impressed many JWs, some of whom have responded to subsequent instruction. Nothing imparts confidence in discussion like knowing where one intends to go, and knowing not only the strength of one's evidence, but that it can be produced when needed.

4. Once the initial "psychological battle" has been won, topics can be selected for subsequent discussion. The fruitfulness of these discussions is often related to the extent to which only *one* area at a time is discussed. Discipline is required not to be led off the issue by subsidiary error drawn in by the JW in support of the proposition under consideration. This appears to be especially true of the "pre-existence" of Christ and the devil.

NATURAL ISRAEL

Isaiah 43:10

"Ye are my witnesses, saith the LORD, and my servant whom I have chosen…"

[7] Great Lakes ASK (Advancement of Scriptural Knowledge), Box 221, Weston Ontario, Canada, published a 32-page reply to this article.
[8] See explanation of wrested scripture, Matt. 23:37,38, on page 95.

93

WRESTED SCRIPTURES

PROBLEM:

JWs interpret this prophecy in a spiritual sense to apply to the Watchtower organization. In a convention of JWs at Columbus, Ohio, 1931, a resolution was proposed and passed in which the following was stated:

"...to make known to the people that Jehovah is the true and almighty God; therefore we joyfully embrace and take the name which the mouth of the Lord God has named, and we desire to be known as and called by the name, to wit, 'Jehovah's witnesses'—Isa. 43:10–12; 62:2; Rev. 12:17."[9]

SOLUTION:

1. The witnesses of this passage cannot be the self-styled "Jehovah's Witnesses" for the following reasons:

   a. The witnesses of this passage are ransomed by the price of Egypt, Ethiopia and Seba (v. 3). JWs claim to be ransomed by the body of Christ.

   b. The witnesses of this passage are condemned: "Yet you did not call upon me, O Jacob; but you have been weary of me, O Israel!...But you have burdened me with your sins, you have wearied me with your iniquities." (Isa. 43:22,24, RSV). When have JWs merited this description?

   c. The witnesses of this passage are condemned for not bringing sheep for sacrifice or honouring God in their sacrifices (v. 23). This verse cannot apply to JWs since they have never offered animal sacrifices.

2. The witnesses of this passage are *unwilling* witnesses. They witness to the truth of God's prophetic Word (Isa. 41:22,23) in their persecution, scattering and regathering (Deut. 28; Lev. 26; Jer. 32:37). But the JWs claim that one who is not a willing witness is "not with the organization".[10]

3. Similarly the "new name" of Isa. 62 is "Hephzibah" (Isa. 62:4) and not "Jehovah's Witnesses". It is the name of a city—Jerusalem (v. 7), not an organization.

4. The following is a useful piece of information to be found in the writing of John Thomas in *Elpis Israel*:[11]

   "The pre-adventual colonization of Palestine will be on purely political principles; and the Jewish colonists will return thither in unbelief of the Messiahship of Jesus, and of the truth as it is in him."

   "I know not whether the men who at present contrive the foreign policy of Britain, entertain the idea of assuming the sovereignty of the Holy Land, and of promoting its colonization by the Jews; their present intentions, however, are of no importance one way or the other; because they will be compelled, by events

---

[9] *Jehovah's Witnesses in the Divine Purpose*, (Brooklyn, NY: Watchtower Bible and Tract Society of NY, 1959), pp.125,126.

[10] *Let God Be True*, (Brooklyn, NY: Watch Tower Bible and Tract Society, 1946), p.237.

[11] John Thomas, *Elpis Israel*, (London: Maran-atha Press, 1858), pp.395,396. (pp.441,442–1958 ed.)—The first edition was printed in 1849.

soon to happen, to do what, under existing circumstances, heaven and earth combined could not move them to attempt."

The fact that this was written 100 years before the establishment of the State of Israel, indicates the part Israel has played in God's divine challenge in Isa. 41:22,23. The "spiritualisations" of the JWs nullify the position of the real witnesses in this challenge. Surely one can hardly use language too strongly in condemnation of this Scripture-whittling practice.

Matthew 23:37,38

"O Jerusalem, Jerusalem...Behold, your house is left unto you desolate."

PROBLEM:

This passage is referred to by JWs as the "irrevocable divorce decree"[12] and is coupled with such passages as Rom. 2:29 to justify the application of the prophecies of restoration of natural Israel in a "spiritual sense".

SOLUTION:

1. "Irrevocable" suggests the exact opposite to what this passage in Matthew affirms. The passage is not an "irrevocable divorce decree", but a *conditional* statement: "Ye shall not see me henceforth, *till* ye shall say, Blessed is he that cometh in the name of the Lord." (v. 39, cf. Ezek. 21:27).

2. This passage has a parallel in Jer. 3:8, in which God gives Israel a bill of divorcement saying: "I had put her away, and given her a bill of divorce..." But God offers *mercy* to her: "I will not cause mine anger to fall upon you: for I am merciful, saith the LORD, and I will not keep anger for ever." (Jer. 3:12, cf. vv. 13–15). God has not cast away his people. (Rom. 11:1). The house of Israel will say, "Blessed is he that cometh in the name of the Lord" (Matt. 23:39), since "blindness in part is happened to Israel, *until* the fulness of the Gentiles be come in." (Rom. 11:25, cf. Isa. 59:20,21; Heb. 8:8; Jer. 31:31–34).

3. Not being infallible, a Bible student may change his mind over the years regarding an interpretation of obscure or highly symbolic passages of Scripture, but JWs, who claim that their instructors are guided by the Holy Spirit, change fundamental doctrines. This is an important point. The JW must afford an explanation as to how his organization can claim to be a theocracy of absolute truth and yet revise its teaching on a Gospel theme which affects one's understanding of hundreds of passages in many Biblical books in both Old and New Testaments.

4. The contradictory teaching of JWs:

---

[12] *The Watchtower*, (Aug. 1, 1962), No. 15, Vol. LXXXVIII, p.475.

What earlier JWs taught	What later JWs teach
"We find statements by both prophets and apostles *which clearly indicate* that in the times of restitution, Israel as a nation will be the first among the nations to come into harmony with the new order of things; that the earthly Jerusalem will be rebuilt upon her own heaps, and that their polity will be *restored* as in the beginning under princes or judges. (Isa. 1:26; Psa. 45:16; Jer. 30:18)." *The Divine Plan of the Ages*, p.294.[13]	"The facts and prophecies *prove* that natural Jews will never again be a chosen regathered people." *Let God Be True*, p.208 (1946 edition)[14]
"Israel is now [1921] being regathered, and is rebuilding Palestine exactly as foretold." *The Harp of God*, p.256.[15]	"Hence the regathering of unbelieving natural Israelites to Palestine cannot be construed as fulfilment of prophecies." *Let God Be True*, p.218. (1952 edition).[16]
"Thus far the Jews have been regathered to Palestine in unbelief. The Lord has graciously held out his hand to them, signifying that the due time has come in which he will again show them favour...God's purpose is to regather Israel into that land that she may become a mighty nation, even greater than in the past." *Comfort for the Jews*, pp.95,96.[17]	"How are events in modern Israel to be viewed? Merely as part of global developments foretold in the Bible. These include war, lawlessness, cooling off of love for God, and love of money—Matt. 24:7; 2 Tim 3:1–5." *Reasoning from the Scriptures*, p.224.[18]

5. It is the claim of JWs that "preaching in harmony with God's revealed Word" is that which "proves [one] to be a minister"[19]. Who then does one take to be the minister, the earlier writers or modern day JWs?

6. Can one "true witness" prove wrong the "clear indications" postulated by another "true witness", and yet *both* remain "faithful and true witnesses"?

7. Fleshly descent constitutes a Jew a *subject* of the kingdom, but confers on him no right to sit and rule on the thrones of the House of David. All Jews and Gentiles who become Jews "inwardly" (Rom. 2:29; 9:6–8) will reign as associate kings with the Messiah. (2 Tim. 2:12; Rev. 5:10). The JWs confuse Israel's national position as subjects in the kingdom with the position of the saints who will be rulers.

[13] Charles T. Russell, *A Helping Hand: Millennial Dawn Vol. 1. The Divine Plan of the Ages*, (Pennsylvania: Watch Tower Bible & Tract Society, 1886), p.294, This publication is still referred to in Watchtower articles. See *The Watchtower*, (March 1, 1965). No. 5, Vol. LXXXVI, p.155.

[14] *Let God be True*, (Brooklyn, NY: Watch Tower Bible & Tract Society, 1946), p.208.

[15] J. F. Rutherford, *The Harp of God*, (Brooklyn, NY: Watch Tower Bible & Tract Society, 1921), p.256.

[16] *Let God Be True*, (Brooklyn, NY: Watch Tower Bible & Tract Society, Inc., 1952), p.218.

[17] *Comfort for the Jews*, (Brooklyn, NY: International Bible Students Association, 1925), pp.95,96.

[18] *Reasoning from the Scriptures*, (Brooklyn, NY: Watch Tower Bible & Tract Society, Inc. 1985), p.224.

[19] Ibid. p.224.

THE "LITTLE FLOCK" AND "THE OTHER SHEEP"

Revelation 7:4
"And I heard the number of them which were sealed: and there were sealed an hundred and forty and four thousand of all the tribes of the children of Israel."

Revelation 14:3
"And they sung as it were a new song before the throne, and before the four beasts, and the elders: and no man could learn that song but the hundred and forty and four thousand, which were redeemed from the earth."

PROBLEM:

These verses are cited by JWs to support the doctrine that most of the 144,000 are now reigning over the earth. This "little flock" of the "anointed remnant", it is claimed, commenced its rule in 1914. Since 1914 members of this group are said to depart to heaven at the instant of death. In Jan. 1969, 10,619 JWs claimed to be living members of this group.[20] A JW publication comments as follows:

> "Those who are called by God to share in such heavenly service are few in number. As Jesus said, they are a 'little flock'. Years after his return to heaven, Jesus made known the exact number in a vision to the apostle John... So the 144,000 are persons who die on earth as humans and are resurrected [at the instant of death, R.A.] to heavenly life as spirit creatures, as Jesus was... Members of the 'little flock' know that God has called them to heavenly life. How? By means of the operation of God's spirit, which implants and cultivates in them the hope of heavenly life."[21]

SOLUTION:

1. It is usually undesirable to begin by saying, "the book of Revelation is primarily symbolic, therefore the 144,000 is a symbolic number". Consistency would demand that the 1,000 years of Rev. 20:4,6 should also be taken figuratively.

2. But, consistency also demands that the JW settle for either a literal or figurative interpretation, but not an indiscriminate mixing of the two to suit a presupposition. If the JW insists on a literal 144,000, then all JWs are excluded from this group because literally the 144,000 only come from the tribes of Israel![22] If, on the other hand, the JW takes the stand that the passage is figurative because the tribes are symbolic, then likewise the 144,000 is a symbolic, and not a literal number.

3. The following evidence from Rev. 14 indicates that the number 144,000 is symbolic, and not literal:

---

[20] *The Watchtower,* (Jan. 1969), No. 1. Vol. XC, p.25.

[21] *The Truth that Leads to Eternal Life*, (Brooklyn, NY: Watchtower Bible and Tract Society, Inc., 1968), pp.77,78.

[22] It should be noted that the tribes of Dan and Ephraim are omitted and the tribes of Levi and Joseph included, which, in itself, suggests a symbolic interpretation of the 144,000.

a. John "looked", v. 1, but could he see a Lamb on Mount Zion from 1,000 miles away on the Aegean Island? (John was on the Island of Patmos, Rev. 1:9). The JW will concede that Jesus is not a literal lamb.

b. Did he *really* hear the harpers playing over the same distance?

c. Were these saints literally virgins? If so, are the firstfruits only bachelors and spinsters? (v. 4).

4. It is usually inconclusive to assert that the 144,000 and the great multitude are two presentations of the *same* redeemed group. There appears to be too much evidence that two different groups are intended. Although it is sometimes stressed that John "heard" the number and "saw" the great multitude, this in itself does not establish that he saw and heard the same group. The two groups have these significantly differing descriptions:

144,000	Great Multitude
—John heard the number	—John saw the great multitude
—precisely numbered as 144,000	—innumerable (7:9)
—sealed out of the tribes of Israel (7:4)	—from all nations, kindreds and people (7:9)
	—have palms in hands

5. A more fruitful approach is to trace the allusions in Scripture. It is suggested that to do so establishes the 144,000 as the firstfruits, i.e., those faithful at Christ's return, and the great multitude, as the final ingathering of the saints at the end of the millennial age.

6. The following is the evidence for identifying the 144,000 with the saints at Christ's return:

a. The 144,000 are said to be "firstfruits" (Rev. 14:4). Two New Testament passages identify the firstfruits:

i. James 1:18—"Of his own will begat he us with the word of truth, that we should be a kind of firstfruits of his creatures."

ii. 1 Cor. 15:22,23—"…in Christ shall all be made alive. But every man in his own order: Christ the firstfruits; afterward they that are Christ's at his coming."

b. The word firstfruits is taken from the Old Testament feasts in Lev. 23. Using the above two quotations to identify the types, the following pattern becomes apparent:

i. The sheaf of the firstfruits, offered during the Passover week, represents Christ in type. (Lev. 23:10). (Notice in 1 Cor. 15:23 that both Christ and the saints are firstfruits, following the similar Old Testament usage in Lev. 23:17 where the two wave loaves are also "firstfruits").

ii. These two wave loaves, offered at Pentecost, seven weeks after Passover, signify the Jew and Gentile composition of the firstfruits. (Lev. 23:17; cf. Eph. 2:12–16).

iii. "The firstfruits unto the LORD" are the saints at Christ's coming. (Lev. 23:17).

7. The evidence that the great multitude, which no man can number, represents the final ingathering of the saints at the end of the millennial age comes from the following:

a. The great multitude have *palms* in their hands. (Rev. 7:9). This is another allusion to Lev. 23. Following the pattern of the types, the great multitude represents the final ingathering of the fruit and the carrying of palms occurs at the *end* of the harvest. (Lev. 23:40).

b. 1 Cor. 15:23–28 supports this interpretation insofar as the firstfruits of the harvest (the loaves of firstfruits) are set out in verse 23. The final ingathering is described from vv. 24–28—"then cometh the end".

c. It is worth noting that a literal reading of the text of Revelation has the 144,000 on the earth (Rev. 7:3,4; standing on Mount Zion, in 14:1) and the "great multitude" in heaven ("before the throne of God...in his temple", 7:15—the opposite of what JWs would have us believe.

8. The symbolic 144,000 reign on the earth (Rev. 5:10)[23] for a period designated as 1,000 years. (Rev. 20:6). Nowhere is their reigning either stated or implied to be in heaven. They will have power over the nations (Rev. 2:26,27), and since they follow the Lamb "whithersoever he goeth" (Rev. 14:4), they will be reigning on the earth—this is where the Lamb will be. As God's accredited representative, "his feet shall stand in that day upon the mount of Olives, which is before Jerusalem on the east..." (Zech. 14:4). He will then sit on David's throne in Jerusalem, the city of the great King. (Luke 1:32,33; Matt. 5:35).

9. The import of the JW teaching on the 144,000 becomes apparent once it is realized that [in 1969,[24] J.A.], 10,619 JWs expect to obtain immortality in heaven at the instant of death, whereas worthies commended for their faith and works, such as Abraham and David, are relegated to second-rate positions of everlasting life on the earth *without* immortality.[25] It is expressly stated that the worthies catalogued in Hebrews 11 died in faith not having received the promises, "God having provided some better thing *for us* [New Testament believers], that they without us should not be made perfect". (Heb. 11:13,39,40). Yet, according to JW teaching, Abraham sleeps unconsciously in

[23] This point is observed in the JW *New World Translation of the Holy Scriptures* which translates this verse "...and they will rule as kings over the earth." The Greek word "*epi*" translated "over" in this text is translated "on the earth" or "upon the earth" in six other places, (Rev. 6:10; 7:1; 11:10; 13:14; 14:6; 17:8, AV), but not "over the earth" so as to suggest remote control. The *Emphatic Diaglott*, until recently a JW publication, renders the text "on the earth". *The Kingdom Interlinear Translation of the Greek Scriptures*, (Brooklyn, NY: Watch Tower Bible & Tract Society, 1969) gives "upon the earth" in the literal, interlinear translation.

[24] The figure is now considerably less. In 1998 it had fallen to 8,795. Interestingly, in 1995 the figure was 8,617. So the number of the 144,000 left on the earth appears to be on the increase! (Figures from the January 1st *Watchtower* for the relevant years, quoted in Doug Harris, *The Jehovah's Witnesses*, London: Gazelle Book, 1998, p.131).

[25] It is sometimes argued by JWs that the kingdom of heaven is for the 144,000, whereas the kingdom of God is for the great multitude on the earth. But Abraham will be in both the kingdom of heaven and kingdom of God, (Matt. 8:11, cf. Luke 13:28), thereby indicating that the terms are used interchangeably and that they are not intended to convey the idea of a "heavenly" and an "earthly" reward.

WRESTED SCRIPTURES

his grave awaiting resurrection to everlasting (not eternal) life on the earth, while thousands of JWs since 1914, said to belong to the 144,000, have gone straight to heaven at the instant of death.

10. The idea of the 144,000 "little flock" and the great multitude "other sheep" has very serious implications. Paul says that there is *one* hope...*one* faith, *one* baptism..." (Eph. 4:4,5). But according to JW teaching the 144,000 are baptized "into Christ" and have a "heavenly hope"; the "great multitude" are baptized merely as a sign of dedication to Jehovah's organization and have "an earthly hope".

THE COMING OF CHRIST

Matthew 24:3
"...what shall be the sign of thy coming, and of the end of the world?"

PROBLEM:

JWs argue that the Greek word *parousia*, translated "coming" in Matt. 24:3,27, should really be rendered "presence". Since, according to JW chronology Jesus returned in 1914, it must be an invisible presence noticed only by those who see him with the eyes of discernment. It is maintained that Jesus will never literally set foot on the earth.

SOLUTION:

1. *Parousia* according to Greek authorities means literally "a presence", being derived from *para* (with) and *ousia* (being, from *eimi*, to be).[26] However, the word itself does not imply that the "presence" is either visible or invisible. The nature of the presence must be obtained from the context in which it occurs. For example, the coming of Titus (2 Cor. 7:6,7); the coming of Stephanas (1 Cor. 16:17); and the coming of Paul (Phil. 1:26) requires the personal presence of these persons. Similarly, the "bodily presence" (Greek: *parousia*) of Paul in 2 Cor. 10:10 is obviously what the record implies—a literal visible presence.

2. Jesus warned against false prophets who would say, "Behold, he is in...the secret chambers," and counselled his disciples, "Believe it not. For as the

---

[26] W. E. Vine, *Expository Dictionary of New Testament Words*, (London: Oliphants, 1940). Also, the Greek word "Parousia" means: "A being alongside, presence". Robert Young, *Analytical Concordance to the Holy Bible*, London: Lutterworth Press, 1965).

[27] It should be noted that many Christadelphians believe that "the presence" (translated "coming" in the AV) of Matt. 24:3,27 refers to the invisible presence of Jesus, supervising the Roman judgement of Israel in AD 70. For example, John Thomas, *Eureka–An Exposition of the Apocalypse*, (Birmingham: 1921 edition), Vol. 2, page 272: "Immediately after the tribulation of those days shall the sun be darkened and the moon shall not give her light, and the stars shall fall from heaven...These were the lights in which there were to be 'great signs and fearful sights', indicative of the parousia, or presence, though invisible, of the Son of Man when the Graeco-Roman army should be sent by him to destroy the city of his murderers." Occasionally one may meet a JW who is aware of this.

100

lightning cometh out of the east, and shineth even unto the west; so shall also the coming of the Son of man be." (Matt. 24:26,27). This verse is directly opposed to a view which states Christ returned to rule invisibly in 1914 (i.e., he's in the secret chambers). Nor does one ordinarily associate lightning, which can be seen across the sky, with an event which is unseen.[27]

3. Jesus will return literally and visibly to the earth. This is proven by the following evidence:

   a. "And his feet shall stand in that day upon the mount of Olives, which is before Jerusalem on the east, and the mount of Olives shall cleave in the midst..."[28] (Zech. 14:4). This passage in itself is conclusive. Christ will be the name-bearer of Yahweh (v. 3, "LORD", i.e., Heb. Yahweh) as was the angel of the Lord. (Exo. 23:20,21). Christ will literally return to the mountain from which he left. (Acts 1:10,11). This event will fulfil the promise of the two men which said, "This same Jesus, which is taken up from you into heaven, shall so come in like manner as ye have seen him go into heaven."[29] (Acts 1:11). He ascended literally and visibly until a cloud received him out of sight from the disciples. This is the "like manner" in which he will return.

   b. The inhabitants of Jerusalem and the house of David will look upon "me whom they have pierced, and they shall mourn for him, as one mourneth for his only son, and shall be in bitterness for him, as one that is in bitterness for his firstborn." (Zech. 12:10; cf. 13:6). How is this to take place unless Christ returns personally to the earth? (Cf. Rev. 1:7—"and every eye shall see him, and they also which pierced him; and all kindreds of the earth shall wail because of him.")

4. *Parousia* is not the only Greek word used to describe the return of Christ. Consider the following:

   a. *Phaneroo*[30]—"And when the chief Shepherd shall *appear*", (1 Pet. 5:4). This word not only means appearing, but also carries the further idea that the person appearing will be seen in his true character. It is the same word used for the appearance of believers before the Judgment Seat of Christ (2 Cor. 5:10), and for the first coming of Christ. (Heb. 9:26).

   b. *Prosopon*[31]—"From the presence of the Lord", (2 Thess. 1:9). This word indicates the actual presence of the one coming and that all are congregated before his face. The same word is used to describe Christ's appearance in heaven before his Father. (Heb. 9:24).

---

[28] JWs attempt to spiritualize the mountain. It only requires one to ask the spiritual intent of the mountain cleaving in two and the formation of the plain from Geba to Rimmon (Zech. 14:10) to indicate that this passage is not figurative.

[29] JWs sometimes reply by stating that the "like manner" refers to the fact that only a few saw him ascend, hence only few would witness his return. It needs to be stressed that the manner of the ascension is indicated in the passage—a cloud received him out of their sight.

[30] "To make manifest", Robert Young, *Analytical Concordance to the Holy Bible*, (London: Lutterworth Press, 1965).

[31] "Face, countenance", *Ibid.*

    c. *Heko*[32]—"Hold fast till I come", (Rev. 2:25). This word means not only coming, but stresses arrival as well. The same word is used for the arrival of Jesus in Galilee from Judea (John 4:47), and for the arrival of the prodigal son back home. (Luke 15:27).

It can be seen, therefore, that the return of Christ must be a *personal* visible return.

THE RANSOM SACRIFICE

1 Timothy 2:5,6

"For there is one God, and one mediator between God and men, the man Christ Jesus; who gave himself a ransom for all, to be testified in due time."

PROBLEM:

On the basis of the undisputed fact that the word "ransom" (Greek *antilutron*) denotes "a corresponding price, or ransom", the following conclusions are drawn:

1. The sacrifice of Jesus has secured the salvation of the whole of mankind.

2. The sacrifice of Jesus was like a commercial transaction, either purchase of goods or settlement of a debt (see section on "Substitution", page 78):

    "If a man pays a debt for a friend but then promptly takes back the payment, obviously the debt continues. Likewise, if, when he was resurrected, Jesus had taken his human body of flesh and blood, which had been given in sacrifice to pay the ransom price, what effect would that have had on the provision he was making to relieve faithful persons of the debt of sin?"[33]

3. For the JW, the doctrine leads to a denial that the body of Jesus was raised from the dead:

    "Disposing of Jesus' physical body at the time of his resurrection presented no problem for God."[34]

SOLUTION:

1. "All" *does not always mean every individual*: When the word "all" occurs in Scripture it must be defined on the basis of the context in which it occurs. For example Jesus said: "*All* that ever came before me are thieves and robbers..." (John 10:8), but clearly this did not include John the Baptist or many Old Testament teachers.

    The context of 1 Tim. 2:5,6 is important. Paul says in the previous verse, "God...will have *all men* to be saved, and to come unto the knowledge of the truth." (1 Tim. 2:4). This does not mean that God wishes to save every individual, for the Scriptures make it plain that the purpose of God is being worked out "according to election" (e.g. Rom. 9:11), i.e., He is choosing. So

---

[32] "To have come, be here", *Ibid.*

[33] *Reasoning From The Scriptures*, Brooklyn: Watch Tower Bible and Tract Society of New York, Inc., 1985, p.217.

[34] *Ibid.* p.217.

that Paul is able to write: "For ye see *your calling*, brethren, how that *not many* wise men after the flesh, *not many* mighty, *not many* noble, are called: but *God hath chosen the foolish* things of the world to confound the wise; and *God hath chosen the weak* things of the world to confound the things which are mighty; and base things of the world, and *things which are despised, hath God chosen*, yea, and things which are not, to bring to nought things that are: that no flesh should glory in his presence." (1 Cor. 1:26–29).

What Paul is saying to Timothy is that it was no longer the case that "salvation is of the Jews". God's purpose was now being worked out with Gentiles as well as Jews—all nations were now being called. And Jesus had died as a ransom for all these kinds of men.

Seen like this the passage does not now contradict Matt. 20:28 which says that Jesus was a ransom for "many" not 'for all': "The Son of man came not to be ministered unto, but to minister, and to give his life a ransom for many." (Matt. 20:28).

2. This teaching that the death of Jesus has secured the redemption of "many" and not of every individual is confirmed by other scriptures: e.g., "By his knowledge shall my righteous servant *justify many*; for he shall bear their iniquities…he hath poured out his soul unto death: and he was numbered with the transgressors; and he *bare the sin of many*, and made intercession for the transgressors." (Isa. 53:11,12). "For this is my blood of the new testament, which is *shed for many* for the remission of sins." (Matt. 26:28).

3. The clear teaching of Scripture is that all mankind will not be saved: "Man that is in honour, and understandeth not, is *like the beasts that perish*." (Psa. 49:20). "For God so loved the world, that he gave his only begotten Son, that *whosoever believeth in him should not perish*, but have everlasting life." (John 3:16). "*He that believeth and is baptized shall be saved*; but he that believeth not shall be damned." (Mark 16:16). "Simeon hath declared how God at the first did visit the Gentiles, *to take out of them a people for his name*." (Acts 15:14).

4. Only a wilful refusal to let the Bible speak for itself can deny the resurrection of the body of Jesus. Note the following:

   a. The women went to the tomb and found it empty: "They entered in, and *found not the body* of the Lord Jesus. And it came to pass, as they were much perplexed thereabout, behold, two men stood by them in shining garments: and as they were afraid, and bowed down their faces to the earth, they said unto them, Why seek ye the living among the dead? *He is not here, but is risen…*" (Luke 24:3–6).

   The women were looking for the body—it was not there, it had been resurrected.

   b. Believers are promised: "For our conversation is in heaven; from whence also we look for the Saviour, the Lord Jesus Christ: *who shall change our vile body*, that it may be fashioned *like unto his glorious body*, according to the working whereby he is able even to subdue all things unto himself." (Phil. 3:20,21).

Since the bodies of the faithful are to be changed and made like the glorious body of Jesus, this implies that Jesus' mortal body was changed. In 1 Cor. 15 which speaks of the bodies of believers being "changed" from mortal to immortal (vv. 51,53), Jesus is referred to as being "the firstfruits" of this resurrection process (vv. 21–23). Again the teaching is that as Jesus' body was raised and changed, so too will the believer's body be raised and changed.

c. Jesus clearly endorsed this: "Jesus answered and said unto them, Destroy this temple, and in three days *I will raise it up*. Then said the Jews, Forty and six years was this temple in building, and wilt thou rear it up in three days? But he *spake of the temple of his body*." (John 2:19–21).

The body of Jesus was raised from the dead. It did not just disappear.

d. Jesus was born to be king on the throne of David, a fact that was referred to by Peter on the Day of Pentecost: "Men and brethren, let me freely speak unto you of the patriarch David, that he is both dead and buried, and his sepulchre is with us unto this day. Therefore being a prophet, and knowing that God had sworn with an oath to him, that of *the fruit of his loins, according to the flesh*, he would raise up Christ to sit on his throne; He seeing this before spake of the resurrection of Christ, that *his soul was not left in hell* [Gk. *hades*, i.e. "the grave"], *neither his flesh did see corruption*." (Acts 2:29–31).

This shows plainly that it was the Jesus descended from David who was to sit on his throne and for this reason the flesh was not allowed to see corruption but was raised from the dead and glorified.

BLOOD TRANSFUSION

Genesis 9:4
"But flesh with the life thereof, which is the blood thereof, shall ye not eat."

PROBLEM:

The JWs cite this reference as proof that blood transfusions are forbidden by Scripture. A Watchtower publication puts it this way:

"Is God's law violated by these medical procedures that involve the use of blood? Is it wrong to sustain life by administering a transfusion of blood or plasma or red cells or others of the component parts of the blood? Yes! The law God gave to Noah made it unlawful for anyone to eat blood, that is, to use it for nourishment or to sustain life. Since this is wrong in the case of animal blood, it is even more reprehensible in the case of human blood. The prohibition includes 'any blood at all'. (Lev. 3:17)".[35]

---
[35] *Blood, Medicine and the Law of God*, (Brooklyn, New York: Watchtower and Tract Society of New York, Inc., 1961), pp.13,14.

SOLUTION:

1. This passage is not *necessarily* binding upon all nations. Circumcision, distinction between clean and unclean animals, and animal sacrifices were all practised by the patriarchs but are not now binding upon believers. (Gal. 6:15; Col. 2:14–17; Heb. 10:11,12).

2. The prohibition of the eating of the blood was later limited to Israel as a part of the Law of Moses. It was not made binding upon all nations.[36] "Ye shall not eat of any thing that dieth of itself: [because the blood had not been poured out as the law required] thou shalt give it unto the stranger that is in thy gates, that he may eat it; or thou mayest sell it unto an alien …"[37] (Deut. 14:21).

3. The changing, inconsistent, and arbitrary nature of the JW prohibition is seen from the following:[38]

   a. In the mid 1940s the Watchtower Organisation initially declared an outright ban on the acceptance of blood in any form, whole or fractional.

   b. Gradually the situation has changed. Now some components of blood are permitted, so that JWs are instructed, "...when it comes to fractions of any of the primary components, each Christian, after careful and prayerful meditation, must conscientiously decide for himself."[39] Thus, whilst whole blood, plasma, white blood cells, red blood cells, platelets, storing a patient's blood for subsequent transfusion are all forbidden, albumin, immunoglobulins, haemophiliac preparations (Factors VIII and IX), diversion of a patient's blood through a heart lung machine, are all allowed if the JWs conscience permits.

   c. Plasma, which is forbidden, consists of 93% water and 7% other components consisting primarily of albumin, globulins, fibrinogen and coagulation factors (used in haemophiliac preparations) that are allowed.

   d. Doctors who are JWs are allowed to take blood and administer blood to patients who are not JWs.

4. Blood used in transfusions is taken from a living, willing donor, not a corpse. Murder is not committed. It was Jesus Christ who said, "Greater love hath no man than this, that a man lay down his life for his friends." (John 15:13). Blood transfusions are given to sustain life, not to take it.

---

[36] See also Psa. 147:19,20: "He sheweth his word unto Jacob, his statutes and his judgments unto Israel. He hath not dealt so with any nation: and as for his judgments, they have not known them…"

[37] It may be thought that Lev. 17:10 conflicts with the instruction given in Deut. 14:21. The apparent conflict is resolved once it is realized that the strangers are different in the two passages. In Lev. 17:10 the strangers were those who "sojourned among" the Israelites as proselytes to the Jewish faith. They observed the law. (Exo. 12:48,49). The strangers in Deut. 14:21 were "strangers in the gates", i.e., foreigners visiting a city in Israel.

[38] This information was derived from Raymond Franz (a former member of the JW Governing Body), *In Search of Christian Freedom*, (Atlanta: Community Press, 1991), pp.286-304, and from Associated Jehovah's Witnesses for Reform on Blood (http://www.ajwrb.org).

[39] *The Watchtower*, 15 June 2000, pp.29-31.

Acts 15:28,29 (21:25)

"For it seemed good to the Holy Spirit, and to us, to lay upon you no greater burden than these necessary things; that ye abstain from meats offered to idols, and from blood, and from things strangled, and from fornication: from which if ye keep yourselves, ye shall do well. Fare ye well."

PROBLEM:

The incident recorded in Acts 15 provides the JWs with one of the main arguments regarding blood transfusion. So we are told:

"The Bible book of Acts sets forth a command to all Christians to 'abstain from blood'...Abstaining from blood is therefore as important for Christians as abstaining from idolatry or fornication." [40]

"The command to 'abstain from blood' was not a mere dietary restriction but it was a serious moral requirement, as seen by the fact that it was as serious to Christians as abstaining from idolatry and fornication."[41]

SOLUTION:

1. Neither in Acts 15 nor any of the Old Testament scriptures on which the recommendations of the Jerusalem Council were based (e.g. Lev. 3:17; 17:14; Deut. 12:23–25) is there any reference to the transfusion of human blood. The problem had to do with the *eating* of *animal blood*—or more precisely to the eating of animal flesh from which the blood had not been properly drained.
2. Blood transfusion is not "feeding on blood" as the JWs maintain. Blood is given for its volume and for its ability to transport oxygen around the body.
3. The Law of Moses on which the advice of the Council was based has been done away as is seen from Col. 2:14; Gal. 3:10–14.
4. The ruling of the Spirit-guided apostles and elders at the Jerusalem Council was for the ecclesias made up of a mix of Jew and Gentile believers. It was given against a background of demands being made by the Jewish element that the Gentiles should be circumcised and observe the Law of Moses (Acts 15:5).

   The Jerusalem Council made it clear that the Gentiles were not required to keep that Law, but "lay upon [them] no greater burden than these necessary things; that ye abstain from meats offered to idols, and from blood, and from things strangled, and from fornication: from which if ye keep yourselves, ye shall do well." (Acts 15:28,29).

   a. This would allow the Jewish believers (many of whom continued to observe the Law) to eat with the Gentiles and thus enjoy fellowship together as brethren (cf. Acts 11:2,3).

---

[40] *Blood Transfusion–Why Not for Jehovah's Witnesses*, [A letter to Members of the Medical Profession from the Governing Body of Jehovah's Witnesses].

[41] *Jehovah's Witnesses and the Question of Blood*, (Brooklyn, NY: Watchtower Bible and Tract Society, 1977), p.12.

b. The demands would, at the same time, place restrictions on the Gentile believers who (many of them being in straitened circumstances) would have been tempted to attend the idol festivals where they could have obtained a free meal from the sacrifices offered to idols, the worship of which was associated with ritual fornication. (Cf. the advice to the Corinthians in 1 Cor. 8:7–15; 10:14–22.)

c. The fact that the restrictions imposed on the Gentile believers had to do with the circumstances local to them in time and place is seen in the prohibition of "fornication". Why no reference to adultery, murder etc.? The fornication, being attached to idolatry and eating flesh with the blood, clearly has reference to the idolatry into which some of them were being tempted.

5. After the Jewish Council the teaching of Paul to the Gentiles made it plain that food in itself was not morally harmful—"I know, and am persuaded by the Lord Jesus, that there is nothing unclean of itself: but to him that esteemeth any thing to be unclean, to him it is unclean" (Rom. 14:14). Of particular relevance is his advice to the Corinthians, "Whatsoever is sold in the shambles, that eat, asking no question for conscience sake: for the earth is the Lord's, and the fulness thereof. If any of them that believe not bid you to a feast, and ye be disposed to go; whatsoever is set before you, eat, asking no question for conscience sake" (1 Cor. 10:25–27).

6. It is worth noting that even under the Law, if one partook of the flesh of an animal that "died of itself" or had been killed by a wild animal the punishment was, "He shall both wash his clothes, and bathe himself in water, and be unclean until the even: then shall he be clean" (Lev. 17:15).

BLOOD TRANSFUSION IN THE FUTURE?

Pressure is being brought to bear on the Watchtower Organisation and some signs are emerging that the stance on blood transfusion is undergoing subtle change.

a. A group of JW elders (and former elders) and members (or former members) of the Hospital Liaison Committee that calls itself "The Associated Jehovah's Witnesses for Reform on Blood" is exerting pressure from within. In their own words, "All have volunteered their time and energies in an effort to bring about an end to a tragic and misguided *policy that has claimed thousands of lives, many of them children.*" They are demanding answers to such questions as: (i) Why is plasma forbidden but all its constituent components are allowed? (ii) Since organ transplants are allowed, and since blood transfusion is essentially an organ transplant, how can it be viewed as eating blood? (iii) How does the Society go about deciding which blood components are allowed and which are barred? There is a possible threat from this quarter of litigation to force the issue.[42]

b. The Christian Association of Jehovah's Witnesses in the 276th Session of the European Commission of Human Rights challenged a 1994 ruling by Bulgaria that the Society would not be recognised as a religion and its activities, and

---

[42] This information obtained from Doug Harris, *The Jehovah's Witnesses*, Gazelle Books, London, 1998, pp.170-173. Further information may be found at: http://www.ajwrb.org.

those of its members, would be suppressed. In what appears to have been an amicable settlement the Bulgarian Government agreed to introduce legislation as soon as possible to provide an alternative to military service for conscientious objectors, and to register the Society as a religion. On its part the Society undertook, concerning its stance on blood transfusion, to draft a statement for inclusion in its statute providing that members should have free choice in the matter for themselves and their children, without any control or sanction on the part of the Watchtower Association.[43]

---

[43] See Doug Harris, op. cit., p.175.
Further information may be found at: http://hudoc.cehr.coe.int/Hudoc1doc/hedec/sift/3642.txt where the following amazing statement occurs:
"In respect of the refusal of blood transfusion, the applicant association submits that while this is part of the religious doctrine of Jehovah's Witnesses, its acceptance depends on the personal choice of the individual concerned. *There are no religious sanctions for a Jehovah's Witness who chooses to accept blood transfusion*" (Emphasis ours). What this last sentence appears to mean is that a JW who decides to have a blood transfusion is no longer disfellowshipped—he is assumed to have unilaterally disassociated himself from the Watchtower Society!
The following AP report sums up the devious attitude of the Society: NEW YORK (AP) 22 June 2000—"The Jehovah's Witnesses will continue to reject members who defy the group's prohibition of most blood transfusions, an official of the denomination said. Spokesman James Pellechia dismissed as misleading news reports that the longstanding policy had been reversed. The group acknowledges that it has ended its practice of "disfellowshipping" —or excommunicating—members who receive blood transfusions. But Pellechia said that a Jehovah's Witness who has a transfusion automatically 'revokes his membership'."

1.6

HERBERT ARMSTRONG'S "BRITISH-ISRAELISM"

PRELIMINARY POINTS:

The progress of British-Israelism[1] over the past three quarters of a century has taken a most unusual path. The year 1936 was held by followers of its teaching to be of great significance when the Prince of Wales (called Prince David) became monarch. It was said at the time that he would live a long prosperous life which would see the advent of the Messiah. The Prince of Wales, however, married the twice-divorced Mrs. Simpson and his abdication dealt a temporary blow to British Israelite doctrine.

In the 1950s, post-war Britain was riddled with agnosticism and had experienced loss of influence in the international world. It seemed unlikely soil for the regrowth of British-Israelism. However in the USA, since the 1930s, a very dynamic individual had been teaching the doctrine and had gathered round him a group of like-minded people who set about the work of proclaiming the British-Israel teaching. This movement, started by Herbert W. Armstrong, began to make amazing progress in large measure due to its worldwide "World of Tomorrow" radio broadcasts. An active, and very successful TV ministry followed, and their *Plain Truth* magazine achieved a circulation of 8 million copies per month. The Worldwide Church of God (WCG), as it was known, had congregations throughout the world. Ambassador College, the centre of its operations, in Pasadena, California, employed 1,000 members.

In the late 1980s the WCG amazingly began to change its teachings. British-Israelism was dropped and evangelical doctrines that had been vigorously rejected by Armstrong were espoused so that by 1997 the WCG was formally accepted into the National Association of Evangelicals. This process of change had a devastating effect on the WCG. Church membership halved, circulation of the *Plain Truth* is now a mere 120,000 and Ambassador College buildings have been sold.[2]

Armstrong's British-Israel views are now proclaimed by a number of groups that splintered from the WCG in its process of 'reform'. These include the United Church of God (publishers of *The Good News* magazine), the Global Church of God, the Living Church of God, the Philadelphia Church of God and many more. We thought it best to group them together in this section since they all owe their origin to the activities of Herbert W. Armstrong.

A number of Bible passages are cited in support of its doctrine and special publications on the subject have circulated since 1954. In brief, British-Israelism (with some variation) is the belief that modern Britain and the Anglo-Saxon

---

[1] The term "British-Israelism" is used instead of "Anglo-Israelism" since Herbert Armstrong's doctrine is popularly known by the former term.

[2] Information obtained from *A Brief History of the Worldwide Church of God*, on the WCG website: www.wcg.org/AboutUs/history.htm.

WRESTED SCRIPTURES

peoples of Canada, the U.S.A., Denmark, Sweden, Holland, France, Germany and north-western European nations comprise the "lost" ten tribes of Israel. The following underpinnings are noteworthy:

1. That the term "Jew" as used in Scripture applies only to the two tribes (Judah and Benjamin) and not to the "House of Israel"—the ten tribes. The terms "Israelite" and "Jew" are not synonymous for British-Israelites.
2. That the return of Jews under Zerubbabel, Ezra and Nehemiah to Palestine from their captivity was limited to the two tribes.
3. That David's throne is presently the throne on which Queen Elizabeth sits in London, England.[3]
4. That the "stone of Israel" of Gen. 49:24 was the pillow used by Jacob and carried by him into Palestine. When Nebuchadnezzar invaded the land of Israel in 606 BC, the daughter of Zedekiah, King of Judah, fled to Egypt with Jeremiah the prophet, taking the stone with her. From Egypt it was shipped by Jews to Ireland, then Scotland and finally found its place in the coronation chair in Westminster Abbey.

Genesis 35:11

"And God said unto him, I am God Almighty: be fruitful and multiply; a nation and a company of nations shall be of thee, and kings shall come out of thy loins."

PROBLEM:

On the basis of this passage Armstrong argues as follows: "The Jews have never been more than one nation. They are not, and never have been many nations…This promise has never been fulfilled in the Jews. So the 'many nations' are eventually to take shape as a nation—one great, wealthy, powerful nation;[4] and another company of nations—a group, or commonwealth of nations allied."[5]

SOLUTION:

1. Armstrong's argument sounds plausible but it is circular. A Jew is first *defined* by him to be a member of the tribe of Judah.[6] He then concludes that the Jews have never been more than one nation. Of course if Jews are *defined* to be

[3] Some astounding conclusions have been drawn from British-Israelite doctrine. Edward Hine, one of the greatest promoters of its teaching said: "It is an utter impossibility for England ever to be defeated. And this is another result arising entirely from the fact of our being Israel." Edward Hine, *The British Nation identified with Lost Israel*, (London: S. W. Partridge & Co. n.d.) p.73. Robert Roberts, former editor of *The Christadelphian*, engaged Hine in a three-nights' debate in Exeter Hall, London, England, 1879. The debate was subsequently published. See, *Are Englishmen Israelites?* (Birmingham: C. C. Walker, 1919).

[4] By "one great wealthy nation" he means the U.S.A., and by "commonwealth" he refers to Great Britain and the British Commonwealth.

[5] Herbert W. Armstrong, *The United States and the British Commonwealth in Prophecy*, (Pasadena: Ambassador College, 1954), pp.2,3.

[6] In the same booklet, Armstrong defines a Jew as follows: "The term 'Jew' is merely a nickname for 'Judah'. It applies to the one nation, or House of Judah only—never to the house of Israel." p.7.

110

members of one tribe they will not be more than one nation. The argument assumes what must first be proven, i.e., that the word "Jew" is used exclusively of one nation in Scripture.

2. The following passages indicate that the word "Jew" is not used exclusively in Scripture for members of the tribe of Judah:

   a. "Brethren the *Jews*" (Neh. 5:1,8,17) is synonymous with "all *Israel*, dwelt in their cities." (Neh. 7:73).

   b. "I am a man which am a *Jew*" (Acts 21:39; 22:3) said Paul. But he also said, "I am an *Israelite* of the tribe of Benjamin." (Rom. 11:1).

   c. The "all Israel" of 1 Chron. 9:1 includes "Judah" and "Benjamin". (1 Chron. 9:3).

   d. "And the days that David reigned over Israel were forty years: seven years reigned he in Hebron, and thirty and three years reigned he in Jerusalem." (1 Kings 2:11). David's kingship over *Judah* in Hebron is counted as part of his reign as king of *Israel*.

   e. Nehemiah, a cupbearer to a Persian king (Neh. 1:11; 2:1) asked one of his brothers "concerning the *Jews* that had escaped, which were left of the captivity, and concerning Jerusalem." (Neh. 1:2). But when Nehemiah arrived in Jerusalem, the enemies of the rebuilding "grieved…exceedingly that there was come a man to seek the welfare of the children of *Israel*." (Neh. 2:10).

   f. Shalmaneser, king of Assyria "took Samaria, and carried *Israel* away into Assyria, and placed them in Halah and in Habor by the river of Gozan, and in the cities of the Medes." (2 Kings 17:6). But when Ahasuerus sent his decree to the 127 provinces of his dominion, it was sent to Jews: "Write ye also for the *Jews*…and it was written according to all that Mordecai commanded unto the Jews…unto every people after their language, and to the Jews according to their writing, and according to their language." (Esther 8:8,9).[7] The decree was not addressed to *Jews* in Babylon and Israelites in Media which one would have expected if British-Israel theory were true.

3. Gen. 35:11 provides *no* proof that the "company of nations" refers to the Anglo-Saxon peoples. Armstrong's case rests merely on assertion, but to assert is not to prove. Any points of alleged identification must rest, therefore, on other evidence which can be considered separately.

4. The land promised to Jacob was the same land promised to Abraham and Isaac (Gen. 35:12). This was "the land of Canaan" (Gen. 17:8) which Abraham as a sojourner was invited to see, but not possess, in his lifetime and which he will ultimately inherit. (Gen. 13:14,15; Heb. 11:8–16; Acts 7:5). It is not the land of Great Britain, U.S.A. and other Commonwealth countries.

5. The blessing upon Jacob cannot be understood to refer merely to the literal descendants—the twelve tribes, since the Apostle Paul's exposition in Rom. 4:16,17 requires an application of the word "nations" to those who share the

---

[7] Peter on the Day of Pentecost addressed "*Jews*, devout men, out of every nation under heaven." (Acts 2:5). Some of these Jews came from Media and Persia (Acts 2:9) and were no doubt descendants of the northern kingdom—*Israelites*. (cf. 2 Kings 17:6).

faith of Abraham: "Therefore it is of faith, that it might be by grace; to the end the promise might be sure to all the seed; not to that only which is of the law, but to that also which is of the faith of Abraham; who is the father of *us all*, (as it is written, I have made thee a father of many nations,)…" (Rom. 4:16,17). The father of many nations refers to "us all" (Jew and Gentile alike) on the basis of faith, not pedigree. Faith, not Anglo-Saxon origin, constitutes one a member of the "many nations".

6. Armstrong argues against the spiritual import of the passage on the following grounds: "It could not pertain to the Church, for there is but one true Church acknowledged in the Bible, and it is not a nation, or a group of nations, but a collection of called-out individuals scattered through all nations."[8] Armstrong is right in saying that there is only one true Church acknowledged in the Bible, but he is wrong in saying that it is not a nation. Peter wrote to the "strangers scattered throughout Pontus, Galatia, Cappadocia, Asia, and Bithynia." (1 Pet. 1:1). Although they were literally scattered in all these areas, Peter addressed them as "a chosen generation, a royal priesthood, an holy *nation*."[9] (1 Pet. 2:9). Similarly "nation" is used in the sense of a "multitude; people living under common institutions"[10] in the following two passages:

   a. "…I will provoke you [i.e. the Jews] to jealousy by them that are no people, and by a foolish nation I will anger you." (Rom. 10:19). What geographical area, or racial characteristics can be ascribed to this nation?

   b. "Therefore say I unto you, The kingdom of God shall be taken from you, and given to a nation bringing forth the fruits thereof." (Matt. 21:43). To what pedigree was Jesus referring by his reference to the "other nation?" What was its geographical location?

Thus believers are a nation (a people living under common institutions) and collectively they form the one Ecclesia (body of called-out ones).

7. Armstrong's conclusion that "'the many nations' are eventually to take shape as a nation—one great, wealthy, powerful nation" is neither stated not implied in either the verse or the context.

Ezra 1:5

"Then rose up the chief of the fathers of Judah and Benjamin, and the priests, and the Levites…to go up to build the house of the LORD which is in Jerusalem."

---

[8] Herbert W. Armstrong, *The United States and the British Commonwealth in Prophecy*, (Pasadena: Ambassador College, 1954), p.3.

[9] *Ethnos*, the Greek word translated "nation" in this passage is the same Greek word used in the Septuagint translation of Gen. 17:5, 35:11 and Paul's citation in Rom. 4:17.

[10] *Goi* the Hebrew word translated "nation" means "a corporate body". In the AV it is translated "Gentile" 30 times, "heathen" 142 times, and "nation" 373 times (Robert Young, *Analytical Concordance to the Holy Bible*, London: Lutterworth Press, 1965 ed.). The Greek equivalent used by the Apostle Paul is *ethnos* which means "a multitude; people, living under common institutions" (E. W. Bullinger, *A Critical Lexicon and Concordance*, London: Bagster and Sons Ltd., 1957 ed.).

Ezra 2:1

"Now these are the children of the province that went up...whom Nebuchadnezzar the king of Babylon had carried away unto Babylon, and came again unto Jerusalem and Judah, every one unto his city."

PROBLEM:

On the basis of these passages Armstrong argues as follows: "Those who returned to Palestine to rebuild the temple and restore worship 70 years after Judah's captivity were all of the House of Judah—all Jews—all of those whom Nebuchadnezzar had carried away. They returned again 'unto Jerusalem and Judah, every one unto his city' (Ezra 2:1). Only those of the tribes of Judah, Benjamin and Levi, who constituted the house of Judah returned at that time. (Ezra 1:5). Consequently those in Jerusalem in the time of Christ were these tribes, not of the House of Israel."[11]

SOLUTION:

1. If the 10 tribes were "lost" at the time of Zerubbabel, why was a sin offering offered for "all Israel"—*twelve* he goats, according to the number of the tribes of Israel"? (Ezra 6:16,17). Under Ezra the "children of those that had been carried away, which were come out of the captivity, offered burnt offerings unto the God of Israel, *twelve* bullocks for *all* Israel..." (Ezra 8:35).

2. Armstrong asserts that, "only those of the tribes of Judah, Benjamin, and Levi, who constituted the house of Judah returned at that time". But this argument neglects to take into account that members of the 10 tribes were also constituents of the Kingdom of Judah in the south. When the captivities took place it was a *mixture* of the tribes which was carried off. Consider the evidence:

   a. The Kingdom of Judah in the south consisted from the start of some of 4 tribes and not just 2 tribes—Levi (2 Chron. 11:13,16) and Simeon (Josh. 19:9) which had its territory in Judah, dwelt with Judah and Benjamin.

   b. There were migrations from the northern to the southern kingdom, as the following passages indicate:

      i. "And he [Asa, King of Judah] gathered all Judah and Benjamin, and the strangers with them out of *Ephraim* and *Manasseh*, and out of *Simeon*: for they fell to him out of Israel in abundance, when they saw that the LORD his God was with him." (2 Chron. 15:9).

      ii. "But as for the children of Israel which dwelt in the cities of Judah, Rehoboam [King of Judah] reigned over them." (1 Kings 12:17; see also 2 Chron. 11:3).

   c. Even after the rebellion which resulted in the setting up of the kingdom of Israel in the north, loyal Israelites to the throne of David migrated south— "...out of all the tribes of Israel such as set their hearts to seek the LORD

[11] Herbert W. Armstrong, *The United States and the British Commonwealth in Prophecy*, (Pasadena: Ambassador College, 1954), p.9.

God of Israel came to Jerusalem [and]...they strengthened the kingdom of Judah..." (2 Chron. 11:16,17).

3. Armstrong reasons that "Consequently those in Jerusalem in the time of Christ were of these tribes (i.e., Judah, Benjamin and Levi), not of the House of Israel." He assumes that the 10 tribes were in Great Britain or migrating across Europe in the direction of Great Britain. But such reasoning is incompatible with the following New Testament evidence:

   a. The disciples were sent to the "lost sheep of the house of Israel." (Matt. 10:6). Since the teaching of the disciples was confined to Palestine, the tribes of Israel must have been in Palestine, not Europe or Great Britain.[12]

   b. Paul informed his hearers that the "12 tribes" were "instantly serving God day and night." (Acts 26:7). This is a thorough refutation of Armstrong's claim that at this time the 10 tribes had lost "their language, their religion, their land."[13]

   c. Jesus stated that he was sent "unto the lost sheep of the house of Israel." (Matt. 15:24). But in carrying out his mission there is no Scriptural record of him journeying to Europe or Great Britain to find the lost 10 tribes. If his teaching was only to the three tribes (Judah, Benjamin, and Levi), then he failed in the greater part of his commission. The fact that the teaching of Jesus was confined to Palestine is in itself proof that the 10 tribes were neither geographically lost nor Anglo-Saxon.

Jeremiah 33:17

"For thus saith the LORD; David shall never want a man to sit upon the throne of the house of Israel..."

PROBLEM:

This passage furnishes the critical link in the British-Israelite argument. Armstrong puts it this way:

"Not only was that throne established for ever, it was to exist continuously for ever—through all generations...If the throne of David ceased with Zedekiah, then it does not exist today. And if it does not exist, how shall Christ sit upon a non-existent throne?"[14]

It is on the basis of this reasoning that appeal is made to the ancient annals of Ireland to attempt to prove that Queen Elizabeth now sits on David's throne. Armstrong after citing Irish tradition, states: "In view of the linking together of Biblical history, prophecy, and Irish history, can anyone deny that this Hebrew princess (Tephi) was the daughter of King Zedekiah of Judah, and therefore heir to the throne of David?—That the aged patriarch was in fact Jeremiah, and his companion Jeremiah's scribe, or secretary, Baruch?...The Royal Family of the

[12] Anna who "departed not from the temple" was from the tribe of Asher (Luke 2:36,37), indicating that Jews from tribes other than Judah, Levi and Benjamin lived in Palestine at the time of Christ.

[13] Herbert W. Armstrong, *The United States and the British Commonwealth in Prophecy*, (Pasadena: Ambassador College, 1954), p.9.

[14] *Ibid.* p.6.

British Commonwealth possesses a chart showing its ancestry, every generation, back to Heremon and Tephi, to Zedekiah, on back to David..."[15]

SOLUTION:

1. If the throne of David has been "overturned" and now exists in London, are the priests and the Levites offering burnt offerings, kindling meat offerings and doing "sacrifice continually?" (Jer. 33:18). British-Israelites only quote the first part of the covenant, but the covenant continues: "Neither shall the priests the Levites want a man before me to offer burnt offerings, and to kindle meat offerings, and to do sacrifice continually." (Jer. 33:18). Notice the similar references in vv. 21,22.

2. The promise, "David shall never want a man to sit upon the throne of the house of Israel" is future, commencing with the reign of Christ and not with the reign of David.[16] Consider the context:

   a. "Behold, the days come..." (v. 14). What days? "In those days, and at that time, will I cause the Branch of righteousness to grow up unto David; and he shall execute judgment and righteousness in the land." (v. 15). The Branch is singular (i.e., "he") and does not, therefore, refer to a successive line of kings and queens. No monarch in the history of Great Britain can be said to have executed judgment and righteousness in the land. This description can only refer to Jesus Christ.

   b. "In those days shall Judah be saved, and Jerusalem shall dwell safely: and this is the name wherewith she shall be called, The LORD our righteousness." (v. 16). Neither Judah, Jerusalem nor Great Britain can be said presently to be "saved" or "dwell safely." Certainly today, Great Britain does not merit the description, "The LORD our righteousness." It has been judged by non-religious men as a decadent, agnostic, atheistic and pseudo-religious society.

3. Scripture never refers to the throne of David being removed from Palestine to any other country. Scripture never refers to a return of David's throne from *any* country to Jerusalem at the time of Christ's return. Such assumptions must be read into Scripture by the British-Israel theory.

4. Jesus will not return to a non-existent throne. David's throne will be re-established in Jerusalem. (Psa. 132:13,14,17,18; Jer. 3:17; Isa. 9:6,7; Luke

---

[15] *Ibid.*, pp.19,20.

[16] Armstrong also cites 2 Sam. 7 in support of his doctrine that there has been an unbroken continuity in the Davidic throne. But the same mistake is made in the interpretation of this reference as in his interpretation of Jer. 33:17. God says: "...thou [David] shalt sleep with thy fathers, I will set up thy seed after thee...and I will stablish the throne of his kingdom for ever. I will be his father, and he shall be my son..." (2 Sam. 7:12–14). These words refer to Jesus Christ and not to Solomon as Armstrong alleges. This is the inspired interpretation given in Heb. 1:5. The continuance of the throne until the promised seed (Christ) would come is *conditional* upon Israel obeying God's statutes. This is stated in David's charge to Solomon: "...*If* thy children take heed to their way, to walk before me in truth with all their heart and with all their soul, there shall not fail thee (said he) a man on the throne of Israel." (1 Kings 2:4). Israel did not walk faithfully and so God removed the diadem and crown. (Ezek. 21:26).

1:32,33). As the prophet, quoted by James, declared: "After this I will return, and will build again the tabernacle of David, which is fallen down; and I will build again the ruins thereof, and I will set it up..." (Acts 15:16).

5. Hosea states clearly that "the children of Israel shall abide *many* days without a king, and without a prince, and without a sacrifice..." (Hosea 3:4). Only in the "latter days" shall the children of Israel "return, and seek the LORD their God, and David their king; and shall fear the LORD and his goodness in the latter days." (Hosea 3:5). The language of these two verses is incompatible with Armstrong's claim that there never has been a break in the Davidic line. Furthermore, it cannot be said of the Commonwealth nations nor of the U.S.A. that in these latter days they "seek the LORD their God."

Jeremiah 43:5-7

"But Johanan...took all the remnant of Judah...and the king's daughters...into the land of Egypt."

PROBLEM:

Armstrong reasons on the basis of these verses that David's throne was preserved by one of King Zedekiah's daughters fleeing to Egypt. The royal seed was then replanted about 580 BC in Ireland, "later overturned a second time and replanted in Scotland, overturned a third time planted in London, from where it cannot be overturned or moved again until the coming of Christ, when it once again shall be overturned and transplanted back in Jerusalem."[17]

The royal party "brought with them some remarkable things, including the harp, an ark, and a wonderful stone called 'Lia-Fail', or 'stone of destiny'...many kings in the history of Ireland, Scotland, and England have been coronated sitting over this stone—including the present queen. The stone rests, today, in Westminster Abbey in London[18], and the Coronation Chair is built over and around it. A sign beside it labels it 'Jacob's pillar-stone' (Gen. 28:18)."[19]

SOLUTION:

1. Even if Zedekiah's daughters had escaped as stated, they were not in the royal line. Zedekiah was an interloper instated by the Babylonians. "And he [Nebuchadnezzar] carried away Jehoiachin [King of Judah] to Babylon, and the king's mother, and the king's wives, and his officers, and the mighty of the land, those carried he into captivity from Jerusalem to Babylon...and the king of Babylon made Mattaniah his father's brother king in his stead, and changed his name to Zedekiah." (2 Kings 24:17). See also the genealogy in Matt. 1:11–13.

---

[17] Herbert W. Armstrong, *The United States and the British Commonwealth in Prophecy*, (Pasadena: Ambassador College, 1954), p.20.

[18] For 700 years the stone rested under the Coronation Chair in Westminster Abbey. However, in 1996 the British Government returned the stone to Scotland where it is now on display in Edinburgh Castle.

[19] Herbert W. Armstrong, *The United States and the British Commonwealth in Prophecy*, (Pasadena: Ambassador College, 1954), p.19.

This evidence completely destroys the case Armstrong is trying to make for the transplantation of the "royal seed."

2. Armstrong presents the escape of the daughters of King Zedekiah as a providential move to preserve the "royal seed". Scripture, however, makes it clear that the move to Egypt was for punishment. "So they came into the land of Egypt: for they obeyed not the voice of the LORD..." (Jer. 43:7). Even while in Egypt their wickedness was manifest: "...ye provoke me unto wrath with the works of your hands, burning incense unto other gods in the land of Egypt..." (Jer. 44:8). All but "a small number" perished since God had declared "they shall all be consumed, and fall in the land of Egypt...they shall die, from the least even unto the greatest, by the sword and by the famine..." (Jer. 44:12,28).

3. Armstrong reasons that the "small number" (Jer. 44:28) included the "royal seed" which departed for Ireland. This conclusion does not follow for these reasons:

   a. The alleged royal seed is not mentioned as escaping. The fact that "all the women" (Jer. 44:15) told Jeremiah that they would not listen to him, but rather preferred the queen of heaven is suggestive that the King's daughters did not escape. (See Jer. 44:16-18).

   b. Those who did escape returned to Judah (Jer. 44:14,28). Scripture is silent about a trip to Ireland.

4. The evidence that the Coronation Stone is the stone Jacob used for a pillow is not conclusive. Consider the following:

   a. The Coronation Stone is *red sandstone*; the stones of Bethel are *white limestone*.

   b. Jacob said, "And this stone, which I have set for a pillar, shall be God's house..." (Gen. 28:22). To set the stone for a pillar is not the kind of language one would ordinarily associate with taking the stone with him on the journey.

5. Ezekiel makes no reference to the throne of David being removed to a different location. This information must be read into the passage. The language employed by Ezekiel is an emphatic denial that the throne of David existed anywhere after the death of Zedekiah. "...and it shall be *no more, until* he come whose right it is..."[20] (Ezek. 21:27, cf. "there shall not be even a trace of it until he comes whose right it is", RSV).

6. "I will overturn, overturn, overturn, it," ("ruin, ruin, ruin" RSV) may be emphatic[21] for the overturning by the Babylonians in the time of Zedekiah, or it may refer to the three invasions by the Babylonians, Antiochus Epiphanes and Titus. The language, "remove the diadem, and take off the crown" (Ezek. 21:26)—symbols of the political government, indicates a termination of the Davidic throne. It would remain so "until he come"—the Lord Jesus Christ.

---

[20] "Abase him that is high" (Ezek. 21:26) is likely a reference to the subsequent degradation suffered by the wicked King Zedekiah at the hands of the Babylonians. (see 2 Kings 25:7). "Exalt him that is low" may refer to the poor left in the land. (See Jer. 40:7).

[21] Note the similarity of emphasis on the word "earth" in Jer. 22:29.

117

Israel was subsequently to remain "many days without a prince, and without a sacrifice". (Hosea 3:4). This language is incompatible with Armstrong's claim that the Davidic throne merely changed location without interruption of continuity.

I.7

THE CHURCH OF CHRIST

PRELIMINARY POINTS:

The Church of Christ[1] is the name of autonomous churches throughout Australia, Canada, and especially the "Bible belt" of the U.S.A.[2] The Church of Christ has similar doctrines to those expounded by Alexander Campbell,[3] an associate of Dr. John Thomas with whom the Doctor broke after a fuller understanding of the elements of the gospel.[4] Members of the Church of Christ have a motto, "Where the Bible speaks we speak, and where it is silent we are silent." They believe in "contending earnestly for the faith" (as they understand the faith), which is interpreted to mean striving as in rivalry or debate. This vigorous approach to Scripture has resulted in debates with Christadelphian lecturers in Indiana, Texas, Manitoulin Island, and Adelaide, Australia.[5]

[1] Not long after the American Civil War one group of members of the original movement proclaimed independence from the main body and has since maintained a separation. It has its headquarters in Nashville, TN, and is the group with which this study is principally concerned. The liberal wing of the Church of Christ is identified as the "Christian Church" in the Midwest and South, and "Disciples of Christ" in the East. See James E. Craig, "Who are the Disciples of Christ?", in *A Guide to the Religions of America*, ed. by Leo Rosten, (New York: Simon and Schuster, 1955), pp.38-46.

[2] When the first edition of this book was published in 1970 the Church of Christ (COC) was little known in the U.K. In 1979 an extremely vigorous offshoot of the COC came into being as a result of the work of Kip McKean, the leader of a COC congregation in Boston, U.S.A. He set himself the task of establishing "pillar churches" in key world cities which would in turn become bases from which other areas could be evangelised. By 1993 the movement, that became known as the International Church of Christ (ICOC), had 130 congregations in different parts of the world. The Central London Church of Christ began in 1982 and by 1998 the church had seven zone churches in the London area. Evangelism in the U.K. continues and there are now churches actively promoting COC teaching in about 25 locations in the U.K.

Their methods of evangelism have been severely criticised. It is considered by some to be the fastest growing cult in the U.K., although it is doubtful if the description 'cult' is fair. Mainstream COC churches tend to distance themselves from the ICOC but the doctrines are essentially the same. The ICOC tends to target college and university campuses. Young inexperienced Christadelphians are advised to take someone of experience with them if invited to meet ICOC evangelists (see Nigel Scotland, *Sectarian Religion in Contemporary Britain*, Carlisle: Paternoster Publishing, 2000, or the ICOC website for further information).

[3] In the "sanctuary" of the Park Avenue Christian Church in New York City, the table is preserved at which Alexander Campbell and Walter Scott presided in their communion services.

[4] See Robert Roberts, *Dr. Thomas: His Life and Work,* 2nd ed., (Birmingham: The Christadelphian, 1873), pp.9-15; 20-84. Also John Thomas, "Confession and Abjuration", *Herald of the Future Age*, 1847, III, pp.73-80.

[5] The Lee-Mansfield debate (1962) is a Christadelphian classic. The debate over six nights between the Church of Christ and the Christadelphians drew an average attendance of 800, and at least six baptisms resulted from people contacted through the debate. Records of the debate have been made available by Logos Publications, West Beach, South Australia.

SUGGESTED STRATEGY:

1. Church of Christ ministers are often schooled debaters. Christadelphians anticipating debating with representatives of this body should have a thorough knowledge of the arguments used by the Church of Christ before the debate. The strength of the Christadelphian position does not rest on the facile tactics of the skilled debater. As the Apostle Paul put it: "[We] have renounced the hidden things of dishonesty, not walking in craftiness, nor handling the word of God deceitfully; but by manifestation of the truth commending ourselves to every man's conscience in the sight of God." (2 Cor. 4:2). Nevertheless, the Christadelphian places himself at a disadvantage if he has no knowledge of logical fallacies in argumentation, or of the desirability of keeping an opponent on the issue in question. Ecclesial mutual improvement classes can help build the needed skills to "mightily convince...and that publicly, showing by the scriptures", as did Apollos. (Acts 18:28).

2. In private discussion, members of the Church of Christ can be a delight to teach. Although they are fundamentalists in their view of inspiration, there is almost an exclusive use of the New Testament. This betrays a fundamental weakness in the Church of Christ position which is often indicated by their confused identification of the Law of Moses with the teaching of the Old Testament prophets. The former served its usefulness as a schoolmaster to bring Israel to Christ (Gal. 3:24), but as a law code it is no longer binding upon believers. This is not, however, to be confused with the many Messianic prophecies referring to the reign of Christ on the earth which still await fulfilment. The Christadelphian must establish the legitimacy of his frequent Old Testament references before the full import of their force registers. The inspired application of more than 630 Old Testament references cited and used by Christ and the Apostles in the New Testament is an authoritative guide to Biblical interpretation.

3. It can be very helpful in discussion with the Church of Christ to keep returning to the following summaries which help to fix in the memory the framework of the kingdom of God:

    a. *The kingdom of God*—its essential elements.
       i. King—Jesus Christ (Luke 1:32,33; John 18:37).
       ii. Rulers—Immortalized saints (Matt. 19:27,28; Rev. 3:21 cf. 2:26,27; 2 Tim. 2:12; Rev. 5:9,10).
       iii. Subjects—Mortal nations surviving wars (Zech. 14:16–18; Micah 4:1–3; Isa. 65:17–25).
       iv. Laws—Righteous (Psa. 72:4,12–14).
       v. Land—Whole earth (Num. 14:21; Hab. 2:14; Isa. 11:9).
       vi. Capital city—Jerusalem (Matt. 5:35, cf. Luke 1:32,33 and 1 Chron. 11:4,5).

    b. *David's throne*—in the past and in the future.
       i. Located in Jerusalem (1 Chron. 11:4,5,7).
       ii. Promised to Christ (2 Sam. 7:12,13,16; cf. Heb. 1:5).

iii. Solomon sat on it (1 Chron. 28:5).

iv. Ceased to exist with removal of Zedekiah (Ezek. 21:26,27).

v. Will be restored by Christ (Luke 1:32,33, cf. Matt. 19:28; Rev. 3:21; Acts 15:16).

THE KINGDOM OF GOD

PRELIMINARY POINTS:

The Church of Christ usually[6] reads "the kingdom of God" in scripture as synonymous with the "Church of Christ".[7] It is appropriate for the Christadelphian, therefore, to show the unscriptural character of this substitution. This can be done by producing Biblical statements about the kingdom which are incompatible with statements about the ecclesia.[8] The following are suggested lines of reasoning:

1. Jesus stated: "When the Son of man shall come in his glory, and all the holy angels with him, then shall he sit upon the throne of his glory: and before him shall be gathered all nations: and he shall separate them one from another, as a shepherd divideth *his* sheep from the goats...Then shall the King say unto them on his right hand, Come, ye blessed of my Father, inherit the kingdom prepared for you from the foundation of the world...Then shall he say also unto them on the left hand, Depart from me...And these shall go away into everlasting punishment: but the righteous into life eternal." (Matt. 25:31,32,34,41,46).

   These conclusions follow:

   a. Jesus has not yet come in the throne of his glory since all nations have not been gathered before him, nor have the "sheep" been separated from the "goats".

   b. Therefore, the faithful are not yet in the kingdom since the invitation to enter the kingdom is not given until *after* the separation of the sheep from the goats.[9]

---

[6] The position outlined is not *invariably* the position of the Church of Christ since considerable variation of belief exists among the autonomous assemblies.

[7] For example, A. R. Main, a member of the Church of Christ makes this identification: "...in denotation the kingdom of God, in so far as it is manifested in visible form on earth, corresponds to the church..." *First Principles*: *Studies in Bible Truth* (Melbourne: The Austral Printing and Publishing Co., 1969), p.67. "The church is the kingdom of God on earth established in approximately 33 AD" (First Principles, ICOC website).

[8] An important distinction should be noted: The Greek word "ecclesia", translated "church", refers to "called out" ones. The word "church" is used today to designate both the building and a religious grouping. The Church of Christ, therefore, is a "church" in the popular usage of the term, but it is not the ecclesia. It is not the ecclesia because of the false doctrines which the Church of Christ teaches. In this analysis careful attention should be given not to confuse the "Church of Christ" (i.e., the religious group known by the name today) with the ecclesia of the first century which held the doctrines presently taught by the Christadelphians.

[9] One does not know before the Judgment Day whether he is for certain a "sheep" or a "goat". The parable of the sheep and goats (Matt. 25:31–46) points out that many who think they are sheep will find out they are goats. The same self-deception is indicated in Matt. 7:22,23.

c. If the faithful[10] are not yet in the kingdom, then the kingdom of God cannot be the "church".

2. Jesus stated that at the Judgment Day men will say, "Lord, Lord, have we not prophesied in thy name? and in thy name have cast out devils? and in thy name done many wonderful works?" (Matt. 7:22). His statement followed the exhortation that "Not every one that saith unto me, Lord, Lord, shall enter into the kingdom of heaven; but he that doeth the will of my Father which is in heaven." (Matt. 7:21). Entry into the kingdom is conditional upon doing the will of God who is in heaven.

These conclusions follow:

a. Since men have not yet been confronted by Jesus to give an account of what they have done (cf. 2 Cor. 5:9,10), they do not know for sure whether they have, in fact, done his will acceptably.

b. But doing the will of God is the requisite for entry into the kingdom of God.

c. Therefore the kingdom of God is not yet established, and cannot be synonymous with the "church".

3. Peter asked Jesus,[11] "Behold, we have forsaken all, and followed thee; what shall we have therefore? And Jesus said unto them, Verily I say unto you, That ye which have followed me, in the regeneration when the Son of man shall sit in the throne of his glory, ye also shall sit upon twelve thrones, judging the twelve tribes of Israel." (Matt. 19:27,28). This passage furnishes a whole array of appropriate questions to lead the Church of Christ contact to the desired conclusions. The following questions require answers:

a. What is the scriptural definition of Christ's "throne of glory"? (See Matt. 25:31; cf. Peter's words in 1 Pet. 5:4).

---

[10] It is sometimes argued that the parable of the sheep and goats refers to sheep and goat nations rather than individuals. Against this interpretation the following should be noted:

• "He shall separate them"—"them" is masculine in gender in the Greek text indicating that it refers to individuals, and not to "nations" which is neuter in gender.

• Those who *inherit* the kingdom are *heirs* of the kingdom. This is the language used of faithful brethren (Gal. 3:29; James 2:5), not of nations.

• The Greek word *ethnos*, translated "nations", is more frequently translated Gentiles (in the AV) implying Christ's stress that Gentiles, and not only Jews from "all *the* nations" will be gathered for the judgment.

• The righteous are commended in the parable for having given food and water to the Master as well as having visited him when sick and in prison. This is the language used elsewhere in the N.T. of believers (Matt. 10:40–42), not nations. Can it be imagined that nations such as Canada, Britain, the USA or Egypt could be commended by the Master, "Inasmuch as ye have done it unto one of the least of these my *brethren*, ye have done it unto me" ("brethren" are defined by Christ to be those who *hear* and *do* his will—Luke 8:21)?

Sheep-like characteristics are attributed to believers and even to the nation of Israel (e.g. John 10:1–28; Ezek. 34), but where in Scripture is it used of other nations?

[11] It is noteworthy that in the context of this conversation Jesus says, "It is easier for a camel to go through the eye of a needle, than for a rich man to enter into the kingdom of God." (Matt. 19:24). If the kingdom of God is the "church," (as the Church of Christ asserts), is it difficult for a wealthy person to enter their church? It is in this context that the kingdom of God is associated with the king coming in "the throne of his glory" in the regeneration. (Matt. 19:28).

b. When will the Son of man sit on this throne? (See Matt. 25:31; cf. Peter's statement, Acts 3:19–21).

c. Where will the throne be located? (See Luke 1:32,33; 1 Chron. 11:4,5 cf. Ezek. 21:26,27; Acts 15:15,16).

d. If the apostles are to sit on twelve thrones, when will this promise be fulfilled? (See Acts 1:6 and Matt. 16:27, cf. Rev. 11:18—the servants are rewarded at the time of the resurrection of the dead "that they should be judged"; Rev. 3:21,22, cf. 2:26,27).

4. The Apostle Paul states, "Now this I say, brethren, that flesh and blood cannot inherit the kingdom of God; neither doth corruption inherit incorruption." (1 Cor. 15:50). This passage in itself is proof that the kingdom is not the "church". Consider the following:

a. "Flesh and blood" persons presently constitute the "church".

b. But, "flesh and blood" cannot inherit the kingdom;

c. Therefore, the kingdom cannot be the "church".

5. Paul wrote to Timothy: "I charge thee therefore before God, and the Lord Jesus Christ, who shall judge the quick and the dead at his appearing and his kingdom." (2 Tim. 4:1). The following questions require answers from the Church of Christ:

a. Is the time designated by "his appearing" the same as the time period indicated by "and his kingdom"?

b. Who are the dead to whom the apostle refers?

c. When will these dead persons be raised? (The event must be future to the time when the apostle wrote to Timothy since he says, "he *shall* judge the quick and the dead". How many quick and dead were judged at the beginning of "the church" and his appearing, if these occurred at Pentecost?)

It is easy to establish by these questions that since the dead have not yet been raised, then the kingdom must yet be future, and, therefore, cannot be the "church".

6. James writes to believers of the "twelve tribes which are scattered abroad". (James 1:1). He speaks of them as "*heirs* of the kingdom which he hath promised to them that love him". (2:5). Since baptized believers are by definition in the "church", in what sense can they be *heirs* of the "church" (if the kingdom is the "church")? Similarly, the Apostle Paul tells believers at Galatia: "Envyings, murders, drunkenness, revellings, and such like: of the which I tell you before, as I have also told you in time past, that they which do such things shall not *inherit* the kingdom of God." (Gal. 5:21). How can believers not inherit the kingdom? If the kingdom is the "church" then believers are already in the kingdom and would have no need to fear failure to reach the promised inheritance, i.e., the kingdom of God.

7. Peter writes to believers in his second epistle, (2 Pet. 1:1). He admonishes them that "...if ye do these things, ye shall never fall: for so an entrance shall be ministered unto you abundantly into the everlasting kingdom of our Lord and Saviour Jesus Christ." (2 Pet. 1:10,11). Since, according to Church of Christ

WRESTED SCRIPTURES

doctrine believers are already in the kingdom, (i.e., the "church"), how is one to understand the *conditional* nature of the entrance? Does the Church of Christ make the virtues listed in verses 5–7 requisites for church membership? How is one to understand the tense—"so an entrance *shall* be ministered … into the everlasting kingdom?" If believers are already in the kingdom into what are they to have a future entrance?

8. The kingdom of God is to bring a reign of judgment, justice and peace. (Isa. 9:6,7; Rom. 14:17). Since the Church of Christ claims to be the kingdom of God one would expect to find judgment, justice and peace in its history. Is such the case? A perusal of COC history shows it to be chequered with internecine strife. If the kingdom of God is the "church", it is not the Church of Christ.[12]

THE ABRAHAMIC COVENANT FULFILLED

Joshua 21:43
"And the LORD gave unto Israel all the land which he sware to give unto their fathers; and they possessed it, and dwelt therein."

Joshua 21:45
"There failed not ought of any good thing which the LORD had spoken unto the house of Israel; all came to pass."

Joshua 23:14
"…not one thing hath failed of all the good things which the LORD your God spake concerning you; all are come to pass unto you, and not one thing hath failed thereof."

PROBLEM:
These verses are usually cited with Neh. 9:8 by the Church of Christ in an attempt to prove that the Abrahamic "land promise" of Gen. 13:15; 15:18 was fulfilled when the land of Canaan was occupied by the twelve tribes under Joshua.

SOLUTION:
1. These passages in Joshua do not refer to the fulfilment of the Abrahamic "land promise" for the following reasons:
   a. Abraham's seed was promised the land from the "river of Egypt [the Nile] to the Euphrates." (Gen. 15:18). The nation of Israel under Joshua never occupied this complete territory.
   b. Abraham was promised the land for ever. (Gen. 13:15). This personal promise has never been fulfilled as the following passages indicate:

---

[12] Dissension still exists between Church of Christ congregations over legalistic interpretations regarding the use of church finances, the use of musical instruments to accompany worship, and the appointment of inter-church committees to promote radio and TV proselytising. These issues are considered matters of faith and fellowship by some Church of Christ congregations.

i. "And he [God] gave him [Abraham] none inheritance in it, no, not so much as to set his foot on: yet he promised that he would give it to him for a possession, and to his seed after him, when as yet he had no child." (Acts 7:5).

ii. "By faith Abraham, when he was called to go out into a place which he should after receive for an inheritance, obeyed...These all died in faith, not having received the promises..." (Heb. 11:8,13).

2. "All[13] the good things" is qualified as the following examples indicate:

a. It was promised, "I will raise them up a Prophet from among their brethren, like unto thee [Moses], and will put my words in his mouth; and he shall speak unto them all that I shall command him." (Deut. 18:18). This promise was not fulfilled, as Peter points out, until the coming of the Messiah. (Acts 3:22).

b. "For if Jesus [Joshua] had given them rest, then would he not afterward have spoken of another day. There remaineth therefore a rest to the people of God." (Heb. 4:8,9).

3. "All the good things" of Josh. 23:14 refers to Exo 3:8,12; Deut. 28:1–14. The "evil things" of Josh. 23:15,16 refers to Deut. 28:15–68; Lev. 26:14–39.

4. The land promised unto the "fathers" alludes to the promise made to Moses (Deut. 11:24) and which referred to land taken by conquest: "Every place that the sole of your foot shall tread upon, that have I given unto you, as I said unto Moses." (Josh. 1:3). This promise was fulfilled when Israel possessed Canaan.

Nehemiah 9:8

"...and madest a covenant with him [Abraham] to give the land...to his seed, and hast performed thy words; for thou art righteous."

PROBLEM:

This passage is used by the Church of Christ in an attempt to prove that the Abrahamic covenant of land inheritance (Gen. 13:15) was fulfilled when the land of Canaan was possessed by Israel under Joshua.

SOLUTION:

1. The promise in Neh. 9:8 refers to the *seed* of Abraham, but it was Abraham *personally* who was promised the land forever in Gen. 13:15. Stephen stated boldly before the Sanhedrin, that God removed Abraham into the land of Palestine, "wherein ye now dwell. And he gave him none inheritance in it, no, not so much as to set his foot on: yet he promised that he would give it to him..." (Acts 7:5). Clearly, then, the words of Nehemiah cannot be interpreted to infer that the Abrahamic covenant was fulfilled in Israel's possession of the land under Joshua.

---

[13] "All" is frequently qualified in Scripture. See for example, "All living" (Gen. 3:20) which refers to humans not animals. Similarly, "all flesh" (Gen. 6:13) did not include those animals and persons saved in the ark.

WRESTED SCRIPTURES

2. The inheritance of the land under Joshua must also be regarded as only a token fulfilment for an additional reason: In the passage to which Nehemiah refers (Gen. 15:13), God promised to give to Abraham's descendants all the land from "the river of Egypt unto the great river, the river Euphrates". Israel never inherited this entire land area. Its fulfilment awaits the future return of the Messiah to bring the first dominion to Zion. (Micah 4:8).

THE KINGDOM NOT ON EARTH

Isaiah 66:1
"Thus saith the LORD, The heaven is my throne, and the earth is my footstool: where is the house that ye build unto me? and where is the place of my rest?"

PROBLEM:

The Church of Christ argues that since the throne of God is in heaven, and the earth is made His "footstool", Christ cannot rule literally on the earth, since this would be the "footstool" of God.

SOLUTION:

1. There are two thrones referred to in Scripture:
   a. God's throne—"To him that overcometh will I grant to sit with me in my throne, even as I also overcame, and am set down with my Father in his throne." (Rev. 3:21).
   b. Christ's throne—"He shall be great, and shall be called the Son of the Highest: and the Lord God shall give unto him the throne of his father David." (Luke 1:32, cf. 1 Chron. 11:4,5). This is the throne that was overturned in the days of Zedekiah, and to be restored when Christ returns: "I will overturn, overturn, overturn, it: and it shall be no more, until he come whose right it is; and I will give it him." (Ezek. 21:27).

      "When the Son of man shall come in his glory, and all the holy angels with him, then shall he sit upon the throne of his glory." (Matt. 25:31). This throne is to be established on the earth, as Luke 1:32, cf. 1 Chron. 11:4,5 indicate. The earth is now the Lord's footstool, but it will become the *dominion* of His Son in the Age to come. (Psa. 72).
2. The "footstool" of Jesus Christ will be his enemies: "The LORD said unto my Lord, Sit thou at my right hand, until I make thine enemies thy footstool." (Psa. 110:1). Since this ruling is said to be from Zion "in the midst of thine enemies" then clearly the reigning is from the earth, not heaven. See Psa. 110:2: "The LORD shall send the rod of thy strength out of Zion: rule thou in the midst of thine enemies."

126

Jeremiah 22:30

"Thus saith the LORD, Write ye this man [Coniah] childless, a man that shall not prosper in his days: for no man of his seed shall prosper, sitting upon the throne of David, and ruling any more in Judah."

PROBLEM:

It is argued that since Christ is of the seed of Coniah (Matt. 1:1–11) he cannot reign in Jerusalem upon the literal throne of David.

SOLUTION:

1. Coniah, called "Jehoiachin" (2 Kings 24:8) and "Jeconiah" (1 Chron. 3:16; Jer. 24:1), perished in Babylon where he was taken as a captive. (2 Kings 25:27–30). Coniah was a descendant of Solomon, but Jesus was a descendant of Nathan (Luke 3:31), therefore what is affirmed of the seed of Coniah does not refer to Jesus Christ.
2. The legal genealogy set out in Matthew's gospel is traced through Joseph. To insist that Jesus is a descendant of Coniah, is likewise to insist that Joseph was his real father. The family tree of Jesus through his mother Mary is set out in Luke 3, not Matthew 1.

THE KINGDOM ESTABLISHED AT PENTECOST[14]

Daniel 2:44

"And in the days of these kings shall the God of heaven set up a kingdom, which shall never be destroyed…"

PROBLEM:

Since the period of these kings is symbolically portrayed as feet of iron and clay, (which is assumed to represent the Roman Empire), then the kingdom of God must have been established during the existence of the Roman Empire—i.e., on the day of Pentecost.

SOLUTION:

1. The period depicted as iron mixed with clay indicates a *disunited period*, having the influence of the iron (Roman influence) but the weakening effect of the miry clay. The Roman Empire was not in this state on the Day of Pentecost, it was rather in the period designated by the legs of iron. (v. 33): later to be divided into east and west, but nevertheless still in the *iron* phase.
2. Even if it be assumed that "in the days of these kings" referred to the Roman Empire, the ecclesia established then did not break in pieces and destroy all other kingdoms. Clearly, the kingdom of God cannot be the ecclesia.

---

[14] Some COC churches believe it was established around AD 33. See footnote 7.

Persecution and death, not "breaking in pieces and destroying" describes the history of the ecclesia. See, for example, Acts 4:17; 5:17,18; 7:58; 8:1; 9:1,2; 16:22,23, etc., Furthermore, Dan. 7:20,21 indicates that the fourth beast would give rise to a horn "that had eyes, and a mouth that spake very great things" which would make war with the saints, and "prevailed against them". Such language indicates the erroneousness of the Church of Christ interpretation which identifies the kingdom of God with the "church".

3. The Babylonian, Persian and Grecian Empires were non-existent as political entities in the period of the political domination of the Roman Empire. Clearly, only the influence of the Babylonian, Persian and Grecian Empires existed within the framework of the Roman Empire as the conquered territories became assimilated. Similarly, the fourth kingdom (Rome) which was "as strong as iron" would be divided into two (eastern and western sections) and would progress to the feet of iron and clay. It is in the ten-toed phase of the Roman Empire that the saints possess the kingdom. This can be shown by the fact that the beasts of chapter 7 represent the same empires as the metals of the image of chapter 2. It is only after the fourth beast gives rise to ten horns (paralleling the ten toes of the image) that the saints possess the kingdom (see Dan. 7:23–27). The Roman Empire formed into its eastern and western "iron-legged" sections after Justinian (AD 529–533), and since the ten-toed phase would be entered after this time, the kingdom could not have been set up at Pentecost.

Daniel 7:7–9

"...behold a fourth beast, dreadful and terrible, and strong exceedingly; and it had great iron teeth: it devoured and brake in pieces, and stamped the residue with the feet of it: and it was diverse from all the beasts that were before it; and it had ten horns...I beheld till the thrones were cast down, and the Ancient of days did sit..."

PROBLEM:

The Church of Christ attempts to argue that the kingdom of God was established at Pentecost (in the time of the Roman Empire). The reasoning goes as follows:

a. The fourth beast refers to the Roman Empire.

b. It is then noted that it is at the time of the fourth beast that the Son of Man receives his kingdom.

Therefore,

c. The kingdom of God must have been established when the Roman Empire existed, i.e., at Pentecost.

SOLUTION:

1. There are a number of assumptions in the above reasoning which are erroneous and invalidate the conclusion. These are as follows:

a. It is not at the time of the fourth beast that the Son of Man receives his kingdom. It is at the time of the *little horn phase* with "eyes like the eyes of man, and a mouth speaking great things" (v. 8). (See vv. 20–22). This phase can be identified with the ten-toed phase of the image of Daniel 2. An examination of Dan. 2 and 7 indicates that the image of the former parallels the four beasts of the latter. This is an important identification since the kingdom is not set up in Daniel 2 until the ten-toed phase. (Dan. 2:44). The Roman Empire formed into its eastern and western "iron-leg" sections after Justinian (AD 529–533), and since the ten-toed phase would be entered *after* this time, then clearly the kingdom was not set up at Pentecost.

    b. The rest of the beasts are said to have had "their dominion taken away: yet their lives were prolonged for a season and a time". (Dan. 7:12). But who would assert that the lives of the Babylonian, Persian and Grecian kings extended even to the time of the Roman Empire? They had been dead for hundreds of years. It was only the influence of the empire within its successor which continued to exist (cf. Dan. 4:15—"the stump" banded with brass and iron).

2. The events outlined in Daniel 7 require a long period of persecution to exist before the setting up of the kingdom. This is indicated by the little horn which would arise to make war with the saints and to prevail against them until the saints possessed the kingdom. (Dan. 7:21,22). Even if it be argued that a persecution arose against believers at the time of Pentecost, such an interpretation must be rejected since the Jewish leaders did not prevail against the believers, and therefore, the persecution must have been subsequent to this time. It can be concluded by implication that the kingdom could not, therefore, have been set up at Pentecost.

3. Dan 7:10 refers to the judgment which was "set" and the "books" were opened. It is known from other parts of Scripture that this time will only occur at the return of Christ to the earth to judge the dead. (See, for example, 2 Tim. 4:1; Matt. 25:21–34; 1 Cor. 15:23; John 5:28,29; 6:39,40,44,54; 11:24).

4. Christ cites Dan. 7:13 ("coming in the clouds") with the words of Psa. 110:1 ("sitting on the right hand of power") and applies them to his second coming. (Matt. 26:64). This application by Christ indicates conclusively that the time for the saints to possess the kingdom is established at his return.

Micah 4:1,2

"But in the last days it shall come to pass, that the mountain of the house of the LORD shall be established in the top of the mountains, and it shall be exalted above the hills; and people shall flow unto it. And many nations shall come, and say, Come, and let us go up to the mountain of the LORD, and to the house of the God of Jacob; and he will teach us of his ways, and we will walk in his paths: for the law shall go forth of Zion, and the word of the LORD from Jerusalem."

PROBLEM:

The Church of Christ places stress upon the use of "last days". It is noted that Peter said that Joel's prophecy concerning the "last days" was being fulfilled at Pentecost. (Acts 2:15–17). It is then inferred that what Micah records was likewise fulfilled at Pentecost and hence the kingdom must have been set up at this time, i.e., the "church".

WRESTED SCRIPTURES

SOLUTION:

1. The following is proof that Micah 4 was not fulfilled on the Day of Pentecost:
   a. There is no indication in Scripture that those assembled at Pentecost said, "Come, and let us go up to the mountain of the LORD, and to the house of the God of Jacob…" (Micah 4:2).
   b. The prophecy in Micah indicates that "many nations shall come" (v. 2), but on the day of Pentecost, "Jews, devout men, out of every nation under heaven" (Acts 2:5) gathered for the celebrations. The descriptions are different. Micah indicates "many nations" is the subject of reference, but in Acts it is recorded that only Jews were present, and these came out of every nation.
   c. Micah states that "in that day…the LORD shall reign over them [the halt, and cast off] in mount Zion from henceforth, even for ever" (Micah 4:7), but this has never been fulfilled. Many wars have since been fought in Palestine and elsewhere. About one hundred years after Pentecost, Hadrian, the Roman Emperor ploughed Jerusalem and sowed it with salt.[15] (cf. Micah 3:12—"therefore shall Zion for your sake be plowed as a field").

2. Peter did not state that Joel's prophecy was completely fulfilled on the day of Pentecost. He omitted the words: "for in mount Zion and in Jerusalem shall be deliverance, as the LORD hath said, and in the remnant whom the LORD shall call" (Joel 2:32). The reason for the omission of this section is that it was not even partially fulfilled on Pentecost, but rather awaits fulfilment when Christ returns to the earth to set up his kingdom. But if the kingdom were, in fact, established on the Day of Pentecost, then this is just the section one would have expected to have been cited.

3. Many prophecies in Scripture have more than one application. Jesus said that John the Baptist was Elijah, Malachi 4:5—"Behold, I will send you Elijah the prophet before the coming of the great and dreadful day of the LORD" (cf. Matt. 11:14; Luke 1:17), and yet an examination of the context of Malachi 4 indicates that the work of John the Baptist was only a partial fulfilment.[16]

4. "Last days" is used for two different time periods in Scripture:
   a. The "last days" of Judah's Commonwealth which was overthrown in AD 70 (cf. Heb. 1:2; 9:26; 1 Pet. 1:20). Peter may well have been using the phrase "last days" in this sense on the Day of Pentecost. The Holy Spirit was indeed poured out upon the early believers during the "last days" of Judah's Commonwealth: less than 40 years later the Romans overturned the nation and scattered the Jews.
   b. The last day (or latter days) which refers to the gathering of the nations to the battle of Armageddon and the raising of the dead. (Ezek. 38:8,16; cf. Dan. 11:40; 12:1,2; John 6:39,40,44,54; Rev. 16:15,16).

[15] See, H. W. Hathaway, *The Bible Today and You*, (London: "The Dawn" Book Supply, 1962), p.72, and William Smith (ed.), *A Dictionary of the Bible*, (London: John Murray, 1863), p.1015.
[16] John the Baptist came in the "Spirit and power" of Elijah. (Luke 1:17). He categorically stated that he was *not* Elijah: "And they asked him [John], What then? Art thou Elias? And he saith, I am not. Art thou that prophet? And he answered, No." (John 1:21).

130

Micah refers to b) as the previous points indicate.

Matthew 3:2

"And saying, Repent ye: for the kingdom of heaven is at hand."

Matthew 4:17

"From that time Jesus began to preach, and to say, Repent: for the kingdom of heaven is at hand."

Matthew 11:12

"And from the days of John the Baptist until now the kingdom of heaven suffereth violence, and the violent take it by force."

Luke 16:16

"The law and the prophets were until John: since that time the kingdom of God is preached, and every man presseth into it."

PROBLEM:

These passages are cited by the Church of Christ in proof of their doctrine that the kingdom of God was established on the Day of Pentecost. Stress is placed on the words "is at hand" to emphasize that the kingdom would not have to wait nearly two thousand years for its establishment at Christ's return.

SOLUTION:

1. The language of these passages must be carefully noted: It is not—"the law and the prophets were until John and since that time the kingdom of God *has been established* and every man presseth into it", but rather the kingdom of God is *preached* and every man presses *towards*[17] it.

2. If the kingdom of God were established at Pentecost, how could every man press into it from the days of John the Baptist? (Luke 16:16). This passage clearly proves too much for the Church of Christ interpretation, for if it is insisted that the kingdom had to be established for every man to press into it, then the passage only serves to show that the kingdom is not the "church" which is said to have been set up at Pentecost. This "church" would have been established in the days of John the Baptist before the death of Christ.

3. Similarly, Jesus stated that "from the days of John the Baptist until now" the kingdom of God suffered violence. (Matt. 11:12). But if the kingdom were not established until Pentecost, how could it suffer violence in the days of John the Baptist? How could violent men take the "church" by *force*?

---

[17] The Greek preposition *eis* translated "into" also means "toward". *"Eis*, into, unto, to, implying motion to the interior..." E. W. Bullinger, *A Critical Lexicon and Concordance to the English and Greek Testament*, (London: Samuel Bagster and Sons Ltd., 1957). *Eis* is translated "toward" 32 times. See, for example: Matt. 28:1; Luke 13:22; John 6:17; Acts 27:40; 28:14.

4. In the preceding verse Jesus stated that "among them that are born of women there hath not risen a greater than John the Baptist: notwithstanding he that is least in the kingdom of heaven is greater than he." (Matt. 11:11). This is in itself proof that the kingdom is not the "church". Consider the following:

   a. Since Jesus says there is none born of women greater than John the Baptist, the greatest in the "church" is not as great as John the Baptist.[18]

   b. But he that is least in the kingdom of heaven[19] is greater than John the Baptist.[20]

   c. Therefore, the "church" cannot be synonymous with the kingdom.

5. How did the kingdom come "nigh" or was "near at hand?" The Greek word *basileia*, translated "kingdom" means "the royal dominion, including the power and form of government, with the territory and the kingdom."[21] When men were confronted with the Royal Majesty of the kingdom in his teaching[22] and power,[23] it is said to be the kingdom coming nigh.

6. The disciples were also confused as to the time of the setting up of the kingdom. It was for this reason that Jesus instructed them that the nobleman must go into "a far country to receive for himself a kingdom, and to return." (Luke 19:11,12). Jesus' instruction is incompatible with the Church of Christ teaching that the kingdom was shortly to be set up at Pentecost.

Mark 9:1

"...Verily I say unto you, That there be some of them that stand here, which shall not taste of death, till they have seen the kingdom of God come with power."

[18] The only way that the logic of this argument can be evaded is for one to argue that by being in the "church" one is greater than John the Baptist. Now this would be a very bold assertion indeed. The work of John the Baptist was a partial fulfilment of the Elijah prophecy (Matt. 11:14, cf. Mal. 4:5,6). John the Baptist was a prophet of God and remained faithful until his death. Is it tenable that *anyone* joining the Church of Christ is greater than John the Baptist? If the kingdom is the "church", then such would be the case. It is a simple matter of observation that many who have joined the Church of Christ have subsequently fallen away. The Church of Christ argument requires that Demas (2 Tim. 4:10), Alexander (2 Tim. 4:14) and Diotrephes (3 John 9) are all greater than John the Baptist by virtue of being in the "church".

[19] The "kingdom of heaven" is synonymous with the "kingdom of God." Compare the following passages: Matt. 11:11 and Luke 7:28; Matt. 8:11 and Luke 13:29.

[20] The possessor of the kingdom (being immortal; 1 Cor. 15:50–54) is greater than John the Baptist who was mortal.

[21] E. W. Bullinger, *A Critical Lexicon and Concordance to the English and Greek Testament*, (London: Samuel Bagster and Sons Ltd., 1957).

[22] E.g. Matt. 3:2.

[23] E.g. Matt. 12:28. The close association of "king" and "kingdom" is indicated in the following parallels in the Synoptic Gospels:

   a. "Behold thy *King* cometh...Hosanna to the Son of David" (Matt. 21:5,9, cf. Zech. 9:9).

   b. "Blessed is he that cometh in the name of the Lord...Blessed be the *kingdom* of our father David" (Mark 11:9,10).

   c. "Blessed be the *King* that cometh in the name of the Lord" (Luke 19:38).

PROBLEM:

If some standing with Jesus would not die until the kingdom was established, then it is argued that the kingdom would not have to wait nearly 2,000 years for its establishment. Hence, it must have been the "church" set up at Pentecost.

SOLUTION:

1. The words, "some of them that stand here...shall not taste of death, till they have seen the kingdom of God come with power" refer to the transfiguration, and not to the Day of Pentecost. Consider the following:

   a. Only *some* were to see the kingdom come with power, but on the Day of Pentecost *all* but Judas were present (Acts 1:23–25; 2:14). The language is entirely appropriate, however, to describe Peter, James and John who accompanied Christ during the transfiguration.

   b. In all three Gospels recording the promise, the transfiguration narrative immediately follows. (See Matt. 17:1; Mark 9:2; Luke 9:28).

   c. Peter refers to the transfiguration in his epistle in such a way as to make the case conclusive: "For we have not followed cunningly devised fables, when we made known unto you the power and coming of our Lord Jesus Christ, but were eyewitnesses *of his majesty*. For he received from God the Father honour and glory, when there came such a voice to him from the excellent glory, This is my beloved Son, in whom I am well pleased. And this voice which came from heaven we heard, when we were with him in the holy mount." (2 Pet. 1:16–18). Thus "the kingdom of God [came] with power" at the *transfiguration*, not at Pentecost. The disciples witnessed this in a vision. (Matt. 17:9).

2. This passage affords evidence that the kingdom of God is not the New Testament "church" as is taught by the Church of Christ.[24] The fact that the kingdom of God came at the transfiguration before Christ had died indicates that the term *kingdom* is not synonymous in this passage with the "church" said to have been set up at Pentecost.

Luke 17:20,21

"And when he was demanded of the Pharisees, when the kingdom of God should come, he answered them and said, The kingdom of God cometh not with observation: neither shall they say, Lo here! or, lo there! for, behold, the kingdom of God is within you."

PROBLEM:

These verses are long-time favourites with those who hold that the kingdom of God is the "church" or the spiritual reign of God in the hearts of believers. The

[24] "The kingdom of God and the church are the same; At Pentecost, the Holy Spirit came, Christ preached, repentance and remission declared in the name of Jesus; men and women saved. The church began, its birthday." Richard Rogers, *The Church of Christ: A Study of the First-Century Church,* (Lubbock, Texas: Sunset School of Preaching), Mimeo., pp.4,9.

language, "cometh not with observation" is taken as proof that the kingdom will not come with the return of Christ accompanied by the "signs of the times". The "kingdom of God is within you" is considered evidence that the kingdom of God is spiritual and not political in character.

SOLUTION:

1. In what sense could the kingdom be within the Pharisees to whom Jesus was speaking? (Luke 17:20). It was the Pharisees who were indicted by the Lord, "...within ye are full of hypocrisy and iniquity". (Matt. 23:28). How can this passage be used to prove that the kingdom of God is a spiritual reign in *believers'* hearts?

2. Those who cite these verses usually attempt to squeeze the Christadelphian into an "either/or" situation. Either the kingdom of God is spiritual or it is political. This dichotomy is unscriptural. The kingdom clearly refers to a divine political rulership in Dan. 2:44; 7:22,27, for example. But the "kingdom" is also used of Christ himself. When Spirit powers of the Kingdom Age were exercised, or Jesus was present, it is spoken of as the "coming nigh of the kingdom". Note the following passages:

   a. "But if I with the finger of God cast out devils, no doubt the kingdom of God is come upon you." (Luke 11:20).

   b. "And heal the sick that are therein, and say unto them, The kingdom of God is come nigh unto you." (Luke 10:9, cf. v.11).

   c. "For it is impossible for those who were once enlightened, and have tasted of the heavenly gift, and were made partakers of the Holy Spirit, and have tasted the good word of God, and the powers of the world to come." (Heb. 6:4,5).

3. The intended sense of the passage is conveyed in the marginal rendering, "the kingdom of God is among you" or "in the midst of you", (RSV). Jesus, the embodiment of the principles of the kingdom—the nucleus of the kingdom—and with the powers of the kingdom, is said to be the kingdom of God.[25]

4. In the context of this passage, the Pharisees asked about the restoration of the kingdom to Israel (the hope of the Jews—Acts 1:6). Jesus replied by using the kingdom in a sense synonymous with himself. (This is indicated by the subsequent verses concerning his coming). The first advent of Jesus was not "with outward show" (AVm.) or "narrow watching". It was said of God's Royal Majesty: "A bruised reed shall he not break, and smoking flax shall he not quench, *till* he send forth judgment unto victory." (Matt. 12:20). When Christ comes the second time, he will come with outward show: "Behold, he cometh with clouds; and every eye shall see him, and they *also* which

---

[25] Hence, the close association in the Gospels of the "king" and the "kingdom". Note the following parallels:

   a. "Behold thy *King* cometh...Hosanna to the Son of David" (Matt. 21:5, 9 cf. Zech. 9:9).

   b. "Blessed is he that cometh in the name of the Lord...Blessed be the *kingdom* of our father David" (Mark 11:9,10).

   c. "Blessed be the *King* that cometh in the name of the Lord" (Luke 19:38).

pierced him: and all kindreds of the earth shall wail because of him. Even so, Amen." (Rev. 1:7). It is at this time that the kingdom will be established, and God will ultimately "perform the mercy promised to our fathers, and to remember his holy covenant; the oath which he sware to our father Abraham". (Luke 1:72,73).

John 18:36

"Jesus answered, My kingdom is not of this world: if my kingdom were of this world, then would my servants fight, that I should not be delivered to the Jews: but now is my kingdom not from hence."

PROBLEM:

The Church of Christ interprets this verse to mean that Christ's kingdom has nothing to do with him reigning from David's throne on the earth, but is rather a spiritual kingdom operating through the "church" since Pentecost.

SOLUTION:

1. The Church of Christ reads, "My kingdom is not of this world" as synonymous with, 'My kingdom is not of this earth'. But "world" and "earth" are not interchangeable. The world Jesus referred to was the constitution or order of things.[26] Certainly, Jesus had neither part nor lot in the world of the Pharisees and the Romans. As Jesus continued, "my kingdom is not from hence", i.e., my kingdom is not from this place. The use of the word "world" is demonstrated repeatedly in John 17:

   a. "…I pray not for the world, but for them which thou hast given me; for they are thine." (John 17:9). Clearly in this reference "world" refers to those who were not followers of the Lord.

   b. "And now I am no more in the world, but these are in the world, and I come to thee." (John 17:11). Jesus was still on the literal earth but he was not a part of the order of things on the earth. (cf. 1 John 2:15–17).

   c. "I have given them thy word; and the world hath hated them, because they are not of the world, even as I am not of the world." (John 17:14). The world that hated the disciples was the world of the Pharisees. The disciples were still in the literal world, but not part of its constitution or order.[27]

   d. See also vv. 14–18.

2. Christ's kingdom is "not of this world" because it is a kingdom from heaven. Its constitution or order is heavenly in origin—designed from the "foundation of the world". (Matt. 25:34). When the disciples thought that the kingdom

---

[26] Young gives the meaning of *kosmos* translated "world" in the AV, as "arrangement, beauty, world". Robert Young, *Analytical Concordance to the Holy Bible*, (London: Lutterworth Press, 1965).

[27] The Apostle Paul uses *kosmos* in a similar way when he writes to the Ephesians: "And you hath he quickened, who were dead in trespasses and sins: wherein in time past ye walked according to the course of this world…the spirit that now worketh in the children of disobedience". (Eph. 2:1,2). The contrast is between two orders or constitutions.

should immediately appear (Luke 19:11), he explained to them in a parable that the nobleman had first to go into a far country to receive for himself a kingdom and then to return (Luke 19:12). Jesus will return to establish his kingdom, as the prophets have written:

a. "Ask of me, and I shall give thee the heathen for thine inheritance, and the uttermost parts of the *earth* for thy possession." (Psa. 2:8).

b. "And there was given him dominion, and glory, and a kingdom, that all people, nations, and languages, should serve him: his dominion is an everlasting dominion, which shall not pass away, and his kingdom that which shall not be destroyed...And the kingdom and dominion, and the greatness of the kingdom *under* the whole heaven, shall be given to the people of the saints of the most High, whose kingdom is an everlasting kingdom, and all dominions shall serve and obey him." (Dan. 7:14,27).

Acts 15:14-17

"Simeon hath declared how God at the first did visit the Gentiles, to take out of them a people for his name. And to this agree the words of the prophets; as it is written, After this I will return, and will build again the tabernacle of David, which is fallen down; and I will build again the ruins thereof, and I will set it up: that the residue of men might seek after the Lord, and all the Gentiles, upon whom my name is called, saith the Lord, who doeth all these things."

PROBLEM:

The Church of Christ reasons that since James quotes the words of Amos 9:11,12 to show that salvation has rightly been preached to the Gentiles, the tabernacle of David must have been established at Pentecost or shortly thereafter with the preaching of the Gospel to the Gentiles.[28] It is then concluded that David's tabernacle must be the spiritual reign of Christ in the believer's heart which will find its ultimate fulfilment in heaven.

SOLUTION:

1. When Acts 15:14–17 is cited with the interpretation outlined in the problem, the onus of proof must rest with those who assert. The following questions, therefore, require *Scriptural* answers:

a. If David's tabernacle were established in heaven, why was David asleep and in his sepulchre on the Day of Pentecost? (Acts 2:29,34).

b. When was the tabernacle of David first built?

c. When did it fall?

d. Where are the ruins?

---

[28] "Amos is predicting that the time would come when God would restore one of David's offspring to a position of reigning monarch...It is not that the literal city of Jerusalem in Palestine was to be rebuilt and restored. But it is a prophecy that in the Messianic age God would erect a kingdom (it began in the day of Pentecost, Acts 2), and then the Gentiles would be gathered into it." (Gareth L. Reese, *Acts*, Joplin, U.S.A.: College Press Publishing Co., 1976, p.542.)

e. Who will build it again?

f. Where will it be built?

2. Proof that David's tabernacle was not restored at Pentecost is indicated from the context of Amos 9. Note the following:

a. "...the plowman shall overtake the reaper, and the treader of grapes him that soweth seed..." (Amos 9:13). The preaching of the gospel to the Gentiles did not affect the fertility of the Palestinian soil. In fact, to the contrary, the land was about to be subjected to centuries of desolation as foretold in Lev. 26:33,34,35,43.[29]

b. "And I will plant them upon their land, and they shall no more be pulled up out of their land..." (Amos 9:15). In AD 70 the Jews were uprooted, expelled and the land made desolate. This passage can only be fulfilled when Christ returns to the Mount of Olives. (Zech. 14:4). This is proven by the fact that Zechariah states that a future invasion of Jerusalem will occur in which half of the population will go into captivity. (Zech. 14:1–5).

3. James may be referring to the Septuagint translation of the Hebrew Old Testament Scriptures.[30] He demonstrated to the Council that it was perfectly acceptable to preach to the Gentiles since prophetically God had declared that Gentiles would be encompassed within the divine plan of salvation. In support of this James selected Amos 9. The restoration of the tabernacle of David, he pointed out, required that the residue of men "upon whom my name is called" be encompassed. If the Gentile, therefore, was to be encompassed in the restoration of David's tabernacle, who then could question the preaching of the gospel to the Gentiles? It is apparent, however, that the actual restoration of David's tabernacle awaits the restoration of the kingdom when the Messiah returns.

Romans 14:17

"For the kingdom of God is not meat and drink; but righteousness, and peace, and joy in the Holy Ghost."

---

[29] "The suppression of Bar Cochba's insurrection, AD 135, marks the final desolation of Judaea, and the dispersion of its inhabitants. The whole of Judaea was made like a desert; about 985 towns and villages lay in ashes, 50 fortresses were razed to the ground; the name of Jerusalem itself was changed into 'Aelia Capitolina'...from entering which (or even viewing from a distance) every Jew was strictly forbidden on pain of death." H.W. Hathaway, *The Bible Today and You*, (London: "The Dawn" Book Supply, 1962), p.72. Hadrian, after his suppression of Bar Cochba's revolt, attempted to obliterate the city of Jerusalem. The ruins which Titus had left were razed to the ground and the plough passed over the foundations of the temple as a symbol of perpetual desolation. (cf. Micah 3:12). William Smith (ed.), *A Dictionary of the Bible*, (London: John Murray, 1863), p.1015; also Henry Milman, *The History of the Jews*, (London: Dent, 1939), p.132.

[30] The LXX reads as follows: "In that day I will raise up the tabernacle of David that is fallen, and will rebuild the ruins of it, and will set up the parts thereof, that have been broken down, and will build it up as in the ancient days; that the remnant of men, and all the Gentiles upon whom my name is called, may earnestly seek me, saith the lord who does all these things." *The Septuagint Version of the Old Testament with an English translation and with various readings and critical notes*, (New York: Samuel Bagster and Sons, Ltd.).

WRESTED SCRIPTURES

PROBLEM:

The Church of Christ argues that the kingdom cannot be political in nature since the apostle says that the kingdom is righteousness, and peace, and joy in the Holy Spirit. Hence, the kingdom must be the "church".

SOLUTION:

1. The passage does not state that the kingdom of God is the "church", and for the Church of Christ argument to stand, it must be shown by its expositors that the language used in this passage is incompatible with belief in a future political kingdom. But can this be done? It cannot. Consider the evidence:

    a. To say that the kingdom of God is righteousness, and peace and joy in the Holy Spirit, is not to say it is *only* these things. Other Scriptures refer to the kingdom as "breaking in pieces" and destroying "all...kingdoms". (Dan. 2:44). The two references are complementary. One provides what the other does not.

    b. Baptized believers of the one Gospel come under the jurisdiction of the King of the kingdom. They are now in training for future rulership. (Rev. 2:26,27). Only upon a faithful completion of the training programme can the believer expect to enter the kingdom. (2 Pet. 1:11; Matt. 25:31–46). Since believers are training for future rulership in the kingdom they are instructed to seek the kingdom and God's righteousness, and peace, and joy in the Holy Spirit for such blessings will constitute the kingdom. (Isa. 9:6,7). It is at the time of the establishment of the kingdom that ultimately those who mourn "*shall* be comforted" (Matt. 5:4); those "that hunger now shall be filled" and those who "weep now shall laugh". (Luke 6:21).

2. It needs stressing to members of the Church of Christ that the believer is an *heir* of the kingdom (James 2:5), not a present possessor. It is only through "much tribulation" that the kingdom will be entered. (Acts 14:22). The kingdom of God is something to be entered, not by joining "the church", but by finishing the race which begins with entry into the ecclesia. (1 Cor. 9:24; 2 Tim. 4:7,8, cf. v. 1; Matt. 24:13; 2 Pet. 1:10,11).

CHRIST REIGNING NOW

1 Corinthians 15:25

"For he must reign, till he hath put all enemies under his feet."

PROBLEM:

It is argued by the Church of Christ that since Christ is to put all things under his feet, he must now be reigning in his kingdom. When Christ returns, it is asserted, he comes to give the kingdom back to God, and not to receive it.

SOLUTION:

1. The text does not read: "he *is* reigning," but rather "he *must* reign". The time of the commencement of the reigning is not stated in verse 25, but this can be inferred from the context: "In Christ shall all be made alive…at his coming." (vv. 22,23, cf. 2 Tim. 4:1). The end of the reign is indicated by the abolition of death (v. 26). This period is designated by Jesus himself to be 1,000 years. (Rev. 20:4–6). Proof that death will not cease at Christ's second coming is indicated by the existence of mortal nations subsequent to his return. (See Zech. 14:4,9,12–19; cf. Isa. 65:17–20). The saints, however, will be immortal, having received their reward (Rev. 3:21; 2:26,27; 22:12).

2. That this is the correct interpretation of 1 Cor. 15, is indicated by Psa. 110:2,5,6 in which the Messiah is depicted as ruling in the *midst of his enemies*. The kingly reign emanates from Zion, not from heaven (v. 2).

Ephesians 1:3
"Blessed be the God and Father of our Lord Jesus Christ, who hath blessed us with all spiritual blessings in heavenly places in Christ."

Ephesians 2:6
"And hath raised us up together, and made us sit together in heavenly places in Christ Jesus."

PROBLEM:

This passage is connected with Col. 1:13 and Rev. 5:9,10 by the Church of Christ in support of their teaching that Christ and the saints are now reigning in a spiritual kingdom.

SOLUTION:

1. The Church of Christ argument rests on a faulty interpretation of Rev. 5:9,10. The kings and priests of these verses could not have been reigning in a spiritual kingdom since Pentecost for the events depicted in the Revelation are said to be things which "must shortly come to pass". (Rev. 1:1). This must be future (to about AD 96), and certainly many years after Pentecost. Furthermore, it is expressly stated elsewhere in Scripture that those who are alive and remain will not precede those who have fallen asleep (died). (1 Thess. 4:15, RSV). The redeemed can only sing the song, therefore, *after* the resurrection at the last day. (See 2 Tim. 4:1; Matt. 25:31,34,46). It can then be inferred that since the dead have not been raised, the song of the redeemed has not yet been sung, and if the song of the redeemed has not yet been sung, then believers are not now reigning as kings and priests.

2. "Heavenly places in Christ Jesus" refers to *status*, and not to location or place. This can be shown from the following:

   a. A contrast runs through the epistle between the position of an alien and that of a believer in Christ. Note the following contrasts:

Before baptism into Christ	*In Christ*
—one is within the principalities and powers of heavenly places that belong to "this world" (3:10; 1:21)	—one is in the heavenlies in Christ Jesus favoured with all spiritual blessing in anticipation of the "world …to come" (1:3,21; 2:6,7)
—dead in trespasses and sins walking according to the course of this world, the spirit which works in the children of disobedience (2:1,2)	—made alive with Christ Jesus (2:6)
—without Christ, aliens from the commonwealth of Israel, strangers from the covenants of promise, having no hope, and without God in the world (2:12)	—fellow citizens with the saints for an habitation of God through the Spirit (2:21,22)

These contrasts are ones of position or status, not of location (i.e., between heaven and earth as if to imply that believers were translated to heaven).

   b. "Heavenlies" ("heavenly places", AV) is used of political systems on the earth (3:10; 6:12 where "high places" is translated from the same Greek word for "heavenlies"), as well as for the exalted position of believers. It can be seen, therefore, that the word relates to position or status and not to location. Although believers are raised with Christ to the right hand of the Father, they are still on the earth, in Ephesus, Corinth, etc. They are transferred from the heavenlies of the world systems for the everlasting kingdom of His dear Son.

3. Rulership in God's kingdom is dependent upon the believer *overcoming*. A believer is raised to heavenly places in Christ Jesus upon his baptism. He is not, however, fitted to rule over the nations until he has suffered (2 Tim. 2:12) and "overcome". As Jesus put it: "And he that overcometh, and keepeth my works unto the end, to him will I give power over the nations: and he shall rule them with a rod of iron; as the vessels of a potter shall they be broken to shivers: even as I received of my Father." (Rev. 2:26,27). Believers have never ruled the nations with a rod of iron. This privilege awaits the return of the King to reign in the midst of his enemies. (Psa. 110:1,2).

Colossians 1:13

"Who hath delivered us from the power of darkness, and hath translated us into the kingdom of his dear Son…"

PROBLEM:

Great stress is placed by the Church of Christ on the words "hath" and "into." It is argued that Colossian believers were already in the kingdom, implying that the kingdom must be the "church" which was set up at Pentecost.

SOLUTION:

1. The "church" was not set up at Pentecost. Stephen refers to the Israelites as the ecclesia.[31] (Acts 7:38). Individuals in all dispensations who walked faithfully before God were members of Christ's ecclesia. It requires stressing that the gospel was preached unto Abraham. (Gal. 3:8).[32]

2. Believers are not changed *into* the kingdom, but *for* the kingdom.[33] The preposition *eis* translated "into" in this verse is translated "for" in verse 16— "all things were created by him and *for* him". The passage in question, therefore, can read: "Who delivered us from the dominion of darkness, and changed us *for* [not into] the kingdom of the Son of his love." This reading is supported by a later reference, "...these only are my fellow workers unto the kingdom of God..." (Col. 4:11). The companions of the apostle were workers "unto", not "in" the kingdom. ("Unto" is translated from the same Greek preposition *eis*) This argument ought to be appreciated by the Church of Christ since their expositors in emphasizing the forgiveness of sins in baptism, stress that *eis* means "for" or "in order to" in Acts 2:38.

That this is the correct interpretation of this passage is supported by the following:

a. The *status* of a baptized believer is changed

From	To
the power of darkness (Col. 1:13)	the power of the risen Christ (1:11)
alienation and an enemy in mind and works (1:21)	reconciliation (1:21), to be presented holy (1:22)
dead in sins (2:13)	dead with Christ to the flesh and rudiments of the world (2:20) spiritually circumcised (2:11,12)
under the old man with his deeds (3:9)	under the new man renewed in knowledge (3:10)

---

[31] "Church" is translated from the Greek word, *ekklesia*. It means "that which is called out." Robert Young, *Analytical Concordance to the Holy Bible*, (London: Lutterworth Press, 1965). The Septuagint (the Greek translation of the Hebrew Old Testament Scriptures in the 3rd century BC) uses the Greek word, *ekklesia*, nearly 100 times in the Old Testament. E.g. Deut. 4:10; 9:10; 10:4; 18:16 and 2 Chron. 30:13.

[32] The Church of Christ fails to appreciate the import of Jesus' ministry to "confirm the promises made unto the fathers" (Rom. 15:8). In part, this deficiency is due to a dismissal of the Old Testament as merely, "a part of God's eternal plan...only a preparation or 'tutor' to bring us to Christ (Gal. 3:24). The New Testament teaches that the Old Testament (or Old Law) was 'blotted out,' taken out of the way and nailed to the cross". Don Morris, *What is the Church of Christ?* (Abilene, Texas; Quality Printing Co., 1956), p.4. A mistaken equation between the Mosaic Law and the Old Testament is part of the faulty foundation of Church of Christ doctrine. The Abrahamic Covenant cannot be too strongly stressed with members of this religious group.

[33] It is translated this way by Benjamin Wilson, *The Emphatic Diaglott*: Containing the original Greek text of what is commonly styled the New Testament. (New York: International Bible Students Ass., Watch Tower Bible and Tract Soc., 1942 ed.).

The effect of the change of status is to transfer the individual for the kingdom of God, the future "reward of the inheritance". (Col. 3:24).

b. Paul speaks of the inheritance in other terms implying its *future* character:

    i. "Knowing that of the Lord ye *shall* receive the reward of the inheritance..." (Col. 3:24). But if, as the Church of Christ contends, that by being baptized, the believer enters the kingdom, then the apostle could not speak of the future nature of the inheritance. Therefore, believers have not yet entered the kingdom.

    ii. "When Christ, who is our life, shall appear, then shall ye also appear with him in glory." (Col. 3:4) Entrance into the glory is only given at the return of Christ, therefore believers cannot now be reigning "spiritually" since the promised thrones are thrones of glory. (cf. Rev. 3:21; Matt. 19:28).

4. Other references in the New Testament likewise indicate that the kingdom is the *future* inheritance of believers. Consider the following:

a. "...Then shall the king say unto them at his right hand, Come, ye blessed of my Father, *inherit* the kingdom..." (Matt. 25:34). The invitation to inherit the kingdom is only given *after* the Shepherd has divided the sheep from the goats. This has not yet happened, and many who now think they are sheep will in the future find out that they are goats. (Matt. 7:22,23).

b. Believers are stated by James to be "heirs of the kingdom which he hath promised to them that love him". (James 2:5). A believer cannot both be a possessor and an heir of the same thing at the same time. The kingdom, therefore, must be a future possession.

c. Peter wrote to believers emphasizing that the kingdom will only be entered by those who bring forth the fruits of the Spirit: "...if ye do these things, ye shall never fall: for so an entrance *shall* be ministered unto you abundantly into the everlasting kingdom of our Lord and Saviour Jesus Christ." (2 Pet. 1:10,11). This statement of Peter indicates the future character of the kingdom of God and implies that believers are changed *for* the kingdom, but are not now *in* the kingdom.

1 Peter 2:9

"But ye are a chosen generation, a royal priesthood..."

PROBLEM:

This verse is connected with Rev. 5:10: "And hast made us unto our God kings and priests: and we shall reign on the earth." It is then argued by the Church of Christ that since believers are a royal priesthood and are to be priests and kings in the kingdom, the kingdom must have been in existence at the time when Peter was writing.

SOLUTION:

1. Peter alludes to Exo. 19:5,6: "…if ye will obey my voice indeed, and keep my covenant, then ye shall be a peculiar treasure unto me above all people…And ye shall be unto me a kingdom of priests, and an holy nation…" But these words were spoken to Israel *before* they were established as a kingdom in the land of promise. Similarly, New Testament believers are spiritual priests (1 Pet. 2:5) offering up spiritual sacrifices *before* entering the land of promise.

2. In Rev. 5:10 the kingdom must be established at the time the saints are said to sing the song. This time must be future to c.AD 96 since the events of the revelation were expressly stated to be "things which must shortly come to pass." (Rev. 1:1).

3. Israelites under the Law were instructed that the "priest's lips should keep knowledge", and that the nation "should seek the law at his mouth" since he was "the messenger of the LORD of hosts". (Mal. 2:7). Similarly, a believer is born of incorruptible seed, by the word of God (1 Pet. 1:23), and is instructed to "desire the sincere milk of the word" that he may "grow thereby". (1 Pet. 2:2). As a priest of the Lord, his responsibility is "to offer up spiritual sacrifices, acceptable to God by Jesus Christ" (1 Pet. 2:5), and to "shew forth the praises of him" who called him out of darkness into his marvellous light. (1 Pet. 2:9). But this priestly function is part of training *for entry* into the kingdom. As Peter put it: "…for *if* ye do these things, ye shall never fall: for so an entrance *shall* be ministered unto you abundantly into the everlasting kingdom of our Lord and Saviour Jesus Christ." (2 Pet. 1:10,11).

Revelation 1:9

"I John, who also am your brother, and companion in tribulation, and in the kingdom and patience of Jesus Christ … "

PROBLEM:

The Church of Christ argues that for John to be in the kingdom requires that the kingdom must have been in existence. The passage is taken, therefore, to support the doctrine that the kingdom is the "church".

SOLUTION:

1. John wrote of the "things which must shortly come to pass". (Rev. 1:1,19). One of the subjects of his writing was the kingdom of God. He pointed out by revelation that it was not until the seventh angel sounded, and the second woe had passed that "the kingdoms of this world are become the kingdoms of our Lord, and of his Christ; and he shall reign for ever and ever". (Rev. 11:15). John was obviously not in this kingdom since the kingdoms of this world have not yet become the kingdom of God.

2. There is never a hint in Scripture that those in the literal kingdom will be in tribulation. The evidence is all the other way. Tribulation is presented as an essential preparation for *entry into* the kingdom. The Apostle Paul said, "Confirming the souls of the disciples, and exhorting them to continue in the

faith, and that we must through much tribulation enter into the kingdom of God." (Acts 14:22). He was not referring to entry into the ecclesia, since he was already in the ecclesia. (1 Cor. 12:13). Since John says that he was a companion in tribulation, in what sense, then, was he in the kingdom? Only in the sense that those who respond to the teaching of its King come under its training for future rulership.

3. John combines the language of fact and *hope* as one companion might say to another, "I am your friend in adversity and in prosperity". One does not infer that the companion must be in adversity and prosperity at the *same* time. Similarly, John was literally in tribulation, but he was only "in" the kingdom in so far as he was under training in hopeful anticipation that he would be in the kingdom in the future age when the kingdoms of the world become the kingdom of God and His Son.

Revelation 5:10

"And hast made us unto our God kings and priests: and we shall reign on the earth."

PROBLEM:

It is argued that since the redeemed saints say thou *hast made* us kings and priests, therefore the kingdom must have been established at the time of writing (i.e., c. AD 96).

SOLUTION:

1. The interpretation outlined in the problem rests on a mistaken inference. The kingdom must be established *at the time* the saints are said to *sing the song*. This time must be future to c. AD 96 since the events of the revelation are expressly stated to be "things which must shortly come to pass." (Rev. 1:1).

2. Since those who "are alive and remain" will not precede those who are dead (1 Thess. 4:15), the redeemed can only sing the song *after* the resurrection at the last day—i.e., the day of Christ's return and establishment of his kingdom. (2 Tim. 4:1; cf. Matt. 25:31,34,46).

MUSICAL INSTRUMENTS

Colossians 3:16

"...teaching and admonishing one another in psalms and hymns and spiritual songs, singing with grace in your hearts to the Lord."

PROBLEM:

It is first questioned, "Is it a good rule to follow that one ought to speak when the Bible speaks and to keep silent where it is silent?" If the answer to this question is, "Yes," then Col. 3:16 is cited along with Eph. 5:19 and Heb. 2:12 to show that the New Testament is explicit, singing is never referred to accompanied by musical instruments. Therefore, it is argued, since it has already been agreed that one ought to keep silent where the Bible is silent, Christians will not have hymn singing accompanied by musical instruments. This conclusion is made an issue of faith, fellowship, and acceptance for eternal life among some Church of Christ assemblies.

SOLUTION:

1. The Church of Christ position is virtually an argument from silence. Since the Bible does not mention singing accompanied by musical instruments, therefore, it is argued, it is wrong. The onus is rather on the Church of Christ to demonstrate that it is forbidden.

2. It is interesting that this legalistic interpretation of Scripture brings problems for the Church of Christ in the following areas:

    a. While musical instruments are decried, congregational singing is often commenced with the aid of a tuning fork or a pitch pipe, but neither of these devices are mentioned in the New Testament.

    b. Four part harmony singing is not mentioned in the New Testament but it is a regular feature of Church of Christ worship today.

    c. Contemporary hymns are sung by the Church of Christ but it is acknowledged that the tune structure of these hymns is not the same, for example, as the Hebrew chants sung in the first century.

3. The Greek word *psalmos*, means "a song of praise (on an instrument)".[34] Bullinger comments on the word as follows: "a touching, twang, e.g., of a bowstring; of stringed instruments, a playing, music; in later usage, a song as accompanied by stringed instruments..."[35] The denotation of the word "psalm" in Col. 3:16 is a complete refutation of the Church of Christ's position. *Psalmos* is also used in Eph. 5:19 and 1 Cor. 14:26.

---

[34] Robert Young, *Analytical Concordance to the Holy Bible*, (London: Lutterworth Press, 1965).
[35] Ethelbert W. Bullinger, *A Critical Lexicon and Concordance to the English and Greek Words*, (London: Samuel Bagster and Sons Limited, 1957), pp.610,611.

I.8

ISLAM

The subject of the Bible and Islam is complex and too vast to be considered in this book. Here we are concerned with Bible passages that are wrested to support the Islamic belief system.

The fact that this section is included reflects the great changes that have taken place in the world since the first edition of this book was issued in 1970. Not only has Islam impacted on the Western world but the gospel is being preached in Islamic countries.

Those who require more information on "Islam and the Bible" will find it in the book of that title by John Thorpe.[1] The Reviser would like to place on record his indebtedness to the author of *The Bible and Islam* for permission to use it as the basis of this section. Alterations and some additions have been made to John Thorpe's original text, but for the most part this section is derived from the book. However, the Reviser must accept full responsibility for the text as it appears.

PRELIMINARY POINTS:

Muslims differ in the esteem in which they hold the Bible. Some place it alongside the Qur'an maintaining that the Jewish Old Testament, the Christian New Testament and the Qur'an are "three concordant books; religious men study all of them and respect them equally."[2] Others believe the Qur'an abrogates all the divinely given books that preceded it.

Even when the Bible is accepted the majority of Muslims maintain that the text of the Biblical scriptures has been changed. This allows them to reject those parts of the Bible that contradict their beliefs and use other parts to bolster their ideas. This indiscriminate and arbitrary use of Scripture can be very frustrating.

ISLAM AND JESUS

1. JESUS—THE SON OF DAVID, NOT THE SON OF GOD

Acts 2:30

"Therefore being a prophet, and knowing that God had sworn with an oath to him, that of the fruit of his loins, according to the flesh, he would raise up Christ to sit on his throne."

---

[1] John Thorpe, *The Bible and Islam* (297 pages).

[2] Muhammad Abdu in Emil Dermengham, *Muhammad and the Islamic Tradition*, trans. Jean M. Watt, (Westport: Greenwood Press, 1974), p.138; quoted Norman L. Geisler & Abdul Saleeb, *Answering Islam*, (Grand Rapids: Baker Book House Co., 1993), p.208.

Romans 1:3

"Concerning his Son Jesus Christ our Lord, which was made of the seed of David according to the flesh."

PROBLEM:

Islam accepts Jesus as a prophet from God but not as God's Son. On the basis of scriptures such as these Muslims argue that since Jesus was truly David's son he could not be the Son of God.

SOLUTION:

1. Because of their exposure to orthodox 'christianity' Muslims often equate the teaching that Jesus is the Son of God with the doctrine of the trinity. It is worth emphasising to the Muslim that the Bible nowhere mentions the "trinity" and that we do not seek to defend this teaching.
2. Jesus is descended from God because God is his father. He is also descended from David because David was an ancestor of Mary the mother of Jesus. The full genealogy is found in Luke 3:23–38.
3. We fully accept the teaching of Romans 1:3—that Jesus was truly David's descendant—but we also accept the clear teaching that "God sent forth his Son, made of a woman…" (Gal. 4:4). The comments of Jesus (regarded by Islam as a prophet) to the Jews in Matt. 22:42–45 are worth noting.

2. JESUS ONLY FOR THE JEWS

Matthew 15:24

"But he [Jesus] answered and said, I am not sent but unto the lost sheep of the house of Israel."

PROBLEM:

Before healing the daughter of the Syrophoenician woman, Jesus said that he was only sent to the lost sheep of the house of Israel. Muslims take this to be confirmation of their view that Jesus was a prophet for the Jews only, and that his disciples were therefore also only sent to the Jews. From this they argue further that the gospel of Jesus is not for Gentiles and therefore, unlike Islam, is not a universal religion.

SOLUTION:

1. Consider the context of the verse. Jesus had deliberately gone to the Gentile area of Tyre and Sidon after being rejected by the Jews (Matt. 15:1–8,21). Although Jesus told the woman that he was not sent to anyone other than Israel, he then commended her for her faith—"O woman, great is thy faith"—and proceeded to heal her daughter. The whole incident was a foreshadowing of the

147

teaching of Jesus that because the Jews rejected him God would turn to the Gentiles (Matt 21:43; John 10:16; 12:32).

2. Jesus gave the apostles the command to preach the gospel in all the world and to everyone without restriction. (Matt. 28:19,20; Mark 16:15; Acts 1:8). This shows that Jesus considered his message to become a universal one for all people.

3. The move to incorporate Gentiles into the early ecclesia did not come until after the resurrection of Jesus. It was produced by a direct revelation from God (Acts 10:9–16) and was confirmed by an outpouring of the Holy Spirit on the converted Gentiles (Acts 10:44–48). In the words of the Apostle Peter, "Of a truth I perceive that God is no respecter of persons: but in every nation he that feareth him, and worketh righteousness, is accepted with him." Clearly from that time the gospel has been a message for Gentiles as well as Jews.

3. JESUS DID NOT DIE A SACRIFICIAL DEATH

Deuteronomy 13:5

"And that prophet, or that dreamer of dreams, shall be put to death; because he hath spoken to turn you away from the LORD your God, which brought you out of the land of Egypt, and redeemed you out of the house of bondage, to thrust thee out of the way which the LORD thy God commanded thee to walk in. So shalt thou put the evil away from the midst of thee."

PROBLEM:

The Law of Moses required that a false prophet should be put to death. Muslims assert that if Jesus had been put to death this would have proved that he was a false prophet. As a true prophet therefore, they argue, he could not have been put to death and the Bible is denigrating him to suggest that he was put to death.

SOLUTION:

1. This is an elementary logical error. A implies B is not the same as B implies A. The fact that Jesus was put to death does not imply that he was a false prophet.

2. Other true prophets were put to death, for example Zechariah (2 Chron. 24:20–22) and Abel (Gen. 4:8). This is a common feature in Jewish history (Matt. 23:29–35). True prophets were often persecuted, and sometimes killed.

Deuteronomy 21:22,23

"And if a man have committed a sin worthy of death, and he be to be put to death, and thou hang him on a tree: his body shall not remain all night upon the tree, but thou shalt in any wise bury him that day; (for he that is hanged is accursed of God;) that thy land be not defiled, which the LORD thy God giveth thee for an inheritance."

PROBLEM:

The Law of Moses states that anyone put to death by hanging (which would include crucifixion) is cursed by God. Muslims assert that God would not have cursed Jesus and that therefore he could not have died by crucifixion.

SOLUTION:

1. The Bible does not say that God cursed Jesus but it does confirm that he "was made a curse for us [i.e. the Jews]" by the Law. By the act of crucifixion he was "hanged on a tree" and thereby came under the curse of the Law (Gal. 3:13). Thus the only man to have kept the Law perfectly was cursed by it. This showed the imperfect nature of the Law as an instrument of salvation. In fact the Law was not given as a means of achieving human salvation but as a means of regulating the national life of Israel because of their waywardness—"It was added because of transgressions, till the seed should come…" (Gal. 3:19).[3]

2. The death of Jesus, an essential part in the process of atonement, also led to the liberation of Israel from the bondage of the Law—"Blotting out the handwriting of ordinances that was against us, which was contrary to us, and took it out of the way, nailing it to his cross…" (Col. 2:14). So Paul could say to those who were seeking salvation by returning to the bondage of the Law covenant, "Wherefore the law was our [i.e. Israel's] schoolmaster to bring us unto Christ…but after that faith is come, we are no longer under a schoolmaster…" (Gal. 3:24,25).

3. Thus, far from the curse proving that the death of Jesus could not have occurred it gives part of the reason for which it did occur—so that the Law of Moses (the Old Covenant) could be abolished.

Hosea 6:6

"For I desired mercy, and not sacrifice; and the knowledge of God more than burnt offerings."

PROBLEM:

On the basis of this verse Muslims argue that God does not wish for sacrifices and that a sacrifice of Jesus would therefore be pointless. (See also Matt. 9:13; 12:7).

SOLUTION:

1. Clearly God did require sacrifice. The Law of Moses, given by God, detailed many sacrifices that the Jews were required to offer. The point in this passage is that, for the individual offering the sacrifice, the sacrifice is without value unless that person also shows mercy.

---

[3] It is worth noting that Galatians 3 confirms the fact that Jesus was for Gentiles as well as Jews. God preached the gospel to Abraham, promising him that the nations would be "justified through faith" (Gal. 3:8). This blessing of justification [i.e. forgiveness of sins, see Acts 3:25,26] would come through Abraham's "seed, which is Christ" (Gal. 3:16).

2. The context shows that this verse refers to individual conduct, not general principle. The meaning of this verse is a matter of idiom. One might therefore read it as, 'I require mercy far more than sacrifice from you.'

Matthew 12:40

"For as Jonas was three days and three nights in the whale's belly; so shall the Son of man be three days and three nights in the heart of the earth."

PROBLEM:

Jesus said that he would be in the belly of the earth just as Jonah was in the belly of the great fish. Therefore, Muslims claim, as Jonah was alive in the belly of the fish, so must Jesus have been alive in the tomb, or the prophecy would not be an exact prediction. This is a frequently raised passage.

SOLUTION:

1. There are clearly limits to the similarities of the two situations. The great fish was alive, and one cannot say the same for the tomb of Jesus. The great fish was in the sea, and the tomb of Jesus was not. Jonah came out of the great fish in a different place to the one where he entered it; Jesus both entered and left the tomb in Jerusalem. Jesus was not buried in a fish.

2. The similarity between the death of Jesus and the swallowing of Jonah by the fish was that both of them were hidden from the light of day. Jonah 2:2 says that when Jonah was swallowed by the fish he was in "hell" (Heb. *sheol*, the grave). Acts 2:27–31 says that after his crucifixion Jesus was in "hell" (Gk. *hades*, the grave. *Hades* is the equivalent of the Heb. *sheol*). Both Jonah and Jesus were in the grave for three days and then brought out again.

3. Three days and three nights. According to the traditional model, Jesus was in the tomb for part of Friday, all of Saturday and part of Sunday, using the Jewish way of reckoning time. Other models exist where Jesus was crucified on the Wednesday, which gives a longer period. However, in Bible times it was common to count a day as a whole day and night (if even the smallest part of it) was included in a period. Examples where both kinds of counting are used include: 1 Kings 22:1,2; 2 Kings 18:9,10; 2 Chron. 10:5,12; Jer. 34:14; Esther 4:16, cf. 5:1; Matt. 17:1, cf. Luke 9:28; Mark 8:31, cf. Matt. 16:21; 27:63,64. In this prophecy Jesus is simply using the inclusive counting system.

4. JESUS DID NOT DIE AND THEREFORE DID NOT RISE FROM THE DEAD

PRELIMINARY POINTS:

1. Muslims regard Jesus as a prophet. However, the Muslim approach to the crucifixion denies the clear teaching of Jesus. Jesus said to his disciples: "Behold, we go up to Jerusalem, and all things that are written by the prophets concerning the Son of man shall be accomplished. For he shall be delivered

unto the Gentiles, and shall be mocked, and spitefully entreated, and spitted on: and they shall scourge him, and put him to death: and the third day he shall rise again" (Luke 18:31–33). This is found in the same gospel to which they appeal to prove that he was not crucified.

2. It should be pointed out that the Old Testament predicted that Jesus would die (Isa. 53:5–10) and this by crucifixion (Psa. 22:16; Zech. 12:10).

3. Predictions that Jesus would be raised from the dead demand that he would first be put to death. E.g. Psa. 16:10, cf. Acts 2:25–31.

Luke 22:41,42

"And he was withdrawn from them about a stone's cast, and kneeled down, and prayed, saying, Father, if thou be willing, remove this cup from me: nevertheless not my will, but thine, be done."

PROBLEM:

Muslims argue that Jesus prayed to God asking that he would not have to die. Because he was a prophet God granted his prayer and Jesus did not die on the cross.

SOLUTION:

1. A prophet's request was not always granted. For example, David's prayer was not granted when his child by Bathsheba died (2 Sam. 12:15–19).[4]

2. In this case, Jesus did not simply and without condition pray that he should not die. Jesus expressed a normal human reaction to the prospect of crucifixion—he would have preferred not to die. But he went on to acknowledge that it was God's will that he should die, and to accept the will of God and allow himself to be put to death. All this within the same prayer. The Muslim case is made by failing to place the request of Jesus in the context of his entire prayer.

Luke 24:39

"Behold my hands and my feet, that it is I myself: handle me, and see; for a spirit hath not flesh and bones, as ye see me have."

PROBLEM:

Muslims assert that resurrected bodies are immaterial. On the basis of this assertion and the words of Jesus in this verse which show that he did have a solid physical body at this point, Muslims argue that Jesus could not have been raised from the dead and hence that he was merely resuscitated.

SOLUTION:

1. There is no reason to suppose that resurrected bodies are immaterial. On the contrary, several verses tell us that they will be real bodies. These include:

[4] David was a prophet, Acts 2:30.

151

WRESTED SCRIPTURES

a. Job 19:25,26—"For I know that my redeemer liveth, and that he shall stand at the latter day upon the earth: and though after my skin worms destroy this body, yet *in my flesh shall I see God.*"

b. Romans 8:11—"But if the Spirit of him that raised up Jesus from the dead dwell in you, he that raised up Christ from the dead shall also *quicken your mortal bodies* by his Spirit that dwelleth in you."

c. John 2:18–21—"Then answered the Jews and said unto him, What sign showest thou unto us, seeing that thou doest these things? Jesus answered and said unto them, Destroy this temple, and in three days I will raise it up. Then said the Jews, Forty and six years was this temple in building, and wilt thou rear it up in three days? But he spake of *the temple of his body.*"

d. Acts 2:31—"He [David] seeing this before spake of the resurrection of Christ, that his soul was not left in hell, *neither his flesh did see corruption.*"

2. It is the fact of Jesus' bodily existence that shows he was really raised. His real body went into the tomb dead, and that same body was raised and changed into "a glorious body" (Phil. 3:21) possessing eternal life. This was no vision of a spirit.

3. Muslims argue that those who are raised have intangible bodies because they are like angels (Luke 20:34–36). There is no reason to suppose that angels have intangible bodies. The angels who came to Abraham were real material beings and were able to eat (Gen. 18:8) and so were the angels that came to Sodom (Gen. 19:1–3).

John 19:14

"And it was the preparation of the passover, and about the sixth hour: and he saith unto the Jews, Behold your King!"

PROBLEM:

Muslims cite this passage, together with passages like Matt. 27:46 which put the death of Jesus at about the ninth hour and deduce that Jesus was on the cross less than three hours. Death by crucifixion would require longer than three hours. Therefore, they argue, Jesus did not die in the crucifixion.

SOLUTION:

1. Jesus was crucified at the third hour, i.e. 9 a.m. (Mark 15:25).

2. At about the ninth hour Jesus shouted loudly (Matt. 27:46). This means that he was not dead at this point. Jesus died shortly after this, quite suddenly (Matt. 27:50). This means that he was on the cross for a little over six hours to his death.

3. The time from unconsciousness to death in crucifixion is very short, less than 20 minutes. Thus if Jesus were still alive but appeared to be dead he would have died within 20 minutes. Jesus was not removed from the cross for burial immediately. It was when evening was come (Matt. 27:57; Mark 15:42–45) that Joseph of Arimathaea came to ask Pilate for the body. Thus Jesus would have

152

been on the cross for another hour or so after his "apparent" death, which would have ensured that he was really dead.

4. After Jesus was found to be dead a spear was thrust into his side (John 19:34) and water and blood came out of the wound. The water could have come from the lungs or the pericardium (the membrane around the heart); the blood could have come from the spleen, the liver or the heart if Jesus had been dead. A spear thrust that pierced lungs or pericardium would kill Jesus if he were not already dead.

5. After his resurrection Jesus walked to Emmaus (7 miles—see Luke 24:13). He wouldn't have been able to do this after crucifixion without a miracle, since his feet had been pierced by nails and his side severely wounded by the spear. This shows that he was not simply resuscitated.

6. The sixth hour of John 19:14 was probably the sixth hour after Jesus' arrest. This shows the shortness of the various trials of Jesus.

John 19:32–34

"Then came the soldiers, and brake the legs of the first, and of the other which was crucified with him. But when they came to Jesus, and saw that he was dead already, they brake not his legs: but one of the soldiers with a spear pierced his side, and forthwith came there out blood and water."

PROBLEM:

The Roman soldiers didn't break Jesus' legs. Muslims claim that this is a sign of the inefficiency of the soldiers. As they were so inefficient, they argue, they couldn't be trusted to be reliable in certifying death. Muslims further argue that as dead men don't bleed, Jesus cannot have been dead. This argument is often embellished by descriptions of blood "gushing" out of the wound.

SOLUTION:

1. The purpose of breaking a victim's legs was to prevent him from raising himself up on them. A victim who could not support his weight on his legs would suffer a pulmonary oedema and die within 20 minutes. As Jesus was, at the very least, unconscious, he would be unable to support himself on his legs and would rapidly die if not dead already. The Romans, with plenty of experience behind them, would know this; breaking the legs would be superfluous.

2. While a superficial wound on a dead body will not bleed, certain organs do bleed for a while after death, albeit at a lesser rate than during life. These organs include the spleen, the liver and the heart.

3. The spear thrust must, at the very least, have pierced Jesus' lungs. If he were not already dead this would have killed him. Leaving him badly wounded and untended in a tomb would certainly have swiftly brought about his death.

4. The record does not say that blood "gushed" out. It says that some blood and some water came out, but this could have been a tiny trickle as far as the text is concerned.

153

WRESTED SCRIPTURES

John 20:17

*"Jesus saith unto her, Touch me not; for I am not yet ascended to my Father: but go to my brethren, and say unto them, I ascend unto my Father, and your Father; and to my God, **and your God.**"*

PROBLEM:

This verse tells us that Jesus had not ascended to God at the time of his resurrection. Muslims assert that whenever someone dies they go back to the Creator. As Jesus had not yet ascended to God, they argue, he could not have died.

SOLUTION:

1. The Muslim interpretation of the passage is based on the false assumption that everyone goes to the Creator immediately after death. There is no passage in the Bible that suggests this. Jesus is the only one who has ascended into heaven (John 3:13; Acts 2:34). All others sleep in the dust awaiting the resurrection (Dan. 12:2; John 5:28,29).
2. Mary was not to touch (some versions say "cling to") Jesus because although he had been raised bodily from the dead it was to be a considerable period of time before he ascended into heaven (Acts 1:3,11).
3. If the Muslim wishes to use this passage to argue that Jesus was not raised from the dead he must accept its words. This means that he must accept that God is the Father of Jesus the prophet.

1 Corinthians 15:31

"I protest by your rejoicing which I have in Christ Jesus our Lord, I die daily."

PROBLEM:

Muslims claim that the Bible uses hyperbolic language to describe suffering. Paul says that he died daily, but he did not literally do so. They claim that where the Bible says that Jesus died (e.g. Matt. 27:50; Luke 9:22; Acts 3:15; Rom. 5:6,8; 8:34; 1 Cor. 8:11; 1 Thess. 2:15; 4:14) it merely refers to a similar symbolic death.

SOLUTION:

1. These passages do not say that Jesus died continually. Many of them state clearly that he died once and rose again (e.g. Matt. 16:21; Mark 8:31; 9:31; Luke 9:22; Acts 3:15; Rom. 14:9; 1 Cor. 15:3,4; 1 Thess. 4:14).
2. One could use the Muslim argument to prove that, as far as the Bible is concerned, no one ever dies—all references to dying being symbolic. This would be equally false.

MUSLIM PRACTICES IN THE BIBLE

According to Muslim tradition the laws of God have never changed since the time of Abraham. Muslims often use passages from the Bible to support this assertion and to try to show that the real teaching of Jesus and the Prophets was the same as current Muslim teaching.

1. CIRCUMCISION

Genesis 17:14

"And the uncircumcised man child whose flesh of his foreskin is not circumcised, that soul shall be cut off from his people; he hath broken my covenant."

PROBLEM:

Muslims note that God gave circumcision to Abraham as the sign of His covenant. This sign was very important and Muslims infer that therefore all believers should be circumcised, even in the present day.

SOLUTION:

1. Muslims tend to be dismissive of the writing of the Apostle Paul.[5] However, the following from the Letter to the Romans is an argument of logic based on other Scripture and does not depend on the inspiration of Romans. Justification is through faith. Abraham was declared righteous [i.e. justified] long before he was circumcised (Rom. 4:9,10), because he believed God [i.e. showed faith], as one can see from Genesis 15:6. Justification was dependent on the faith of Abraham, and on nothing else. "The covenant of circumcision" (Acts 7:8) was given later (Gen. 17:9–14) as a sign of Abraham's covenant status (Rom. 4:11). Circumcision did not affect justification in the sight of God as this was already in force because of Abraham's faith in the covenant promises, as Genesis 15 shows. Therefore there is no need to be circumcised in order to be forgiven and justified in the sight of God.

2. Circumcision was always, even in the Old Testament period, a sign of humbleness of heart before God (Deut. 30:6; Jer. 4:4). The true follower of God needs to be circumcised in the mind (Rom. 2:29). Bodily circumcision was a sign that pointed forward to the work of Jesus. So true believers are said to be "circumcised with the circumcision made without hands, in putting off the body of the sins of the flesh by the circumcision of Christ" (Col. 2:11). Jesus destroyed the flesh and through him his followers can destroy it too. The sign of circumcision is now fulfilled.

John 7:22,23

"Moses therefore gave unto you circumcision; (not because it is of Moses, but of the fathers;) and ye on the sabbath day circumcise a man. If a man on the sabbath

[5] According to Muslims the Apostle Paul corrupted much of the teaching of Jesus.

WRESTED SCRIPTURES

day receive circumcision, that the law of Moses should not be broken; are ye angry at me, because I have made a man every whit whole on the sabbath day?"

PROBLEM:

Muslims see this passage as one in which Jesus showed approval of circumcision. He points out that a priest carrying out circumcision on the Sabbath is blameless; this, they argue, shows that the law of circumcision had not been removed.

SOLUTION:

1. The verse cited is absolutely clear that circumcision, although originally given to Abraham, was incorporated into, and became an integral part of, the Law of Moses. Jesus was born "under the law" (Gal. 4:4 RV), was himself circumcised according to the Law (Luke 2:21) and throughout his life observed the Law. But the Law having been fulfilled by Jesus (Matt. 5:18) was then removed (Col. 2:14).
2. The context of the passage shows that the argument involved was about priorities. Jesus had healed a man on the Sabbath day and the Pharisees were accusing him of breaking the Law of Moses. The point that Jesus was making was that even within the Law of Moses, some actions took precedence over others. Thus the argument was within the framework of the Law of Moses under which Jesus and the Pharisees were living. Since the Law has been removed it is not binding on Gentile believers (Col. 2:13,14; Gal. 3:24,25; Rom. 10:4).

2. PILGRIMAGE TO MECCA

Psalms 84:6

"Who passing through the valley of Baca make it a well; the rain also filleth the pools."

PROBLEM:

This Psalm describes pilgrims ascending to the house of God and in verse 6 tells us that they pass through the valley of Baca. In Q 3:96 the word Bakkah (Becca in some translations) appears as a name for Mecca. Muslims identify the well in Psa. 84:6 with the well Zam-zam in Mecca which has ritual significance during the Hajj. On the strength of this, they assert that this Psalm is a description of pilgrims going to Mecca for the Hajj. Since the Psalm was written considerably before the time of Christ, this shows that Mecca was a centre of pilgrimage to the true God long before the time of Muhammad.

SOLUTION:

1. The psalm is speaking about the temple—the house of God in Jerusalem—with its "courts" and its "altars" (vv. 3,4). Verses 5–7 describe the last part of the ascent of pilgrims to this house.

156

2. This is the only occurrence of the word "Baca" in the Bible. It signifies "weeping".[6] The RV gives "Passing through the valley of weeping they make it a place of springs…" There may of course be a reference to a literal valley encountered by the pilgrims on the high way to Jerusalem. However, the sense appears to be that the path to God's presence leads the pilgrims through a vale of tears.

3. The end of the pilgrimage is Zion (v. 7). This is, of course, Jerusalem and not Mecca.

4. Psa. 84:6 describes a well made by the pilgrims. The well Zam-zam in Mecca was not made by pilgrims.

5. The valley is filled with pools of water by the rains. Mecca is very dry all the year round; it virtually never finds itself surrounded by pools of standing water left by rains.

3. PRAYING IN A PROSTRATE POSITION

Matthew 26:39

"And he went a little further, and fell on his face, and prayed, saying, O my Father, if it be possible, let this cup pass from me: nevertheless not as I will, but as thou wilt."

PROBLEM:

Islamic tradition requires that Muslims should pray by bending their faces to the ground. They cite this verse (and its parallel in Mark 14:35) to "prove" that Jesus followed this tradition in the way that he prayed.

SOLUTION:

1. The fact that Jesus prayed once in this attitude does not mean that he always did so.

2. This was not the time of the ritual prayers of Islam; it was long after midnight, the last supper being ended. (John 13:30 tells us that it was already night during the last supper).

3. The words of Jesus' prayer did not resemble any Muslim traditional formula; among other things he addressed God as his "Father".

4. Jesus taught the disciples how to pray in Matt. 6:5–15. This passage does not specify any posture at all and leaves out almost every element of Muslim ritual prayer. Further, it requires that we address God as "Father".

[6] It is also found in the plural form in 2 Sam. 5:23,24 and 1 Chron. 14:14,15 where it is translated in the AV "mulberry trees", but which almost certainly refers to a Balsam bush because of the "tears" of balsam obtained from it. This has led some to identify "the valley of Baca" with the valley of Rephaim where the battle between David and the Philistines was fought, as recounted in 2 Sam. 5 and 1 Chron. 14.

4. WOMEN'S HEAD COVERINGS

1 Corinthians 11:5,13

"But every woman that prayeth or prophesieth with her head uncovered dishonoureth her head: for that is even all one as if she were shaven."

"Judge in yourselves: is it comely that a woman pray unto God uncovered?"

PROBLEM:

Muslims teach that both men and women should cover their heads during prayer (and that women should cover all of their bodies at other times). They cite this passage in support of their assertion that this practice was taught by the early church.

SOLUTION:

1. The passage does not require the women to cover their heads other than during the acts of prayer and prophesying.
2. Verses 4 and 7 of this same chapter say that men should keep their heads uncovered during prayer. If the second part of the commandment (that women should cover their heads) is from God, then Muslims should also accept the first part of the commandment and male Muslims should pray with heads bared.
3. Here is clear guidance that women should cover their heads when praying and prophesying in the ecclesia. Muslims should acknowledge that this passage comes from God, which means that Paul is a prophet.

MUHAMMAD IN THE BIBLE

Although Muslims maintain that the Bible is corrupt, they do claim that certain passages have in fact retained their original form and these, they assert, are passages that witness to the prophethood of Muhammad. There is a series of such passages, and anyone likely to spend time talking to Muslims will need to be aware of these. This section looks at the more common passages cited by Muslims as alleged prophecies of Muhammad.

Genesis 49:10

"The sceptre shall not depart from Judah, nor a lawgiver from between his feet, until Shiloh come; and unto him shall the gathering of the people be."

PROBLEM:

Muslims assert that Shiloh is a name for Muhammad. They do this on the basis that Shiloh means "Peace", which is also a possible meaning of the word Islam. Further, by some strange reasoning it is maintained that Shiloh could not be a Jew since after his time the sceptre would depart from Judah.

SOLUTION:

1. The passage is about a ruler; it makes no reference to a prophet. One cannot claim it to be a prophecy about Muhammad who is held by Muslims to be a prophet rather than a king.

2. The word "Shiloh" does not mean peace[7] and there is no justification for connecting it with the word "Islam".

3. Shiloh is to rule the nations ("people" in the AV). Muhammad never ruled more than a few tribes but Jesus will rule the whole world in his kingdom.

4. There is no reason to suppose that Shiloh would not be a Jew. The king's sceptre was to remain with Judah until the coming of Shiloh; Shiloh was to be the last of the kings of Judah appointed by God. After Shiloh there were to be no more. (See Ezek. 21:27 where many Hebraists associate the phrase "he...whose [right] it is" with the word "Shiloh" which means "he to whom it belongs"). The passage prophesies that the kingship of Israel would pass down the generations in the lineage of Judah until Shiloh, the last king of this line who would rule the nations. Jesus is a fulfilment of this prophecy, being a descendant of David who was of Judah.

Deuteronomy 18:18,19

"I will raise them up a Prophet from among their brethren, like unto thee, and will put my words in his mouth; and he shall speak unto them all that I shall command him. And it shall come to pass, that whosoever will not hearken unto my words which he shall speak in my name, I will require it of him."

PROBLEM:

Muslims claim that the prophet referred to in this passage is Muhammad. They support their claim by producing an impressive list of ways in which Muhammad was like Moses and in which Jesus was not like Moses. This list includes the following:

	Moses	Jesus	Muhammad
Rejected by his people and then accepted	Yes	No	Yes
Became a national leader	Yes	No	Yes
Miraculous birth	No	Yes	No
Encountered enemies in battle	Yes	No	Yes
Family—married with children	Yes	No	Yes

---

[7] There is disagreement among Hebrew scholars with respect to the meaning of "Shiloh". The prevailing opinion appears to be that it means "he to whom it belongs". Thus the RSV renders Gen. 49:10: "The sceptre shall not depart from Judah, nor the ruler's staff from between his feet, *until he comes to whom it belongs*; and to him shall be the obedience of the peoples." The NIV also has "The sceptre will not depart from Judah, nor the ruler's staff from between his feet, *until he comes to whom it belongs* and the obedience of the nations is his."

SOLUTION:

1. There are a number of ways in which Moses was like Jesus, but unlike Muhammad:

	Moses	Jesus	Muhammad
Unusual death and has no tomb.[8]	Yes	Yes	No
Inaugurated a new covenant with God	Yes	Yes	No
Came out of Egypt[9]	Yes	Yes	No
Was an Israelite	Yes	Yes	No
Brought up by own mother[10]	Yes	Yes	No
Performed miracles	Yes	Yes	No
Saved by God as a baby[11]	Yes	Yes	No
Transfigured[12]	Yes	Yes	No
Gave prophecy which was later fulfilled	Yes	Yes	No
Offered himself to God in atonement[13]	Yes	Yes	No

Even at this level of argument there are more points of similarity between Jesus and Moses than there are between Muhammad and Moses. Also, some of the points where Jesus seems to be different from Moses only appear because the Muslims have not considered the whole of the life of Jesus. For example, Jesus was rejected by his people and has not been accepted by them yet. But the time will come when they will "look on me whom they have pierced" (Zech. 12:10) and God will cleanse them (Ezek. 36:26–31). Similarly, Jesus will become a national leader and will encounter his enemies in battle (Zech. 14:3; Psa. 2:6 which is applied to Jesus in Acts 13:33 & Heb. 1:5).

2. In Deut. 18:18 God tells Moses to inform Israel that the prophet was to be "from among their brethren", which means that he would have to be an Israelite. The Muslim response that, as the Arabs are the brothers of the Jews, this refers to an Arab, has no scriptural support. The Arabs are never called the brethren of the Jews in the Bible. There are a few verses where Edom is described as the brother (singular) of Israel (e.g. Num. 20:14; Deut. 23:7; Amos 1:11), but the word brethren (plural) is never used. In any case, Muhammad is not a descendant of Edom but of Ishmael, who is never referred to as the brother of Israel. The passage can only mean that the prophet like unto Moses was to be an Israelite.

---

[8] Moses had no known tomb, but died on Mount Nebo (Deut. 34:6).

[9] Moses came out of Egypt at the Exodus, and Jesus went to Egypt as a baby and returned (Matt. 2:15).

[10] Moses was brought up by his mother as a nurse in Pharaoh's household, and Jesus was brought up by Mary, but Muhammad was an orphan.

[11] Moses was saved as a baby in the rushes; Jesus was saved when God told Joseph to take him to Egypt.

[12] Moses was transfigured on Mt. Sinai (Exo. 34:29) and the transfiguration of Jesus is described in Matt. 17:1–6.

[13] Moses offered to take the sins of Israel on himself in Exo. 32:30–32; Jesus was sacrificed for the sins of mankind.

3. To list the similarities and differences between Jesus, Muhammad and Moses is a rather inconclusive and contrived way of looking at Deuteronomy 18. Rather than devising lists of ways that Muhammad is, or is not, like Moses, it is better to let the passage itself say in what ways the prophet would be like Moses:

> "And if thou say in thine heart, How shall we know the word which the LORD hath not spoken? When a prophet speaketh in the name of the LORD, if the thing follow not, nor come to pass, that is the thing which the LORD hath not spoken, but the prophet hath spoken it presumptuously: thou shalt not be afraid of him." (Deut. 18:21,22).

The prophet's message would be validated by the manifestation of a promised sign (or miracle) or the fulfilment of a prophecy. There is no doubt that Jesus performed signs (or miracles); even the Qur'an admits this (e.g. Q 5:115). However, Muhammad never performed a miracle and the set of predictions claimed for him is singularly unimpressive (he is said to have predicted that his followers would win the battle of Badr—probably a method of encouraging them to fight more fiercely, and self-fulfilling as one would never have heard of the prediction if the battle had been lost). The lack of signs from Muhammad is also commented upon in the Qur'an with words like: "They say: Why not a sign sent down to him from his Lord?" (Q 10:20; see also Q 6:109; Q 13:7; Q 17:59; Q 21:5,6). There is only one reason that the Qur'an would record passages like these, and that is because Muhammad never gave a prophecy or performed a miracle.

4. Muslims cannot have things both ways. Either the passage in Deuteronomy 18 is from God, in which case they must believe it and reject Muhammad because he does not fulfil Scripture, or it is not from God, in which case they cannot claim it as a prediction of Muhammad.

5. Deut. 18:18 is cited in Acts 3:22,26. Here the Apostle Peter, speaking words from God through the Holy Spirit, identifies the prophet like Moses as being Jesus Christ and not Muhammad.

Psalm 110:1

"The LORD said unto my Lord, Sit thou at my right hand, until I make thine enemies thy footstool."

PROBLEM:

Muslims ask, "How could this refer to Jesus, since he is David's son; the person referred to is called 'my Lord' by David?" They answer this question by suggesting that the Lord of David is in fact Muhammad.[14]

SOLUTION:

1. In Matt. 22:42–44 Jesus himself tells us that this verse refers to him; it cannot therefore refer to Muhammad.

14 Baagil H. M., *Muslim-Christian Dialogue*, (Birmingham, U.K.: Islamic Propagation Centre International UK, 1984), p.50.

2. David calls Jesus "Lord" because he is not only the son of David but also the Son of God.

Song of Songs 5:16

"His mouth is most sweet: yea, he is altogether lovely. This is my beloved, and this is my friend, O daughters of Jerusalem."

PROBLEM:

The word "lovely" is the Hebrew *machmaddim*. Muslims claim that this word is a reference to Muhammad for two reasons:

1. When spoken the word *machmad* (singular of *machmaddim*) sounds a bit like the name Muhammad.
2. The word *machmad* means "the praised one" (i.e. the one worthy of praise); this, they assert, must be Muhammad!

SOLUTION:

1. The logic of the assertion that the word *machmad* is Muhammad because the two words sound similar is somewhat specious. The name *John* sounds a bit like the Arabic *Jinn*, but there is no connection between the two. Similarly a connection on the grounds that the word means "the praised one" (even if this were true) falls short of a guaranteed logical link; has only one person in the world ever been praised?
2. The context of the passage identifies the person described as *machmadim* as someone in the time of Solomon (Song 3:11) who is loved by a Shulamite (Song 6:13). He is red-haired (Song 5:10). None of these descriptions fits Muhammad who never visited Shunem in his life.
3. A search of all the occurrences of the word *machmad* in the Bible shows that the word has nothing to do with praise. It simply refers to whatever is desirable for whatever reason and is derived from the root *chamad*, which means "to delight in".
4. When all the scriptural occurrences of the term *machmad* are examined it is easy to see why Muslims only refer to this one in Song of Songs 5:16. The others say that *machmad* was destroyed (2 Chron. 36:19), was to be laid waste (Isa. 64:10,11), has been taken captive by an enemy (Lam. 1:10), has been traded for food (Lam. 1:11), has been slain by God (Lam. 2:4; Hos. 9:16), has been removed by God (Ezek. 24:16), is to be profaned by God (Ezek. 24:21), is to be buried in nettles (Hos. 9:6) and been carried away by pagans into their temples (Joel 3:5). None of these have anything to do with Muhammad.

Isaiah 11:1,2

"And there shall come forth a rod out of the stem of Jesse, and a Branch shall grow out of his roots: and the spirit of the LORD shall rest upon him, the spirit of wisdom and understanding, the spirit of counsel and might, the spirit of knowledge and of the fear of the LORD."

PROBLEM:

Muslims maintain that the name "Jesse" is a contraction of "Ishmael". On this basis they claim that the prophecy is of a descendant of Ishmael and not of Jesse. The prophecy says that he would be a success as a statesman and a leader of men. This, they assert, could only be Muhammad. To further support this claim they then ask why Jesus would be referred to as a son of the relatively obscure Jesse when he could have been described as a son of David.

SOLUTION:

1. The name Jesse is not a contraction of Ishmael. Ishmael is derived from the Hebrew root *shama*, "to hear"[15]. Jesse is derived from the Hebrew *yesh*, which means "substance or wealth" and is related to the name Issachar.[16] In the Bible record Jesse and Ishmael are distinct and different people. Ishmael the son of Hagar is never called Jesse and Jesse the father of David is never called Ishmael. Thus the prophecy is of someone descended from Jesse the father of David.

2. The descendant of Jesse was to accomplish the following:

   a. Bring in a kingdom of complete peace (Isa. 11:6–9).

   b. Regather the nation of Israel into the land of Palestine (Isa. 11:12–16).

The return of Jesus will see these prophecies fulfilled, but Muhammad did not and never will fulfil them.

Isaiah 21:7

"And he saw a chariot with a couple of horsemen, a chariot of asses, and a chariot of camels; and he hearkened diligently with much heed."

PROBLEM:

Muslims argue: "Who was the rider on the ass? Every Sunday school student will know him. That was Jesus (John 12:14). Who, then, is the promised rider on a camel? This is the Prophet Muhammad...If this is not applied to him then the prophecy has yet to be fulfilled. That is why Isaiah mentioned further in the same chapter (Isa. 21:13) the burden upon Arabia which means the responsibility of the Arab Muslims, and now of course of all Muslims, to spread the message of Islam."[17]

SOLUTION:

1. The passage does not describe one man riding on a donkey at all. In the AV it describes a chariot pulled by donkeys. In the RSV it is translated "riders on

[15] Alfred Jones, *The Proper Names of the Bible,* (London: Samuel Bagster and Sons, 1856), p.165.

[16] *Ibid*, p.198.

[17] Baagil H. M., *Muslim-Christian Dialogue*, (Birmingham, U.K.: Islamic Propagation Centre International UK, 1984), p.46

asses, riders on camels…" and other modern versions likewise. When Jesus rode into Jerusalem he had no chariot, and in any case, following the later versions, the prophecy states that several riders would be involved. Similarly with respect to the camels the choice is either "a chariot of camels" (AV) (Muhammad never used a chariot) or "riders on camels" (RSV and other modern versions), i.e. several riders.

2. The passage also refers to a third group—a chariot of horses. This group finds no place in the Muslim interpretation; for an adequate interpretation of a prophecy all the elements have to be explained.

3. In fact the prophecy is about Babylon. "The desert of the sea" (v. 1) is an area of the Babylonian empire (now in southern Iraq). In verse 9 we read the outcome, "And he answered and said, Babylon is fallen, is fallen; and all the graven images of her gods he hath broken to the ground." The prophecy is of a successful invasion of Babylon from Persia by way of the desert of the sea, and was fulfilled long before the time of Jesus.

4. The burden of the Arabs (vv. 13–17) describes the fall of the children of Kedar (Arab tribes who were troubling Judah) within a year of the prophecy being given by Isaiah.

The Muslim interpretation of this prophecy does not fit and it is difficult to think why they should use it.

Isaiah 29:12

"And the book is delivered to him that is not learned, saying, Read this, I pray thee: and he saith, I am not learned."

PROBLEM:

Muslims claim that Muhammad was illiterate and could not read or write (although some *ahadith*[18] suggest that he could read and write a little). They ask who the prophet was who could not read, and say that since all the Biblical prophets could read and write this must refer to Muhammad.

SOLUTION:

1. This is a prophecy about a false prophet. Consider the context, "For the LORD hath poured out upon you the spirit of deep sleep, and hath closed your eyes: the prophets and your rulers, the seers hath he covered." (v. 10). The prophet was unable to read the words of the prophecy because God had made him illiterate. He had done this because the prophet was teaching man's ideas and not the word of God (v. 13).

2. Since the prophet in this prophecy is a false prophet, if it refers to Muhammad it shows him to be a false prophet.

---

[18] *Ahadith* are stories about Muhammad that date from AD 800–900.

Isaiah 42:1

"Behold my servant, whom I uphold; mine elect, in whom my soul delighteth; I have put my spirit upon him: he shall bring forth judgment to the Gentiles."

PROBLEM:

Muslims assert that this messenger is not Jesus, but Muhammad. This claim is based on the titles that have been given to Muhammad. These include: The slave servant of God and his elected messenger, a title given to Muhammad five times every day in the Muslim liturgy of prayers. Other claims from the chapter include:

ISAIAH 42	CLAIMS FOR MUHAMMAD
"He shall not fail nor be discouraged, till he have set judgment in the earth" (v. 4).	It is claimed that as Jesus was rejected by Israel and did not set up a worldwide government this cannot be Jesus.
"[the LORD] will keep thee" (v. 6).	It is claimed that this is a statement that no other prophet would come after!
"and give thee for a covenant of the people, for a light of the Gentiles" (v. 6).	Many Gentiles from all nations converted to Islam and Muslims claim that this is prophesied here.
"Sing to the LORD a new song, and his praise from the end of the earth" (v. 10).	Muslims claim that the song is new because it is in a different language (Arabic), and that it refers to the Muezzins singing praise to God from minarets throughout the Islamic world.
"Let them...declare his praise in the islands" (v. 12).	Muslims assert that these islands are in the South China Sea and in the Caribbean, where Islam has taken root.
"He shall prevail against his enemies" (v. 13).	Muslims assert that Jesus did not prevail against his enemies, but Muhammad has done so. Hence, they argue, this verse must refer to Muhammad and not to Jesus, and the rest of the prophecy must therefore also refer to Muhammad.[19]

SOLUTION:

1. The titles given to Muhammad were given after the event (possibly long after). They reflect titles in the Bible because titles were plundered from the Bible to give to Muhammad.
2. The prophecies describe the servant as ruling the world, and giving judgment for it. Muhammad died before his armies had left Arabia and he never judged even Jerusalem, let alone the rest of the world. Jesus has not judged the world yet, but he is to return and do so. At this time he will prevail against his enemies. (Psa. 110:1; Rev. 11:15 etc.).

[19] Baagil H. M., *Muslim-Christian Dialogue*, (Birmingham, U.K.: Islamic Propagation Centre International UK, 1984), p.48,49.

3. In verse 6 the prophecy states that the servant is to be given for a covenant of the people, a light of the Gentiles. In what way was Muhammad given? Jesus was given as a sacrifice at his crucifixion. (John 3:16; 6:51).

4. This chapter cannot be taken alone. It is part of the servant cycle prophecy of Isaiah and any interpretation must fit the whole of the prophecy. This is an embarrassment to Muslims as the cycle ends with the suffering servant prophecy of Isa. 53, which can be applied only to Jesus:

   a. rejected (v. 3)

   b. sins of mankind laid upon him (vv. 5,6)

   c. killed (v. 8)

   d. died with the wicked and was buried with the rich (v. 9)

   e. did no violence (v. 9)

   f. raised from the dead (v. 11)

   None of these fits Muhammad who was a man of war.

5. Isa. 42:1 is applied to Jesus in Matt. 12:18,19.

Jeremiah 28:9

"The prophet which prophesieth of peace, when the word of the prophet shall come to pass, then shall the prophet be known, that the LORD hath truly sent him."

PROBLEM:

Muslims assert that this is a prophecy of a specific prophet to come, a prophet that would prophesy peace. This, they say, is not Jesus because he did not come to bring peace (Luke 12:51–53). The word Islam can be interpreted to mean peace (it comes from the same root as *Salaam*) so Muslims claim that this prophet was to be he who brought Islam, i.e. Muhammad.

SOLUTION:

1. To understand this prophecy it is important to look at the context. This is a confrontation between Jeremiah and Hananiah at the time of the Babylonian captivity of the Jews. Jeremiah, speaking God's word, said that the captivity would last for 70 years (Jer. 25:11,12). Hananiah, the false prophet, contradicted Jeremiah and said that the captivity would be over in two years (28:3). In these circumstances to prophesy peace was the hallmark of a false prophet.

2. Jeremiah states that the prophet who prophesied imminent peace is a false prophet because all the faithful prophets predicted that Israel's sins would be visited by war, evil or pestilence (v. 8). He had made a similar rebuke of the false prophets in Jer. 14:13,14.

3. The peace of Jer. 28:9 is not inner tranquillity. It is the absence of war, and this can be seen clearly from the context. Muhammad may have prophesied peace, but peace did not come. From the Battle of Badr to the present day Islam has

always been involved in political conflict, both internally and externally. Therefore, by Jeremiah's test, Muhammad is a false prophet.

Matthew 3:11

"I indeed baptize you with water unto repentance: but he that cometh after me is mightier than I, whose shoes I am not worthy to bear: he shall baptize you with the Holy Spirit, and with fire."

PROBLEM:

These words of John the Baptist are taken by Muslims to be a prediction of the coming of Muhammad. According to Baagil[20] the person referred to by John the Baptist was not Jesus, because if it had been Jesus then John would have followed him and become his disciple. Therefore there had to be a great prophet after Jesus, and this could only be Muhammad.

Dawud argues, "the very preposition 'after' clearly excludes Jesus from being the foretold prophet [since] they [Jesus and John] were both contemporaries and born in one and the same year."[21]

SOLUTION:

1. John the Baptist was a prophet. He had a mission from God to baptize and to preach repentance to Israel. Because he submitted to the will of God (a concept familiar to Muslims) he could not leave his God-given task to follow Jesus, no matter how much he would like to have done so.
2. Jesus was born six months after John (Luke 1:36). The beginning of John's ministry is recorded in Matt. 3:1. Jesus did not begin his ministry until after his baptism (Matt. 3:16,17) and temptations in the desert (Matt. 4:1–11). In fact, although Jesus chose disciples and visited Jerusalem he did not begin his main Galilean ministry until after the imprisonment of John (Matt 4:12–17; Mark 1:14). Thus whilst they were contemporary, Jesus definitely was born after John and began his ministry after John had completed his.
3. Jesus did baptize people with the Holy Spirit and with fire. His disciples received the Holy Spirit (Acts 2:1–4) and became prophets in their own right. Muhammad, on the other hand, never gave the gift of the Holy Spirit to anyone. None of his followers became a prophet. Thus Muhammad could not possibly be the person described by John the Baptist.

Matthew 5:9

"Blessed are the peacemakers: for they shall be called the children of God."

[20] Baagil H. M., *Muslim-Christian Dialogue*, (Birmingham, U.K.: Islamic Propagation Centre International UK, 1984), p.50,51.

[21] Dawud, Addul Ahad, *Muhammad in the Bible*, (Kuala Lumpur: Pustaka Antara, 1979), page158 quoted in Norman L. Geisler & Abdul Saleeb, *Answering Islam*, (Grand Rapids U.S.A.: Baker Book House Co., 1993), p.151.

WRESTED SCRIPTURES

PROBLEM:

As part of the Beatitudes, Jesus said, "Blessed are the peacemakers" (Matt. 5:9). Muslims note Jesus' statement, "I came not to send peace on earth, but a sword" (Matt. 10:34), and argue from this that Jesus did not refer to himself when he spoke of "peacemakers". They argue that Muhammad is the only alternative and support this by stating that the word *Islam* comes from the same root as *Salaam*, which means "peace".

SOLUTION:

1. Jesus talks about "peacemakers" (plural). The phrase does not describe one person, but many. It therefore cannot be a reference to Muhammad alone.
2. The passage is part of the Sermon on the Mount, which sets out the qualities of character that should be seen in the true children of God. All the qualities are to be seen in each of God's children—this includes meekness (Matt. 5:5). Muhammad was not meek; he was a ruthless and successful military leader. Neither can it be said that Muhammad showed love to his enemies (v. 44) or followed the instructions for prayer laid down in the Sermon on the Mount (Matt. 6:6–13), which include praying in private and addressing God as Father.
3. Islam has a poor claim to be a peacemaker. More wars have been fought in the name of Islam than in almost any other cause, even more than in the cause of mainstream Christianity.

Matthew 11:11

"Verily I say unto you, Among them that are born of women there hath not risen a greater than John the Baptist: notwithstanding he that is least in the kingdom of heaven is greater than he."

PROBLEM:

Jesus described John the Baptist as equal to the greatest prophet. Nevertheless, Jesus promised that the least in the kingdom of God would be greater than he. Muslims take the word *least* to be a chronological reference and argue that the *least* in the kingdom of God would be the *last* of the prophets. They further assert that this is Muhammad.

SOLUTION:

1. Jesus does not say that "the least in the kingdom of God *would be* greater than" John Baptist. He says. He that *is* [i.e. now as I am speaking to you] least in the kingdom of heaven *is* [now] greater than he." This must exclude Muhammad who was not born until centuries later.
2. If the word "least" indicates the time of the prophet's appearing, then according to this Muslim way of looking at things the "least" is the "last". John was the last prophet before Jesus came offering the kingdom of heaven to the Jewish nation—"Repent: for the kingdom of heaven is at hand" (Matt. 4:17).

By the Muslim argument, John being the last of the prophets, he should be called the "least" and not the "greatest" as Jesus says he was! Thus the term "least" refers to status and not to time. If, as Muslims maintain, Muhammad is the least in the kingdom of God, then he is less important than Jesus, Paul or even Agabus.

3. The greatness of John the Baptist lies in the relationship he occupied to the Son of God. He was raised up specifically to be "my messenger…which shall prepare thy way before thee" (Matt. 11:10). He was the one "spoken of by the prophet Esaias, saying, The voice of one crying in the wilderness, Prepare ye the way of the Lord, make his paths straight". (Matt. 3:3). For the exercise of this great responsibility he was unique among the Old Covenant prophets in being "filled with the Holy Spirit, even from his mother's womb" (Luke 1:15).

4. Jesus is not talking about the future kingdom of God. Jesus sent his apostles out to take his message to Israel—"The kingdom of heaven is [now] at hand" (Matt. 10:7). Jesus was the divinely appointed king of that kingdom (Luke 1:32,33) and the apostles were told, "In the regeneration when the Son of man shall sit in the throne of his glory, ye also shall sit upon twelve thrones, judging the twelve tribes of Israel" (Matt. 19:28). Thus the administration of the future kingdom—king and government of the twelve tribes—was there, then, in the midst of Israel offering the kingdom to them—an offer that was rejected. These chosen men, the nucleus of God's future kingdom, were blessed with over three years' association with the Son of God. These blessed disciples were given the ability to perform miracles in support of their message (which John was not), and the promise that in their future preaching they would do even greater works than the Lord himself (John 14:12). They were witnesses of his resurrection and were with him for almost six weeks afterwards being taught by him about the coming kingdom (Acts 1:1–3). The least of these favoured men was, then, because of this association with the Lord, greater than John the Baptist.

John 1:20,21

"And he confessed, and denied not; but confessed, I am not the Christ. And they asked him, What then? Art thou Elias? And he saith, I am not. Art thou that prophet? And he answered, No."

PROBLEM:

Muslims argue that there are three people referred to in this passage, Christ, Elijah and The Prophet. Thus, they argue, the prophet is not Christ or Elijah. They go on to claim that the prophet here is the prophet like Moses from Deut. 18:18,19, and that this is a major prophet following Christ, who can only be Muhammad.

SOLUTION:

1. The Muslims are correct when they see in this passage reference to Messiah, Elijah and "the prophet like unto Moses".[22] The Jews were asking John the Baptist if he was one of these three.

2. The fact that John denied being "that prophet" does not mean that the prophet must therefore be Muhammad. This conclusion can only be reached by misunderstanding Deut. 18:15–19. See notes on this on page 150.

3. The prophet like unto Moses was Jesus as a perusal of Acts 3:22,26 confirms.

John 14:16,17

"And I will pray the Father, and he shall give you another Comforter, that he may abide with you for ever; even the Spirit of truth; whom the world cannot receive, because it seeth him not, neither knoweth him: but ye know him; for he dwelleth with you, and shall be in you."

PROBLEM:

Muslims claim that the Comforter described in this passage is Muhammad. The word "Comforter" is a translation of the Greek *paracletos*. Muhammad is referred to in the Qur'an as Ahmad (Gk. *periclytos*), which they take to be the correct rendering of the word *paracletos* in John's Gospel. Jesus shows in John 14 that his work was not complete, but that something else would be sent to complete it. Muslims believe that many of the things that were left for the Comforter (Greek: *paracletos*) to do were things that were done by Muhammad.

SOLUTION:

1. If Muslims quote this passage they must be prepared to take its teaching seriously as something sent from God.

2. The names, titles, etc. applied to Muhammad were given after the event by Muslims who would be aware of them from accounts of the Bible which had reached Arabia.

3. The New Testament clearly identifies the Comforter as the Holy Spirit (John 14:26).

4. The task of the Comforter was to enable the disciples to call to mind all the words of Jesus (John 14:26). Muhammad could not do this since he never heard Jesus speak. He did not relate any of the words of Jesus (the words that appear in the Qur'an and purport to come from Jesus really came from late apocryphal sources).

5. Muhammad cannot have been the "Spirit of truth" (John 14:17; 16:13). He was not a spirit but a normal man of flesh.

---

[22] There is another view that sees "the prophet" as being Elijah's prophet, i.e. Elisha, but this is difficult to sustain. The same words are used of Jesus in John 6:14 where there can be little doubt that "the prophet like unto Moses" is intended.

6. The world could not receive the Comforter (John 14:17). Muhammad was not only received but founded a great empire.

7. The Comforter was sent by Jesus from God (John 15:26; 16:7). In what way did Jesus send Muhammad? The Muslims should note that if they maintain that Jesus sent Muhammad this implies that Jesus is greater than Muhammad.

8. The Comforter was to give prophecy (John 16:13). Muhammad never gave any prophecy.

2.1

THE IMMORTALITY OF THE SOUL

PRELIMINARY POINTS

1. It is useful in discussion to lead the conversation by well-chosen questions which guide the disputant to the desired conclusion without having to tell him so. This approach reduces the "loss of face" which can be a barrier to further profitable discussion. This is especially true of discussion on the death state in which the loss of loved ones may prejudice a reasoned consideration of the evidence. The following questions are samples:

   a. How can it be said that Christ brought immortality to light (2 Tim. 1:10) if man has been immortal since Adam?

   b. How can immortality be sought for (Rom. 2:7) if it is already a present possession?

   c. If Adam had an immortal soul, why was he thrust out of the garden that he might not "live for ever"? (Gen. 3:22,23).

   d. If the souls of the righteous go to heaven at death, why a resurrection? (Usually the reply is, "for the purpose of judgment," but this implies that souls are rewarded first, and *then* judged!)

   e. In an ongoing discussion, when this subject is raised, it is worth giving the antagonist the time to discover for himself that the Bible never mentions immortal souls—"When we meet next week why not bring a list of all the Bible references which mention immortal soul(s)?" More than one person has embraced the Truth as a result of this exercise.

2. The doctrine of the immortality of the soul destroys the arguments whereby the New Testament writers affirm the resurrection of the dead.

   a. "If Christ be not raised...then they also which are fallen asleep in Christ are perished." (1 Cor. 15:17,18). But how can these dead saints be said to be sleeping if their souls (the *real* saints) are already in heaven, and how can it be said that these saints would perish unless Christ be raised, if their immortal souls go to bliss at death?

   b. The Apostle Paul said, "If after the manner of men I have fought with beasts at Ephesus, what advantageth it me, if the dead rise not?" (1 Cor. 15:32). If the soul is immortal (and hence can enjoy heavenly bliss when separated from the body) why does the apostle stress "if the dead rise not"? Why the concern for the body if the soul can enjoy bliss without the body?

Genesis 35:18

"And it came to pass, as her soul was in departing, (for she died)."

172

PROBLEM:

It is argued from this passage that at death the soul departs. Since it must depart *to* somewhere, the somewhere is said to be either heaven or hell.

SOLUTION:

1. To say that the souls of dying persons depart is to say nothing about whether or not the soul is immortal, or to where, if any place, it might depart.
2. In everyday speech it is appropriate to say "X lost the sight in his right eye" or "X lost his hearing after the accident." To use these expressions is not to imply that the eyesight was removed to another location or that the hearing departed to another abode. Likewise, "her soul was in departing" does not imply that the soul went to heaven, hell or anywhere else. The expression is synonymous with "her life was ebbing".
3. The Hebrew word, *nephesh* rendered "soul" in this passage is translated "life" in one hundred other passages, e.g., Gen. 1:30 (NB animals, birds and creeping things have *nephesh*); Exo. 4:19; 21:23; 21:30.

1 Samuel 28:8–15

"Saul disguised himself...came to the woman by night: and he said, I pray thee, divine unto me by the familiar spirit, and bring me him up, whom I shall name unto thee...Then said the woman, Whom shall I bring up unto thee? And he said, Bring me up Samuel. And when the woman saw Samuel, she cried with a loud voice: and the woman spake to Saul, saying, Why hast thou deceived me? for thou art Saul. And the king said unto her, Be not afraid: for what sawest thou? And the woman said unto Saul, I saw gods ascending out of the earth. And he said unto her, What form is he of? And she said, An old man cometh up; and he is covered with a mantle. And Saul perceived that it was Samuel, and he stooped with his face to the ground, and bowed himself. And Samuel said to Saul, Why hast thou disquieted me, to bring me up? And Saul answered, I am sore distressed; for the Philistines make war against me, and God is departed from me, and answereth me no more, neither by prophets, nor by dreams: therefore I have called thee, that thou mayest make known unto me what I shall do."

PROBLEM:

This passage is used by Spiritualists to give Scriptural support to their idea that living people can communicate with the souls of the "departed".

SOLUTION:

1. This passage neither provides evidence for "heaven going" nor "immortal soulism".
   a. Samuel (a righteous man) came "up" out of the earth, not down from heaven. (v. 15).
   b. The witch said that she saw an old man, not an intangible soul. (v. 14).

173

   c. Samuel said, "Why hast thou disquieted me…?" This indicates that he was not enjoying the bliss of heaven, but rather the sleep of death (cf. Job 3:17; Eccl. 9:5,10; John 11:11).

2. Some have suggested that this passage in Samuel is really a fake séance. The following evidence is usually given:

   a. The king saw *nothing*.

   b. The woman would almost certainly have seen through Saul's attempt at disguise, bearing in mind that "he was higher than any of the people from his shoulders and upward" (1 Sam. 10:23).

   c. The witch said that she saw an old man with a mantle. (1 Sam. 28:14). This was an ambiguous description. Was Samuel the only old man to wear a mantle?

   d. Samuel was buried at Ramah, not Endor. (1 Sam. 25:1).

   e. Some reject this explanation, because of its inability to explain the predictions ostensibly made by Samuel (1 Sam. 28:19). However, it is quite possible that God used the woman to convey a message to Saul, as he had used the unfaithful prophet Balaam to convey a message to the king of Moab (Numbers 23 & 24; 2 Pet. 2:15).

3. Another possible explanation to the events in this chapter is the following:

   a. God raised Samuel for the occasion in order to rebuke a fool according to his folly.[1]

   b. This accounts for the precise predictions of verses 15–19, as well as the surprise of the witch (when "she cried with a loud voice", v. 12), when suddenly confronted by an *unexpected* Samuel.

However, two objections to this explanation must be considered:

   c. Would God raise Samuel in these circumstances after instructing Israel: "Regard not them that have familiar spirits, neither seek after wizards, to be defiled by them: I am the LORD your God"? (Lev. 19:31). God could have used the witch as He did the lying prophet of Bethel. (1 Kings 13). In so doing, it no more implies sanction to the witch's activities than it does to Beelzebub in Jesus' allusion (Matt. 12:27) or to the belief of the Pharisees in Luke 16:19–31.

   d. Samuel was buried at Ramah, not at Endor where the resurrection would have taken place. The rejoinder to this is simply that for God, there is no more difficulty in reassembling Samuel in Endor than to transport Philip from the Gaza Road to Azotus. (Acts 8:39,40).

1 Kings 17:21

"And he stretched himself upon the child three times, and cried unto the LORD, and said, O LORD my God, I pray thee, let this child's soul come into him again."

---

[1] God punished Saul with death. "So Saul died for his transgression which he committed against the LORD, *even* against the word of the LORD, which he kept not, and also for asking counsel of one that had a familiar spirit, to inquire of it; and inquired not of the LORD: therefore he slew him, and turned the kingdom unto David the son of Jesse." (1 Chron. 10:13,14).

PROBLEM:

Only the hard-pressed resort to this passage to prove the immortality of the soul. It is argued that when the child's soul left him, his immortal entity departed to heaven.

SOLUTION:

1. The passage neither states nor implies that the soul described is immortal or that it would depart to heaven. Such views must be read into this passage. They are assumptions for which this passage offers no support.
2. The personal pronoun "him" describes the lifeless body. If the real child was the immortal soul tabernacling in a mortal, earthly body, then the pronoun should have been descriptive of the soul and not (as it is) of the body.
3. It was not the child that had departed, neither was it the child which returned. The child was dead. He died when life was lost; he became living when life was restored. The Hebrew word, *nephesh* translated "soul" in this passage, is translated "life" in Gen. 1:30; 9:4; Lev. 17:11; Deut. 12:23 and dozens of other places.
4. If, as some argue, the soul of the child went immediately to bliss in heaven, would it not have been better for the prophet to have left the soul of the child to enjoy bliss in heaven rather than to recall it to the travail of earthly life, and possible later consignment to the fires of hell?

Ecclesiastes 12:7

"The spirit shall return unto God who gave it."

PROBLEM:

This passage is cited as evidence that man's immortal spirit (or soul) leaves the body at death and returns to God.

SOLUTION:

1. The point needs to be made here, and in all other places where the immortal soulist uses passages about the spirit to support his case, that "soul" and "spirit" are not interchangeable terms. Paul writes, "I pray God your whole spirit and soul and body be preserved blameless..." (1 Thess. 5:23). The spirit is not the same as the soul.
2. The passage makes no distinction between "good" and "bad" spirits—the spirits of all men, good or bad, go to God.
3. If the spirit is to return to God, it must have come from God. But who would suggest one has a conscious existence before the earthly life begins? Therefore, there is no reason to expect a conscious existence when this life ends.
4. The word "spirit" (Heb. *ruach*) is the same as in Eccl. 3:19 (Heb. *ruach*, translated "breath"). Would any argue that beasts have, or are, immortal "spirits"?

WRESTED SCRIPTURES

5. The writer of Ecclesiastes emphatically teaches the mortality of man (see Eccl. 9:5,6,10; 3:19,20).

Matthew 10:28

"And fear not them which kill the body, but are not able to kill the soul: but rather fear him which is able to destroy both soul and body in hell."

PROBLEM:

This passage is cited by Pentecostals and Evangelicals as the foundation proof that man is really an indestructible soul clothed with an earthly body.

SOLUTION:

1. "Rather fear him which is able to *destroy*[2] both body and soul in hell" is proof that the soul is destructible and therefore, not immortal.
2. Since both soul and body can be destroyed in hell (Gk. *Gehenna*—the garbage dump outside the walls of Jerusalem), this indicates that the soul is as destructible as the body since both can be destroyed in the same place. Is this what the immortal soulist wants from this passage?
3. What is meant by "not able to kill the soul"? Simply, 'Fear not (for an instant) them which kill the body, but are not able to destroy you utterly and finally.' As far as the disciple is concerned, his name being written "in the book of life" (Phil 4:3; Rev. 21:27), his life is "hid with Christ in God" (Col. 3:3) and although men may kill the body, in the resurrection this life will be given back to the body. (See Col. 3:4).
4. The Greek word, *psuche,* translated "soul" in this verse has the meaning of "life". In Matt. 16:25, *psuche* is translated "life": "For whosoever will save his life [*psuche*] shall lose it: and whosoever will lose his life [*psuche*] for my sake shall find it."[3] (In the RSV *psuche* is translated "life" in v.26: "For what will it profit a man, if he gains the whole world and forfeits his *life*.") The similarity of context suggests that "life" in Matt. 10:28 should be read for "soul".

Luke 16:19–31

"There was a certain rich man, which was clothed in purple and fine linen, and fared sumptuously every day: and there was a certain beggar named Lazarus, which was laid at his gate, full of sores, and desiring to be fed with the crumbs which fell from the rich man's table: moreover the dogs came and licked his sores. And it came to pass, that the beggar died, and was carried by the angels into Abraham's bosom: the rich man also died, and was buried; and in hell he lift up

[2] It is sometimes argued that "destroy" means to "afflict" or "torment" but not to annihilate. The Greek word, *apollu,* translated "destroy" means to "destroy utterly"—see Ethelbert W. Bullinger, *A Critical Lexicon and Concordance to the English and Greek Testament,* (London: Samuel Bagster and Sons Ltd., 1957), p.220. There is not the slightest suggestion of torment in any of the places where *apollu* is translated "destroy" in the AV (e.g. Matt. 2:13; 12:14; 21:41; 22:7; 27:20).

[3] Obviously if the words "immortal soul" were substituted for "life" in this reference, the result would be absurd.

176

his eyes, being in torments, and seeth Abraham afar off, and Lazarus in his bosom. And he cried and said, Father Abraham, have mercy on me, and send Lazarus, that he may dip the tip of his finger in water, and cool my tongue; for I am tormented in this flame. But Abraham said, Son, remember that thou in thy lifetime receivedst thy good things, and likewise Lazarus evil things: but now he is comforted, and thou art tormented. And beside all this, between us and you there is a great gulf fixed: so that they which would pass from hence to you cannot; neither can they pass to us, that would come from thence. Then he said, I pray thee therefore, father, that thou wouldest send him to my father's house: for I have five brethren; that he may testify unto them, lest they also come into this place of torment. Abraham saith unto him, They have Moses and the prophets; let them hear them. And he said, Nay, father Abraham: but if one went unto them from the dead, they will repent. And he said unto him, If they hear not Moses and the prophets, neither will they be persuaded, though one rose from the dead."

PROBLEM:

This is a stock passage cited by many religious groups to prove that souls of the departed go to torment in hell or bliss in heaven.

SOLUTION:

1. It is noteworthy that this passage mentions neither heaven nor souls.
2. Since this passage is cited as a literal description of actual events (and not as a parable) it is helpful to show that even the immortal soulist cannot take this passage as a literal description. The following is the evidence:
   a. The passage speaks about bodies not souls. e.g., eyes, bosom (v. 23) tip of finger and tongue (v. 24).
   b. Souls are said to be immaterial (the material body being left in the grave), how then could Lazarus (if really a soul) be carried by angels? (v. 22).
   c. The passage states that there was a great gulf fixed between Abraham and the rich man, yet they could both see and converse with each other (v. 26). Is the great gulf to be taken literally?
   d. Is heaven literally a place where conversations can be carried on between those enjoying bliss and those agonizing in hell?
   e. How could Lazarus go literally to Abraham's bosom? Abraham (as now) was unquestionably dead and without his reward. (Heb. 11:8,13,39,40).
3. It is sometimes asserted that parables are simple stories. It is then argued that they should be read simply (i.e., literally), therefore Lazarus and the rich man must be historical figures and the narrative must have occurred as written. Such a view is not supported by the Master's statements about his parables:
   a. "Unto you it is given to know the mystery of the kingdom of God: but unto them that are without, all these things are done in parables: that seeing they may see, and not perceive; and hearing they may hear, and not understand..." (Mark 4:11,12).

177

    b. "But without a parable spake he not unto them: and when they were alone, he expounded all things to his disciples." (Mark 4:34).

4. Stress is often placed upon words "there was a certain rich man" to emphasize the historical character of the language used. But in Luke 16:1 the parable of the unjust steward commences with the same language. Must this parable be read literally? (Similar language is used in other parables—see Luke 12:16).

5. Some take exception to Jesus using a false idea of the Pharisees[4] as a basis for his teaching. But it should be noted that the truth or falsity of the story in a parable is immaterial[5]. The lesson conveyed through the story is the intended point. Jesus makes reference to Beelzebub, "the lord of the fly", but this does not commit him to a belief in a real "lord of the fly". (Matt. 12:27).

6. Further objection to reading this passage as a parable is argued on the grounds that Jesus did not definitely call it a parable. This objection is not valid since only 11 of the 26 parables recorded in Luke's gospel are actually named parables.

7. Religious bodies like the Church of Christ hold the view that disbelievers go to hell (left hand side of the divided state of hades) whereas idol worshippers go straight to the lake of fire. It should be pointed out that this view puts Abraham in the lake of fire and not in hades since it is recorded that Abraham "was gathered to his people" (Gen. 25:8) and his people were idol worshippers. (Josh. 24:2).

8. In an effort to support their interpretation of Luke 16, Church of Christ preachers assert that bodies never go to hades. This assertion is false. In Acts 2:27,31 Peter cites Psa. 16:10 where the word for "hell" is *sheol,* the Hebrew equivalent of the Greek *hades.* The Hebrew parallelism (where the writer expresses the same thought in slightly different words) of verse 10 indicates that "thou wilt not leave my soul in hell" is equivalent to, "neither wilt thou suffer thine Holy One to see corruption". Clearly then, "my soul" is synonymous with "thine Holy One". Therefore, bodies are placed in hades.

9. Although the issue to be settled in a consideration of this passage is whether or not it provides support for the doctrine of the immortality of the soul and heaven the place of reward for the righteous, it is useful to be able to explain what the passage does mean. The following is a suggested exposition:

---

[4] The Pharisaical character of the narrative is indicated by the rich man praying (v. 27) to "father" Abraham (cf. the encounters between Jesus and the Scribes and Pharisees in John 8:31–59). The reference to Josephus' *Discourse to the Greeks Concerning Hades* that appeared in the first edition, has been removed from this note since it is now the opinion of informed scholarship that this was wrongly attributed speculatively to Josephus by the 9th Century Greek theologian, Photius. It is actually a quotation from a work by Hippolytus of Rome (AD 160–235). However, perusal of John Lightfoot, *Commentary on the New Testament from the Talmud and Hebraica*, (Hendrickson, 1995 reprint), Vol. 3, pp.165-176, will show that the parable of Jesus was based on Jewish superstition.

[5] Similarly, the Old Testament parable of Jotham (Judg. 9:7–15) does not require the trees of the forest to enter into political discussion and finally invite a bramble to be king.

THE IMMORTALITY OF THE SOUL

vv. 14,15—The Pharisees deride Jesus after his attack on materialism. The Pharisees were noted for their asceticism[6] regarding externals, but Jesus pointed out their covetous designs.

v. 16—The Pharisees had long been locked with the Sadducees in a bitter disputation over the oral and written traditions. Their conduct had resulted in the exclusion of publicans, sinners, and the Lazarus class from spiritual food which ought to have been provided by the chief priests. They had taken away the key of knowledge. (Luke 11:52). But with the coming of John, the kingdom was preached and every man pressed into it. (See Luke 16:16). Even the Pharisees and Sadducees, desirous no doubt, of a kingdom in which they would be prominent, went out to hear John. They were indicted as a "generation of vipers" and told to "bring forth therefore fruits meet for repentance." (Matt. 3:2,7–10).

v. 17—But lest it be thought that God's demands on men had slackened with the teaching of the kingdom and every man pressing into it, Jesus told his hearers, "It is easier for heaven and earth to pass, than one tittle of the law to fail."

v. 18—Jesus cites the teaching of the law on adultery as an example, and in so doing, condemns the notorious loose-living of the Sadducees.

v. 19—"Which was clothed" is in the imperfect tense and means to be habitually clothed.

a. Purple is a colour which is used in Scripture for the following: priestly garments (Exo. 39:2,24,29); royal apparel (Judg. 8:26; Esther 8:15); and is synonymous with wealth in Rev. 18:16.

b. Fine linen was used extensively in the priestly garments such as the ephod, robe, mitre, and bonnet. (Exo. 39). Linen is used as a symbol of wealth in Rev. 18:16.

c. Only one class in Israel was habitually clothed in purple and linen and fared sumptuously *every* day[7]—the high priestly class of Sadducees.[8] Caiaphas is likely the unnamed (for obvious reasons) rich man.

v. 20—Lazarus is the only character personally named in the parables of Jesus, implying that Lazarus must have been known to the audience. This parable of Jesus might have been uttered after he received news of the death of his friend, Lazarus. The parable was given in Peraea, east of the Jordan at Bethabara

[6] See, for example, Matt. 9:14; 23:23; Luke 18:12. Also Flavius Josephus, *Antiquities*, Book XVIII, chap. 1, section iii, pp.376,377 in Josephus: *Complete Works*, trans. by William Whiston, (Grand Rapids: Kregel Publications, 1966).

[7] Some interpretations suggest that the rich man represented the Pharisees, but the Pharisees did not fare sumptuously every day. They generally lived austere lives and fasted twice a week. (Luke 18:12).

[8] At the time of Jesus the Sadducees had much political power derived from their wealth, office and political connections. They were unpopular with the public because of their avaricious spirit. Special hatred was felt toward the chief representative, the family of Annas. See Flavius Josephus, *Antiquities*, Book XIII, chapter 10, section vi, p.281 and Book XVIII, chapter 1, section iv, p.377; also *Wars of the Jews*, Book 11, chapter 8, section xiv, p.478, in Josephus: *Complete Works*, trans. by William Whiston, (Grand Rapids: Kregel Publications, 1966). The Sadducees had installed booths in the outer court of the temple in Jerusalem which increased their wealth by currency exchange and sale of sacrificial animals. (See John 2:13–16; Matt. 21:12,13).

(where news of Lazarus' death came to him, John 11:6, cf. John 10:40; 1:28). It was an easy day's journey from Bethabara to Bethany.

v. 21—Lazarus was typical of most Jews of his day. They were deprived of even the most meagre crumbs of the bread of life from the rich man's table (i.e., the High Priestly class, but Caiaphas in particular). However much Lazarus might patiently await the rich man's (Caiaphas') condescension, the high priest was incapable of dispensing even spiritual crumbs."[9]

vv. 22–31—Lazarus dies and in the parable the premature death of Caiaphas is made to follow. In hades they meet but in situations reversed. Caiaphas requests Abraham (with whom he claimed privilege by virtue of ancestry—Matt. 3:9) to warn his five brothers. The five brothers are the five brothers-in-law of Caiaphas, the Sadduceean high priest.[10] Caiaphas was son-in-law of Annas who had been deposed by the Romans for openly resisting them. The request is refused on the grounds that they had not heard Moses and the Prophets (e.g. in their attitude to adultery and resurrection, Luke 16:18; 20:27–38), nor would they respond if one rose from the dead. The resurrection of Lazarus further incensed the Pharisees, chief priests[11] and Caiaphas who feared their loss of power. (John 11:47–57).

10. The parable condemns Caiaphas the chief Shepherd of Israel for his selfish irresponsibility in neglecting the spiritual and material needs of Jews in Israel. Lazarus represents this neglected class.[12] The parable is a further indictment of the Sadducees (who denied the resurrection of the body and were about to reject the miraculous resurrection of Lazarus) in their disbelief of Moses and the prophets. The parable is presented in terms of the popular belief of the Pharisees about the death state.

Acts 7:59,60

"And they stoned Stephen, calling upon God, and saying, Lord Jesus, receive my spirit. And he kneeled down, and cried with a loud voice, Lord, lay not this sin to their charge. And when he had said this, he fell asleep."

[9] The Lazarus class was like the Gentile dogs who hoped for crumbs from their Master's table. (Matt. 15:27).

[10] Josephus records, "Now the report goes, that this elder Ananus [Annas] proved a most fortunate man; for he had five sons, who had all performed the office of a high priest to God, and he had himself enjoyed that dignity a long time formerly, which had never happened to any other of our high priests…" *Antiquities*, Book XX, chapter 9, section i, p.423. Elsewhere, Josephus gives the names of Annas' five sons as Eleazar, Jonathan, Theophilus, Matthias, and the younger Annas.

[11] If as Josephus records, the five brothers were to succeed to the high priesthood after Caiaphas, they would be the most eminent members of "the chief priests." (In addition to the ex-high priests the title was applied to members of those families from which the high priests were usually chosen.) See J. D. Douglas ed., *The New Bible Dictionary*, (Grand Rapids: Wm. B. Eerdman's Book Co., 1962), p.1124.

[12] Ezekiel's condemnation of the priests of his day appropriately underlies Jesus' censure of Caiaphas: "Woe be to the shepherds of Israel that do feed themselves! should not the shepherds feed the flocks? Ye eat the fat, and ye clothe you with the wool, ye kill them that are fed: but ye feed not the flock. The diseased have ye not strengthened, neither have ye healed that which was sick…but with force and with cruelty have ye ruled them." (Ezek. 34:2–4).

PROBLEM:

It is frequently understood from this passage that Stephen expected Jesus Christ immediately to receive his "immortal soul" in heaven.

SOLUTION:

1. This is talking about the "spirit" not the "soul".
2. If the *real* Stephen was the spirit, what is the "he" of verse 60 which "fell asleep"? The personal pronouns are associated with the body, not something inside the body. This use of the pronouns is fatal to the idea that the real Stephen was an immortal essence within the body.
3. "Sleep" is a scriptural expression describing the unconsciousness of death and implying the waking at the Resurrection Day. For this there is unimpeachable evidence in John 11; esp. vv. 11,14,24, cf. Dan. 12:2; 1 Cor. 15:6,18. The fact that Stephen fell asleep indicates he did not immediately go to his reward. (See 1 Thess. 4:13–16.)
4. One could handle the problem of what Stephen meant by the expression "Lord Jesus receive my spirit" by taking the following approach:
   a. Show scripturally *when* the righteous (and hence Stephen) will receive their reward, e.g., 1 Cor. 15:22,23.
   b. Indicate the uses of spirit—e.g., that the "spirit" is not the immortal part of man, but the life-force which God gives (Job 34:14,15; Gen. 7:21,22 — "the breath of the spirit of life" mg.).
   c. Then finally show that Stephen had the confidence that as God sent forth His Spirit and raised Jesus, likewise he would be raised. In the death state Stephen's life would be "hid with Christ", and when Christ appears the second time, then Stephen would appear with him in glory. (Col. 3:3,4).
5. Jesus uttered similar words to those of Stephen, "Father, into thy hands I commend my spirit". (Luke 23:46). But Christ went to hell[13], not heaven. (Acts 2:27; cf. John 20:17—"I am not yet ascended to my Father").

1 Thessalonians 5:23

"And the very God of peace sanctify you wholly; and I pray God your whole spirit and soul and body be preserved blameless unto the coming of our Lord Jesus Christ."

PROBLEM:

It is inferred from this verse that in addition to a body one has a soul and a spirit. In some way this is supposed to endorse the concept of the immortality of the soul.

---

[13] The Greek word *hades* translated "hell" in Acts 2:27 simply means "the grave". This can be proven from other passages which state that after his crucifixion, Jesus was placed in the tomb. (Matt. 12:40; Acts 10:38–40; 1 Cor. 15:4,5. *Hades* is translated "grave" in 1 Cor. 15:55).

SOLUTION:

1. The words, "spirit" (Gk. *pneuma*) and "soul" (Gk. *psuche*) are used in a variety of ways in Scripture. However, they are never referred to as conscious immortal entities within man.
2. It is likely that in the passage under consideration by "spirit" is meant "mind"[14] and by "soul" is meant "life". The expression, "spirit and soul and body" is synonymous with the whole person. Consider the following:
    a. Spirit, soul and body are synonymous with the whole person since the preceding words, "And the very God of peace sanctify you *wholly*" imply a parallelism between the two expressions.
    b. The word "spirit" is used elsewhere by the Apostle Paul as synonymous with the "mind". For example:
        i. "For I verily, as absent in body, but present in spirit ..." (1 Cor. 5:3).
        ii. "That ye stand fast in one spirit, with one mind ..." (Phil. 1:27).
        iii. See also 1 Cor. 7:34; 2 Cor. 7:1.
    c. The word "soul" is used elsewhere by the apostle for "life". For example:
        i. "So being affectionately desirous of you, we were willing to have imparted unto you, not the gospel of God only, but also our own souls, because ye were dear unto us." (1 Thess. 2:8).[15]
        ii. "Moreover I call God for a record upon my soul..." (2 Cor. 1:23).[16]
3. A corpse is a body without life. Someone born with severe brain damage may well be a body with a soul (life), but with only an improperly functioning spirit (mind). It is the person with spirit and soul and body—the whole person, which Paul prays may be "preserved blameless unto the coming of our Lord Jesus Christ."
4. If the body is destroyed, then necessarily the life and mind cease to function. In death there is complete dissolution of being. (Eccl. 9:5,6; Psa. 146:4).

Hebrews 12:23

"To the general assembly and church of the firstborn, which are written in heaven, and to God the Judge of all, and to the spirits of just men made perfect."

[14] J. B. Phillips in his translation renders the Greek word *pneuma* (translated "spirit" AV) in this verse by "mind". J. B. Phillips, *The New Testament in Modern English*, (London: Geoffrey Bles, 1960).

[15] Benjamin Wilson translates the Greek word *psuche* (translated "soul" AV) in this verse by "lives". Benjamin Wilson, *The Emphatic Diaglott: Containing the Original Greek Text of What is Commonly Styled the New Testament*, (Brooklyn, New York: International Bible Students Ass., 1942).

[16] There is another approach to this passage which sees in the apostle's prayer a reference to the Old Testament way of looking at the whole man as consisting of:
    a. His "heart" (his objective, thinking, powers, e.g. "understand with their heart", Isa. 6:10).
    b. His "soul" (the seat of his subjective feelings—his emotions and appetites that he shares with the other creatures, e.g. "Why art thou cast down, O my soul?" Psa. 42:5).
    c. His "strength, or might"—his physical body. This last is combined with the other two to give the complete man in Deut 6:4,5—"Thou shalt love the LORD thy God with all thine *heart*, and with all thy *soul*, and with all thy *might*."

PROBLEM:

It is argued by Evangelicals that the "spirits of just men made perfect" refers to the immortal spirits (or souls) of the departed.

SOLUTION:

1. The immortal soulist, as so frequently is the case, assumes that soul and spirit are identical terms. Paul says they are not in 1 Thess. 5:23.

2. The same writer to the Hebrews expressly states that the great cloud of witnesses catalogued in the 11th chapter, "having obtained a good report through faith, received not the promise: God having provided some better thing for us, that they without us *should not be made perfect.*" (Heb. 11:39,40). In chapter 12 the writer uses the perfect tense to describe an event yet future, but assured—"the Spirits of just men *made* perfect". This mode of expression is a common feature of Scripture and is clearly stated in Rom. 4:16,17. (See also Rev. 13:8—Christ was not literally slain from "the foundation of the world"; Matt. 25:34—but the kingdom is not yet established.)

3. When will the spirits of "just men" be made "perfect"? Not until after resurrection and judgment when immortality is granted. (2 Cor. 5:10, cf. Phil. 3:9–12—"Not as though I had already attained, either were already perfect"). A person is justified (made righteous) by appropriating the great salvation of the gospel at his baptism. (Rom. 6:3,4, cf. vv. 17,18; 4:24). The Law of Moses could not make the offerer of sacrifices perfect (Heb. 10:1), but Christ "by one offering...hath perfected for ever them that are sanctified." (Heb. 10:14). The spirit or life of the believer is not made perfect until he has endured unto the end, overcoming the world (Matt. 24:13; Rev. 2:26,27), but God can speak of believers coming unto the spirits of "just men made perfect" since known to Him are all His works from the "beginning of the world." (Acts 15:18). In actuality the spirits will not be made perfect until the granting of immortality at the Lord's return.

4. It is difficult to define precisely the meaning of "spirits" in this passage. "Lives" seems to be a fair approximation. In Heb. 12:9 the writer states: "Shall we not much rather be in subjection unto the Father of spirits, and live?" This verse appears to allude to Num. 16:22; 27:16—the intent of these references being that God is the giver of life, and therefore must be respected when He chastens or punishes. But the life of a person is manifested in the kind of life lived (i.e., the character of the person), hence "spirits made perfect", refers to the lives of persons made perfect.[17]

---

[17] Another possibility arises by noting that in verse 9, according to the RVm, NIV and Rotherham, the contrast is between "fathers of our flesh" and "the Father of *our* spirits". In this case the "spirit" referred to is that "inner man", "new man" [of the mind], or "Christ in you", that has been created in the believer by the gospel—"Of his own will begat he us with the word of truth, that we should be a kind of firstfruits of his creatures" (James 1:18). This spiritual man, having been born, must then grow—"As newborn babes, desire the sincere milk of the word, that ye may grow thereby..." (1 Pet. 2:2). This is only possible because of the sacrifice of Jesus who "by one offering...hath *perfected* for ever them that are sanctified" (Heb. 10:14). "The spirits of just men made perfect" then refers to this process of regeneration and rebirth which is the consequence of believing the gospel.

WRESTED SCRIPTURES

1 Peter 3:19

"By which also he went and preached unto the spirits in prison."

PROBLEM:

This passage is frequently cited by Mormons and Evangelicals to prove the conscious existence of the dead as "disembodied spirits". It is alleged that when Jesus died, he preached to these spirits in prison.

SOLUTION:

1. How can the "spirit" go back to God who gave it, as taught in Eccl. 12:7, and yet be imprisoned in Hades?

2. The word "spirits" never signifies disembodied persons in Scripture.[18] Even angels who are called "spirits" (Heb. 1:7) are bodily beings. Lot called them "men" (Gen. 19:1,8) and Jacob wrestled with one of them. (Gen. 32:24). Similarly, the Apostle John admonishes believers to "try the spirits" (1 John 4:1), but the same verse identifies the spirits with false prophets.

3. "Spirits in prison" is an expression for a person in bondage to sin and death. Prison has this association in the following passages:

   a. "I the LORD have called thee [Christ] ... to open the blind eyes, to bring out the prisoners from the prison, and them that sit in darkness out of the prison house." (Isa. 42:6,7).

   b. "The Spirit of the Lord GOD is upon me; because the LORD hath anointed me to preach good tidings unto the meek; he hath sent me to bind up the broken-hearted, to proclaim liberty to the captives, and the opening of the prison to them that are bound." (Isa. 61:1).

   c. See also Eph. 2:1,2—Prior to becoming believers, Paul told the Ephesians: "And you hath he quickened, who were dead in trespasses and sins; wherein in time past ye walked according to the course of this world, according to the prince of the power of the air, the spirit that now worketh in the children of disobedience."

4. The Mormon and Evangelical interpretations of this passage are shown to be false since they both require an opportunity for dead persons to respond to instruction. Scripture is clear: "It is appointed unto men once to die, but after this the judgment" (Heb. 9:27); "They that go down into the pit cannot hope for thy truth" (Isa. 38:18); "The dead know not anything". (Eccl. 9:5). The "dead" in 1 Pet. 4:6 were alive when preached to by Noah, but dead at the time of Peter's writing.

5. The "spirits in prison" proves too much for the Mormons. Mormons practise proxy baptisms only for relatives who die in ignorance of the gospel. The "spirits in prison" however, were not ignorant, but *disobedient*, condemned by the preaching of Noah. (1 Pet. 3:19,20, cf. 2 Pet. 2:5; Heb. 11:7). Why was

---

[18] Luke 24:37,39 might be cited as an exception since the Greek word *pneuma* signifies a spirit in this passage. The context, however, offers no proof that spirits actually exist. The disciples mistakenly thought they had seen a spirit when they actually saw the risen Master.

184

Christ's mission confined to those disobedient in the days of Noah (who had a preacher—Noah) at the expense of all the ignorant who died before and after the time of Noah?

6. The passage does not state that Jesus personally preached to the spirits in prison, but rather, "*by which* also he went and preached unto the spirits in prison." (v. 19). It was the "Spirit of Christ" in Noah which preached to the spirits in prison (live persons in bondage to sin and death) many years before Jesus was born in the days of Herod the King. (Matt. 2:1). By means of the Holy Spirit given to the prophets (2 Pet. 1:21) they were able to speak as though they were Christ. Consider the following passages:

   a. "For thou wilt not leave my soul in hell; neither wilt thou suffer thine Holy One to see corruption." (Psa. 16:10, cf. Acts 2:26,27).

   b. "Behold, I and the children whom the LORD hath given me." (Isa. 8:18, cf. Heb. 2:13).

   c. "A body hast thou prepared me." (Heb. 10:5, cf. Psa. 40:6).

   Literally there was no flesh and body of Christ when these words were written. The Spirit of Christ in the prophets enabled them to testify "beforehand the sufferings of Christ, and the glory that should follow." (1 Pet. 1:11). Noah, "a preacher of righteousness" (2 Pet. 2:5) "being warned of God of things not seen as yet, moved with fear, prepared an ark to the saving of his house; by the which he condemned the world, and became heir of the righteousness which is by faith." (Heb. 11:7).

7. Peter by inspiration draws a figure. He says "the like figure whereunto even baptism doth also now save us…" (1 Pet. 3:21). The whole human race stands as a community of prisoners condemned to death on account of sin. Even while awaiting the inexorable judicial sentence they are "all their lifetime subject to bondage". (Heb. 2:15). The way of escape from this prison is by baptism into Jesus Christ, the anti-typical ark. "For as many of you as have been baptized into Christ have put on Christ." (Gal. 3:27).

Revelation 6:9

"And when he had opened the fifth seal, I saw under the altar the souls of them that were slain for the word of God, and for the testimony which they held."

PROBLEM:

This passage is quoted to support the teaching of Evangelicals that souls of the dead depart to heaven.

SOLUTION:

1. It is generally taught that souls which go to heaven enjoy a state of bliss, but this passage speaks of souls *crying* "with a loud voice." (v. 10).

2. Instead of this passage supporting the doctrine of the immortality of the soul, the context shows the passage to be directly opposed to it. The souls are given white robes. (v. 11). Can immaterial souls be clothed?

3. The souls in this text are under the altar. Is this where immortal souls are said to reside?

4. It is a principle in Scripture that "the life (Heb. *nephesh*, soul) of the flesh is in the blood". (Lev. 17:11). By personification, a slain person's blood is said to "cry" or "speak". (Gen. 4:10, cf. Heb. 12:24). The Revelation contains over 500 references to the Old Testament, and in this text the allusion is to the blood of the burnt offering which was poured at the base of the brazen altar. (Lev. 4:7). The passage, therefore, refers to the lives of martyrs given as a testimony to their faith. (Paul makes a similar allusion: "For I am already on the point of being sacrificed ['poured out'[19]]; the time of my departure has come." (2 Tim. 4:6 RSV).

---

[19] The Greek word, *spendomai* translated "offered" in the AV means, "to be poured out". Robert Young, *Analytical Concordance to the Holy Bible*, (London: Lutterworth Press, 1965).

2.2

HEAVEN—PLACE OF REWARD

Matthew 5:12

"Great is your reward in heaven."

PROBLEM:

This passage is understood by Evangelicals and Pentecostals to teach that the righteous go to heaven at death, or are rewarded later in heaven.

SOLUTION:

1. If the reward is in heaven, then there are two possibilities:
   a. The righteous go to heaven to obtain it.
   b. The reward comes from heaven to the righteous (here on earth).
2. The following passages are conclusive—the reward comes to the righteous:
   a. The reward is *"reserved* in heaven" (1 Pet. 1:4) "and *when* the chief Shepherd *shall appear*, ye shall receive a crown of glory that fadeth not away." (1 Pet. 5:4).
   b. "For the Son of man shall come in the glory of his Father with his angels; and *then* he shall reward every man according to his works." (Matt. 16:27).
3. See also 1 John 5:11, cf. Col. 3:2–4 and Rev. 22:12.

Matthew 17:3

"And, behold, there appeared unto them Moses and Elias talking with him."

PROBLEM:

This passage is used to prove that the reward of the righteous will be in heaven since Elijah, taken in a whirlwind, was still alive many hundreds of years later, and conversed with Jesus in the transfiguration.

SOLUTION:

1. It is assumed that Elijah lived from the time he was taken to heaven in a whirlwind until the time he appeared to Jesus in the transfiguration, but the passage does not state this to be the case. Moses was present, but there is no doubt that he died (Deut. 34:5). Therefore, the fact that Elijah was alive (assuming that he was bodily present) at the transfiguration, is not in itself proof that he continued to live after he was taken to heaven in a whirlwind. He may have died and been raised for the occasion.

187

WRESTED SCRIPTURES

2. Even if Elijah was bodily present at the transfiguration, having been miraculously preserved since he was caught up in a whirlwind, his experience offers no grounds for present believers to expect a similar privilege. God has not promised to do for present believers what he did for Elijah.

3. There is evidence that Elijah was back on earth after he was taken away in the whirlwind. It can be shown that a letter was received by Jehoram, King of Judah, from Elijah, *after* Elijah was taken to heaven. Either the letter was written before he went to heaven and delivered by a messenger on earth (unlikely), or Elijah was "caught away" as was Philip from the Gaza Road to Azotas (about 17 miles, Acts 8:39,40) for an unspecified purpose and returned to the earth. Consider the evidence:

   a. Elijah had been taken to heaven in a whirlwind. (2 Kings 2:11).

   b. Elisha had taken over the duties of Elijah in the reign of Jehoshaphat. (2 Kings 3:10,11).

   c. Jehoram received a letter from Elijah, the prophet. (2 Chron. 21:1,9–12). King Jehoram reigned after Jehoshaphat. (2 Chron. 21:1).

4. Elijah did not ascend to the heavens (the dwelling place of God)[1] since it is expressly stated: "no man hath ascended up to heaven." (John 3:13).

5. Matthew's account records Jesus' instruction to his disciples: "Tell the *vision*[2] to no man, until the Son of man be risen again from the dead." (Matt. 17:9). These words may mean simply, 'Do not tell what you have seen', or they may imply that Elijah and Moses were not bodily present but what occurred, transpired as a subjective experience. A vision does not necessarily have objective reality (e.g., Acts 10:3,10,17; notice the contrast in Acts 12:9 where what was objective, was thought by Peter to be merely subjective), although it may, as when the Lord appeared to Paul on the road to Damascus (Acts 26:19, cf. vv. 13–18)[3] and possibly when the women at the tomb of Christ saw a "vision of angels". (Luke 24:23, cf. v. 4).

6. Those who use this scripture to prove heaven-going at death believe that it is the soul that goes to heaven. This account seems to be talking about the bodily presence (whether real or in vision) of Moses and Elijah with Jesus.

Matthew 22:32; Luke 20:38

"God is not the God of the dead, but of the living."

---

[1] "Heaven" is used in Scripture for the place where the birds fly (Gen. 7:23), where the stars are located (Gen. 1:16,17), and where God dwells (Psa. 115:16).

[2] The Greek word, *horama* means "a sight, vision". Robert Young, *Analytical Concordance to the Holy Bible*, (London: Lutterworth Press, 1965). *Horama* is translated "sight" (Acts 7:31) in a context which requires objective reality—an angel really did appear to Moses "in a flame of fire in a bush". (Acts 7:30).

[3] In this verse a different Greek word, *optasia* is translated "vision". *Optasia* means, "a sight, apparition, vision". *Ibid.*

188

PROBLEM:

This verse is considered to be proof that Jesus meant to teach that Abraham, Isaac, and Jacob are alive in heaven.

SOLUTION:

1. Such reasoning indicates a complete disregard for the context. The conversation is between Jesus and the Sadducees who denied the resurrection of the *body*. Jesus said, "But as touching the resurrection of the dead..." (Matt. 22:31). The passage has nothing to do with immortal souls alleged to be in heaven.
2. If Abraham, Isaac and Jacob are alive, as the immortal soulist asserts, how does Jesus' argument prove the resurrection of the dead?
3. The essence of Jesus' argument is as follows: God is a God of living people and not of dead people, therefore the fathers Abraham, Isaac and Jacob, must one day rise from the dead.
4. Abraham, Isaac and Jacob, although heirs of the same promise, "all died in faith, not having received the promises." (Heb. 11:13, cf. vv. 8,9,39,40).

Luke 23:43

"Jesus said ... Verily I say unto thee, To day shalt thou be with me in paradise."

PROBLEM:

This passage is used principally by Evangelicals to prove the immortality of the soul and the departure of the "saved" to heaven at death.

SOLUTION:

1. This passage mentions neither souls nor heaven.
2. The thief did not request a place in heaven. He said, "Lord, remember me *when* thou comest into ["in" not "into" RSV] thy kingdom." (v. 42). The same hope was expressed by the Apostle Paul. (2 Tim. 4:1,8). The thief was not thinking of going to be with the Lord, he was requesting a place in the *future* kingdom of God.
3. Jesus answered in words that can be paraphrased: 'You ask me to remember you then, but I say unto you now...' (Luke 23:43). This repunctuation is not merely tinkering with the text. The Greek word *semeron* translated "today", "this day" is used as a term of emphasis.[4] In the following references *semeron* qualifies the preceding verb: Luke 2:11; 22:34; Acts 20:26; 26:29; 2 Cor. 3:14,15. Rotherham in his translation places the comma after "this day"[5] and there are a

---

[4] Bullinger repunctuates and comments as follows: "'And Jesus said to him, Verily, to thee I say this day, with Me shalt thou be in Paradise.' The words to-day being made solemn and emphatic." Ethelbert W. Bullinger, *A Critical Lexicon and Concordance to the English and Greek New Testament*, 8th ed., (London: Samuel Bagster and Sons Ltd., 1957, p.811).

[5] Joseph Rotherham, *The Emphasized Bible: A translation designed to set forth the exact meaning, the proper terminology, and the graphic style of the sacred original*, (Grand Rapids, Michigan: Kregel Publications, 1967).

large number of passages in the *Septuagint* translation in which the Greek construction corresponds to that of Luke 23:43: "I say unto you this day" corresponds to the emphatic, "I testify unto you this day", e.g., Deut. 6:6; 7:11; 8:1; 10:13; 11:8,13,28.

4. If the argument on repunctuation proves ineffective, the disputant can still be led to the desired conclusion by assuming that by "today", Jesus meant the thief would go to paradise the day he died. But where did the thief go that very day? (Since the thief was promised a place with Jesus, by establishing where Jesus went the day he died, it follows that the thief went to the same place.) Most will quickly assert that Jesus went to heaven. The Christadelphian need only demand proof to show that this assertion is foundationless.

5. The disputant should be pressed for an explanation to the following passages:

   a. Jesus said, "So shall the Son of man be three days and three nights in the heart of the earth." (Matt. 12:40, cf. Matt. 16:21). How could the Son of man be both in heaven and in the earth at the *same* time?

   b. Jesus after his resurrection, said, "Touch me not; for I am not yet ascended to my Father." (John 20:17).

6. Since Jesus lay dead in the grave on the day of his crucifixion, this passage offers no proof for the immortality of the soul, nor for the belief that the thief went that day to heaven. Like the Lord the thief also was in the grave. By implication, if the expression "Verily I say unto thee, today shalt thou be with me in paradise" be read as meaning the thief went with Jesus to the grave, then the grave must be paradise. Is that what the immortal soulist believes?

7. Hopefully at this stage in the discussion the merit of repunctuation will have become evident. It remains to be shown that Jesus really did answer the thief's request to be remembered in his kingdom. Paradise in Scripture is always associated with a place on earth, never in heaven. Consider the following:

   a. Those who overcome will "eat of the tree of life, which is in the midst of the paradise of God." (Rev. 2:7). The allusion to the Garden of Eden is unmistakable. The Garden of Eden (paradise) is often used to describe the paradise-like condition of the earth in the kingdom of God. (See Gen. 13:10; Isa. 51:3; Ezek. 36:35).

   b. Paradise is translated from the word *paradeisos* which Bullinger says was used by the Greeks "to describe a large pleasure-garden with trees, or park of an Eastern monarch."[6] The word itself, therefore, is descriptive of an idyllic place on earth, not in heaven.[7]

8. Jesus taught that eternal life is preceded by the resurrection and judgment of the *last* day.

   a. "For the Son of man shall come in the glory of his Father with his angels; *and then* he shall reward every man according to his works." (Matt. 16:27).

   b. Those that have done good come forth "unto the resurrection of life ... " (John 5:29). They are raised up at the "last day". (John 6:39,40,44,54).

---

[6] Ethelbert W. Bullinger, *A Critical Lexicon and Concordance to the English and Greek New Testament*, 8th ed., (London: Samuel Bagster and Sons Ltd., 1957).

[7] The *Septuagint* translation uses the Greek word *paradeisos* for the garden of Eden (e.g. Gen. 2:8).

c. The righteous go "into life eternal" after the judgment. (Matt. 25:31–46).

The thief will receive his reward, therefore, at the last day, when Christ comes in his kingdom.

John 14:2

"In my Father's house are many mansions… "

PROBLEM:

The "many mansions" are understood to refer to a dwelling place in heaven to which the righteous depart at death.

SOLUTION:

1. The passage teaches nothing of the kind. Every reference to God's house in Scripture is to His house *on the earth*. See John 2:16; 2 Kings 20:5; Micah 4, esp. vv. 1,2. It is a false assumption to read into this passage that the Father's house is in heaven.

2. The passage does not refer to literal mansions in the ordinary sense of the word as understood today, for a mansion is larger than a house. How then can one have mansions in a house? The simple solution is that the house referred to is a spiritual house. Consider the following passages:

   a. "Ye also, as lively stones, are built up a spiritual house, an holy priesthood, to offer up spiritual sacrifices, acceptable to God by Jesus Christ." (1 Pet. 2:5).

   b. "Him that overcometh will I make a pillar in the temple of my God, and he shall go no more out: and I will write upon him the name of my God…" (Rev. 3:12). "And Moses verily was faithful in all his house, as a servant, for a testimony of those things which were to be spoken after; but Christ as a son over his own house [God's house, RSV]; whose house are we, if we hold fast the confidence and the rejoicing of the hope firm unto the end." (Heb. 3:5,6).

   c. "Ye…are built upon the foundation of the apostles and prophets, Jesus Christ himself being the chief corner stone; in whom all the building fitly framed together groweth unto an holy temple in the Lord: in whom ye also are builded together for an habitation of God through the Spirit." (Eph. 2:19–22).

   God's house is a spiritual one in which are many abiding places.[8]

3. Heaven is not an unprepared place. It is the Father's throne (Psa. 115:16; Matt. 5:34) where His will is done. (Matt. 6:10). Christ is preparing a place for his followers by his high priestly mediation in the house of God. (Heb. 3:1–6). Under God, he is building the house of believers, preparing the stones for right and left-hand places of honour in his kingdom; God being judge of their

---

[8] The Greek word translated "mansions" is *mone* and means "abode" or "abiding place." Robert Young, *Analytical Concordance to the Holy Bible*, 8th ed. (London: Lutterworth Press, 1965). *Mone* is translated "abode" in John 14:23, and translated "abiding places" in John 14:2 RV.

191

worthiness. Jesus said to the mother of Zebedee's children: "To sit on my right hand, and on my left, is not mine to give, but it shall be given to them for whom it is *prepared* of my Father." (Matt. 20:23).

4. If Christ's disciples went to heaven at death, then Christ's assurance, "I will come again, and receive you unto myself" would be a separation and not a reunion. (John 14:3).

5. Some have mistakenly interpreted the "going away" to refer to Christ's crucifixion, and the "coming again" to his resurrection. The correct interpretation is that Christ was going away to his Father, and would come again to the earth.[9] This can be shown from the following:

   a. Jesus said, "...and as I said unto the Jews, Whither I go, ye cannot come; so now say I to you." (John 13:33). Earlier Jesus had said to the Jews: "Yet a little while am I with you, and then I go unto him that sent me. Ye shall seek me, and shall not find me: and where I am, thither ye cannot come." (John 7:33,34). See also John 8:21. Since God is in heaven (Matt. 6:9), Jesus must have been referring to his going away to heaven.

   b. In John 14:12, Jesus said, "I go unto my Father."

   c. Also in John 14:28, Jesus said, "I go unto the Father."

6. "I will come again and receive you unto myself" is interpreted by Evangelicals to mean that Christ comes to gather the saints together and take them to heaven. But nowhere is his reign spoken of as being in heaven. See Luke 1:32,33; cf. Dan. 2:44; Psa. 2:6 and Isa. 2:3.

7. It is sometimes pointed out that Jesus said to Peter, "Whither I go, thou canst not follow me now; but thou shalt follow me afterwards." (John 13:36). From this verse it is implied that Peter at his death would follow Christ to heaven. Two points require stressing;

   a. Peter was promised a place on the earth, not in heaven. "Then answered Peter and said unto him, Behold, we have forsaken all, and followed thee; what shall we have therefore? And Jesus said unto them...when the Son of man shall sit in the throne of his glory, ye also shall sit upon twelve thrones, judging the twelve tribes of Israel." (Matt. 19:27,28). Jesus will sit in his throne at Jerusalem (Luke 1:32,33) when he returns. (See also Matt. 25:31,32).

   b. Jesus did not make contradictory assertions within the short space of four verses. It is known what John 13:36 does not mean. It does not mean that Peter would go to heaven. What does it mean? That Peter would follow his Master's death. Jesus told Peter what death he was to die. (John 21:18,19).

---

[9] The allusion in John 14:1–3 appears to be that of the high priest's atonement for the sin of the people (Lev. 9). Likewise, Jesus must first offer the sacrifice, then present it in the divine presence and in due course come forth to bless the people in the name of the Lord. (Heb. 9:28). The literal going away requires a literal return.

2 Corinthians 5:8

"We are confident, I say, and willing rather to be absent from the body, and to be present with the Lord."

PROBLEM:

This passage is a standard proof text, used by Evangelicals to prove that Paul's desire was to leave behind his mortal body and for his soul or spirit to depart to be with Christ in heaven. The inference is drawn that all the saved will go to be with their Lord in heaven.

SOLUTION:

1. This passage is usually misquoted to read, 'to be absent from the body is to be present with the Lord.' What the apostle says is that he is "willing rather to be absent from the body and to be present with the Lord." The former reading assumes an instantaneous transition from death to be with Christ; the latter allows for the interval of "sleep" in the grave, resurrection and judgment. The following passages indicate the teaching of the Apostle Paul:

    a. Sleep of death—1 Cor. 15:6,18,20,51 (cf. Dan. 12:2); 1 Thess. 4:13,14.

    b. Resurrection and judgment—2 Tim. 4:1,8; 2 Cor. 4:14, cf. 5:10.

2. To be "unclothed" does not mean to leave behind the mortal body and depart as an immortal soul or spirit. If it did, Paul would have desired to be "unclothed". But he says, "not for that we would be unclothed, but *clothed* upon, that mortality might be swallowed up of life." (v. 4).

3. Verse 10 needs forthright emphasis: "For we must all appear before the judgment seat of Christ; that every one may receive the things done in his *body* according to that he hath done, whether it be good or bad." Appropriate questions can be advanced on the basis of this verse. For example:

    a. When does Scripture teach that believers must appear before the Judgment Seat?

    b. What will faithful believers receive after judgment?

4. It requires stressing that an exposition of this passage must be in line with other statements of the apostle in his epistles. This is a safe guide to follow since the Apostle Paul speaks of "things in which are some things hard to be understood, which they that are unlearned and unstable wrest, as they do also the other scriptures, unto their own destruction." (2 Pet. 3:16).

5. 2 Cor. 5:1 provides the contrasts between "our earthly house of this tabernacle" which can be dissolved (temporary mortality) and "a building of God, an house not made with hands, eternal in the heavens" (the permanent immortality reserved with Christ, but to be brought at his return).[10]

6. Verses 2–4 indicate that the interpretation of verse 1 is the correct one. Note the following:

---

[10] See, for example, 1 Pet. 1:4,5; 2 Tim. 4:8, cf. 4:1; Col. 3:3.

a. "For we that are in this tabernacle do groan." (v. 4). Paul groaned for the redemption of the body. "Even we ourselves groan within ourselves, *waiting for* the adoption, to wit, the redemption of our body." (Rom. 8:23, cf. 2 Cor. 4:14). But when does the redemption of the body take place? Not at death, for at death the body undergoes the very opposite of the process of "redemption". Not until the resurrection is the body raised to incorruption. (1 Cor. 15:53–55).

b. "Not for that we would be unclothed, but clothed upon, that mortality might be swallowed up of life." (v. 4). The Apostle Paul contrasts two states, mortality and life (in 1 Cor. 15:44 he calls the two states "a natural body" and "a spiritual body"), but he never desires disembodiment. "Mortality...swallowed up of life" (2 Cor. 5:4) is synonymous with his earlier words: "We shall all be changed, in a moment, in the twinkling of an eye, at the *last trump*...for this corruptible must *put on* incorruption, and this mortal must *put on* immortality." (1 Cor. 15:51–53).

7. The apostle's manifest desire to be "absent from the body, and to be present with the Lord" was a desire to be free from the imperfections of mortality (e.g., 2 Cor. 4:16–18) and to be with Christ in an immortal nature. The apostle expresses this hope elsewhere. For example:

a. "Our commonwealth is in heaven, and from it we await a Saviour, the Lord Jesus Christ, who will change our lowly body to be like his glorious body..." (Phil. 3:20,21 RSV).

b. "Now this I say, brethren, that flesh and blood [i.e., mortality] cannot inherit the kingdom of God; neither doth corruption inherit incorruption." (1 Cor. 15:50, cf. 1 Cor. 15:19–22).

2 Corinthians 12:2–4

"Caught up to the third heaven...caught up into paradise, and heard unspeakable words, which it is not lawful for a man to utter."

PROBLEM:

This passage is pressed into service by Evangelicals for the following reasons:

a. Since Paul's friend could exist without body, this proves that the real person is not the body, but the immortal soul within the body.

b. Since Paul's friend was taken to be with his Lord in paradise (heaven), this implies that all the saved go to be with their Lord at death.

SOLUTION:

1. Paul said that he wasn't sure if the man he knew was in the body or out of the body. (vv. 2,3). If the inspired apostle didn't know for certain, how can this reference be cited to *prove* that one can, in fact, exist outside his body?

2. Two assumptions advanced in the problem require proof. These are as follows:

a. It is assumed that the man Paul knew died; the passage does not say so.[11] Until it is proven that he did die, there is no warrant for the sweeping generalisation that the souls of any righteous dead persons go to heaven.

b. It is assumed that to be in the third heaven is to be "with the Lord". Until it is proven that to be in the third heaven is to be with the Lord, there is no warrant for asserting that the man Paul knew, or any, go "to be with their Lord" at the instant of death.

3. The contextual evidence strongly suggests that the man Paul knew was none other than Paul himself. Consider the evidence:

a. The apostle says, "And lest I should be exalted above measure through the abundance of the revelations, there was given to me a thorn in the flesh, the messenger of Satan to buffet me, lest I should be exalted above measure." (v. 7). If the visions and revelations which occupy the preceding verses were those of the man Paul knew (and not Paul himself) why should the apostle be chastened lest *he* be exalted above measure? Surely the concern ought to be for the recipient of the visions and revelations.

b. The Apostle Paul claims: "I am become a fool in glorying; ye have compelled me: for I ought to have been commended of you: for in nothing am I behind the very chiefest apostles, though I be nothing." (v. 11). Such a comment is entirely appropriate if the subject of the glorying (v. 1) has been Paul. It is difficult to see how such a comment follows from a consideration of the glory of a person other than Paul.

c. Paul's authority was being undermined in Corinth. (2 Cor. 10:10,11; 11:4,12–15). Even the ecclesia had demanded proof that Christ was speaking in him. (2 Cor. 13:3). The apostle vindicates his rightful position in the following ways:

i. By an open attack on the adversaries. (2 Cor. 10:11,12; 11:4,5,13).

ii. By challenging the ecclesia to demonstrate his lack of integrity. (2 Cor. 11:7).

iii. By becoming a "fool" (2 Cor. 11:1,17; 12:11) in boasting of his accomplishments as a disciple. (2 Cor. 11:21–29).

iv. By citing personal acts of divine favour. (2 Cor. 11:30–33).

v. By recounting his personal privilege and glory in receiving visions and revelations. (2 Cor. 12:1–4).

It can be seen that if the man Paul knew was none other than Paul himself, then the appeal to visions and revelations is an integral part of the apostle's argument. It is difficult to see how the experiences of glory of any other person would complement Paul's argument vindicating his authority in the Corinthian ecclesia.

---

[11] Some Evangelicals, like the Gospel Hall, teach that the man Paul knew was Paul himself, but they speculate that the visions were received when he died by stoning at Lystra. The record in Acts does not state that Paul actually died—"having stoned Paul, drew him out of the city, *supposing* he had been dead." (Acts 14:19). If the apostle were the victim of stoning to death, then it is certain that he did not receive any visions at this time since the "dead know not anything." (Eccl. 9:5, cf. Psa. 146:3,4).

WRESTED SCRIPTURES

4. "Whether in the body, or out of the body, I cannot tell: God knoweth." (vv. 2,3). Various interpretations of these words have been proposed. The following one has the advantage of fitting the context: Paul did not know for certain whether he was transported to participate objectively in the visions and revelations, as did Daniel (Dan. 10), or whether his experience was subjective, as was Peter's vision of the sheet let down from heaven. (Acts 10:10,11,17). Later, when Peter was led out of prison by an angel he "wist not that it was true which was done by the angel; but thought he saw a vision." (Acts 12:9). Peter thought his objective experience might only be subjective—that what was actually occurring might only be transpiring in his mind. When Peter was "come to himself, he said, Now I know of a surety..." (Acts 12:11). Similarly, Paul was unable to know for certain whether he was in the body (actually participating) or out of the body (whether the events transpired only in a vision in the mind).

5. The Greek verb *harpazo,* translated "caught up", does not denote direction. It can be translated, "caught away".[12]

6. Paradise[13] is descriptive, not of a place in heaven, but on the earth. The following passages show this:

   a. Luke 23:43—the thief requested a place in the kingdom. (Luke 23:42). But the kingdom is to be on the earth. (Dan. 2:44; 7:27).

   b. Rev. 2:7—A symbolic allusion to the Garden of Eden.

   c. The Septuagint translation uses the word *paradeisos* for the Garden of Eden. See Gen. 2:8; cf. also Ezek. 28:13; 36:35.

Since Paul says that the man he knew was caught away to the third heaven (v. 2) and caught away to paradise (v. 4) it can be inferred that the two locations are synonymous. Since it is known that paradise refers either to the Garden of Eden or to paradise-like conditions on the earth, by implication it is also known that the third heaven refers to the same thing. The word "heavens" is used figuratively elsewhere in Scripture. See 2 Pet. 3:13, cf. Isa. 65:17.

Colossians 1:5
"For the hope which is laid up for you in heaven..."

PROBLEM:

This passage is cited by Evangelicals and Pentecostals to support their belief that heaven is the promised place of reward for the righteous.

---

[12] *Harpazo*, the verb translated "caught up", means to "snatch away". Robert Young, *Analytical Concordance to the Holy Bible*, 8th ed., (London: Lutterworth Press, 1965). Bullinger comments: "In 2 Cor. 12:4 the verb is... 'catch away', not, 'up'." Ethelbert W. Bullinger, *A Critical Lexicon and Concordance to the English and Greek New Testament*, 8th ed., (London: Samuel Bagster and Sons Ltd., 1957), p.569. See the use of the same verb, "to pluck", for example, in John 10:28,29.

[13] This conclusion is further borne out by the meaning of the word "paradise". *Paradeisos*, the Greek word translated "paradise", means "a park, garden ground". Robert Young, *Analytical Concordance to the Holy Bible*, 8th ed., (London: Lutterworth Press, 1965).

SOLUTION:

1. The passage does not say that believers go to heaven, it only asserts that the believer's hope is *laid up* in heaven.
2. What is the hope which is laid up for believers in heaven? It is immortality which Christ will give to the faithful at their resurrection in the last day and his return. Consider the evidence:
   a. The "hope which is laid up for you in heaven" is the "hope of the gospel" (v. 23), "the hope of glory" (Col. 1:27), "For ye are dead [i.e., to sin], and your life is hid with Christ in God. When Christ, who is our life, shall appear, then shall ye also appear with him in glory." (Col. 3:3,4).
   b. Paul elsewhere identifies this hope with the resurrection:
      i. "Even we ourselves groan within ourselves, waiting for the adoption, to wit, the redemption of our body. For we are saved by hope...But if we hope for that we see not, then do we with patience wait for it." (Rom. 8:23–25). See also 1 Cor. 15:19–22; Titus 1:2; 2:13; 3:7; 1 John 3:2,3.
      ii. "But this I confess...believing all things which are written in the law and in the prophets: and have hope toward God...that there shall be a resurrection of the dead, both of the just and unjust." (Acts 24:14,15, cf. Acts 23:6).
3. The "lively hope" in "an inheritance incorruptible, and undefiled, and that fadeth not away, *reserved* in heaven for you, who are kept by the power of God through faith unto salvation ready to be revealed in the *last time*." (1 Pet. 1:4,5). The "last time" is a Scriptural expression for the period when "the Son of man shall come in the glory of his Father with his angels; and *then* he shall reward every man according to his works." (Matt. 16:27, cf. 2 Cor. 5:10; John 6:39,40,44,54).
4. The hope of the believer is with the Saviour, Jesus Christ in heaven. (1 Tim. 1:1). But the believer is not going to heaven to see his hope fulfilled. The Scriptures make it clear that the hope (i.e., eternal life) is brought with Christ when he returns. Unto those who look for him, he shall "appear the second time without sin unto salvation." (Heb. 9:28).

Philippians 1:21–23

"For to me to live is Christ, and to die is gain...I am in a strait betwixt two, having a desire to depart, and to be with Christ; which is far better."

PROBLEM:

This passage is a stock proof text of Evangelicals. It is argued that since death for Paul would be gain, he was not thinking of sleep in the grave but rather of departure of the soul or spirit to be with his Lord. It is inferred that all the saved have the same expectation of being with the Lord at the instant of death.

WRESTED SCRIPTURES

SOLUTION:

1. It is mistakenly assumed by such expositors that "to depart" means to be *immediately* with Christ. Evangelicals should be pressed hard for justification of this assumption. Elsewhere in the same letter the Apostle Paul indicated where his hope lay for being in the presence of the Lord. This was in the return of Christ and the resurrection. Note the following passages:

   a. "Until the day of Jesus Christ." (Phil. 1:6,10; 2:16).

   b. "If by any means I might attain unto the resurrection of the dead." (Phil. 3:11).

   c. "We look for the Saviour, the Lord Jesus Christ: who shall change our vile body, that it may be fashioned like unto his glorious body…" (Phil. 3:20,21).

2. Peter, referring to the letters of the Apostle Paul, said that there were "some things hard to be understood, which they that are unlearned and unstable wrest, as they do also the other scriptures, unto their own destruction." (2 Pet. 3:16). It is a wise guide to follow therefore, in interpreting a disputed passage, to consult the other writings of the Apostle Paul. When did the apostle expect to be with Christ? At the return of Christ following resurrection and judgment. Consider the following evidence:

   a. "Knowing that he which raised up the Lord Jesus shall raise up us also by Jesus, and shall present us with you." (2 Cor. 4:14).

   b. "We must all appear before the judgment seat of Christ." (2 Cor. 5:10).

   c. "Henceforth there is *laid up* for me a crown of righteousness, which the Lord, the righteous judge, shall give me at that day: and not to me only, but unto all them also that love his appearing." (2 Tim. 4:8, cf. 4:1).

3. The time sequence must be capable of Scriptural verification. Paul did not look for an instantaneous arrival into the presence of Christ. The apostle knew he would "sleep" as other saints until the Resurrection Day,[14] (1 Cor. 15:51–53), unless his Master returned while he was still alive. (1 Cor. 15:6,18,20,51; 1 Thess. 4:13,14, cf. Dan 12:2,3).

4. In what sense would "to depart" (to die) be gain? In the death state "the dead know not anything." (Eccl. 9:5, cf. 3:20). The apostle would, therefore, have relief from his suffering. (2 Cor. 11:23–28). He realised, however, for the sake of the work he could do among the Philippians it would be better to "abide in the flesh" (i.e., to continue to live). (Phil. 1:24–26).

5. There is another possibility. Paul was in a strait between wanting to die (and escape the severe tribulations of his life; see 2 Cor 11:23–33) and wanting to live (to carry on his ministry). But more than either of these he had a desire "to depart, and to be with Christ; which is far better" [i.e. better than life or death]. The word "depart" in the Greek is literally "the departing". The words [Gk. *to analusai*] denote "the loosing again" or "the returning" as in the *Emphatic*

---

[14] This explains the juxtapositioning of "depart", and "to be with Christ". From the point of view of the Apostle Paul, the next conscious moment after his departure would be the resurrection and judgment seat of Christ. After this he would "ever be with the Lord." (1 Thess. 4:17).

Diaglott. More than life or death, he desired the return of Jesus when he would be with the Lord in his kingdom.

Philippians 3:20

"For our conversation is in heaven…"

PROBLEM:

It is noted by Evangelicals that "conversation"[15] is more accurately translated "citizenship". It is then argued that the real person (i.e., the immortal soul) must belong in heaven, its homeland, where it returns at the death of the body.

SOLUTION:

1. The apostle is silent about souls leaving the body and departing to heaven at death. His hope is the resurrection of the dead at the return of Christ. Note the context:

    a. "If by any means I might attain unto the resurrection of the dead." (Phil. 3:11).

    b. "For our conversation is in heaven; from whence also we look for the Saviour, the Lord Jesus Christ: who shall change our vile body, that it may be fashioned like unto his glorious body…" (Phil. 3:20,21).

2. In what sense is the believer's citizenship in heaven? Philippi was a colony of the Roman Empire. On Paul's second journey his company landed at Neapolis, "and from thence to Philippi, which is the chief city of that part of Macedonia, and a colony[16]…" (Acts 16:12). A Roman colony was a miniature Rome, a reproduction and outpost of the city.[17] The Roman citizens attempted to reproduce the life and customs of Rome. Their citizenship and commonwealth was in Rome. This background information forms the basis of Paul's instruction. He says, "Let your conversation [literally, citizen life] be as it becometh the gospel of Christ." (Phil. 1:27). The citizen life to which the apostle refers is not that of Rome but of a higher relationship. Philippian believers had become "fellow-citizens with the saints, and of the household of God." (Eph. 2:19). Paul contrasts those whose interests are fixed on the earth (Phil. 3:19) with those whose citizenship is in heaven. (Phil. 3:20). Just as the Philippian colonist was a part of an outpost of Rome, so the believer looked to heaven as the centre of his government from whence would come the Saviour,

---

[15] "Conversation" as the word is used today, means "speech", "talk". This specialised use of the word is different from its meaning at the time of the King James translators (1611). The word then meant "behaviour". The Greek word, *politeuma*, translated "conversation" in the AV means "commonwealth" (RSV) or "citizenship" (RV).

[16] A colony of the Roman Empire, like Philippi, was only a city and not a country as were the colonies of Great Britain.

[17] See Dictionary of the Bible, James Hastings ed., (New York: Charles Scribner's Sons, 1963), p.763.

the Lord Jesus Christ. (Phil. 3:20). Ecclesial and individual life were therefore to be patterned after the heavenly, not after Rome.[18]

1 Thessalonians 4:17

"Caught up...in the clouds, to meet the Lord in the air: and so shall we ever be with the Lord."

PROBLEM:

This passage is the foundation text for the Evangelical doctrine of the "rapture of the church", i.e., that at the second coming, Christ will gather the saints together, take them to heaven, and rule *over*, but not on the earth.

SOLUTION:

1. Nowhere does this pasage state that the saints are taken to heaven. The evidence is the other way, since "the Lord shall descend *from* heaven" (v. 16).
2. "And so shall we ever be with the Lord." Where? On the earth, not in heaven. This is the testimony of the Apostle Paul elsewhere in his writings. (Rom. 4:13, cf. Gen. 13:15 and Gal. 3:27–29) and the teaching of scores of Biblical references (e.g., Dan. 7:18–27 esp. verse 27; Psa. 37:11,22,29; Matt. 5:5; Rev. 5:10.)
3. Even if the passage be taken literally, the meeting of the Lord and the saints is said to be in the air. But the air extends upwards for 600 miles (a generous estimate). Are the saints to spend eternity suspended in mid-air? If it is contended that the saints only meet the Lord and are then taken up to heaven, then proof that such is the case is required. It does not come from this passage.
4. The Greek word, *harpazo* translated "caught up" does not in itself denote direction (either up or down). It simply means, "to snatch away."[19] Its usage is illustrated in the following references where the same verb occurs:
   a. "The spirit of the Lord *caught away* Philip." (Acts 8:39).
   b. "The wolf *catcheth* them, and scattereth the sheep." (John 10:12).
   c. "No man is able to *pluck* them out of my Father's hand." (John 10:29).
5. What is meant by "the clouds"? Three possibilities exist. These are as follows:
   a. The saints are caught away in literal clouds. Jesus was taken from the disciples' gaze by a cloud. (Acts 1:9). He will return with the same literal clouds. See Rev. 1:7, cf. Dan. 7:13; Matt. 24:30.

---

[18] Believers were commanded by Jesus to "be ye therefore perfect, even as your Father which is in heaven is perfect." (Matt. 5:48). The disciples were instructed to pray for the kingdom to come that God's will might be done on earth as it is in heaven. (Matt. 6:10). In so doing, believers were "outposts" of heaven. Moffatt, in his translation paraphrases Phil. 3:20—"We are a colony of heaven."

[19] Robert Young, *Analytical Concordance to the Holy Bible*, 8th ed., (London: Lutterworth Press, 1965). Bullinger comments: "To snatch away, to carry off (suddenly and by force) esp., of wild beasts." Ethelbert Bullinger, *A Critical Lexicon and Concordance to the English and Greek Testament*, 8th ed., (London: Samuel Bagster and Sons Ltd., 1957) p.138.

b. The clouds refer to large numbers of saints. The Greek text does not contain the definite article. The passage reads, therefore: "Then we which are alive and remain shall be caught away in clouds" (i.e., clouds of saints). Support for this interpretation is found in Heb. 12:1 where a similar image is used: "Wherefore seeing we also are compassed about with so great a cloud of witnesses … " (i.e., the faithful listed in Heb. 11). Saints are compared with the innumerable water droplets comprising a great cloud. Some have seen the further image of the saints being exhaled from the sea of nations by the powerful beams of the Sun of Righteousness.

c. The clouds are those of divine glory, indicating the divine presence. It is stated in Matt 24:30 that the Son of man will come "in the clouds of heaven with power and great glory", but it is not certain that the great glory refers to the clouds of heaven. One disadvantage with this interpretation is that the divine cloud is invariably one cloud.[20] The word "clouds" in 1 Thess. 4:17 is plural. It was *the* cloud which covered Mt. Sinai (Exo. 34:5) and guided Israel during the wilderness journeyings. (Exo. 13:21; 14:19). Similarly, it was *the* cloud of glory which filled the Tabernacle (Num. 9:15,16) and the Temple of Solomon (1 Kings 8:11).

Hebrews 11:5

"By faith Enoch was translated that he should not see death…"

PROBLEM:

This passage is cited to prove that the souls of the righteous depart to heaven at the instant of the death of the body.

SOLUTION:

1. It is difficult to see how this passage can prove either that man has an immortal soul, or that at death the soul departs to heaven. The passage mentions neither souls nor heaven.
2. Enoch was translated that he might not see death, but how can his experience be cited as proof for what will happen to those who have died, or will die?
3. It is probable, but not certain, that Enoch is dead. Consider the evidence:
   a. The writer to the Hebrews includes Enoch[21] when he says, "These all died in faith, not having received the promises…" (Heb. 11:13).
   b. "Death reigned from Adam to Moses." (Rom. 5:14). No exceptions are noted in the context to this categorical assertion of the kingship of death.
4. Enoch did not ascend to heaven—the dwelling place of God, since it is expressly stated: "No man hath ascended up to heaven". (John 3:13).

[20] The parallel passage in Luke 21:27 reads: "And they shall see the Son of man coming in *a* cloud with power and great glory."

[21] It might be argued that Enoch merits exception because of the specific statement earlier in the chapter that he was "translated that he should not see death". (v. 5).

5. Enoch is an example of the unknown in Scripture. It is not known for certain in what way he was "translated" or changed. Neither is it known where he went, when God took him. (Gen. 5:24). Only the hard-pressed will resort to this passage to prove either the immortality of the soul or heaven the home of the righteous. The exhortation of Deut. 29:29 is appropriate: "The secret things belong unto the LORD our God: but those things which are revealed belong unto us..."[22]

2 Peter 3:10

"...the elements shall melt with fervent heat, the earth also and the works that are therein shall be burned up."

PROBLEM:

It is argued that since the earth is to be destroyed by fire, the future inheritance of the righteous must be in heaven, and not on the earth.

SOLUTION:

1. Peter states that "the heavens being on fire shall be dissolved." (v. 12). Are those who argue for the literal burning up of the earth prepared to allow the literal dissolution of the heavens? What in the literal heavens is burnable?

2. The literal earth will not be destroyed. This is proven from Peter's quotation from Isa. 65:17 and Isa. 66:22. The "new heavens and a new earth, wherein dwelleth righteousness" (2 Pet. 3:13) is portrayed in Isaiah as a time on the earth when Jerusalem will be a rejoicing and the nature of the animals changed. (Isa. 65:18–25). The prophecy requires the continued existence of the earth.

3. The "heavens" and "earth" (2 Pet. 3:10,12) is figurative for a constitution or order on the earth. This is also proven by Peter's quotation from Isa. 65:17. Since the new heavens and earth is the creation of "Jerusalem a rejoicing, and her people a joy" in which "they shall not hurt nor destroy in all my holy mountain" (Isa. 65:18–25), the heavens and earth which are destroyed must be prior constitutions or orders on the earth which are removed for the establishment of the new.

4. Peter says that the "world"[23] in the days of Noah perished. (2 Pet. 3:6). The literal earth or "world" did not perish, only the "everything living" (RSV) of

---

[22] One possibility arises from the fact that Enoch was "the seventh from Adam" in the line of Seth (Jude 14). Jude also (v. 15) describes the way in which Enoch severely rebuked the ungodly of his day. In Genesis 4 we read of the ungodly attitude of Lamech who was the seventh from Adam in the line of wicked Cain. He boasts to his wives, "I will slay a man for wounding me, and a young man for bruising me..." (Gen. 4:23 RV margin). Since Enoch and Lamech were contemporary it may well be that Enoch was the man who wounded Lamech by severely rebuking him for his ungodliness. Lamech planned to slay Enoch but God removed him from the scene—"He was not, for God took him" (Gen. 5:24).

[23] The Greek word *kosmos* translated "world" literally means "order, i.e., regular disposition and arrangement." Ethelbert W. Bullinger, *A Critical Lexicon and Concordance to the English and Greek Testament*, (London: Samuel Bagster and Sons Ltd., 1957), p.900.

Gen. 7:21 perished. Similarly, "I will destroy them with the earth" (Gen. 6:13) did not mean the literal destruction of the planet, but only the wicked order of things on the earth.

5. The burning up of the earth is an Old Testament expression for the destruction of a wicked order, but not the literal earth. Consider the following:

   a. "...my determination is to gather the nations, that I may assemble the kingdoms, to pour upon them mine indignation, even all my fierce anger: for all the earth shall be devoured with the fire of my jealousy." (Zeph. 3:8). The prophet continues, however, to tell of the day when the people would speak a pure language and "from beyond the rivers of Ethiopia my suppliants, even the daughter of my dispersed, shall bring mine offering." (Zeph. 3:9,10).

   b. "And the mountains shall be molten under him, and the valleys shall be cleft, as wax before the fire..." (Micah 1:4). The prophet continues, however, to speak about the day when the law of the LORD would go forth from Zion and Jerusalem. (Micah 4:1,2).

6. Rather than being destroyed in a great conflagration, the earth is to become filled with the glory of the Lord. (Num. 14:21; Hab. 2:14; cf. Eccl. 1:4; Isa. 45:18).

Revelation 5:10

"...we shall reign on the earth."

PROBLEM:

This verse is translated "over" rather than "on" by the Plymouth Brethren, and the Jehovah's Witnesses, in an attempt to evade the difficulty of having the righteous live and reign on the earth.

SOLUTION:

1. The JW *Kingdom Interlinear Translation*[24] at this place has, "they are reigning upon the earth" in the literal interlinear column, but changes it to "they are to rule over the earth" in the *New World Translation* column. In six other places in Revelation, which do not impinge on the location of the kingdom, the identical phrase in both the *Interlinear* and the *New World Translation* columns is translated "on the earth" or "upon the earth", but not "over the earth" as though suggesting remote control. (See Rev. 6:10; 7:1; 11:10; 13:14; 14:6; 17:8).

2. Even if "over" were the correct translation, it is said that the Queen reigns *over* the United Kingdom without suggesting that she reigns *above* it.

---

[24] *Kingdom Interlinear Translation of the Greek Scriptures...together with the New World Translation of the Christian Greek Scriptures*, (Brooklyn, NY: Watch Tower Bible and Tract Society, 1969).

2.3

HELL—PLACE OF TORMENT

Matthew 25:46

"And these shall go away into everlasting punishment."

PROBLEM:

This passage is used to prove the eternal torment of the wicked. It is argued that since the same Greek word, *aionios* is used for the duration of life for the righteous as for the punishment of the wicked, therefore the wicked are subject to eternal torment.

SOLUTION:

1. The punishment is everlasting, but it is not conscious eternal torment. The punishment will be final and complete cutting off. (Psa. 37:9,34). Life eternal is reserved for the righteous, but the wicked are to die "the second death" (Rev. 21:8) which in Scriptural terms means to be without thoughts. (Psa. 146:3,4; Eccl. 9:5). The word "everlasting" is used of a *result*, not a process. Similarly, "eternal judgment" (Heb. 6:2) and "eternal redemption" (Heb. 9:12) do not mean that judgment and redemption will continue throughout eternity, but rather that their results are eternal.

2. The wicked are to suffer torment at the Judgment Day (Matt. 8:12; 13:30,40–42,49,50; Luke 12:47,48), but this is not eternal torment. Other Scriptures either state or imply a termination of the torment. For example:

   a. Speaking of those who "know not God, and that obey not the gospel of our Lord Jesus Christ", the Apostle Paul states that they "shall be punished with *everlasting destruction* from the presence of the Lord, and from the glory of his power." (2 Thess. 1:9).

   b. Jesus stated that "if a man abide not in me, he is cast forth as a branch, and is withered; and men gather them, and cast them into the fire, and they are burned." (John 15:6). To be "cast forth as a branch" and "burned" suggests termination of the burning when that which is burnable is consumed.

   c. "And many of them that sleep in the dust of the earth shall awake…to shame and everlasting contempt." (Dan. 12:2, cf. John 5:29). It is the contempt or damnation which is everlasting, not the conscious torment.

3. Even if by "everlasting punishment" is meant "everlasting conscious torment", this passage in itself does not prove the eternal torment of the wicked since the Greek word, *aionios*, can mean either limited or unlimited duration.[1] Although the New Testament nearly always uses *aionios* with the meaning of unlimited

---

[1] *Aionios* means 'age-lasting', Robert Young, *Analytical Concordance to the Holy Bible*, (London: Lutterworth Press, 1965).

duration,[2] there are a number of occurrences in the Septuagint[3] (where the Hebrew equivalent *olam* is translated *aionios*) in which a limited duration is obviously intended. For example:

a. "The lasting [*aionios*] hills"; "The eternal God is thy refuge, and underneath are the everlasting [aionios] arms." (Deut. 33:15,27). The intended meaning of *aionios* is limited duration in the first reference whereas in the same chapter the second reference is to unlimited duration.

b. The Aaronic priesthood is termed, "an everlasting [*aionios*] priesthood throughout their generations." (Exo. 40:15). Limited duration is intended in this reference since the Aaronic priesthood was later to change (Heb. 7:12) when that which "waxed old" was ready to "vanish away". (Heb. 8:13).

c. See also Gen. 49:26; Exo. 12:17; 21:6; Jonah 2:6; Hab. 3:6 ("perpetual hills" = *aionios* hills).

4. Many passages in Scripture teach that eternal life is the reward for the righteous (e.g. Luke 20:35,36). There are also many passages which teach that the ungodly and wicked will be destroyed or perish (e.g., 1 Thess. 4:13, cf. John 3:16; 2 Thess. 1:9). It is not therefore, merely an arbitrary decision to choose endless duration for *aionios* life of the righteous and limited duration for *aionios* punishment of the wicked. The decision has been based on the use of the Greek word elsewhere in Scripture and the teaching of other passages on the respective rewards of the righteous and wicked.

5. The word "punishment" is translated from the Greek word, *kolasis* which means 'a pruning'. It comes from the verb, *kolazo* which means "to curtail, dock, prune, but usually like Lat., *castigare,* to keep within bounds, check, chastise."[4] This denotation is in complete harmony with the Scriptural teaching on the punishment of the wicked. Jesus said that the wicked would be cast like branches into the fire. (John 15:6). The Psalmist said they would be "cut off" (Psa. 37:9) and "shall not be". (Psa. 37:10). Malachi states that the wicked will be burnt like stubble leaving them "neither root nor branch" (Mal. 4:1), like "ashes" to be trodden under foot. (Mal. 4:3). This is not the kind of language one would associate with immortal souls in torment for eternity.

Mark 9:43–48

"The fire is not quenched."

---

[2] Two NT passages should be noted: The "eternal fire" (Gk. *aionios*) which consumed Sodom and Gomorrha (Jude 7) is not now burning (cf. Lam. 4:6; 2 Pet. 2:6; Deut. 29:23). Similarly, Philemon is instructed to receive Onesimus "for ever" (Gk. *aionios*). (Philemon 15).

[3] In the 3rd century BC, the Greek king Ptolemy of Egypt commissioned the translation of the Hebrew Scriptures into Greek. This translation is now known as the "LXX" or the *Septuagint* Version.

[4] Ethelbert S. Bullinger, *A Critical Lexicon and Concordance to the English and Greek Testament,* (London: Samuel Bagster and Sons Ltd., 1957), p.612. *Kolasis* is translated "torment" in 1 John 4:18 and "torment" is one of the meanings given for *kolasis* in James Strong, *Strong's Exhaustive Concordance of the Bible,* (New York: Abington Press, 1951).

WRESTED SCRIPTURES

PROBLEM:

This passage is argued vigorously by Holiness-Fire Pentecostals and other Evangelical bodies as positive proof that the souls of the wicked will spend eternity suffering the torment of hell-fire.

SOLUTION:

1. Pentecostals insist on taking "the fire is not quenched" literally, but what about "where their worm dieth not"? Are there immortal worms in hell? Similarly, is one to take literally the cutting off of hand (v. 43), foot (v. 45) and the plucking out of one's eye (v. 47)?

2. Jesus is almost certainly quoting from Isa. 66:24: "And they shall go forth, and look upon the carcases of the men that have transgressed against me: for their worm shall not die, neither shall their fire be quenched; and they shall be an abhorring unto all flesh." But this unquenchable fire is not the hell-fire of Pentecostal teaching. Note the differences:

   a. The fire is located outside Jerusalem in Israel. (Isa. 66:20). This is not the location of the hell-fire of Pentecostal and Evangelical teaching.

   b. Travellers will observe the *carcasses* of the men that have transgressed against God. Pentecostal teaching consigns souls, not bodies, to hell.

3. The Greek word, *Gehenna* translated "hell" comes from the Hebrew, *Ghi Hinnom*,[5] the name of the valley to the south of Jerusalem[6] where the kings Ahaz and Manasseh offered their sons to the god Molech. (2 Chron. 28:3; 33:6; Jer. 32:35). The area was polluted by Josiah (2 Kings 23:10) and was called Topheth (altar).[7] It subsequently became the city's garbage dump, where dead animals were thrown and refuse burned.[8] What remained from the fire was consumed by the worm. Jesus, therefore, uses the word *Gehenna* as a symbol of complete and utter destruction, not as a term denoting eternal preservation in torment.

4. Fire is used in Scripture for utter destruction, not for preservation in torment. Consider the following:

   a. Sodom and Gomorrha were destroyed by fire and brimstone and are now set forth as "an example, suffering the vengeance of eternal fire." (Jude 7 cf. Gen. 19:24). But are these cities still burning? Scripture affirms that these cities were overthrown in a moment. (Lam. 4:6) and turned to ashes. (2 Pet. 2:6, cf. Deut. 29:23).

   b. Nadab and Abihu (sons of Aaron) were "devoured" and died by fire which came out from the Lord. (Lev. 10:1,2).

---

[5] Ethelbert W. Bullinger, *A Critical Lexicon and Concordance to the English and Greek New Testament*, (London: Samuel Bagster and Sons Ltd., 1957), p.367.

[6] See Josh. 15:8.

[7] Robert Young, *Analytical Concordance to the Holy Bible*, (London: Lutterworth Press, 1965). Young comments: "A place in the valley of Hinnom where sacrifices were offered and the dead bodies buried or consumed."

[8] James Hasting, (ed.) *Dictionary of the Bible*, (New York: Charles Scribner's Sons, 1963), p.319.

c. A fire from the Lord "consumed" the 250 men who illegally offered incense in the rebellion of Korah, Dathan and Abiram. (Num. 16:35).

d. Fire came down from God out of heaven and "consumed" the messengers from the King of Samaria during the time of the Prophet Elijah. (2 Kings 1:10).

5. "Unquenchable fire" is an apparently absolute expression which is limited in application (i.e., until that which is the subject of reference, is totally and utterly consumed). Two passages serve as an illustration:

a. "Behold, mine anger and my fury shall be poured out upon this place, upon man, and upon beast, and upon the trees of the field, and upon the fruit of the ground; and it shall burn, and shall not be quenched." (Jer. 7:20 and note the interesting reference to "the valley of the son of Hinnom" in the context, v. 32). Nevertheless God will have mercy upon Zion when the "set time is come". (Psa. 102:13). Jerusalem will be the city of the great King. (Matt. 5:35, cf. Luke 1:31–33).

b. The Lord "will kindle a fire in the gates thereof, and it shall devour the palaces of Jerusalem, and it shall not be quenched." (Jer. 17:27). The fire was not quenched until it had consumed all that could be burned. The fire is not now burning.

Revelation 14:10,11

"He shall be tormented with fire and brimstone in the presence of the holy angels, and in the presence of the Lamb: and the smoke of their torment ascendeth up for ever and ever."

Revelation 19:3

"And her smoke rose up for ever and ever."

Revelation 20:10

"And the devil that deceived them was cast into the lake of fire and brimstone, where the beast and the false prophet are, and shall be tormented day and night for ever and ever."

PROBLEM:

These verses are stock references quoted in proof of eternal hell torment for the wicked.

SOLUTION:

1. "Fire and brimstone" is used figuratively, not literally in Revelation. Consider the evidence:

a. In the first occurrence of the expression, "fire and brimstone" is said to issue from horses' mouths. (Rev. 9:17). This is certainly no hell-fire.

b. If literal torment in hell were intended, then the language of the passage would require Jesus to be with his angels in hell, since it is stated: "He shall

207

be tormented with fire and brimstone in the *presence* of the holy angels... and the Lamb." (Rev. 14:10).

   c. Consistency demands that if "tormented with fire and brimstone" is literal, so must "the same shall drink of the wine of the wrath of God, which is poured out without mixture into the cup of his indignation". (Rev. 14:10). But the latter is an obvious figure drawn from Jer. 25:15. Why then insist on literal fire and brimstone?

   d. A figurative interpretation of "fire and brimstone" is in keeping with the general symbolic character of the Revelation. The woman is "that great city" (Rev. 17:18); waters are "peoples" (Rev. 17:15); the Lamb similarly represents Jesus Christ. (Rev. 17:14).

2. Fire is used in Scripture for utter destruction, not for preservation in torment. Sodom and Gomorrha were destroyed by fire and brimstone and are now set forth as "an example, suffering the vengeance of eternal fire". (Jude 7, cf. Gen. 19:24). But are these cities still burning? Scripture affirms that these cities were overthrown in a moment (Lam. 4:6) and turned to ashes. (2 Pet. 2:6; Deut. 29:23). See also Lev. 10:1,2; Num. 16:35; 2 Kings 1:10).

3. "And her smoke rose up for ever and ever" (Rev. 19:3) is no hell-fire torment for the scene is the destruction of "Babylon the great", and is witnessed by lamenting merchants and shipmasters. (Rev. 18:8–10,15,18). "For ever and ever" emphasizes complete destruction.

4. Rev. 19:3 appears to draw its symbol from Isa. 34:10. In this passage a fire from the Lord on Idumea (Idumea—"Edom" RSV v. 6) "shall not be quenched night nor day; the smoke thereof shall go up for ever." (Isa. 34:10). But again, this is no hell-fire since the prophet Isaiah continues to speak of the land lying waste, a dwelling place for the owl and raven. (v. 11).

Revelation 19:20
"These both were cast alive into a lake of fire burning with brimstone."

Revelation 20:14
"And death and hell were cast into the lake of fire."

Revelation 21:8
"But the fearful ... shall have their part in the lake which burneth with fire and brimstone: which is the second death."

PROBLEM:

These verses are cited by Pentecostals and Evangelicals to prove that hell is a literal place of torment.

SOLUTION:

1. The non-literal character of "the lake of fire" is established by the following considerations:

a. Death is cast into the lake of fire. (Rev. 20:14). How can death literally be cast into a lake of fire?

b. Hell is cast into the lake of fire. (Rev. 20:14). Therefore hell is not the same place as the lake of fire.

c. Frequently in the Revelation symbols are interpreted. For example: "the woman" is "that great city" (Rev. 17:18); "waters" are "peoples" (Rev. 17:15). Similarly, the "lake of fire" is interpreted to be "the second death". (Rev. 20:14; 21:8).

2. The "lake of fire and brimstone" expressed figuratively what is stated literally—"the second death." To die means to have no thoughts (Psa. 146:4), and to "know not anything." (Eccl. 9:5). This Scriptural definition of death is incompatible with the interpretation that the lake of fire and the second death refer to conscious eternal torment.

2.4

IMMORTAL EMERGENCE AND RESURRECTIONAL RESPONSIBILITY

IMMORTAL EMERGENCE

1 Corinthians 15:52

"The dead shall be raised incorruptible."

PROBLEM:

It is argued on the basis of this passage that the righteous "sheep" are known of the Shepherd during their life and therefore there is no need for them to appear before the Judgment to obtain immortality. They will rise from the grave immortal.

SOLUTION:

1. The dead shall be "raised incorruptible", but this is not the same as saying the "dead shall come out of their graves immortal." The word "raised" (translated from the Greek, *egeiro*) does not in itself imply immortal emergence. Lazarus was raised (*egeiro*) (John 12:1), but he did not come forth immortal.[1] Neither does *egeiro* denote an instantaneous change from mortality to immortality. The following examples indicate this:

   a. Luke 1:69: "And hath raised up an horn of salvation for us in the house of his servant David."

   b. Acts 13:23: "Of this man's [David—v. 22] seed hath God according to his promise raised unto Israel a Saviour, Jesus."

   c. Romans 9:17 (speaking of Pharaoh): "Even for this same purpose have I raised [Gk. *exegeiro*] thee up…"

   Therefore, when Paul says the "dead shall be raised incorruptible", he is not using a word (raised) which in itself denotes an instantaneous transformation in which the dead come forth immortal.

2. In 1 Corinthians 15:35, the question asked is: "How are the dead raised up? and with what body do they come?"[2] The answer given compares the raising of the

---

[1] Lazarus could not have come forth immortal, since Christ was the "firstfruits of them that slept". (1 Cor. 15:20,45). This obviously applies to Christ's resurrection to immortality since he was not the firstfruits by virtue of being raised only. Many resurrections preceded his.

[2] In answer to these questions the apostle sets out two arguments: a. The life to come is not merely the continuation of life as it now is—life in the resurrection is different in kind; b. Resurrection preserves personal identity; there is a continuity of personal identity before and after resurrection.

Two analogies are cited in support of these two arguments: a. When grain is sown ("bare grain"—v. 37) it produces a different seed bearing plant from the original seed, yet the distinctiveness of the grain is preserved—corn produces corn seed, not wheat or barley; b. There are different kinds of flesh—human, animals, birds, and fish, yet each is flesh. (v. 39).

dead with the raising of wheat. To raise a crop of wheat implies the whole process of sowing, cultivating and reaping. As Jesus said: "For the earth bringeth forth fruit of herself; first the blade, then the ear, after that the full corn in the ear." (Mark 4:28). Likewise, "the dead shall be raised incorruptible" is a process. It commences (as the parable of the sower indicates) when the word is heard, understood, and obeyed. (Matt. 13:23). The process involves the resurrection of the dead from their graves (1 Cor. 15:42; Isa. 26:19) and judgment with the subsequent granting of immortality. (Matt. 25:31–34,46; Rom. 14:10; 2 Cor. 5:10). The process is complete when believers are given a "spiritual body".

3. It is sometimes argued that believers are "sown" when at the resurrection their mortal bodies are made alive. But this interpretation must be rejected since at the resurrection believers are reaped, not sown. Jesus said, "the harvest is the end of the world; the reapers are the angels." (Matt. 13:39). The "sowing" is the life of the believer in a nature which tends to corruption, dishonour, and weakness (inherent in the natural body). (Gal. 6:7,8; 1 Cor. 15:42,43). Jesus further employed the analogy of the seed in the context of resurrection: "Verily, verily, I say unto you, Except a corn of wheat fall into the ground and die, it abideth alone: but if it die, it bringeth forth much fruit. He that loveth his life shall lose it; and he that hateth his life in this world shall keep it unto life eternal." (John 12:24,25). Likewise, Paul protested, "I die daily". (1 Cor. 15:31). The dying in these two passages cannot be restricted to mere physical death. The dying is a continuous process in the life of the believer in which the "old man" of the flesh is crucified with his lusts and affections. (Gal. 5:24; Rom. 6:6).

4. "It is sown a natural body" (v. 44) cannot refer to the dead body in the ground (as is required by the doctrine of immortal emergence) since the Greek for natural body is *psuchikon soma* which means a living body.[3] This point becomes even stronger once it is noted that Paul compares the natural body and Adam (a living soul, not a dead body) with a spiritual body and Christ. The contrasts are as follows:

It is sown in	It is raised in
corruption, dishonour, weakness,	incorruption, glory, power
a natural body	a spiritual body or quickening spirit
first that which is natural	afterwards that which is spiritual
Adam	Christ

5. Although the judgment of believers is not detailed in this section of the epistle, it is in 2 Cor. 5:9,10. The consideration here is with those whose privilege it is to inherit the kingdom, not with those who are unfaithful. Similarly, although Paul asserts we "shall *all* be made alive" (1 Cor. 15:22) and "we shall *all* be changed" (1 Cor. 15:51), these statements do not nullify his earlier teaching that believers can be destroyed, can perish and become castaways. (1 Cor. 3:17; 8:11; 9:27).

---

[3] cf. Gen. 2:7, Adam was made a "living soul" (*psuche* being the equivalent of the Hebrew word, *nephesh*).

6. It requires stressing that the righteous go *"into* life eternal" (and therefore are not already immortal). (Matt. 25:46). The invitation to enter into eternal life is preceded by the Judgment which determines who are sheep and who are goats. The "sheep" (i.e. the righteous) come forth mortal, therefore, and not immortal. Similarly, Jesus stated that those in the graves who hear his voice will come forth "unto the resurrection of life." (John 5:28,29). The righteous come forth *to* eternal life, not *with* eternal life.

Philippians 4:3

"...my fellowlabourers, whose names are in the book of life."

PROBLEM:

This passage is used to support the idea that the faithful sheep are known by the Good Shepherd, hence in the resurrection there is no need for judgment as candidates for eternal life. Since their names are written in the book of life, these faithful come forth from their graves immortal.

SOLUTION:

1. Names of the faithful are written in the book of life, but names can also be removed from the book of life. (Rev. 3:5). It is the purpose of the Judgment to make manifest which names have been retained and which deleted.
2. One cannot know for certain whether he is in fact a sheep or goat until the Judgment Seat of Christ. Many passages emphasize this. Consider the following:
   a. The Laodiceans considered themselves rich, increased with goods and in need of nothing. From the divine point of view, they were "wretched, and miserable, and poor, and blind, and naked." (Rev. 3:17).
   b. Many are to come in the Day of Judgment and say: "Lord, Lord, have we not prophesied in thy name? and in thy name have cast out devils? and in thy name done many wonderful works?" And then he will profess unto them, "I never knew you..." (Matt. 7:22,23).
   c. In the parable of the sheep and goats, some of those who thought they were sheep, found out they were goats. (Matt. 25:31–46).
3. The Apostle Paul, the recipient of an abundance of revelations from the Lord, (2 Cor. 12:7), at the *end* of his life could say, "I have fought a good fight, I have finished my course, I have kept the faith..." (2 Tim. 4:7). But caution should be exercised in assessing one's spiritual standing with the same confidence as did the Apostle Paul. He had earlier written, "I am not aware of anything against myself, but I am not thereby acquitted." (1 Cor. 4:4, RSV). He also wrote: "Therefore judge nothing before the time, until the Lord come, who both will bring to light the hidden things of darkness, and will *make manifest* the counsels of the hearts: and then shall every man have praise of God." (1 Cor. 4:5).

4. God, of course, knows whose names are retained in the book of life and whose names are not. The believer is commanded not to judge; it is the Lord Jesus Christ who makes manifest the verdict.

1 John 1:9

"If we confess our sins, he is faithful and just to forgive us our sins, and to cleanse us from all unrighteousness."

PROBLEM:

It is argued that the righteous dead are raised immortal since they have already received the forgiveness of sins in this life. The judgment to which the righteous are subject is said to be the dispensing of rewards and not a trial for eternal life.

SOLUTION:

1. It is apparent that this passage says nothing about the righteous dead coming forth immortal from the grave. This conclusion is only inferred. The conclusion inferred is invalid because its premises are false. It is assumed that the righteous are *ipso facto* accepted because of forgiven sins. This assumption is false. Consider the evidence:

    a. Peter, writing to believers, stated: "And beside this, giving all diligence, add to your faith virtue; and to virtue knowledge...for if these things be in you, and abound, they make you that ye shall neither be barren nor unfruitful in the knowledge of our Lord Jesus Christ. But he that lacketh these things is blind, and cannot see afar off...for if ye do these things, ye shall never fall: for so an entrance shall be ministered unto you abundantly into the everlasting kingdom of our Lord and Saviour Jesus Christ." (2 Pet. 1:5–11). Entrance into the kingdom is conditional not only on having sins forgiven but on producing fruit. Stewards of the Lord must show the result of their stewardship, the results of trading with the Lord's pounds and talents.

    b. Paul said, "It is a very small thing that I should be judged by you [Corinthians] or by any human court. I do not even judge myself. I am not aware of anything against myself, but I am not thereby acquitted. It is the Lord who judges me. Therefore do not pronounce judgment before the time, before the Lord comes, who will bring to light the things now hidden in darkness and will disclose the purposes of the heart. Then every man will receive his commendation from God." (1 Cor. 4:3–5, RSV). A believer may have sins of ignorance, therefore he is not acquitted until the Lord pronounces judgment. The judgment of the Lord is to make manifest even the secret purposes of the heart.

Forgiveness of sins at baptism and throughout one's probationary period is one of the most precious assurances given to believers. But to maintain that forgiveness of sins merits immortal emergence from the grave is to indicate a mistaken view of the nature of judgment. There is *everything* to judge except the sins which are forgiven.

213

2. Jesus said that the righteous go "into life eternal". (Matt. 25:46). But the invitation to enter into eternal life is preceded by the Judgment which determines who are sheep and who are goats. The "sheep" (i.e. the righteous) come forth mortal, therefore, and not immortal. By implication, the purpose of the Judgment cannot be merely to dispense rewards since at its conclusion, the righteous are invited to enter into life eternal.

3. The purpose of the Judgment Seat of Christ is not merely to pass sentence without trial as is sometimes assumed. The meaning of the Greek word, *bema*,[4] translated "judgment" is illustrated in Acts 25. A "hearing" took place in which Festus on his judgment seat (Acts 25:17) heard the charges of the Jews and the defence of Paul. Similarly, in statements about the Judgment Seat of Christ, believers will all appear to receive good or evil, according to what they have done in the body. (2 Cor. 5:10). The fact that some will receive "evil" indicates that the judgment is not merely the distribution of rewards but a trial for eternal life.

RESURRECTIONAL RESPONSIBILITY

Psalm 50:5

"Gather my saints together unto me; those that have made a covenant with me by sacrifice."

PROBLEM:

This passage is used in an attempt to prove that only those who are in covenant relationship with God (the Jews or baptized believers) will be at the Judgment Seat. It is argued that there would be no purpose in God raising "enlightened rejectors"[5] since they have neither part nor lot in the eternal scheme of things. Since they will not be given immortality, and their fate is known by God before the resurrection, why raise the enlightened rejector for a few hours, days or weeks and then consign them back to the eternal grave?

---

[4] The Greek word *bema* translated "Judgment seat" (AV) is translated "tribunal" (RSV). *Bema* is used of the Judgment Seat of Christ in 2 Cor. 5:10 and Rom. 14:10.

[5] "Enlightened rejector" refers to a person who understands but rejects the call of the Gospel to be baptized. Only God, however, knows precisely when a person understands sufficiently to be accountable to the Judgment Seat. The word "enlightened" is taken from John 3:19–21 and Psalm 119:130. The principle that knowledge brings responsibility is well-founded in Scripture. See for example:
- Rom. 3:20—"By the law is the knowledge of sin."
- Rom. 4:15—"Where no law is, there is no transgression." (cf. Rom. 5:13).
- Rom. 7:7—"I had not known sin, but by the law: for I had not known lust, except the law had said, Thou shalt not covet."
- John 9:41—"If ye were blind, ye should have no sin: but now ye say, We see; therefore your sin remaineth."
- John 15:22—"If I had not come and spoken unto them, they had not had sin: but now they have no cloke for their sin."

214

SOLUTION:

1. Psa. 50:5 states who will be gathered[6] — those who have made a covenant *by sacrifice*. It is evident that this applies to the Jews but how does this apply to New Testament believers?

    This passage can only be used to prove who will be gathered, not to state who will not be gathered. To argue otherwise is to make a mistake in logic. It is like arguing:

    If crows are black birds,

    Then all black birds are crows.

    (But, some black birds are pigeons)

    The parallel is as follows:

    If saints will be gathered,

    Then all the gathered are saints.

3. It is not always a sufficient answer to say that these enlightened rejectors will be raised because God has promised that He would do so (although this is, of course, perfectly true). This answer often implies that it is a great privilege to be raised from the dead. Indeed it is a joy for the accepted saints, but it is anguish, sorrow and gnashing of teeth for the rejected. (Matt. 8:11,12).

4. The answer lies in the ideal Scriptural attitude of mortal man toward his Maker. This attitude is commanded to be one of reverence. (Psa. 89:7; Heb. 12:9; —a perfect blend of love and fear).

    This attitude can be discerned in the relationship of an obedient son to an earthly father. The father loves his son and the son loves his father—but in reserve—he has a healthy fear of his father. This fear may involve punishment for disobedience.

    Human nature being what it is, requires two things to keep it in the way of obedience:

    —Offer of reward

    —Fear of punishment

    These two things are like two blades of a pair of scissors; linked together, they act as a strong instrument of action.

5. Although humans cannot state with certainty which persons are enlightened rejectors, it is clear that Scripture teaches that enlightened rejectors are resurrectionally responsible. Enlightenment, not baptism, is the ground of accountability. The following is a summary of the relevant passages which indicate that "enlightened rejectors" will be at the Judgment Seat of Christ:

    a. John 12:48 (cf. John 15:22; John 9:41): "He that rejecteth me, and receiveth not my words, hath one that judgeth him: the word that I have spoken, the same shall judge him in the last day." Notice that the occasion which evokes this statement of Jesus was the failure of the believing Pharisees to break with their traditions (v. 42). The following require stressing:

---

[6] This is assuming that the gathering is to Judgment, which is by no means certain, since the Judgment Seat is not under consideration in the context.

  i. There is no more evidence that this passage applies only to Jews in covenant relationship than does the parable of the Good Samaritan. Note the emphasis of Deut. 18:18,19, "*Whosoever* will not hearken"—this is not limited only to Jews.[7]

  ii. There can be no doubt that this passage applies to the Day of Judgment. See its similarity with Matt. 12:36; Luke 12:1–9.

  iii. "The word that I have spoken, shall judge him in the last day" is sometimes understood to refer to the judgment of Christ on Israel in AD 70. This interpretation is most unlikely since the "last day" in John's Gospel refers exclusively to the resurrection and judgment. See John 6:39,40,44,54; 11:24. The only exception is in John 7:37 where the expression refers to the last day of the feast.

b. Rom. 2:12–16—Notice especially "as many as have sinned in the law shall be judged by the law" (then follows a parenthetical section until verse 16). "In *the day* when God shall judge the secrets of men by Jesus Christ according to my gospel." The words of this passage are addressed to Jews and Gentiles: "Therefore thou art inexcusable, O man, *whosoever* thou art..." (v. 1) Notice, too, that law existed before the Mosaic law. Law was given to Adam and Eve (Gen. 2:16,17), to Noah (Gen. 6:14), and to Abraham (Gen. 26:5).

c. Acts 24:25—Felix trembled when Paul reasoned of "righteousness, temperance, and judgment to come". Why did Felix (a Roman) tremble unless he became aware of his personal accountability to Christ's Judgment Seat? (Note v. 22—"Felix having a rather *accurate knowledge* [cf. v. 15] of the Way", RSV).

d. 1 Pet. 4:3–6 (see RSV)—Peter refers to Gentiles as the ones who shall "give account to him that is ready to judge the quick and the dead." Are these baptized believers?

e. Rev. 21:8—"But the fearful, and unbelieving, and the abominable, and murderers, and whoremongers, and sorcerers, and idolaters, and all liars, shall have their part in the lake which burneth with fire and brimstone: which is the *second death*." The second death requires a first death and resurrection. Are the ones raised in this verse baptized believers?

f. Matt. 12:41,42—"The men of Nineveh shall rise in judgment with this generation, and shall condemn it...The queen of the south shall rise up in the judgment with this generation, and shall condemn it..." These verses require that men of Nineveh and the queen of the south be present at the Day of Judgment. Were they believers in covenant relationship with God?

g. Rom. 2:8—"But unto them that are contentious, and do not obey the truth ..." The Greek word *apeitheo* translated "not obey" is always used of the unbaptized (e.g. Rom. 11:30,31; 15:31 —in each of these references the word translated "not believe" is *apeitheo*)[8], yet these unbaptized, who obey

---

[7] Compare these other "Whosoever" passages: Rom. 10:11–13; Rom. 9:33; Acts 2:21.

[8] The one exception only occurs in the AV of Gal. 3:1. The RSV, RV, and *Nestle Greek Text* omit the words "that ye should not obey the truth".

not the truth, will be judged "in the day when God shall judge the secrets of men by Jesus Christ." (Rom. 2:16).

Hebrews 13:20

"Now the God of peace, that brought again from the dead our Lord Jesus, that great shepherd of the sheep, through the blood of the everlasting covenant."

PROBLEM:

This is the principal verse cited to prove the theory that only the baptized will be raised to the Judgment Seat of Christ. This conclusion is based on the following premises:

1. That Jesus himself was raised from the dead by the blood of the everlasting Abrahamic covenant. (Heb. 13:20).
2. That this blood was his own blood which ratified and confirmed the covenant. (Rom. 15:8).

Therefore, unless a mortal man enters into the everlasting covenant by means of baptism (in this dispensation) and thereby is washed in the blood of Christ, he *cannot* rise from the dead since the agency of resurrection (namely the blood of Christ) is not available to him.

SOLUTION:

1. This theory distorts the significance of the blood of Christ and the scriptural teaching on the resurrection which is a means, or an instrument to an end—the distribution of rewards and punishments. The actual rising forth out of the ground is only an incidental event. This is proved by the fact that at the appearing of Christ, living saints will go into the kingdom without experiencing death and resurrection (1 Thess. 4:15–17), yet all these have been washed in the blood of the Lamb. (Rev. 5:9; 7:14).
2. When the writer to the Hebrews declared that the Lord Jesus was brought again from the dead, he was not referring *merely* to the rising forth out of the ground, but of the whole great and glorious bestowal of immortality. To confine the meaning of this verse to a mere rising out of the ground is a narrow, mechanical, and erroneous view of the whole process.
3. The following two passages indicated the way in which resurrection is not confined to a mere emergence from the ground, but rather a means to what follows thereafter:
   a. When Paul declared, "of the hope and resurrection of the dead I am called in question" (Acts 23:6), he was not confining his hope to mere emergence from the ground, but rather he was looking forward to being bestowed with the crown of life which fadeth not away. (Cf. 2 Tim. 4:8; Phil. 3:20,21.)
   b. "In the resurrection whose wife of them is she?" (Luke 20:33). Would any assert that the meaning here is only the rising from the ground? It is obvious that the meaning here has to do with conditions *after* the actual raising from the dead has been accomplished.

4. Whatever interpretation is given to explain the blood of Christ as the agent for bringing again the *dead*, must also be the same explanation to apply to the *quick* (living). On the day appointed for the appearing of the Lord two classes of saints will be gathered at the voice of the archangel and the trump of God:

a. first—the dead

b. second—those who are alive and remain. (1 Thess. 4:13–17).

Whatever efficacy the blood of Christ has, it is just as efficacious for the *quick* as it is for the dead.

5. Even if it could be proven (which it cannot) that this passage means that all those touched with the blood of Christ will come out of the ground, it does not necessarily follow that *only* those touched with the blood of Christ will rise out of the ground. The logic involved in this theory is:

1. If all baptized will be raised,

2. Then all the raised are the baptized.

Which is like saying:

1. If crows are black birds,

2. Then all black birds are crows.

(Obviously all black birds are not crows, some are pigeons.)

6. This legalistic theory of the blood of Christ which in fact means that God *cannot* raise those not baptized must be rejected as infringing on the sovereignty of God. It allows that mortal man can decide by his own act (or failure to act, i.e. to be baptized) whether or not he will make himself accountable to his Creator. What more pernicious and erroneous theory than that which teaches a teenager that it rests in his own hands whether or not he *makes himself* accountable to God?

1 Corinthians 15:22

"For as in Adam all die, even so in Christ shall all be made alive."

PROBLEM:

It is argued that since all men are born "in Adam" and therefore subject to death, the only way they can come out of the grave is to become "in Christ" (i.e. to be baptized).[9] Hence it is said that only the baptized will be raised for judgment; those not baptized will remain eternally in the grave.

SOLUTION:

1. The chief fallacy in the above interpretation is the assumption that baptized believers are no longer "in Adam". The erroneousness of this assumption is evidenced by the fact that baptized believers still experience the pull of fleshly desires and are subject to death. (cf. Rom. 7:18–25). The deliverance at baptism is potential, not actual. It is not actual until believers are freed from the "law of sin and death" (Rom. 8:2) when their mortal bodies are redeemed from its

[9] Or by sacrifices in patriarchal and Mosaic dispensations.

218

power by change to an immortal nature. Deliverance begins at baptism and the process continues through the probationary period until resurrection to judgment, and if faithful, the granting of immortality.

2. Believers are baptized for the forgiveness of *their own sins*, and not for the sin of Adam. This is indicated by the following passages:

   a. "...and hath forgotten that he [the believer] was purged from *his* own sins." (2 Peter 1:9).

   b. "And now [Paul] why tarriest thou? arise, and be baptized, and wash away *thy* sins, calling on the name of the Lord." (Acts 22:16).

   c. "...Repent, and be baptized every one of you in the name of Jesus Christ for the remission of sins..." (Acts 2:38, cf. 3:26; 5:31).

   Believers (along with the rest of humanity) inherit the *effects* of Adam's sin, but not the guilt.

3. Resurrections have occurred in the past of those who evidently were neither Jews nor baptized. (Elijah raised the son of the widow of Zarephath, a Phoenician city between Tyre and Sidon—1 Kings 17:21–23). Baptism, therefore, cannot be the deciding factor by which God raises the dead, nor does He regard the Adamic sentence of death as a barrier to His raising the unjustified dead.

Matthew 2:17,18

"Then was fulfilled that which was spoken by Jeremy the prophet, saying, In Rama was there a voice heard, lamentation, and weeping, and great mourning, Rachel weeping for her children, and would not be comforted, because they are not."

PROBLEM:

This passage is quoted by JWs in support of their belief that children will be raised to a life of opportunity in the kingdom of God. It is reasoned by them, that Jer. 31:15,16 indicates that resurrection cannot be limited to the "responsible" since these babes will come back from the land of the enemy and Rachel will be rewarded for her labours.[10]

SOLUTION:

1. "The land of the enemy" (Jer. 31:16) is not the grave but the countries in which natural Israel has been scattered. This is indicated by the context:

   a. Natural Israel is punished for unfaithfulness to God. (vv. 15,18,28, cf. also 30:12–15; 32:42).

   b. God will extend forgiveness to unfaithful Israel. "I will build thee, and thou shalt be built", Jer. 31:3,4; "I will turn their mourning into joy, and will comfort them, and make them rejoice from their sorrow", v. 13; "I will surely have mercy upon him [Ephraim] saith the LORD", v. 20, cf. 30:17.

[10] See *The Watchtower*, (August, 1962), No. 15, Vol. LXXXIII, p.475.

WRESTED SCRIPTURES

   c. Natural Israel will be restored to the land of Israel. (Jer. 31:8,10,28, also vv. 11–13,21).

2. Rachel and Leah "did build the house of Israel". (Ruth 4:11). In this sense Rachel is the "mother" of Israel. Some of her sons "are not" because of God's punishments through Herod. But comfort is extended to Rachel (Jer. 31:16) with the promise that her scattered sons will return from the lands of the enemy to the land of Israel (cf. Ezekiel chapters 36 & 37). This passage has nothing to do with the resurrection of babies.

3. The destiny of children who die before the age of accountability is illustrated in the death of David's child by Bathsheba: "While the child was yet alive, I fasted and wept: for I said, Who can tell whether God will be gracious to me, that the child may live? But now he is dead, wherefore should I fast? can I bring him back again? I shall go to him, *but he shall not return to me.*" (2 Sam. 12:22,23, cf. Acts 2:34 which shows that David did not have heaven in mind!) See also Job 10:18,19; 3:11–13.

John 5:28,29

"Marvel not at this: for the hour is coming, in the which all that are in the graves shall hear his voice, and shall come forth; they that have done good, unto the resurrection of life; and they that have done evil, unto the resurrection of damnation."

PROBLEM:

These verses are cited to support the doctrine of universal resurrection. Stress is placed on the words of Jesus that *all* in the graves shall hear his voice and come forth from their graves.

SOLUTION:

1. The "all" are those who *hear* the voice of the Son of God and are, therefore, responsible to his Judgment. (v. 24). There is, however, a large segment of humanity that has never heard the words of Jesus and will not come forth in the resurrection. (Isa. 26:14; Jer. 51:57; Psa. 49:19,20). These are the dead that God remembers "no more". (Psa. 88:5).

2. "All" is frequently qualified by the context in which it occurs. The following are examples:
   a. Luke 2:1—"All the world should be taxed" referred to the Roman world and not the areas of North, Central and South America.
   b. John 10:8—"All that ever came before me are thieves and robbers", but this did not include John the Baptist and other prophets.
   c. Rom. 1:7—"All that be in Rome" referred to the beloved of God—those called to be saints, and not to the populace.

Similarly, in the passage under consideration, the "all" refers only to those who hear the words of the Son of God and not to unenlightened adults and children.

220

1 Corinthians 7:14

"For the unbelieving husband is sanctified by the wife, and the unbelieving wife is sanctified by the husband: else were your children unclean; but now are they holy."

PROBLEM:

JWs reason that children of believers who die before reaching the age of accountability would not be termed "holy" if their destiny was that of perishing with the rest of the ignorant.[11]

SOLUTION:

1. "Holy" in the New Testament means, "separate, set apart".[12] It is used with this meaning in the following two passages:

   a. "Every male that openeth the womb shall be called holy to the Lord." (Luke 2:23).

   b. Israel is spoken of as the "holy" firstfruit. (Rom. 11:16).

   But neither passage carries the implication that *all* Israelites or *all* firstborn sons have a resurrectional destiny with the faithful.[13]

2. The context of 1 Cor. 7:14 is a consideration of the status of a Christian believer having previously married a pagan partner. The marriage may have been anything but a Christian union[14] when contracted, but Paul affirms that the children of such a union are legitimate. The believing partner would have the responsibility to bring the children up "in the nurture and admonition of the Lord". (Eph. 6:4). For this reason, and for the sake of the believing parent, the children are "set aside" or "separate" under God's special care. In the Old Testament the whole house of Abraham was blessed for Abraham's righteousness and Paul indicates to the believers in Corinth the effect of the same principle.[15] But the passage nowhere states that "holy" has any application to resurrection.

---

[11] See "The Watchtower", (August, 1962), No. 15, Vol. LXXXIII, p.475.

[12] The Greek word *hagios* translated "holy" means "separate, set apart, holy." Robert Young, *Analytical Concordance to the Holy Bible*, (London: Lutterworth Press, 1965).

[13] The Apostle states that the unbelieving partner is "sanctified" by the believing mate. (1 Cor. 7:14). But "sanctified" comes from the same root word in the Greek as does "holy". Does this imply the resurrection of all or even some unbelieving partners? JWs indicate the inconsistency in their argumentation since in their literature no claim is made for the resurrection of all unbelieving partners. See *The Watchtower*, (March 1, 1965), No. 5, Vol. LXXXVI, pp.146-148. No doubt some mates would be Gentiles "without hope". (1 Thess. 4:13; Eph. 4:18,19; 2:11,12).

[14] Marriage is *not* a sacrament of the ecclesia. Marriage between believers and unbelievers is still a marriage and binding in God's sight.

[15] The same principle is illustrated in Gen. 39:5: "And it came to pass from the time that he [Potiphar] had made him [Joseph] overseer in his house, and over all that he had, that the LORD blessed the Egyptian's house for Joseph's sake; and the blessing of the LORD was upon all that he had in the house, and in the field" (cf. also Gen. 30:27).

221

WRESTED SCRIPTURES

1 John 2:2

"And he is the propitiation for our sins: and not for ours only, but also for the sins of the whole world."

PROBLEM:

This passage is cited by JWs in proof of their doctrine that God will raise those who are ignorant of His great salvation to a life of opportunity in the paradise-like conditions on the earth.[16]

SOLUTION:

1. The redemption effected by the sacrifice of Christ is now available to all the world, but for it to have benefit for an individual, belief of the gospel is required. "For God so loved the world, that he gave his only begotten Son, that whosoever *believeth* in him should not perish, but have everlasting life." (John 3:16). Those who do not believe—"perish", or are destroyed.

2. Scripture states that the Gentiles who perish have their "understanding darkened, being alienated from the life of God through the ignorance that is in them, because of the blindness of their heart". (Eph. 4:18). They perish, "without Christ", "aliens from the commonwealth of Israel", "strangers from the covenants of promise, having *no hope*, and without God in the world". (Eph. 2:12).

3. Those who come forth at the resurrection do so for *judgment* unto "life" (if they have done good) or unto "damnation" (if they have done evil). (John 5:29). There is no opportunity for a third group of ignorant individuals to come forth since they cannot be commended for having done good. "It is appointed unto men once to die, but after this the *judgment*" (Heb. 9:27). Therefore, only those responsible, who do "good" or "bad" will rise for judgment.

4. There are many statements in Scripture which either state or imply that those ignorant of God's salvation will sleep a "perpetual sleep" in the grave. See Isa. 26:13,14, cf. with believers v. 19; Jer. 51:39,57; 1 Thess. 4:13.

5. The divine purpose today requires the visiting of the Gentiles to take out of them a "people for his [God's] name". (Acts 15:14). The "taking out" has been made possible by the sacrifice of Christ, but his propitiation "for the whole world" does not require the resurrection of those who have their "understanding darkened". (Eph. 4:18). It is difficult for religionists to understand that in the divine appraisal "all flesh is grass, and all the goodliness thereof is as the flower of the field" for "surely the people is grass". (Isa. 40:6,7). "All nations before him are as nothing; and they are counted to him less than nothing, and vanity." (Isa. 40:17).

---

[16] "The Watchtower," (Feb. 1, 1965), No. 3, Vol. LXXXVI, pp.85-87; also (Aug. 1, 1962), No. 15, Vol. LXXXIII, p.475.

THE REST OF THE DEAD

Revelation 20:5

"But the rest of the dead lived not again until the thousand years were finished. This is the first resurrection."

PROBLEM:

Many religious groups separate the resurrection of the righteous and the wicked. The righteous, it is argued are raised at the return of Christ but the wicked, i.e. "the rest of the dead" are not raised until the thousand years are finished.

SOLUTION:

1. The word "lived" in verse 4: "And they lived and reigned with Christ a thousand years" refers to *eternal* life. See this use of the Greek word *zao* in Rev. 1:18; 4:10; 5:14; 10:6; and 15:7.
2. Similarly "lived" in verse 5 has the force of "eternal life". The dead are the righteous dead as is indicated by the context in verse 4. The dead under consideration are those who sit upon thrones and reign with Christ (cf. Matt. 19:27,28), hence the rest of the dead must be the remainder of the *righteous* dead. These are the rest of the class seen in the vision. The "firstfruits" are those who are raised before the 1,000-year period, and the "harvest", those who are faithful during the 1,000-year period and ingathered at the end of the millennium. (Rev. 14:1–5; 7:9).
3. "But the rest of the dead lived not again until the thousand years were finished" should be read as parenthetical. "This is the first resurrection" refers not to the rest of the dead, but to those who "lived and reigned with Christ a thousand years" (vv. 4 and 6)—i.e. those immortalized at Christ's return.
4. In the parables of Jesus, the wicked and righteous are judged at the same time—when he appears. (Matt. 25:31–46—the righteous and wicked converse with Jesus at the time designated: "when the Son of man shall come in his glory, and all the holy angels with him, then shall he sit upon the throne of his glory"; cf. Luke 13:24–30—the sitting down in the kingdom is presented in the same context as the casting out of the wicked, thereby indicating that there is not a 1,000-year interval between the resurrection of the just and unjust).

2.5

INFANT BAPTISM

Mark 10:14

"Suffer the little children to come unto me, and forbid them not: for of such is the kingdom of God."

Matthew 18:4

"Whosoever therefore shall humble himself as this little child, the same is greatest in the kingdom of heaven."

PROBLEM:

These references are cited to justify the widespread practice of "baptizing" infants. The United Church of Canada puts it this way:

> "...if the Kingdom belongs to little children, they cannot be denied baptism which is the sacrament of initiation into that kingdom...If even adult candidates for baptism have to become like little children, how can baptism be refused to the children whom they are supposed to imitate?"[1]

SOLUTION:

1. Infant sprinkling is not mentioned in these passages or any other in the New Testament.

2. If the United Church interpretation were the correct one, then the doors of the kingdom would be shut to all but baptized infants since Jesus said, "Verily I say unto you, Whosoever shall not receive the kingdom of God as a little child, he shall not enter therein." (Mark 10:15).

3. "Of such" and "as" ("like", see RSV, Mark 10:14,15) indicate that Jesus is making a comparison. Unless the adult has childlike qualities the doors of the kingdom will be shut. Childlike qualities are stressed elsewhere in Scripture, e.g. "Brethren, be not children in understanding: howbeit in malice be ye children, but in understanding be men." (1 Cor. 14:20); "Wherefore laying aside all malice, and all guile, and hypocrisies, and envies, and all evil speakings, as newborn babes, desire the sincere milk of the word, that ye may grow thereby." (1 Pet. 2:1,2).

---

[1] "The Doctrine and Practice of Infant Baptism", *Church Membership: Doctrine and Practice in The United Church of Canada*: A report presented and accepted at the Twentieth General Council in 1962. (Toronto: The Board of Evangelism and Social Service, and The Board of Christian Education, 1963), p.25. It was a stated objective of the report to "be of use in helping the Church come to a clearer understanding of God's purpose and a more faithful obedience to his will."

4. The Matthew account leaves no doubt as to the intent of Jesus' words: "Except ye be converted, and become *as* little children, ye shall not enter into the kingdom of heaven. Whosoever therefore shall humble himself *as* this little child, the same is the greatest in the kingdom of heaven." (Matt. 18:3,4). See verses 10 and 14—"little ones" are the disciples.[2]
5. In the Mark account Jesus refers to his disciples as "children." (Mark 10:24).

Mark 7:4

"And when they come from the market, except they wash..."

Luke 11:38

"And when the Pharisee saw it, he marvelled that he had not first washed before dinner."

PROBLEM:

Since the Greek word *baptizo* is translated "wash" and "washed" in these passages, it is argued that one cannot insist that the form of baptism must be immersion.

SOLUTION:

1. These are the only two passages in the AV where *baptizo* is translated other than baptism. In 74 other passages *baptizo* is translated by "baptize".[3] The Greek word, *rhantizo*, which means "sprinkle", is never translated "baptize".
2. The word *baptizo* comes from *bapto* which means, "to cover wholly with a fluid...to fully wet...by implication, to stain (as with a dye): dip".[4]
3. The descriptive language of Biblical baptisms clearly implies immersion. For example:
   a. John the Baptist—"John also was baptizing in Aenon near to Salim, because there was *much* water there." (John 3:23).
   b. Jesus—"Jesus, when he was baptized, went *up* straightway *out* of the water ..." (Matt. 3:16).
   c. Eunuch—"...and they went down both *into* the water, both Philip and the eunuch; and he baptized him. And when they were come *up out* of the water..." (Acts 8:38,39).
4. Baptism is likened to a burial in Rom. 6:4 (cf. Col. 2:12): "Therefore we are *buried* with him [Jesus Christ] by baptism into death." The figure of death and burial is preserved in immersion in water; it is not preserved in sprinkling or pouring.

[2] The reference to "the little ones" harks back to Num. 14 where the unfaithful were condemned to die in the wilderness, but the faithful (Joshua, Caleb with "the little ones" vv. 30,31) were to enter the promised land.

[3] The Greek word *baptismos* is translated "washing" in the AV of Mark 7:4,8 and Heb. 9:10. Even in these there is no suggestion of a mere sprinkling; the "washing" would have involved immersion of the part(s) washed.

[4] James Strong, *Strong's Exhaustive Concordance of the Bible*, (New York: Abingdon Press, 1965).

John 4:2

"Though Jesus himself baptized not, but his disciples."

PROBLEM:

Since Jesus did not baptize, it is reasoned that baptism cannot be necessary for salvation.

SOLUTION:

1. It should be immediately apparent that the conclusion, "baptism cannot be necessary for salvation" does not follow from the statement, "Jesus himself baptized not," since his disciples *did* baptize.

2. It is a mistaken idea that baptism is less important when performed by the disciples than if performed personally by Jesus Christ. John records, "After these things came Jesus and his disciples into the land of Judaea; and there he tarried with them, and *baptized*." (John 3:22). The disciples were the instruments by which the baptismal act was performed. Similarly, Jesus told his disciples "He that receiveth you receiveth me..." (Matt. 10:40). He later told the seventy, "He that heareth you heareth me." (Luke 10:16).

3. Many Biblical passages record instructions for candidates to be baptized (e.g. Acts 2:38; 8:38; 10:48) yet no prescriptions are set out as to who should perform the baptism. The historical narratives indicate that the immerser (when identified) was always a believer, e.g. Philip (Acts 8:38); Peter (Acts 10:47,48); Paul or Silas (Acts 16:31–33).

4. Baptism is essential for salvation. The following passages indicate this:

   a. Jesus himself said, "Go ye into all the world, and preach the gospel to every creature. He that believeth *and is baptized* shall be saved..." (Mark 16:15,16). Who has the authority to whittle Jesus' instruction to mean that one can be saved without water baptism?

   b. "Be baptized every one of you in the name of Jesus Christ for the remission of sins..." (Acts 2:38). This implies that until baptism one does not have forgiveness of sins.

   c. "For *as many* of you as have been baptized into Christ have put on Christ." (Gal. 3:27). Baptism, therefore, is the divinely appointed way to "put on Christ."

   d. Paul was told, "And now why tarriest thou? Arise, and be baptized, and *wash away thy sins*..." (Acts 22:16). This implies that even though Paul had confessed: "What shall I do, Lord?" (v. 10), he was "in" his sins until they were washed away in baptism.

   e. "...the longsuffering of God waited in the days of Noah, while the ark was a preparing, wherein few, that is, eight souls were saved by water. The like figure whereunto even baptism *doth also now save us*..." (1 Pet. 3:20,21). Were any saved outside the ark of Noah? Since baptism is a "like figure" can one be saved outside of the divine provision of baptism?

Romans 10:9

"That if thou shalt confess with thy mouth the Lord Jesus, and shalt believe in thine heart that God hath raised him from the dead, thou shalt be saved."

Romans 10:13

"For whosoever shall call upon the name of the Lord shall be saved."

PROBLEM:

These passages are used primarily by Evangelicals who teach that all that is needful for salvation is to "Accept the Lord Jesus and take him as your own personal Saviour". The assumption is made that baptism is an outward sign of an inward change, but is not essential for salvation.

SOLUTION:

1. These verses in Romans must be understood against the background of other clear Scriptural teaching. Baptism is essential as the plain evidence of Matt. 3:13–15; Mark 16:16; John 3:5; Acts 2:38; 10:48; 22:16; 1 Pet. 3:21 shows.
2. Is Paul going to suggest that baptism is not essential after writing so powerfully about it in the sixth chapter? (Rom. 6:3–5).
3. Can one really be a believer and disallow the plainest and simplest (so far as ease of obedience goes) of Christ's commandments?
4. A permissible rendering of Rom. 10:13 is, "Whosoever shall call the name of the Lord upon himself shall be saved". See James 2:7 (RVm.) and Acts 22:16, where the same form of the Greek verb is used. How does one call the name of the Lord upon himself except by baptism?
5. The same phrase, "Whosoever shall call on the name of the Lord shall be saved", is used in Acts 2:21 and here was certainly followed by baptism on the part of those who "gladly" received Peter's words. (Acts 2:40,41).
6. Sometimes in an endeavour to prove that doctrine is not essential Evangelicals quote Acts 8:37: "I believe that Jesus Christ is the Son of God." The following points require stressing:
   a. These words are not in the majority of New Testament Greek manuscripts. They are deleted by RSV, RV, ESV, NIV, Rotherham's *Emphasized Bible*, NEB, and *Nestle Greek Text*.
   b. To "preach Christ" is a comprehensive expression. This is indicated by a comparison of Acts 8:5 and Acts 8:12. "Then Philip went down to the city of Samaria, and preached Christ unto them", but in verse 12 Philip is preaching "the things concerning the kingdom of God, and the name of Jesus Christ ..."
   c. Even to believe that Jesus is Lord requires an understanding of his nature and sacrifice. Similarly, to believe that God raised him from the dead requires an understanding of hell, soul, spirit, and quickening spirit.

d. As false doctrines and perversions increased with the growth of the Truth in the first century, this made necessary negative as well as positive teaching. (See for example: 1 Cor. 15:35,36; 1 Tim. 1:19,20: 2 Tim. 2:17,18; 1 John 4:1–3; Titus 1:14).

1 Corinthians 1:17

"Christ sent me not to baptize, but to preach the gospel."

PROBLEM:

This passage is quoted to prove that baptism is not necessary for salvation.

SOLUTION:

1. Such an interpretation is sheer perversion of the context for Paul says he did baptize Crispus, Gaius and the household of Stephanas (vv. 14–16), which would mean Paul writes his own condemnation if "Christ sent me not to baptize" be understood to be a prohibition of him baptizing converts.

2. The context shows that there was a partisan spirit in Corinth. Converts were saying "I am of Paul", "I am of Apollos" (1 Cor. 1:12), but Paul would have none of it. Hence his sigh of thankfulness: "I thank God that I baptized none of you...lest any should say that I had baptized in mine own name." (vv. 14,15).

3. This passage indicates that no special virtue is associated with the baptizer.[5] Paul himself was commissioned by Christ to be, first and foremost, a preacher of the gospel. Whether he personally undertook the baptism of converts was a matter of no importance.

4. That baptism is essential to salvation is evident from Mark 16:16; John 3:5; 1 Pet. 3:21; Gal. 3:27; Acts 2:38; 22:16; 16:30–33.

---

[5] Jesus did not personally baptize; this was done by his disciples. (John 4:2).

2.6

ETERNAL SECURITY—
"ONCE SAVED, FOR EVER SAVED"

PRELIMINARY POINTS:

There are likely very few Christadelphians who have not at some time or another been confronted by those who argue for "eternal security". Usually these individuals can cite hour and place when "saved". Christadelphian open-air speakers are often challenged by these Evangelicals, "Have you accepted the Lord Jesus as your personal Saviour? Have you been born again and washed in the blood of the Lamb? Are you a saved man?" These zealots are quick to testify: "Hallelujah! Praise the Lord! I'm a saved man!" Little headway is made in such an exchange until the Christadelphian speaker insists on the questioner explaining what he means by "saved". There is, for example, a temporary and an ultimate sense in which "saved" can be used.

The following illustration shows the differing, but related ways in which "saved" can be used: Imagine a downed bush pilot in the Canadian Arctic desperately attempting to maintain his body heat in -60°F weather. Weakened by loss of blood and broken bones, the cold of the icy blasts drives like nails through the folds of his anorak. At night the circle of half-starved wolves becomes increasingly brazen. But suddenly in the few hours of daylight, a noise is heard out of the skies and overhead a rescue plane is seen coming in the direction of the downed craft. "Thank God, I'm saved," cries the bush pilot. But he is not completely out of danger. The rescue craft may be unable to land on the rough ice surface and by the time a rescue team travels several miles the pilot may perish from loss of blood or fall victim to the wakeless sleep of the Arctic cold. Even when rescued by the team and placed in the rescue aircraft he is not "saved" in the strict sense of the term. The rescue craft may lose a ski on a protruding chunk of ice or may itself be ruined from carburettor-icing or a down-draft. Not until the bush pilot is safely back at the base and fully recovered from his ordeal, can he be said in the fullest sense to be "saved".

Similarly in the Bible, Jude states that God "having saved the people out of the land of Egypt, afterward destroyed them that believed not." (Jude 5). "Having saved" is not used in the ultimate sense of eternal salvation.

Three distinct uses of "saved" occur in Scripture. Care in their use is required to avoid the misleading and disastrous conclusions of Evangelicals.

1. "Saved" in the *past tense* referring to the sacrificial work of Christ or when the believer avails himself of that sacrifice at his baptism.

    a. "Who hath saved us, and called us with an holy calling, not according to our works, but according to his own purpose and grace, which was given us in Christ Jesus before the world began." (2 Tim. 1:9). The reference here is to the sacrifice of Christ in the plan of God.

    b. "Not by works of righteousness which we have done, but according to his mercy he saved us, by the washing of regeneration, and renewing of the Holy Spirit." (Titus 3:5). This verse refers to the believer's acceptance of divine salvation at baptism; therefore the past tense is used.

2. "Saved" in the *present tense* (continuous tense in the Greek). These passages indicate that salvation is a continuing process throughout the whole of the believer's life.

    a. "...And the Lord added to the church daily such as should be saved [were being saved, RSV]." (Acts 2:47).

    b. "For the preaching of the cross is to them that perish foolishness; but unto us which are [being, RSV] saved , it is the power of God." (1 Cor. 1:18).

    c. "By which [belief of the gospel] ye are saved, if ye keep in memory what I preached unto you..." (1 Cor. 15:2).

    d. "For we are unto God a sweet savour of Christ, in them that are saved [are being saved, RSV]..." (2 Cor. 2:15).

3. "Saved" in the *future* tense and ultimate sense.

    a. "...but he that endureth to the end shall be saved." (Matt. 10:22).

    b. "If any man's work shall be burned, he shall suffer loss: but he himself shall be saved; yet so as by fire." (1 Cor. 3:15). This passage refers to salvation at the Day of Judgment.

    c. "To deliver such an one unto Satan for the destruction of the flesh, that the spirit may be saved in the day of the Lord Jesus." (1 Cor. 5:5). This passage likewise refers to salvation at the Day of Judgment.

    d. "Take heed unto thyself, and unto the doctrine; continue in them: for in doing this thou shalt both save thyself, and them that hear thee." (1 Tim. 4:16). Timothy had been appointed leader of the ecclesia by Paul. According to Evangelical teaching Timothy was "a saved man". But note, the Apostle Paul writes of Timothy's salvation as yet future *and conditional* on giving heed to the doctrine.

In the past, God manifested His great salvation in the person and work of Christ. This is appropriated by the believer at his baptism. A life of discipleship follows in which the salvation is worked out in fashioning a new creation. It is not until the Day of Judgment that one is ultimately saved. It is, therefore, presumptuous for a man to consider himself unalterably reserved for eternal life before that time.

SUGGESTED STRATEGY:

1. Once clarification has been successfully undertaken on the word "saved", a very strong group of passages can be mustered against the view "once saved, for ever saved" or "eternal security". One approach is to argue as follows from the Epistle to the Hebrews:

    a. Read Heb. 3:12–14; 6:4–6 and 10:26–29. There is no way the "saved" Evangelicals can evade the force of these passages. Were or were not these believers saved? Since the references specifically state that they were "brethren", were "partakers of Christ", "enlightened, and have tasted of the heavenly gift, and were made partakers of the Holy Spirit…and have tasted …the powers of the world to come", it is idle for Evangelicals to evade the issue by saying they never were in the way of life or "saved".

b. The second question follows: Since these believers were in the way of life, did (or could) they fall away? The fact that a "sorer punishment" and "fiery indignation" awaited such reprobates (of whom it is said that it is impossible to renew them again to repentance since they crucify afresh the Son of God and put him to an open shame—Heb. 6:6) is proof that either the believers had committed such offences, or were about to. Either is fatal to Evangelical claims that believers are irrevocably reserved for eternal blessedness.

c. The logic of the above reasoning may be summarized as follows:

   i. Believers in the way of life had either fallen or were about to fall from their calling.

   ii. Upon such a "sorer punishment" will come.

   iii. But if believers are to be punished, then they are not irrevocably reserved for eternal favour, and by implication believers have no justification for claiming "eternal security".

2. Another approach is to argue from the life and statements of the Apostle Paul:

   a. Was the apostle "saved" when he confessed, "What shall I do, Lord?" (Acts 22:10). (The Evangelical answer is inevitably, "Yes.") Then why was he told, "And now why tarriest thou? arise, and be baptized, and wash away thy sins, calling on the name of the Lord"? (Acts 22:16). If he were "saved" (having had his sins washed away when he said, "What shall I do, Lord?"), why was he told not to tarry but to arise and *wash* away his sins?

   b. If the apostle was "eternally secure", how is one to understand the following language: "That I may know him, and the power of his resurrection, and the fellowship of his sufferings, being made conformable unto his death; *if by any means I might attain unto* the resurrection of the dead. *Not as though I had already attained*, either were *already* perfect…Brethren, I count not myself to have apprehended…" (Phil. 3:10–13).

   c. Similarly: "But I keep under my body, and bring it into subjection: lest that by any means, when I have preached to others, I myself should be a *castaway*." (1 Cor. 9:27). Is this the language of a man who knows that his eternal blessedness is already fully assured?

   d. The Apostle Paul said, "That being justified by his grace, we should be made heirs according to the *hope* of eternal life." (Titus 3:7). But the apostle defined hope explicitly: "hope that is seen is not hope: for what a man seeth, why doth he yet hope for?" (Rom. 8:24). If the apostle had already been assured of eternal security, why was he in *hope* of eternal life?

John 3:36

"He that believeth on the Son hath everlasting life: and he that believeth not[1] the Son shall not see life; but the wrath of God abideth on him."

---

[1] "Believeth not" should be translated "does not obey" as in RSV and *Nestle Greek Text*, (London: Samuel Bagster and Sons Ltd., 1967).

WRESTED SCRIPTURES

John 6:47

"Verily, verily, I say unto you, He that believeth on me hath everlasting life."

John 6:54

"Whoso eateth my flesh, and drinketh my blood, hath eternal life; and I will raise him up at the last day."

1 John 5:11

"And this is the record, that God hath given to us eternal life, and this life is in his Son."

1 John 5:13

"These things have I written unto you that believe on the name of the Son of God; that ye may know that ye have eternal life, and that ye may believe on the name of the Son of God."

PROBLEM:

These verses are stressed by the Gospel Hall groups, Pentecostals and Evangelicals. Since the past tense, "hath eternal life" is used by John, it is argued that believers have eternal life as a present possession—their eternal security assured.

SOLUTION:

1. Almost without exception, those who claim to have "eternal security" also believe in the immortality of the soul. But if believers and non-believers alike have immortal souls, what is the eternal life that Jesus said he would give to believers?

2. If it is argued that by "getting saved" one is immune from hell-fire and the lake of fire, where is this taught in John's Gospel or Epistles?

3. What objective evidence is there that a "saved man" is really saved? He may say that he is saved, but how is one to know for certain that his profession is true?

4. The "saved" arguments in the above passages rest on a mistaken understanding of the use of the tenses in the writings of John. The past tense is used by John of *future* events, to emphasise the certainty of their outcome. Consider the following examples:

   a. "The Father loveth the Son, and hath given all things into his hand." (John 3:35). But the writer to the Hebrews explicitly states, "But now we see not yet all things put under him." (Heb. 2:8).

   b. "I have overcome the world." (John 16:33). But Gethsemane lay ahead.

   c. "I have finished the work which thou gavest me to do." (John 17:4). Jesus had yet to die "for our sins according to the Scriptures." (1 Cor. 15:3).

d. "And the glory which thou gavest me I have given them…" (John 17:22). But believers are not ultimately glorified until the return of Christ and the granting of immortality. (Col. 1:27, cf. 2 Tim. 2:10–12).

e. "…That they may behold my glory, which thou hast given me…" (John 17:24). Jesus was not glorified until after his resurrection. (Luke 24:26; 1 Tim. 3:16).

f. See also: Rom. 4:17–21 (Isaac was not born at the time of the promise) and 2 Tim. 1:10 (but people still die; not until the end of the millennium will death be abolished, cf. 1 Cor. 15:24–28).

5. Similarly, eternal life is spoken of as a present possession, when it is still future—to be given "at the last day." This is proven in two ways: a) by showing that John refers to eternal life to be given at the last day and b) by citing other references in the New Testament which show that eternal life and ultimate salvation are still future. The following is the evidence:

a. Eternal life is to be given at the "last day":

i. "And this is the Father's will which hath sent me, that of all which he hath given me I should lose nothing, but should raise it up again at the *last day*." (John 6:39).

ii. "And this is the will of him that sent me, that every one which seeth the Son, and believeth on him, may have everlasting life: and I will raise him up at the *last day*." (John 6:40).

iii. "Whoso eateth my flesh, and drinketh my blood, hath eternal life; and I will raise him up at the *last day*." (John 6:54).

Eternal life is promised (1 John 2:24,25) but resides with the Son (1 John 5:11) until the "last day" when it will be given to the faithful.

b. Other passages which indicate that eternal life is not a present possession of believers:

i. "In *hope* of eternal life, which God, that cannot lie, promised before the world began." (Titus 1:2).

ii. "That being justified by his grace, we should be made heirs according to the *hope* of eternal life." (Titus 3:7, cf. Rom. 8:24: "hope that is seen is not hope: for what a man seeth, why doth he yet hope for?").

iii. "And these shall go away into everlasting punishment: but the righteous *into* life eternal." (Matt. 25:46, cf. Dan. 12:2). The context of this passage indicates the righteous are first judged and then invited to enter into life eternal. (Matt. 25:31–46). This implies that the righteous do not have eternal life before entering into life eternal.

c. Salvation is an ultimately future experience:

i. "…for now is our salvation *nearer* than when we believed." (Rom. 13:11). If salvation was nearer than when saints believed, it was obviously not a present possession.

ii. "Are they not all ministering spirits, sent forth to minister for them who shall be *heirs* of salvation." (Heb. 1:14). An heir is not a present possessor.

WRESTED SCRIPTURES

    iii. "For a helmet, the *hope* of salvation." (1 Thess. 5:8). One does not hope for that which he already possesses.

John 10:28

"And I give unto them eternal life; and they shall never perish, neither shall any man pluck them out of my hand."

PROBLEM:

This passage is cited by Evangelicals to prove that those who "accept the Lord as their personal Saviour" are eternally secure, their future salvation being assured.

SOLUTION:

1. This passage applies to those who are Christ's sheep, but who is to know before the Day of Judgment who is a "sheep" or a "goat"? (Matt. 25:33).
2. Many who think they are "sheep" will find that they are really "goats". (Matt. 25:41–46; 7:21–23; Luke 13:26,27).
3. "And they shall never perish" does not mean "they shall never die". For the disciple, death is not a perishing, but a sleep. (John 11:11–14; 1 Cor. 15:6,18; 1 Thess. 4:13). It is the unbeliever who is consigned to perish. (John 3:16; Luke 13:3,5; cf. Jer. 51:53,57).
4. Note the steps Christ outlines in John Chapter 10. The sheep:

    a. "hear my voice" (v. 27)   —response
    b. "follow me" (v. 27)   —discipleship
    c. "I give unto them eternal life" (v. 28)   —resurrection[2]
    d. "They shall never perish" (v. 28)   —security *in the kingdom*
    e. "neither shall any man pluck them
       out of my hand" (v. 28)   —security from false prophets[3]

Evangelicals make the mistake of placing step 'd' before 'c'.

John 11:26

"And whosoever liveth and believeth in me shall never die."

PROBLEM:

This passage is cited by Pentecostals and Evangelicals as proof that when one "accepts the Lord Jesus as his personal Saviour", he is saved for eternity.

---

[2] Faithful disciples alive at the return of Christ will be transformed to immortality without experiencing the sleep of death. (John 11:26; 1 Cor. 15:51; 1 Thess. 4:13–17).

[3] The same Greek word *harpazo* translated "pluck" (vv. 28,29) is translated "catcheth" in verse 12. The "wolf" represents false teachers. (cf. Acts 20:28–30).

234

SOLUTION:

1. Jesus said "whosoever *liveth* and believeth in me shall never die." He refers to living believers who will be transformed directly from mortality to immortality without experiencing death.

2. This interpretation is supported from the context:
   a. Verse 24—speaks of the resurrection at the last day.
   b. Verse 25—refers to believers who die before the last day, "though he were dead, yet shall he live."
   c. Verse 26—completes the picture. Faithful disciples alive at the Lord's return will put on immortality without experiencing the sleep of death. Cf. 1 Cor. 15:51 where the Apostle Paul makes the same point.

3. The Apostle Paul stated: "I am not aware of anything against myself, but I am not thereby acquitted. It is the Lord who judges me. Therefore do not pronounce judgment before the time, before the Lord comes, who will bring to light the things now hidden in darkness and will disclose the purposes of the heart. Then every man will receive his commendation from God." (1 Cor. 4:4,5 RSV). Similarly, Jesus indicated in his parables that many who think they are "sheep" will find out that they are rejected as "goats". (Matt. 25:41–46, cf. 7:21–23; Luke 13:25–30). It is presumptuous, therefore, for one to declare "before the time" that one is irrevocably reserved for eternal favour.

Ephesians 2:8,9

"By grace are ye saved...it is the gift of God...not of works, lest any man should boast."

PROBLEM:

This passage is used by Evangelicals to justify their doctrine of "eternal security" when "Jesus comes into the heart". This "eternal security" is said to be independent of subsequent works.

SOLUTION:

1. Let it be said at the outset that one cannot obtain salvation as a return for works done. The law witnessed to the truth of this (Rom. 3:21; 5:21; Gal. 2:21).

2. There are two sides to salvation. The divine side, which is *grace*, and the human side, which is obedient faith. Evangelicals argue that if one "works" for salvation then the reward is paid as wages rather than a gift. This is an over-simplification. God gives us food, but we must work for it. God gave Joshua the city of Jericho, but he was still commanded to march around the walls for seven days. (Josh. 6:2,4). Likewise salvation is the free gift of God, but man must comply with the conditions. The Ephesian letter proceeds to make this very point: "We are his workmanship, created in Christ Jesus unto good works, which God hath before ordained that we should walk in them" (Eph. 2:10).

3. It is true to say that no man can ever be saved without the grace of God, but there are other characteristics required in the receiver of grace, for salvation. The following is a representative list:

   a. "For we are saved by *hope*." (Rom. 8:24).

   b. "Therefore being justified by *faith*, we have peace with God…" (Rom. 5:1).

   c. "And being made perfect, he became the author of eternal salvation unto all them that *obey* him." (Heb. 5:9).

   d. "The like figure whereunto even *baptism* doth also now save us…" (1 Peter 3:21).

   e. "But *if we walk in the light*, as he is in the light, we have fellowship one with another, and the *blood* of Jesus Christ his Son cleanseth us from all sin." (1 John 1:7).

   f. "…*Work* out your own salvation with fear and trembling." (Phil. 2:12).

   g. "Ye see then how that by *works* a man is justified, and not by faith only." (James 2:24).

   h. "*Save yourselves* from this untoward generation." (Acts 2:40).

   i. "By which also ye are saved, *if ye keep in memory* what I preached unto you…" (1 Cor. 15:2).

   Grace involves three things: a giver, a gift, and a receiver. From these passages it is clear that the receiver must evidence hope, faith, obedience, baptism, a walking in light, works, and that, by his response to God's grace, he also saves himself.[4]

4. Ultimate salvation is not now a present possession. The following passages indicate this:

   a. "…he that endureth to the end shall be saved." (Matt. 10:22).

   b. "…the gospel…by which ye also are saved, *if* ye keep in memory what I have preached unto you…" (1 Cor. 15:1,2).

   c. "…give diligence to make your calling and election sure: for if ye do these things, ye shall never fall." (2 Pet. 1:10).

   d. "Take heed, brethren, lest there be in any of you an evil heart of unbelief, in departing from the living God…lest any of you be hardened through the deceitfulness of sin. For we are made partakers of Christ, *if* we hold the beginning of our confidence steadfast unto the end." (Heb. 3:12–14).

5. Evangelical logic has a superficial impressiveness. When examples are cited of "saved" members who have fallen away (e.g. drunkards, who will be excluded from the kingdom, Gal. 5:19–21), Evangelicals reply by stating that such individuals were never really "saved". This is sheer logical emptiness. Security has been purchased at the price of truth.

[4] The question as to which single characteristic saves the man is an abstraction. An illustration is helpful. A man who has fallen into the river screams for help. A man on the bank runs with a rope and throws it to the man in the river. He catches hold and is pulled to safety. What saved him? Was it his scream? Was it the rope? Was it the man on the bank? Did he save himself? Or was it all of these working together?

6. Almost without exception, those who are quick to stress Eph. 2:8 are the very ones who dismiss baptism as a mere outward sign of an inward change. When such occasions arise Gal. 3:27 should be emphasised—"For as many of you as have been baptized into Christ have put on Christ". It is also impressive to cite the baptism of Paul, since it can be shown that a man can be "converted" (Acts 22:10), but does not have his sins washed away until baptized. (Acts 22:16, cf. Acts 2:38,41).

2.7

THE DEVIL AND SATAN

PRELIMINARY POINTS:

1. Wrested scripture on the devil may be categorized into three areas:

   a. Passages which are cited to prove that the devil is a fallen angel. (E.g. Job ch. 1; Rev. ch. 12).

   b. Passages which are quoted to prove that the devil is a personal superhuman being. (E.g. Matt. 4).

   c. Passages in which demons, alleged to be angels of the devil, are said to "possess" humans. (E.g. Matt. 12:22). This aspect of the subject will be considered in the next chapter.

2. The devil and the pre-existence of Christ are two areas of discussion which often bog down and sometimes generate more heat than light. A discussion on these two areas, unless strictly regimented, inevitably brings in subsidiary evidence which becomes impossible to clarify because of the number of unproven assertions and counter assertions. It is often advantageous in these two areas to assume the negative and let the non-Christadelphian select the passages which he considers prove the proposition. This is a productive way in which to sift the evidence passage by passage—"Does or does not passage 'x' prove that the devil is a rebel angel?"

3. In such discussions it is sometimes advantageous to withhold expositional knowledge. Assuming for example, that it has been shown that Rev. 12 does not prove the proposition that the devil is a rebel angel, it may be far more appropriate either to advance to another passage which the non-Christadelphian considers does prove the proposition, or to expound the Bible's teaching on the devil. To expound the meaning of the woman, man-child, sun, moon, and stars, etc. of Rev. 12 will probably afford too many opportunities for irrelevant considerations.

4. The following are passages which should be a part of every Christadelphian's arsenal:

   a. Origin of sin—James 1:13–15; Mark 7:20–23, cf. Jer. 17:9.

   b. The meaning of *satan* (a word of Hebrew origin that means 'adversary')— the following are referred to as "satan" or "adversary":

i. God	—2 Sam. 24:1, cf. 1 Chron. 21:1.
ii. An obedient divine angel	—Num. 22:22.
iii. Hadad the Edomite	—1 Kings 11:14.
iv. Peter	—Matt. 16:23.

   c. The meaning of "devil" (accuser; calumniator)—the following are referred to as a "devil" or "slanderer":

i. Judas	—John 6:70.
ii. Women	—1 Tim. 3:11, cf. Titus 2:3.
iii. Men	—2 Tim. 3:3.
iv. "Sin in the flesh"	—See comments on Heb. 2:14 below.

5. Heb. 2:14 is a key passage—"Forasmuch then as the children are partakers of flesh and blood, he also himself likewise took part of the same; that through death he might destroy him that had the power of death, that is, the devil..." The following should be noted:

   a. Heb. 2:14 teaches that *the devil* has the power of death. Cf. Rom. 5:21; 6:23, which show that *sin* has the power of death.

   b. Heb. 2:14 teaches that Jesus destroyed *the devil* by his death. Cf. Heb. 9:26, which shows that Jesus destroyed *sin* by his death.

   c. The following comparison is very useful in reinforcing the connection between the devil and sin:

Hebrews 2:14	Romans 8:3
"As the children are partakers of flesh and blood, he also himself likewise took part of the same...	"God sending his own Son in the likeness of sinful flesh...
...that through death...	...and for sin (AVm. & RV "by a sacrifice for sin")...
...he might destroy...	...condemned...
...him that had the power of death, that is, the devil..."	...sin in the flesh."

   d. The Romans 8:3 passage provides a bridge to Romans 7:17–23 which shows the true nature of the biblical devil.

Genesis 3:4,5

"And the serpent said unto the woman, Ye shall not surely die: for God doth know that in the day ye eat thereof, then your eyes shall be opened, and ye shall be as gods, knowing good and evil."

PROBLEM:

A typical interpretation of these verses is given in the following quotation:

"What the serpent said to Eve, did it think up and say of its own accord? Impossible! We know that no serpent has the brains of a man to understand God's command...[and] to converse with man in man's own language...Who, then, caused the serpent to talk to Eve? ...It must have been some superhuman invisible intelligent creature...It must have been...[an] angelic son...now turned traitor to his own heavenly Father...Because of developing a greed for power over mankind, this rebellious son of God actually took steps to turn mankind away from obedience to God and to line mankind up on his side as rebels against Jehovah God."[1]

SOLUTION:

1. If angels can become such rebels what guarantee is there that believers who are to be made like them (Luke 20:35,36) will not likewise become rebels?

2. God deals with three parties in the fall of mankind: Adam, Eve and the serpent. An alleged fourth—the devil—is not mentioned in the Genesis narrative.

3. God said to the serpent, "*Thou* hast done this". (v. 14). Paul likewise says, "the *serpent* beguiled Eve through his subtilty". (2 Cor. 11:3). Now this language is entirely appropriate if the serpent were the guilty party, but the language is totally inappropriate if the helpless serpent had merely been used as a tool by a powerful angel. Why the curse on the serpent: "thou art cursed above all cattle, and above every beast of the field; upon thy belly shalt thou go, and dust shalt thou eat all the days of thy life", (Gen. 3:14)—a victim used by the devil for his own ends when the devil, the instigator, gets off scot-free?

4. The interrogation of Adam by God resulted in a typically human projection of the blame:

   a. Adam blamed Eve (and God?): "The woman whom thou gavest to be with me, *she* gave me of the tree, and I did eat". (v. 12).

   b. The woman blamed the serpent: "The serpent beguiled me, and I did eat". (v. 13).

   c. The serpent blamed no one. The blame was not placed on a fallen angel, because there was no fallen angel to be blamed.

5. It is objected that serpents cannot talk because they lack man's brain power. Of course, serpents as they are known today do not talk, neither do asses. But an ass did speak in Biblical times: "the dumb ass speaking with man's voice forbad the madness of the prophet." (2 Pet. 2:16; see Num. 22:28). It is carefully outlined that the serpent was more "subtle" or "crafty" (Septuagint) than any beast of the field (Gen. 3:1), its propensities being used to provide a trial of the integrity of the first parents.

6. Since the fall of man the serpent has been symbolically identified with sin. Thus sin is referred to in 1 Cor 15:56 as a creature whose sting causes death and men who are given over to sin are designated as the serpent's seed (e.g. Matt. 23:33).

Genesis 6:2

"...the sons of God saw the daughters of men that they were fair; and they took them wives of all which they chose."

---

[1] *Things In Which It Is Impossible For God To Lie*, (Brooklyn, New York: Watchtower Bible and Tract Society of N.Y., Inc., & Int. Bible Students Ass., 1965), pp.158,159.

PROBLEM:

The "sons of God" are claimed by JWs and others to have been angels who had sinned and spread evil by marrying the daughters of men. A JW publication puts it this way:

> "To marry the daughters of men, those heavenly sons of God [angels] materialized human bodies, clothing themselves with fleshly bodies like those of men on earth...When the Flood came, those disobedient sons of God could not get into Noah's ark, and so, to escape from the floodwaters, they dematerialized, dissolved their assumed human bodies, and returned to the spirit realm. They were not admitted back to the heavenly family of God's perfect, sinless sons. They were degraded to a very low state that the Bible calls 'Tartarus'... [JWs teach that they became the spirits in prison, 1 Peter 3:19,20.] In view of this form of imprisonment those disobedient spirit 'sons of the true God' cannot materialize anymore and live like husbands with women. But they still keep as close as they can to mankind, especially to women, whom they prevail upon to serve as spirit mediums, fortune-tellers, clairvoyants, and so forth."[2]

SOLUTION:

1. All existence in Scripture is bodily existence. Nothing is known in Scripture of materializing and dematerializing assumed bodies. JWs should be pressed hard for evidence to justify such a doctrine.

2. Luke 20:35,36 is conclusive—angels do not marry: "But they which shall be accounted worthy to obtain that world, and the resurrection from the dead, neither marry, nor are given in marriage: neither can they die any more: for they are equal unto the angels; and are the children of God, being the children of the resurrection."

3. "Sons of God" can refer to angels as it may in Job 38:7, but the expression is also used of men. (See Deut. 14:1, RSV; Hosea 1:10; Luke 3:38; John 1:12; 1 John 3:1). In Gen. 6:2 the "sons of God" were the righteous line of Seth (Gen. 4:26)[3] becoming apostate and intermarrying with evil Cainites.

4. It is sometimes contended that only angel-human offspring could produce *nephilim* (a Hebrew word meaning, 'mighty ones or giants' as in Gen. 6:4). But the sons of Anak (Num. 13:33) were also giants (Heb. *nephilim*) and these were certainly not angel-human offspring, as they existed long after the Flood.

5. Divine angels cannot sin. They are "ministering spirits, sent forth to minister for them who shall be heirs of salvation". (Heb. 1:14). These angels are not rebels, but do God's commandments, "hearkening unto the voice of his word...ministers of his, that do his pleasure." (Psa. 103:20,21).

6. The "spirits in prison" passage in 1 Pet. 3:19,20 is considered elsewhere in this handbook.

---

[2] *Things In Which It Is Impossible For God To Lie*, (Brooklyn, New York: Watchtower Bible and Tract Society of N.Y., Inc., Int. Students Ass., Brooklyn, N.Y., 1965) pp.167-169.

[3] See the AVm.: "Or, to call themselves by the name of the LORD."

WRESTED SCRIPTURES

Job 1:6

"Now there was a day when the sons of God came to present themselves before the LORD, and Satan came also among them."

PROBLEM:

This passage is usually connected with Rev. 12 to prove that the devil is a fallen angel. A JW publication puts it this way:

"...an angelic son of God in the heavens had rebelled against Jehovah God, thus making himself Satan ('Resister')".[4]

"At a conference of the angelic sons of God in heaven, Satan the Devil came also 'from roving about in the earth and from walking about in it.' So Jehovah God called Satan's attention to a man down there on earth, Job in the land of Uz, as being different from all others, 'a man blameless and upright, fearing God and turning aside from bad'."[5]

SOLUTION:

1. Nowhere in the book of Job is Satan explicitly stated to be a fallen angel. The argument that Satan is a fallen angel is an inferred one, and involves the following assumptions:
   a. That the "sons of God" refers to angels. The expression is possibly identified with angels in Job 38:7, but is used of humans elsewhere in Scripture: Deut. 14:1 RSV; Psa. 82:6 RSV; Hosea 1:10, Luke 3:38; John 1:12; 1 John 3:1.
   b. That Satan was a son of God. The passage only states that he "came among them", but not that he was himself a son of God.
2. It is inferred that a conference took place in heaven from the following two references: "To present themselves before the LORD" (Job 1:6); "so went Satan forth from the presence of the LORD" (Job 2:7). But note the following:
   a. The conference need not have taken place in heaven. When men came before God's accredited representatives on earth (e.g. the judges), they were said to be standing "before the LORD". The following are two examples:
      i. "Then both the men, between whom the controversy is, shall stand before the LORD, before the priests and the judges, which shall be in those days." (Deut. 19:17).
      ii. "...Take heed what ye do: for ye judge not for man, but for the LORD, who is with you in the judgment." (2 Chron. 19:6).
   b. To leave the presence of the Lord (Job 1:12) does not require Satan ("adversary", AVm. Job 1:6) to have had access to the dwelling place of God in heaven. Cain "went out from the presence of the LORD" (Gen. 4:16) and he certainly was not in heaven. The adversary was well travelled on the

[4] *Things In Which It Is Impossible For God To Lie*, (Brooklyn, New York: Watchtower Bible And Tract Society of N.Y. Inc., Int. Bible Students Ass. Brooklyn, N.Y., 1965), p.48.
[5] *Ibid.*, p.299.

242

earth: "going to and fro on the earth, and from walking up and down on it." (Job 1:7, RSV). (Is walking the usual mode of locomotion for a mighty angel?)

3. It is impossible that a rebel angel could have had access to the dwelling place of God in heaven for the following reasons:

   a. God does not tolerate evil: "Evil may not sojourn with thee." (Psa. 5:4,5, RSV); "Thou art of purer eyes than to behold evil, and canst not look on iniquity…" (Hab. 1:13). How then could a rebel angel have access to heaven from before the creation of Adam and Eve until 1914? Or if, as it is sometimes asserted that Satan was cast out of heaven before the creation of Adam and Eve, how did he manage to regain access to heaven?

   b. If Satan were a rebel angel with access to heaven until 1914 (as JWs assert), this would invalidate the Lord's prayer. Jesus prayed: "Thy kingdom come. Thy will be done in earth, as it is in heaven." (Matt. 6:10). Did Jesus believe that heaven was the seat of revolution, intrigue, and disorder, and later to be the scene of a great war?

4. Job never attributed his afflictions to a rebel angel. His declaration was simply: "The hand of God hath touched me". (Job 19:21, cf. 2:10). Even Job's brethren, sisters and acquaintances acknowledged that the evil was brought upon Job by the Lord: "they bemoaned him, and comforted him over all the evil that the LORD had brought upon him." (Job 42:11).

5. Although it can be shown what the passage does not mean, an attempt need not be made to identify the adversary. Scripture does not provide a positive identification, and although some evidence might be deduced, ultimately "the secret things belong unto the LORD our God: but those things which are revealed belong unto us". (Deut. 29:29). The onus of proof rests with those who cite this passage as proof that Satan is a fallen-angel devil. To this issue the discussion should be confined, since to do otherwise allows too many red-herring opportunities in which considerations irrelevant to the main issue are soon dragged in, resulting in a tangle of unresolved propositions and assertions.

Isaiah 14:12–14

"How art thou fallen from heaven, O Lucifer, son of the morning! how art thou cut down to the ground, which didst weaken the nations! For thou hast said in thine heart, I will ascend into heaven, I will exalt my throne above the stars of God…I will be like the most High."

PROBLEM:

This verse is used to prove that Satan is a fallen angel. A SDA book of official doctrine puts it this way:

"As to Satan, or the devil, we hold the uniform teaching of the Word to be that he is definitely a personal being—the supreme adversary of God and man… He was, however, once an angel of light, the highest of the angels. He was named Lucifer, son of the morning (Isa. 14:12–14). But he fell from his high estate (Ezek. 28:13–18; Luke 10:18; John 8:44), and drew down with him a host of angels, first unto disaffection and then into open rebellion against God and His government…"[6]

SOLUTION:

1. This passage nowhere mentions the terms "devil", "satan" or "fallen angel". The argument in support of a fallen angel is, therefore, an *inferred* argument.

2. Lucifer is identified in the narrative, but not with a rebel angel. It is explicitly stated: "Take up this proverb[7] against *the king of Babylon*, and say, How hath the oppressor ceased!" (v. 4). (The preceding chapter is a prophecy against Babylon itself, but now the prophecy is directed against the king of Babylon.)

3. Some questions require answering:

   a. Is Satan really accompanied by the noise of viols (sound of harps, RSV)? (v. 11).

   b. Is Satan to be covered by worms in the grave (v. 11) or is he not rather to be cast into the lake of fire? (Rev. 20:10).

   c. Why is Satan desirous of a place "in the sides of the north"? (v. 13).

   d. If Satan is a rebel angel, why is he called "the man"? (v. 16).

   e. What land has Satan possessed, the destruction of which merits him dishonourable burial? (v. 20).

   f. Where are Satan's people *buried*? (v. 20). Is not the lake of fire said to be the common receptacle of Satan and his cohorts?

   g. When did Satan have charge over a prison, refusing to let the people go home? (v. 17 RSV).

4. Lucifer means "Day Star" (RSV) and the verse employs the figure of the brilliant planet Venus which appears low in the sky just before dawn and climbs higher and higher in the sky until unseen in the daylight.[8] The same bright planet is also an "evening star" seen at sunset and going lower and lower until lost beneath the horizon. Hence the figure of Lucifer, king of Babylon, rising in power to his zenith and saying in his heart, "I will ascend into heaven, I will exalt my throne above the stars of God" (which parallels the arrogance of

---

[6] *Seventh-day Adventists Answer Questions on Doctrine: An Explanation of Certain Major Aspects of Seventh-day Adventist Belief*, (Washington, D.C.: Review and Herald Publishing Ass., 1957), pp.618,619.

[7] The "proverb" was a "taunting speech" (mg.) in which trees spoke (v. 8), and the dead in hell were made to speak when the king died with his pomp and glory. (vv. 9,10).

[8] See James Hastings (ed.), *Dictionary of the Bible*, (New York: Charles Scribner's Sons, 1963), p.936. *The Amplified Old Testament*, (Michigan: Zondervan Publishing House, 1962), comments in a footnote to Isaiah 14 as follows: "…the application of the name Lucifer to Satan, in spite of the long and confident teaching to that effect, is completely erroneous… Nowhere in the Bible is Satan called Lucifer. The misapplication of the name has existed since the third century AD, and is based on the false supposition that Luke 10:18 is an explanation of Isaiah 14:12…It is the satanic king himself who is being addressed." (p.503).

Interestingly, the JWs have recognized the force of these arguments and now, in their official publications, no longer refer to Satan as Lucifer, nor is Isaiah 14 cited in support of their belief that Satan is a fallen angel.

another king of Babylon—Nebuchadnezzar—who said: "Is not this great Babylon, that I have built for the house of the kingdom by the might of my power, and for the honour of my majesty?" (Dan. 4:30). The "evening star" seen at sunset going lower and lower until lost beneath the horizon portrays the demise of Lucifer—"brought down to hell, to the sides of the pit." (v. 15).

5. "Ascending to heaven" is a Biblical idiom for increase in pride or exaltation, and "falling from heaven", an idiom for complete humiliation. See Jer. 51:53 (refers to Babylon); Lam. 2:1; Matt. 11:23 (refers to Capernaum).

Ezekiel 28:13–15

"Thou hast been in Eden the garden of God...Thou art the anointed cherub that covereth...Thou wast perfect in thy ways from the day that thou wast created, till iniquity was found in thee."

PROBLEM:

This passage is cited to prove that Satan is a fallen angel. A SDA publication puts it this way:

"Thus we believe Satan to be but a created being, though of the highest rank. He was once called the 'anointed cherub that covereth' (Ezek. 28:14). He was described as 'full of wisdom, and perfect in beauty' (verse 12). He was the embodiment of created perfection, and apparently led the worship of the universe. He was in the 'mountain of God,' where God manifests His glory, and was 'perfect' in his ways until 'iniquity' developed in him (verses 14,15). His heart became lifted up because of his beauty, and his wisdom was corrupted because of his brightness (verse 17). Unholy ambition and jealousy ruined him, and he led a host of angels in rebellion against God and Christ (Rev. 12:7–9). As a result he was 'cast' out of the mountain of God (Ezek. 28:16), and down to the 'ground', or earth (verse 17; Isa. 14:12)."[9]

SOLUTION:

1. This passage nowhere mentions the terms "devil", "satan", or "fallen angel". The argument in support of a fallen angel interpretation, is therefore, an *inferred* argument.

2. The anointed cherub (accepting the AV translation)[10] is identified in the passage, but not with a rebel angel: "Son of man, say unto the prince[11] of Tyrus..." (v. 2).

---

[9] *Seventh-day Adventists Answer Questions on Doctrine: An Explanation of Certain Major Aspects of Seventh-day Adventist Belief,* (Washington, D.C.: Review and Herald Publishing Ass., 1957), p.619.

[10] The AV rendering of this verse identifies the cherub with the "king of Tyrus". The RSV translates this verse as follows: "With an anointed guardian cherub I placed you"—in which case the guardian cherub does not refer to the king of Tyre.

[11] Or "king of Tyrus". (v. 12). "Prince" is translated from the Hebrew word *nagid* which means 'leader'. It is translated most often by "ruler" in the AV; "king" is translated from the Hebrew word *melek* which means 'king, counsellor'. Robert Young, *Analytical Concordance to the Holy Bible,* (London: Lutterworth Press. 1965).

In chapters 26 and 27 prophecies recorded the then impending doom of the city of Tyre.

3. Some questions require answering:

a. In chapters 26 and 27 of Ezekiel's prophecy the destruction of Tyre is recorded—and literally enough, since today the site of ancient Tyre is like "the top of a rock...a place to spread nets upon" and has never been rebuilt. (Ezek. 26:14). The remainder of chapter 28 is a prophecy directed against Sidon and the future restoration of Israel. Why, in this context, would the prophet introduce a revelation about the origin of Satan?

b. If Satan is a rebel angel, why is he called "a man"? (vv. 2,9 RSV).

c. Does Satan the devil really traffic in riches—gold and silver? (vv. 4,5). Is not his concern for humans?

d. It is said by JWs that Satan rebelled "because of developing a greed for power over mankind."[12] But how is this to be squared with vv. 4,5, "and thine heart is lifted up *because of thy riches*"?

e. Since Jesus stated that angels do not die: "neither can they [children of the resurrection] die any more: for they are equal unto the angels" (Luke 20:36), how is Satan to die "by the hand of strangers" (v. 10), to be devoured by fire and brought "to ashes" (v. 18), and "to be no more for ever" (v. 19, RSV)?

4. "There is no secret that they can hide from thee." (v. 3). This is an illustration of the way in which "the children of this world are in their generation wiser than the children of light." (Luke 16:8). The king of Tyre was wise in his ability to increase his riches through trade (v. 5; Zech. 9:2), but this does not mean that he was wiser than Daniel in divine matters.

5. "Thou has been in Eden the garden of God." (v. 13). It is reasoned that the real character must have been Satan the devil since the king of Tyre could not have lived contemporary with Adam and Eve. But the passage does not require the King of Tyre to have lived contemporary with Adam and Eve. It just requires the king to have been in Eden, the garden of God, but without specification as to time. Eden appears to have been an extensive area in which the garden was placed in the east. (Gen. 2:8; cf. Ezek. 27:23). In figurative language, Pharaoh, king of Egypt is depicted as being a cedar in Lebanon taller than any of the other trees of Eden (trees are used here symbolically for nations). (Ezek. 31:2,3, RSV, 8,9,16,18). But this reference to Eden does not imply that Pharaoh must have lived contemporary with Adam and Eve.

6. "Thou wast perfect in thy ways from the day that thou wast created, till iniquity was found in thee." (v. 15). It is sometimes argued that the passage cannot refer to the literal king of Tyre since he was not perfect. The Hebrew word *tamim* translated "perfect" means 'perfect, plain, whole, complete'.[13] Noah was a "just man and perfect (Heb. *tamim*)" (Gen. 6:9—same Hebrew word), but there is no question of his being an angel.

[12] *Things In Which It Is Impossible For God To Lie*, (Brooklyn, New York: Watchtower Bible and Tract Society of N.Y., Inc., Int. Bible Students Ass., 1965), p.159.

[13] Robert Young, *Analytical Concordance to the Holy Bible*, (London: Lutterworth Press, 1965).

7. It is sometimes argued that the literal king of Tyre would have been procreated, not created (vv. 13,15), therefore, the passage must refer to an angel. But the Hebrew word, *bara* translated "create" means "to be prepared, formed, created."[14] The same word is used for the creation of people (Psa. 102:18) and the Ammonites (Ezek. 21:30). Clearly in these passages the word cannot imply the creation of angels.

8. Tyre occupied a privileged position in its relationship to Israel. David and Hiram had been close friends (2 Sam. 5:11; 1 Kings 5:1,6,7,10) and Hiram and Solomon had made a league in which Hiram supplied materials for the building of the temple. (1 Kings 5:12,17,18). The language of Ezek. 28:13–18 is taken from Israelitish worship and used symbolically for the relationship of Israel and Tyre (by implication suggesting the divine favour which rested upon Tyre because of its association with Israel). Consider the following:

   a. "Every precious stone was thy covering" (v. 13); "thou hast walked up and down in the midst of the stones of fire." (v. 14). This is an allusion to the stones set in the breastplate of the high priest of Israel. (Exo. 39:10–14). They were "stones of fire" because of the way they would shine when exposed to the brilliance of the Shekinah glory of the sanctuary. They symbolized the twelve tribes of Israel. (Exo. 39:14). The king of Tyre walked in the midst of these stones of fire when he moved among the children of Israel (as in the preparation of the materials for the temple). The position of Israel in the divine purpose provided a "covering" for Tyre on the basis of the decree in Gen. 12:3: "I will bless them that bless thee, and curse him that curseth thee." God blessed the house of Potiphar because of Joseph: "...the LORD blessed the Egyptian's house for Joseph's sake; and the blessing of the LORD was upon all that he had in the house, and in the field." (Gen. 39:5). Similarly, Tyre was "covered" by Israel.

   b. "Thou art the anointed cherub that covereth." (v. 14). The cherubim were figures of beaten gold at either end of the mercy seat. (Exo. 37:7–9). Their wings overshadowed the mercy seat with which they were of one piece. (Exo. 25:19,20). Although the translation of the Hebrew is uncertain, (accepting the AV), the suggestion may be that Tyre as a great mercantile power was privileged to cast its "wings" over Israel.[15] It was the abuse of this exalted position that was a factor in the ruin of Tyre. (vv. 4,5).

   c. "Thou wast upon the *holy* mountain of God." (v. 14). This holy mountain is Mount Zion, the future site of God's house of prayer for all people. (Isa. 2:2,3; 56:7). This "holy mountain of God" is on the earth, not symbolically in heaven as JWs assert. (See Ezek. 20:40).

   d. "Thou hast defiled thy sanctuaries by the multitude of thine iniquities." (Ezek. 28:18). This verse may imply that Tyre had set up forms of worship similar to that of Israel. Hiram was "ever a lover of David" and rejoiced with

---

[14] *Ibid.*

[15] Wings suggest protection. See Matt. 23:37; Psa. 36:7; 91:4. The Hebrew word *kanaph* (the usual Hebrew word for the wings of the cherubim) carries the meaning of wings as covering and protecting. See Robert Young, *Analytical Concordance to the Holy Bible*, (London: Lutterworth Press, 1965).

Solomon in the building of the temple. (1 Kings 5:1–12). The king of Tyre would no doubt have learned about God's kingdom in Israel from these two kings of Israel. Or, the verse may be interpreted this way: Tyre's sanctuaries were in Israel where the divine presence and favour were manifest. But Tyre failed to appreciate its privileged association with Israel. When Nebuchadnezzar came down into Jerusalem (586 BC), the prince of Tyrus said: "Aha, the gate of the peoples is broken, it has swung open to me; I shall be replenished, now that she is laid waste." (Ezek. 26:2 RSV). In so saying, Tyre had spoken her own nemesis according to the decree of Gen. 12:3: "I will…curse him that curseth thee." Tyre, in her self-centered mercantile interests, had profaned the sanctuaries and was herself to be reduced to ashes.

e. "I [will] bring forth a fire from the midst of thee, it shall devour thee, and I will bring thee to ashes upon the earth in the sight of all them that behold thee." (v. 18). Tyre could not with impunity violate her privileged relationship with Israel. When Nadab and Abihu treated the sacred as secular, "there went out fire from the LORD, and devoured them, and they died before the LORD." (Lev. 10:2). Similarly, Tyre had failed to make a difference between the holy and unholy. It was, therefore, to be reduced to ashes—devoured like Sodom and Gomorrah. (Gen. 19:24,25).

Matthew 4:1–11

"Then was Jesus led up of the Spirit into the wilderness to be tempted of the devil…"

PROBLEM:

This is a stock proof-text cited in support of the belief that Satan is a personal being—a fallen angel.

SOLUTION:

1. If the devil were a fallen angel, why would the Holy Spirit lead the Son of God into the wilderness to be tempted of the devil?
2. The essence of a temptation rests in its subtlety, not in its obviousness. If Jesus had been confronted by a fallen angel the obviousness of the temptation would have vitiated its power.
3. Jesus "was in all points tempted like as we are" (Heb. 4:15), but who today is ever engaged in discussion by a fallen angel devil?
4. A temptation, to be a temptation, must be plausible, but if a fallen angel offered to Jesus all the kingdoms of the world and their glory, Jesus would know he were a fake. God, "the most High [not a fallen angel], ruleth in the kingdom of men, and giveth it to whomsoever he will." (Dan. 4:32). Jesus knew his Old Testament.

5. There is considerable evidence that the temptations were subjective (i.e. that the conflicts within Jesus are presented in the narratives as if there was a dialogue between Jesus and Satan, when in effect Satan is only a personification[16] of the pull of the desires of Jesus—(cf. James 1:13–15). Consider the following:

a. Mark states that Jesus was "there in the wilderness forty days, tempted of Satan" (Mark 1:13), but at least one of the temptations is said to have taken place in the holy city—Jerusalem. If Jesus literally went to the holy city, then the accounts appear contradictory.

b. Where is the mountain in the wilderness which is high enough to view all the kingdoms of the world and their glory in a moment of time? (Matt. 4:8, cf. Luke 4:5).

c. Jesus had been baptized by John and given the Holy Spirit. (Matt. 3:16). How was the power to be used? To make life easy by using the power for selfish purposes (making stones into bread)? By converting Israel through dazzling displays of divine power (by casting himself down from the pinnacle of the temple)? By avoiding the agony and humiliation of crucifixion and death by taking the kingdoms of the world (his miracles would have assured this—cf. John 6:14,15)?

Luke 10:18

"...I beheld Satan as lightning fall from heaven."

PROBLEM:

This passage is connected with Isaiah 14:12 to support the doctrine that Satan, a rebel angel, was cast from heaven after a great war with the forces of the Almighty. A SDA book of official doctrine, for example, puts it this way:

"As to Satan, or the devil, we hold the uniform teaching of the Word to be that he is definitely a personal being—the supreme adversary of God and man... He was, however, once an angel of light, the highest of the angels. He was named Lucifer, son of the morning (Isa. 14:12–14). But he fell from his high estate (Ezek. 28:13–18; Luke 10:18; John 8:44), and drew down with him a host of angels, first unto disaffection and then into open rebellion against God and His government..."[17]

SOLUTION:

1. It is usually argued that Satan was cast out of heaven prior to the events of Gen. 1–3, or that he was cast out of heaven in 1914 (as JWs assert), but this passage squares with neither, since Jesus said, "I *beheld* Satan as lightning fall from heaven". (This was about AD 30.)

---

[16] Personification is commonly used in Scripture. For example: death is personified as reigning (Rom. 5:14), sin as a person (Rom. 7:11), and riches as a master (Matt. 6:24).

[17] *Seventh-day Adventists Answer Questions on Doctrine*: An Explanation of Certain Major Aspects of Seventh-day Adventist Belief, (Washington, D.C.: Review and Herald Publishing Ass., 1957), pp.618,619.

2. The passage does not state either that Satan was in heaven or that he fell from heaven. Jesus makes a comparison indicated by the simile "as". The comparison is not that as lightning falls from heaven so Satan fell from heaven. The point of the comparison is rather that the swiftness of the fall of Satan is as lightning falling from heaven.

3. The context indicates that the casting out of demons and not the fall of a rebel angel is the subject of reference. (v. 17).

4. Satan (meaning: "adversary")[18] is used by Jesus to describe the binding effect of sin through diseases. A number of passages indicate this:

   a. Luke 11:14–23—The cause of dumbness (which was attributed to demon possession in the vernacular of the time—v. 14) was associated with the "house" of Satan. (vv. 17,18). The subsequent cure was said to be the "kingdom of God" coming, since the power of the King was present. (vv. 20–22).

   b. Luke 13:10–17—Jesus healed a woman who had "a spirit of infirmity eighteen years". (v. 11). But this same healing is described as "a daughter of Abraham, whom Satan hath bound, lo, these eighteen years". (v. 16).

   Hence, the victory of the seventy over demons and other diseases resulted in the dethronement of Satan (the adversary) in his "house". The cures effected by the disciples were so complete and rapid as to be compared to lightning falling from heaven. Despite this victory over the powers of sin and its effect—disease, Jesus instructs his disciples to rejoice rather that their names were written in heaven. (Luke 10:20).

Luke 22:3

"Then entered Satan into Judas surnamed Iscariot, being of the number of the twelve."

Luke 22:31

"And the Lord said, Simon, Simon, behold, Satan hath desired to have you, that he may sift you as wheat."

John 13:2

"And supper being ended, the devil having now put into the heart of Judas Iscariot, Simon's son, to betray him."

John 13:27

"And after the sop Satan entered into him."

PROBLEM:

These verses are cited to prove that Satan is a superhuman being.

---

[18] Robert Young, *Analytical Concordance to the Holy Bible*, (London: Lutterworth Press, 1965).

SOLUTION:

1. Which is the superhuman being, Satan, or the Devil? In John 13:2 the *devil* put the thought of betrayal into Judas' heart, but after the sop, *Satan* entered into him. (John 13:27). Does Satan enter one who is already captured by the devil? (Cf. "have not I chosen you twelve, and one of you is a *devil*"?—John 6:70). The distinction between "the devil" (John 13:2) and "Satan" (John 13:27) may suggest that the former was sown by some emissary of the chief priests. The latter may indicate complete abandonment to sin. (cf. John 12:6—Judas' problems began before the crucifixion: "he was a thief, and had the bag".)

2. "Satan hath desired to have you [plural]" (Luke 22:31): it is possible that the chief priests were looking for two or more of the disciples who they could use for their own evil purposes; or it may suggest that they contemplated rounding up all the disciples.

3. There is a parallel passage in Acts 5:3,4: Peter said to Ananias, "Why hath Satan filled thine heart...?" But the next verse explains: "Why hast *thou* conceived this thing in thine heart?" When an individual gives himself over to sin, it is said to be Satan (adversary) entering into his heart.

John 12:31; 14:30; 16:11

"Now shall the prince of this world be cast out."

PROBLEM:

Since Jesus refers to "the prince of this world", this passage is cited to prove the personal existence of Satan.

SOLUTION:

1. The JWs teach that Satan was cast out of heaven in a great war in 1914. Others assert that he was cast out before the fall of Adam, but this passage squares with neither of these, for it emphasizes: *"Now* shall the prince of this world be cast out".

2. "The prince of the power of the air" is identified with sin in Eph. 2:1–3. Notice the parallel structure: "And you hath he quickened, who were dead in *trespasses and sins*; wherein in time past ye walked according to the course of this world, [Greek: *aion* of this *kosmos*] ...the prince of the power of the air, the spirit that now worketh in the children of disobedience." "The prince of this world" which had nothing in Christ was sin. The outward appearances in the death of Christ were deceptive since it appeared as if he were condemned, when it was the sin which was cast out and condemned. (Rom. 8:3). This personification of sin is in the pattern of other Scriptures. Sin is compared with a master who pays wages (Rom. 6:23), a slave owner from whom men are emancipated that they might serve God (Rom. 6:17), a reigning monarch (Rom. 5:21), and as indwelling with men (Rom. 7:17).

251

WRESTED SCRIPTURES

3. The world rulers (Herod and Pontius Pilate) and the chief priests were the embodiment of the "prince of this world". The latter were shortly to be "cast" from their office by the sacrificial death of Christ (his "lifting up", John 12:32).

2 Corinthians 11:14

"And no marvel; for Satan himself is transformed into an angel of light."

PROBLEM:

This passage is interpreted as a description of the subtle nature of a personal superhuman being—Satan the Devil. A SDA publication puts it this way:

> "The unsaved are in the 'power of Satan' (Acts 26:18), and the wicked world lies in his evil embrace (1 John 5:19, RSV). He has many subtle 'devices' (2 Cor. 2:11), even transforming himself into an angel of light (2 Cor. 11:14)."[19]

SOLUTION:

1. How can Satan be transformed into an angel of light when it is taught that he was transformed *from* an angel of light because of his rebellion?
2. The Satan of this passage is not a rebel angel but rebel Jewish adversaries who were undermining the Apostle Paul's influence in the Corinthian ecclesia (see 2 Cor. 10:2,10–18; 11:3–26). As Paul said: "for such *men* are false apostles, deceitful work*men*, disguising themselves as apostles of Christ. And no wonder for even Satan [the chief leader] disguises himself as an angel of light. So it is not strange if his servants [misguided supporters] also disguise themselves as servants of righteousness". (vv. 13–15, RSV). The same Satan is referred to in 2 Cor. 2:11: "Lest Satan should get an advantage of us: for we are not ignorant of his devices."

1 Peter 5:8

"Be sober, be vigilant; because your adversary the devil, as a roaring lion, walketh about, seeking whom he may devour."

PROBLEM:

This passage is cited in support of the doctrine that the devil is a rebel angel.

SOLUTION:

1. The passage does not state that the devil is a rebel angel. The devil is compared to a roaring lion, but elsewhere in Scripture lion-like characteristics are ascribed to men, not angels (e.g. Psa. 22:12,13; 57:4; Prov. 28:15).

[19] *Seventh-day Adventists Answer Questions on Doctrine*, (Washington, D.C.: Review and Herald Publishing Ass., 1957), p.620.

252

2. The Greek word *antidikos* translated "adversary" means "an adversary in law"[20] and the Greek word *diabolos* translated "devil" means "accuser, calumniator".[21] Hence, "the roaring lion" was an opponent at law who maliciously accused. This was none other than the Roman magistracy. The persecution of the ecclesia under Nero and Diocletian is well documented.

3. If it is argued that the devil was really behind the persecution, then proof that such is the case is required from the narrative.

4. Peter's first epistle expresses concern for the steadfastness of the ecclesia because of the imminent period of suffering that the ecclesia was about to enter. He exhorted: "Resist him, firm in your faith, knowing that the same experience of suffering is required of your brotherhood throughout the world"; "Beloved, think it not strange concerning the fiery trial which is to try you, as though some strange thing happened unto you." (1 Pet. 5:9 RSV; 4:12). See also 4:16–19.

5. Paul had a similar encounter with a roaring lion (2 Tim. 4:17): this lion was not a fallen angel, but Caesar's tribunal (vv. 16,17) from which Paul was delivered at the first trial. Paul was also delivered, not from a rebel angel, but from persecutions and afflictions at Antioch, Iconium, and Lystra of which he wrote: "...but out of them all the Lord delivered me. Yea, and all that will live godly in Christ Jesus shall suffer persecution...But evil *men* and seducers shall wax worse and worse, deceiving, and being deceived." (2 Tim. 3:11–13).

Jude 9

"Yet Michael the archangel, when contending with the devil he disputed about the body of Moses, durst not bring against him a railing accusation, but said, The Lord rebuke thee."

PROBLEM:

This verse is cited to prove that the devil is a personal superhuman being.

SOLUTION:

1. It is generally taught that the devil is concerned with souls or humans, but this devil is concerned with the body of Moses. Why should the devil want custody of a corpse?

---

[20] Robert Young, *Analytical Concordance to the Holy Bible*, (London: Lutterworth Press. 1965).
[21] *Ibid.*

2. It is sometimes argued that the devil wished to lead Israel into idolatry through veneration of the body of Moses, but this conjecture must be rejected for lack of Scriptural support. It is also argued that Jude alludes to an apocryphal writing "The Assumption of Moses"[22] but there is no certain evidence that Jude wrote his epistle later than the apocryphal work.[23] Some critics suggest that Jude refers to the "Targum of Jonathan", but this work makes no reference to the devil or to any contention concerning the body of Moses.

3. There are two lines of evidence which indicate that the devil of this passage is human and not superhuman. Jude and 2 Peter have so many similarities that Jude 8,9 can be read as an amplification of 2 Peter 2:10–12. It is clear that the description in Peter's account is about humans, therefore the same must be true of the parallel account in Jude. (See footnote 23a, and cf. Jude 16,19.)

4. The second line of reasoning seeks to show that "the body of Moses" is Joshua the high priest in the time of Ezra and Zechariah, and that the devil is the group of disaffected priests debarred from priestly office. It is evident that Jude alludes to Zech. 3:2 from the following similarities:

Zechariah 3	Jude
An angel of the Lord	Michael the archangel
Satan	the devil
The LORD that hath chosen Jerusalem rebuke thee	The Lord rebuke thee
a brand plucked out of the fire	Pulling them out of the fire (v. 23)

5. The children of the priests were debarred from priestly office because they were unable to provide proof of descent. (Ezra 2:62). It can be inferred that this disaffected group was the devil. The priests would likely turn on Joshua. "Then what of you as high priest? Where is your priestly attire?" (no doubt lost during the Babylonian captivity). Hence the angel's remark: "Take away the filthy garments from him. And unto him he said, Behold, I have caused thine iniquity

---

[22] The text extant as quoted by early "Christian" writers reads as follows: "Moses having died in the mount, the archangel Michael is sent removing the body. The devil therefore, wishing to cheat him, withstood him saying, 'The body is mine as lord of all material things' or because of his slaying of the Egyptian blaspheming against the holy man and proclaiming him a murderer. The angel, not enduring this blasphemy against the holy one, said to the devil, 'God rebuke thee!' " H.W., "The Apocryphal Associations of the Epistle of Jude", *The Testimony Magazine*, (June 1964), Vol. 34, No. 402, pp.188,189.

[23] There are further reasons for rejecting the claim that Jude quotes from "The Assumption of Moses". These are as follows:

   a. Nearly every verse in Jude has its counterpart in 2 Peter. (It can be inferred that Jude wrote after Peter since Jude 17,18 is taken from 2 Peter 3:2,3.) Peter's equivalent phrase to "the devil" in Jude's account is "railing accusation against them" (2 Peter 2:11), thereby indicating that "the devil" in Jude's account is plural, and not singular, as it is in "The Assumption of Moses".

   b. The contention alluded to by Peter is "before the lord" (2 Peter 2:11), whereas "The Assumption of Moses" locates it on top of the mountain where Moses died.

   c. If Jude were alluding to the apocryphal work, then this argument would be pointless. How is the self-restraint of a mighty angel in refraining from rebuking a superhuman devil a reason why a "servant of Jesus Christ" should "earnestly contend for the faith which was once delivered unto the saints"? (Jude 3).

to pass from thee, and I will clothe thee with change of raiment." (Zech. 3:4). Jude alludes to this event in attacking the would-be corrupters of the Faith.

6. The "body of Moses" likely refers to Joshua the high priest. The Greek word *soma* can be translated "slave" as it is in Rev. 18:13. Compare Heb. 10:5 with Psa. 40:6 where the allusion is to the binding of slaves to their masters by the piercing of the ear (Exo. 21:2–6); also Rom. 6:6 where "body of sin" means, "slave of sin". Joshua the high priest was Moses' servant (slave) in a figure, since he served the law which Moses gave.

Revelation 12:7–9

"And there was war in heaven...and the great dragon was cast out, that old serpent, called the Devil, and Satan, which deceiveth the whole world: he was cast out into the earth, and his angels were cast out with him."

PROBLEM:

This passage is a stock proof text for those who argue that the devil is a rebel angel. A JW publication puts it this way:

"In Eden, Satan used the serpent. And so the Bible identifies the Devil, or Satan, as 'the original serpent,' hence the one who really introduced rebellion and wickedness into the universe.—Rev. 12:9".[24]

"Christ would then oust Satan from heaven [1914], the seat of government, hurling him down to the vicinity of the earth, in preparation for putting him completely out of action. In the heavens the grand announcement would then be made: 'Now have come to pass the salvation and the power and the kingdom of our God and the authority of his Christ.' But for the earth, what? 'Woe...because the Devil has come down to you, having great anger, knowing he has a short period of time.' (Rev. 12:5,7–10,12)"[25]

SOLUTION:

1. Rev. 12 is the key text on which JWs & SDAs build their doctrine that the devil is a fallen angel. Since the devil is associated with the serpent (v. 9) it is argued that the devil used the serpent to obtain the fall of man (Gen. 3). It is further argued that the devil must be a fallen angel since his cohorts are called angels (v. 9). At the outset the weakness of the total argument should be indicated: Why would the disclosure of the devil's identity be reserved for the last book of scripture, and in a symbolic setting? (Even the most ardent fallen-angel devil expounder must concede the symbolic character of the dragon. A seven-headed, ten-horned red dragon isn't the kind of description one would ordinarily associate with an angel—fallen or otherwise.) Many passages describe in detail warnings to Israel about apostasy (e.g. Exo. 32; Lev. 26; Num. 16; Deut. 28), but none of these narratives contains a warning about what would, according to

[24] *The Truth that leads to Eternal Life*, (Brooklyn, New York: Watchtower Bible and Tract Society of N.Y., Inc., Int. Bible Students As., 1968), p.57.

[25] *Ibid.*, p.83.

JW and SDA teaching, be the real instigator—Satan the Devil. Similarly, in the New Testament comprehensive attention is given to sin and the nature of man (e.g. Rom. 7) and just where one would expect the devil of JW and SDA teaching to place prominently, the narratives contain no hint of such a creature. It can be expected, therefore, with such poverty of evidence in contexts where evidence is most to be expected, the recourse must be taken by SDAs and JWs to the symbolic language of Revelation.

2. The devil of Rev. 12 is nowhere stated to be a fallen angel. Satan in the narrative is a red dragon, not a fallen angel, and if the red dragon is symbolic of a fallen angel, then proof that the symbol should be interpreted this way is required. The argument that Satan is a fallen angel is therefore *inferred*, since it is not stated that such is the case in the passage.

3. For those who teach that Satan was cast out of heaven *before* the creation of man, it only needs to be pointed out that this is an anachronism since the Revelation was written about AD 96, and its contents are expressly stated to be about "things which [were] shortly [to] come to pass" (i.e. future to that time). (Rev. 1:1).

4. A discussion on Rev. 12 requires that a clear distinction be made between the literal and the figurative and that a criterion or reason by which to make the choice be established *before* the discussion. By a fast-and-loose treatment of the figurative and literal in a predominantly symbolic book, one can make a passage support nearly any presupposition.

5. Failure to distinguish the literal and the figurative is at the root of all arguments which press Rev. 12 into service to prove that the devil is a rebel angel. This is indicated in the following approach in which the aim is to establish step by step that the dragon, heavens and war are all symbolic and are not to be taken literally:

   a. The devil of this passage is a "great red dragon, having seven heads and ten horns, and seven crowns upon his heads. And his tail drew the third part of the stars of heaven, and did cast them to the earth" (vv. 3,4). Is, or is not, this a *literal* description of the fallen-angel devil?[26]

   b. Assuming that it is conceded that the dragon is figurative, is the heaven of v. 7 also figurative? (The answer is inevitable: "No".) The use of the word "heaven" in the preceding verses must then be examined to show whether or not there is consistency in this reply (remembering the distinction between the literal and figurative set out at the beginning of the discussion). Is the heaven of v. 1 figurative? (The reply must be "yes" since the woman is clothed with the sun and the moon is under her feet, which would be a literal impossibility). Is the heaven of verse 3 the same heaven, or a different heaven from the heaven of verse 1? (Consistency demands that the answer again be "yes", but if the answer is "no", then it must be shown by the non-Christadelphian on what basis he decides between the literal and the figurative.) Is this the same criterion as set out before the discussion began? Assuming that it is conceded that the heaven of verse 3 is also figurative, it

---

[26] If any should argue that it is, the impossibility of casting one of the literal stars to the earth can be shown.

only remains by the same reasoning to establish that the heaven of verse 7 is the same heaven, and therefore, is also figurative.

    c. Since the dragon and heaven are figurative, then the war (v. 7) must also be figurative, since one cannot have a literal war when the locale and one of the combatants are figurative.

6. Jesus did not believe the heavens to be the seat of angelic rebellion and subsequent war, since he taught his disciples to pray, "Thy kingdom come. Thy will be done in earth, *as it is in heaven.*" (Matt. 6:10).

7. If Satan had access to heaven until 1914 as JWs teach, how did the devil manage to last so long since God is of "purer eyes than to behold evil"? (Hab. 1:13; Psa. 5:4).

8. If the devil were a rebel angel[27] against the will of God, what guarantee is there that believers who will be glorified with Christ, and "made equal unto the angels" (Luke 20:35,36), will not similarly rise against the authority of the Almighty once they have tasted the blessings of immortality?

9. The issue is—Does or does not this passage teach the existence of a fallen-angel devil? Although an exposition of the chapter might be attempted, it frequently allows too many red herrings to be dragged into the discussion without settling the main issue.

---

[27] It should be noted that the Greek word *aggelos* translated "angels" (vv. 7,9), can refer to either human or divine angels. The word means "messenger, agent". Robert Young, *Analytical Concordance to the Holy Bible*, (London: Lutterworth Press, 1965). *Aggelos* refers to human messengers or agents in the following passages: Matt. 11:10; Luke 7:24,27; 9:52; and James 2:25.

2.8

DEMONS AND DEMON POSSESSION

This is a difficult subject that the Christadelphian should not lightly dismiss or treat with complacency. Sadly, too often our approach is along the lines, "We know that there are no such beings as demons, therefore demons do not exist." We must do better than this.

EXISTENCE OF DEMONS

PRELIMINARY POINTS:

Belief in demons is still a prominent doctrine among the Evangelical churches and groups like the JWs and SDAs. They consider them to be wicked spirit beings responsible for doing untold harm to mankind. Wars, civil unrest and the progress of evil political ideologies are all considered to be the result of demon activity. They are held to be capable of entering into the body or mind of an individual when the demon can destroy faith, induce bodily sickness or make the individual mad. People who believe in the existence of demons give different explanations as to their origin. There appear to be four popular ideas which the Christadelphian may be called upon to refute:

1. **Demons are the immortal spirits of wicked people who have died**: This idea may be instantly dismissed since according to the Bible neither wicked men nor good men possess immortal spirits. The Bible teaches that when men die they are really dead. (Gen. 3:19–22; Psa. 146:3,4; Eccl. 9:5–10).

2. **Demons are the spirits of the inhabitants of a pre-adamic earth**: It is possible that there was a race of beings on the earth prior to the creation of Adam (suggested, perhaps, by the command to Adam and Eve to "be fruitful, and multiply, and *replenish* the earth"—Gen. 1:28), but there is not the faintest hint in the Bible that if this race did exist, its members had immortal spirits or that demons are the wicked of that race.

3. **Demons are the offspring of angels and antediluvian women**: This theory rests entirely on an interpretation of Gen. 6:2, which, speaking of the wickedness of the generation that was destroyed by the flood, says, "The sons of God saw the daughters of men that they were fair; and they took them wives of all which they chose". It is said that the "sons of God" in this verse refers to angels who contracted marriages with human women and that the progeny of these marriages are the demons.[1]

---

[1] This idea is said to go back to the second century BC. It is set out in the apocryphal Book of Enoch, ch. 15. Details may be found in Merrill F. Unger, *Biblical Demonology*, (Wheaton, Ill., Scripture Press, 1967), p.46.

A variation of this idea is set out by the JWs in their publications. They maintain that it was the angels who contracted these marriages who became the demons:

"In the days of Noah, disobedient angels did take on human form. They actually married, and they fathered children."[2]

"They are no longer counted among the sons of God, because they have made demons of themselves. They have become the angels of the great symbolic dragon, Satan the Devil, the first demon. As the leader in demon activities, he has become their prince or ruler. The Bible speaks of him as the 'the ruler of the demons.' As such, he was given the name Beelzebub."[3]

Whilst it is true that occasionally in the Bible the phrase "sons of God" does refer to angels (e.g. Job 38:7) it usually has reference to members of the human race, who have a special relationship with God. For example, writing to members of the early church the apostle declares, "Beloved, now are we *the sons of God*, and it doth not yet appear what we shall be" (1 John 3:2). See also John 1:12; 11:52; Gal. 3:26; Heb. 12:7,8; Rom. 8:14; Deut. 14:1; Isa. 1:2. The "sons of God" in Gen. 6 we take to be those descendants of Seth referred to in Gen. 4:26, who are said to "call upon the name of the LORD",[4] whilst "the daughters of men" refers to the descendants of wicked Cain. Gen. 6 is thus describing the apostasy from the Truth of the children of God of those days, and their punishment by the flood.

Another compelling reason for rejecting this idea of marriages between angels and women is the clear teaching of Jesus that angels "neither marry, nor are given in marriage" (Mark 12:25).

4. **Demons are fallen angels**: Closely related to the foregoing is the idea that at some time in the remote past a company of angelic beings led by Satan (who is identified with Beelzebub the prince of the demons, Matt. 12:24–26) rebelled against God and were cast out of heaven. These angels, it is said, are referred to by Peter when he says, "God spared not the angels that sinned, but cast them down to hell, and delivered them into chains of darkness, to be reserved unto judgment" (2 Pet. 2:4 and see Jude 6). These angels that sinned are said to be the demons. For the approach to these see the entries under these references.

Reasons for rejecting the idea that Satan is a fallen angel are to be found in the previous chapter.

SUGGESTED STRATEGY:

When faced with Scripture that is "hard to be understood, which they that are unlearned and unstable wrest..." (2 Pet. 3:16), the time honoured Christadelphian approach is to seek out the basic Bible teaching on the subject and bring this to bear on the difficult passage. So, for example, when we are faced with, "We

---

[2] *Reasoning from the Scriptures*, (Brooklyn, N.Y., Watch Tower Bible and Tract Society of New York Inc., 1985), p.388.

[3] *Things In Which It Is Impossible For God To Lie*, (Brooklyn, New York: Watchtower Bible and Tract Society of N.Y., Inc., Int. Bible Students Ass., 1965), p.169.

[4] The Authorised Version margin gives an alternative translation—"Called themselves by the name of the LORD"—i.e. they were His children.

are…willing rather to be absent from the body, and to be present with the Lord" (2 Cor. 5:8), we first of all establish the basic Bible teaching about the mortality of man. It is easy to show that in death man simply ceases to exist. Therefore the verse cannot be saying that men go to heaven when they die. With this established we then seek out the meaning of the passage.

We must adopt this approach to the subject of demons. The basic Bible teaching about demons is simple and must be grasped before trying to explain the difficult demon passages.

1. The Old Testament mentions demons on a number of occasions:

   a. Speaking of the apostasy of the people of Israel we are told that, "They sacrificed unto devils [RV, "demons"],[5] not to God; to gods whom they knew not…" (Deut. 32:17).

   b. Of the way in which apostate Israel offered their own children as sacrifices to pagan gods the Psalmist writes, "They sacrificed their sons and their daughters unto devils [RV, "demons"]" (Psa. 106:37).

   Thus in the Old Testament the clear, simple teaching is that demons are the objects of pagan worship—pagan gods.

2. This is also the teaching of the New Testament:

   a. Speaking of certain wicked people, Rev. 9:20 says, "The rest of the men which were not killed by these plagues yet repented not of the works of their hands, that they should not worship devils [Gk. *daimonia*]…", showing that demons were objects of worship—i.e. pagan gods.

   b. Warning the Corinthian believers that they should not continue to be involved with the idolatrous system around them, Paul writes, "Wherefore, my dearly beloved, flee from idolatry…the things which the Gentiles sacrifice, they sacrifice to devils [demons], and not to God: and I would not that ye should have fellowship with devils [demons]. Ye cannot drink the cup of the Lord, and the cup of devils [demons]: ye cannot be partakers of the Lord's table, and of the table of devils [demons]" (1 Cor. 10:14,20,21).

   c. When Paul visited the Greek city of Athens he saw that the city was "given to idolatry" (Acts 17:16). When these pagans heard Paul speak about Jesus they said, "He seemeth to be a setter forth of strange gods [Gk. *daimonion*]" (v. 18). The Athenians thought that in preaching Jesus, Paul was speaking about the same kind of demon-god as the deities they worshipped. In the same chapter the apostle, amazed at the multitude of their gods, declared, "I perceive that in all things ye are too superstitious" (v. 22). The word translated "superstitious", is *deisi-daimon-esterous* which means that they were extremely devoted to their demon-gods.

   Thus in the New Testament also, demons are presented to us in such a way to lead to the conclusion that they are pagan deities.[6]

---

[5] The Old Testament was, of course, written in Hebrew. But in the Septuagint (the ancient Greek translation of the Old Testament) the word "devils" here is *daimonion*—demons.

[6] This conclusion is in keeping with the basic meaning of the Gk. *daimon*. E.g. (a) "In Gk. auth. a god, a goddess; an inferior deity, whether good or bad…" Joseph H. Thayer, *Greek-English Lexicon of the New Testament*, (Peabody, Mass.: Hendrickson Publishers Inc., 1996), p.124. (b) "We may

3. This next point is vital. We can be absolutely sure that pagan gods have no real existence. In Isaiah 44, Yahweh, the true God asks, "Is there a God beside me?" The answer comes, "There is no God; I know not any" (Isa. 44:8).

Since the Bible declares demons to be pagan gods and since pagan gods have no real existence, it follows that demons do not exist.

Matthew 12:24–26

"But when the Pharisees heard it, they said, This fellow doth not cast out devils, but by Beelzebub the prince of the devils (demons). And Jesus knew their thoughts, and said unto them, Every kingdom divided against itself is brought to desolation; and every city or house divided against itself shall not stand: And if Satan cast out Satan, he is divided against himself; how shall then his kingdom stand?"

PROBLEM:

When Jesus healed the demoniac (Matt. 12:22) the Pharisees said that Jesus cast out demons by Beelzebub the prince of the demons (v. 24). Although Jesus denied this, he does not deny the existence of Beelzebub (who he identifies as Satan— v.26) and his demon minions.

Therefore, it is argued, since Jesus accepted the existence of Beelzebub and the demons so should we.

SOLUTION:

1. The fact that Jesus did not see fit to deny this belief of the Pharisees cannot be taken as proof that he believed in the real existence of Beelzebub and his demons. Jesus recognized no other gods but the one true God (John 17:3) and certainly did not believe in the real existence of Beelzebub (AVm., Beelzebul), the Philistine god of dung and flies. Of all such pagan deities the Scriptures state clearly: "All the gods of the nations are idols (Heb. *elilim*, things of nought)…" (Psa. 96:5)—this includes Beelzebul!
2. The fact that Jesus equated Beelzebul with Satan proves only that the belief system of the Pharisees was opposed to the Truth. Jesus also described Peter as "Satan" when he opposed God's purpose in Matt. 16:23.
3. The Pharisees were giving expression to the most blasphemous sentiments a man could utter. They were saying that the wonderful manifestation of Israel's God through the Lord Jesus, accomplished in all the power of the Holy Spirit, was in fact accomplished by the co-operation of Jesus with a filthy pagan god.

There comes a time in God's dealing with an apostate people that has willingly closed its eyes to the wonder of His ways, when God gives them a helping hand in the direction of blindness: "For the heart of this people is waxed gross, and their ears are dull of hearing, and their eyes have they closed; lest they should see with their eyes, and hear with their ears, and understand with their heart, and

---

begin with the solid fact that the term *daimon* is used for both deity or minor deity…" Gerhard Kittel, Ed., *Theological Dictionary of the New Testament*, (Grand Rapids, Mich.: Wm. B. Eerdmans Publishing Co., 1964), Vol. 2, p.1.

should be converted, and I should heal them." (Acts 28:27; cf. Isa. 6:9,10). For this reason Jesus spoke to them in parables: "that seeing they may see, and not perceive; and hearing they may hear, and not understand; lest at any time they should be converted, and their sins should be forgiven them" (Mark 4:12). Thus Jesus, in the Matt. 12:24–26 passage, accepted their apostasy as being beyond recall and contented himself with confounding their argument and rebuking their blasphemy.

Matthew 25:41

"Then shall he say also unto them on the left hand, Depart from me, ye cursed, into everlasting fire, prepared for the devil and his angels."

PROBLEM:

This verse is said to teach that the demons (Satan's angels) will be destroyed along with the devil himself at the time of the coming of Jesus.

SOLUTION:

1. The verse does not mention demons.
2. This understanding is based on the unfounded assumption that the devil referred to is the leader of a group of sinful angels, and on a further assumption that these fallen angels are demons. (See the relevant section on "The Devil").
3. The word "angels" (Gk. *aggelois,* the equivalent of the Heb. *malachim*) denotes simply, "messengers", and in itself does not imply whether the angels are human (as, for example, in Ezek. 30:9, Luke 7:24) or divine (as in Psa. 103:20,21; Mark 8:38).
4. There are a number of Scriptures where "the devil" refers to the political manifestation of sin in the flesh. E.g. the Roman authorities referred to in 1 Pet. 5:8 and the authorities in Smyrna who cast some of the believers into prison in Rev. 2:10. This appears to be the way it is used in Matt. 25:41 (see point 6 below).
5. "Everlasting fire" denotes divine punishment that is enduring in its effect such as the judgement poured out on the Jews by the Babylonians in the time of Jeremiah: "Thus saith the Lord GOD; Behold, mine anger and my fury shall be poured out upon this place, upon man, and upon beast…and *it shall burn*, and shall *not be quenched*." (Jer. 7:20). Similarly, the future judgment of "them that know not God" (unbelievers) and "them [RV] that obey not the gospel" (the unfaithful believers) is described thus: "…the Lord Jesus shall be revealed from heaven with his mighty angels, *in flaming fire* taking vengeance on them that know not God, and that obey not the gospel of our Lord Jesus Christ: who shall be punished with *everlasting destruction* from the presence of the Lord, and from the glory of his power." (2 Thess. 1:7–9).
6. This verse in Matt. 25 is speaking of the fate of those on the left hand who are rejected at the judgment—those "who obey not the gospel" who will be turned away to suffer the fate of those ungodly nations who oppose the Lord Jesus at his coming—"them that know not God", described here as "the devil and his

angels." The fate of these ungodly nations is the subject of many prophecies: e.g. "For, behold, the LORD will come *with fire*, and with his chariots like a whirlwind, to render his anger with fury, and his rebuke *with flames of fire*. For *by fire* and by his sword will the LORD plead with all flesh: and *the slain of the LORD shall be many.*" (Isa. 66:15,16).

1 Corinthians 8:5

"For though there be that are called gods, whether in heaven or in earth, (as there be gods many, and lords many)..."

1 Corinthians 10:19,20

"What say I then? that the idol is any thing, or that which is offered in sacrifice to idols is any thing? But I say, that the things which the Gentiles sacrifice, they sacrifice to devils (demons), and not to God: and I would not that ye should have fellowship with devils (demons)."

PROBLEM:

Amazingly, in spite of the apostle's very emphatic declaration in 1 Cor. 8:4 that "an idol is nothing in the world ["has no real existence" RSV], and that there is none other God but one", his statement concerning the pagan world that "there be gods many, and lords many" (1 Cor. 8:5) is taken as proof that these gods really do exist—they are the demons of 1 Cor. 10, the gods that are represented by the idols. Such scriptures as, "There is no God beside me" (Isa. 45:5) are said to be teaching merely that Yahweh is the *true* God.

SOLUTION:

1. Those who believe that the demon-deities had real existence maintain that the gods worshipped by pagans were *represented* by their idols—the gods themselves were demons with real spirit existence. But this does not agree with such scriptures as: "There ye shall serve gods, *the work of men's hands*, wood and stone, which neither see, nor hear, nor eat, nor smell" (Deut. 4:28). "Ye shall not *make* with me *gods* of silver, neither shall ye *make* unto you *gods* of gold." (Exo. 20:23). In this connection we are told that Israel made a golden calf and said, *"This* is thy *god*, O Israel" (Exo. 32:4 RVm.). In great detail the prophet Isaiah argues the folly of heathenism. From part of a tree a man makes a fire and from another part of the same tree, "He *maketh* a god...and worshippeth it...and prayeth unto it, and saith, Deliver me; for *thou art my god*" (Isa. 44:15,17).

2. From these scriptures it is clear that what they made *was* the god. Clearly, any powers it possessed could have existed solely in the minds of the worshippers. This accords with Paul's description of apostasy from the Truth in Romans chapter 1—"They...became vain in their reasonings...and changed the glory of the incorruptible God for the likeness of an image of corruptible man, and of birds, and fourfooted beasts and creeping things...and worshipped and served

the creature rather than the Creator" (verses 21–25 RV)—there is no indication that in reality they were worshipping demon-spirit beings.

3. Time and again the fact that these gods did not exist in any real sense is proclaimed from Scripture: "The gods of the peoples are idols [Hebrew, *elilim, things of nought*]" (1 Chron. 16:26 RV). "Thy children have forsaken me, and sworn by them that are no gods" (Jer. 5:7). "Shall a man make unto himself gods, which yet are no gods?" (Jer. 16:20 RV).

4. Isaiah is particularly emphatic: "Before me there was no God formed, neither shall there be after me" (43:10). The context of this is *Yahweh* versus *pagan gods* and has no bearing on the purpose of the Deity to bring "many sons to glory" of whom Jesus, the "mighty God" of Isa. 9:6, is the firstborn. The theme of this section of Isaiah is that the gods of the nations have no real existence—not that they exist but are not the true God. So, "the workman melteth a graven image…He that is so impoverished…chooseth a tree…he seeketh unto him a cunning workman to prepare a graven image…" etc. (40:19,20). To the gods thus manufactured Yahweh challenges, "Shew the things that are to come hereafter, that we may know that ye are gods…Behold, ye are of nothing, and your work of nought" (41:23,24). "Is there a God beside me? Yea, there is no God; I know not any" (44:8). "I am God, and there is none else" (45:22).

Of course, those who worshipped these pagan gods believed in their real spiritual existence, and the phenomenon of possession (see page 268) that took place at their frenzied worship gave credence to this belief. But as far as the Bible is concerned the gods did not exist in any real sense, just as today we deny the real existence of, say, the Voodoo deities, in spite of the possession phenomena that can be observed in their worship.

James 2:19

"Thou believest that there is one God; thou doest well: the devils [Gk, daimonia, 'demons', RSV] also believe, and tremble."

PROBLEM:

This passage is widely quoted to prove the existence of demons.[7]

SOLUTION:

1. This passage appears to be an allusion by James to the demons cast out by Christ and the disciples. (E.g. Mark 3:11; Luke 4:33,34,41).

2. The context of this passage in James indicates a concern for the relationship between faith and works. (vv. 14–18). The demoniacs or demon-possessed persons had sufficient sanity to acknowledge, trembling, that Jesus was the Son of God, but this faith was not demonstrated in acceptable works. The Gadarene

---

[7] E.g. *The Watchtower*, (Aug. 1962), No. 15, Vol. LXXXIII, p.477. Anthony Buzzard, *Demon Really Does Mean Demon*, (Oregon, Ill.; Restoration Fellowship, n.d.) p.3. (The Restoration Fellowship has a great deal in common with Christadelphians, but this article distributed in the U.S.A. and the U.K. was directed at our beliefs with respect to demons).

demoniacs were, for example, "exceeding fierce, so that no man might pass by that way." (Matt. 8:28). Unless believers to whom James addressed his epistle, demonstrated their faith in appropriate works, their professions of faith were in effect no better than those of a demoniac.

3. There is no indication elsewhere in Scripture that demons literally believed and trembled. It was the *individual* possessed with demons who did the speaking. (See Mark 5:9—"And *he* answered, saying, My name is Legion: for we are many.") To be possessed of demons is equivalent to madness. (John 8:48; 10:20). Similarly, demon possession described infirmities of the body (e.g. blindness—Matt. 12:22; epilepsy—Mark 9:17–22; dumbness—Matt. 9:32,33). See section on "Demon Possession", page 268.

4. The following points may be helpful:

   a. There is frequently employed in the Bible a figure of speech where one name or noun is used instead of another. E.g. Job 32:7: "Days should speak, and multitude of years should teach wisdom". In this verse clearly "days" means "men who have days", and "years" means "men who have years". By the same figure, in "the devils also believe and tremble", devils stands for "men who have devils".

   b. Luke 11:14 says that Jesus "was casting out a devil, and it was dumb". Here the demon is said to be dumb but in fact it was the man who was dumb for "when the devil was gone out, the dumb spake".

   c. Luke 4:41 reads, "Devils [i.e. demons] also came out of many, crying out; and saying, Thou art Christ the Son of God". Again, bearing in mind the above, a common sense reading of the passage is that when the demons were cast out, the people, out of whom they had been cast, declared Jesus to be the Son of God.

Jude 6

"And the angels which kept not their first estate, but left their own habitation, he hath reserved in everlasting chains under darkness unto the judgement of the great day."

2 Peter 2:4

"For if God spared not the angels that sinned, but cast them down to hell, and delivered them into chains of darkness, to be reserved unto judgment..."

PROBLEM:

A JW publication interprets these verses as follows:

"...before the flood of Noah's day some of these spirit 'sons of God' materialized as men, that is, they left their place in heaven as spirit creatures and clothed themselves with fleshly bodies. And why? To enjoy human passions by marrying the good-looking daughters of men...When the global flood of Noah's day destroyed all the wicked humans, the unfaithful angels dissolved their fleshly bodies and returned to the spirit realm. But they were not allowed to become part of God's organization of holy angels again. Instead, they were confined in a debased condition of spiritual darkness (2 Peter 2:4). Since the flood, God has not permitted these demonic angels to materialize in the flesh as they did before then. Yet they can still exercise dangerous power over men and women. In fact, with the help of these demons Satan is 'misleading the entire inhabited earth'. (Rev. 12:9)."[8]

SOLUTION:

1. The above publication assumes without proof the following:
   a. That the angels which sinned were spirit creatures. The Greek word *aggelos* translated "angel" means "messenger, agent",[9] and is used of both human and divine messengers. It is used of humans in the following places: Matt. 11:10; Luke 7:24,27; 9:52; and James 2:25.
   b. That "sons of God" must refer to divine angels. (It refers to humans in Deut. 14:1, RSV; Psa. 82:6, RSV; Hosea 1:10; Luke 3:38; John 1:12; 1 John 3:1.)
   c. That evil power can still be exercised by the "angels that sinned" despite the fact that they are "reserved in everlasting chains". (Why bother to chain these angels, if as the JW publication contends, they can still "exercise dangerous power over men and women"?)
2. The angels in this passage are human, not divine angels. This is proven by the following:
   "The wages of sin is death." (Rom. 6:23).
   If divine angels were sinners, then they would die.
   But Jesus said angels do not die. (Luke 20:36).
   Therefore, the angels which sinned were human, not divine angels.
3. All existence in Scripture is bodily existence. JWs should be pressed hard for Scriptural evidence for asserting bodies can be "materialized" and "dissolved".
4. There is evidence that the human angels were the 250 princes of the Israelitish congregation which were led in rebellion by Korah, Dathan and Abiram. (Num. 16). Consider the following:
   a. They were *aggeloi* (angels) since they were assigned to "minister" to the congregation. (Num. 16:9).
   b. Their "first estate" or "principality" (Jude 6 AVm.) was that of "princes" or "leaders" RSV (Num. 16:2).
   c. They left this "first estate" when they sought the priesthood. (Num. 16:10).
   d. They were delivered into "chains of darkness" when they were swallowed alive by the earth. (Num. 16:31–33).[10]

[8] *The Truth that leads to Eternal Life*, (Brooklyn, New York: Watchtower Bible and Tract Society of N.Y. Inc., Int. Bible Students Ass., 1968), pp.58,59.

[9] Robert Young, *Analytical Concordance to the Holy Bible*, (London: Lutterworth Press, 1965).

[10] The Greek word for "hell" in 2 Pet. 2:4 is *tartarus* which only occurs in this passage. In popular mythology *tartarus* meant lower than hell (*hades*). This is exactly where Korah, Dathan, and Abiram went when swallowed up by the earth. See James Hasting (ed.), *Dictionary of the Bible*, (New York: Charles Scribner's Sons, 1963), p.319.

e. They were "sinners" in arrogating to themselves the priesthood. (Num. 16:10,38).

f. The judgment is that which will be administered by Christ. (2 Tim. 4:1).

5. It will be noted that in Peter's epistle, the phrase "the angels that sinned" is placed chronologically *before* the time of Noah (2 Pet. 2:4,5), whereas in Jude's epistle, it is placed *after* the exodus of Israel from Egypt. (Jude 5,6). There are too many similarities between the two epistles to conclude that the accounts refer to two different occasions on which angels sinned. Rather Jude's epistle must be regarded as setting out the chronological order of events since in verse 6 the Greek text is syntactically connected with verse 5,[11] thereby implying the historical sequence. But why the reversal of historical allusions in Peter's account? Because verse 4 in Peter's account is connected with verse 1. "But there were false prophets also among the people [i.e. Israel of old],[12] even as there shall be false teachers among you..." Verses 2 and 3 are a warning of false teachers to come in the future, but verse 4 reverts to verse 1 and illustrates the judgment of God upon false prophets in Israel. In verses 5–7, Peter guided by the Holy Spirit, selects two additional illustrations from Old Testament history.

Revelation 16:13,14

"I saw three unclean spirits like frogs come out of the mouth of the dragon, and out of the mouth of the beast, and out of the mouth of the false prophet. For they are the spirits of devils, working miracles, which go forth unto the kings of the earth and of the whole world, to gather them to the battle of that great day of God Almighty."

PROBLEM:

This passage is widely used to support the idea that Satan through his demons controls the movements of men and nations. The unclean propaganda that emanates from the mouths of the beast, dragon and false prophet is said to consist of "expressions inspired by demons" (NWT). Demons are thus very influential in end-time events. "Just before the end of the age [Satan's] sinister spirits of demons influence the nations, gathering them together for the great day of God Almighty."[13]

SOLUTION:

1. The main objection to this use of Scripture must be the symbolic nature of the record. Is the record talking about a literal dragon, a literal beast and a literal false prophet? If so do these "spirits of demons" come out of their literal mouths?

---

[11] 2 Peter 2:5,6 uses the normal disjunctive *kai*, but Jude uses *te* which is copulative in character, and indicates the connection between Jude 5 and 6.

[12] Note the connection between 2 Peter 2:1 ("among the people") and 2 Peter 1:21 ("holy men of God"—i.e., in Israel), cf. Acts 4:27.

[13] *Seventh-day Adventists Answer Questions on Doctrine*, (Washington, D.C.: Review and Herald Publishing Ass., 1957), p.621.

2. Clearly it is necessary to interpret the dragon, beast and false prophet in order to understand the record. Surely it is necessary to interpret what their mouths represent and what the "spirits of demons" are that emanate therefrom.

3. The clear teaching that God is in control of the movements of men and nations is relevant too: "…the most High ruleth in the kingdom of men, and giveth it to whomsoever he will, and setteth up over it the basest of men." (Dan. 4:17).

DEMON POSSESSION

Demon possession is never mentioned throughout the entire Old Testament period. In the New Testament it is mainly confined to the Gospels. But, what is demon possession?

SUGGESTED STRATEGY:

There are many references in the Gospels that appear to teach demon possession. For example, we read that "Jesus rebuked the devil (Gk. *daimonion*); and he departed out of him: and the child was cured from that very hour" (Matt. 17:18). To many, Scriptures such as this are proof that demons do exist and that they are able to enter into people. However, demons are pagan gods and as such have no real existence and are therefore unable to possess anyone. (See pages 263,264).

The key to understanding the accounts of possession is to be found in the way demons (false gods) were worshipped by the pagans.

Whilst we can be absolutely sure that demons (pagan gods) do not exist in any real sense, it is equally certain that something most unusual did happen to the worshippers, which they interpreted to be possession by the god. In fact, such things still happen today. For example, it is possible to visit West Africa and to observe ceremonies devoted to the worship of the various Voodoo deities where individuals *apparently* become possessed by the god.[14] But these gods do not exist! What then is this observable and very real phenomenon of 'possession'?

EXPLANATION OF 'POSSESSION'

What follows is a brief and simplified explanation of the phenomenon of 'possession'. Under normal circumstances everything we see, hear or touch is received by the brain, which acts as a computer. The brain-computer then compares the new information with all other recorded experiences from the past that might have a bearing on it. To a great extent this is an automatic process not requiring conscious effort.

When the brain is put under great stress, changes in brain function occur that alter the way in which information is received, analysed and recorded. It is this alteration in brain function that leads to the possession state. At a pagan religious festival people are put under such stress. By rhythmic clapping, drum beating and dancing; by

---

[14] Dr. Wm. Sargant, *The Mind Possessed*, Heinemann, London, 1973. In this book the author describes many ceremonies visited by himself and others in Africa, Brazil, Jamaica, Barbados, Haiti, the U.S.A. and elsewhere, in which demon possession phenomena were observed and photographed.

exhaustion of the body; by inducing pain; and even by the use of drugs, the brain is progressively exhausted until the stage is reached where it no longer critically computes the information it receives. At this point any ideas fed into the brain are accepted without question and the worshipper, surrounded by an expectancy of possession, becomes possessed. Thus 'possession' is not due to possession by the spirit of a pagan god but is due to brain exhaustion.[15] Such 'possession' is usually accompanied by unconsciousness, convulsions or a trance-like state.[16]

Matthew 17:14–18

"...there came to him a certain man, kneeling down to him, and saying, Lord, have mercy on my son: for he is lunatick, and sore vexed: for ofttimes he falleth into the fire, and oft into the water. And I brought him to thy disciples, and they could not cure him. Then Jesus answered and said, O faithless and perverse generation, how long shall I be with you? how long shall I suffer you? bring him hither to me. And Jesus rebuked the devil (demon); and he departed out of him: and the child was cured from that very hour."

PROBLEM:

Here is an example of Jesus casting out a demon. He is said to have rebuked the demon, which implies its personality, and the demon is said to have departed out of the child confirming its reality.

SOLUTION:

1. Note that the father desired that the disciples "cure" his child and that as a result of the ministrations of Jesus "the child was cured." The use of the word "cure" implies that the condition from which the child suffered was an illness.[17]

---

[15] This is dealt with in greater detail by Dr. Wm. Sargant, "The Physiology of Faith", *British Journal of Psychiatry,* 1969, pp.505-518. Also his *Battle for the Mind*, (London: Heinemann, 1957), pp.1-41, is helpful. It should be noted that Sargant, who rightly observed that modern "charismatic" possession by the "holy spirit" is exactly the same phenomenon as demon possession, wrongly proceeded to equate the modern "charismatic" experience with the New Testament outpouring of the Holy Spirit.

[16] Possession by something called "the holy ghost" in response to the excitement generated at Pentecostal meetings is exactly the same phenomenon. Those possessed may fall down unconscious and even convulse ('slain by the spirit'), may behave strangely such as laughing uncontrollably (the so-called 'Toronto blessing') or may pass into a trance-like state and make incoherent noises ('speaking in tongues').

[17] The connection between demon possession and illness is beyond all reasonable doubt. Examination of the Gospel records shows that:
1. TO BE POSSESSED WITH A DEMON WAS EQUIVALENT TO BEING ILL
(a) Jesus told the twelve, "Heal the sick, cleanse the lepers, raise the dead, cast out devils" (Matt. 10:8). Thus the casting out of demons was a part of the healing ministry. In answer to the comment that the verse distinguishes demon possession from sickness, it must be pointed out that it also distinguishes leprosy from sickness. (b) In Matt. 9:32 and Luke 11:14 dumbness is said to result from demon possession. (c) In Matt. 12:22 demon possession is said to cause both blindness and dumbness. (d) It is clear that when the Jews used the term of Jesus they thought that he was mentally disturbed: "He hath a devil and is mad" (John 10:20. See also John 8:48,52.).

2. The fact that Jesus rebuked the demon and the demon departed cannot be taken as proof of the personality of the demon. When Jesus healed Peter's mother-in-law we are told, "[Jesus] rebuked the fever; and it left her…" (Luke 4:39). This does not imply the personality of the fever.

3. The AV describes the child as being "lunatick". The RV and RSV say he was "epileptic" and the description given by the father of the child falling into the fire and into the water is consistent with a description of epilepsy.

4. The cause of epilepsy was unknown. The behaviour of the epileptic was to all intents and purposes identical with the behaviour of the person who fell down convulsing as he worshipped his demon at the idol festival. It was quite understandable that the disease of epilepsy should have been equated with the 'possession' that occurred at the pagan festivals.

5. The same is true of all the diseases that are described as being due to possession by a demon. The bizarre behaviour of the mentally ill, the grunting and vacant staring of the blind and dumb man and the behaviour of the epileptics, all resembled the behaviour of those who reached the point of brain exhaustion and were 'possessed' by the demon-god at the idol festival. These unexplainable diseases were therefore described as being due to demon possession. Jesus used the language of his day in describing these illnesses.

6. The following is an analysis showing that what was attributed to demon possession at the time of Jesus is today described in different terminology but involves the same symptoms. Jesus simply used the vernacular of the times:

Description	Vernacular at the time of Jesus	Diagnosis Today
Matt. 12:22: "Then was brought unto him one possessed with a devil [Gk. *daimonizomai*; demoniac, RSV], blind, and dumb: and he healed him, insomuch that the blind and dumb both spake and saw."	"possessed with a devil [demon]"	blind and dumb
Mark 5:1–5: "No man could bind him…because that he had been often bound with fetters and chains, and the chains had been plucked asunder by him, and the fetters broken in pieces…And always, night and day, he was in the mountains, and in the tombs, crying, and cutting himself with stones."	"a man with an unclean spirit"	insanity, schizo-phrenia?
Mark 9:17–27: "He teareth him: and he foameth, and gnasheth with his teeth, and pineth away…and ofttimes it hath cast him into the fire, and into the waters, to destroy him."	"hath a dumb spirit"	epilepsy
Luke 13:11–17: "A woman which had a spirit of infirmity eighteen years, and was bowed together, and could in no wise lift up herself."	"spirit of infirmity"	Arthritis or severe osteoporosis

2. TO CAST OUT A DEMON WAS TO HEAL AN ILLNESS

(a) In Matt. 4:24 we are told, "They brought unto him all sick people that were taken with divers diseases and torments, and those which were possessed with devils, and those which were lunatick (RV epileptic) and those that had the palsy; and he healed them." (Also Mark 3:15). (b) Of the blind and dumb man it is said, "Then was brought unto him one possessed with a demon, blind, and dumb: and he healed him, insomuch that the blind and dumb both spake and saw". (Matt. 12:22; also see Matt. 9:32). (c) Of the faithful Canaanitish woman whose daughter was grievously vexed with a demon it is said, "Her daughter was healed from that hour." (Matt. 15:22,28 RV).

See also John 10:20 & Mark 3:21, where "he hath a devil and is mad" means "he is beside himself".

7. Patients today with the same symptoms as those said to be possessed with demons in New Testament times, respond to chemotherapy. This is significant, for if indeed the ailment were due to demon possession, as some suggest, how can the patient's recovery through medicine and therapy be explained? Can pills cast out demons?

8. Although the narratives appear to indicate that the "spirits" cried out, it is clear that the vocalization of the sounds came from the demoniac. This is implied in the shift of pronouns in Mark 5:7,9: "What have I to do with thee?"[18] Cf. "I adjure thee by God that thou torment me not". Cf. "My name is Legion: for we are many."

9. After the miraculous cure by Jesus, Legion is described as "clothed, and in his right mind". (Mark 5:15). This implies that his affliction was insanity and not the influence of a fallen angel. (The request that the unclean spirits enter the swine is characteristic of some kinds of schizophrenics who fear the return of the insanity.)

Matthew 12:43–45

"Then goeth he, and taketh with himself seven other spirits more wicked than himself, and they enter in and dwell there: and the last state of that man is worse than the first ..."

PROBLEM:

This verse is cited to prove the existence of unclean spirits or demons that are able to possess humans. Unclean spirits are said to be emissaries of Satan the Devil, "the god of this system of things."[19]

---

[18] This should read: "What have you to do with *me*... ?" "I" is not in the Greek text. See *The Interlinear Greek-English New Testament: The Nestle Greek Text*, 2nd ed. (London: Samuel Bagster and Sons Ltd., 1967). NIV renders it, "What do you want with me?"

[19] All manner of evil has been wrought by the teaching that demons are invisible spirit-creatures. Augustine, revered by the Roman Church, taught that "all diseases of Christians are to be ascribed to demons, chiefly do they torment the fresh baptized, yes, even the guiltless new-born infant". Gregory the Great solemnly related that a nun, having eaten some lettuce without making the sign of the cross, swallowed a devil, and that when the devil was commanded to come forth by a "holy man" it did so and is reported to have said: "How am I to blame? I was sitting on the lettuce, and this woman, not having made the sign of the cross, ate me along with it." Men who then cast out devils were very careful to keep their mouths closed while carrying out their exorcism, lest the devil should jump from the mouth of the patient into their own mouth. See Howard W. Haggard, M.D., *Devils, Drugs, & Doctors: The Story of the Science of Healing from Medicine-Man to Doctor*, (New York: Pocket Books, Inc., 1959), pp.310,311. Under the belief that possession by devils causes disease, the sick during epidemics were carried to churches (often bound a dozen at a time), and thrown upon the floor of the church where they remained until they died or the devils expelled. Needless to say, recoveries were not frequent under this treatment, but the patient and not the treatment bore the blame. Projection of blame has also resulted. In France, during the Middle Ages, male demons were blamed for violating women, most of whom were nuns. Pope Innocent VIII issued a bull to provide the faithful with an efficacious formula for exorcising incubuses (these demons). In 1637 a formal public

SOLUTION:

1. Why should a powerful angel (angels "excel in strength"—Psa. 103:20) walk through dry places seeking *rest*? (v. 43).
2. The narrative concerning the unclean spirit concludes: "Even so shall it be also unto this wicked generation." (v. 45). This conclusion indicates that the preceding is a parable of comparison and not to be taken literally.
3. The nation of Israel had experienced a cleansing by the teaching of John the Baptist. There "went out to him Jerusalem, and all Judaea, and all the region round about Jordan, and were baptized of him in Jordan, confessing their sins." (Matt. 3:5,6). The house was cleaned—"swept, and garnished" (Matt. 12:44), but it was without its real occupant—the Messiah. "He came unto his own ["own home", RSV], and his own received him not." (John 1:11). The refusal of Israel to respond to the teaching of the Christ merited the description: "and the last state of that man [Israel] is worse than the first" [prior to the cleansing of John's teaching]. (Matt. 12:45).

WHY DEMON POSSESSION IN THE MINISTRY OF JESUS?

Those who believe in the real existence of unclean spirit demons will inevitably respond, "If there are no such beings as demons, why did not Jesus set the record straight. Why for example did he go along with the ideas about demon possession and address the demons? Why did he refer to unclean spirits in his teaching?" The following suggested strategy depends on a prior grasp of the Bible teaching about the nature of demons and demon possession.

SUGGESTED STRATEGY:

1. Demon possession is never mentioned in the entire Old Testament period. In the New Testament, demon possession is principally to be found in the synoptic Gospels with an occasional mention in the Acts. From this it would seem that the Almighty saw no need to instruct Israel in the Old Testament period about demon possession, neither did the apostles in their writings see the need to instruct the New Testament Ecclesia in the matter. Demon possession appears in the Gospels as a local and transitory way of speaking about certain diseases and is not a doctrine of Old Testament or New Testament belief. This being the case, it is not surprising that Jesus could accept the current way of referring to illness. A doctrine of demon possession forms no part of the Christian gospel[20] and there is no reason why Jesus should consider it from a theological standpoint. The only reason why it is necessary for us to examine the subject today is because of the theological absurdities that have become associated with it.

discussion took place in Paris on the subject. More recently, in Ontario Canada (Jan. 1969), a woman convicted of driving on the wrong side of a highway attributed the blame to "unseen forces" which placed the car in the opposite lane. She was fined and lost her driver's licence.

[20] "Doctrines of demons" is one of the characteristics of apostasy—"the Spirit speaketh expressly, that in the latter times some shall depart from the faith, giving heed to seducing spirits, and doctrines of devils [demons]" (1 Tim 4:1).

2. For Jesus to use such language when describing certain diseases, does not imply that he believed in the real existence of demons—he certainly did not accept the existence of any God save his Father whom he described as "the only true God" (John 17:3). He simply accommodated himself to the language of his day. He no more believed in the existence of demons as real beings causing disease than we believe men are really affected by the moon when we call them *lunatics*; or that demons are responsible for a state of confusion when we speak of *pandemonium*.[21]

3. However, there was a reason why Jesus was so ready to use the language of his day and refer to epileptics, insane people and the dumb as being demon possessed.

   a. When he spoke in parables there was nothing haphazard about them; there was always a reason why he spoke the parable. So, for example, the parable of the sower in Luke 8:4–15 was given to illustrate the different responses in Israel to his teaching. To understand the parables it is necessary to interpret them. This is often straightforward as in the parable of the sower, but it sometimes proves to be a most difficult exercise.

   b. One such difficult parable is that found in Matt. 12:43–45. (See page 271): "When the unclean spirit is gone out of a man, he walketh through dry places, seeking rest, and findeth none. Then he saith, I will return into my house from whence I came out; and when he is come, he findeth it empty, swept, and garnished. Then goeth he, and taketh with himself seven other spirits more wicked than himself, and they enter in and dwell there: and the last state of that man is worse than the first. Even so shall it be also unto this wicked generation." Whatever the detailed explanation might be, the inescapable 'punch line' of the parable, which comes in the final sentence, is that Jesus would have us view the Jewish nation at that time in their history as being like a demon possessed man—"Even so shall it be also unto *this wicked generation*."

   c. Just as the parables of Jesus were the *words* of God through His Son, so the miracles of Jesus were the works of God. Thus he said, "The works which the Father hath given me to finish, the same works that I do, bear witness of me, that the Father hath sent me" (John 5:36). So, the cursing of the fig tree

---

[21] It is frequently argued that Jesus would never have accommodated himself to the language of the day since this would have conveyed the impression that he accepted the pagan ideas about demons. To this it may be said: (a) Jesus did not try to counter the idea of Beelzebub (the god of the fly) but used it as an argument against the Jews (Luke 11:19). If he used the idea of the "prince of the demons" which was manifestly pagan, why should he not in his teaching also accommodate himself to the current ideas on demons generally? (b) The parable of the rich man and Lazarus in Luke 16 provides further evidence that Jesus did not hesitate to use current Jewish theological ideas that had a pagan origin in his reasoning with the unbelieving Jews. (See pp.176-178, where this parable is considered). (c) The reason for the above may well lie in God's attitude towards Israel in the time of Jesus' ministry. In Isaiah chapter 6, which is a prophecy about Jesus it is said, "Go, and tell this people, Hear ye indeed, but understand not; and see ye indeed, but perceive not. Make the heart of this people fat, and make their ears heavy, and shut their eyes; lest they see with their eyes, and hear with their ears, and understand with their heart, and convert, and be healed" (Isa. 6:9,10, cf. John 12:37–41). To use the language of the day about demons was one of the ways of shutting their eyes.

(Matt. 21:19,20) was really an act of teaching in which Jesus was conveying to his disciples an important message about the nation of Israel. Israel was the fig tree that had leaves but no fruit. Because Israel had failed to bring forth the fruit of righteousness before God, it was cursed as a nation. (Cf. Luke 13:7–9).

    d. In a similar way the miracles of Jesus that had to do with the casting out of demons, were intended to teach the disciples something about the nation of Israel, for we have already seen from the parable of the man with the unclean spirit, that Jesus wanted them to view that "wicked generation" as demon possessed.

What a fitting representation this was. God had predicted through Moses that Israel would forsake Him and turn aside "unto *devils* [i.e. demons], and not to God; to gods whom they knew not, to new gods that came newly up..." (Deut. 32:17). The consequence of their unfaithfulness was that "The LORD shall smite thee with *madness*, and *blindness*, and astonishment of heart..." (Deut. 28:28). This was precisely the situation at the time of Jesus. They had turned aside to the foolish superstitions of the Gentile world and had embraced ideas and forms of worship that were opposed to God's truth.[22] The pagan ideas of the Gentiles had entered into the body politic of Israel—Israel had become possessed of the pagan demons. They were so blind that they did not recognise Jesus and so insane that they crucified him. Thus the nation was fittingly represented by a blind man, a mad man or an epileptic, which, according to the superstitions of the day, were illnesses attributed to demon possession. This lies at the root of the teaching of Jesus with the demoniacs.

4. The healing of the epileptic in Matt. 17 / Luke 9 is a good example of the way in which the healing of the demoniacs contained important parabolic teaching, usually about the unfaithful nation of Israel.

    a. The body politic of Israel throughout its history had repeatedly been possessed by Gentile demon-gods. E.g. "They left all the commandments of the LORD their God, and made them molten images, even two calves, and made a grove, and worshipped all the host of heaven, and served Baal. And they caused their sons and their daughters to pass through the fire, and used divination and enchantments, and sold themselves to do evil in the sight of the LORD, to provoke him to anger..." (2 Kings 17:16,17). Because of this, like the demon possessed boy, they were repeatedly "thrown down" (Luke 9:42)—by the Assyrians and the Babylonians, and they were soon to be thrown down by the Romans in AD 70.

    b. But like the epileptic boy who was "sore vexed: [and] ofttimes [fell] into the fire and the water" (Matt. 17:15) Israel was not fatally injured. God had said: "When thou *passest through the waters*, I will be with thee; and through the rivers, they shall not overflow thee: when thou *walkest through the fire*, thou shalt not be burned; neither shall the flame kindle upon thee." (Isa. 43:2).

---

[22] For example, under the heading "Beelzubub, lord of the fly" Young's Concordance states, "A heathen deity to whom the Jews ascribed supremacy among evil spirits"—which is of course confirmed by Matt. 12:24.

c. Israel's casting down is not yet over. "The time of Jacob's trouble" out of which he will be saved by the returned Messiah (Jer. 30:7–9) is yet to happen. Then, like the boy, brought face to face with Messiah, the demons will be cast out: "It shall come to pass in that day, saith the LORD of hosts, that I will cut off the *names of the idols* out of the land, and they shall no more be remembered: and also I will cause the prophets and the *unclean spirit* to pass out of the land." (Zech. 13:2). "For I will take you from among the heathen, and gather you out of all countries, and will bring you into your own land. Then will I sprinkle clean water upon you, and ye shall be clean: from all your filthiness, and from all *your idols*, will I cleanse you." (Ezek. 36:24,25).

2.9

PRE-EXISTENCE AND DEITY OF CHRIST

PRELIMINARY POINTS:

1. The passages which are used to support the pre-existence[1] of Christ can be grouped into the following two classes:

   a. Those which refer to Christ as the Creator.

   b. Those which refer to Christ as existing before his birth.

   Group a) passages are easily explained once it is shown that the creative work of Christ refers to the making of new men and women, and not to the creation of animals, trees etc. of Genesis 1. Christ is the firstborn of the *new* creation.

   Group b) passages require an understanding of the divine point of view that God "calleth those things which be not as though they were." (Rom. 4:17, cf. Isa. 46:9,10). Through His foreknowledge, God speaks in the present and past tenses of events yet future. This emphasizes the certainty of the outcome.[2] As the Great Architect, God can envisage the glory of the saints, the kingdom, and Christ before their actual existence. (See Acts 15:18; Matt. 25:34; John 17:5,24; Eph. 1:4; Heb. 4:3).

2. Belief in the pre-existence of Christ has inevitable effects on one's understanding and appreciation of the Saviour's redemptive work. Consider the following:

   a. If Jesus was conscious of having existed in heaven as the glorious Creator, how could he in any sense be tempted the same way as are his brethren? (Heb. 4:15).

   b. If Christ pre-existed the force of the argument in 1 Cor. 15:46 is lost. Paul says, "Howbeit that was not first which is spiritual, but that which is *natural*; and *afterward* that which is *spiritual*." But if Christ pre-existed, then for him, this divinely appointed order is reversed—first spiritual, then natural. How then is he "the firstborn among many brethren" (Rom. 8:29), if indeed his experience is the very reverse of theirs?

3. It requires stressing that the description of the birth of Christ precludes the possibility of his having a prior existence. Note the following:

   a. The words used to describe his birth indicate the beginning of existence, (e.g. "birth", "conceive", Matt. 1:18,20; Luke 1:31,35; 2:21). If a change from one form of existence to another were intended, such words as 'transform' or 'incarnate' would have been used.

---

[1] The term 'pre-existence' is contradictory since one cannot exist before he exists. It is retained here because of its current usage. 'Pre-human existence' would ordinarily be a more accurate term.

[2] Although God has divine foreknowledge of the way humans will exercise their free will, it should not be inferred that He makes them act the way they do.

b. The divine action involved in the coming of God's Son into the world is not kept secret or made mysterious. Instead, it is plainly explained in Luke 1:34,35; Matt. 1:18,20. The description of these passages indicate the creation of a new person by means of God's power acting on Mary, and thereby rules out any possibility that Christ personally existed in some manner prior to his birth.

4. The passages used to support the trinity (i.e. that 'God the Son' is the second person in the Godhead, co-equal and co-eternal with God the Father)[3] can also be grouped into two classes:

   a. Those which confer divine titles on Christ, e.g. "His name shall be called …the mighty God, the everlasting Father." (Isa. 9:6).

   b. Those which record Christ exercising divine prerogatives such as accepting worship and forgiving sins.

In general, both a) and b) passages require an understanding of God-manifestation—the principle outlined in Old and New Testaments in which God carries out His divine activity through accredited representatives who bear His name. For example, an angel went before Israel. The Israelites were instructed: "Beware of him, and obey his voice, provoke him not; for he will not pardon your transgressions: for my name is in him." (Exo. 23:20,21). Although Jesus is worthy of divine honour as the manifestation of God in the flesh (1 Tim. 3:16), it must be shown that he is not a person within a triune Godhead, co-equal and co-eternal with the Father.

SUGGESTED STRATEGY:

The following approach is an attempt to order a discussion on the relationship of Jesus to his Father:

1. Jesus Christ cannot be 'Very God' (i.e. of one person with the Father) since statements about Jesus Christ are contradictions of statements about God, his Father. Consider the following:

Jesus Christ	God (his Father)
a. Was tempted (Heb. 2:18)	Cannot be tempted with evil (James 1:13)
b. Died (Rev. 1:18)	Cannot die (1 Tim. 6:16)
c. Seen by men (Acts 1:3)	Cannot be seen by men (1 Tim. 6:16)

2. Jesus Christ is a separate person from his Father. This is further indicated by the following references:

   a. Jesus ascended to his Father and *his* God. (John 20:17). Since Jesus *after* his resurrection ascended to his God,[4] then clearly he was not himself 'Very God'.

   b. He prayed to his Father indicating a distinction and independence of will. "Not as I will, but as thou wilt." (Matt. 26:39).

   c. He is referred to as a *man*, *after* his ascension into heaven. (1 Tim. 2:5).

[3] The Holy Spirit is also said to be co-equal and co-eternal with the other persons in the Godhead. The Holy Spirit is considered in the next chapter.

[4] See also Luke 6:12; Eph. 1:17; 1 Pet. 1:3. Since Jesus has a God, he is not himself 'Very God'.

3. Jesus is not co-equal with his Father. This is indicated by the following passages:

   a. God is the head of Christ. (1 Cor. 11:3).

   b. Christ is approved by God—the greater. (Acts 2:22).

   c. Christ himself states that his Father is greater. (John 14:28).

   d. Christ is to be subject to the Father. (1 Cor. 15:28). This passage is often the single most effective quotation in setting forth the relationship of Jesus to God. It shows his position of delegated authority in the kingdom (v. 27) and subsequent subjection to the Father. (v. 28). Can one person in the Godhead be *subject* to another and yet all persons be co-equal?

   e. See also Mark 10:18 and John 5:19,30.

4. Pointing out the clear teaching that Jesus needed to be saved from death, and that he benefited personally from his own sacrificial death, provides a very powerful argument against the trinity. Note the following:

   a. Heb. 5:7—"Who in the days of his flesh, when he had offered up prayers and supplications with strong crying and tears unto him that was able to save him from death, and was heard in that he feared…And being made perfect, he became the author of eternal salvation unto all them that obey him". This clearly teaches that the Father saved Jesus from [RV "out of"] death, which is not consistent with Jesus being God the Son.

   b. Heb. 9:11,12—"Christ… by his own blood he entered in once into the holy place, having obtained eternal redemption." (RV). This clearly teaches that Jesus benefited from his own sacrificial death. Again, if he had been God the Son he would not have needed "redemption".

   c. Heb. 13:20—"Now the God of peace, that brought again from the dead our Lord Jesus…through the blood of the everlasting covenant…" God delivered Jesus out of death as a consequence of Jesus' blood being shed.

   d. Psa. 89:26,27—"He shall cry unto me, Thou art my father, my God, and the rock of my salvation. Also I will make him my firstborn, higher than the kings of the earth." This is very powerful:

      i. The birth of Jesus was in the future—therefore the Father and the Son were not co-eternal.

      ii. Jesus would acknowledge the Father as his God—therefore they were not co-equal.

      iii. God would bring about the salvation of His firstborn—therefore clearly Jesus was not God.

Genesis 1:26

"And God said, Let us make man in our image, after our likeness…"

PROBLEM:

It is pointed out that the verse reads, "God said", yet the plurals "us" and "our" indicate a plurality within a unity. It is argued that this refers to the trinity since Jesus at the time of the creation was a spirit creature.

SOLUTION:

1. The Jews, of all people, have been fiercely monotheistic. The Hebrew word, *elohim*, translated "God", and the plurals "us" and "our", never suggested trinitarian ideas to them. Nor is there any New Testament allusion to indicate that in their interpretation of this passage they were mistaken.
2. The trinitarian argument on this passage is only an inferred argument. It is stated that the "us" and "our" refer to either Jesus or to the Holy Spirit.
3. The plurals in the passage refer to God performing his creative work through his angels. Consider the evidence:
   a. Men bear the physical image of angels. Angels were mistaken for men by Lot. (Gen. 18:2,22, cf. 19:1,15)[5]. Hence the admonition: "Be not forgetful to entertain strangers: for thereby some have entertained angels unawares." (Heb. 13:2). If faithful, saints will bear the *nature* of angels in the resurrection. (Luke 20:35,36).
   b. Divine activity is said to be done by God, although actually executed by the angels. Note the following examples:
      i. The LORD appeared to Moses in the burning bush. (Exo. 3:4–8). But Stephen says Moses was with "the *angel* which appeared to him in the bush." (Acts 7:35, cf. v. 30). The Exodus account also reveals that it was an angel. (Exo. 3:2).
      ii. God came down onto Mt. Sinai (Exo. 19:18) and gave the ten commandments to Moses (Exo. 20:1–17). Note: "I am the LORD thy God" (20:2), "me" (20:3); "for I the LORD thy God" (20:5), etc. But Stephen says it was the angel "which spake to him in the mount Sina, and with our fathers: who received the lively oracles to give unto us." (Acts 7:38).
      iii. Jacob said that he had "seen God face to face, and my life is preserved." (Gen. 32:30). Hosea states, however, that he wrestled with an angel. (Hos. 12:3,4, cf. Gen. 32:1,2).
   c. The Hebrew world *elohim* translated "God" is an elastic word, much like "soul" or "spirit". It is translated "goddess" (1 Kings 11:33), "judges" (Exo. 21:6), and applied to pagan idols in Judg. 16:23; 1 Kings 11:33. It is generally acknowledged that it comes from a root meaning 'power' or the 'strong one'.[6] The plural *elohim* means 'powerful ones' or 'strong ones'. This is precisely the description of the angels. "Bless the LORD, ye his angels, that excel in strength, that do his commandments, hearkening unto the voice of his word." (Psa. 103:20).
   d. Although the usual Hebrew word for "angel" is *malak*, the Hebrew word *elohim* is translated "angels" in Psa. 8:5. Since the writer to the Hebrews quotes this passage in Heb. 2:7, cf. v. 9, and translates the word *elohim* by the Greek *aggelous* (angels), it can be inferred that the intended meaning of *elohim* in Psa. 8:5 is also "angels".

[5] See also Gen. 32:24—Jacob wrestled with a "man". This "man" was an angel. (Hos. 12:3,4).

[6] Jas. Hastings (ed.), *Dictionary of the Bible*, Revised ed., (New York: Charles Scribner's Sons, 1963), p.334.

WRESTED SCRIPTURES

Isaiah 6:8

"I heard the voice of the Lord, saying, Whom shall I send, and who will go for us? Then said I, Here am I; send me."

PROBLEM:

It is argued that since the plural pronoun "us" is used by the "Lord", the passage implies a plurality of persons in the Godhead.

SOLUTION:

1. In the first instance the "me" in the phrase, "Here am I; send me" is Isaiah the prophet, but it is also a prophecy of the work of Jesus. The one who is sent takes the message of verses 9 and 10 to Israel. Matt. 13:13 shows that this work was done by Jesus—"Therefore speak I to them in parables: because they seeing see not; and hearing they hear not, neither do they understand", which is a clear reference to Isa. 6:9,10. If Jesus was the "me" of Isa. 6:8 he could not be one of the "us" and the argument for the trinity based on this passage is shown to be faulty.
2. When was Jesus sent in fulfilment of the phrase, "Here am I; send me"? A comparison of Isa. 61:1 and Luke 4:18–21 shows that it was during his ministry. It is necessary to make this point because of the trinitarian misinterpretation of Isa. 48:16 (see facing page).
3. Who then comprise the "us"? Surely the "LORD" and the "seraphim" of verse 2.

Isaiah 9:6

"His name shall be called...The mighty God, The everlasting Father, The Prince of Peace."

PROBLEM:

Since Isaiah refers to Christ as "The mighty God, The everlasting Father", this passage is quoted to prove the deity of Christ.

SOLUTION:

1. Isaiah states that he *"shall* be called" (i.e. in the Kingdom Age, v. 7), not that he is now "The mighty God, The everlasting Father." Although the work of this kingdom is executed by Christ, it is "the zeal of the LORD [Yahweh] of hosts [which] will perform this." (Isa. 9:7). As Christ said: "I can of mine own self do nothing". (John 5:30).
2. "Mighty God"—Jesus Christ will be the "mighty God" in the Kingdom Age when he comes with the power and glory of his Father. (Matt. 16:27). Christ is altogether worthy of this title. Of an angel, it is written, "my name is in him", (Exo. 23:21).[7] But the Son of God has obtained a more excellent name than the

---

[7] Similarly, Christ came in his Father's name. (John 5:43).

280

angels (Heb. 1:4, RSV) and is, therefore, worthy to bear the divine titles. But this does not imply he is 'Very God' any more than it did for the angel who bore the divine name before the children of Israel.

3. "Everlasting[8] Father"—Christ in his reign as King will bear the title, "everlasting Father" for at least the following two reasons:

a. He will be a father to the mortal nations in the Kingdom Age. Isaiah prophesied, "he shall be a father to the inhabitants of Jerusalem, and to the house of Judah...and they shall hang upon him all the glory of his father's house." (Isa. 22:21–24). Like the relationship between a father and son, Christ will exercise justice, wisdom, might, and knowledge (Isa. 11) toward the mortal population. Father-like characteristics are illustrated in the letters of the Apostle Paul: "I write not these things to shame you, but as my beloved sons I warn you. For though ye have ten thousand instructors in Christ, yet have ye not many fathers ... " (1 Cor. 4:14,15); "Ye know how we exhorted and comforted and charged every one of you, as a father doth his children." (1 Thess. 2:11).

b. Although believers are usually referred to as "brethren" (e.g. 1 Thess. 2:14; Heb. 2:11) it is not inappropriate to term them "children". For example: "I and the children which God hath given me." (Heb. 2:13, cf. Isa. 8:17,18). Christ is the father of these children since he is the means whereby they are born anew. (John 3:3,7).[9] This is the seed which Christ shall see and be satisfied. (Isa. 53:10,11, cf. Psa. 45:16—The Messianic character of this psalm is indicated by v. 6 and Heb. 1:8,9 where it is quoted in a context referring to Christ.)

4. 1 Cor. 15:22–28 provides an explanation of Isa. 9:6. The Father gives the Son *delegated* authority and power for a limited duration of time. "For he [God] hath put all things under his [Jesus'] feet. But when he saith all things are put under him, it is manifest that he is excepted, which did put all things under him. And when all things shall be subdued unto him, then shall the Son also himself be *subject* unto him [God] that put all things under him [Jesus], that God may be all in all." (vv. 27,28). Since the Son is to be subject unto the Father, then he is clearly not co-equal with the Father, and by implication not a person within the Godhead.

Isaiah 48:16

"...the Lord GOD, and his Spirit, hath sent me."

PROBLEM:

It is said that this passage refers to all three persons of the trinity—"the Lord God", "his Spirit", and "me", i.e. Jesus.

---

[8] "Everlasting" means "duration; continuity". Robert Young, *Analytical Concordance to the Holy Bible*, (London: Lutterworth Press, 1965). The same Hebrew word *ad*, is used of mountains in Hab. 3:6. It does not follow, therefore, that "everlasting Father" means "eternal Father."

[9] The living word of God is the active agent in effecting the new birth. (Heb. 4:12; James 1:18; 1 Pet. 1:23).

WRESTED SCRIPTURES

SOLUTION:

1. This just will not do. In Deut. 6:4 we are told that "…the LORD our God is one LORD". Trinitarians argue that the Lord is indeed one but He is three in one. However, if the Lord God be three, then in this Isaiah passage there are also "his Spirit" and "me", which make five!

2. Many trinitarian commentators see the "me" as referring to Isaiah himself, at least in the first instance, as in Isa. 6:8 (Jamieson, Fausett and Brown; Lange; Pulpit; Barnes all see it in this way). Calvin, writing concerning attempts to prove the trinity from this verse says, "Such forced and violent interpretations are to be avoided".

3. If it is maintained that the "me" is Jesus, then it should be pointed out that this does not support the trinitarian concept, for it would teach that 'God the Son' was *sent* by 'God the Father' and 'God the Holy Spirit'. There is no 'co-equality in this.

4. The verse may well, like Isa. 6:8, reach forward into the future and speak of the work of Jesus. Jesus was indeed sent by God as is clear from Isa. 61:1 (which is applied to the work of Jesus in Luke 4:18)—"The *Spirit of the Lord GOD* is upon me; because the LORD hath anointed me to preach good tidings unto the meek; he hath *sent* me to bind up the broken hearted" etc. Note: "the Spirit", "the Lord GOD" and "me" are all mentioned as in Isa. 48:16, and note, too, that Isa. 61:1 speaks as though it was happening at that time, but Luke 4:18–20 shows that it did not happen until the ministry of Jesus.

5. John 5:30,36 and John 3:34 show when Jesus was sent.

Thus Jesus was sent by the "LORD" (Yahweh) who is the only true God. Being the sender, He is greater than the sent. In any case the sending of Jesus was not in Isaiah's day but during the ministry of Jesus. The verse proves neither co-equality nor co-eternity of the Father and the Son.

Micah 5:2

"Thou Bethlehem…out of thee shall he come forth unto me that is to be ruler in Israel; whose goings forth have been from of old, from everlasting."

PROBLEM:

That this refers to Jesus there can be no doubt (Matt. 2:6). The verse is said to prove the eternal pre-existence of 'God the Son'.

SOLUTION:

1. "From of old, from everlasting" does not imply eternity. The Hebrew word translated "from of old" is *mikedem* which signifies "from of old, anciently"[10], and the word "everlasting" is the Hebrew *olahm* which denotes an indefinite period of time: "what is hidden; especially hidden time, long; the beginning or

---

[10] Samuel Prideaux Tregelles, *Gesenius Hebrew and Chaldee Lexicon*, (Grand Rapids, Mich.: Wm. B. Eerdmans Publishing Co.,1969), p.724.

end of which is uncertain or else not defined...”[11] The same two words occur together in Isa. 51:9, rendered “as in the ancient days (*kedem*), in the generations of old (*olahm*)” and this refers to the time of the Exodus. Thus whatever is meant by the “goings forth” of Messiah it does not imply his eternal pre-existence. (The RSV renders the phrase “from of old, from ancient days”).

2. “Goings forth” is plural. If it refers to the begettal of the Son of God then it contradicts Heb. 1:5, “Thou art my Son, *this day* have I begotten thee”—a single begettal at a definite point in finite time.

3. “Goings forth”, is the Hebrew *motsaah*, feminine plural from *yatsa,* “to go forth”[12], which is the word used in Gen. 15:4 where, speaking of Messiah, Abraham is promised, “he that shall come forth (Heb. *yatsa*) out of thine own bowels shall be thine heir”. It is also used of Messiah in 2 Sam. 7:12, “I will set up thy seed after thee, which shall proceed (Heb. *yatsa*) out of thy bowels...” These were the promises “from of old, from ancient days” (RSV). From Abraham *came forth* Isaac; from Isaac *came forth* Jacob; from Jacob *came forth* Judah; from Judah ultimately *came forth* David; from David finally there *came forth* “the handmaid of the Lord” (is this why the feminine plural is used, because Jesus was to be the seed of the woman?)—i.e. many “goings forth” until finally the virgin “brought forth” Jesus. (Luke 2:7).

Matthew 1:23

“Behold, a virgin shall be with child, and shall bring forth a son, and they shall call his name Emmanuel,[13] *which being interpreted is, God with us.”*

PROBLEM:

This passage is said to show that Jesus was God, in the trinitarian sense.

SOLUTION:

1. At the time of the Exodus we are told that God remembered His covenant (Exo. 2:24; 3:7,8). Having thus remembered the covenant the record proceeds to tell us that God:

a. Came down—“I am come down to deliver them” (3:8).

b. Visited His people—“I have surely visited you.” (3:16).

c. Was therefore to be with them—“I will be with thee.” (3:12). [Note: the word here is from the same root as Immanuel; “with thee” is the Heb. *imarch*, “with us” is the Heb. *imanu*.]

In all of this God acted by manifestation in an angel. He did not personally come down, visit, be with them (see Exo. 3:2), but the record speaks of God Himself as doing these things (Exo. 3:4,8).

[11] *Ibid.* p.612.

[12] F. Brown, S. R. Driver, A. Briggs, *Hebrew and English Lexicon*, (Peabody, Mass.: Hendrickson Publishers, 1996), p.425.

[13] “Immanuel” in Isa.7:14.

2. In the New Testament period God again came to Israel (Mark 1:3) and visited His people (Luke 1:68). "Blessed be the Lord God of Israel; for he hath visited...his people." But again He did not come personally. He raised up Jesus who, like the angel (cf. Exo. 23:20,21) came in the Father's name (John 5:43), spoke God's words (John 3:34) and did the Father's works (John 5:36).

It was in this sense that Jesus was Immanuel—God with us. Paul puts it in a nutshell—"God was manifest in the flesh..." (1 Tim. 3:16). John says, "No man hath seen God at any time; the only begotten Son, which is in the bosom of the Father, he hath declared him" (John 1:18). Jesus showed men what God was like. He manifested the Father in all that he did, his teachings, his healings, his manner of life.

Matthew 28:19

"...baptising them in the name of the Father, and of the Son, and of the Holy Spirit."

PROBLEM:

It is argued that here we have a clear reference to the trinity. All the 'persons of the trinity' are mentioned and they have one name.

SOLUTION:

1. This is the only passage in the Bible where the Father, Son and Holy Spirit are mentioned in the same verse. (2 Cor. 13:14 is usually linked with this passage but see comments on this verse on page 301). The word "God" occurs 1,326 times in the New Testament without any suggestion of a plurality of persons in the Godhead. The authenticity of this verse is questioned by some, but there is no need to rely on textual criticism for an answer to the problem, and the verse can be understood as being in harmony with the truth.

2. Whilst the Father, Son and Holy Spirit are all mentioned in the verse, the verse does not imply either their co-equality or their essential unity in the trinitarian sense.

3. The name referred to is without question the name of the Father (i.e. Yahweh), for Jesus said to the Father, "I have manifested *thy name* unto the men which thou gavest me..." (John 17:6). Since Isa. 45:5 says "I am the LORD (Yahweh), and there is none else, there is no God beside me", and since 1 Cor. 8:6 says, "To us there is but one God, the Father..." the truth of Jesus' words is borne out—one God, i.e. the Father, and His name is Yahweh.

4. Jesus is said to have come in his Father's name (John 5:43, cf. the angel in Exo. 23:20,21), to have manifested the Father's name (John 17:6) and to have been given the name after his resurrection—"God highly exalted him, and gave unto him the name which is above every name; that at the name of Jesus [Yah-shua] every knee should bow...and every tongue confess that Jesus Christ is Lord, to the glory of God the Father." (Phil. 2:9–11 RV). Thus the name of the Father was associated with the Son—but it was the Father's name, which He gave to the Son, not the name of a triune God.

284

5. The manifestation of the Father by the Son (John 17:6; 1 Tim. 3:16) was accomplished by means of the Holy Spirit (Luke 1:35; John 3:34).

Luke 1:68

"Blessed be the Lord God of Israel; for he hath visited and redeemed his people."

Luke 7:16

"God hath visited his people."

PROBLEM:

Since the work of Jesus is spoken of as God visiting His people, it is said that the verses imply that Jesus was God before he appeared on the human stage.

SOLUTION:

1. For God to visit His people does not involve His personal presence. When God visited Israel in Egypt (Exo. 3:16; 4:31) it was by an angel (Exo. 3:2,7,8).
2. The appearance of Jesus, born in a miraculous way (Luke 1:35), speaking God's words (John 3:34), doing the Father's work (John 5:36; 9:4), was God visiting His people. But this does not make Jesus himself God, any more than it makes the angel of Exodus 3 God.
3. As in so many of these verses, the key is the doctrine of God manifestation (1 Tim. 3:16; John 1:18).

John 1:1–3

"In the beginning was the Word, and the Word was with God, and the Word was God. The same was in the beginning with God. All things were made by him; and without him was not any thing made that was made."

PROBLEM:

This passage is usually the chief reference on which the pre-existence and deity of Christ are argued.

SOLUTION:

1. Christ was not literally the Word. He was "the word...made flesh". (v. 14). The Greek word *logos* translated "Word" expresses the divine intention, mind, or purpose.[14] Young defines *logos* as "a word, speech, matter, reason."[15] In the AV, *logos* is translated by more than 20 different English words and is used for utterances of men (e.g. John 17:20) as well as those of God (John 5:38).

[14] This can be supported by evaluating all references to *logos* in the New Testament and the Septuagint.

[15] Robert Young, *Analytical Concordance to the Holy Bible*, (London: Lutterworth Press, 1965).

2. "In the beginning was the Word...All things were made by him."[16] *Logos* does not in itself denote personality. It is personified by the masculine gender in the AV; the *Diaglott* avoids confusion by translating the pronouns in the neuter— "through it every thing was done."[17] An Old Testament parallel to the personification of *logos* is the personification of wisdom: "The LORD possessed me in the beginning of his way, before his works of old. I was set up from everlasting, from the beginning, or ever the earth was." (Prov. 8:22,23). In this passage, wisdom is personified as a woman. (vv. 1,2).

3. "All things were made by him"—John is apparently alluding to the creation recorded in Genesis. God spoke, and it was done (e.g. "And God said, Let there be light: and there was light."—Gen. 1:3. Notice another allusion—John 1:7,8). But this creation was not accompanied by Christ, but by the *logos* of God. This is indicated by several passages:

   a. "By the *word* of the LORD were the heavens made; and all the host of them by the *breath* of his mouth...For he *spake*, and it was done; he *commanded*, and it stood fast." (Psa. 33:6,9). See also Psa. 107:20; 147:15,18,19; Isa. 55:11.

   b. "...by the *word* of God the heavens were of old, and the earth standing out of the water and in the water...But the heavens and the earth, which are now, by the same word are kept in store, reserved unto fire against the day of judgment and perdition of ungodly men." (2 Pet. 3:5,7).

   c. See also Heb. 11:3, cf. Jer. 10:12,13.[18]

4. Angels, prophets and Christ have been vehicles by which God has expressed His *logos*. Christ is the complete manifestation of the *logos*—"in him dwelleth all the fulness of the Godhead bodily." (Col. 2:9). It was the *logos* which was in the beginning with God, not Christ. When the "Word was made flesh" (John 1:14) then, and then only, Christ became the "Word". Christ is called the Word (Rev. 19:13, cf. 1 John 1:1; Luke 1:2) since his doctrine and words came from his Father (John 7:16; 17:14). He was the *logos* lived out in speech and action, not merely written on scrolls.

John 3:13

"And no man hath ascended up to heaven, but he that came down from heaven, even the Son of man which is in heaven."

---

[16] It is sometimes argued that the "beginning" referred to in John 1:1 is the beginning of Christ's ministry. 1 John 1:1 is offered in support of this interpretation. It should be noted, however, that John's allusions in John 1 are drawn from Genesis 1 as point 3 outlines, thereby implying that the beginning refers to the same narrative and not to the ministry of Christ.

[17] Benjamin Wilson, *The Emphatic Diaglott*, (Brooklyn: International Bible Students Ass., Watchtower Bible and Tract Society, 1942).

[18] It is also noteworthy that although the writer to the Hebrews speaks in exalted terms of Christ (e.g. "express image of his [God's] person"—Heb. 1:3), *logos* is used of God's message, and not of Christ himself. See Heb. 2:2; 4:2,12; 7:28; 12:19 and 13:7,22.

PROBLEM:

Since Christ is said to have come down from heaven, he must have had an existence in heaven prior to his birth as a human on the earth.

SOLUTION:

1. This passage proves too much. It is argued that 'God the Son' pre-existed as a spirit creature in heaven prior to his 'incarnation', but the passage in John reads, "even the Son of *man* which is in heaven". Did the Son of *man* literally come down from heaven?

2. This passage is one of the many in John's gospel which employs the Old Testament language of theophany (God appearing). A manifestation of divine power is referred to as God "coming down". The completion of the theophany is God "going up" or "ascending". (See Gen. 11:5; 18:21; Exo. 3:7,8; 19:11,18,20; 34:5; Psa. 18:9,10; Isa. 64:1.)

3. Christ did not literally come down from heaven. His origin was heavenly (as the context states—John 3:31), since he was conceived by the Holy Spirit sent from heaven, and his teaching was not his own but his Father's. (Luke 1:35; John 7:16; 17:14).

4. "Even the Son of man which is in heaven" is likely the comment of John and not part of the conversation between Jesus and Nicodemus.

John 5:18

"He...said also that God was his Father, making himself equal with God."

PROBLEM:

It is argued that the Jews understood Jesus to be claiming equality with the Father in the trinitarian sense.

SOLUTION:

1. Not only did Jesus say God was his Father; he also said that his Father was his God—which denies the trinitarian doctrine of the co-equality of persons within the Godhead (John 20:17; John 17:1–3).

2. Jesus expressly denied equality with the Father—"The Son can do nothing of himself, but what he seeth the Father do" (John 5:19). Also his declaration that the Father "will show him (Jesus) greater works than these" (John 5:20) illustrates that the Son was not equal with the Father.

3. The statement of Jesus in John 5:30 is conclusive—"I can of mine own self do nothing." If he could do nothing without the sanction and help of his Father then clearly he was not co-equal with Him.

4. The statement in verse 43—"I am come in my Father's name"—shows that, like the angel (Exo. 23:20,21), he was God's representative speaking His words and performing His works (cf. also John 12:13).

5. See Jesus' answer to the same accusation in John 10:33–36.

John 5:23
"That all men should honour the Son, even as they honour the Father. He that honoureth not the Son honoureth not the Father which hath sent him."

Hebrews 1:6
"Let all the angels of God worship him."

Revelation 1:6
"To him be glory and dominion for ever and ever."

Revelation 5:12
"Worthy is the Lamb..."

PROBLEM:

These verses are cited with Matt. 4:10 in which Jesus says to Satan, "Thou shalt worship the Lord thy God, and him only shalt thou serve", to show that since Jesus instructs men to honour himself, then the Son must be 'Very God'.

SOLUTION:

1. The context to this verse is sufficiently emphatic that Christ is not co-equal with the Father. Consider the following:
   a. John 5:19—"The Son can do nothing of himself, but what he seeth the Father do." Jesus specifically repudiates the claim that he is making himself "equal with God". (v. 18).
   b. v. 22—"For the Father...hath committed all judgment unto the Son."
   c. v. 23—"...the Father which hath sent him."
   d. v. 27—"And hath given him authority to execute judgment also, because he is the Son of man."
   e. v. 30—"I can of mine own self do nothing...I seek not mine own will, but the will of the Father which hath sent me."
   f. v. 36—"For the works which the Father hath given me to finish."
   g. These verses indicate that the Father has *delegated* authority and power to the Son. This power and authority is not the right of the Son by virtue of his being 'God the Son', but rather is an exercise of the divine prerogatives of the Father. Even when the Son returns, he does so "in the glory of his Father." (Matt. 16:27).
2. The worship of Jesus needs to be considered from two standpoints:
   a. The worship of Jesus AFTER his resurrection—all the above passages refer to Jesus after his resurrection.

i. The fact that Jesus receives worship implies neither his co-equality nor co-eternity with the Father.

ii. The worship given to Jesus by the angels is commanded by the Father—"When he bringeth in the first begotten into the world, he saith, And let all the angels of God worship him" (Heb. 1:5,6). This is against the idea of the Son being equal to the Father.

iii. Similarly in John 5:22,23—"The Father...hath committed all judgment unto the Son: that all men should honour the Son, even as they honour the Father." Again the honouring of the Son is at the behest of the Father, which denies that the two are co-equal.

iv. The worship thus afforded to the Son after his resurrection is "to the glory of God the Father" (Phil. 2:11).

b. The worship of Jesus BEFORE his resurrection—the passages which record this happening are of an altogether different nature from those quoted above.

i. Jesus was "worshipped" during days of his flesh by a leper (Matt. 8:2), the ruler whose daughter had died (Matt. 9:18), and by the wise men from the east who had heard of his birth (Matt. 2:2). There are other similar references. None of them implies that they worshipped him as God. They simply paid him an act of reverence such as one man would pay to a superior.

ii. For similar occurrences see 1 Chron. 29:20 where David was worshipped, Rev. 3:9 where the Philadelphians were to be worshipped, and Matt. 18:26 where the servant in the parable worshipped his master.

John 6:33
"For the bread of God is he which cometh down from heaven."

John 6:38
"I came down from heaven."

John 6:51
"I am the living bread which came down from heaven."

John 6:58
"This is that bread which came down from heaven."

PROBLEM:

These passages are considered to be proof that Jesus existed in heaven prior to his coming to the earth.

WRESTED SCRIPTURES

SOLUTION:

1. The words of chapter 6 were a "hard saying" (v. 60) and as a result "many of his disciples went back and walked no more with him". (v. 66). An understanding of the analogy with the manna provides the key to the right understanding of this passage.

2. The bread "from heaven" (v. 31) did not mean that it was actually manufactured in heaven and descended through the atmosphere, but rather that it was produced on the earth by God's Holy Spirit power. "From heaven", therefore, emphasizes the divine origin of the bread. [Cf. "The baptism of John, was it from heaven, or of men?" (Luke 20:4)].

3. Similarly, Christ came down from heaven, not literally, since it was the Holy Spirit which descended upon the virgin Mary to effect the conception. (Luke 1:35). "From heaven" emphasizes his divine origin as a person (i.e. his father was God) and the divine origin of his teaching. Unlike the manna, which profited only temporarily, his words were "spirit" and "life". (v. 63).

John 6:62

"What and if ye shall see the Son of man ascend up where he was before?"

PROBLEM:

It is argued that if the Son of man could ascend up to where he was before, then clearly he must have pre-existed before his 'incarnation' on earth.

SOLUTION:

1. This passage proves too much. It is argued that 'God the Son' pre-existed as a spirit creature in heaven prior to his 'incarnation', but the passage in John reads, "What and if ye shall see the Son of *man* ascend up where he was before?" Did the Son of *man* literally come down from heaven?

2. The context indicates that verse 62 is part of a discourse in which Jesus compares himself to the manna which God provided for Israel. The fact that this manna was referred to as "bread from heaven" (v. 31) did not mean that it actually descended from heaven through the great expanse of space to the earth, but rather that it had its *origin* in heaven. Similarly, Christ was of divine origin—"from heaven", since the Holy Spirit was sent from heaven to effect his conception in the womb of Mary. (Luke 1:35). He later ascended to heaven. (Acts 1:10,11).

John 8:23

"...Ye are from beneath; I am from above: ye are of this world; I am not of this world."

PROBLEM:

It is argued that since Christ was not of this world but rather came from above, he must therefore have existed prior to his birth on earth.

SOLUTION:

1. Jesus said, "I know whence I came, and whither I go." (John 8:14), but he did not literally come down from heaven. It was the Holy Spirit which came down from heaven and overshadowed the virgin Mary. The result was the conception of Jesus. (Luke 1:35). Jesus referred to his divine origin when he declared: "If God were your Father, ye would love me: for I proceeded forth and came from God; neither came I of myself, but he sent me." (John 8:42).
2. Jesus was also "from above" in the following ways:
   a. The things he spoke came from his Father: "I speak to the world those things which I have heard of him." (John 8:26, cf. v. 28).
   b. His Father honoured and bore witness to him: "The Father that sent me beareth witness of me…It is my Father that honoureth me…" (John 8:18,54).
3. Jesus instructed his followers that they too must be "born from above". (John 3:3,7 AVm.). Obviously believers could not be born from above physically, as was Jesus. Only in a spiritual sense could they be born from above. By contrast, the Pharisees were motivated by the wisdom which did not come down from above, but which was "earthly, sensual, devilish." (James 3:15).
4. Jesus was "not of this world" because its constitution was the "lust of the flesh, and the lust of the eyes, and the pride of life". (1 John 2:16). "If any man love the world," John said, "the love of the Father is not in him." (1 John 2:15). Similarly, Jesus said, "My kingdom is not of this world." (John 18:36). By this he did not mean that it had nothing to do with the earth, but rather that it was a heavenly kingdom whose constitution was not of the Jewish and Roman arrangements[19], but was designed by the Father from the "foundation of the world." (Matt. 25:34).

John 8:56

"Your father Abraham rejoiced to see my day: and he saw it, and was glad."

PROBLEM:

It is argued that if Abraham saw Jesus then Jesus must have existed in the time of Abraham. This is held to support the idea of the pre-existence of Jesus.

SOLUTION:

1. The RVm. gives "Abraham rejoiced that he should see my day…" which undoubtedly gives the true sense, i.e. that Abraham looked forward to the

[19] The meaning of the Greek word *kosmos,* translated "world", is "arrangement, beauty, world". Robert Young, *Analytical Concordance to the Holy Bible*, (London: Lutterworth Press, 1965).

coming day of Jesus who was the seed that had been promised to him (Gen. 22:17:18, cf. Gal. 3:16). It is the connection of the words of Jesus with the events described in Gen. 22 that provides the solution to the problem.

2. The offering up of Isaac was an acted prophecy about the providing of a sacrifice for men's sins. This is why "Abraham called the name of that place Jehovah-jireh: as it is said to this day, In the mount of the LORD it [i.e. the lamb of God's providing] shall be seen" (Gen. 22:14). So Abraham was looking to the future when the Lamb of God would appear as a sacrifice.

3. This is why he said to Isaac as they journeyed to Moriah, "God will provide himself the lamb for a burnt offering" (Gen. 22:8 RV). Remember, Abraham was a prophet (Gen. 20:7; Psa. 105:15).

4. Thus Abraham looked forward to the coming of Jesus. But he also saw it acted out in a prophetic drama. When Isaac was bound on the wood on the altar, Abraham was about to kill Isaac when he heard a voice behind him. He turned and saw a ram caught in a thicket by his horns. The ram was, on divine instruction, offered instead of Isaac (Gen. 22:13).

Thus a sacrifice was provided and Isaac was delivered. Heb. 11:19 tells us that this was a figure or type of Isaac's death and resurrection. The ram, then, was a type of the true sacrifice that makes resurrection possible. It represented Jesus.

How would Abraham have felt when he heard the voice and saw the ram and Isaac was spared?—Glad!

Thus not only did Abraham look forward to the day of Jesus, in a figure "he saw it and was glad".

John 8:58

"...Before Abraham was, I am."

PROBLEM:

This passage is connected with Exo. 3:14 where God says to Moses, "I AM THAT I AM". From these references two conclusions are drawn:

1. Since Christ was before Abraham, Christ must have existed prior to his birth on earth.

2. Since Christ says, "I am" he is alluding to the divine name, thereby in effect telling the Jews that he is 'Very God'.

SOLUTION:

1. Christ's reference to Abraham is to affirm his (Christ's) pre-eminence, not pre-existence. The Jews had claimed that Abraham was their father (v. 39) and so Christ establishes his pre-eminence in the divine purpose by stating that before Abraham was, "I am". He did not say, "Before Abraham was, I was" as it is frequently misread. But the Jews, like modern-day trinitarians, misunderstood Jesus. He was not claiming to be literally older in years than Abraham. This is indicated by his prior remark, "Your father Abraham rejoiced to see my day: and he saw it, and was glad." (v. 56). Abraham, to whom the gospel was

preached (Gal. 3:8), "saw" the day of Christ through the eye of faith. Christ was "foreordained before the foundation of the world, but was manifest in these last times". (1 Pet. 1:20). He was foreordained in the divine purpose, but not formed. Similarly in the divine purpose he was the "Lamb slain from the foundation of the world" (Rev. 13:8), but literally he was not slain until his crucifixion in the time of Pilate.

2. There is no proof that Christ alludes to the divine name (imperfectly rendered by the AV, "I AM THAT I AM"). Jesus simply uses the present tense of the verb "to be". Even if this verse were intended to be read as an allusion to the divine name, this is not proof that Christ was claiming to be 'Very God'. The divine name declared, "I WILL BE WHAT I WILL BE". (Exo. 3:14 RSVm. & NIVm.). The name was a prophetic declaration of the divine purpose. Jesus Christ was "God manifest in the flesh" (1 Tim. 3:16); "the word" (Greek: *logos*) "made flesh" (John 1:14). As such, he was the expression of the divine character, "full of grace and truth" (John 1:14, cf. Exo. 33:19; 34:6), and became the "firstborn among many brethren" (Rom. 8:29). Christ was the result of the word made flesh, not the originator of the divine plan. As he himself said, "I proceeded forth and came from God; *neither came I of myself*, but he sent me." (John 8:42).

John 10:17,18

"...I have power to lay it down [my life], and I have power to take it again..."

PROBLEM:

It is argued by trinitarians that if Jesus had power to lay down his life and take it again, then the 'God part' ('God the Son') must have continued while the body (the 'Son of Man') lay dead in the grave.

SOLUTION:

1. The trinitarian argument mistakenly rests on the word "power". The Greek word *exousia*[20] translated "power" is rendered "authority" in 29 other references (e.g. Matt. 7:29; 21:23; Luke 7:8; John 5:27). Weymouth renders this passage as follows: "No one is taking it away from me, but I myself am laying it down...I am *authorized* to receive it back again."[21] This translation is in harmony with the following statements of Jesus:

   a. "...The Son can do nothing of himself..." (John 5:19).

   b. "I can of mine own self do nothing..." (John 5:30).

---

[20] *Exousia* means privilege or authority: Robert Young, *Analytical Concordance to the Holy Bible*, 8th ed., (London: Lutterworth Press, 1965). Bullinger gives the meaning of *exousia* as follows: "delegated authority, liberty or authority to do anything." Ethelbert W. Bullinger. *A Critical Lexicon and Concordance to the English and Greek New Testament*, 8th ed., (London: Samuel Bagster and Sons Ltd., 1957). p.593.

[21] Richard F. Weymouth, *The New Testament in Modern Speech*, (London: Jas. Clarke & Co., Ltd.).

Jesus had authority to take his life again because as he himself said: "This commandment have I received of my Father". (v. 18). It is not, therefore, Jesus who does something for himself.

2. In many places the New Testament writers refer to the resurrection of Christ. Not one writer, however, states that Jesus raised himself from the dead. In *every* reference it is God who raises Christ, not 'God the Son' who raises the 'Son of Man'. Note the following passages:

   a. "Whom God hath raised up, having loosed the pains of death..." (Acts 2:24).

   b. "This Jesus hath God raised up..." (Acts 2:32).

   c. See also Acts 3:15; 5:30; 10:39,40; and 1 Cor. 15:15.

3. The personal pronoun "him" when referring to the death and resurrection of Christ always means the body which lay in the grave. It never refers in Scripture to 'God the Son', who it is hypothesized, survived the death of the body. For example, Acts of the Apostles records the following: "...whom they slew and hanged on a tree: him God raised up the third day, and shewed him openly." (Acts 10:39,40). The "him" that was hanged is the same "him" that was raised. This evidence is fatal to the trinitarian view that the real 'him' was 'God the Son' who continued to exist after the death of the body. Jesus stated plainly, "*I am he that liveth, and was dead.*" (Rev. 1:18). This statement was made after his resurrection.

4. Jesus was unable to do anything for himself once dead because "the dead know not any thing." (Eccl. 9:5).

John 10:30

"I and my Father are one."

PROBLEM:

This passage is understood by trinitarians to be a clear assertion that Christ claimed to be a person within the Godhead.

SOLUTION:

1. Jesus said, "I and my Father are one" but the Jews misunderstood him, thinking he was claiming to be equal with God. (v. 33). Trinitarians make the same mistake. The oneness referred to is not a declaration by Christ that he is 'Very God', but rather unity of purpose. Consider the evidence:

   a. Jesus subsequently prayed for his disciples, "that they may be one, even as we are." (John 17:11,21,22). These words require that the unity referred to, be also extended to the disciples. Obviously the unity is not that of the powers of the Godhead but unity resulting from sanctification through the word of God. (John 17:14,17,18).

   b. See also John 17:22,23: "...that they may be one, even as we are one: I in them, and thou in me, that they may be made perfect in one..." Likewise, these words require a relationship between the disciples and Christ which exists between the Son and his Father—a unity, or perfection with the divine purpose.

2. Elsewhere in John's gospel, Jesus clearly affirms that he is not co-equal with the Father: "The Son can do nothing of himself, but what he seeth the Father do." (John 5:19); "I can of mine own self do nothing: as I hear, I judge: and my judgment is just; because I seek not mine own will, but the will of the Father which hath sent me" (John 5:30); "My Father is greater than I." (John 14:28).

John 14:9

"Jesus saith, ... he that hath seen me hath seen the Father..."

PROBLEM:

This verse is quoted by trinitarians as a clear declaration that Jesus Christ was God Almighty incarnate.

SOLUTION:

1. Jesus did not mean by these words that when men saw him, they were literally beholding his Father. Consider the following:

   a. Physically, Jesus was not the image of his Father. Isaiah wrote: "he hath no form nor comeliness; and when we shall see him, there is no beauty that we should desire him". (Isa. 53:2). It is unthinkable that the Father would be less comely than His creation.

   b. Jesus told the Jews that they had "neither heard his [the Father's] voice at any time, nor seen his shape." (John 5:37). This would have been untrue if Jesus were himself the Father.

   c. The Father dwells "in the light which no man can approach unto; whom no man hath seen, nor can see." (1 Tim. 6:16; cf. 1 John 4:12). Those who saw Jesus, did not, therefore literally see the Father.

2. John comments, "No man hath seen God at any time; the only begotten Son, which is in the bosom of the Father, he hath declared him." (John 1:18). The Son "declared" the Father by the words which he spoke and the works which he performed. Jesus told Philip: "the words that I speak unto you I speak not of myself: but the Father that dwelleth in me, he doeth the works." (John 14:10). It was in this sense that Jesus meant, "he that hath seen me hath seen the Father."

3. Jesus employed the language of 'God manifestation' characteristic of the Old Testament. Accredited representatives exercising divine power and authority bore the divine name. (See Exo. 23:20,21—"I send an Angel ... my name is in him.") Jesus was the supreme manifestation—"God was manifest in the flesh." (1 Tim. 3:16). Although not 'Very God', he was justified in saying "he that hath seen me hath seen the Father" since he lived out the character of the Father and since the Father had delegated this authority and power to him. (See John 1:18; 5:19,22,23,30).

WRESTED SCRIPTURES

John 16:27–30

"...I came out from God. I came forth from the Father, and am come into the world: again, I leave the world, and go to the Father...We believe that thou camest forth from God."

PROBLEM:

Here for the trinitarian is a clear statement of the eternal pre-existence of the Son.

SOLUTION:

1. The way in which Jesus came forth from the Father is clearly defined in such Scriptures as Matt. 1:18; Luke 1:35; John 1:14. Nowhere in Scripture are we told that God the Son became incarnate.
2. Compare John 6:51—"I am the living bread which came down from heaven: if any man eat of this bread, he shall live for ever: and the bread that I will give is my flesh, which I will give for the life of the world."
   a. What part of Jesus was "the bread...which came down from heaven"? The verse says it was the "flesh". Did the flesh of Jesus really come down from heaven, or is this a way of saying that it was of divine origin? Obviously the latter.
   b. Note that the manna, too, is said to have come down from heaven, i.e. it was of divine origin. (John 6:31,32).
3. It was the changed, resurrected body of Jesus that left the world and went to the Father (Mark 16:6; John 20:17; Acts 1:11). No trinitarian would argue that the literal, flesh body of Jesus came down from heaven. But the Bible clearly teaches that the Son of man, i.e. the baby born to Mary—the body—did come down from heaven (John 6:62; 3:13) in the sense that he was of divine origin.

John 17:5

"And now, O Father, glorify thou me with thine own self with the glory which I had with thee before the world was."

PROBLEM:

If Christ had glory with God before the world was, then obviously it is argued he must have existed before his birth on earth.

SOLUTION:

1. Stress is often placed on Jesus' statement that he had glory with the Father. The JWs in their *New World Translation of the Holy Scriptures* translate this verse as follows: "So now you, Father, glorify me *alongside* yourself with the glory that I had *alongside* you before the world was."[22] But the Greek preposition

---

[22] *New World Translation of the Holy Scriptures*, (Brooklyn, New York: Watchtower Bible and Tract Society of New York, Inc., 1961).

para translated "with" in the AV and "alongside" in the NWT also occurs in John 1:6: "There was a man sent from [Greek: *para*] God, whose name was John." If the preposition in John 17:5 requires the literal pre-existence of Christ, then likewise it requires the literal pre-existence of John the Baptist.[23] It is interesting that the NWT inconsistently translates John 1:6 as follows: "There arose a man that was sent forth as a representative of God: his name was John." There is no hint of pre-existence here.

2. How could Jesus have glory with his Father "before the world was" if he did not literally pre-exist? An illustration is helpful: An architect sees and knows the beautiful details of his proposed construction before the site is prepared, or the foundation stone laid. But God is the great Architect and in His divine plan, Christ was "the Lamb slain from the foundation of the world" (Rev. 13:8)—the chief cornerstone "foreordained before the foundation of the world" (1 Pet. 1:20). The building will duly be "fitly framed together" (Eph. 2:21) to perform its role in the "kingdom prepared...from the foundation of the world." (Matt. 25:34). Christ was "foreordained", but not formed until born of the virgin Mary in the days of Herod the king. Likewise, the glory he had with his Father was in the divine plan of the great Architect. It was the subject of prophetic testimony "when it [the Spirit of Christ] testified beforehand the sufferings of Christ, and the glory that should follow." (1 Pet. 1:11, cf. John 12:41).

3. Scripture speaks as if others pre-existed, as well as Christ. Consider the following:

   a. Of believers, Paul wrote:
      i. "Whom he did foreknow." (Rom. 8:29).
      ii. "He had afore prepared [note the past tense] unto glory." (Rom. 9:23, cf. 2 Tim. 1:9).
      iii. "He hath chosen us in him before the foundation of the world." (Eph. 1:4).

   b. Of Jeremiah, the Lord said: "Before I formed thee in the belly I knew thee; and before thou camest forth out of the womb I sanctified thee, and I ordained thee a prophet unto the nations." (Jer. 1:5).

But who would contend for the pre-existence of Jeremiah and other believers because the language employed states that God knew them before they were born? Similarly, the language of John 17:5 must be understood in terms of this background. Unless the principle is recognized that God "calleth those things which be not as though they were" (Rom. 4:17), confusion will result in Biblical interpretation, as it does with the wrested pre-existence interpretation given to this passage in John's gospel.

4. The context is sufficiently clear that Christ is not 'Very God'. His power and authority are derived, not innate: "As thou hast given him [Christ] power over

---

[23] The Greek preposition *para* in John 17:5 takes the dative case and means "beside and at, with or near a person; with, i.e., in the estimation or power of." But in John 1:6 *para* takes the genitive case and means "from beside, beside and proceeding from." See Ethelbert W. Bullinger, *A Critical Lexicon and Concordance*, (London: Samuel Bagster and Sons Ltd., 1957), p.888.

all flesh, that he should give eternal life to as many as thou hast given him." (John 17:2).

5. Since Jesus says in verse 3 that the Father is the "only true God", this itself shows that Jesus did not consider himself to be God.

John 20:28
"My Lord and my God."

PROBLEM:

Since Jesus is addressed by Thomas as "My Lord and My God", this passage is considered by trinitarians to prove the 'deity of Christ'—that he is 'God the Son'.

SOLUTION:

1. Thomas' confession is an acknowledgment that Jesus had indeed risen from the dead, but it is not a declaration that Jesus is 'God the Son'. Thomas, a Jew, used a mode of expression common to the Old Testament in which accredited representatives of God are referred to as God. Angels are called "God" in the following passages: Gen. 16:7, cf. v. 13; 22:8,11,15, cf. v. 16; Exo. 23:20,21. Moses is referred to as a "god" to Pharaoh. (Exo. 7:1, "god" is translated from the Heb. *elohim*). *Elohim*, translated "God" in Gen. 1:26 (and many other passages), refers to the judges of Israel in Psa. 82:1,6, cf. John 10:34. It is also translated "judges" in Exo. 21:6; 22:8,9 and "gods" (AVm. "judges") in Exo. 22:28.

2. Earlier in this chapter, Jesus told Mary, "I ascend unto my Father, and your Father; and to my God, and your God." (v. 17). Since Jesus was to ascend to his God, then clearly he was not himself 'Very God'.

Acts 20:28,29
"...the church of God, which he hath purchased with his own blood".

PROBLEM:

It is argued that since the Church was purchased with the blood of Jesus, this passage teaches that Jesus Christ was God and hence supports the trinity.

SOLUTION:

1. Literally the verse may be rendered, "the church of God which he hath purchased with the blood of his own one."[24] The Greek *idios*, "own", is being used in the sense of the Hebrew *yachid*, "only", as in Gen. 22:2, "thine *only* son"; Zech. 12:10, "*only* son".

2. Some MSS have "blood of his own Son".

---

[24] F. F. Bruce, *Commentary on the Book of Acts*, (London: Marshall, Morgan & Scott Ltd., 1954), p.416.

3. God does not have blood—this is a property of flesh (Lev. 17:11–14).
4. Note the RVm, which states, "Many ancient authorities read the church of the Lord, which he hath purchased" etc., meaning the Lord Jesus Christ.

Romans 8:3

"God sending his own Son..."

PROBLEM:

It is argued that if God sent his Son, then Jesus was there in heaven to be sent.

SOLUTION:

1. God sent John the Baptist (John 1:6) but he did not pre-exist in heaven.
2. The sender is greater than the sent and this is a denial of the idea of co-equality of Father and Son. Cf. John 14:28 where Jesus confirms this by saying, "My Father is greater than I".
3. Rom. 1:3,4 puts the order: "His Son Jesus Christ our Lord, which was made of the seed of David according to the flesh; and declared to be the Son of God with power, according to the spirit of holiness, by the resurrection from the dead..." Note: seed of David first and then he became Son of God with power—not the reverse. The trinity teaches that the Son of God with power became the seed of David.
4. This agrees with 2 Sam. 7:14—"I *will be* his father and *he shall be* my son" and with Psa. 89:27.

Romans 9:5

"...Christ came, who is over all, God blessed for ever."

PROBLEM:

This passage is cited by trinitarians to prove that Christ is 'Very God'.

SOLUTION:

1. The trinitarian argument rests on the punctuation of this passage. The RSV translates as follows: "They are Israelites...to them belong the patriarchs, and of their race, according to the flesh, is the Christ. God who is over all be blessed for ever. Amen." There is no evidence in this translation in support of the trinitarian assertion.
2. The passage appears to allude to Psa. 41:13: "Blessed be the LORD God of Israel from everlasting, and to everlasting. Amen, and Amen." This psalm concludes Book II of the Psalms and is a fitting climax to the apostle's argument in Romans. Paul enumerates the spiritual privileges of Israel: the Sonship, the glory (Shekinah glory), the covenants, the law, the temple worship, the promises, the patriarchs, and the Messiah himself of Jewish lineage. The apostle

then concludes with a thankful ascription of praise to God for all that He has done for Israel.

3. Even if it be insisted that the passage be read as in the AV it is appropriately explained on the basis of God-manifestation. Christ is "over all, God blessed for ever" because this power and authority has been delegated to him. (John 5:19,30; 1 Cor. 15:24–28). Those who act for God are referred to as "God" in the Old Testament. (See Exo. 23:20,21).[25] Paul elsewhere makes it clear, however, that "the *head* of Christ is God." (1 Cor. 11:3). Therefore the Son cannot be 'co-equal' with the Father.

2 Corinthians 5:19

"God was in Christ, reconciling the world unto himself."

PROBLEM:

Since the apostle says that "God was in Christ", it is alleged that this supports the trinitarian idea of the incarnation of 'God the Son'.

SOLUTION:

1. What part of God was in Christ? The doctrine of the trinity says it was 'God the Son'. "God" in 2 Corinthians is defined as "the Father of our Lord Jesus Christ" (2 Cor. 1:3). The Bible clearly teaches that it was *the Father* who was in Jesus, e.g. John 14:10, and note especially John 14:9: "He that hath seen me hath seen the Father."

2. It should be pointed out that:

   a. God was in the temple, but this did not make the temple God.

   b. God is said to be in the believers (2 Cor. 6:16), but this does not make the believers God.

   c. Thus, because God was in Christ, this does not make Jesus God.

3. Jesus spoke the Father's words (John 3:34; John 8:28) and performed His works (John 14:10). In this, Jesus was a manifestation of the Father (John 1:18; John 17:6). God was in Christ by means of His Spirit as in John 3:34.

2 Corinthians 8:9

"Our Lord Jesus Christ…though he was rich, yet for your sakes he became poor."

PROBLEM:

This is held to teach the incarnation of God the Son who gave up his heavenly position of power and assumed human form.

---

[25] It is worth noting again that angels are called "God" in the following passages: Gen. 16:7, cf. v. 13; 22:8,11,15, cf. v. 16. Moses is referred to as a "god" to Pharaoh. (Exo. 7:1; "god" is translated from the Heb. *elohim*). *Elohim* translated "God" in Gen. 1:26 (and many other passages) refers to the judges of Israel in Psa. 82:1,6, cf. John 10:34. It is also translated "judges" in Exo. 21:6; 22:8,9, and "gods" (AVm. "judges") in Exo. 22:28.

SOLUTION:

1. This verse says nothing at all about incarnation or the eternal pre-existence of Jesus. The time when Jesus was rich is not defined and must be discovered from other Scripture.

2. But did Jesus (even accepting for a moment the trinitarian concept) leave the riches of the Godhead behind? The trinitarians say that Jesus was God during his ministry—if so, what part of the Godhead did he leave behind? Did the God part of Jesus die on the cross? If not, then it is difficult to see what the riches of the Godhead were that Jesus is said to have left behind.

3. Christ's riches may be scripturally ascertained and they started with birth and did not exist before:

   a. He was the rightful heir to David's throne and could have assumed this position then (Matt. 1:1; Luke 1:32; John 6:15).

   b. He could have made stones into bread (Matt. 4:3) and performed many other similar miracles had he chosen so to do.

   c. He could have called on twelve legions of angels to come to his aid (Matt. 26:53).

   All these things he refused and instead he "endured the cross, despising the shame" (Heb. 12:2) becoming "a man of sorrows, and acquainted with grief" (Isa. 53:3). Thus, the suffering of the Lord was his poverty by which we may become rich.

2 Corinthians 13:14

"The grace of the Lord Jesus Christ, and the love of God, and the communion of the Holy Spirit..."

PROBLEM:

Here, it is said, is a clear statement of the existence of the trinity.

SOLUTION:

1. Note that it does not say Jesus, the Father and the Holy Spirit, but Jesus, God and the Holy Spirit. Thus this verse does not support the trinity for it shows that Jesus is separate from God and by implication it teaches that the Father alone is God as in 1 Cor. 8:6—"To us there is but one God, the Father...and one Lord Jesus Christ..."

2. The verse does not suggest or imply in any way that there is equality or perfect unity in the trinitarian sense existing between Jesus, God and Holy Spirit—this has to be read into the verse.

3. See notes on Matt. 28:19, page 284.

Ephesians 4:8–10

"Wherefore he saith, When he ascended up on high, he led captivity captive, and gave gifts unto men. (Now that he ascended, what is it but that he also descended

first into the lower parts of the earth? He that descended is the same also that ascended up far above all heavens, that he might fill all things.)"

PROBLEM:

This verse is connected with 1 Pet. 3:18–20 in an attempt to prove that when he died the 'divine' part of Jesus survived the death of the body, and preached to disobedient spirits and took "a host of captives" (RSV) on high (alleged to be Old Testament worthies taken to Paradise). If Jesus were able to preach and release these individuals, then it is argued, he must have been conscious when dead, and hence 'Very God'.

SOLUTION:

1. At his resurrection, Jesus did not take Old Testament worthies to paradise, since David, who is commended as "having obtained a good report through faith" (Heb. 11:39, cf. v. 32), did not go there. Peter, on Pentecost (about seven weeks after Christ's resurrection), said explicitly: "Men and brethren, let me freely speak unto you of the patriarch David, that he is both dead and buried, and his sepulchre is with us unto this day...For David is not ascended into the heavens..." (Acts 2:29,34).

2. The interpretation outlined in the problem nullifies the power of the resurrection of Christ. Jesus said: "...I lay down my life, that I might take it again." (John 10:17). But according to the above interpretation, the real Jesus Christ never did die. Jesus said plainly: "I am he that liveth, and was dead; and, behold, I am alive for evermore, Amen..." (Rev. 1:18). To die, in the Biblical sense, means to go to one place—the grave (Eccl. 3:20), and to be without consciousness (Eccl. 9:5,6; Psa. 146:4). At death Jesus was therefore without life and dependent upon resurrection for life.

3. Scripture never refers to Jesus as a 'God part' and a 'body'—the 'human part'. The personal pronouns in Acts of the Apostles indicated that Jesus—*the person* was dead, and that he became alive by resurrection when God raised him by His Holy Spirit power. Note the following:

   "And when they had fulfilled all that was written of *him*, they took *him* down from the tree, and laid *him* in a sepulchre. But God raised *him* from the dead...But *he*, whom God raised again, saw no corruption." (Acts 13:29,30,34,37). Who would be so bold as to assert that the pronoun "him" refers, in the former, to the body, and in the latter to the 'God part'?

4. Eph. 4:8 quotes Psa. 68:18, and an understanding of this passage requires an examination of the Psalm. The following attempts to show the significance of the Psalm in the context of Ephesians 4:

   a. "When he ascended up on high..." (Eph 4:8), upon which Paul comments, "Now that he ascended, what is it but that he also descended first...?" (Eph. 4:9). —When God exercised His power for the deliverance of His people, it is said in Scripture, to be God coming down. Note the following:

302

i. "And the LORD said (to Moses at the bush), I have surely seen the affliction of my people... and I am come down to deliver them out of the hand of the Egyptians..." (Exo. 3:7,8).

ii. "And be ready against the third day: for...*the LORD will come down* in the sight of all the people upon mount Sinai". (Exo. 19:11).

iii. "And mount Sinai was altogether on a smoke, because the LORD *descended upon* it in fire...And the LORD *came down upon* mount Sinai, on the top of the mount..." (Exo. 19:18,20; see also Exo. 33:9; 34:5; Neh. 9:13, cf. Acts 7:34).

iv. At the conclusion of the deliverance, it is said in Scripture, to be God going up—see Psa. 47:5.

Thus God "descended", manifesting Himself in an angel, bringing the plagues on Egypt, in order to deliver natural Israel from Egyptian bondage and captivity (Psa. 68:17,31–35).

He also descended by His Holy Spirit power (Luke 1:35) to effect the miraculous birth of His Son (Luke 1:35), and to instruct His Son in the things which he spoke (John 7:16) and the works which he performed (John 10:36,37). Thus the work of redemption was effected, which enabled bondslaves of sin (Rom. 6:16–20; Heb. 2:15) to come out of that which is "spiritually called...Egypt" (Rev. 11:8), and become spiritual Israelites. (Gal. 3:27,29, cf. Gal. 6:16). God then "ascended", in the language of theophany, when Christ was "received up into glory". (1 Tim. 3:16).

b. "He led captivity captive"—The RSV translates this, "he led a host of captives". Assuming this is the correct translation, the host of captives in the Old Testament deliverance from Egypt, were those Israelites who faithfully kept the Passover and were led by the angel out of the land of bondage. In the deliverance effected through the Lord Jesus they are those who respond to the invitation to come out of the captivity and bondage of sin. Christ "led" the host of captives since he was the first to destroy the devil (i.e. overcome sin) and become the firstfruits of them that slept. (Heb. 2:14,15; 4:15; 1 Cor. 15:20, cf. Col. 1:18).

c. "And gave gifts unto men"—It is apparent that there is a difference in the wording of the Psalm ("hast received[26] gifts") and its quotation in Ephesians ("gave gifts"). The difference is significant. The Levites were a gift *from* God to the nation of Israel ("the rebellious also"—cf. 1 Cor. 10:5–10), but they were also a gift *to* God. (Num. 8:9–19, cf. 3:5–10). It is likely that the Levites are the "gifts" alluded to in Psa. 68:18—"that the LORD God might dwell among them". The Apostle Paul in his inspired comment brings out what the Psalm does not. Just as the Levites were a gift by God to Aaron and his sons, so God provided for his spiritual Israel by the gift of apostles,

---

[26] The Hebrew word *laqach* can carry the meaning of "receiving" and "giving". It is translated 62 times "receive" and 793 times "take away". See Robert Young, *Analytical Concordance to the Holy Scriptures*, (London: Lutterworth Press, 1967).

prophets, evangelists, pastors and teachers (as distinct from the *gifts* of the Spirit, e.g. tongues, administrations, etc.).[27]

Philippians 2:6,7

"Who, being in the form of God, thought it not robbery to be equal with God: but made himself of no reputation, and took upon him the form of a servant, and was made in the likeness of men."

PROBLEM:

This is one of the most frequently used passages to support the trinity and pre-existence. Great stress is placed on *morphe* (the Greek word for "form") by trinitarians and others like the JWs who teach that Christ had a pre-human existence. It is argued that "in the form of God" means that Christ had the *nature* of God before his birth, and it was this that he sacrificed in coming to the earth to live as a human. The NIV rendering, "Who, being in very nature God..." is frequently used to support this argument.

SOLUTION:

1. If "in the form of God" means the very nature of God, then Christ could not have been 'Very God' while on earth, as trinitarians assert, since this is what he is said to have sacrificed and left behind in coming to the earth.
2. The NIV translation is inexcusable and betrays the theological position of the translators. The Greek word *morphe* (translated "form" in the AV) does not refer to "essential nature" as the trinitarian cause requires. This is proven by the following:
   a. If Paul wanted to convey the idea that Jesus was God why did he not say just that? Why use the expression that Jesus was in "the form" of God?
   b. *Eidos*, not *morphe* is the Greek word which conveys the idea of "essential nature". As Liddell and Scott point out in their lexicon, *morphe* means form, shape, fine, beautiful form or shape, figure, fashion, appearance, outward form or semblance. It is opposed to *eidos*, which means "true form". Thayer states, *morphe* is "the form by which a person or a thing strikes the vision; the external appearance"[28]

   [In this instance it is not wise to place too much emphasis on lexicons. The majority of lexicographers blatantly import into their explanation of this

---

[27] Another approach is to note that God, in angelic manifestation, came down to deliver Israel (Exo. 3:8) and having delivered the captives from Egyptian bondage (a task that involved descending "into the lower parts of the earth"—the depths of the Red Sea) He "ascended up on high", i.e. on Mount Sinai (Exo. 19:20). Following this He gave spirit gifts to Bezaleel and Aholiab to enable them to build the tabernacle (Exo. 31:1–6) so that "I may dwell among them" (Exo. 25:8). In like manner the resurrected Jesus "gave gifts" of Holy Spirit—i.e. "apostles...prophets...evangelists... pastors...teachers" (Eph. 4:11)—to the First Century Ecclesia to help them in the work of building up the "spiritual house" of God, in which God will dwell (Eph. 2:21,22).

[28] Joseph H. Thayer, *Greek-English Lexicon of the New Testament*, (Peabody, Mass.: Hendrickson Publishers, 1996), p.418.

word their belief in the trinity. Trinitarians will be able to muster far more lexicon articles in support of their views.]

c. The context is all-important. The apostle is urging us to consider the attitude of Jesus *in his life*. "Let this mind be in you, which was also in Christ Jesus" (v. 5). We are not being exhorted to emulate a pre-existent person of the trinity who gave up his divinity—how could we possibly do this? The apostle is exhorting us to follow the example of Jesus in the way he lived as recorded in the gospels. In the context of this passage, it is stated that Christ "took upon him the form of a servant" (v. 7). But what is the "form" of a servant (Gk. *doulos*, a slave)? Not the 'essential nature' for the essential nature of a slave is the same as that of any other human being. The "form", therefore, must refer to the semblance or demeanour of a slave as the distinguishing characteristic.

d. *Morphe* occurs in only one other place in the New Testament—Mark 16:12, and here it clearly does not mean 'essential nature'. Some time after his resurrection Jesus appeared "in another form", but this could not refer to a change of his essential nature since the reason why he appeared to be in another form was because the disciples' "eyes were holden". (Luke 24:16, cf. v. 31). Not even a trinitarian or a JW would be prepared to say that the essential nature of the resurrected and glorified Jesus was subsequently changed again.

3. How was Christ "in the form of God"? He had the semblance and demeanour of the Father mentally and morally. His character was "the express image" of his Father's person. (Heb. 1:3).

4. Sometimes trinitarians stress that Christ was *originally* in the form of God—i.e. "being" in the form of God is taken to mean that he was in fact 'Very God' before his supposed 'incarnation'. The Greek verb *huparchon*, "being", is in the continuous tense and although this involves a pre-existent state it does not in any way imply eternal pre-existence. Note the use of *huparchon* in the following passages:

a. Luke 16:23—"In hell [the rich man] lift up his eyes, being [Gk. *huparchon*] in torments, and seeth Abraham afar off, and Lazarus in his bosom." He was in torments then and had been in torments for some time before. But this does not imply he had been eternally in torment. He was in fact not in torment at all before he died.

b. Acts 7:55—"But [Stephen] being [Gk. *huparchon*] full of the Holy Spirit, looked up steadfastly into heaven, and saw the glory of God, and Jesus standing on the right hand of God..." He was full of the Holy Spirit then and had been full of it for some time before. But there is no suggestion that he had always been full of it. He was not full of it before he was anointed with it.

c. Acts 2:30—"Therefore being [Gk. *huparchon*] a prophet" does not mean "being originally before birth a prophet", but rather, "being a prophet from the time when he was given the prophetic gift". He was therefore a prophet when he wrote Psalm 16, and continued to be such.

d. Gal. 2:14—"If thou, being [Gk. *huparchon*] a Jew..." does not mean "being originally before his birth a Jew", but rather, "If you a Jew now and a Jew from birth and continuing to be a Jew..."

Christ "being in the form of God" does not take us back into eternity. It takes us back to that point in finite time when he began to be in the form of God. Throughout his life he never ceased to be in the form of God since, in semblance and demeanour, he habitually exemplified his Father's character.

5. "He thought it not robbery to be equal with God." Understood in the trinitarian sense the apostle's words are reduced to a nonsense; since, according to the trinitarian Christ is God, which has the apostle saying that Christ thought it not robbery to be equal with himself!

The statement may be approached in two ways:

a. Accepting the AV rendering of the Gk. *harpagmos* in the active sense as "robbery",[29] which is quite reasonable, the words may be understood in the light of John 14:9—"He that hath seen me hath seen the Father." Jesus lived out to perfection the character of his Father and it was not "robbery" for him to claim this. The character he displayed was the character of God.

b. Many consider the AV to be a poor translation and render *harpagmos* in the passive sense denoting "a thing seized". The RSV reads: "He did not count equality with God a thing to be grasped." Unlike Eve who grasped after the fruit which was to be desired to make one like God (the *elohim*) to know good and evil, Jesus refused to take the kingdoms of the world without the crucifixion of the flesh and the declaration of the righteousness of his Father. In the Garden of Gethsemane he subjected his will to his Father's, not arrogating to himself prerogatives that rightly belonged to his Father. (Matt. 26:39).

6. How did Christ take the form of a servant (slave)? Two passages supply the answer:

a. "If I then, your Lord and Master, have washed your feet; ye also ought to wash one another's feet." (John 13:14; see also Matt. 20:28).

b. "Though he were a Son, yet learned he obedience by the things which he suffered. And being made perfect, he became the author of eternal salvation unto all them that obey him." (Heb. 5:8,9).

Although Christ was in the form of God in his semblance and demeanour, he "humbled himself" and voluntarily took on him the semblance and demeanour of a slave.

7. "He made himself of no reputation"; "he emptied himself" RSV (v. 7), refers to Christ's deliberate choice to submit his will to that of his Father. These words are quoted from Isa. 53:12, he "poured out his soul unto death." This making himself of no reputation, the pouring out of his soul, was not done when he supposedly left his divine state and took on human form; it was done during his life and led finally to the cross. His example was a powerful lesson in humility to the Philippians. But if Christ "being originally, before his birth, while he was

---

[29] G. Abbott-Smith, *Manual Greek Lexicon of the New Testament*, (Edinburgh: T. & T. Clarke, 1937), p.60—"*Harpagmos*...the act of seizing, robbery."

in heaven in the form (essential nature) of God thought at his birth, when he descended into the womb, not to be equal with God, but left the form of God",[30] where is humility demonstrated?

Colossians 1:15,16

"Who is the image of the invisible God, the firstborn of every creature: for by him were all things created..."

PROBLEM:

This passage is understood by JWs to teach that Jehovah created His Son as His first creative act, and then subsequently performed all creative acts by His Son. Other religious bodies merely assert that this passage proves that Christ existed prior to his birth on the earth, since all the creative acts are ascribed to him.

SOLUTION:

1. The Messianic prophecy in Psa. 89:27 indicates that the JW assertion, that Jehovah created his Son as his first creative act, is unscriptural. "Also I *will make* him my firstborn, higher than the kings of the earth"[31] proves that Christ was not the firstborn prior to the creation narrative in Genesis 1 and 2, but rather Christ was not to be made firstborn until many years *after* the Psalmist penned his words. (The Messianic character of the Psalm. is indicated by comparing the following: Psa. 89:26, cf. 2 Sam. 7:14; Heb. 1:5 and Psa. 89:35–37, cf. Psa. 72:1–8.)

2. "The firstborn of every creature (RV all creation)" is qualified in verse 18 to be "the firstborn from the dead". Frequently an apparently absolute declaration is limited in application. Consider the following examples in which "all" is clearly to be understood in a restricted sense:

   a. "...there went out a decree from Caesar Augustus, that *all* the world should be taxed." (Luke 2:1). The "all" refers to the Roman world, not the areas of South, Central and North America.

   b. "*All* that ever came before me are thieves and robbers ... " (John 10:8). The "all" does not refer to John the Baptist and other prophets.

   c. See also Gen. 3:20 where "all living" did not include the beasts; Gen. 6:13 where "all flesh" did not include Noah and the creatures taken into the ark.

3. The creation of which Christ is the firstborn is the creation of new men and women, and not the creation of light, dry land, etc. of Genesis. "Create" and

---

[30] This is the way in which Phil. 2:6 is read by trinitarians. See A. B. Bruce, *The Humiliation of Christ*, (Edinburgh: T. & T. Clarke, 1889), pp.1-23.

[31] The force of this point is obscured in the JW *New World Translation of the Holy Scriptures*, (Brooklyn, New York: Watchtower Bible and Tract Society of N.Y., Inc., 1961). It reads as follows: "Also, I myself shall *place* him as first-born, the most high of the kings of the earth."

It should be noted that in this prophetic Psalm 89 the "firstborn" speaks of his "Father" as "my God, and the rock of my salvation" (v. 26). Since the Father was to be his God and since Jesus would need saving [out of death, Heb. 5:7 RVm.] then clearly Jesus was not himself God.

307

"creation" are used of the work of Christ in this regenerative sense. Consider the following:

a. "For we are his workmanship, created in Christ Jesus unto good works, which God hath before ordained that we should walk in them." (Eph. 2:10, cf. 4:23,24).

b. "...for to make in himself of twain one new man, so making peace." (Eph. 2:15).

c. See also Col. 3:9,10 RSV; Gal. 6:15; James 1:18; 2 Cor. 5:17.

4. The inspired apostle, employing the Old Testament background of the first-born, is ascribing to Christ his position, rank, and status in the divine purpose. The following is a summary of this background:

a. The firstborn succeeded his father as head. (2 Chron. 21:2,3).

b. He received a double portion of the inheritance. (Deut. 21:17).

c. A younger son could be elevated to the position of firstborn if there were personal unworthiness in the eldest. (1 Chron. 5:1).

Adam lost this privilege because of his personal unworthiness, but the last Adam became perfect, through things which he suffered, and inherited the "double portion". He became the "firstfruits of them that slept"—the "firstborn among many brethren"—"the head of the body, the church...that in all things he might have the preeminence." (Col. 1:18; 1 Cor. 15:20; Rom. 8:29).

5. "Who is the image of the invisible God." This is an obvious allusion to Gen. 1:26, "Let us make man in our image". Christ who was "full of grace and truth" demonstrated that he was the "image of the invisible God" by his faithfulness to death. In him both earthly and heavenly creatures are "created" because in him they have a new function in the divine purpose. The angels who "minister for them who shall be heirs of salvation" (Heb. 1:14) have been instructed to pay him homage—"let the angels of God worship him." (Heb. 1:6).[32]

6. Colossians 1, rather than supporting the trinitarian doctrine, is opposed to it. Consider the following:

a. If Christ is the "*image* of the invisible God" (Col. 1:15), then he is a replica, not the original.

b. Christ is the "firstborn of every creature". (Col. 1:15). "Firstborn" implies a beginning; therefore Christ is not the 'eternal Son of God' of the trinitarians.

Colossians 2:9

"In him dwelleth all the fulness of the Godhead bodily."

---

[32] Another approach to Col. 1:16—"By him were all things created, that are in heaven (RV the heavens), and that are in earth..."—is to see this as referring to the "new heavens and... new earth" of the Kingdom (Isa. 65:17; 2 Pet. 3:13). Those who are described as "new creature[s]" (2 Cor. 5:17) are already part of the "heavens" of this new order of things having been exalted by God and "made [to] sit in heavenly places in Christ Jesus: that in the ages to come he might show the exceeding riches of his grace in his kindness toward us through Christ Jesus" (Eph. 2:6,7). The "earth" of the new order will be the regenerated remnant of Israel—the "her people" of Isa. 65:18. See comments on Heb. 1:10–12, page 311.

PROBLEM:

This appears to teach the divinity of Jesus and, to the trinitarian, that He was, and is, 'Very God'.

SOLUTION:

1. The word "Godhead" (Gk. *theotes*) denotes 'deity'. It may be compared with the word 'manhood'.
2. The word "fulness" is used in Eph. 3:19 and Eph. 4:10 where the apostle clearly states that we can be filled with the "fulness of God". Therefore for Jesus to be filled with this fulness does not imply that he was part of the Godhead before his birth, any more than for us to be filled with it implies that we were part of the Godhead before our birth.
3. The fulness of God is that with which God is full—His nature both moral and physical.

Jesus exhibited the moral fulness of his Father during his ministry (John 1:14; 14:9). Physically Jesus was filled with the fulness of divine nature after his resurrection (Eph. 1:17,20,23; Col. 1:18,19; Phil. 2:9).

Titus 2:13

"The glorious appearing of the great God and our saviour Jesus Christ."

PROBLEM:

To the trinitarian here is clear proof that Jesus is God.

SOLUTION:

1. Like John 17:3 and 1 Cor. 8:6 which clearly teach that there is one God and that this God is to be identified with "the Father", so the letter to Titus clearly teaches that the Father alone is God. Paul commences the letter, "To Titus…from God the Father and the Lord Jesus Christ our Saviour" (Titus 1:4).
2. Note the RVm. rendering—"appearing of the glory of the great God and our Saviour Jesus Christ", which agrees with Matt. 16:27—"the Son of man shall come in the glory of his Father."
3. The glory of the Father is seen in Jesus (2 Cor. 4:6; John 1:14; Phil. 2:11).

Hebrews 1:2

"[God] hath in these last days spoken unto us by his Son, whom he hath appointed heir of all things, by whom also he made the worlds."

PROBLEM:

This passage is cited to prove the pre-existence of Christ since God made the worlds by him. It is argued that if the worlds were made by Christ, then he must be an eternal Person within the Godhead.

SOLUTION:

1. There is no case in this verse to be made for the contention that the Son was an 'eternal Person' within the Godhead. The Son is *"appointed* heir" (v. 2)—his position of power and authority is delegated and not innate. It is by "inheritance" (v. 4) that he has obtained a more excellent name, not by virtue of being (as is supposed), a co-equal person within the Godhead.

2. "By whom [*"through* whom", RSV] he made the worlds [Gk. *Aion*, 'ages', as in RVm.]". "The worlds" does not refer to the earth and the other planets but rather to the ages or dispensations on the earth. The Greek word translated "worlds" is not the usual word for world—*kosmos*, but *aion* which means, "age, indefinite time, dispensation".[33] Jesus Christ is the chief cornerstone of all ages—whether antediluvian (before the flood), patriarchal (Abraham, Isaac, Jacob, etc.), Mosiac, Gentile, or Millennial. The Seed was promised to Eve (Gen. 3:15) and Abraham looked forward to Christ's day with the eye of faith. (John 8:56, cf. Gal. 3:8). Even the sacrifices of animals under the Law of Moses only had their effectiveness because they pointed to the sacrifice that would be offered once for all time.[34] (Heb. 10:4,10). The law was a schoolmaster ("custodian", RSV) to bring men to Christ. (Gal. 3:24). The worlds (ages) were made or constituted through Christ since it is in him that they have their meaning and ultimate realisation.

3. Although Christ was the "chief corner stone" (1 Pet. 2:6) in the divine purpose, "foreordained before the foundation of the world" (1 Pet. 1:20), he was not formed or manifest until "these last times". (1 Pet. 1:20). He had no personal existence until he was born of the virgin Mary. (Luke 1:31–35).

Hebrews 1:8

"But unto the Son he saith, Thy throne, O God, is for ever and ever: a sceptre of righteousness is the sceptre of thy kingdom."

PROBLEM:

Since the Father addresses the Son, "O God", this is taken by trinitarians as proof that the Son is 'Very God'.

SOLUTION:

1. There is some uncertainty as to the precise translation of this verse. Two possibilities exist:

   a. "Thy throne, O God, is for ever and ever" (AV)

   b. "God is thy throne for ever and ever" (RSVm.)

   Since only the first of these translations is useful for the trinitarian, it will be assumed that this is the correct translation.

---

[33] Robert Young, *Analytical Concordance to the Holy Bible*, (London: Lutterworth Press, 1965).

[34] Animal sacrifices in the temple of the Kingdom Age (Ezek. 44:27) will point back to the sacrifice of Christ.

2. "Therefore God, even *thy God*" (v. 9) is evidence that Christ is not the 'eternal Son'. Since the Father is the God of Jesus, then clearly Jesus is not himself 'Very God'. (See also John 20:17).

3. Heb. 1:8 is a quotation from Psa. 45:6. In this Psalm the Hebrew word *elohim* is translated "God". *Elohim* is used of Moses' relationship with Pharaoh: "And the LORD said unto Moses, See, I have made thee a god [*elohim*] to Pharaoh". (Exo. 7:1). It also is used of the judges of Israel. (Psa. 82:6, cf. John 10:34; Exo. 22:9,28). Persons who are divinely appointed and made strong by Yahweh are referred to as "God", but this does not imply they are persons within the Godhead.

4. In "the world to come" (Heb. 2:5), the Son will be called "The mighty God" (Isa. 9:6), although "now we see not yet all things put under him." (Heb. 2:8). In the Kingdom Age, the Son will reign with the power and authority of his Father. (1 Cor. 15:24–28). The writer to the Hebrews points out, however, that the "more excellent name" obtained by the Son is by virtue of his personal worthiness and elevation by his Father, and not by the Son reclaiming divested powers of the Godhead, as trinitarians assert: "Thou hast loved righteousness, and hated iniquity; therefore God, even thy God, hath anointed thee with the oil of gladness above thy fellows." (Heb. 1:9).

Hebrews 1:10–12

"And, Thou, Lord, in the beginning hast laid the foundation of the earth; and the heavens are the works of thine hands: they shall perish; but thou remainest; and they all shall wax old as doth a garment; and as a vesture shalt thou fold them up, and they shall be changed: but thou art the same, and thy years shall not fail."

PROBLEM:

The writer to the Hebrews quotes from Psa. 102:25–27. It is argued that the Father is the creator of heaven and earth in this Psalm. Since the writer to the Hebrews applies this Psalm to Christ to show that he has a more excellent name than the angels, therefore, it is argued, he must be the creator of the universe, and hence 'Very God'.

SOLUTION:

1. The Psalm does not refer to the literal heavens and earth since these will not perish. Many Bible passages either state or imply the continued existence of the earth. (Isa. 45:18, cf. Isa. 11:9, Num. 14:21, Hab. 2:14; Eccl. 1:4; 1 Chron. 16:30; Psa. 93:1; 104:5). The "heavens and earth" are used figuratively elsewhere in Scripture (e.g. 2 Pet. 3:12,13, cf. Isa. 65:17; 66:22 where it is apparent that the literal earth is still in existence).

2. Psa. 102 is Messianic. It was written for the "generation to come: and the people which shall be created". (v. 18, cf. vv. 13–16). The Messiah is now making new men and women for his kingdom. In the New Testament, "create" is frequently

used in reference to this regenerative work of the Lord. (Eph. 2:10,15; 4:23,24; Gal. 6:15,[35] 2 Cor. 5:17; James 1:18).

3. The heavens and earth which were to pass away, rolled up like a garment, are the Mosaic heavens and earth. This is indicated by the following:

   a. The writer to the Hebrews elsewhere in his epistle alludes to the language of Psa. 102:26 in describing the termination of the Mosaic order: "Now that which decayeth and waxeth old is ready to vanish away." (Heb. 8:13).

   b. The people "which shall be created" (Psa. 102:18) refers to those in the new covenant. It was prophesied of Christ: "Lo, I come to do thy will, O God. He taketh away the first [old covenant], that he may establish the second. By the which will we [believers] are sanctified through the offering of the body of Jesus Christ once for all." (Heb. 10:9,10). Again, the context indicates the termination of the Mosaic order.

   c. The argument in Hebrews 1 is that the Son hath by inheritance obtained a more excellent name than the angels. (Heb. 1:4). The reference to the Mosaic "heavens and earth" is an effective argument since angels administered this constitution. (Acts 7:38,53; Gal. 3:19; Heb. 2:2). This was the constitution to be folded up as a garment by the Son—therefore the Son must have a more excellent name than the angels.

Hebrews 2:16

"...he took not on him the nature of angels; but he took on him the seed of Abraham."

PROBLEM:

According to the trinitarian view of Jesus this verse presents him as becoming God incarnate in Abraham's seed.

SOLUTION:

1. The nature of angels is spirit (Psa. 104:4). God also is spirit (John 4:24). If, as is alleged, Jesus pre-existed then he was not spirit, for this passage when read through trinitarian spectacles implies that he could have taken the nature of angels, but he did not. If he was not spirit he was not God, for God is spirit.

2. A comparison of the RV ("For not of angels doth he take hold, but he taketh hold of the seed of Abraham"), with Isa. 41:8,9 RV shows that Paul is here quoting from that passage in Isaiah—"But thou, Israel, art my servant, Jacob whom I have chosen, the seed of Abraham my friend; *thou whom I have taken hold of* from the ends of the earth..." The clear sense of Isaiah is that Yahweh is the One who, in the outworking of His purpose, "took hold" of the seed of

---

[35] The Greek word *ktisis* means "a making, thing made" and is translated by the word "creature" in this passage. See Robert Young, *Analytical Concordance to the Holy Bible*, (London: Lutterworth Press, 1967). In the other references cited, the Greek word is *ktizo*, which means 'to make, produce'. *Ibid.*

Abraham, i.e. Jesus who was descended from Abraham through his mother but divinely begotten. (Gal. 3:16; Gal. 4:4; Matt. 1:1).

3. With this in mind it is clear that the "he" of Heb. 2:16 is the "him" of 2:10, i.e., "It became him [the Father]...in bringing many sons unto glory, to make the captain of their salvation perfect through sufferings...for verily not of angels doth he take hold, but he taketh hold of the seed of Abraham".

Hebrews 7:3

"Without father, without mother, without descent, having neither beginning of days, nor end of life; but made like unto the Son of God; abideth a priest continually."

PROBLEM:

This passage is cited to prove the deity of Christ, since the writer says he was "without beginning of days, nor end of life".

SOLUTION:

1. This passage shows the likeness of the priesthood of Christ to the priesthood of Melchizedek, in order to demonstrate that the priesthood of Christ is superior to the Aaronic priesthood. It does not have reference to the nature of the origin of Christ. This can be shown from the following:

   a. Jesus did have a mother (Mary) and a father (God)[36]. (Luke 1:35). His family line is the subject of the early chapters of both Matthew's and Luke's gospels. (Matt. 1; Luke 3).

   b. Jesus had an end of life when he died. After his resurrection he declared: "I am he that liveth, and was dead." (Rev. 1:18). He is now alive "for evermore" since his Father raised him from the dead. (Acts 13:29,30).

2. The superiority of the priesthood of Christ over the Aaronic, Levitical priesthood is established in the Epistle to the Hebrews by the following arguments:

   a. The Levitical priesthood depended upon descent (e.g. Ezra 2:61,62), but Scripture is silent about the family tree of Melchizedek. He appears in the Genesis narrative without antecedents and nothing is said about his subsequent life. He is, therefore, a type of the priesthood of Christ. The writer to the Hebrews states that Christ "has become a priest not according to a legal requirement concerning bodily descent but by the power of an indestructible life." (v. 16, RSV). Hence the superiority of Christ's priesthood—he "abideth a priest continually" (v. 3); his priesthood is not dependent upon inherited qualifications.

   b. The Levitical priests received tithes according to the Law. (v. 5). But their inferior status is implied, since in a figure they paid tithes to Melchizedek while in the loins of Abraham, their father. (vv. 9,10).

---

[36] It is said of Esther that she had "neither father nor mother." (Esther 2:7). Likewise, this did not mean that she had no natural parents, but rather that they were dead.

WRESTED SCRIPTURES

Hebrews 10:5

"Wherefore when he cometh into the world, he saith...a body hast thou prepared me."

PROBLEM:

It is argued that since the passage states that a body was prepared for Christ when he came into the world, this implies his existence prior to his 'incarnation'.

SOLUTION:

1. Even if the passage be read as trinitarians suggest, it results in a negation of the very point the inspired writer is making. The *eternal* effectiveness of the sacrifice of Christ is contrasted with the ineffective sacrifices offered under the Law of Moses. (vv. 3–12). But trinitarians assert that by "body" is meant a flesh and bone tabernacle for 'God the Son', in which case the sacrifice has no merit, since 'God the Father' *prepared* the body which housed 'God the Son'. On the basis of this reasoning, 'God the Father' did not provide His Son for a sacrifice, but provided merely a flesh and bone body ('God the Son' continuing to exist while the body remained in the tomb).[37] How then is this sacrifice any more effective than the shed blood of bulls and of goats under the Law?

2. The writer to the Hebrews quotes Psa. 40:6–8. But this Psalm reads differently in the Old Testament than in the New: "Mine ears hast thou opened ["digged" AVm.]" It is apparent that the Psalm alludes to the piercing of the ear of a servant who voluntarily desired to serve his master for life. (Exo. 21:2–6). The substance of this Psalm provides the background for the argument in Hebrews. Consider the following:

   a. "Prepared" (Heb. 10:5) denotes 'to fit or adjust thoroughly'[38] Christ willingly complied with the divine purpose. (Matt. 26:39). He "made himself of no reputation, and took upon him the form of a servant [Greek: *doulou*, a slave[39]]...and became obedient unto death, even the death of the cross." (Phil. 2:7,8).

   b. In bringing about this great salvation, Christ "learned...obedience by the things which he suffered." (Heb. 5:8).

   Rather than asserting the pre-existence of Christ, this passage is a declaration of the faithfulness of the Son to his Father, like the slave to his master, and hence the merit of his sacrifice "once for all" (v. 10).

Hebrews 13:8

"Jesus Christ the same yesterday, and to day, and for ever."

---

[37] Which in effect denies the resurrection of Christ. Scripture states that it was "him" that God raised. (Acts 13:29,30).

[38] Robert Young, *Analytical Concordance to the Holy Bible*, (London: Lutterworth Press, 1965).

[39] *Ibid.*

PROBLEM:

This verse is held to support the doctrine of the trinity that Jesus was God, is God, and ever shall be God.

SOLUTION:

1. There is nothing in this verse to suggest that Jesus existed before he was born or that he was the second person of the trinity. How far back "yesterday" goes must be determined from Scripture.

2. Jesus, before his resurrection was not the same as the Jesus after his resurrection. He is "the captain (one who goes first) of our salvation" (Heb. 2:10) and "the firstfruits of them that are asleep" (1 Cor. 15:20 RV).

   When those who are asleep are raised from the dead they "shall all be changed" (1 Cor. 15:51). If Jesus is the one who goes first, the firstfruits of them that are asleep, he too must have been changed at his resurrection. Paul confirms this when he says that Jesus was "declared to be the Son of God with power...by the resurrection from the dead" (Rom. 1:4).

3. The "yesterday" goes back to that definite point in time when Jesus was raised from the dead and became the Son of God with power.

Revelation 1:8; 22:12,13 (and see 1:17)

"I am Alpha and Omega, the beginning and the ending."

PROBLEM:

Rev. 1:8 says that the "Alpha and Omega, the beginning and the ending" is "the Lord...the Almighty." This agrees with the Old Testament which applies the title of "the first and the last" to Yahweh, the God of Israel (Isa. 44:6; 48:12). But in Rev. 1:17 and 22:13 Jesus claims to be the first and the last, i.e. the Alpha and Omega. This, the trinitarian argues, shows that Jesus is part of the Godhead.

SOLUTION:

1. The phrase "Alpha and Omega" (the first and last letters of the Greek alphabet) has its origin in Isa. 41:4; 44:6; 48:12. In these passages, it is Yahweh who is declared to be the first and the last—He is the only true God—"Thus saith the LORD (Yahweh)...I am the first, and I am the last; and beside me there is no God" (Isa. 44:6 and see Isa. 45:21). Yahweh in the Old Testament is identified with the Father in the New Testament, as the following verses clearly show:

   a. Isa. 45:5, cf. 1 Cor. 8:6; John 17:3.

   b. Psa. 110:1, cf. Heb. 1:3–5, 13; Eph. 1:17–20.

   c. Joel 2:27,28, cf. Luke 24:49; Acts 1:4,5; 2:33.

   Since the Father is the only true God and since He is the "LORD" (Yahweh) of the Old Testament, then He is clearly "the first and the last".

2. In the Revelation Jesus is distinguished from the Alpha and the Omega. In chapter 1:4 John sends greetings to the seven churches: "from him which is, and which was, and which is to come...*and* from Jesus Christ." In Rev. 1:8 the Alpha and Omega is said to be "the Lord, which *is*, and which *was*, and which *is to come, the Almighty.*" From this it is clear that Jesus is not the Alpha and the Omega. The Alpha and Omega is God himself—the Almighty. Thus again the Father is seen to be the first and the last.

3. The Revelation is about Jesus after his resurrection when he had manifested *the Name* (John 17:6), had been given *the Name* (Phil. 2:9 RV) and is waiting to come again "*in the Name* of the Lord" (Matt. 23:39). In view of this, it is correct to speak of Jesus as Yahweh and therefore as "the first and the last", but only because he is a manifestation of the Father. It is clear that the Father never died, but, of the Father manifest in the Son it could be said: "I am the first and the last [Yahweh]: I am he that liveth, and was dead [manifestation of Yahweh in the Son]" (Rev. 1:17,18). Note the similar reference to two parties in Zech. 12:10—"They shall look upon me [Yahweh] whom they have pierced, and they shall mourn for him [the Son]."

Revelation 3:14
"...These things saith the Amen, the faithful and true witness, the beginning of the creation of God."

PROBLEM:

This passage is usually quoted with Colossians 1 by JWs to prove that Christ was the first of God's creation, and that all subsequent creation (e.g. trees and animals of Genesis 1) is the work of Christ. Therefore, it is argued, Christ existed before his birth in the days of Herod the King.

SOLUTION:

1. This creation is not the creation of trees and animals as recorded in Gen. 1, but rather the "creation" of new men and women. "Create" and "creation" are frequently used in this regenerative sense in the New Testament. See, for example, the following: Eph. 2:10,15, cf. 4:23,24; Col. 3:9,10 RSV; Gal. 6:15; James 1:18; 2 Cor. 5:17.

2. Rev. 3:14 refers to this new creation and not to the creation of Genesis 1. This is indicated by the context:

   a. "...hold that fast which thou hast, that no man take thy crown." (Rev. 3:11).

   b. "Him that overcometh *will I make* a pillar in the temple of my God...and *I will write* upon him the name of my God, and the name of the city of my God, which is *new* Jerusalem...and *I will write* upon him my *new* name." (v. 12).

   c. "To him that overcometh will I grant to sit with me in my throne..." (v. 21).

The "making", "writing" and "granting" refer to the *"new"* Jerusalem and the *new* name—the ultimate regeneration of believers, and not to the creative acts on the earth of Genesis 1.

3. Jesus is the "beginning" of this new creation—the first to live, die and to receive life for evermore. (Rev. 1:18). As Paul puts it: "And he is the head of the body, the church: who is the beginning, the *firstborn from the dead*; that in all things he might have the preeminence." (Col. 1:18).

4. A further proof (but more lengthy to develop) that "the beginning of the creation of God" refers to Christ as "the firstborn from the dead", and not as the creator of the universe, can be deduced by noting that Rev. 1:18, "I am he that liveth, and was dead; and, behold, I am alive for evermore, Amen" is a commentary on Rev. 3:14. If this can be shown then clearly Rev. 3:14 refers to the creation which commenced with Christ's death and resurrection. The proof rests in a comparison of the introductory statements about Jesus which begin each of the letters to the seven ecclesias with the description of Jesus in the first chapter. Consider the following:

   a. To Ephesus—"These things saith he that holdeth the seven stars in his right hand, who walketh in the midst of the seven golden candlesticks." (Rev. 2:1). Cf. Rev. 1:20.

   b. To Smyrna—"These things saith the first and the last, which was dead, and is alive." (Rev. 2:8). Cf. Rev. 1:11,18.

   c. To Pergamos—"These things saith he which hath the sharp sword with two edges." (Rev. 2:12). Cf. Rev. 1:16.

   d. To Thyatira—"These things saith the Son of God, who hath his eyes like unto a flame of fire, and his feet are like fine brass." (Rev. 2:18). Cf. Rev. 1:14,15.

   e. To Sardis—"These things saith he that hath the seven Spirits of God, and the seven stars…" (Rev. 3:1). Cf. Rev. 1:4.

   f. To Philadelphia—"These things saith he that is holy, he that is true, he that hath the key of David, he that openeth, and no man shutteth; and shutteth, and no man openeth." (Rev. 3:7). Cf. Rev. 1:18.

Therefore,

   g. To Laodicea—"These things saith the *Amen*, the faithful and true witness, the beginning of the creation of God" (Rev. 3:14); cf. "I am he that liveth and was dead; and, behold, I am alive for evermore, *Amen*; and have the keys of hell and of death." (Rev. 1:18). Clearly, "the beginning of the creation of God" = "I am he that liveth and was dead" (i.e. "the firstborn from the dead"). (Col. 1:18).

317

2.10

THE HOLY SPIRIT

In this chapter we shall consider Scriptures that are wrested in connection with—
(1) The Personality of the Holy Spirit: (2) The Work of the Holy Spirit.

1. THE PERSONALITY OF THE HOLY SPIRIT

PRELIMINARY POINTS:

1. No attempt is made in this handbook to consider each of the passages wrested in an effort by trinitarians to prove that the Holy Spirit is a person with the Godhead. To do so would result in many repetitious solutions. Instead, a list of the evidence against the trinitarian position is tabulated.

2. The Holy Spirit is the power of God. (Luke 1:35). Consequently, what the Holy Spirit does is really what God is doing. For example, the "Comforter, which is the Holy Spirit...shall teach you all things" (John 14:26) means simply: "God shall teach you all things through His divine power." Similarly, although the Scriptures cannot literally 'say' anything, it is written: "For the Scripture *saith* unto Pharaoh." (Rom. 9:17). God said this, and His human penman, guided by Holy Spirit power, reliably recorded it. In this quotation there is a merging of what 'God says' with what 'Scripture says'. Likewise, the Holy Spirit is said to "speak", "bear witness", and to be a "comforter" when in actuality it is God doing the speaking, bearing witness and comforting, *by* his power—the Holy Spirit.

John 14:26

"But the Comforter, which is the Holy Spirit...he shall teach you all things, and bring all things to your remembrance, whatsoever I have said unto you."

John 15:26

"But when the Comforter is come, whom I will send unto you from the Father, even the Spirit of truth, which proceedeth from the Father, he shall testify of me."

John 16:13,14

"Howbeit when he, the Spirit of truth, is come, he will guide you into all truth: for he shall not speak of himself; but whatsoever he shall hear, that shall he speak: and he will shew you things to come. He shall glorify me: for he shall receive of mine, and shall shew it unto you."

Acts 5:3

"But Peter said, Ananias, why hath Satan filled thine heart to lie to the Holy Spirit, and to keep back part of the price of the land?"

Acts 5:9

"...How is it that ye have agreed together to tempt the Spirit of the Lord?"

Acts 5:32

"And we are his witnesses of these things; and so is also the Holy Spirit, whom God hath given to them that obey him."

Acts 8:16

"(For as yet he was fallen upon none of them: only they were baptized in the name of the Lord Jesus.)"

Acts 10:19

"While Peter thought on the vision, the Spirit said unto him, Behold, three men seek thee."

Acts 13:2

"As they ministered to the Lord, and fasted, the Holy Spirit said, Separate me Barnabas and Saul for the work whereunto I have called them."

Acts 15:28

"For it seemed good to the Holy Spirit, and to us, to lay upon you no greater burden than these necessary things."

Acts 16:6

"Now when they had gone throughout Phrygia and the region of Galatia, and were forbidden of the Holy Spirit to preach the word in Asia..."

1 Corinthians 12:11

"But all these worketh that one and the selfsame Spirit, dividing to every man severally as he will."

Hebrews 3:7

"Wherefore as the Holy Spirit saith, To day if ye will hear his voice..."

PROBLEM:

On the basis of these passages trinitarians argue that the Holy Spirit is a co-equal and co-eternal Person within the Godhead.

SOLUTION:

1. The Holy Spirit can be shown to be a power by a careful comparison of the following passages:

    a. Gen. 1:1,2—"In the beginning God created the heaven and the earth... And the *Spirit* of God moved upon the face of the waters." But other references to creation attribute the work to God's power. Consider the following:

    i. "I have made the earth, the man and the beast that are upon the ground, by my great *power* ... " (Jer. 27:5).

    ii. "He hath made the earth by his *power* ... " (Jer. 51:15, cf. 10:12).

    iii. "By the *word* of the LORD were the heavens made; and all the host of them by the breath [Heb. *ruach*, spirit] of his mouth..." (Psa. 33:6). The latter is understandable if the Holy Spirit is a power, but the language is inappropriate if, in fact, the Holy Spirit is a mighty, omnipotent, and omniscient Personage within the Godhead.

  b. Heb. 6:4,5—"For it is impossible for those who were once enlightened, and have tasted of the heavenly gift, and were made partakers of the *Holy Spirit*, and have tasted the good word of God, and the *powers* of the world to come..." The Holy Spirit is associated with the "powers of the world to come."

  c. Luke 1:35—"The *Holy Spirit* shall come upon thee, and the *power* of the Highest shall overshadow thee..." The parallel structure indicates that the "Holy Spirit" is equivalent to "power of the Highest".

  d. Isa. 11:2—"The spirit of the LORD shall rest upon him..." This is interpreted in the New Testament to be "God anointed Jesus of Nazareth with the *Holy Spirit* and with *power*". (Acts 10:38).

2. It was the *power* of the Highest which "overshadowed" Mary. (Luke 1:35). But if the Holy Spirit were a Person within the Godhead, then the Holy Spirit, and not the Father, is the real father of Jesus. This is inescapable and should be pressed. Matthew writes, "[Mary] was found with child of the Holy Spirit...that which is conceived in her is of the Holy Spirit" (Matt. 1:18–20).

3. Jesus breathed on the disciples and they received the Holy Spirit. (John 20:22). This language is understandable if a power were conveyed, but inappropriate if the Holy Spirit were a divine Person.

4. Similarly, the Holy Spirit was transmitted by the laying on of hands. (Acts 8:17–19). Was this the transmission of a divine Personage within the Godhead?

5. The Holy Spirit was given "without measure" to Jesus. (John 3:34). "Without measure" is an appropriate description of Holy Spirit power, but it is not the kind of language ordinarily associated with a person. (cf. Acts 10:44, "The Holy Spirit *fell* on all them which heard the word". Also Acts 2:17, "I will *pour out* of my Spirit".)

6. God sent the Holy Spirit to anoint Jesus. (Matt. 3:16; Luke 4:18; cp. Acts 10:38). Is it credible that 'God the Father' sent 'God the Holy Spirit' to anoint 'God the Son' with 'God the Holy Spirit'?

7. In 17 epistles opening with an invocation of grace and peace, in only one is the Holy Spirit referred to, and then as the *means* of sanctification,[1] and not the source of grace. Why the invocation to God and Christ, and not to the Holy

---

[1] 1 Peter 1:2. [Even here it is doubtful if Peter is referring to the Holy Spirit as the means of sanctification. The expression Peter used was simply "sanctification of spirit" (See *Emphatic Diaglott* or any interlinear Greek NT). The words may well refer to the sanctification of the believer's spirit (or mind) which is the result of believing the gospel and which leads to obedience. The same expression is used in 2 Thess. 2:13 where the process of salvation is said to be "sanctification of spirit

Spirit, if the latter were a Personage within the Godhead? Similarly, in the 11 occurrences of thanksgiving or blessing which follow the invocations in the epistles, not one contains any mention of the Holy Spirit.

8. The divine order is set out in 1 Cor. 11:3. "But I would have you know, that the head of every man is Christ; and the head of the woman is the man; and the head of Christ is God." Why is there no mention of the Holy Spirit if he were a person?

9. Jesus gave commandments by the Holy Spirit (e.g. Acts 1:1,2) Was this one 'co-equal' commanding another 'co-equal'?

10. Although it is stated that the Holy Spirit (i.e. the "Comforter") would make his abode in the disciples (John 14:16,17), this does not necessarily imply the personality of the Holy Spirit, since both the Father and the Son (in the same context) were also to make their abode in the disciples. (John 14:23). Clearly then, God and his Son would abide through the Holy Spirit power. As Jesus said, "But when the Comforter is come, whom I will send unto you from the Father, even the *Spirit of truth*, which proceedeth from the Father, he shall testify of me." (John 15:26).

11. The Holy Spirit appeared as a dove, (Matt. 3:16), as cloven tongues of fire, (Acts 2:3), and was accompanied by the sound of a rushing mighty wind (Acts 2:2). If the Holy Spirit were a Person, why are the theophanies so unlike those of the Father? (Exo. 33:18–23; 34:5–7).

12. Why is the Holy Spirit not shown as sitting on God's throne? (See Rev. 7:10— "Salvation to our God which sitteth upon the throne, and unto the Lamb." Also Acts 7:55,56). Why no mention of the Holy Spirit?

13. The personality of the Holy Spirit is sometimes inferred from Luke 12:10— "And whosoever shall speak a word against the Son of man, it shall be forgiven him: but unto him that blasphemeth against the Holy Spirit it shall not be forgiven." But this passage proves too much. Orthodox trinitarians claim that the Holy Spirit is co-equal with the Father and the Son[2], but their interpretation of this passage places the Holy Spirit *above* the Father and the Son, since it is a greater offence to sin against the Holy Spirit, than against either the Father or the Son.

14. The word "spirit" (*pneuma*) in the Greek text is neuter in gender, and does not therefore, in itself, denote personality. This point can be illustrated in the text of Acts 8:15,16: "…who came down and prayed for them that they might receive the Holy Spirit; for it had not yet fallen on any of them, but they had only been baptized in the name of the Lord Jesus." (RSV) The immediate antecedent to the pronoun is "spirit" which is neuter in gender, hence the neuter pronoun. Many other translations give "it" rather than "he" (as does the AV). See for example: NWT, Diaglott, Rotherham's, *Emphasized Bible*.

and belief of truth" (following the Greek as in the *Emphatic Diaglott*). The agent of a believer's sanctification is "the truth" (John 17:17–19) which finds its focus in the sacrifice of Jesus (Heb. 10:10,14,29).]

[2] The Athanasian Creed reads as follows: "…But the Godhead of the Father, of the Son, and of the Holy Ghost, is all one: the Glory equal, the Majesty co-eternal…But the whole three Persons are co-eternal together: and co-equal." *Book of Common Prayer*, (Oxford: Oxford University Press, n.d.).

2. THE WORK OF THE HOLY SPIRIT

It should be remembered that those who maintain that there is a current activity of Holy Spirit in the lives of men and women are arguing that the third person of the Godhead is active in the experience of believers. Showing that the Holy Spirit is not a person therefore to some extent undermines their case.

The activity of the Holy Spirit may be considered from two standpoints;

a. The work of the Holy Spirit in producing conversion.

b. The gift of the Holy Spirit subsequent to conversion.

A. THE WORK OF THE HOLY SPIRIT IN PRODUCING CONVERSION

PRELIMINARY POINTS:

1. Many mainstream churches believe that it is impossible for a person to believe the gospel unless God first acts on the individual's mind by the Holy Spirit to enable him/her to believe. This 'evangelical' position is eloquently stated by Packer:

   > "...man's mental 'eyes' are blind through sin, and he can discern no part of God's truth till the Spirit opens them."[3]

   > "Without the Spirit's help there can be no grasp of the meaning of Scripture, no conviction of the truth of Scripture and no faith in the God of Scripture. Without the Spirit, nothing is possible but spiritual blindness and unbelief."[4]

   This work of God in enabling men to believe is frequently referred to as 'prevenient grace' or 'preventing grace'.

2. In contrast to this is the teaching of the Bible that faith (i.e. belief [5]) is a man's voluntary response to the gospel preached. Abraham is set before us in the Bible as an example of a man who showed faith. The sequence of events in Abraham's life was:

   a. God made promises to Abraham (e.g. Gen. 15:4,5).

   b. Abraham believed (showed faith) in the promises (Gen. 15:6).

   c. God then counted Abraham righteous because of his faith (Gen. 15:6; Rom. 4:3).

   Abraham is a living example of the teaching of the apostle that "Faith cometh by hearing, and hearing by the word of God." (Rom. 10:17).

---

[3] J. I. Packer, *Fundamentalism and the Word of God*, (Grand Rapids, USA: Wm. B. Eerdmans Publishing Co., 1988), p.118.

[4] *Ibid*, p.112.

[5] It is important to note that "faith" and "belief" in the New Testament are two English words used to translate the same Greek word *pistis*. It is necessary to use two words because there is, in English, no verbal form for the word faith. So we have to say, "He that believeth" rather than, "He that faitheth". But "faith" and "belief" are exactly the same thing.

There is nothing mysterious about faith. It is simply knowledge of the gospel of salvation and a conviction that it is true.

3. This act on God's part of counting Abraham righteous in response to his faith— i.e. forgiving his sins, is called "grace"[6]. The word "grace" [Gk. *charis*] means "gift"—God gives this wonderful blessing of forgiveness to those who believe the gospel. "Therefore being *justified* (Gk. *dikaioo*, declared righteous) *by faith* (as Abraham was) we have peace with God through our Lord Jesus Christ: by whom also we have access *by faith* into *this grace* wherein we stand, and rejoice in hope of the glory of God." (Rom. 5:1,2).

Acts 16:12–15

"Philippi...is the chief city of that part of Macedonia, and a colony: and we were in that city abiding certain days. And on the sabbath we went out of the city by a river side, where prayer was wont to be made; and we sat down, and spake unto the women which resorted thither. And a certain woman named Lydia, a seller of purple, of the city of Thyatira, which worshipped God, heard us: whose heart the Lord opened, that she attended unto the things which were spoken of Paul. And when she was baptized, and her household, she besought us, saying, If ye have judged me to be faithful to the Lord, come into my house, and abide there. And she constrained us."

PROBLEM:

This is a principle passage used to argue that men cannot believe unless acted on by the Holy Spirit. It is argued that Paul preached the gospel to the women by the riverside, but this was not enough to secure Lydia's salvation. It was necessary for God to act directly on Lydia—to open her heart—so that the preaching might be effective.

SOLUTION:

1. The example of Abraham should be kept in mind: God made promises to him (e.g. Gen. 15:4,5); Abraham believed (Gen. 15:6); God then counted Abraham righteous because of his faith (Gen. 15:6; Rom. 4:3).

2. The idea of direct Holy Spirit action on Lydia's mind is not in the Acts 16 text, but is easily read into it if the reader has this idea already in his mind. What the text says is:-

   a. Paul *preached* and Lydia *heard*;

   b. *the Lord opened her heart*;

   c. with the result that she *attended to the things* preached.

   The opening of Lydia's heart was accomplished by the preaching of the gospel. In its natural state Lydia's heart was in that state described by Paul—"having the *understanding darkened*, being alienated from the life of God through...ignorance." (Eph. 4:18). By the word preached, her understanding

---

[6] The word "grace" is used in other ways in the New Testament, but here we are only concerned with the grace of God in forgiving sins and counting men righteous.

was illuminated—i.e. her heart was opened—to the goodness of God's salvation. She then had to respond if she was to be saved. The record says that she did. For she "attended to" the things preached. The words "attended to" imply far more than a mere listening to the things preached, but involved her response to the word, which included her baptism.

3. There is confirmation that it was indeed by the gospel that Lydia's heart was opened, in the words of Jesus concerning the ministry of the apostle who preached the word to her. Jesus said, "I send thee (to the Gentiles), to *open their eyes*, and to turn them from darkness to light..." (Acts 26:17,18). The opening of the eyes and the opening of the heart are both figures for divine enlightenment (see, for example, John 12:40 where to "see with the eyes" is the same as to "understand with the heart"). In the process of enlightenment—of opening eyes or heart—God uses means. The means He has chosen is "the foolishness of preaching." In the case of Lydia it was accomplished by the Lord sending Paul to preach the gospel. Thus it was indeed the Lord who opened Lydia's eyes, heart, or understanding. He did so by means of the word Paul preached. (Cf. the Lord Jesus who appeared to his disciples and opened their understanding by showing them the things written in the Law, the Prophets and the Psalms concerning him—Luke 24:45,46.)

1 Corinthians 12:8,9

"For to one is given by the Spirit the word of wisdom; to another the word of knowledge by the same Spirit; to another faith by the same Spirit; to another the gifts of healing by the same Spirit..."

PROBLEM:

Here, it is maintained, is the clear teaching of Scripture that man, unaided, cannot believe the scriptures unless God acts directly on his mind enabling him to believe. Faith results from the operation of the Spirit on man—it is in fact a gift of the Spirit.

SOLUTION:

1. Two serious errors of exposition are made in thus applying the 1 Corinthians 12 text:
    a. The gifts of the Spirit of which Paul is writing in 1 Corinthians 12, with the exception of Cornelius and his house (and this was for a very special reason), were given to those who had already believed and been baptized. Thus those who received the gifts *had already shown their faith* by responding to the gospel message. The subsequent "gift of faith" was manifestly something quite different, and therefore to use this scripture as evidence that faith today is a gift from God is entirely without foundation.
    b. The chapter proceeds to state, "To another the gifts of healing by the same Spirit; to another the working of miracles; to another prophecy..." etc. (1 Cor. 12:9,10). To divide the gifts of the Spirit into non-miraculous gifts (knowledge, wisdom, faith), which are available today, and miraculous gifts

324

(healings, miracles, tongues etc.), which are not available today, is without any scriptural support. In 1 Cor. 13:1,2, alongside tongues and prophecy, Paul refers to the Holy Spirit gift of faith. We may not understand what, exactly, the Holy Spirit gift of faith was (any more than we understand what the Spirit gifts of "helps" and "governments" [1 Cor. 12:28] were), but since the faith which we are required to manifest "cometh by hearing and hearing by the word of God" this latter is clearly something quite different from that which was miraculously conferred.

2. The gifts of the Spirit listed in 1 Cor. 12:8–11 were given to the believers in Apostolic times for the purpose of establishing the Ecclesia. They were withdrawn when that work was done. On this see "Gifts of the Spirit", pages 79–84.

Ephesians 2:8

"For by grace are ye saved through faith; and that not of yourselves: it is the gift of God…"

PROBLEM:

Here, it is said, in words that cannot be misunderstood, is the teaching that faith is a gift from God and hence, unaided, we cannot manifest faith.

SOLUTION:

1. This interpretation of Eph. 2:8 contradicts the clear teaching of Scripture, exemplified by Abraham, that faith is man's response to the gospel preached. The process is set out clearly in Rom. 10:14—"How then shall they call on him in whom they have not believed? and how shall they believe in him of whom they have not heard? and how shall they hear without a preacher?" The order of events is:

a. Preaching

b. Hearing

c. Belief

2. *"That* not of yourselves: *it is the gift of God"* refers not to 'faith' but to 'salvation'. Prof. F. F. Bruce who subscribed to the evangelical belief that "we could never exercise saving faith did not the Holy Spirit persuade and enable us to embrace Jesus Christ…" comments on Eph. 2:8, "The fact that the demonstrative pronoun 'that' is neuter in Greek (*touto*), whereas 'faith' is a feminine noun (*pistis*), combines with other considerations to suggest that it is the whole concept of salvation by grace through faith that is described as the gift of God."[7]

---

[7] F. F. Bruce, *The Epistle to the Ephesians*, (London: Pickering & Inglis Ltd., 1961), p.51.

B. THE GIFT OF THE HOLY SPIRIT SUBSEQUENT TO CONVERSION

PRELIMINARY POINTS:

1. Some churches, e.g. the Pentecostals, maintain that the miraculous gifts of the Holy Spirit are still available today and claim to be able, for example, to heal the sick and speak with tongues. The passages used to support these assertions have been examined in *Section One*, pages 85–90.

   However, whilst most denominations reject such extravagant claims, many still believe that believers are given the gift of the Holy Spirit. This widely held belief is but an extension of the view (looked at in Section A, page 322) that men cannot believe the gospel unless the Holy Spirit first acts on their mind enabling them to believe. The gift of the Holy Spirit, it is maintained, is also necessary after conversion to enable men to resist temptation and to live the Christian life. The Spirit is said to be active in "enforcing truth, restraining from evil, exciting to do good, imparting wisdom or strength, when, where, and in what measure seemeth to Him good."[8]

   The part played by the Word of God in the process of regeneration and the living of the Christian life, is thus subordinated to the influence of the Holy Spirit. So we are told:

   "The great judgment which ever hangs over the impenitent hearers of the Gospel is that God may withhold His Holy Spirit, leaving them to themselves and to the *mere* power inherent in the truth."[9]

2. This is a denial of the clear teaching of Scripture that the power of salvation is in the gospel itself. "I am not ashamed of the gospel of Christ: for it is the power of God unto salvation to every one that believeth; to the Jew first, and also to the Greek." (Rom. 1:16). "The preaching of the cross is to them that perish foolishness; but unto us which are saved it is the power of God." (1 Cor. 1:18).

3. Before looking at some of the passages used to support this view, it will be helpful to summarise the Bible teaching about the nature of "the inner man". It is the confusing of passages that refer to the inner man, with passages that refer to the miraculous gifts of the Holy Spirit that leads to so much misunderstanding.

   When a man hears the gospel and signifies his acceptance of its message by being baptized, the Bible says that he has "been born again, not of corruptible seed, but of incorruptible, by the word of God, which liveth and abideth for ever." (1 Pet. 1:23). This new birth clearly is not a new birth of the person's flesh and blood body. The "word of God" has created in his mind something that did not exist before he heard the gospel. That 'something' is a mental and moral likeness of the One who "of his own will begat...us with the word of truth" (James 1:18), or, since Christ is "the image of the invisible God" (Col. 1:15), a mental and moral likeness of Jesus Christ. This new man of the mind is variously referred to in the Bible as "a new creature" (2 Cor. 5:17), "the

---

[8] Charles Hodge, *Systematic Theology*, Volume 2, p.667.

[9] *Ibid*, p.663. [Emphasis ours].

inward man" (Rom. 7:22), "Christ in you" (Col. 1:27), "the mind of Christ" (1 Cor 2:16). It is also referred to as "the spirit of God" or "the spirit of Christ" (Rom. 8:9), meaning "the mind of God" or "the mind of Christ." Because it is referred to as "the spirit" it is frequently confused with "the gift of the Holy Spirit".

4. In this connection the teaching in Acts 8 is useful and the protagonist of this view should be taken through the following steps:-

   a. Philip went to Samaria and "preached Christ" to the Samaritans (8:5).

   b. The Samaritans believed and were baptized (8:12).

   c. Since they had believed and been baptized, they had been born again into God's family and were "in Christ" for says Paul, "Ye are all the *children of God* by faith in Christ Jesus. For as many of you as have been baptized *into Christ* have put on Christ". (Gal. 3:26,27).

   d. If they were "in Christ" and had "put on Christ" they clearly belonged to Christ. This the apostle confirms by saying, "And *if ye be Christ's*, then are ye Abraham's seed, and heirs according to the promise" (Gal. 3:29).

   e. Since they belonged to Christ they had the spirit of Christ, for we are told, "Ye are not in the flesh, but in the Spirit, if so be that the Spirit of God dwell in you. *Now if any man have not the Spirit of Christ, he is none of his*." (Rom. 8:9). This is referring to the results of the new birth into the family of God—to the new creation, the inner man, the mind of Christ and not to the "gift of the Holy Spirit" for these Samaritans did not have the Holy Spirit.

   f. It was some time later that the Apostles Peter and John visited Samaria so that the Samaritan believers "might receive the Holy Spirit" (Acts 8:15). Only when the apostles laid their hands on them did they receive the Holy Spirit (Acts 8:17).

This distinction between the miraculous "gift of the Holy Spirit" and "the spirit of Christ" needs to be kept in mind. When the Scriptures simply refer to "the spirit" it is necessary to determine which of these is being referred to by careful examination of the context.

Luke 11:13

"If ye then, being evil, know how to give good gifts unto your children: how much more shall your heavenly Father give the Holy Spirit to them that ask him?"

PROBLEM:

This, it is said, is a clear reference to the giving (gift) of the Holy Spirit. Jesus says that God will give it to all who ask.

SOLUTION:

1. In the context it appears to refer to Holy Spirit gifts needed by the disciples to fulfil their preaching activities as in Luke 10:17.

2. However, it may be an anticipation of the outpouring of the spirit after the ascension of Jesus. God had promised to give the Holy Spirit (Joel 2:28,29).

WRESTED SCRIPTURES

Jesus had reinforced this (e.g. John 14:26) and did so again after his resurrection (Acts 1:4,8). The Holy Spirit was poured out on the Day of Pentecost (Acts 2). But subsequently, as the need arose, requests were made for further gifts of Holy Spirit to support them in their work. So, for example, they prayed, "Now, Lord, behold their threatenings: and grant unto thy servants, that with all boldness they may speak thy word, by stretching forth thine hand to heal; and that signs and wonders may be done by the name of thy holy child Jesus." Their prayer was answered, for "when they had prayed, the place was shaken where they were assembled together; and they were all filled with the Holy Spirit, and they spake the word of God with boldness." (Acts 4:29–31).

3. Since the Holy Spirit gifts have been withdrawn (see page 79 etc.) it is not according to God's will for present day believers to ask for this and God only responds to prayer that is according to His will (1 John 5:14).

Acts 2:38

"Then Peter said unto them, Repent, and be baptized every one of you in the name of Jesus Christ for the remission of sins, and ye shall receive the gift of the Holy Spirit. For the promise is unto you, and to your children, and to all that are afar off, even as many as the Lord our God shall call."

PROBLEM:

It is maintained by some, that since the miraculous gifts are not available today and since this is a promise of the gift of the Holy Spirit to all believers for all time, then it must refer to the special power that comes from God into a believer's heart to strengthen him and help him live the Christian life.

SOLUTION:

1. The phrase "the gift of the Holy Spirit" only occurs on two occasions in the Bible. Here, where the context is the pouring out of the spirit on the Day of Pentecost, causing the believers to speak in foreign languages, and in Acts 10:45 which records that "on the Gentiles also was poured out the gift of the Holy Spirit" causing them to speak in tongues. Thus on both occasions it had to do with the miraculous gifts.

2. This connection is reinforced by Acts 11:17 where the gift poured out on the Gentiles in Acts 10 is referred to as "the like gift" that was poured out on the Jews in Acts 2. This was the same Holy Spirit:

   a. Promised by Jesus to the apostles (Acts 1:5).

   b. Given to the ecclesia on the Day of Pentecost (Acts 2:1–4) enabling them to speak in tongues.

   c. That caused the believers to speak the word with boldness (Acts 4:8,31).

   d. That enabled Philip to work miracles (Acts 6:3,5; 8:13).

   e. That was given subsequently by "the laying on of apostles' hands" (Acts 8:18; Acts 19:6; 2 Tim. 1:6).

328

f. That was poured out on Cornelius and his fellow Gentiles causing them to speak in tongues—as a sign to the Jews that it was right to baptize believing Gentiles (Acts 10:44–48; 11:15).

g. That caused the Ephesians to speak in tongues and prophesy (Acts 19:6) and caused other believers to prophesy (Acts 20:23; 21:11).

3. Acts 2:38,39 is not promising these miraculous gifts to all believers for all time. They are not available today. On this see further notes on Acts 2:38, pages 79–82.

Romans 5:5

"...and hope maketh not ashamed; because the love of God is shed abroad in our hearts by the Holy Spirit which is given unto us."

PROBLEM:

It is held that this shows that men are able to show true Christian love only because of the operation of God's spirit on their hearts.

SOLUTION:

1. "The love of God" was the substance of the gospel to which the apostle has just been referring—the fact that they were "justified by faith" and had "peace with God through our Lord Jesus Christ" and that through him they had "access...into this grace wherein we stand, and rejoice in hope of the glory of God" (vv. 1,2). Because of this experience of the love of God the apostle says he was able to endure and even rejoice in his trials (vv. 3,4).

2. The correct rendering of this passage is given in the RV—"The love of God *hath been* shed abroad in our hearts through the Holy Spirit *which was given* unto us."

3. In what way had "the love of God...been shed abroad in [their] hearts *by the Holy Spirit*"? In those days they possessed the miraculous gifts to help them in the preaching of the gospel. It was by means of these gifts that the gospel was preached and Peter refers to this when he writes of those who "have preached the gospel unto you with the Holy Spirit sent down from heaven..." (1 Pet. 1:12).

Romans 14:17

"For the kingdom of God is not meat and drink; but righteousness, and peace, and joy in the Holy Spirit."

PROBLEM:

This verse is used to teach that the Kingdom of God is in the here and now. Jesus rules in the hearts of men. He does so by the Holy Spirit dwelling in them causing righteousness, peace and joy.

WRESTED SCRIPTURES

SOLUTION:

1. For an answer to the use of this verse to argue that the Kingdom of God is in the here and now, see page 131.

2. Paul is dealing with a local situation in the Roman ecclesia. Some believed that "they could eat all things", but others were unable to bring themselves to eat meat that might have been offered to idols. This type of person "eateth herbs" (v. 2). Paul is trying to get them to exercise love and forbearance to each other.

3. The point he is making is that the Kingdom of God will not be attained on the basis of partaking of, or abstaining from, certain foods. It will be attained as a result of a manifestation of righteousness (see 1 Cor. 6:9), peace and joy (see Gal. 5:21).

4. These qualities of character were the evidence of 'a holy spirit' (there is no definite article and no capital letters in the Greek). The "holy spirit" here referred to is the spirit of Christ, the inner man. Thus the verse is an exhortation to the Romans to "Put off concerning the former conversation the old man, which is corrupt according to the deceitful lusts; and be renewed in *the spirit of your mind*; and that ye put on the *new man*, which after God is created in *righteousness* and true *holiness*." (Eph. 4:22–24).

Galatians 5:16–18,22,23

"This I say then, Walk in the Spirit, and ye shall not fulfil the lust of the flesh. For the flesh lusteth against the Spirit, and the Spirit against the flesh: and these are contrary the one to the other: so that ye cannot do the things that ye would. But if ye be led of the Spirit, ye are not under the law...the fruit of the Spirit is love, joy, peace, longsuffering, gentleness, goodness, faith, meekness, temperance: against such there is no law."

PROBLEM:

On the basis of this passage it is said that the Holy Spirit influences men to do good, and only those who are led by the inner prompting of the Holy Spirit can manifest love, joy, peace etc.

ANSWER:

1. This is not what Paul is saying. He is stating what every disciple knows by experience—"I delight in the law of God after the inward man: but I see another law in my members, warring against the law of my mind, and bringing me into captivity to the law of sin which is in my members." (Rom. 7:22,23). "The flesh" in Gal. 5 corresponds to "the law of sin...in my members" in Romans 7. "The spirit" in Gal. 5 corresponds to "the inward man", "the law of my mind" in Romans 7.

2. Thus Galatians 5 is not talking about the direct influence of the Holy Spirit in the life of a believer but of the influence of the gospel creating in a person's mind the spirit or mind of Christ.

3. The fact that spirit of Christ—the new man—does indeed exist and is alive and well, is shown by the reformed life of the believer. "Love, joy, peace, longsuffering, gentleness, goodness, faith, meekness, temperance"—such are the effects of the mind of Christ: the fruit of the spirit.

Ephesians 1:17

"That the God of our Lord Jesus Christ, the Father of glory, may give unto you the spirit of wisdom and revelation in the knowledge of him…"

Colossians 1:9–11

"For this cause we also, since the day we heard it, do not cease to pray for you, and to desire that ye might be filled with the knowledge of his will in all wisdom and spiritual understanding; that ye might walk worthy of the Lord unto all pleasing, being fruitful in every good work, and increasing in the knowledge of God; strengthened with all might, according to his glorious power, unto all patience and longsuffering with joyfulness…"

PROBLEM:

These verses are held to teach that the Christian can expect the spirit to work within him, opening his eyes to a greater appreciation of the purpose of God and strengthening him to live faithfully.

SOLUTION:

1. Today the only source of information about the purpose of God—the only source of knowledge, revelation, wisdom and spiritual understanding—is to be found in the Word of God, i.e. in the Scriptures.

2. These early brethren did not have the completed Scriptures. They had the Old Testament and perhaps part of the New Testament. But they did not have the Scriptures as we have them today. However, new revelation was being given to them as the apostles, prophets and teachers used their Holy Spirit gifts to instruct the believers. An example of this is seen in Eph. 3:5 where the spirit was revealing new truth about the part to be played by Gentiles in the purpose of God.

3. In the verses under examination the apostle is praying that the brethren in Ephesus and Colosse might be given the Holy Spirit gifts of wisdom (1 Cor. 12:8) and revelation (1 Cor. 14:26) which would be utilised in their ecclesias to instruct the believers and make them strong in faith.

4. The gifts are no longer available. We have the completed Scriptures. The Word of God in its written form is no less powerful than it was when it was spoken "with Holy Spirit sent down from heaven" by spirit-gifted brethren.

Ephesians 3:14–21

*"For this cause I bow my knees unto the Father of our Lord Jesus Christ, of whom the whole family in heaven and earth is named, that he would grant you, according to the riches of his glory, to be **strengthened with might by his Spirit** in the inner*

*man; that Christ may dwell in your hearts by faith; that ye, being rooted and grounded in love, may be able to comprehend with all saints what is the breadth, and length, and depth, and height; and to know the love of Christ, which passeth knowledge, that ye might be filled with all the fulness of God. Now unto him that is able to do exceeding abundantly above all that we ask or think, according to **the power that worketh in us**, unto him be glory in the church by Christ Jesus throughout all ages, world without end."*

PROBLEM:

This passage is frequently used to support the idea that in order to live the Christian life it is necessary to have an indwelling of the Holy Spirit—"the power that worketh in us"—and in particular that in some unexplainable mysterious way God will grant inner strength to believers who ask for it.

SOLUTION:

1. Paul's prayer for the Gentiles in Ephesus was that as a result of their being "strengthened with might by his Spirit in the inner man…Christ might dwell in their hearts *by faith*" (vv. 16,17). The end product was Christ in their hearts by faith. The apostle says, "Faith cometh by hearing, and hearing by the word of God" (Rom. 10:17). Here then is strong presumptive evidence that being strengthened with might by the Spirit actually has reference to the Word of God working faith in them.

2. This is confirmed by the context. Paul has already in this chapter spoken of the way in which new revelation was being given to the apostles and prophets at that time by the Spirit [i.e. by the exercise of the special gifts then available] (Eph. 3:5), and thus it is reasonable to conclude that it is this same Spirit to which he refers when he prays for the Gentiles that they might be strengthened with might by his Spirit in the inner man (v.16). That which strengthened was the revelation, or the word, spoken by means of the Spirit as the apostles, prophets, evangelists, pastors and teachers exercised their Spirit gifts—as they ministered instruction, counsel and guidance to meet the needs of the ecclesia.

   The "inner man" which Paul prays might be strengthened is "the new man" (Eph. 4:24) which is conceived by the Word of God (1 Pet. 1:23), brought forth by the Word (James 1:18 RV) and which is strengthened and nourished by the Word (1 Pet. 2:2). The Word of God, whether spoken or written, is living and powerful (Heb. 4:12).

3. Paul's final ascription of praise in this chapter again needs to be considered in the first century context in which it was written. "Unto him that is able to do exceeding abundantly above all that we ask or think, according to the power that worketh in us ("among" NEB)", has reference to those gifts of the Holy Spirit that were present in the ecclesias at that time and experienced by the Ephesians to whom Paul writes these words.

Philippians 2:13

"For it is God which worketh in you both to will and to do of his good pleasure."

PROBLEM:

This passage is frequently used in an endeavour to show that the only way a man can be saved is for the Holy Spirit to act on the will to enable him live the Christian life.

SOLUTION:

1. The verse says nothing about any direct inward activity by the Holy Spirit.
2. Of course salvation is of God. He promised and provided His Son as the means of man's redemption; He has graciously given His Word that we might know and appreciate His purpose in Christ; He extends His grace to those who respond in faith to His invitation. But without man's response there can be no salvation. In the previous verse the apostle exhorts, "Wherefore, my beloved, as ye have always obeyed, not as in my presence only, but now much more in my absence, work out your own salvation with fear and trembling." (Phil. 2:12).
3. Acceptance of the gospel message has a dramatic effect on the lives of believers. Such no longer seek to please themselves but try to please their Heavenly Father after the example of Jesus (Eph. 5:1,2), seeking to "shine as lights in the world" (Phil. 2:15). It is in this way that "God...worketh in us" as Paul elsewhere writes, "When ye received *the word of God* which ye heard of us, ye received it not as the word of men, but as it is in truth, the word of God, *which effectually worketh also in you* that believe." (1 Thess. 2:13).

3.1

MIRACLES[1] AND THE UNIFORMITY OF NATURE[2]

PROBLEM:

Many today reject the Biblical accounts of miracles because men of science, having examined nature with great care, have discovered that it has certain laws which it obeys. It is reasoned that if miracles were to be permitted, this regularity would not be observed, and one could never tell what would happen the next day.

SOLUTION:

1. It is not a question of nature obeying laws but of behaving (from the human point of view) in a predictable and reducible way. The fact that uniformity is observed in the large is not a reasonable objection against there having been deviations from it on certain exceptional occasions.

2. The concept of order, regularity, and in *general*, uniformity of natural order is a Biblical concept. God promises the regularity of seed time and harvest, cold and heat, summer and winter, day and night. (Gen. 8:22). Jeremiah affirms that the sun, moon and stars fulfil their function because they move according to the ordinances which God controls. (Jer. 31:35,36). The regularity of night and day is called a covenant of God which cannot be broken. (Jer. 33:20). See also Job 38:8–11; Psa. 104:8,9; Prov. 8:2.

3. Men have discovered that in most of their researches it is possible to discover nature doing precisely the same things in precisely the same circumstances. But it cannot be assumed from this that "all things have continued as they were from the beginning of creation". (2 Pet. 3:4, RSV).[3] That is, one cannot logically extrapolate to say that there is an inviolable set of laws, which it is impossible for events to transgress. There is not the knowledge required to justify such a statement. Scientific law is a systematized approach to the complex

---

[1] "Miracle" as used here, refers to the direct operation of God's power in such a manner as to be an arresting deviation from the ordinary sequence of nature.

[2] Uniformity of nature is the belief that the way everything is occurring today is the way that it has always occurred in the past—that present causes solely have operated in the past. The concept was popularized by Charles Lyell in his text, *Principles of Geology*, 11th ed. rev. (New York: D. Appleton and Co., 1892) I, pp.317,318. Darwin built his theory of organic evolution upon the uniformitarian foundation.

[3] The concept of the uniformity of nature is the foundation upon which all evolutionary theory is built. Accepting, for the sake of argument, that uniformity of nature is a fact produces some interesting situations. For example, scientists estimate that the sun is decreasing in size at a rate of 0.1 percent every 100 years, i.e. about 5 feet/hour. It does not take a genius to calculate that if uniformitarianism applies, 100,000 years ago the sun would have been twice the size it is today. One million years ago the size of the sun would have rendered life on earth impossible. 20 million years ago (a figure not unusual in evolutionary circles) the sun would have been so big it would have touched the earth! Thus, in fact, uniformitarianism is the enemy of evolution.

interrelations of the universe. It is not a handbook to tell us what cannot happen. The relativity of scientific law is illustrated in the revision of Newtonian laws which was required by Einstein's theory of relativity.

4. Belief in the uniformity of nature is in itself an act of faith and not of logic. It requires the projection backwards of the regularity observed in the present as well as predicting future events on the basis of the past. Although many regularities in nature are observed, these observations only cover a minute fraction of the events that actually go on and have gone on. The observations are, therefore, of no use unless one believes in the uniformity of nature—i.e. that nature behaves in the same way when it is not being observed.[4]

5. Biblical claims of miracles cannot, therefore, be dismissed *a priori* (beforehand) as violations of a supposed law of uniformity of nature. Uniformity of nature is a belief, not a scientific law.

6. The principal opponents of the reality of miracles are those who believe that there is no God. In this connection observe that atheism is also a "belief". If the believer in miracles can argue for the existence of an omnipotent God who sustains the world and is able to act according to His divine will, then he has produced evidence that justifies a belief in miracles. The atheist must admit the *possibility* of miracles unless he can *prove* atheism to be true.

Genesis 1:16
"And God made two great lights ..."

PROBLEM:

In an effort to show the mythical character of the first eleven chapters of Genesis, liberal clergymen of the United and Anglican Churches cite this passage. They point out that on the first day, God made light (Gen. 1:3–5), but He did not make the sun and moon until the fourth day (Gen. 1:16–19). Therefore, it is argued, the days in Genesis 1 cannot be understood as literal days.

SOLUTION:

1. The Hebrew word *asah*[5] translated "made" can be rendered "appoint" or "ordain". It is translated this way in Psa. 104:19—"He *appointed* the moon for seasons". On the basis of this translation, God did not literally make the sun and

[4] C. S. Lewis in *Miracles*, (London: Collins Clear-Type Press, 1947) makes the same point as follows: "Experience, therefore, cannot prove uniformity because uniformity has to be assumed before experience proves anything. It is no good saying, 'each fresh experience confirms our belief in uniformity and therefore, we reasonably expect that it will always be confirmed', for that argument works only on the assumption that the future will resemble the past—which is simply the assumption of uniformity under a new name. Can we say that uniformity is at any rate very probable? Unfortunately not, we have just seen that all probability depends on it. Unless nature is uniform, nothing is either probable or improbable, and clearly the assumption which you have to make before there is any such thing as probability cannot itself be probable ..." (pp.106,107).
[5] *Asah* is also translated "appointed" in Job 14:5. It is translated "ordained" in Num. 28:6, 1 Kings 12:32,33.

moon on the fourth day. In fact these are said to have been formed "in the beginning" (an unspecified period of time in the past—Gen. 1:1).

2. The sun, moon and stars were "appointed" on the fourth day to give light upon the earth. It is likely that prior to the fourth day light was diffused on the earth as on a misty or cloudy day, without being able to see the sun. Light could be distinguished from darkness but not until the fourth day did the atmosphere become sufficiently clear for the heavenly bodies to be seen.

Genesis 3:1

"Now the serpent was more subtil than any beast of the field ..."

PROBLEM:

Religious bodies (such as United Church of Canada) in an attempt to rationalize the miraculous elements in the Biblical record of Genesis, while retaining the fall of mankind, view the serpent, not as a literal beast of the field, but as part of a myth in which the evil desires within Eve are symbolized.

SOLUTION:

1. If the literalness of Adam and Eve is retained, but a non-literal serpent suggested, the following questions need answering:

   a. How is Gen. 3:1 to be understood: "Now the serpent was more subtil than any *beast* of the field which the LORD God had made"? Are the beasts in this verse also figurative? If the serpent is only a symbol of sinful thinking, why the allusion to all the beasts of the field?

   b. If the serpent is a non-literal element, are the special trees, the disobedient eating, the shameful nakedness, the covering, concealment, subsequent questioning, and expulsion also allegorical?

   c. If these details are literal (as many religious persons would concede) then why the demand for a non-literal serpent?[6] If a talking serpent is too great a tax on one's credulity, what then of the tree of knowledge of good and evil, and of the tree of life?

   d. How can one consistently hold a literal Adam and Eve (as some do) and yet have a figurative environment?[7] This leaves the non-literal serpent position with no alternative but to view the whole narrative as a symbolic fall which actually took some other form than described.[8]

---

[6] If this is the basis on which a literal serpent is rejected, the problems become cumulative. How is one to interpret Balaam's ass speaking, "And the LORD opened the mouth of the ass, and she said unto Balaam, What have I done unto thee, that thou hast smitten me these three times?" (Num. 22:28). Peter endorses the account: "the dumb ass speaking with man's voice forbad the madness of the prophet." (2 Pet. 2:16).

[7] The geographic location of the garden is carefully specified in Gen. 2:9–14.

[8] It is not possible to maintain this view since the historicity of the fall of man is reaffirmed in the New Testament. (1 Tim. 2:13,14; Rom. 5:12,14). Allusions to the early chapters of Genesis in the New Testament occur in contexts in which the arguments require a belief in the historicity of the narratives. See for example, 1 Cor. 11:7–9 (the prior creation of Adam); Matt. 19:4,5; Matt. 23:35; Heb. 11:4; 1 John 3:12 (the death of Abel).

e. How is one to understand the curse on the serpent, "Because *thou* hast done this, thou art cursed above *all cattle* ..." (Gen. 3:14)?

2. There is a relevant comment by Paul on the serpent in his writing to the Corinthian Ecclesia. He says: "I fear, lest by any means, as the serpent beguiled Eve through his subtilty, so your minds should be corrupted from the simplicity that is in Christ." (2 Cor. 11:3). The full force of Paul's argument requires a literal serpent in the Garden of Eden.

His argument rests on parallels:

Serpent lied— (Gen. 3:4)	False teachers lied— (2 Cor. 11:13)
Serpent was subtle— (Gen. 3:1)	False teachers were beguiling— (2 Cor. 11:3,13)
Eve was seduced— (2 Cor. 11:3)	Corinthians in danger of being seduced— (2 Cor. 11:3)
Eve's fall was disastrous— (1 Tim. 2:14)	Corinthians in danger of disaster— (2 Cor 11:3)

The full force of the parallels requires a literal serpent. If the serpent were merely a symbol of Eve's unworthy thoughts, then Eve (created "very good", Gen. 1:31) was tempted *within*, yet the Corinthians (fallen descendants of Adam) were tempted from without. What force would there be in Paul's allusion to the serpent?

3. If the *primary* incitement came of the woman's inner fleshly insubordination to divine law, then how could it be said that she was made "very good"? The next logical step required by those who hold a non-literal view of the serpent would be to have God condemning in Christ (the seed of the woman) what He had Himself created—the "nature" which Eve bore. Adam, described as "very good" could not say as did Paul, "In me (that is, in my flesh,) dwelleth no good thing". (Rom. 7:18). Nor could he speak of "the law of sin" which is "in my members". (Rom. 7:23).

4. Sometimes stress is placed on Gen. 3:15 where the serpent and its seed are used symbolically to represent sin. It is then reasoned that the preceding verses referring to the serpent must also be symbolic. To suggest this is to miss the point that a symbol must have its basis in prior fact. The symbolic use of the serpent elsewhere in scripture is intelligible because of the literal serpent in the Garden of Eden.

Joshua 10:13

"And the sun stood still, and the moon stayed ... "[9]

PROBLEM

There are two problems arising from this verse:

---

[9] It is reported that there is independent historical confirmation of a long day in the writings of other people. See Arthur Gook, *Can A Young Man Trust His Bible?*, (London: Pickering and Inglis Ltd.). Gook comments as follows: "There were three ancient nations in the East which kept records of their history—the Greeks, the Egyptians and the Chinese. Each of these nations has a record of an unnaturally long day. Herodotus, 480 BC, a Greek who is called 'the father of history', tells us that

WRESTED SCRIPTURES

1. If the Bible is a divinely inspired book, why does it use Ptolemaic language implying a geocentric concept of the solar system (i.e. that the sun goes around the earth), rather than Copernican language which would imply a heliocentric concept of the solar system (i.e., that the earth revolves around the sun)?

2. Even if one accepts that a heliocentric concept was in fact merely being presented in geocentric terms, if the spin of the earth was slowed this would have caused catastrophe and therefore it could not have happened.

SOLUTION:

Considering the above two problems in turn:

1. a. The language of the Bible is often phenomenal (i.e., it pertains to appearances). The Bible describes the heavenly bodies, and classifies the animal world by appearance. Likewise data in sociology, education and psychology, as well as many other disciplines, are collected on the basis of observation. Other attempts to order data may involve classification according to other criteria such as internal structure.

   b. Popular expressions include the phenomenal approach. The sun is still spoken of as 'rising' and 'setting'. One still hears idioms like: 'From every corner of the earth' and 'from all quarters of the globe'. Such expressions are entirely serviceable in everyday communications as vehicles of meaning. Their use does not imply postulation about the actual or absolute relationships of heavenly bodies to the earth. The Bible no more errs in its use of the phenomenal approach than a contemporary person does in his use of similar idioms.

2. a. The argument in Problem 2 is based on a prior assumption that miracles cannot happen. The God who made the solar system is quite capable of making the sun shine for a longer period.

   b. How God achieved this event which is described from the standpoint of the observer as the sun standing still, we cannot know. Slowing the spin of the earth (with all the necessary adjustments) or refracting the light from the sun so that it shone longer on the earth are possible explanations. The fact that we do not know how the Almighty produced the effect does not mean that we cannot know that He did perform the miracle.

   c. That Joshua did not experience a long day cannot be proven scientifically or in any other way.

---

some priests in Egypt showed him a record telling of the lengthening of a day far beyond the twenty-four hours. In the Chinese ancient writings it is plainly stated that such an occurrence took place in the reign of their Emperor Yeo, and their genealogical tables show that an Emperor of this name was reigning in China in the time of Joshua. Lord Kingsborough, who has made a special study of the aboriginal Indians in America, states that the Mexicans, who reached a high state of civilization long before America was discovered by Europeans, have a record that the sun 'stood still' for a whole day in the year which they call 'seven rabbits'. Now, the year 'seven rabbits' corresponds exactly with the time that Joshua and the Israelites were conquering Palestine." (p.43).

3.2

EVOLUTION

PRELIMINARY POINTS

Most Bible students, it would seem, are far more comfortable instructing friends who accept the authority of the Bible, rather than those for whom this remains to be demonstrated. But it is likely that the latter group of questioners and students will make up an increasingly large number of contacts.

One of the main factors in the general decline in belief of Biblical inspiration is the widespread acceptance of evolution as the 'scientific' explanation for the origin and development of life.[1] As one writer observed:

> "The tale could be told a thousand times, of a Christian[2] church or school or mission society or some other organization, founded by men of strong Biblical faith (belief in the verbal, plenary, and infallible inspiration of Scripture)...slowly but steadily drifting off its foundations and gradually sinking in the sands of modernism and secularism. This tragedy repeated times without number, almost always begins with a questioning of Biblical creationism. The Scriptural account of origins must somehow be accommodated to the latest scientific theories of origins (which are always evolutionary). This accommodation inevitably and necessarily leads to a softening of the doctrine of Biblical inspiration and infallibility. Other creative acts of God (that is, the recorded miracles) begin to be questioned, and a view of Biblical inspiration which allows for cultural limitations and even for outright contradictions becomes adopted...The proper activity for modern Christians eventually becomes more 'social action', striving to help in the future evolution of the social order into a more advanced and enlightened humanistic society."[3]

Many Christians feel an uneasiness about tackling an evolutionist on his own ground. There is usually good reason for this, since one may lack familiarity with the specialized language and data of a particular area of science. The Bible student is far more competent to expound the great truths of the written Word. Amateur

---

[1] Theoretical framework, evolutionary in nature, has been widely employed in the behavioural sciences such as psychology, anthropology, and sociology as well as in biology. Sir Julian Huxley, the famous British biologist, has emphasized the all-inclusive character of evolutionary philosophy: "the concept of evolution was soon extended to other than biological fields. Inorganic subjects such as the life-histories of stars and the formation of the chemical elements on the one hand, and on the other hand subjects like linguistics, social anthropology, and comparative law and religion, began to be studied from an evolutionary angle, until today we are enabled to see evolution as a universal all pervading process." Julian Huxley, "Evolution and Genetics", in *What is Science*. ed. by J. R. Newman, (New York: Simon and Schuster, 1955), p.272.

[2] The term 'Christian' is used by the author in the popular sense of a person "following Jesus Christ". It is preferable to use the term 'Christian' only for believers in the one gospel (the basic elements of which are outlined in the *Christadelphian Birmingham Amended Statement of Faith*).

[3] Henry Morris, *The Twilight of Evolution*, (Michigan: Baker Book House Co., 1963), preface.

WRESTED SCRIPTURES

though he may be, there is no monopoly on logic. Every believer should equip himself with sufficient knowledge to formulate clearly the kind of evidence which would be required reasonably to support evolution. Any evidence which may be raised (even if previously unknown) may then be considered in discussion on evolution to avoid the wrangling which can occur over insignificant or even irrelevant considerations. The ground can then be cleared for constructive Biblical teaching to follow.

SUGGESTED STRATEGY:

1. Insist on a definition of the term evolution. Biology texts use the term in the following three ways:

   a. The gradual change in the characteristics of species over the course of time. The Christadelphian need not concern himself with this definition of evolution, since minor changes do occur within species without a change in their essential nature.

   b. 'Horizontal differentiation'—the diversification of a single type into a number of types of creatures with similar characteristics. Again, the Christadelphian need not concern himself with this definition since different types of dogs may have come from one dog type, but they are still dogs.

   c. 'Vertical evolution'—the development of existing forms[4] from a few primitive forms with increasing complexity and development through the ages. It is this definition which conflicts with the *special creative acts* of God outlined in Genesis.

---

[4] It is helpful to know that there are currently at least 1,000,000 species of animals and 250,000 species of plants described in biological literature—and this is almost certainly an underestimate. Taxonomic categories usually follow the structure set out by Linnaeus, a Swedish botanist. The classification uses the following categories:

    Kingdom—either plant or animal

    Phylum—related classes

    Class—families with common fundamental characteristics

    Family—a cluster of genera (the plural of genus)

    Genus—species with common characteristics

    Species—kinds of plants and animals, "the individuals of any one kind differing from each other only in minor traits, except sex; sharply separated in some traits from all other species; and mutually fertile, but at least partially sterile when crossed to other species". Edward O. Dodson, *Evolution: Process and Product*, (New York: Reinhold Publishing Corporation, 1960), p.28.

The classification of two birds, the red-headed woodpecker and the red-winged blackbird would, for example, be classified as follows:

Taxonomy	Red-winged blackbird	Red-headed woodpecker
Kingdom	Animalia	Animalia
Phylum	Chordata	Chordata
Class	Aves	Aves
Family	Passeriformes	Piciformes
Genus	Icteridae	Picidae
Species	Agelaius phoeniceus	Melanerpe erythrocephalus

Evidence for a) and b) is often mistakenly advanced in support of c).

2. It is useful to anticipate that the evidence for 'vertical evolution' is usually taken from four major areas:[5]

A. Palaeontology—the study of fossil remains of extinct animals and plants, including traces of their existence (e.g. footprints in slate, clay, or coal). It attempts to establish the order in which things lived. It is worth noting that the fossil record provides the only objective evidence of what actually did happen. All other arguments for evolution are based on what might have happened.

B. Morphology and Comparative Anatomy—the study of the comparison of living and dead things for resemblances and differences which might suggest relationships between them and indicate whether one form might have been derived from another.

C. Embryology—the study of developing creatures before their birth. Comparisons are made between the adult or developing forms of other creatures.

D. Genetics—the study of how the characteristics of parents are transmitted to their offspring, and how variations in these characteristics can arise. It is also concerned experimentally with breeding research in which new variables are produced and specialized.

3. In general, the evidence produced in discussion can be critically evaluated in terms of the following schema:

A. *Palaeontological*

a. *Evidence required*—A reasonable argument in support of vertical evolution must show that there is a finely graded sequence from simple to complex over a long period of evolutionary history.[6]

b. *Evidence lacking*

i. At best palaeontological enquiry can only show that one form of life came after another (granting the very generous assumption that all inverted orders of fossil deposits can be explained). Present palaeontological enquiry does not prove descent.

---

[5] Evidence for evolution is sometimes taken from biogeography (the study of geographical distribution of plants and animals) and taxonomy (the science of the classification of organisms). These, however, are not usually the crucial arguments. When arguments of classification are advanced by evolutionists it requires stressing that it is the *evolutionist*, and not the fossils, which orders the single celled amoeba, first, and next to it places a multicellular hydra, a three-layered worm, an amphioxus, and then a fish, an amphibian, reptile, lower mammal, lower ape, higher ape, and man. The order is a synthetic one. It no more proves that one form of life came from another than the arrangement of books on a shelf from simple to complex proves that the books "evolved". Both simple and complex may have been produced simultaneously. Arguments from the classification *assume* the very thing which must be proved.

[6] This argument is considered in greater detail in an excellent article by C. E. A. Turner, *Phantom Ancestors*. The article is an abstract from a pamphlet published by the Evolution Protest Movement under the title, *Horse Sense about Horse Evolution*. See Science Section ed. by D. A. B. Owen, *The Testimony*, 34, No. 401, (May, 1964), pp.171-173.

ii. The fossil record does not show a finely graded sequence from simple to complex.[7] Its record is one of discontinuity. Types spring suddenly in the Cambrian deposits.

iii. If evolution were true the fossil record should show creatures with the beginnings of new structures—e.g. giraffes with necks half as long as at present or birds with beaks evolving from reptile jaws. Such are completely absent.

B. and C. *Morphological, Anatomical,*[8] and *Embryological*

a. *Evidence required*—It must be shown that x and y are part of an historical sequence of progressive changes, or that x can be made to give birth to y by this or that genetic modification.

b. Evidence lacking

i. Comparing the anatomy of the wing of a bird, the paddle of a whale and the arm of a man, certain similarities of structure can be observed. But resemblances of structure are just as capable of indicating a common designer as ancestry from prior forms.

ii. Morphological, anatomical and embryological evidence depend on palaeontological and genetic claims. It depends on whether the fossil record shows a finely graded progression from simple to complex, and whether the study of genetics provides the mechanisms by which creatures would move over time from simple to complex.

D. *Genetic*

a. *Evidence required*—Experimental evidence to prove that chance factors can elaborate the structural complexities of creatures.

---

[7] Alfred Norris notes, "Of course specific instances to the contrary are claimed. In particular, much is made of the evolution of the horse from a primitive, dog-sized and multitoed *eohippus* ('dawn horse') to our modern large and single-toed-equus. Here we can, if we wish, join 'deceitful delusion', and exploit the differences which exist between those who try to arrange the fossils in sequence. But it is much more profitable, to my mind, to point out that even if the sequence were absolutely demonstrated we begin with a placental mammal of a particular type, and we finish with a placental mammal of the same type. It is bigger in size (but no one calls *that* evolution), and it has fewer toes (which needs no comment), but it is utterly valueless in providing any sort of presumption that less complex creatures evolve into more complex ones; for nothing of the kind has happened in this instance. Nor has it in any other for which the sequence is claimed to be sufficiently complete to justify a belief in demonstrated descent." Alfred Norris, "Where Science and Religion Meet: Is Evolution a Fact?" *The Christadelphian*, 102, No. 1208, (Feb., 1965), pp.59-62.

[8] Sometimes vestigial organs (useless representatives of organs which in other animals serve a useful purpose) are presented as proof of evolution. It is argued that these useless organs like the coccyx (last vertebral column of man and said to be the vestigial tail) or the appendix have no function in humans but functioned in the ancestors of humans. The argument assumes that if no purpose is known for organs that no purpose exists. Weidersham listed 180 of such organs which he considered "useless luggage". Recent research has shown that only a small number of organs now have no known purpose at some stage in the human life. Many evolutionists are critical of the vestigial proof for evolution as the "useless luggage" becomes increasingly smaller. See H. Enoch, *Evolution or Creation*, (London: Evangelical Press, 1968), pp.14-21. To make a case for evolution, it must be shown that nascent organs are in evidence (organs newly acquired by an animal, but which did not exist in its ancestors). Such proof has not yet been found.

b. *Evidence lacking*

   i. Although it is true that selective breeding has produced many varieties of plants and animals which may, under carefully controlled conditions, breed true to their new type, the fact that almost without exception, such new types would not be viable in nature[9] is very strong presumption that evolution is unlikely to have been much helped by such processes.

   ii. Indications of diversity on the same level of organization (e.g., Drosophila—the fruit fly) do not prove that present organization has proceeded from single-celled creatures to complex placentae. Extensive mutation experiments with the fruit fly produced only malformed fruit flies—i.e. they always remained fruit flies (often morphologically and functionally compromised).

   iii. Years of labour, and millions of dollars of research have gone into unlocking the secrets of genetic codes. The results of this research indicate deliberate planning and highly intelligent understanding behind the formation of the codes. These DNA codes are extremely complicated and they lock each type of creature into its own pattern. Against this background the evolutionist has the problem of proving that chance origin of species and change across species could occur.

BIBLIOGRAPHY

A. CHRISTADELPHIAN PUBLICATIONS

The Finger of God: Evolution or Creation?, Evington, Leicester: The Testimony, 1963.

   This 106-page booklet is useful in its analysis of the diverse specializations of the animal and plant worlds. The cumulative effect of the booklet is an argument against the probability that chance factors could produce the highly complex specializations of organic life.

Creation or Chance?, Herald of the Coming Age, Vol. 40 No. 2 March, 1994.

   This is a compact 16-page booklet designed for distribution to friends. Requests for back copies should be addressed to Logos Publications, Box 220, Findon, South Australia, 5023.

The Bible and Modern Thinking—Assent or Dissent?, The Testimony, Vol. 35, No. 417, (Sept. 1965).

   This 114-page special issue of the magazine ought to be read by every Christadelphian. Its articles cover a wide range of the conflicts between

---

[9] It is generally accepted that the genes (heredity determiners) tend to keep species constant. However, the genes are capable of undergoing a change (mutation), so that the trait determined is different from the original and is just as stable. Since mutations form the basis of heredity they are thought by evolutionists to provide the raw material or mechanism for evolution. Nearly all such mutations result in inferior survival chance in nature. "Indeed inasmuch as a living cell is an exceedingly complex, very finely adjusted whole, it is to be expected that any permanent change in cellular properties would be more or less disruptive and harmful." Paul Weisz, *The Science of Biology*, (New York: McGraw-Hill, 1960), p.690.

science and the Bible. On pages 402,403 the magazine has a bibliography of books considered helpful by the editors.

Collyer, John V., *Creation, Evolution and Science*, The Testimony, Norwich, 1993.

A 139-page book considering the evidence for creation and against evolution. Originally appeared as a series of articles in the *Testimony* magazine 1990-1991.

Hellawell, John M., *Creation or Evolution*, Birmingham: CMPA, 2004.

A 24-page booklet that argues the case for the Biblical creation. Useful for giving to interested friends.

Pearce, David, *Evidence for Design*, Birmingham: CMPA, 2004.

A 31-page booklet that convincingly uses the design argument to show the paucity of the theory of evolution. Again, useful for giving to interested friends.

B. NON-CHRISTADELPHIAN PUBLICATIONS[10]

Life–How Did it Begin: By Creation or Evolution? Brooklyn, New York: Watchtower Bible and Tract Society of New York, Inc., 1985, pp.1-198.

This book is available from the Jehovah's Witnesses. It is well documented and very easy to read. The latter chapters contain a little J.W. theology.

Enoch, H. *Evolution or Creation*. Pennsylvania: Evangelical Press, London, 1968.

This is one of the most thorough and systematic examinations of the claims of evolutionists. This book is a *must* for every Christadelphian entering university.

Ferril, Vance, *The Evolution Cruncher*, Altamont, TN, USA: Evolution Facts Inc., 2001.

A 928-page paperback containing a simple presentation of an amazing amount of scientific and other argument against evolution. Also available online at http://evolution-facts.org. Also on this website is the three-volume work on which the "Evolution Cruncher" is based: *Creation-Evolution Encyclopedia*.

McLean, G. S., Oakland, R., McLean, L., *The Evidence for Creation*, Whitaker House: Springdale, PA, 1989.

An excellent and concise argument of the case for creation, with scientific evidence against evolution. Excellent for those with no scientific background. Contains a little 'evangelical' theology in the Introduction and the Epilogue.

Morris, Henry. *The Twilight of Evolution*. Grand Rapids, Mich., Baker Book House, 1966, pp.1-74.

---

[10] It must be realised that these textbooks are recommended only for their analysis of evolution. The books must be read with discernment since the writers, while believing in the verbal, plenary and infallible inspiration of Scripture, have occasionally misunderstood its teaching on basic doctrines.

This small book has one of the best analysis of the inroads of evolution within the Evangelical movement. Morris is an hydrologist who co-authored the book, *The Genesis Flood*.

Wells, Jonathan, *Icons of Evolution: Science or Myth?*, Washington, DC: Regney Publishing Inc., 2000.

A very incisive review of the principle lines of evidence used to support evolutionary theory. The author shows that all of them are false or misleading.

Behy, Michael J. (1996) *Darwin's Black Box. The Biochemical Challenge to Evolution*, Touchstone, Simon & Schuster, New York, 307 pages.

Demonstrates that biological systems, at the biochemical level, have an irreducible complexity and therefore any simpler system as postulated in evolution would be ineffective.

RADIOMETRIC DATING METHODS

PROBLEM:

The theory of evolution requires very long periods of time for all its postulated changes to have taken place. Evolutionists talk in terms of billions of years for the beginning of the solar system and the emergence of living things on the earth. Evidence for this is garnered from the radioactive dating of rocks and the fossils contained in them.

The most common methods employed for the dating of inorganic material such as rock strata are:

The uranium-lead method.

The rubidium-strontium method.

The potassium-argon method.

In each of these methods the first mentioned element is said to be the 'parent' element and the second is the 'daughter' element. Over time the 'parent' element undergoes radioactive decay and is gradually changed to the 'daughter' element of the system. Using a mass spectrometer the ratio of 'parent' to 'daughter' element can be measured. The known radioactive decay rate of the system can then be used to calculate how long the decaying process has been taking place and hence the age of the specimen being examined.

By these methods it is said that the age of the earth can be calculated and the results suggest that it is billions of years old—plenty of time for evolution to have occurred!

SOLUTION:

1. There are three assumptions[1] that must be made if the accuracy of the results of such measurements are to accepted:

---

[1] The significance of these assumptions may be seen from the following examples of radiometric dating:

    a. *The Journal of Geophysical Research*, volume 73, July 15, 1968, reported that lava rocks formed in 1800 and 1801 in Hawaii (i.e. they were known to be 168–169 years old) were dated by the potassium-argon method and showed an age of formation of 160 million to 3 billion years.

    b. In *Science*, volume 162, October 11, 1968, volcanic rocks known to be less than 200 years old were dated by a radiometric dating method and showed ages of 12 to 21 million years.

(Both examples quoted in McLean, G. S., Oakland, R., McLean, L., *The Evidence for Creation*, [Whitaker House: Springdale, Penn. 1989] p.38.)

In the light of this, when we are told, with respect to Skull 1470 found by Richard Leakey, that "layers of volcanic tuff, datable by the potassium-argon method have led scientists to fix the age of the level that yielded the '1470' skull at 2.8 million years" (*National Geographic*, June 1973, p.824), we have good reason to be sceptical.

a. The system being examined (e.g. the uranium-lead system) must have been initially made up of all 'parent' element; there must have been no 'daughter' element present. But this is not possible. There is just no way that we can know that when the particular specimen being examined came into existence all the uranium-238 had no lead-206 in it.

b. The rate of radioactive decay must have been constant from the very moment when the decaying process started. This is impossible to prove and unreasonable to assume. There are many things that can change the rate of radioactive decay. Pressure, temperature, electric and magnetic fields, for example have all been shown to affect decay rates[2]. The sedimentary rock strata were laid down under tremendous pressure and would have been associated with great temperature changes thereafter.

c. The system being measured must have operated as a 'closed system' with nothing being added to it and nothing taken away from it. There is no such thing as a closed system in nature and to make measurements on the assumption that such a system existed renders the measurements unreliable.

2. These assumptions arise out of the unsustainable and more fundamental assumption of the uniformity of nature. (See pages 334,335).

CARBON-14 (^{14}C) DATING

PROBLEM:

All living things contain the element carbon. Carbon-14 dating is a method of estimating the age of organic matter such as fossils. It is said that this method proves that man has been on the earth for at least 30,000 years. This age for man conflicts with Biblical chronology which dates the beginning of man's existence on the earth about six thousand years ago.

SOLUTION:

1. In order to appraise critically the claim that ^{14}C "definitely proves" the age of man to be at least 30,000 years, a description of ^{14}C dating is required:

The ^{14}C method of dating is used to determine the age of vegetable and animal remains. The procedure rests on the fact that cosmic radiation in the upper atmosphere leads to the formation of a radioactive isotope of carbon with an atomic weight of fourteen, instead of the normal weight of twelve (carbon-14 instead of the normal carbon-12). Atmospheric carbon contains a small amount of radioactive ^{14}C which decays at a fixed known rate, but is continuously replaced by the formation of more ^{14}C. The rate of breakdown is calculated in terms of the 'half-life' which for carbon is 5,568 (plus or minus 30) years. After this amount of time, only half the original amount of ^{14}C will be left; after about 11,400 years, a quarter. Plants, by means of photosynthesis, and animals, by

[2] Dudley, H. C., "Radioactivity Re-Examined", *Chemical and Engineering News*, April 7, 1975, p.2, quoted in Ferrell, V., *The Evolution Cruncher*, (Evolution Facts Inc.: Altamont, TN, 2001), p.180.

respiration and feeding on plants and one another, incorporate atmospheric carbon into their tissues, a process that is assumed to cease when the tissues die. As the ^{14}C disintegrates in the dead tissues and is not replaced, the ratio of non-radioactive carbon-12 to carbon-14 will slowly change, and its value at any time will depend on the time that has elapsed since the tissues died. Thus the age of the tissues can in principle be determined by comparing the ratio of non-radioactive carbon to ^{14}C in the tissue and in the atmosphere.[3]

2. As with other methods of radiometric dating, the ^{14}C dating method is only reliable if the general assumption of the uniformity of nature[4] is valid. Uniformity of nature is the belief that present causes solely have operated in the past. Within this general assumption are a number of particular assumptions:

   a. That the amount of radioactive carbon in the earth's atmosphere and in the oceans has been constant and that fossilized creatures when living had as much ^{14}C as similar things have today.[5]

   b. That the rate of decay of ^{14}C has remained constant (i.e. that the rate of decay has not changed in the interval from when the fossilized creatures lived to the present day).

   c. That no contamination of the specimen containing ^{14}C has occurred since the death of the organism.

3. There are a number of technical problems involved in ^{14}C dating which suggest that the above assumptions are not valid:

   a. It requires relatively small effects to change the level of ^{14}C. For example the burning of coal and oil which contain virtually no ^{14}C has, during the past century and a half, lowered the proportion of ^{14}C in the atmosphere by an amount equivalent to at least 400 years. The explosion of hydrogen bombs between 1955 and 1961 increased the amount of ^{14}C by an amount equivalent to an estimated 1,500 years.

   b. The fossils are often contaminated by carbon from their surroundings—carbonates, humic acid, etc. Materials recovered from wet earth inevitably have been invaded by water containing carbonates, humic acid and even pitch. All these must be extracted from the sample with acid, alkali and

[3] See John Watts, "Carbon 'Fourteen' Dating", in "The Bible and Modern Thinking—Assent or Dissent?" *The Testimony*, Vol. 35, No. 417 (Sept. 1965), pp.352,353.

[4] Lyell, sometimes referred to as "the high priest of uniformitarianism" and author of the famous textbook, *Principles of Geology*, wrote: "... all theories are rejected which involve the assumption of sudden and violent catastrophes..." Charles Lyell, *Principles of Geology*, 11th. ed. rev., (New York: D. Appleton and Co., 1892), 1,317-318. Uniformitarianism has been accepted in all major centres of scientific learning. Darwin built his theory of organic evolution upon the uniformitarian foundation which Lyell had laid. But the Apostle Peter denounces uniformitarianism (i.e., the belief that "all things continue as they were from the beginning of the creation", 2 Peter 3:4). He cites God's divine intervention in the violent catastrophe of the Noahic flood (2 Peter 3:6) as evidence of its falsity.

[5] This assumption was noted at a conference of radiocarbon experts: "Throughout the conference emphasis was placed on the fact that laboratories do not measure ages, they measure sample activities. The connection between activity and age is made through a set of assumptions...one of the main assumptions of ^{14}C dating is that the atmospheric radiocarbon level has held steady over the age-range to which the method applies." *Science Digest*, (Dec. 10, 1965), p.1490.

organic solvents, and even after this some degree of contamination is possible. This invalidates the results.

c. Chemical and/or biological changes may have been going on in the fossil over the centuries changing its composition. The amount of ^{14}C in a fossil (for example, 6,000 years old) is a very small part of the total carbon, and contamination can have a big effect.

d. It is known that the earth's magnetic field has decreased by about 14 per cent in the past 130 years. This has allowed an increase in cosmic radiation penetrating the earth's atmosphere thus increasing ^{14}C formation. This mitigates against the rate of ^{14}C formation having been constant in the past.

4. Even if it be shown that there is a high degree of correlation between independent dating methods, this does not in itself prove the age of man on the earth. The appearance of age may be due to the following factors:

a. God's creation was in equilibrium, hence the appearance of age.[6]

b. Conditions have not been uniform on the earth. The record in Genesis 1:6 states that on the second day the waters were divided into two parts, water below the heaven and water above the heaven. The accumulation of water above the heaven would form an outer band round the atmosphere. But this does not exist today, therefore it cannot be assumed that the cosmic ray intensity has been constant. Nor can it be assumed that there has been a stable equilibrium condition between atmospheric ^{14}CO$_2$ (Carbon-14 dioxide) and the reservoirs, primarily the oceans. Genesis 7:12; 8:2 state that in the great Noahic flood the heavens were opened for 40 days and presumably the above-the-heaven water returned to the earth. (Vast quantities of water are now stored as ice in the frozen polar regions.) The blanket of water vapour around the earth prior to the flood would be expected to reduce the ionising power of the sun's rays and the amount of ^{14}C in living things would be less than now.[7] If ^{14}C in living things was less than it is now, then the geologists' assumption of the uniformity of nature and hence the age postulated for fossils on the basis of these dating methods will be erroneous—the original amount of ^{14}C being smaller than they calculate.[8]

c. The rate of decay of ^{14}C may also have been different under conditions before the Noahic flood.

---

[6] The record in Genesis presents Adam as a fully developed man when newly made. Similarly the birds, animals and plants were created full grown. This implies that the soil in which the plants were to grow was already formed. Similarly the ocean would contain the salt and other chemicals to support its marine life. In other words, there must have been an equilibrium among the innumerable and complex interrelationships between the plant and animal kingdoms, the organic and inorganic realms. This can only mean that the world when created had the appearance of age. Obviously the apparent age of the world would not be the same as the real or actual age of the world.

[7] *Science Digest* of Dec. 1960 reported that if the ^{14}C level in the atmosphere has not remained steady, "…it would most certainly ruin some of our carefully developed methods of dating things from the past…If the level of ^{14}C was less in the past, due to a greater magnetic shielding from cosmic rays, then our estimates of the time that has elapsed since the life of the organism will be too long." p.19.

[8] See G. Pearce, "The Weakness of Science Concerning the Origin of Man", *Logos*, Vol. XXXII, No. 12, (Nov. 1966), pp.411-419.

3.4

THE DAYS OF CREATION

Genesis 1:5
"...And the evening and the morning were the first day."

PROBLEM:

In attempting to reconcile the creative acts of Genesis 1 with the great ages currently postulated for life on the earth, some scholars have interpreted the creative days to mean geological epochs or '1,000-year days'.[1] Support for this position is taken from 2 Peter 3:8—"One day is with the Lord as a thousand years". Some who profess to be 'Christians' even argue that God has used the process of evolution as the means of creation.

SOLUTION:

1. In Exo. 20:11 (also Exo. 31:17) God commanded Israel to observe the Sabbath as a sign of the covenant: "For in six days the LORD made heaven and earth, the sea, and all that in them is, and rested the seventh day: wherefore the LORD blessed the sabbath day, and hallowed it." Would an Israelite receiving the instruction to rest one day because God had rested after six days of work, understand the six days as six "geological epochs" of unspecified length, or six one-thousand year periods?

2. If one day = 1,000 years, then Adam must have lived at least 1,000 years before dying. Even if he was created at the very end of the sixth day (1,000 year period) it is inconceivable that his fall occurred on the Sabbath (the next 1,000 year period), since God sanctified the Sabbath (Gen. 2:3), and "everything" was declared "very good" on the sixth day. (Gen. 1:31). The record states that Adam lived only 930 years (Gen. 5:5), therefore, the days of creation cannot be '1,000-year days'.

3. Plants were created on the third day (Gen. 1:11,13), but insects did not appear until the sixth day. (Gen. 1:24–31). If one day = 1,000 years, how did certain specialized plants requiring insect pollination (the maple tree, the strawberry, the blackberry, the honeysuckle, and the poppy) continue to exist without the ability to reproduce?

4. The Genesis record informs us that birds were created on the same day as fish and other marine life. (Gen. 1:20–23). Evolution maintains that birds evolved from reptiles millions of years after the appearance of fish. Clearly any attempt to reconcile creation and evolution is doomed to failure.

---

[1] The JWs for example are among this group. They reason as follows: "...the Bible tells of six 'days' during which life appeared. But the Bible's use of 'day' here means a period of time and not a twenty-four hour day." *Did Man Get Here By Evolution Or By Creation?* (New York: Watchtower Bible and Tract Society, Inc., 1967), p.97.

5. To argue that God used evolution as the means of creation is unsupportable and fails to explain the appearance of death in the human experience. If man took millions of years to be created by some evolutionary process there must have been death throughout that process. This would be in denial of the teaching of Genesis 3 which is endorsed by the New Testament—"...by one man sin entered into the world, and death by sin; and so death passed upon all men, for that all have sinned..." (Rom. 5:12). Denial of this fundamental teaching then makes the process of salvation incomprehensible.

6. Proof is required that Gen. 1:5 alludes to Peter's statement that one day is with the Lord as a thousand years, and a thousand years as one day (2 Pet. 3:8). There is no *necessary* connection between the two passages.

Genesis 2:4

"These are the generations of the heavens and of the earth when they were created, in the day that the LORD God made the earth and the heavens."

PROBLEM:

In attempts to make the six days of Gen. 1 into a longer period of time (in keeping with dates currently postulated for life on the earth), the word "day" in Gen. 2:4 is used to support a longer day than the period bounded by the "evening and the morning" of Gen. 1.[2]

SOLUTION:

1. "Day" in scripture is sometimes used to represent an unspecified length of time.[3] The Hebrew word *yom,* translated "day" in this passage, is translated "time" elsewhere (e.g. Gen. 4:3; 26:8 38:12). But when second, third, etc., occur as they do in Genesis 1, the word refers to a literal day, defined in Genesis by the "evening and the morning".

2. As used in Genesis 2, *yom* covers the whole period when the Lord God "made the earth and the heavens". (Gen. 2:4). Failure to distinguish between these two uses of "day" has led to faulty interpretations of Genesis 1. The days of Genesis 1 are determined by light and darkness, evening and morning.

Genesis 4:14

"...every one that findeth me shall slay me."

[2] JWs use this argument: "... the Bible tells of six 'days' during which life appeared. But the Bible's use of the word 'day' here means a period of time and not a twenty-four hour day. Gen. 2:4 indicates this by speaking of the 'day' that Jehovah God made earth and heaven when previously it called each of six periods included in that same time a 'day'." *Did Man Get Here By Evolution Or By Creation?* (New York: Watchtower Bible and Tract Society of New York, Inc. 1967), p.97.

[3] For example, "the day of temptation" (Psa. 95:8), "the day of adversity" (Prov. 24:10), "the day of vengeance" (Isa. 61:2), but when Scripture refers to "the fifteenth day of the same month" (Lev. 23:6), the seven days of Unleavened Bread, or the fifty days until Pentecost, the word "day" can mean only a 24-hour period.

WRESTED SCRIPTURES

PROBLEM:

In an attempt to reconcile the account of creation of Adam with evolutionary explanations, this passage is cited by the clergy of the United Church of Canada and of the Anglican Church to support the idea that pre-Adamites lived on the earth. It is argued that Cain alludes to these pre-Adamites.

SOLUTION:

1. There were no pre-Adamites in the earth at the time of Adam. This is indicated from the following:
   a. "And Adam gave names to all cattle, and to the fowl of the air, and to every beast of the field; but for Adam there was not found an help meet for him." (Gen. 2:20). Two questions arise:
      i. Why only the mention of beasts which Adam named, if pre-Adamite humans existed?
      ii. Why no mention of pre-Adamite women?
   b. Jesus, in reply to the Pharisees' question on divorce, said, "Have ye not read, that he which made them at the beginning made them male and female, and said, For this cause shall a man leave father and mother, and shall cleave to his wife: and they twain shall be one flesh?" (Matt. 19:4,5). Jesus states that the 'making' was from the "beginning of creation". (Mark 10:6). This is not the kind of language to describe the gradual evolution of man over a 30,000-year period.
   c. Until the creation of Adam, the narrative states: "there was not a man to till the ground". (Gen. 2:5). Would this be true if there were other man-like creatures?
2. Adam and Eve "begat sons and daughters". (Gen. 5:4). Cain would, therefore, fear death at the hands of his brethren.

Genesis 4:16,17

"And Cain went out from the presence of the LORD, and dwelt in the land of Nod ...and Cain knew his wife."

PROBLEM:

This passage is used to support evolutionary interpretations of the origin of man. It is argued that there were other humans on the earth beside the descendants of Adam and that Cain found one of these in the land of Nod.

SOLUTION:

1. The passage does not say that Cain went to Nod and there found a wife. Cain could have taken his wife with him to Nod.
2. Adam begat sons *and daughters*. (Gen. 5:4). Cain would, therefore, marry one of his sisters.

3. Other Biblical references make it plain that all humans are descendants from *one* original pair. Consider the following:

   a. "And he made from *one* every nation of men to live on all the face of the earth ... " (Acts 17:26, RSV).

   b. Rom. 5:12—"by *one* man sin entered into the world, and death by sin."

   Rom. 5:16—"for the judgment was by *one* to condemnation."

   Rom. 5:18—"by the offence of *one* judgment came upon all men to condemnation."

   Rom. 5:19—"by *one* man's disobedience many were made sinners."

   c. "The *first* man Adam was made a living soul." (1 Cor. 15:45).

4.1

PARTIAL INSPIRATION

PROBLEM:

The most widely accepted view of inspiration in Protestant circles is that inspiration was an enlightening of the Biblical authors which, while it gave them moral and spiritual insight and made their work 'inspiring' (or, as some say, a vehicle of God's word to their readers), it did not guarantee doctrinal or historical trustworthiness to all they actually wrote. This has led partial inspirationists to reject much of the historical information in the Bible as being unreliable, for example:

> "The Holy Spirit who inspired the Bible knew that these little details of genealogies and battles and such like, in the history of Israel, were not a whit more important to us than similar details in the history of England."[1]

SOLUTION:

1. If inspiration of the Biblical writers "did not guarantee doctrinal or historical trustworthiness to all they actually wrote" how does one distinguish the trustworthy pronouncements from those which are not trustworthy? If the writers were liable to err in historical writing, how can they be trusted in *anything* they wrote?[2]

2. The Bible records God's purpose and interaction with men. As such, the historical facts have a *doctrinal* content. For example, God revealed himself to Israel as "I am the LORD thy God, which have brought thee out of the land of Egypt..." (Exo. 20:2). The assertion is not only historical in character but doctrinal.

3. Biblical writers never make a difference between 'non-essential detail' and 'divine principles'. The New Testament writers frequently allude to historical events (e.g. Matt. 12:42; Luke 17:27), and regard them as factual records of divine instruction. Historical illustrations are cited as 'admonition' and 'examples'. (1 Cor. 10:11; Heb. 3:7–19). As the Apostle Paul expressed it: "Whatsoever things were written aforetime were written for our learning". (Rom. 15:4).

4. The often recurring expression, "He did that which was evil in the sight of the LORD" (e.g., 2 Kings 17:2), is history, but it is also a moral judgment from the

---

[1] J. Paterson Smyth, *How God Inspired the Bible*, (London: Sampson Low, Marston & Co. Ltd., 1910), p.145.

[2] Instead of Scripture dictating what human thoughts ought to be, human thoughts are elevated by partial inspirationists to the position of deciding what is human and what is divine in the records. A partly divine and partly human Bible would only be of value if the human mind were sufficiently enlightened and infallible to distinguish between the human and divine parts.

divine point of view. Again, the distinction between 'spiritual insight' and 'historical trustworthiness' is an abstraction not borne out by the record itself.

5. It is questionable whether the Biblical writers were always, or necessarily, given 'moral and spiritual insight'. Often they wrote down God's words yet did not necessarily understand the moral teaching.

   a. Jonah received revelations from God, yet "it displeased Jonah exceedingly, and he was very angry...I do well to be angry, even unto death." (Jonah 4:1–9).

   b. Daniel was also the recipient of revelation but the meaning was not fully revealed to him. "The words are closed up and sealed till the time of the end." (Dan. 12:9).

   c. Peter stated that the prophets did not fully understand what they wrote. "Of which salvation the prophets have enquired and searched diligently ...searching what, or what manner of time the Spirit of Christ which was in them did signify, when it testified beforehand the sufferings of Christ, and the glory that should follow..." (1 Peter 1:10,11).

6. We should be able to mount a sustained offence when a "partial inspirationist" is encountered. All too often the Christadelphian is put on the defensive and his inability to explain all difficulties is taken as evidence that no explanation is possible. A discussion of this sort does not do justice to the case the Bible presents for itself. Scripture teaches a doctrine of inspiration just as it contains a doctrine of baptism, resurrection and the kingdom.

7. The following evidence provides ammunition for the Christadelphian arsenal (since many religionists revere Jesus it is usually advantageous to begin with this common ground):

   a. Jesus quoted the Old Testament as completely authoritative and definitive. In so doing, he never once regarded the authority of the Law, Prophets, or Psalms as in any way dependent upon the personality of the human writers, or on the conditions under which they wrote.[3]

   b. Jesus cited the Old Testament in such a way as to establish its inspiration as infallible (without error), verbal (applying to the words used to convey the message) and plenary (extending to all parts alike). For example:

   i. Jesus answered the Jews, "Is it not written in your law, I said, Ye are gods? If he called them gods, unto whom the word of God came, and the scripture cannot be broken..." (John 10:34,35). Jesus argued on the basis of *one* word in this quotation from Psa. 82:6. He further affirms that Scripture "cannot be broken".

   ii. Jesus equated what Moses said with what God said:

   Mark 7:10—"*Moses* said, Honour thy father and thy mother..."

   Mark 7:9—"Full well ye reject the commandment of *God*..." (also v.13, "the word of God").

---

[3] This point is especially noteworthy in terms of the modern interest in hermeneutics (i.e., the interpretation of Scripture giving consideration to the environment and cultural conditions thought to influence the author's work).

Similarly, Mark 12:26,27: "Have ye not read in the book of *Moses*…?" and Matt. 22:31,32: "But…have ye not read that which was spoken unto you by *God*?"

c. The extent of Jesus' use of Old Testament Scripture and the authority which he gave to it can be shown from the following passages:

New Testament Reference	Words of Jesus	Old Testament Cited by Jesus
Matt. 4:4,7,10	"It is written…"	Deut. 8:3; 6:13,16
Matt. 12:3	"Have ye not read what David did…?"	1 Sam 21:1–6
Mark 12:10,11	"Have ye not read this scripture…?"	Psa. 118:22,23
Matt. 19:4–6	"Have ye not read, that he which made them at the beginning…?"	Gen. 1:27; 2:24
Matt. 22:31,32	"Have ye not read…I am the God of Abraham…?"	Exo. 3:6
Mark 12:36	"David himself said by the Holy Spirit…"	Psa. 110:1
Luke 4:18–21	"This day is this scripture fulfilled…"	Isa. 61:1,2
Luke 22:37	"This that is written must yet be accomplished in me…"	Isa. 53:12
Luke 16:31	"If they hear not Moses and the prophets…"	
Luke 24:25–27	"O fools, and slow of heart to believe all that the prophets have spoken…"	General references to the Old Testament
Luke 24:44	"All things must be fulfilled, which were written in the law of Moses, and in the prophets, and in the Psalms, concerning me."	

d. Four points illustrate the position of the Apostle Paul on inspiration:

i. Paul asserts that "All scripture is given by inspiration of God…" (2 Tim. 3:16,17). By inspiration, Paul means "God-breathed" Scripture.[4]

---

[4] "Inspiration" is translated from the Greek word, *theopneustos*, which means, 'God-breathed'. Robert Young, *Analytical Concordance to the Holy Bible*, (London: Lutterworth Press, 1965). In reading poetry one might feel 'inspired', but this is not what the apostle means when he states the Scriptures are inspired. The Scriptures are inspired because of their divine origin, which makes their inspiration independent of the way in which they might affect any given reader.

    ii. Paul wrote, "Now to Abraham and his seed were the promises made. He saith not, And to seeds, as of many; but as of one, And to thy seed, which is Christ." (Gal. 3:16). Paul is arguing his case on the basis of *one* word from the Old Testament. (Gen. 13:15).

    iii. Quotations from Moses, the Psalms and Prophets are considered authoritative pronouncements. For example, compare the following:

    Rom. 15:9 from Psa. 18:49

    Rom. 15:10 from Deut. 32:43

    Rom. 15:11 from Psa. 117:1

    Rom. 15:12 from Isa. 11:10

    iv. Rom. 9:17—"For the *scripture saith* unto Pharaoh, Even for this same purpose have I raised thee up, that I might shew my power in thee, and that my name might be declared throughout all the earth." The Scripture cannot literally 'say'. God said this (Exo. 9:16) and Scripture reliably records it.

  e. New Testament writers consider the Holy Spirit to be the author of Old Testament passages:[5]

    i. Heb. 3:7—"The Holy Spirit saith..." quoting Psa. 95:7–11.

    ii. Heb. 10:15—"The Holy Spirit also is a witness to us: for after that he had said before..." quoting Jer. 31:33,34.

    iii. See also Acts 1:16—"The Holy Spirit by the mouth of David spake..." Psa. 69:25; 109:8.

    iv. Acts 28:25—"Well spake the Holy Spirit by Esaias the prophet..." citing Isa. 6:9,10.

8. The prophets when inspired by God were at times *compelled* to speak what they spoke. Their human reactions were sometimes either to refrain from speaking or to utter words other than those directed by God. Two prophets serve as examples:

  a. Balaam—"If Balak would give me his house full of silver and gold, I cannot go beyond the word of the LORD my God, to do less or more... have I now any power at all to say any thing? the word that God putteth in my mouth, that shall I speak." (Num. 22:18,38).[6]

  b. Jeremiah—"Then I said, I will not make mention of him, nor speak any more in his name. But his word was in mine heart as a burning fire shut up in my bones, and I was weary with forbearing, and I could not stay." (Jer. 20:9).

9. The partial inspiration position outlined in the problem has resulted in scepticism and barrenness. A spirit of unconcern about doctrine has resulted

---

[5] The writer to the Hebrews expresses the abiding authority of Scripture in his citation of the words of Psa. 95:7–11 and Jer. 31:33. He cites these passages using the present tense—"The Holy Spirit saith, (not 'said') (Heb. 3:7). Likewise, the "Holy Spirit bears [not bore] witness to us". (Heb. 10:15, cf. RSV).

[6] See also Ezek. 2:7. To put words in someone's mouth is to tell him exactly what to say. (See, for example, 2 Sam. 14:2,3,19).

WRESTED SCRIPTURES

since on so many issues it is thought to be anyone's guess as to what is true. Perplexities about the Holy Scriptures have discouraged lay reading of the Bible and the idea has spread that the Bible is a book full of pitfalls which only the learned can hope to avoid. Sometimes it is considered virtuous to censure predecessors for being too definitive and dogmatic. New thought is complimented as being open-minded, flexible, and free from obscurantism. It should be noted that those who are "tossed to and fro, and carried about with every wind of doctrine" (Eph. 4:14) and "ever learning, and never able to come to the knowledge of the truth" (2 Tim. 3:7) are not commended in the New Testament.

1 Corinthians 7:25

"Now concerning virgins I have no commandment of the Lord: yet I give my judgment, as one that hath obtained mercy of the Lord to be faithful."

PROBLEM:

This verse is interpreted by many of the clergy of the Anglican and United Churches to mean that Paul is giving a personal opinion which may or may not be the right advice. Therefore, it is argued, the Bible cannot be plenary (fully, completely) inspired.

SOLUTION:

1. Paul's point is not that he is giving advice which may, or may not be right, but that he cannot quote the Lord Jesus as having already pronounced on this subject. Notice the context:
   a. Verse 10—"And unto the married I command, yet not I, but the Lord, Let not the wife depart from her husband." (Paul refers to the Master's teaching in Matt. 19.) Paul then deals with a matter concerning which the Lord has made no particular pronouncement. So he says, "I have no commandment of the Lord: yet I give my judgment as one that hath obtained mercy of the Lord to be faithful."
   b. Verse 40—"I think also that [as well as others] I have the Spirit of God." Paul points out that although there was no specific commandment of the Lord he can be trusted.
2. The Apostle Paul, in 1 Cor. 14:37, sets forth his claim to Holy Spirit guidance as a criterion by which other claimants to Spirit possession might be judged: "If any man think himself to be a prophet, or spiritual, let him acknowledge that the things that I write unto you are the commandments of the Lord."
3. Plenary inspiration affirms that "all scripture is given by inspiration of God". (2 Tim. 3:16). It does not assert that statements made by wicked men and recorded in Scripture are inspired, but only that their statements are accurately recorded because God in His wisdom chose such to be the case for the reader's learning and admonition. (Rom. 15:4; 1 Cor. 10:11). It is inspired that such should be recorded.

4.2

NON-PROPOSITIONAL REVELATION

PROBLEM:

Most of the clergy of the United and Anglican Churches (Episcopalian in the U.S.A. and the Church of England in the U.K.) hold the following view of revelation expressed by William Temple:

> "There are truths of revelation, that is to say propositions which express the results of correct thinking concerning revelation, but they are not themselves directly revealed."[1]

God is viewed as revealing Himself by illuminating chosen observers of 'significant events' so that they perceived what the events meant in terms of the divine character and plan. The events, therefore, are considered to gain revelatory status through the divine enlightenment (i.e., through the observer's heightened intuitive and reflective capacities, and sharpened moral and spiritual perceptions). Revelation is not considered to be the act of God communicating words, i.e., propositions. This view of revelation is sometimes referred to as "non-propositional".

SOLUTION:

1. The non-propositional view of revelation destroys Biblical faith which honours God in trusting what He has said. When Abraham (whom the New Testament sets forth as an example of the man of faith *par excellence*) believed God, "it was counted unto him for righteousness". (Rom. 4:3; Gal. 3:6, cf. Gen. 15:6). The object of Abraham's faith was a specific promise, a seed which would become as numerous as the stars of heaven. (Gen. 15:1–6). But according to Temple's theory of revelation there never was an objective revelation of promise to Abraham. However, the Abrahamic promise consisted of informative statements, but *informative statements are propositional*; therefore, revelation *is* propositional.

2. If revelation is in the event rather than in the interpretation, revelation can be re-shaped according to one's subjective whims. For example, C. H. Dodd dismisses the divine words of commission which Jeremiah heard (Jer. 1:4–19) as "actual hallucinations".[2] Dodd's view requires that a "thus saith the Lord" be read as "I feel quite certain that if God spoke He would say..."[3]

3. The view of revelation outlined in the problem nullifies the claim of Scripture for its prophecies. In fact, it must disallow even the claim made in Isaiah, "I am

---

[1] William Temple, *Nature Man and God*, (New York: St. Martin's Press, 1934), p.317.

[2] C. H. Dodd, *The Authority of the Bible*, (London: Harper, 1958), p.83.

[3] The "death of God" theology is the legitimate offspring of its liberal parents who fed upon such views of the non-objective character of divine revelation.

God, and there is none else...declaring the end from the beginning, and from ancient times the things that are not yet done..." (Isa. 46:9,10). It might prove enlightening for such expounders to account for the prophecies concerning the Jew in Deut. 28 and Lev. 26, or Tyre in Ezek. 26, and Babylon in Isa. 13.

4. The non-propositional view of revelation in effect makes Jesus a fraud. If there were no revealed truths, then the statements made by Jesus Christ are not revealed truths. But Jesus claimed to have received revealed truths:

   a. "My doctrine is not mine, but his that sent me..." (John 7:16).

   b. "I do nothing of myself; but as my Father hath taught me, I speak these things." (John 8:28).

   c. "For I have not spoken of myself; but the Father which sent me, he gave me a commandment, what I should say, and what I should speak... whatsoever I speak therefore, even as the Father said unto me, so I speak." (John 12:49,50).

5. Furthermore, Jesus claimed to have received not just a message from God but the actual words of the message: "For I have given unto them the words (Gk. *rhema*) which thou gavest me; and they have received them, and have known surely that I came out from thee, and they have believed that thou didst send me...I have given them thy word (Gk. *logos*); and the world hath hated them, because they are not of the world, even as I am not of the world." (John 17:8,14).

6. Since revelation is not considered to be a direct communication of information (in the non-propositional view of revelation), reliance is usually placed on the 'assured results' of criticism. This amounts to a kind of papalism—the 'infallibility of the scholars' from whom one can learn the 'assured results'.[4] The task of the scholar then becomes that of reconstructing Biblical history (i.e., what really happened). From the Biblical narratives and the reconstruction, assessment is made of the adequacy of the interpretation of history which Biblical writers have recorded. Attempts at reconstruction, from the 'modern' point of view square more easily with a naturalistic, evolutionary, anti-miraculous, uniformitarian outlook, than with the belief that biblical history has been chequered by God revealing information (content) otherwise unknowable.

7. The Greek word for "reveal" is *apokalupto* which means "to uncover, or unveil".[5] Revelation is the process whereby God disclosed to chosen men things otherwise unknowable (e.g., Dan. 2:22; 8:27; 10:1; 1 Cor. 2:9,10; Eph. 3:3–5; Rev. 1:1).

8. Revelation is a divine activity, "God...hath...spoken". (Heb. 1:1,2). It was verbal ("hath...spoken") and cumulative ("by the prophets...by his Son"). Revelation is not, therefore, a human flash of insight or the emergence of a bright idea.

[4] This point is expanded in J. I. Packer, *God Hath Spoken: Revelation and the Bible*, (London: Hodder and Stoughton, 1965), pp.12-18.

[5] Robert Young, *Analytical Concordance to the Holy Bible*, (London: Lutterworth Press, 1965).

9. The chief fallacy in viewing revelation as other than propositional is the assumption that man can read God's mind, learn His character, guess His motives and predict His movements by unaided brainwork.[6] Modern theology has yet to learn, "My thoughts are not your thoughts, neither are your ways my ways, saith the LORD. For as the heavens are higher than the earth, so are my ways higher than your ways, and my thoughts than your thoughts." (Isa. 55:8,9). "How unsearchable are his judgments, and his ways past finding out! For who hath known the mind of the Lord...?" (Rom. 11:33,34).

---

[6] Denial of the Virgin birth of Jesus, his miracles and his bodily resurrection is the end-product of current theological speculations.

4.3

ALLEGED CONTRADICTIONS
AND INACCURACIES

A number of supposed contradictions and inaccuracies in the Bible are regularly advanced by critics and partial inspirationists to bolster the claim that the Bible is not inspired.

PRELIMINARY POINTS

1. The basis of the believer's approach to alleged contradictions may be summarised:
   a. *God cannot err.* A partial inspirationist will accept the existence of God and logically must concede that God cannot err. A God who errs is no God.
   b. *The Bible is the word of God.*—A fact stated repeatedly by prophets, Jesus and the apostles (Isa. 1:11,18; Jer. 26:2; 34:1,2; Matt. 4:4; John 10:35; 2 Tim. 3:16).
   c. *Therefore the Bible does not err.* Any errors in the text of our modern Bibles must be due to translation or transcription. (This is not to deny that the Bible contains difficulties.)

2. Many of the alleged contradictions in the Bible do not qualify as such since a contradiction requires an affirmation and denial of the same proposition. The inscriptions on the cross are often cited as contradictory. Upon an examination of the accounts in the gospels, it will be seen that none of the writers denies what one of the other gospel writers affirms. The claim that the accounts are contradictory is a spurious one, since the evidence does not satisfy the definition of a contradiction.[1] If, however, one talks about a sun that is always light, yet dark, contradictory statements are made. By definition that which is *always* light cannot be dark. Nor can one talk about a square circle, since by definition a circle is round and not square. The property of squareness precludes the possibility of a square being a circle.

3. Many of the alleged inaccuracies (between parallel narratives in the gospels, for example) which are argued against belief in the verbal and infallible inspiration of Scripture, indicate a misunderstanding of the nature of verbal inspiration. Divine penmen were not obliged to record all details of an event. For the purposes of his gospel, Mark only refers to the healing of one blind man as Jesus left Jericho (Mark 10:46–52), whereas Matthew includes the healing of two blind men. (Matt. 20:29–34). All writers are selective in the information they record. John commented: "And there are also many other things which Jesus did, the which, if they should be written every one, I suppose that even the world itself could not contain the books that should be

---

[1] Contradiction: "The act of denying the truth of something, or stating the opposite of something ..." *Webster's Illustrated Dictionary*, (New York: Books, Inc., 1955).

written."² (John 21:25). Similarly, a contemporary 'uninspired' historian may choose to ignore certain data and include others which are relevant to his purpose and classification.

4. Most apparent contradictions are easily resolved by a careful reading of the passages in question in their contexts, and by clearly defining what is, and what is not, said. For example, it is written of both Hezekiah and Josiah that "after him was none like him among all the kings of Judah, nor any that were before him". (2 Kings 18:5; 23:25). As these statements read, they appear contradictory until it is noted in what respect "after him was none like him… nor any that were before him". It will be seen that Hezekiah is commended because he *trusted*, and Josiah because he *turned* to the Lord. Since mutually exclusive statements are not made, the two statements are not contradictory. The problem is resolved by merely noting precisely what the records do say.

5. In certain instances not all problems may be resolved by a careful reading of the contexts and a clarification of what is, and what is not, claimed by the narratives. Such ought not to be the source of undue embarrassment. The fact that no resolution of a problem is immediately possible is not proof that the right solution is not available. Humility is required that one does not confine the divine inspiration of Scripture to the level of one's own intellectual attainments.

Exodus 6:3

"And I appeared unto Abraham, unto Isaac, and unto Jacob, by the name of God Almighty [El Shaddai] but by my name Jehovah [Yahweh] was I not known to them."

PROBLEM:

There is an apparent contradiction between what God says to Moses in this passage and Abraham's use of the divine name, for example, in Gen. 14:22. (The divine name, Yahweh, occurs 165 times in Genesis.)

SOLUTION:

There are two ways of approaching this:

1. It is not said that Abraham, Isaac and Jacob did not use the divine name, but that they did not *know* it. Pharaoh said, "Who is the LORD [Yahweh], that I should obey his voice to let Israel go? I know not the LORD, neither will I let Israel go." (Exo. 5:2). Pharaoh came to know the power of the name when the Egyptians said, "Let us flee from the face of Israel; for the LORD fighteth for them against the Egyptians." (Exo. 14:25). Yahweh had declared: "The

---

² This in itself may be held by some to mitigate against the inspiration of the Bible. How could it be possible for one person in the space of a three year ministry do so many things that it would be impossible for the whole world to contain the books required to record them. John uses the word "world" [Gk. *kosmos*] to refer to the Jewish nation (e.g. John 7:4; 9:39). What John is saying is that the synagogue libraries in the Jewish nation would not have room for all the scrolls that would be needed to record the things that Jesus did during his ministry.

Egyptians shall know that I am the LORD [Yahweh], when I stretch forth mine hand upon Egypt..." (Exo. 7:5, cf. also 8:10,22; 14:18).

2. "God Almighty" [El Shaddai] is not a *name* of God but a *title*. Exo. 6:3 actually says, "I appeared unto Abraham...as El Shaddai"—the words "by the name of" are not in the Hebrew text as the italics in the AV show. In fact Genesis only records one occasion when God appeared to Abraham as El Shaddai (Gen. 17:1), never to Isaac (although Isaac uses the title in Gen. 28:3) and once to Jacob (Gen. 35:11). But many times God declares to the patriarchs, "I am Yahweh" and calls Himself "Yahweh God of Abraham" (Gen. 28:13). Abraham is said to have "called upon the name of Yahweh" in his worship (Gen. 12:8; 13:4; 21:33) and he named the altar at Moriah "Yahweh Yireh" (Gen. 22:14). Likewise Isaac and Jacob worshipped Yahweh, the God of Abraham (Gen. 25:21; 26:25; 28:16,21).

The name of Yahweh was linked with the covenant that God made with the patriarchs (e.g. Gen. 15:7). The context in which these words of Exo. 6:3 are found is that God had remembered the covenant made with Abraham (to which he had attached His name). "I am Yahweh...and I have established my covenant with them." (Exo. 6:2,4).

In view of this it is perhaps better to read Exo. 6:3 as a question: "I am Yahweh: I appeared unto Abraham, unto Isaac, and unto Jacob, as El Shaddai, but by my name Yahweh *was I not known to them*? And I have also established my covenant with them..." There are sound grammatical reasons for doing this.[3] Read in this way there is no contradiction at all.

Exodus 33:11

"And the LORD spake unto Moses face to face, as a man speaketh unto his friend..."

Exodus 33:20

"...Thou canst not see my face: for there shall no man see me, and live."

PROBLEM:

These two references are cited as contradictions in the Bible. The one verse says that God spoke to Moses face to face and yet nine verses later the writer says that no man can see God's face and live.

SOLUTION:

1. Moses did not see Yahweh ("the LORD") literally "face to face". This is indicated by the following New Testament passages:
   a. "[God] who only hath immortality, dwelling in the light which no man can approach unto; *whom no man hath seen*, nor can see..." (1 Tim. 6:16).

---

[3] The case for doing this is set out in, Martin, W. J., *Stylistic Criteria and the Analysis of the Pentateuch*, (Tyndale Press: London, 1955), p.19.

b. "Now unto the King eternal, immortal, invisible, the only wise God…" (1 Tim. 1:17, cf. Heb. 11:27).

c. "No man hath seen God at any time…" (John 1:18).

2. It is clear from Stephen's exposition in Acts 7 that Moses spoke face to face with God's accredited representative, an angel, and not to God Himself. Note these verses:

a. v. 30—"there appeared to him…an angel"

b. v. 35—"the angel which appeared to him in the bush"

c. v. 38—"the angel which spake to him in the mount Sina"

d. v. 53—"who have received the law by the disposition of angels" (cf. Gal. 3:19, "ordained by angels")

3. The principle of 'God-manifestation' is illustrated in Exo. 33, and elaborated in Stephen's commentary in Acts 7. When God acts through accredited representatives, the work is accomplished by God although executed by chosen messengers. An example is recorded in Exo. 23:20,21: "Behold, I send an Angel before thee [Israel], to keep thee in the way, and to bring thee into the place which I have prepared. Beware of him, and obey his voice, provoke him not; for he will not pardon your transgressions: for my name is in him." Moses, therefore, conversed with an angelic messenger, "face to face" and not with the invisible Creator who dwells in light unapproachable by mortal man.

4. God-manifestation in the angel which spake unto Moses is illustrated in Acts 7 in the shift from "an angel" (v. 30), to "the voice of the Lord" (v. 31), and "then said the Lord to him". (v. 33).

1 Samuel 15:35

"And Samuel came no more to see Saul until the day of his death…"

1 Samuel 19:24

"[Saul]…prophesied before Samuel…"

PROBLEM:

If the Bible is an inspired record from God, how are these two passages (apparently contradictory) to be explained?

SOLUTION:

1. A contradiction requires an affirmation and denial of the same proposition. The two passages are not the same proposition. One says Samuel came no more to see Saul, but this is not the same as saying Samuel saw Saul no more.

2. When Saul prophesied before Samuel, the narrative makes it clear that it was Saul who went to Ramah where Samuel lived (1 Sam. 19:22,23), and not Samuel who went to see Saul.

1 Kings 15:14

"But the high places were not removed…"

2 Chronicles 14:5

"Also he [Asa] took away out of all the cities of Judah the high places and the images…"

PROBLEM:

These two passages are cited as contradictions in the Bible. The one passage says that the high places were not removed; the other passage says they were removed.

SOLUTION:

1. In 1 Kings 15:14 and 2 Chron. 15:17 the reference is to the complete removal of the high places. Notice 2 Chron. 15:17 says the high places were not taken *out of Israel*. This implies that in Judah, where the King had authority,[4] the high places were removed, but in Israel where he did not have control, the high places remained.
2. Asa, therefore, took away out of all the cities of *Judah* the high places and the images (2 Chron. 14:5), but was unable to complete his reform in Israel, hence: "But the high places were not taken away out of *Israel*…" (2 Chron. 15:17). The allusion might also be to the high places not removed in the *country* areas as distinct from the *cities* of Judah.

2 Kings 18:5

"He [Hezekiah] trusted in the LORD God of Israel; so that after him was none like him among all the kings of Judah, nor any that were before him."

2 Kings 23:25

"And like unto him [Josiah] was there no king before him, that turned to the LORD with all his heart, and with all his soul, and with all his might, according to all the law of Moses; neither after him arose there any like him."

PROBLEM:

It is argued that mutually exclusive statements are made, therefore, both statements cannot be true. Both kings cannot "be like no other king before or after" in the same respect.

SOLUTION:

1. A careful reading is all that is necessary to indicate that there is no contradiction. Hezekiah is commended because he "trusted" (2 Kings 18:5);

---

[4] A state of war existed between Asa, King of Judah, and Baasha, King of Israel (1 Kings 15:32), as there had been between Abijam, King of Judah (the father of Asa) and Jeroboam, King of Israel. (1 Kings 15:7).

Josiah is commended because he "turned" (2 Kings 23:25). Mutually exclusive statements are not made.

2. It is also noteworthy that David is the *rule* by which the later kings are evaluated, e.g., 1 Kings 11:33,38; 14:8. He is, therefore, excluded from comparative statements about Josiah and Hezekiah, that "like unto him was there no king before him."

THE DEATH OF JEHOIAKIM

2 Kings 24:6
"So Jehoiakim slept with his fathers…"[5]

2 Chronicles 36:6
"Against him came up Nebuchadnezzar king of Babylon, and bound him in fetters, to carry him to Babylon."

Jeremiah 22:18,19
"He shall be buried with the burial of an ass, drawn and cast forth beyond the gates of Jerusalem."

Jeremiah 36:30
"…and his dead body shall be cast out in the day to the heat, and in the night to the frost."

Ezekiel 19:9
"And they put him in ward [in a cage RV] in chains, and brought him to the king of Babylon: they brought him into holds, that his voice should no more be heard upon the mountains of Israel."[6]

PROBLEM:

It is argued that these passages are apparently contradictory since Jehoiakim is said to be carried off to Babylon and yet cast beyond the gates of Jerusalem.

SOLUTION:

The passages are capable of being harmonized. Consider the following:

a. Jehoiakim was captured by Nebuchadnezzar and taken to Nebuchadnezzar's headquarters near Jerusalem (but not to Babylon).

---

[5] In Scripture, "he slept with his fathers" means simply that "he died". See, for example: 2 Kings 13:9,13; 14:16; 15:7,38. Frequently in the record of the kings of Judah the place of burial is stated. However, in Jehoiakim's case this is not done which tends to confirm that he was not buried in Jerusalem.

[6] Although Jehoiakim is not specifically mentioned it is almost certain that he is the one to whom Ezekiel refers.

WRESTED SCRIPTURES

b. Jehoiakim was put in a cage, as stated by Ezekiel, and bound in fetters to be carried to Babylon. (None of the passages asserts that he was actually taken to Babylon.)
c. Jehoiakim died before leaving for Babylon[7] so his body was dumped outside the walls of Jerusalem.[8]

Matthew 2:1
"...Jesus was born in Bethlehem of Judaea in the days of Herod the king..."

Luke 2:4
"And Joseph also went up from Galilee, out of the city of Nazareth, into Judaea unto the city of David, which is called Bethlehem..."

PROBLEM:
It is maintained that Matthew indicates that Mary and Joseph lived at Bethlehem, but Luke says that they returned to Bethlehem for the census. Therefore, it is argued, there is an apparent discrepancy.

SOLUTION:
1. Jesus' birth in Bethlehem is no more proof that his parents lived there, than the statement that "I was born at sea" implies that mine lived in a ship.
2. A reading of Luke 2:1–7 shows that while at Bethlehem for the census, Jesus was born. Mary had lived at Nazareth in Galilee before the journey to Bethlehem. (Luke 1:26,27).

Matthew 17:1
"And after six days Jesus taketh Peter, James, and John his brother, and bringeth them up into an high mountain apart."

Mark 9:2
This is the same as Matthew's account.

Luke 9:28
"And it came to pass about an eight days after these sayings, he took Peter and John and James, and went up into a mountain to pray."

---

[7] Perhaps he died from exposure while awaiting transportation to Babylon. It has been suggested that the AV of 2 Chron. 36:8, "Now the rest of the acts of Jehoiakim, and his abominations which he did, and that which was found in him" be read literally, "that which was found *upon* him." The abomination upon him might refer to extraordinary tattooing which would explain why he would be put into a cage and transported as an exhibition piece to Babylon.
[8] This would serve as a further humiliation to the Jews.

368

PROBLEM:

If the Bible is indeed an inspired revelation of God to man, then why the discrepancy between the numbers of days in Matthew, Mark, and Luke?

SOLUTION:

1. Notice that Luke says "about"—an approximation.
2. There are several ways of accounting for the difference in the number of days. The most probable one is that Luke uses the Jewish method of counting, in which case he would count the remaining part of the day on which Jesus spoke (see v. 27) as one day, as well as the early part of the day before they went up into the mountain. These two days, plus the intervening six of Matthew and Mark's record, account for the eight days.

Matthew 19:16

"...Good Master, what good thing shall I do, that I may have eternal life?"

Mark 10:17 and Luke 18:18

"...Good Master, what shall I do that I may inherit eternal life?"

PROBLEM:

It is argued that the Bible cannot be verbally inspired since the gospel writers do not quote the same words in the dialogue between Jesus and the young man.

SOLUTION:

1. Verbal inspiration does not require a writer to record a complete conversation unless this is essential to the purpose of the record.
2. The Biblical doctrine of inspiration requires the writers to record faithfully the information selected, although for the purpose of the narrative only a section of a dialogue may be reproduced. The complete request of the rich young man may have been: "Good Master, what good thing shall I do, that I may inherit eternal life?"

Matthew 20:29–34

"And as they departed from Jericho, a great multitude followed him. And, behold, two blind men...cried out...so Jesus had compassion on them, and touched their eyes: and immediately their eyes received sight, and they followed him."

Mark 10:46–52

"And they came to Jericho: and as he went out of Jericho...blind Bartimaeus... began to cry out...And Jesus said unto him, Go thy way; thy faith hath made thee whole."

WRESTED SCRIPTURES

Luke 18:35–43

"And it came to pass, that as he was come nigh unto Jericho, a certain blind man ...cried, saying, Jesus, thou Son of David, have mercy on me...And Jesus said unto him, Receive thy sight: thy faith hath saved thee."

PROBLEM:

a. In Matthew's account *two* blind men are healed, whereas in the accounts of Mark and Luke only one blind man is mentioned.

b. Matthew and Mark place the healing when Jesus was departing *from* Jericho, whereas Luke places the healing when Jesus was coming *to* Jericho.

SOLUTION:

1. If two blind men were healed, then certainly one was healed. This is not the only place where Matthew records that two people were involved when the other gospels mention only one. E.g. the healing of the Gadarene demoniac. (Matt. 8:28, cf. Mark 5:2).
2. The gospel writers did not include all that Jesus did and said. (cf. John 21:25).
3. It is perfectly possible that Jesus healed "a certain blind man" as he was come nigh to Jericho (Luke's account), and then healed two more blind men (one of whom was blind Bartimaeus, Mark's account) as he was leaving Jericho.
4. Another possibility is that blind Bartimaeus cried out to Jesus as the Master entered the city but was either not heard or ignored (cf. the woman from Tyre, Matt. 15:23). Undeterred Bartimaeus was waiting for the Lord the next morning as he departed and continued to appeal for help, upon which the Lord granted his request.

Matthew 27:6,7

"And the chief priests took the silver pieces... and they took counsel, and bought with them the potter's field, to bury strangers in."

Acts 1:18

"Now this man [Judas] purchased a field with the reward of iniquity..."

PROBLEM:

If the Bible is a divinely inspired record, why does Matthew state that the chief priests bought the field, whereas in the Acts account Judas is said to have purchased the field?

SOLUTION:

A number of possible solutions have been advanced which are capable of harmonising the two records. The following are two:

1. It may be that two different purchases were involved. The word for "field" in Matthew's account is *argros*,[9] which is the usual word for field in the New Testament. The chief priests purchased this field with the 30 pieces of silver. It could be that Judas purchased a different field, a "little space or place", [Greek: *chorion*].[10] The money for this purchase need not have come from the 30 pieces of silver, but from money Judas had stolen from the bag. (John 12:6). The account merely states that the field was purchased "with the reward of iniquity" without specifying where the money came from.

2. Another possibility is that the words, "This man purchased a field" might be elliptical for the more lengthy explanation that the money Judas had obtained from the betrayal of the Master was used to purchase a field, although the actual transaction was effected by the chief priests. In John 19:1 we are told that "Pilate therefore took Jesus, and scourged him", but we have no difficulty in seeing that the scourging would have been done by Roman soldiers and that Pilate didn't actually scourge Jesus himself.

A variation of this is that the priests may have bought the field in Judas' name since the thirty pieces of silver were his. The emphasis in Acts lies in the fact that the field purchased by Judas' money was obtained by the reward of iniquity.

Matthew 27:37

"And set up over his head his accusation written, THIS IS JESUS THE KING OF THE JEWS."

Mark 15:26

"And the superscription of his accusation was written over, THE KING OF THE JEWS."

Luke 23:38

"And a superscription also was written over him in letters of Greek, and Latin, and Hebrew, THIS IS THE KING OF THE JEWS."

John 19:19

"And Pilate wrote a title, and put it on the cross. And the writing was, JESUS OF NAZARETH THE KING OF THE JEWS."

PROBLEM:

It is argued that the Bible cannot be verbally inspired since the gospel writers do not quote the same superscription on the cross.

[9] Robert Young, *Analytical Concordance to the Holy Bible*, (London: Lutterworth Press, 1965).
[10] *Ibid.*

SOLUTION:

1. Verbal inspiration does not require the writers of the gospels to record the *complete* inscription unless such would be relevant to the purpose of their gospels.
2. There is no contradiction in the words of the inscription. This can be seen by the following comparison:

Matt. 27:37	THIS IS JESUS		THE KING OF THE JEWS
Mark 15:26			THE KING OF THE JEWS
Luke 23:38	THIS IS		THE KING OF THE JEWS
John 19:19		JESUS OF NAZARETH	THE KING OF THE JEWS

Thus the complete superscription would almost certainly have read: "THIS IS JESUS OF NAZARETH THE KING OF THE JEWS."

Matthew 28:7

"...he [Christ] goeth before you into Galilee; there shall ye see him..."

Luke 24:33

"And they rose up the same hour, and returned to Jerusalem, and found the eleven gathered together, and them that were with them."

PROBLEM:

There is an apparent contradiction, for how could the disciples be in both Galilee and Jerusalem at the same time?

SOLUTION:

1. Neither passage implies that the disciples were to be in Galilee and Jerusalem *at the same time*.
2. Jesus was forty days upon the earth after his resurrection (Acts 1:3). The gospels record at least ten appearances of the Lord to his disciples during this period. Two of these were in Galilee (John 21:1; Matt. 28:16). Since it is not more than a two or three day's journey between Galilee and Jerusalem, appearances in both places are perfectly possible.

Mark 2:26

"...[David] went into the house of God in the days of Abiathar the high priest, and did eat the shewbread, which is not lawful to eat..."

1 Samuel 21:1–6

"Then came David to Nob to Ahimelech the priest...so the priest gave him hallowed bread..."

PROBLEM:

Mark quotes Jesus as saying that Abiathar was the high priest, but the account in Samuel to which Jesus refers, says that Ahimelech was the high priest. Therefore, it is argued, one, or both accounts, is in error.

SOLUTION:

Whilst this is one of the most difficult problems to resolve it does not really prove that one of the divine penmen (either Mark or the author of 1 Samuel) erred. There are a number of possible explanations, but it is unwise to be dogmatic as to which is the correct one. The following are among those that have been suggested:

1. The apparent inaccuracy may be resolved once it is realized that Abiathar and Ahimelech may have been the names of *both* father and son as suggested by comparison of the following passages:

    a. 1 Sam. 14:3—"And Ahiah, [AVm. called Ahimelech] the son of Ahitub."
    b. 1 Sam. 22:20—"And one of the sons of Ahimelech the son of Ahitub, named Abiathar, escaped, and fled after David."
    c. 2 Sam. 8:17—"And Zadok the son of Ahitub, and Ahimelech the son of Abiathar, were the priests..."
    d. 1 Chron. 18:16; 24:6—same as 2 Sam. 8:17.
    e. The following diagram illustrates the point:

Ahitub (1 Sam. 14:3)	Ahitub (2 Sam. 8:17)
father	father
of	of
Ahimelech (1 Sam. 14:3; 22:20)	Abiathar (2 Sam. 8:17; 1 Chron. 18:16)
father	father
of	of
Abiathar (1 Sam. 22:20)	Ahimelech (2 Sam. 8:17; 1 Chron. 18:16; 24:6)

    Jesus and the account in Samuel refer to Ahimelech (or Abiathar, his other name), the son of *Ahitub*. According to this reasoning there is, therefore, no inaccuracy. Jesus uses one name, and the Samuel account uses the other name, for the *same* individual.

2. An alternative possible explanation is that both Ahimelech and Abiather were there when David ate the shewbread. Soon after the incident Ahimelech and his family were killed by Doeg at Saul's behest apart from Abiathar who escaped. Abiather then became high priest. For Jesus to describe the well known and respected Abiathar as "high priest" before he assumed the office is not unusual.

373

For example we are told that "Jesse begat David the king" (Matt. 1:6) when in fact Jesse begat David, who many years later became king.

3. The third explanation worthy of consideration rests on the fact that the words translated in the AV "*in the days of* [Gk. *epi*] Abiathar the high priest" may be translated "*about the time* of Abiathar the high priest". The same construction in the Greek text is found in Matt. 1:11 where we are told that "Josias begat Jechonias and his brethren *about the time* [Gk. *epi*] they were carried away to Babylon". This allows Jesus (as recorded by Mark) to identify this incident by reference to the better known priest, but leaves open the possibility that he did not intend to say that Abiathar was actually the high priest at the time.

Mark 16:7,8

"[Mary Magdalene, Mary the mother of James, and Salome]...tell his disciples and Peter that he goeth before you into Galilee: there shall ye see him, as he said unto you. And they went out quickly, and fled from the sepulchre; for they trembled and were amazed: neither said they any thing to any man; for they were afraid."

Luke 24:8,9

"And they remembered his words, and returned from the sepulchre, and told all these things unto the eleven, and to all the rest."

PROBLEM:

The Mark record says the women said nothing "to any man", and yet the Luke narrative says the women "told all these things unto the eleven, and to all the rest". It is argued, therefore, that the two accounts are contradictory.

SOLUTION:

The apparent contradiction is resolved by the following:

1. The Lord's first appearance was to one woman only—Mary Magdalene. (John 20:13–17; cf. Mark 16:9).
2. The other women had only seen the bodiless tomb with a young man in it. As these women were on their way to tell the disciples ("with fear and great joy"), they were met by Jesus. (Matt. 28:9). It was Jesus who further encouraged the women to tell the news to the disciples. (Matt. 28:10). Until this encounter with Jesus, they had not said "any thing to any man; for they were afraid".

THE CLEANSING OF THE TEMPLE

John 2:13–16

"...Take these things hence; make not my Father's house an house of merchandise."

Matthew 21:12,13

"...My house shall be called the house of prayer; but ye have made it a den of thieves."

PROBLEM:

Since John places the cleansing of the temple at the beginning of Christ's ministry, and Matthew and the other gospels place it at the end of his ministry, it is argued that the compilations of the gospels could not have been divine.

SOLUTION:

1. It is true that John places the cleansing at the beginning of Christ's ministry and the other gospels place it just prior to the crucifixion. The reason for this is that there were *two*, and not just one cleansing of the temple.
2. A comparison of the contexts of these two passages indicates the contrast in events preceding and following the temple cleansings. In John's gospel the cleansing occurs at the beginning of Christ's miracles at Cana of Galilee. (John 2:11). Jesus journeyed from Capernaum to Jerusalem in this gospel. The cleansing is then followed by the Jews' request for a sign. In Matthew's gospel, Jesus comes to Jerusalem from Judaea beyond Jordan (Matt. 19:1), and enters Jerusalem on an ass to the cries of "Hosanna" from the populace. (Matt. 21:9). The cleansing of the temple is then followed by the cursing of the fig tree. (Matt. 21:18,19). It follows, therefore, that two different cleansings occurred.
3. It is appropriate that the cleansing of the temple at the end of Christ's ministry should prohibit the carrying of vessels in the temple: "And [he] would not suffer that any man should carry any vessel through the temple." (Mark 11:16). The outer court of the temple was called 'The Court of the Gentiles'. It was a large open area, the only area of the temple to which the Gentiles had access. But this area had become a shortcut route for persons travelling to and from the north end of the city. The prohibition of Jesus was in effect a symbolic declaration that the outer court was also holy, and that the Gentile as well as the Jew was now acceptable before God. There was to be "neither Jew nor Greek...neither bond nor free"—all the baptized were to be "one in Christ Jesus". (Gal. 3:28).

James 1:13

"...God cannot be tempted with evil, neither tempteth he any man."

Genesis 22:1

"...God did tempt Abraham..."

PROBLEM:

Apparently contradictory statements are made since James says God tempts no man, and yet in Genesis God is said to have tempted Abraham.

375

SOLUTION:

1. The Greek word *peirazo* and its Hebrew equivalent, *nasah,* carry the meaning of "to try, prove",[11] as well as to "tempt". The RSV translators preserve the distinction between "test" and "tempt", thereby removing the confusion: "After these things God *tested* Abraham..." (Gen. 22:1, RSV). See also the use of the same word in Exo. 16:4, "Behold, I will rain bread from heaven for you; and the people shall go out and gather a certain rate every day, that I may prove [Heb. *nasah*] them, whether they will walk in my law, or no."

2. The RSV also makes a distinction in James 1:2,3 between "trial" and "temptation": "Count it all joy, my brethren, when you meet various trials (temptations, AV), for you know that the testing of your faith produces steadfastness." This translation is in harmony with a similar point made by Peter. (cf. 1 Pet. 1:6,7).

3.   Similarly, an apparent contradiction exists between James 1:13 and Psa. 78:18,56; 95:9; 106:14, but in each of these Old Testament references the RSV renders the Hebrew word *nasah* by "tested" rather than "tempted" (as does the AV).

---

[11] Robert Young, *Analytical Concordance to the Holy Bible*, (London: Lutterworth Press, 1965). According to Young, *nasah* is rendered in the AV 20 times "prove" and 12 times "tempt". *Peirazo* is rendered in the AV 4 times "try" and 29 times "tempt".

SCRIPTURE INDEX

WRESTED SCRIPTURES

WRESTED SCRIPTURES

2 Kings *Ezra*

WRESTED SCRIPTURES

382

Matt (handwritten)

John

J ohn

Acts

1 COR

2 COR

1 TIM   *2 TIM*

HEB

398

REV.